History and Landscape

History and Landscape

The Guide to National Trust Properties in England, Wales and Northern Ireland

Lydia Greeves

Foreword by HRH The Prince of Wales

 THE NATIONAL TRUST

First edition, by Robin Fedden and Rosemary
Joekes, published by Jonathan Cape, 1973
Revised editions published 1977 and 1984
Second edition, by Lydia Greeves and Michael
Trinnick, published by The National Trust, 1989

This edition published in Great Britain in 2004 by
National Trust Enterprises Ltd,
36 Queen Anne's Gate, London SW1H 9AS
www.nationaltrust.org.uk

ISBN 0 7078 0369 1

Thanks to the late Michael Trinnick, who died in 1994, and who wrote much of the original
countryside text, which has been updated for this edition.

Cataloguing in Publication Data is available from the British Library.

Project Management: Fiona Screen
Editorial: Emma Dickens, Wendy Vallance
Picture research: Fiona Screen, Shirley Kenyon
Designed and typeset in Adobe Caslon and Helvetica Neue by Bridget Heal

Maps © Maps in Minutes ™2002 Crown Copyright, Ordnance Survey & Ordnance Survey
Northern Ireland 2002 Permit No NI 1675 & © Government of Ireland Ordnance Survey Ireland.

Cover design: Bridget Heal

Printed and bound in Italy by G. Canale & C.s.p.A

Half-title page: The delicate cast-iron
balustrade of the staircase at Mount
Stewart in County Down.

Frontispiece: Looking down the
graceful spiral staircase at
The Homewood in Surrey. The feature
at the bottom of the well is a sunken
spotlight, one of many original touches
which make this house so individual.

Contents

Foreword

As President of The National Trust, I never cease to be amazed by the uniquely varied activity with which it is involved: it is custodian of an extraordinary range of our national heritage, from beautiful countryside and coastline, to fine gardens and country houses. Yet the Trust is not only about the "great and the grand"; it looks after many unexpected treasures too, such as the exquisite sixteen-sided A La Ronde in Devon, or the last working spade mill, Pattersons, in Northern Ireland, or even the Workhouse at Southwell in Nottinghamshire, which reflects the day-to-day life of the very poorest in the nineteenth century. All these buildings, and the huge tracts of countryside in the care and management of the Trust, are show-cased in this book, the National Trust's bible for members and visitors alike.

My late Grandmother, The Queen Mother, was President of the National Trust for many years – and I was enormously proud to be her vice-President. I was therefore delighted to become President in her place because the National Trust has meant a great deal to me over the years.

I believe I have become President at a very interesting time in the National Trust's history as it builds on its foundation in the nineteenth-century, its development through the twentieth-century and now faces the new challenges of the twenty-first. It has to represent continuity, but also far-sightedness, just as the landscape gardeners of the eighteenth century planned for the future as they laid out gardens like Stourhead and Croome Park, both now looked after by the Trust.

While there is an increased understanding and appreciation of precious landscape and architecture, there continues to be a growing concern about the impact of the constant expansion of urban areas, of roads and airports. These twin concerns – the positive and the negative – are expressed in television and radio programmes, campaigns and protests and also in the growing membership of the National Trust itself. Some years ago it was believed that the Trust's membership would 'plateau', but in 2002–03 more members joined than at any time during the previous decade and membership, which reached three million in 2002, is growing still.

I believe the Trust's work is no less important in the countryside: it owns some 250,000 hectares and has many farmers as tenants, often in the remotest parts of the country where farming is financially precarious. Here the Trust's mission to support local communities to maintain continuity, while conserving the natural environment for this and future generations to enjoy, is so vital. During the horrors of the Foot and Mouth outbreak, the Trust played a particularly important role in helping its tenants through those bleak days. Since then, a range of initiatives has put the Trust at the forefront of encouraging the "small family farmer": Whole Farm Plans, local sourcing and the encouragement of farm shops – and other diversification – have been a great success.

I hope that, like me, inspired by this attractive book, you will have the opportunity of exploring the huge variety of beautiful places in the care of the National Trust. Members will find some unexpected and new treasures, while others will, I hope, discover a wealth of beauty and history on their doorstep and, as a result, perhaps be moved to support the work of the National Trust in preserving the best of our heritage for future generations to enjoy and, you never know, even be inspired enough to understand the continuing need for an "organic", sympathetic building tradition when it comes to the way we build the future heritage in our precious countryside today.

Robert Adam's imposing Saloon at Kedleston Hall in Derbyshire is a huge domed rotunda, lit from above. Over each of the doors hangs a large painting of a Roman ruin by William Hamilton, and the grisaille is one of several by Biagio Rebecca showing scenes from English history.

Introduction

The gift of a 1.8-hectare (4-acre) stretch of cliffland overlooking Cardigan Bay in 1895 and the purchase of a little pre-Reformation clergy house in Alfriston in Sussex in 1896 were the start of a great enterprise which has grown, over a century later, into an organisation that is Europe's largest conservation charity, with well over 3 million members. The infant Trust, which was registered under the Companies Act in January 1895, and given statutory authority with the passing of the National Trust Act in 1907, was rooted in a growing appreciation of and concern for our wilder countryside and open spaces, and increasing awareness of how easily the beauty of a landscape could be diminished. Half a century earlier, William Wordsworth had been horrified by the rash of villas which sprung up on the eastern shore of Windermere when the lake could first be reached by rail. The Trust's three indomitable founders, Octavia Hill, Canon Hardwicke Rawnsley and Sir Robert Hunter, were all involved in other early conservation bodies; Hill and Hunter in the Commons Preservation Society, founded in 1865, and Rawnsley in the Lake District Defence Society, which he initiated. And in 1875 Octavia Hill had lost a major campaign to prevent the development of Swiss Cottage Fields, which would have been a valuable urban lung for London.

From small beginnings, the Trust has grown to be the largest private landowner in the country, currently protecting some 260,000 hectares – over a thousand square miles – in England, Wales and Northern Ireland (Scotland has its own Trust). This is an area seven times the size of the Isle of Wight, or roughly equivalent to the county of Dorset, and it includes over 600 miles of coastline, some 18 per cent of the total, and over 150,000 hectares (370,500 acres) of farmland, worked by some 2,000 tenant farmers. In its first half century or so, the accent was very much on the acquisition of coast and countryside, and the historic buildings which did come to the Trust were generally small, like Alfriston Clergy House, or the tiny fourteenth-century dwelling known as the Old Post Office at Tintagel, which was bought in 1903. From the late 1930s, and particularly after the Second World War, when the owners of large houses faced rising costs, increasing taxes and the impact of death duties, more and more of these properties passed to the Trust, a process greatly eased by a second National Trust Act in 1937, which enabled the Trust to hold land and investments to provide for the upkeep of these properties. This was the start of the Country Houses Scheme, by which owners could transfer their houses to the Trust, together with a suitable endowment, while continuing to live there. Many more followed after 1946, when the government decided to accept houses and land *in lieu* of death duties and to hand suitable properties over to the Trust. As a result the Trust today is custodian of over 160 historic houses, from the Elizabethan Hardwick Hall, standing high on a Derbyshire ridge, and the medieval Ightham Mote, hidden away in a Kentish valley, to a number of lavish and romantic creations built by the *nouveaux riches* of the nineteenth and earlier twentieth centuries, among them Cragside in Northumberland, Castle Drogo in Devon and Wightwick Manor, on the outskirts of Wolverhampton.

As time has gone on, too, the Trust's sphere of interest has widened and the scope of its portfolio is now immense. Countryside properties include large areas of woodland, moorland and fell, lakes and waterfalls, bridges and canals and over 40,000 archaeological sites, among them the great henge at Avebury in Wiltshire and a number of prehistoric hill-forts, barrow cemeteries, hut circles and field systems. There are the ruins of once-great castles, wind and water-mills, barns and dovecotes, thousands of farms, cottages and other vernacular buildings and even a number of whole villages. In recent years a former workhouse on the edge of Southwell in Nottinghamshire, the home and studio of the celebrated photographer E. Chambré Hardman in Liverpool, the last courtyard of back-to-backs in Birmingham,

The Cherry Garden at Ham House in Surrey, where cones of box punctuate the beds of lavender and santolina.

a couple of early and significant examples of modern architecture – The Homewood in Surrey and 2 Willow Road in London – and the childhood homes of two icons of popular music, John Lennon and Sir Paul McCartney, have taken the Trust into areas of which its founders probably never dreamt. On top of this there are the many works of art and other objects in the Trust's care, ranging from paintings by masters such as Rembrandt, Turner and Titian, and furniture designed by Kent and Adam, to garden sculpture, costumes worn by the great actress Ellen Terry and collections of lawnmowers, spinning wheels and early bicycles.

The philosophy and principles of the Trust remain unchanged. Most importantly, as its founders recognised, it is completely independent of government subsidy, relying for its income on the generosity of the public together with support from bodies such as the Historic Buildings Council and the National Heritage Memorial Fund, which may recommend a grant to make up an endowment or help meet the cost of a major acquisition. Increasingly, too, local authorities have provided financial assistance. Nevertheless, although rich in terms of what it holds, the Trust is always short of money. When faced with the need for a huge sum at short notice, as when Tyntesfield, a major example of Victorian Gothic, was due to be sold by public auction in 2001, or when the important Snowdonia estate of Hafod y Llan came on the market in 1998, the necessary funds were secured by whirlwind appeals. Through these campaigns, £3.65 million, including a £1 million donation from Sir Anthony Hopkins, was raised for Hafod y Llan and over £20 million for Tyntesfield, including a vital contribution from the National Heritage Memorial Fund. More general concerns spawned Enterprise Neptune, launched in 1965 to capture as much undeveloped and beautiful coastline as possible, and the South Downs Appeal, relaunched in 1991, as a result of which the Trust now protects a substantial acreage of fragile downland.

Secondly, and as a result of the 1907 Act, the Trust has the unique power to declare its properties inalienable, which means they cannot be sold or mortgaged. This is a priceless asset, enabling donors to feel confident that what they are offering will be safeguarded for ever.

Thirdly, and again this has been a principle since its early days, the Trust exists to preserve places and buildings for the nation – it is for all of us to enjoy what it offers. But there is a conflict here between the demands of access and preservation, a problem that grows larger with each passing year. Given the reasons for its being set up in the first place, preservation must come first. This raises dilemmas of which the Trust is acutely aware, and accounts for, for example, the very low light levels in some rooms, the closure of paths, and restrictions placed on visitor numbers.

In the countryside, the Trust has both safeguarded and enhanced some of our most beautiful and unspoilt landscapes. Before the days of planning control, substantial areas were threatened by building development, including such prominent and glorious sites as the Devil's Punch Bowl at Hindhead in

Surrey, Pentire Head on the north coast of Cornwall, Haresfield Beacon on the Cotswold escarpment in Gloucestershire, and the woods at Glencoyne in the Ullswater Valley. Similarly, open land that we now take for granted, such as the Lake District fells, has been saved from conifer plantations by the Trust. Enhancement has taken many forms. There have always been telephone or electric cables to bury or re-route, huts and other eyesores to clear away, like the clutter of shacks which once disfigured Stonehenge Down, and prominent caravan sites and car parks have been resited so that they are hidden from view or unobtrusive.

A consequence of the Trust's work, and one that was probably not foreseen by its founders, is that it has helped to preserve a sense of the distinctive character of different regions. In an age when standard building styles, ever more commercial agriculture and the spread of the chain store have ironed out the individuality that was once based on the local architectural vernacular and farming practices, the Trust maintains traditional farm buildings and perpetuates now outdated farming systems where this is necessary to preserve historic and much-loved landscapes. The characteristic Lake District scene, with tiny fields edged by stone walls in the valley bottoms and rugged open fell above, reflects the enduring pattern of sheep farming. A way of life that once provided a livelihood for the farmer is now barely viable, and the Trust's decision to encourage the continuance of old forms of land use for the sake of the landscape has involved accepting little or no financial return from estates here. This does not mean, however, that the Trust expects its tenant farmers in general to farm uneconomically, but on all its farmland changes are made, and new buildings erected, as sensitively as possible, with big new barns sited inconspicuously and perhaps shielded by a copse, and new uses found for redundant farms and cottages. As Prince Charles mentions in his Foreword, diversification and new initiatives to augment farming incomes are encouraged.

This kind of approach goes hand in hand with management for wildlife conservation. Downs, cliffs and heaths have been cleared of invading scrub and trees, eroded sand dunes restored, grazing regimes controlled, and flowery meadows and peat bogs conserved. Some of the Trust's properties, such as Wicken Fen in Cambridgeshire, Blakeney Point in Norfolk and the Farne Islands in Northumberland, are specifically concerned with nature conservation, the wetland character of Wicken Fen now having to be artificially maintained as drainage has lowered the level of the surrounding agricultural land. Practices can work at a micro scale. The riverside meadows of Ty'n y Coed Uchaf, a smallholding in the Snowdonia National Park, are rich in orchids and other wild flowers, and even the humblest copse can nurture a diverse flora and fauna. Domesticated animals, too, come within the Trust's sphere of interest. Rare breeds farms, such as those established at Wimpole Hall in Cambridgeshire and Shugborough in Staffordshire, are designed to foster forms of livestock which have no part to play in current agricultural regimes and which are threatened with extinction. At Wimpole, for example, there are a dozen rare breeds of sheep, including the Manx Loghtan, the Golden Guernsey and the primitive Soay, with its heavy double horns and dark brown fleece.

All this reflects the nation's growing appreciation for the historical importance of our rural landscapes. As well as a wealth of prehistoric remains, the countryside also holds less obvious clues to past settlement and land use, in the pattern of field boundaries and lanes, in ancient coppice and old pollarded trees, in patches of rough common and the lynchets of medieval agriculture. Visitors to Wimpole Hall in Cambridgeshire can follow a 'hollow way' or sunken track which appears on a map of 1638, and see the banks and ditches outlining the site of the medieval settlement of Bennall End and the pattern of ridge and furrow in an area of old pasture marking part of the open-field system which once surrounded the village. Similarly, on the Trust's newly acquired Godolphin estate, in Cornwall, the many layered landscape includes prehistoric remains, the walls of an ancient deer-park, and the shafts, gullies and ruined buildings of tin and copper mining. These precious survivals show how much has been lost, ploughed out or buried under ever-expanding towns and cities and their satellite villages.

By such means the Trust preserves irreplaceable clues to past landscapes and ways of life. But its properties are in no sense dry museum pieces of interest only to historians. They are there to be enjoyed, to be wandered round at the visitor's own pace. Some people relish viewing a collection of paintings or porcelain. Others prefer to spend an afternoon strolling through a garden and relaxing in one of the Trust's many tea-rooms. And there are huge stretches of open country where the seeker after solitude can find peace of mind by spending the day walking across fells and moors or through fields and woods.

The Trust continues to grow and change with each passing year, with much ongoing restoration and re-appraisal of existing properties as well as acquisition of new ones. Although the great country houses and gardens continue to form the central plank of what the Trust has to offer, in recent years there has been a shift to enabling visitors to appreciate the wider setting of these places, with the opening of new footpaths and circular walks around the estate. At the same time, a more general concern with heritage as a whole has led to a widening of the property portfolio.

As well as describing all properties accessible to the public and all stretches of coast and countryside of any size and significance, this book also offers fourteen pictorial essays on themes which are intended to give visitors fresh perspectives and enrich their appreciation of what the Trust has to offer. Some explore the history of the landscape, others focus on an important individuals or key aspect of house design and furnishing. As well as giving a sense of the wider historical context, these pieces are designed to show the common threads running through properties.

Although encyclopedic, this book is not exhaustive. It has not been possible to cover every minor holding: some are only the size of a field or a copse. Buildings not open to the public, open for only a few days a year, or visible only by appointment have also been excluded. The maps on pages 442–45 show the locations of all properties mentioned in the text and map references are included for each property. Opening times and other practical information – such as admission fees and the availability of tea-rooms and facilities for the disabled – are in the National Trust Handbook, published every year and given free to Trust members. Information about the countryside in the Trust's care can be found in the introductory sections to each region in the Handbook, and in the Coast and Countryside Handbook (obtainable from the Membership Department or via the website – see jacket flap for contact details).

As always, I am greatly indebted to all who have helped me with this book. Several individuals within the Trust have listened patiently to my queries and have provided me with the information I needed. Outside the Trust, I am very grateful to Brian and Dill Hughes and Tom and Lis Greeves who allowed me to use their houses as hotels while visiting properties, and I owe particular thanks to Lucy Taylor, who time and again resolved problems to do with the limitations of my word processor.

Lydia Greeves
LONDON 2004

History and Landscape

A la Ronde DEVON

2 miles north of Exmouth on A376 [442 D7]

On the northern fringes of Exmouth, with views right across the Exe estuary, is a delightfully uninhibited late eighteenth-century cottage ornée. Looking rather like a human dovecote, A la Ronde is a small sixteen-sided, three-storey house, with rough limestone walls and a steeply pitched conical roof – now tiled but originally thatched – topped off with tall brick chimneys. Dating from a time when Exmouth was a fashionable resort, it was built, almost certainly to designs by the Bath architect John Lowder, for two resourceful spinsters: Jane Parminter, daughter of a Barnstaple wine merchant, and her younger cousin Mary, who had both just returned from a nine-year Grand Tour. The design of the house, with wedge-shaped main rooms divided by triangular lobbies, and curious diamond-shaped windows on the exterior angles, is unusual enough; even more so are the decorative schemes of the Parminters, rare survivals of the kind of time-consuming, intricate techniques involving paint and paper, shell and feathers, sand and seaweed, much indulged in by Regency ladies but which, due to their fragility, have mostly been lost. The interior stands out, too, for the skilful use of awkward angles and corners, and for the survival of its original contents.

The main rooms are arranged around a central octagon, with marbled yellow and green architraves to the eight doors off, ingenious seats folding down over the openings, and unique painted chairs with octagon-shaped seats. The west-facing drawing room has its eighteenth-century tub chairs and sofa, the original marbled skirting and painted pelmet and the Parminters' feather frieze, with a delicate pattern of downy concentric circles.

Pictures here include a large silhouette group of the Parminter family in 1783 and landscapes of paper, sand and seaweed, with feathery trees stretching out microscopic branches. A chimney board with shellwork surrounding a watercolour of St Michael's Mount (*see* p.328) is a prelude to the gallery at the top of the house. Alas, so fragile that it can only be viewed on video, this is the Parminters' *tour de force*, with shell-encrusted recesses and a zig-zag frieze setting off feathery bird portraits resting on moss and twigs.

Jane died in 1811, Mary in 1849. Partly due to Mary's will, which aimed to keep the house as it was and to allow only unmarried kinswomen to inherit, A la Ronde survived remarkably unaltered, despite the attentions of its only male owner, the Rev. Oswald Reichel, who added the third-storey dormer windows and roofline catwalk and introduced a dark Victorian note to some of the rooms. The family struggled to keep the property intact until increasing difficulties brought it to the Trust in 1991.

Aberconwy House CONWY

At junction of Castle Street and High Street in Conwy [444 F7]

When Edward I built his great castle at Conwy in 1283, he invited English settlers to colonise the little walled town established at its feet. This medieval house dating from the fourteenth century occupies what would have been a prime site in the new settlement, at the junction of High Street and Castle Street, the two principal thoroughfares, and close to the gate through which most of the town's trade passed down to the quay on the river. Now the oldest building in Conwy after the castle and the church, it is probably typical of the prosperous burgess houses which formed the body of the town, with two lower floors of stone supporting a half-timbered upper storey jettied out over the street. Furnished rooms illustrate life from different periods and there is a Trust shop.

Aberdulais Falls
NEATH AND PORT TALBOT

On the A4109, 3 miles north-east of Neath [442 D4]

Upstream from Neath, the Trust holds about an acre of the narrow wooded gorge through which the turbulent River Dulais runs into the main valley. The spectacular falls are at the northern end, where the dark green waters of the Dulais pour over ledges and lips of sandstone in the river bed. A place of great natural beauty, this narrow leafy valley is also important as an early site of water-powered industry, with some picturesque remains still to be seen.

The earliest, the first Welsh copper smelter, was built here by the Mines Royal in *c.*1590, and fed with ore shipped across the Bristol Channel from the rich Cornish mines. Copper smelting was replaced by iron working, fulling and dyeing, and in the eighteenth century the falls were used to run a large corn mill which supplied flour to the growing industrial towns of the Welsh valleys. This was when the valley was recorded in the romantic vision of a number of painters, J.M.W. Turner, Henry Gastineau, Penry Williams and de Loutherbourg among them. The present ivy-clad ruins, including a tall chimney, are the

Above: Aberconwy House is a survivor from the medieval town which grew up beside Conwy Castle.

Opposite: The whimsical A la Ronde once had dovecotes hanging from the eaves.

Previous page: The glorious ridge of Catbells rising above Derwentwater in the Lake District, as seen from the heights of Castlerigg Fell on the eastern shore, where the Trust has a substantial holding.

remains of a nineteenth-century tinplate works, which ceased operations in the 1880s.

Now the falls are harnessed once again, in a unique hydroelectric scheme introduced by the Trust. An 8-metre (27-foot) overshot water-wheel installed in the original wheel-pit for the tinplate works now produces all the power needed for the property, while a twentieth-century water-powered turbine feeds up to 200kw of electricity into the national grid. Also built into the system is a new fish pass, enabling salmon and sewin to reach the upper Dulais for the first time. Visitors can see all these features, with a memorable view down on to the falls and water-wheel, from the roof of the turbine house.

The turbulent waters of the Dulais pouring over outcropping sandstone at Aberdulais Falls.

Aberglaslyn Pass GWYNEDD

Extending south for 1½ miles from Beddgelert, along both sides of the pass (the A487 and the A498) [442 C1]

Near the village of Beddgelert is this dramatic pass, where the turbulent River Glaslyn forces its way through the hills to reach the sea at Porthmadog. With mountains crowding the three valleys which meet at Beddgelert, and the great shoulder of Snowdon 4 miles away to the north, the setting is dramatic: the gorge planted with pine and larch, the river a mountain stream should be. And above the pass, to the east, is Moel y Dyniewyd, with panoramic views from its 382-metre (1254-foot) summit.

The Trust owns a thousand acres here, with a network of paths. A circular route passes the romantic spot where Prince Llywelyn is said to have buried his faithful hound, Gelert, and the narrow and more treacherous Fisherman's Path leads along the rugged west bank of the Glaslyn.

Abergwesyn Common POWYS

West of Llandrindod Wells [442 D3]

To the west of the River Wye, covering 16,187 hectares (40,000 acres) between Llangurig and Rhayader, lie the great gathering grounds of the Elan Valley reservoirs, built to serve the thirsty industrial towns of the West Midlands. Ten miles to the west is now the enormous Tywi Forest, straddling the valley of the River Tywi, while to the south the Irfon Forest does likewise for the River Irfon.

Between the Elan gathering grounds and these great conifer forests is Abergwesyn Common, which has survived as open unfenced country among spruce plantations because its commoners graze it extensively and had registered their legal rights to do so. Its 6,677 hectares (16,500 acres) run for 12 miles west from Newbridge-on-Wye.

Walking is difficult, as the ground is boggy, tussocky and largely trackless, so much of the common's peaceful wilderness is only seen by grazing sheep. Its undisturbed quietness means that ravens, kites and buzzards can be found, as well as bog plants and insects.

An 8-mile walk from Llanwrthwi in the Wye Valley leads up to the 600-metre (1,968-foot) summit of Y Gamriw, south-east to Drum-ddu and back, with unforgettable views north to Plynlimon and south to the Brecon Beacons. Streams tumble off the common into the River Irfon, to the west, and the walk from there up Drygarn Fawr, on the common's northern boundary, opens a wide prospect over the vast grassy wastes above the reservoirs.

Acorn Bank Garden CUMBRIA

Just north of Temple Sowerby, 6 miles east of Penrith on the A66 [445 H4]

This little garden on the north side of the Eden Valley is set below the bleak moors of the Pennines, the peaty heights of Cross Fell rising to almost 915 metres (3,000 feet) only a few miles to the north. On a little bluff above the fast-flowing Crowdundle Beck sits the old manor house, a welcoming building of warm red sandstone.

The heart of Acorn Bank is the seventeenth-century walled garden to the south-east of the house, now planted as an orchard with apples, pears, medlars and quinces. In spring the long grass beneath the trees is alive with wild flowers, including the double wood anemone, the yellow wild tulip and the pheasant's eye narcissus, while in May heavy blossom weighs down the cherry avenue which bisects the orchard. Espaliered fruit trees interspersed with clematis and climbing roses line the walls. A gateway leads south-west into the walled herb garden, where 250 species of medicinal and culinary herbs have been established in the last twenty years, ranging from balm and the gentle evening primrose to the more sinister hemlock and opium poppy, and to such oddities as gipsywort, used by gipsies to darken their skin.

One of the most tranquil parts of the garden is the beautiful wooded bank falling steeply to the little beck, covered with the ancient oaks which gave the house its name and which now provide shelter for a wildflower and bird reserve. Over 60 varieties of daffodil are planted here.

Although the old walled garden was first laid out in the seventeenth century, it was much restored in the 1930s by Dorothy Una Ratcliffe, the Yorkshire travel writer and folk historian, and her second husband, Captain Noel McGrigor Phillips. Dorothy Ratcliffe created the reserve on the bank above the stream and was responsible for introducing the ornamental iron gates which add so much to the charm of the garden. The Trust established the now famous herb collection, thought to be the largest in the north of England.

Alderley Edge CHESHIRE

On south-east of Alderley Edge, 4½ miles north-west of Macclesfield, astride the B5087 [445 I7]

In a countryside which is a dormitory for Manchester and Stockport, the red sandstone ridge of Alderley Edge rises up sharply to form an escarpment at 183 metres (600 feet), giving views north to Wilmslow and the South Lancashire plain. To the south the hill, wooded with beech and pine, drops gently back to the rich pastures of Cheshire.

Building would have encompassed the Edge had it not belonged to the Stanleys of Alderley. Although it was originally common land, Lord Stanley planted the area from 1745, and enclosed it with hedges in 1779, but always allowed access to the people of Manchester who thronged here on high days and holidays. In 1938 the Stanley estates were sold, and with great public spirit the 89 hectares (220 acres) of the Edge were bought by the Misses Pilkington,

A display of opium poppies set against the mellow brick of Acorn Bank's 17th-century walled garden.

Beech woodland on the sandstone escarpment of Alderley Edge.

Alfriston Clergy House in a dilapidated state in 1893; three years later it was the first building to be acquired by the infant National Trust.

Allen Banks and Staward Gorge
NORTHUMBERLAND

3 miles west of Haydon Bridge, ½ mile south of the A69
[445 H3]

The Allen, one of the fast-flowing rivers that drains the high Northumbrian moors, tumbles into the Tyne through a deep ravine. Mature deciduous woodland – a mix of beech, oak, sweet chestnut and ash – clinging to the banks is threaded with a network of paths, with a suspension bridge to take visitors over the peaty waters of the river. The walks and much of the planting date from the eighteenth and nineteenth centuries, when the area was laid out as part of the pleasure grounds of Ridley Hall. To the south, where the Allen races through Staward Gorge, the terrain is wilder and contains the dramatic ruins of Staward Pele, a fortified medieval tower-house. There are extensive views from here and also from the walk leading out onto the open landscape of the Pennines, while there are deer and woodland birds to be seen amongst the trees.

Anglesey GWYNEDD

Off the North Wales coast, approached by either the Britannia or Telford suspension bridges, Bangor [444 E7–F7]

At the north-west tip of Anglesey, Mynydd-y-Garn overlooks the Trust's 6 miles of coast from Clegir Mawr in Holyhead Bay, north round Carmel Head and east to Cemlyn. The view south-eastward is right across the island to the mountains of Snowdon.

The coast is wonderfully varied, with little beaches, rocky inlets and islands, a salt-blasted pine wood, remains of copper mines, the Skerries reef and lighthouse offshore, and the pool behind the pebble beach in Cemlyn Bay, where the five species of tern which breed in Britain have all been spotted.

Anglesey Abbey CAMBRIDGESHIRE

In the village of Lode, 6 miles north-east of Cambridge on the B1102 [443 J3]

An interest in horse racing led Huttleston Broughton, later 1st Lord Fairhaven, to purchase Anglesey Abbey in 1926. A typical stone Jacobean manor house with mullioned windows and tall chimneys, it was conveniently placed for Newmarket and the stud he owned with his brother at Bury St Edmunds. Apart from the vaulted canon's parlour,

with help from Cheshire County Council, and later vested in the Trust.

Alderley Edge was once a prehistoric settlement. There is evidence of copper, lead and cobalt workings on the slopes, and mining tools as well as weapons and Bronze Age pottery have been unearthed.

Alfriston Clergy House EAST SUSSEX

4 miles north-east of Seaford, just east of the B2108, in Alfriston village [443 J6]

Despite its name, this low, timber-framed thatched building, delightfully situated on the green of a leafy South Downs village, was probably built for a well-to-do farmer, becoming known as the Clergy House because it was subsequently owned by the Church. However, it may have been the vicarage at some time in its history. Constructed in about 1350, it is typical of its date, with a central hall rising to the rafters flanked by two-storey blocks on either side, one containing the family's private apartments, the other service quarters. The hall has a rammed chalk floor of a kind local to Sussex, the lumps of chalk being laid and sealed with sour milk.

Bought in 1896 for only £10, Alfriston Clergy House was the first building to come to the Trust, and is one of only a very few fourteenth-century houses surviving in such a little-altered state. It is surrounded by a small cottage garden.

now the dining room, few traces remained of the Augustinian priory founded here in 1135 from which the house takes its name.

Over the next 40 years this comfortable gentleman's residence was transformed. Although his sporting pursuits were never neglected, Lord Fairhaven devoted most of his time and energy to collecting fine and decorative art, a passion he had inherited from his wealthy mother, the American heiress Cara Leyland Rogers. The result is an outstanding and wide-ranging collection of works of art, for which he adapted and extended the house. More remarkably, 40 hectares (98 acres) of unpromising fen were used to create an imaginative and individual garden.

The interior of the house is an Aladdin's cave of priceless furniture, silver, paintings, clocks, tapestries and statuary, seeming to include examples of every style and period from all the countries of the world. An inlaid Louis XV commode supporting a pair of oriental bronze candlesticks in the shape of deer stands below a Suffolk coastal scene, a rare seascape by Gainsborough. Close by, a Spanish seventeenth-century walnut table is used to display an Egyptian bronze cat dating from about 500 BC, two eighteenth-century mortars and a pair of silver Dutch tobacco boxes. It also holds a medieval wooden carving of Jerome and the lion, which depicts the beast looking up at the saint affectionately. With so many interesting and beautiful pieces set so close together, each one can only be fully appreciated by mentally isolating it from its companions.

Lord Fairhaven had a particular liking for nudes by the fashionable Victorian painter William Etty, about twenty of which now hang in the house. He also acquired a unique collection of views of Windsor, where he lived for a time in the Great Park. Displayed in the two-storey gallery he built on to the house in 1955, these paintings faithfully record changes in landscape and architecture over 350 years, ranging in style from the toy castle depicted in an early seventeenth-century canvas to William Daniell's mistily romantic view down the Long Walk. Many consider the jewels of the collection to be two superb paintings by Claude Lorraine, examples of the sublime landscapes which inspired the naturalistic gardens of the eighteenth century. In *The Landing of Aeneas*, each slave rowing the boat carrying the Trojan leader is an individual, two looking over their shoulders to see how far they are from the shore.

Whereas the sumptuousness and muted lighting of the house suggest exotic influences, the garden is quintessentially English. Like the great gardens of three centuries ago, it is conceived on a generous scale, a striking contrast to the inward-looking intimacy of the contemporary layouts at Sissinghurst and Hidcote (*see* pp.341 and 182). Majestic avenues and walks, such as the wide grassy ride lined by double rows of horse chestnuts which runs for half a mile to the west of the house, provide a geometric framework for areas of very different character. Some are sweeping compositions in trees and grass or grand set pieces, like the curved border in the herbaceous garden, a D-shaped plot giving a spectacular display in late June and July. Others are more intimate and enclosed, such as the small sheltered lawn where William Theed's *Narcissus* contemplates his image in the still waters of a pond, or the leafy secluded terrace circling the pool in the old quarry, with views to the picturesque water-mill on the River Lode (*see* p.228) at the northernmost tip of the garden. Recently, a mile-long circuit walk displaying plants that make their emphasis during the winter months was added to celebrate the centenary of the birth of Lord Fairhaven.

The wide-ranging collection at Anglesey Abbey includes 18th-century bird paintings by Charles Collins hung against linenfold panelling (below) and this delightful cat (above) set on an Italian pillar veneered with lapis lazuli.

A wide variety of trees, such as the planes, alders, elms, sycamores and willows lining the river, act as shelter belts and backdrops, while many rare and unusual species are displayed on the arboretum lawns, including the Hungarian oak, the Indian chestnut, the Judas tree and the Japanese hop hornbeam. Changes in perspective and scale are enhanced by carefully planned contrasts between the formal and the naturalistic, as if Lord Fairhaven deliberately set out to create his garden from the best of the past. 'Capability' Brown would have approved of the Temple Lawn, where 'islands' of trees are subtly sited to enhance rather than destroy the sweep of the grass and planted to give a range of tone and texture, from the grey and gold of willows, elder and privet to the red and purple of violet willow and purple cotinus. In the centre of the lawn two recumbent lions guard the entrance to a circular yew enclosure surrounding ten Corinthian columns of Portland stone.

Statues, urns and other classical features are used throughout the garden to close vistas and punctuate lawns and avenues. Father Time presides over the Hyacinth Garden, his lichen-stained figure bending over the sundial as if to urge the hours on; haughty stone griffins greet visitors to the Dahlia Garden. Along the grassy Emperor's Walk, over 402 metres (1,319 feet) long, twelve busts of Roman emperors on marble plinths are incongruously set against a wall of Norway spruce. And always there is the backdrop of the East Anglian sky, with towering cloudscapes forming and dissolving over the expanse of the Fens.

Antony CORNWALL

5 miles west of Plymouth via Torpoint car ferry, 2 miles north-west of Torpoint, north of the A384, 16 miles south-east of Liskeard, 15 miles east of Looe [442 C7]

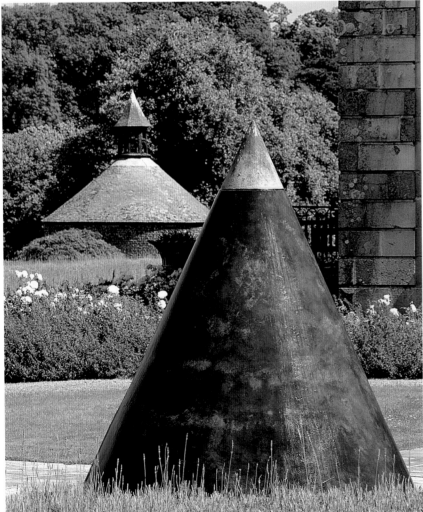

Antony stands at the end of the long neck of land forming the far south-east corner of Cornwall, an isolated peninsula bounded by the estuaries of the rivers Tamar and Lynher to the east and north and by the sea to the south. The best way of approaching Antony is by boat, as it has been for centuries, crossing to Cornwall by the car-ferry from Plymouth to Torpoint rather than taking the much longer route by road over the Tamar bridge.

The setting of the house is superb. The entrance front faces up a slight rise crowned by a wrought-iron screen, but at the back the ground falls away from a flight of terraces across a sweep of grass. In the distance attractively grouped clumps of trees frame glimpses of the Lynher and of the prodigious arches of Brunel's Saltash railway bridge crossing the Tamar estuary.

The Antony estate has been the property of the Carews, and their descendants the Pole-Carews and Carew Poles, since the early fifteenth century. The main block of the present house, a deceptively simple two-storey rect-angle faced with silver-grey stone, was built by Sir William Carew between 1718 and 1729. Red-brick colonnaded wings enclosing a courtyard on the south front were possibly added by the architect James Gibbs. Antony is a charming and entirely satisfying house, one of the best of its date in the West Country. It is not large: modest, oak-panelled rooms lead off the hall and upstairs there are only five principal bedrooms, the space for a sixth being taken up by the magnificent staircase.

Antony is also exceptional for the quality of its furnishings, many of which are contemporary with the house, and for the collection of family and other portraits, including works by Reynolds. Most memorable is the portrait of Charles I painted at his trial which hangs in the hall. The king is shown dressed in black wearing a large beaver hat, his sad eyes pouched with weariness. This is the last of a number of portraits which record Charles's final days and only here has the famous pointed beard turned grey. John Carew, who had sat in judgement on Charles, was himself executed at the Restoration. His tragic elder brother Alexander, whose portrait hangs in the library, suffered the same fate at the hands of the Parliamentarians, dying with a troubled and divided mind, uncertain which cause was right.

No such doubts assailed the historian Richard Carew, author of the great *Survey of Cornwall*, who inherited the estate in 1564. His striking portrait, painted in 1586 when he was 32, faces Charles across the hall. Two years later he must have seen the Armada sail up the Channel along the coast for which, as deputy lieutenant of the county, he was responsible.

Antony's landscaped setting, with tree-framed lawns sweeping down to the water and views across to the opposite bank, is partly due to Humphry Repton, who was consulted in 1792 and produced one of his earliest Red Books at the house. But the clumps of ilexes framing the grass were planted a few years earlier, and some significant specimen trees, such as a cork oak and black walnut, may date from the same time. The terraces above the lawns were once planted with parterres and there is a more formal garden to the west. Here, clipped yew hedges a long walk punctuated by a Burmese bell, one of a number of eastern ornaments acquired by General Sir Reginald Pole-Carew, and forms the tall wigwam-like shape, originally intended as a yew arbour, which rises conspicuously to one side.

Another axial walk following the wall of the old kitchen garden is bordered by espaliered fruit trees and a row of magnolias. An arch in the yew hedge leads to the sheltered flower garden, which provides a colourful summer display at the same time as the roses on the terraces are in bloom, and there is also a knot garden with interweaving lines of box and germander. An eighteenth-century dovecote squats by the house, some striking modern sculptures were commissioned by Sir Richard Carew Pole, who lives in the house, and hidden in a tangle of woodland beside the Lynher (not owned by the Trust) is a bath house of 1784, with a plunge bath.

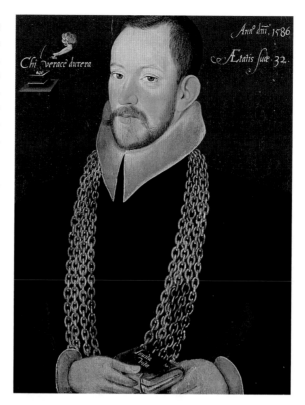

Among the family portraits at Antony is this painting of Richard Carew, dated 1586 (left). As deputy lieutenant of Cornwall, Carew was responsible for defences against the Armada and he wrote a great survey of the county, one of the first of its kind, which gives a portrait of Cornwall in Elizabethan times. In recent years the garden at Antony (opposite below) has been enlivened by a stainless-steel fountain by William Pye, its conical shape chiming in with the 18th-century dovecote beyond.

Opposite above: This bearded Pan, an Italian herm of *c.*1850, is part of an extensive collection of historic sculpture in the gardens of Anglesey Abbey.

Ardress House CO. ARMAGH

7 miles from Portadown on the B28 Moy road, 5 miles from Moy, 3 miles from Loughgall, intersection 13 on the M1
[444 C4]

Ardress House is not quite what it seems. The long two-storey entrance front with an impressive array of Georgian sash windows is partly a sham, one end of the façade being nothing more than a wall with false openings added in the interests of symmetry, while the pedimented portico giving dignity and importance to the front door is not placed centrally between the windows on either side. Both features betray the rather piecemeal approach to the gentrification of what was originally a simple seventeenth-century Irish farmhouse, one room deep.

Ardress's finest feature is the elegant late eighteenth-century drawing room on the garden front, which seems to have strayed from a Dublin town house. Adam-style decoration in muted greens, pinks and yellows dominates the room, the central plaster medallion on the ceiling being the focus of an intricate pattern of intersecting circles and arcs. Whirls of foliage here are echoed in more extravagant loops and chains framing the oval plaques on the walls. Plaster cherubs along the frieze stand with the right leg

Above: The entrance hall of the Argory is dominated by the cast-iron stove, topped by an urn, which heated the centre of the house. There is still no electricity here and the hanging lamp, originally oil-powered, is lit by gas.

Below: Originally an Irish farmhouse, Ardress House was gentrified with sash windows and the curving screen walls which flank the garden front.

crossed behind the left, except in one corner of the room, where the stance is reversed. The work of the Dublin stuccadore Michael Stapleton, known for his magnificent interiors in the Irish capital, this decoration was carried out for the architect George Ensor some ten years after his marriage to the heiress of Ardress in 1760. Having executed several commissions in Dublin himself, Ensor probably knew Stapleton well.

George Ensor II's additions to the house, including the extended entrance façade and the curving screen walls flanking the garden front, are less happy. The cavernous dining room below the library in which he may have written his many provocative works on politics and religion is reached only by a door in the yard at the back of the house. It is now hung with paintings from the collection of the Earl of Castle Stewart, including a rare signed picture by the seventeenth-century Flemish artist J. Myts. The diminutive haloed figure of Our Lord on the road to Emmaus is portrayed in a Northern European setting, with gentlemen in frock coats and a cluster of steep-roofed half-timbered houses in the little town in the distance.

French windows lead out to the lawn which slopes down to a sunken rose garden. Behind the house outbuildings set round a cobbled yard are filled with reminders of the working farm Ardress once was, including a dairy, a smithy, a cow byre and a threshing barn complete with horse-powered thresher.

The Argory CO. ARMAGH

4 miles from Moy, 3 miles from the M1, exit 14 [444 B4]

The barrister Walter McGeough Bond's decision in the 1820s to build on his newly inherited land at Derrycaw was influenced by the terms of a very curious will. He and his three sisters had been left the bulk of their father's fortune, their unfortunate elder brother inheriting only £400, but Walter was not allowed to live at Drumsill, the family house, while two of his sisters remained unmarried. He was wise to provide himself with an alternative establishment, as two of his sisters died in Drumsill, rich and eccentric old spinsters.

Walter McGeough Bond's house is a modest two-storey stone building set on a rise overlooking the Blackwater river, its plain Neo-classical façades given added interest by the lengthened centre windows added on the west and south in the late nineteenth century. The Argory was designed by the relatively obscure Arthur and John Williamson, who may have been employed on the recommendation of the much more famous Dublin architect Francis Johnston and whose work betrays traces of Johnston's influence.

The largely original interiors powerfully evoke the lifestyle of the Irish gentry during the early nineteenth century, with mahogany furniture, sumptuous curtains and upholstery, potted plants, an abundance of cushions and *objets* and fur-draped chairs in the drawing room. The family traditionally entertained at tea-time and the white cloth on the dining-room table is set with china and silver as if awaiting guests. Tea was also occasionally taken at the round walnut table in the organ lobby on the first floor, dominated by the magnificent instrument Walter commissioned from James Bishop of London in 1822. Three surviving 6-foot barrels hold a selection of music chosen on the advice of Samuel Sebastian Wesley, nephew of the founder of Methodism, a mixture of suitably uplifting hymn tunes such as 'See, the conquering hero comes' and excerpts from *The Magic Flute*. The instrument is also playable manually.

Personal possessions in the bedrooms suggest the family has only just left. A wardrobe is filled with Lady Bond's early twentieth-century outfits, including fashionable narrow-waisted jackets and tiny Italian shoes. Another holds her hats. Ugly gas lamps disguised as candles on the dressing-tables are examples of the Argory's early nineteenth-century lighting arrangements, the most impressive being the six fittings with pale green conical shades which hang low over the billiard table. Originally oil, the fittings were subsequently converted to gas, run from the plant still to be seen in the stable yard, installed by the Sunbeam Acetylene Gas Company of Belfast in 1906 at a cost of £250. Although the gas lighting has not been restored, there is still no electricity in the house.

A little Victorian rose garden, with small-flowered polyantha and China roses in box-edged beds, leads into the pleasure ground sloping down to meadows fringing the Blackwater river. There is a pair of garden pavilions, of the same date as the house, linked by a long curving walk. A wide lawn is studded with two yew arbours and a handkerchief tree and framed by borders planted with a collection of shrubs and other plants raised or introduced by Leslie Slinger of the Slieve Donard Nursery.

Arlington Court DEVON

7 miles north-east of Barnstaple on the A39 [442 C6]

The plain, grey stone façades of this Neo-classical house are no preparation for the cluttered Victorian interior, with boldly patterned and coloured wallpaper, mahogany furniture and display cabinets overflowing with shells, snuffboxes, model ships, pewter and precious objects. The setting of this Aladdin's cave was created in 1820 for Colonel John Chichester by the Barnstaple architect Thomas Lee, who had just completed the Wellington

Monument in Somerset (*see* p.422). But the collections themselves are all the work of Rosalie Chichester, the last of the Chichesters of Arlington, who lived here for 84 years until her death in 1949.

Only child of the flamboyant and extravagant Bruce Chichester, who created the opulent staircase hall hung with yachting pictures more suited to a gentleman's club than a private house, Rosalie had been taken on two world cruises in her father's schooner *Erminia* before she reached her teens. Perhaps fired by these early experiences, she was always an enthusiastic traveller, one of the many delightful photographs on display showing her with her diminutive companion in New Zealand, both of them in sensible shoes and heavy suits with skirts down to their ankles. She was also a collector, acquiring tea caddies, candle snuffers and paperweights to add to the Pacific shells and other mementoes she brought back from her travels. Although her stuffed birds, Maori skirts and African clubs are no longer in the house, Arlington is still full of her treasures, with her favourite piece, a slightly malevolent red amber elephant from China, prominently displayed in the White Drawing Room, one of three sunny rooms on the south front which form a long gallery. In the ante-room next door hangs the mystical watercolour by William Blake which was found on top of a cupboard at Arlington in 1949.

On the first-floor landing another watercolour, of Miss Chichester's parrot Polly, reflects her passionate love of all living plants and creatures. This undoubtedly eccentric lady kept budgerigars and canaries in brass cages in the house and allowed her parrots to fly free, causing incalculable damage to the curtains. The Jacob sheep and Shetland ponies still in the park are the descendants of those she established as part of a wildlife refuge.

Shady lawns surrounding the house are planted with specimen trees, including an ash collection. Some distance away is a small formal garden laid out in 1865, where a delightful conservatory against a high brick wall at one end looks down over three grass terraces and a fountain pool guarded by metal herons, the birds of the Chichester crest. A more informal note is struck by the wilderness pond hidden in a huge clump of rhododendrons further down the hill and by the walk which threads its way to the lake on the River Yeo half a mile below the house, where two great piers are all that was built of the suspension bridge Rosalie's father had planned to carry his grand new drive. He also constructed the imposing colonnaded stable block west of the house, beyond the little parish church filled with Chichester memorials. With the images of the

Above left: This period hip bath at the Argory is in one of the rooms that formed the master bedroom suite in the late 19th century.

The Victorian interiors of Arlington Court display the exotic collections of the eccentric Rosalie Chichester, who lived in the house for 84 years. Among her treasures is a display of model ships (top), to which the Trust has added a likeness of *Gypsy Moth IV*, the tiny boat in which Rosalie's nephew Sir Francis Chichester made his solo voyage round the world in 1967. The portrait of Rosalie as a child with her mother (above), from *c.*1870, is one of many family photographs on show in the house.

family photographs still strongly in mind, it is easy to imagine Miss Rosalie seated in one of the well-preserved carriages now displayed here, although the collection, one of the finest in the country, was brought together after the Trust took over the house.

Arlington is the centre of a thriving agricultural estate, as it has been ever since the Chichester family came here in the sixteenth century. Hidden within the farmland is a 2½-mile stretch of the thickly wooded valley of the River Yeo, a haven for wildlife, as Miss Rosalie intended. Early or late in the day there may be glimpses of wild red deer among the trees from the rides and paths along the Yeo and up the two re-entrant valleys leading to North Woolley and Coombshead; a hide has been erected on the lake below the house so the wild duck and other birds which congregate here can be observed without disturbance. Neglected by Miss Rosalie because she hated felling trees, the woods have now been rejuvenated by the Trust.

Ascott BUCKINGHAMSHIRE

½ mile east of Wing, 2 miles south-west of Leighton Buzzard, on south side of the A418 [443 H4]

Entrepreneurial talent rarely passes from generation to generation, but Mayer Amschel Rothschild (1744–1812), who founded the family banking business in Frankfurt during the Napoleonic Wars, was blessed with five sons whose drive and ambition matched his own. While one inherited his father's mantle, the others dispersed to Paris, Naples, Vienna and London to set up branches of the firm. The wealth generated by the activities of this extraordinary clan financed the collection in this rambling neo-Jacobean house overlooking the Vale of Aylesbury as well as the more flamboyant magnificence of Waddesdon a few miles away (*see* p.411).

Ascott is the creation of Leopold de Rothschild, great-grandson of the founder of the family fortunes and son of Baron Lionel, the first Jewish MP. The little Jacobean half-timbered farmhouse he took over in 1876 is now buried in the gabled ranges added by the architect George Devey in the years that followed, transforming the house into a massively overgrown cottage. But, despite Ascott's size, the rooms are pleasingly domestic in scale, with the intimate atmosphere of a beautifully furnished private house.

Predominantly Dutch and English paintings include Aelbert Cuyp's panoramic *View of Dordrecht*, its wide shallow canvas filling one wall of the low-ceilinged dining room. The town lies on the left, a low sun lighting up a row of gabled houses on the glassy river and giving a warm glow to the clouds heaped overhead. A faint mark in the centre of the painting shows where the canvas was once divided to be sold in two halves. Gainsborough's supposed portrait of the Duchess of Richmond, her flaming red curls set off by the silky sheen of her blue satin dress, is one of a number of fine English portraits at Ascott. There are three of Stubbs's distinctive horse studies, including the only known canvas in which he shows mares without any foals, and a major work from the Italian Renaissance, Andrea del Sarto's arresting *Madonna and Child with St John*. Elegant eighteenth-century English furniture, such as the two oval pie-crust tables and the walnut and mahogany chairs covered with tapestry and needlework in the library, contrast with the contemporary French pieces elsewhere.

Leopold's son Anthony, besides acquiring paintings and English furniture, also introduced the oriental porcelain now such a prominent feature of the house. This starts with ceramics from the Han (206BC–AD220), Tang tufa grotto adds a romantic note at one end. The highlight of a wealth of topiary and clipped hedges is the giant sundial set out at the east end of one of the terraces. Roman figures in box encase the central egg-shaped gnomon of golden yew grafted on to Irish stock, while an outer circle of yew spells out the legend 'Light and shade by turn but love always', an echo of the Victorian proverbs carved on a cornice in the house. An alternative route back to the car park leads down a wide serpentine walk to the sheltered lily pond.

Ashdown House OXFORDSHIRE

2½ miles south of Ashbury, 3½ miles north of Lambourn, on west side of the B4000 [443 G5]

Set high up on the rolling, windswept Berkshire Downs, some 2 miles from the nearest village, this bizarre seventeenth-century building most closely resembles a gigantic doll's house. Diminished by distance, it looks as if the front might come off to reveal a series of beautifully furnished miniature rooms. This air of unreality derives from the square plan with four almost identical honey and cream façades and from the fact that the house is extraordinarily tall and narrow, its height increased by the crowning cupola. It is as if one of the contemporary town houses that fight for ground space along the canals of Amsterdam had been suddenly uprooted and put down in this isolated spot. Ashdown would look even more strange were it not for the fact that its starkness is softened and broadened by detached pavilions on either side, possibly added some twenty years after the main block was built.

Ashdown was created for William, 1st Lord Craven, in about 1663. One of the richest figures of the seventeenth century, Lord Craven is remembered particularly for his devotion to Charles I's unlucky sister, Elizabeth of Bohemia, who reigned for only one winter before being forced into exile by the defeat of her husband's forces by the Habsburg Emperor. There is a family tradition that Lord Craven chose the site of his house so Elizabeth would have a refuge from plague-ridden London, but sadly she contracted a fatal disease without ever seeing the completed building.

Today Lord Craven's devotion to the Winter Queen is reflected in the portraits of her and her family which the Treasury presented to the Trust from the Craven Collection in 1968 to hang in the hall and on the staircase rising the height of the building. With three exceptions, all the works are by, or after, two Dutch artists, Michel

(618–906) and Sung (906–1280) dynasties, with the cream of the collection, in deep rich colours, from the Ming (1368–1644) and K'ang Hsi (1662–1722) periods. These were the centuries which produced sophisticated, three-colour ware in vibrant shades of blue, purple and burnt yellow, such as the elegant vases decorated with flowing chrysanthemums.

The extensive Victorian gardens were laid out by the leading Chelsea nursery of James Veitch & Sons. An abundance of evergreen trees and shrubs probably reflects the fact that Leopold originally intended to use Ascott mainly in the winter, as a hunting lodge. Terraced lawns with panoramic views to the Chilterns fall away from the house, planted with widely spaced specimen and ornamental trees, predominantly chosen for their coloured and variegated foliage. Clipped yew hedges and a high retaining wall like a ha-ha beyond the lawns conceal an unexpected formal garden. A long herbaceous walk ending in a colonnaded pavilion looks over the circular lawn framing Waldo Story's Venus fountain, with winged seahorses pulling the goddess's shell-chariot. Another Story fountain crowns the long, narrow Dutch garden, where circular beds are planted for summer show and a

Miereveldt and Gerard van Honthorst, echoing the strong associations of the exterior.

The architect of the house is not known, but it was probably built by William Winde, who spent his early years with exiled Royalists in Holland and would have seen similar buildings in Leiden, Amsterdam and The Hague. The west front of the house is now set off by a formal parterre based on a seventeenth-century engraving, such as Winde might have designed. The twists and curves of box and gravel are best seen from the roof and from here there are also spectacular views over the woodland round the house and to the Berkshire Downs beyond. Long breaks cutting through the trees mark the north-south ride which shows clearly on Kip's engraving of 1724.

Ashleworth Tithe Barn
GLOUCESTERSHIRE

6 miles north of Gloucester, 1¼ miles east of Hartpury on the A417, on west bank of River Severn, south-east of Ashleworth [442 F4]

Ashleworth barn stands in a group of picturesque buildings on the banks of the River Severn, only metres from a riverside inn and a fine medieval house and just west of the largely fifteenth-century parish church. Although smaller than Great Coxwell or Middle Littleton (*see* pp.167 and 242), this 38.5-metre (126-foot) limestone building with two projecting wagon porches is still impressive, an immense stone-tiled roof supported on timber trusses stretching the width of the barn. It was built in about 1500, probably by the canons of St Augustine's, Bristol, who were lords of the manor here.

Ashleworth Tithe Barn, built of local limestone and with a stone-tiled roof, dates from *c*.1500.

Attingham Park SHROPSHIRE

4 miles south-east of Shrewsbury, on Telford road [442 E2]

Few family mottoes can be more apposite than that of Noel Hill, 1st Lord Berwick: 'Let wealth be his who knows its use.' This wily politician, who obtained his peerage through expedient loyalty to William Pitt the Younger, poured the fortune he inherited into this grandiose classical house, set, like Wallington (*see* p.414), in full view of a public road, from which it was devised to look as magnificent as possible.

Designed in 1782 by the individual Scottish architect George Steuart, and a rare survival of his work, Attingham consists of a main three-storey block linked by colonnaded corridors to pavilions on either side, with a classical portico running the full height of the house on the entrance front. Seen from the bridge taking the road over the River Tern, the façade stretches 122 metres (400 feet) from pavilion to pavilion, while inside there are 80 rooms, an unusually large number for a house of this period. The layout of the interior is equally singular, with the rooms on the west side, including the library and dining room, making up a set of masculine apartments, and those on the east, including the drawing room, a set of feminine rooms.

On the 1st Lord's untimely death at the early age of 44, Attingham passed successively to his two elder sons, who were responsible for the splendid Regency interiors which are now such a feature of the house. Acquisitions during a lengthy Grand Tour in Italy formed the basis of an extensive collection built up by the 2nd Lord, who also commissioned John Nash to add the grand picture gallery in 1805–7. One of the first to be built in a country house, this room is notable for the revolutionary use of curved cast-iron ribs supporting the windows in the roof, a forerunner of the design of the Crystal Palace. Although the paintings for which the gallery was designed were largely dispersed in the sale following the 2nd Lord's bankruptcy in 1827, the mixture of Italianate landscapes and copies of Old Masters now hanging two and three deep conjures up the splendour of the original collection. A pair of Neapolitan landscapes by Philipp Hackert (1737–1807) includes a view of Pompeii showing the small extent of the excavated area at the end of the eighteenth century and the garlanded vines still seen in this part of Italy. The Regency flavour is similarly strong in the dining room, bold red walls with moulded panels picked out in gold being overshadowed by the display on the ceiling, where a lacy plaster wreath of vine leaves stands out dramatically white against the background red. Frail tendrils of foliage and medallions depicting cherubs set against rose-tinted clouds on the domed ceiling of the tiny boudoir are from an earlier age, part of one of the most delicate late eighteenth-century schemes to survive in England.

The paintings and furniture now seen in the house were collected by the diplomatist 3rd Lord – described by Byron as the only Excellence who was really excellent – during his 25 years in Italy. He was responsible for the elegant pale-blue drawing room filled with white and gold Italian furniture, some of which may have come from Napoleon's sister's Neapolitan palace, and for the glittering silver displayed in the old wine cellars, once stocked with some 900 bottles of sherry, port and madeira.

Parkland dotted with mature oaks, elms, beeches and pines slopes gently down to the Tern. The initial layout, of 1769–72, was by Thomas Leggett, but the planting schemes reflect the hand of Humphry Repton, who produced a Red Book for Attingham in 1797. A grove of Lebanon cedars marks the start of the Mile Walk, bright with wild flowers in spring and with rhododendrons later in the year.

Avebury WILTSHIRE

6 miles west of Marlborough, 1 mile north of the A4 Bath road, at junction of the A361 and the B4003 [443 G5]

The picturesque village of Avebury, set in a shallow valley below the ridge of the Marlborough Downs, lies at the centre of a rich and diverse prehistoric landscape. Over about 1,500 years, between *c.*3500 and *c.*2000BC, Neolithic peoples transformed this open downland with an impressive sequence of works. Most obvious is the great stone circle now enmeshed with the village, like some surreal sculpture park, with a massive bank and ditch enclosing the remains of a ring of sarsens. Nearly a mile in circumference, this vast composition can be seen as a whole only from a hill above the village; at close quarters, its extent is obscured by buildings and trees. The bank, originally measuring 15 metres (50 feet) from crest to ditch, screens Avebury from the world. Built only with the aid of antler picks and ox shoulder-blade shovels, such as those now displayed in the little site museum, Avebury must represent tens of thousands of hours of labour. The stones are unworked, unlike those at Stonehenge, but there were originally 98 in the main circle, plus two smaller circles, and the largest boulders are some 6 metres (20 feet) high. Over the centuries, many of the stones were broken up and incorporated in the village, with grassy hollows marking

A marble statue of Venus, a copy of a sculpture by Canova, presides over the elegant drawing room at Attingham. The mirror behind her reflects a corner of the Adam-style ceiling and one of the Italian paintings – a landscape by Philipp Hackert, a German artist who worked in Naples).

where they once stood, and in the superstitious Middle Ages the circle was deliberately buried. Most of the 30 or so stones seen standing today were re-erected in the 1930s by the innovative amateur archaeologist Alexander Keiller, who bought several of the Avebury sites.

From the top of the bank, the north-east horizon is closed by the bushy crest of Fyfield Down, from where the sarsens – the remains of a sheet of hard sandstone which once capped this landscape – were dragged 2 miles or so down to Avebury; there are views over the rounded humps of Bronze Age barrows, their outlines transformed into giant hedgehogs by nineteenth-century plantings of beech trees; and, to the south-east, the remains of what was once an impressive stone avenue, originally consisting of about a hundred pairs of stones, meanders gently uphill into the distance.

Most of the outlying monuments are more elusive than the circle. The course of the Avenue leads 1½ miles from the village to a field on the ridge of the Downs by the main A4 Marlborough road, where a series of low concrete blocks and stubby posts marks out the tight concentric circles of

The sarsen stones which make up the great stone circle at Avebury were collected from the downland round about and were probably dragged to the site on wooden rollers. They were used in their natural state, without being shaped in any way, and it seems as if the builders were particular about the shapes they selected, favouring stones which were columnar or triangular.

what is known as the Sanctuary, originally a composition in wood and stone thought to date from *c.*3250BC. The long-distance prehistoric route known as the Ridgeway starts here, three-quarters of a mile of which, together with a group of seven Bronze Age barrows, is now in Trust hands. Beside the A4 too, seen from a viewing platform by the road, is the enigmatic Silbury Hill. Set strangely low in the landscape, in the valley of the Kennet, this huge man-made mound, the largest in Europe, is a steep-sided grassy pudding, its purpose unknown. Standing 42 metres (130 feet) high, and thought to have taken 18 million man-hours to build, it is as arresting now as it must have been when first constructed, *c.*2700BC. On the crest of the Downs just to the south, reached by a stiff 10-minute climb from the road, is the atmospheric West Kennet long barrow. This tapering grassy mound was a place of burial, in constant use for perhaps a thousand years from *c.*3700BC. At the east end, confronting visitors as they reach the top of the hill, is the opening to the interior, where massive sarsens – one, flanking the entrance, showing the grooves of Neolithic axe sharpening – frame a central passage and five burial chambers. It seems the dead were buried here mostly in a disarticulated state, after the flesh had gone, and that those honoured in this way represented a select group within prehistoric society, marked out by birth rather than achievement. A wall of sarsens almost blocking the entrance was a later addition, after the barrow was no longer in use. In the gathering dusk of a late winter's afternoon this is a haunting place, stirring the imagination.

Most elusive are the Neolithic remains on grassy Windmill Hill, to the north-west of the village. On the northern side of the gently swelling summit low bumps and indentations in the sward and, in one place, a well-defined ditch and bank, the result of excavations by Keiller and others, mark the site of a large causewayed camp, originally consisting of three concentric banks and ditches. These earthworks were never impressive and were frequently broken by the causewayed approaches which give the monument its name. Unlike the later Iron Age hill-forts, this was not a defended position, but a place where Neolithic farmers came to trade, gossip and make contacts. Excavations have found remains of young animals, nuts, berries and ears of grain, suggesting the site was in use almost throughout the year. Windmill Hill is the most insubstantial of the Neolithic sites, but the views are well worth the climb: the village is half obscured by trees in the valley below, but beyond it, to the south, is the hard outline of Silbury, while to north and north-west is a panorama over sparsely populated countryside, with the crest of Cherhill Down marked by the assertive finger of the Lansdowne Monument (*see* p.89) closing the western horizon. The Trust now owns or manages all these prehistoric sites, and has devised a series of walks, some taking only an hour or so, others involving half a day or longer, round the village and out into the wider landscape.

With the exception of the Iron Age, Avebury has links

with almost every period of settled man. A Roman road, a section of which is now owned by the Trust, ran past Silbury Hill, and an early Saxon and medieval village stood close to the Kennet, with the church between it and the pagan circle. In the centuries following the Reformation, as the mists of superstition gradually cleared, the village crept eastwards into the circle, where the narrow street is now lined with some fine eighteenth-century houses. The Trust owns most of this later development, and also the old manor on an originally monastic site outside the circle bank. A charming classical gateway is approached through what was the manor farmyard, past a thatched and weather-boarded great barn and a moss-encrusted sixteenth-century dovecote. Set back across a stretch of grass is a long, asymmetrical, many-gabled range, with tall chimneys and some stone-mullioned windows. This is the eastern wing of a rambling building set round three sides of a small courtyard, which developed from a medieval hall house. The earliest part, facing south, has a delightful eighteenth-century façade, with a parapet instead of the original gables and a classical porch with fluted pilasters. The eastern range is partly an addition of 1548, with the later incorporation of an old brew-house at the northern end, while the western side of the house is a 1920s library in the same spirit as the medieval and Tudor building, with a pretty flight of stone steps leading down into the garden.

The picturesque assemblage is the backdrop to the extensive compartmental garden developed by Colonel and Mrs Jenner, who lived here from 1900 to 1935 and restored the house, adding on the library. Using an existing framework of medieval, Tudor and eighteenth-century walls in stone and mellow red brick, Mrs Jenner devised a series of formal, strongly architectural layouts, each different but all featuring clipped yew and box. A rose garden with box-edged beds is overlooked by the pinnacled tower of St James's church just beyond the garden wall; topiary yew surrounds the orchard, newly planted with Wiltshire varieties of apples; and there is a yew walk and a serene pond garden, where geometric topiary echoing the designs of the plaster ceilings inside the house encloses a rectangular pool. In season, lilies flower profusely here. Most memorable, perhaps, is a long half moon of yew with box buttressing set against a gently curving, lichen-spotted brick wall.

This is a garden of surprises and unexpected vistas, with echoes of Lytes Cary (see p.236), where Mrs Jenner probably had a hand in her brother-in-law's design, and of Sissinghurst (see p.341), whose chatelaine, Vita Sackville-West, was a frequent visitor to Avebury.

Badbury Rings DORSET

4 miles north-west of Wimborne Minster, 6 miles south-east of Blandford Forum, immediately east of the B3080 [442 F6]

This is one of the larger and more impressive Iron Age hill-forts in Britain, with three tiers of concentric ramparts enclosing a wooded interior. From the air, Badbury looks like a coral atoll, with an 'island' of trees surrounded by chalky 'reefs'. Bronze Age burial mounds and field systems surround the hill-fort and Badbury was also of significance in Roman times, lying at the junction of routes from Bath, Old Sarum and Dorchester.

The chalk grassland is rich in butterfly-attracting downland plants, among them the greater butterfly, frog and bee orchids, bastard toadflax, adder's tongue fern and knapweed broom rape. The clump of trees which is now such a feature of the fort was first planted back in the eighteenth century and has been re-established in recent years.

Badbury Rings is part of the extensive estate which came to the Trust with the seventeenth-century mansion of Kingston Lacy (*see* p.204).

Baddesley Clinton WARWICKSHIRE

¾ mile west of the A41 Warwick–Birmingham road, at Chadwick End, 7½ miles north-west of Warwick, 15 miles south-east of central Birmingham [443 G2]

This perfect medieval manor house set in an ancient park lies in a remnant of the Forest of Arden. Although only 15 miles south of Birmingham, the surrounding countryside still has an essentially medieval character, criss-crossed by a network of sunken lanes and with the waves of ridge and furrow visible in fields now under grass.

The present house, built round three sides of a courtyard, dates from the fifteenth century, but it is encircled by a thirteenth-century moat, all that remains of the farmstead built here when the forest was first cleared. The only way in is over the two-arched, red-brick, eighteenth-century bridge which leads to the crenellated gatehouse. Grey walls punctuated with mullioned windows fall sheer to the water on either side, tall red-brick Elizabethan chimneys forming splashes of colour against the roof. Despite its guarded appearance, this is not a forbidding place. Its small panelled rooms filled with mostly seventeenth- and eighteenth-century oak furniture are intimate and homely. The house is a rare survival from the world of the lesser gentry.

Baddesley Clinton is a remarkable survival. From the 15th century until 1980, when it came to the Trust, this romantic moated house was lived in by generation after generation of the Ferrers family, who managed to hang on to the manor, its contents and the estate, despite financial pressures. In 1939, when the house was first offered for sale, the estate lands were the same as those shown on a map of 1699.

For most of its history Baddesley Clinton has been connected with the Ferrers family, who lived here from the early sixteenth century until 1939. The remarkable Elizabethan antiquary, Henry Ferrers, did much to enlarge and embellish the house he inherited, introducing rich oak panelling and highly decorated overmantels in many of the rooms. He also emblazoned his descent through several generations in rich armorial glass. He was the first of many in his family to suffer for his Roman Catholicism and this remote house became a haven for recusants in the late sixteenth century, when Catholics were persecuted with severity. Looking at the hiding place formed out of an old drain in the kitchen – one of three in the house – it is difficult to believe that nine men evaded capture here in October 1591, standing motionless with their feet in water for four hours. The simple little sacristy above is another testimony to the faith which took men to their deaths. Fined heavily for their religious beliefs, the family was also impoverished by the Civil War, in which they supported the king. The shortage of funds which so plagued the Ferrers ensured that Baddesley survived unchanged.

The medieval atmosphere of the house was particularly appreciated by the extended family group who lived here at the end of the nineteenth century. Marmion Edward Ferrers married the talented Rebecca Dulcibella Orpen, whose romanticised portraits of her friends and life at Baddesley now enhance the house. For financial reasons the couple were joined by Rebecca's literary aunt, Lady Chatterton, well known as a romantic novelist, and her husband Edward Dering. All four revelled in the antiquity of the place and re-created a Catholic chapel, sumptuously fitted out with leather hangings decorated with flowers and birds in gold, pink and blue. Both Lady Chatterton and Rebecca liked to paint in the bay window of the great parlour, where, today, the high barrel ceiling, sparse furnishings and rippling reflections from the moat create a sense of airy spaciousness contrasting with the dark intimacy of the rest of the house.

Barrington Court SOMERSET

2 miles north of the A303 between Ilchester and Ilminster, at east end of Barrington village, ½ mile east of the B3168
[442 E6]

Twisted finials and chimneys reaching skywards from every gable and angle transform Barrington's roofline into a forest of stone fingers. Although not as grand as Montacute only 10 miles or so to the east (*see* p.245), which it predates by about 40 years, this fine sixteenth-century house has the same indefinable charm, a blend of romance, fantasy and age. Built to a characteristic Elizabethan E-plan, with long wings projecting either side of the original entrance court on the south front, the honey-coloured façades with their generous mullioned windows and buttressed gables are typical of the best architecture of the day. Barrington's flamboyant roofline, reminiscent of the extravagant self-advertisement of Francis I's contemporary French châteaux, heralds more fully developed Renaissance features at Montacute. And the connection between the two houses is not only architectural, as Barrington was briefly owned by the Phelips family of Montacute in the early seventeenth century.

But, unlike its grander neighbour, Barrington was not designed for a high-flying politician. Although the Daubeney family who owned the estate in the early sixteenth century were ambitious members of the Tudor court, Sir Giles serving as Henry VII's Ambassador to France and his son a participant in the Field of Cloth of Gold, it seems they were content with the moated medieval house they inherited and that the new building was commissioned by William Clifton, a prosperous London merchant to whom the property was sold in 1552. William Strode, whose father had acquired Barrington in 1625, was responsible for the fine late seventeenth-century stable block in the style of Wren only a stone's throw away from the house, its tall red-brick chimneys echoing the Elizabethan roofline.

Barrington still preserves a largely sixteenth-century layout, although few original internal features survive. Deceptively authentic oak panelling and other decoration, including a remarkable honeycomb of wooden ribs covering the ceiling of the small dining room, was brought here between the First and Second World Wars as part of the restoration initiated by Colonel A. Lyle, who took over the house in 1920 when it was a gutted shell and filled it with his collection of interior fittings from contemporary derelict buildings. Barrington is now leased to Stuart Interiors for the display of period and reproduction furniture and is arranged as a series of showrooms.

The enchanting formal garden, laid out as a series of outdoor rooms within the warm brick walls of Elizabethan cattleyards, is another twentieth-century creation. Originally planted to plans by Gertrude Jekyll, the raised beds bordering the fountain pond in the Lily Garden still reflect her colour schemes, with azaleas, wallflowers, marigolds and dahlias flowering orange and red in vivid displays. A brick path leads through an arch to the restful Iris Garden

flowering pink, blue and purple round a sundial, and to the cool White Garden planted with a range of silver-foliaged and pale-blossomed herbaceous and annual species. Two arms of the moat enfold the house, one bridged by the path which brings visitors from the car park, the other forming a long lily-encrusted corridor bordering the grassy entrance court. Espaliered apples, pears and plums are trained along the high brick walls of the large kitchen garden, thriving in the sun which turns the Ham stone of the house to gold.

Above: The lively skyline and E-shaped south façade of Barrington Court, as captured in a photograph of the 1890s when it was being used as a farmhouse. Not long afterwards, in 1907, it was acquired by the Trust and let to Colonel Lyle, who restored it. West of the house, walls of mellow brick and stone shelter a flower garden laid out to plans by Gertrude Jekyll and a substantial kitchen garden, where pears and other fruit trees are espaliered against the walls (left).

Opposite: The little sacristy at Baddesley Clinton is a reminder of the staunch Catholicism of the Ferrers family. During the anti-Catholic mania of the 16th century, which was fuelled by war with Spain, priests were harboured here, hiding in an old shaft accessible from this room when men came to search the house.

The grandest interior at Basildon Park is the Octagon Drawing Room, where the great windows looking out towards the Thames are balanced by a pair of huge pier glasses and gilt console tables on the inner walls. The tables have marquetry tops and are supported by carved caryatids.

Basildon Park BERKSHIRE

Between Pangbourne and Streatley, 7 miles north-west of Reading, on west side of the A329 [443 H5]

This Neo-classical mansion standing high above the River Thames a mile or two upstream from Reading was built between 1776 and 1783 by the Yorkshire architect John Carr. Ranked as one of his masterpieces and his only house in the south of England, it was commissioned by another Yorkshireman, Francis Sykes, who had bought the Basildon property in 1771. Sykes, later 1st Baronet, was one of the successful men who returned from India with vast fortunes accumulated in the service of the East India Company. Although less corrupt than many, he appears

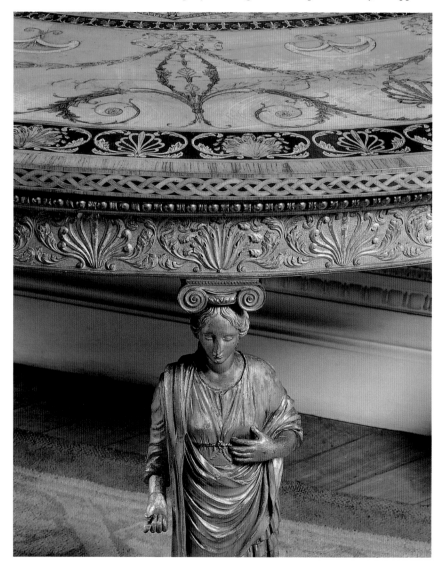

to have been particularly wealthy, and was able to spend lavishly on his new house. Several other nabobs lived in the tranquil countryside round about, including his friend Warren Hastings, and Lord Clive himself had tried to purchase Basildon in 1767.

John Carr's Palladian villa, built out of beautiful honey-coloured Bath stone, is both restrained and suitably grand. The main three-storey block dominated by a pedimented portico – the massive columns etched white against the shadowy recess behind on sunny days – is separated by courtyards from the two-storey pavilions on either side. Although all three parts of the house were originally linked internally, this is no longer so and the windows and doors on the exterior walls of the courtyards are only dummies.

Carr's Neo-classical decoration in the hall, with its delicate plasterwork ceiling subtly coloured like expensive wrapping paper in pink, lilac, green and stone, survives unaltered. His magnificent staircase is little changed, lit by graceful lunettes from above and with an elegant wrought-iron balustrade curving gently upwards. But Francis Sykes did not finish his new house, perhaps because he never recovered from the investigation into his dealings in India, which lost him his parliamentary seat and left him £11,000 poorer, or because of his disappointment in his sons, one dying young, the other a spendthrift. In 1838 the decline in the family fortunes forced his grandson to sell to the Liberal MP James Morrison, a self-made man whose upward path in life had been eased by marriage to his employer's daughter. Now a merchant prince, he needed a suitably grand setting to display his considerable collection of pictures. Morrison employed his architect-friend J.B. Papworth to complete the house and he and his ten children lived here in style. This was Basildon's golden age. A fast train link with London brought many distinguished visitors, J.M.W. Turner and Bishop Samuel Wilberforce among them.

Sadly, with the death of Morrison's daughter Ellen in 1910, the contents were dispersed and the house remained empty for over 40 years. During this period Basildon survived a scheme to re-erect it in America (no purchaser could be found) and lost some sections of plasterwork, which were sold to the Waldorf Astoria Hotel in New York. It was saved by the 2nd Lord and Lady Iliffe, who bought it in 1952, restored it with great skill and filled it with period furnishings and paintings, including portraits by Lely, Hoppner and Mytens as well as one or two twentieth-century works, such as Frank Salisbury's lovely painting of Lady Iliffe in a simple white dress. One of the glories of the house today is the Octagon Drawing Room, with its three great windows looking out over the Thames and the beech woods beyond. Pompeo Batoni's vivid portrayals of seven of the apostles and God the Father clustered round the doors on either side of the room are typical of the fine Italian paintings that Sir Francis Sykes might have acquired on a Grand Tour, and the deep red of the walls on which they are displayed is in accord with eighteenth-century taste.

Parkland studded with carefully placed chestnuts, beeches and limes still comes right up to the entrance front, as it did in Sir Francis Sykes's day. James Morrison added the balustraded terrace walk which now frames a lawn at the back of the house, and he also introduced the pair of carved stone dogs on the north side of the grass, which he bought on a trip to Italy in 1845–6. Lord and Lady Iliffe were responsible for most of the other garden ornaments and the present sympathetic planting, such as the white rambling rose on the terrace balustrade and the magnolia on the house.

Bateman's EAST SUSSEX

½ mile south of Burwash on the A265; approached by road leading south from west end of village or north from Woods Corner [443 J6]

Bateman's is a modest Jacobean house of local sandstone, with six brick columns forming a massive central chimney-stack above the gabled façades. The date 1634 over the porch almost certainly records the year in which it was completed. In the early seventeenth century this part of southern England was benefiting from the wealth created by the Wealden iron industry, then at its height, and there is a tradition that the house was built by a local ironmaster.

The particular interest of this modest building lies in its association with Rudyard Kipling, who bought the property in 1902 and lived here until his death in 1936. The great man broods over the stairs in a painting by John Collier, his dark three-piece suit slightly too big for him, the eyes behind the glasses tinged green and blue. In tune with Edwardian appreciation of seventeenth-century furniture and design, he and his wife created interiors that perfectly complement the building and which are still as the Kiplings left them. The heart of the house is the book-lined study at the top of the stairs, where Kipling wrote at the long early seventeenth-century walnut refectory table under the window, flinging himself down on the day-bed when inspiration deserted him. His tidily arranged 'writing tools' look as if he has just gone out for the afternoon, with

the fur seal he used as a paperweight and his boxes of pins and clips flanking the blotter. The large Indian wastepaper basket to the right of the desk has just been emptied, awaiting further discarded drafts of the stories and poems that Kipling wrote and rewrote conscientiously to produce what are now classics of the English language.

Kipling wrote some of his greatest works here, including *Puck of Pook's Hill*, called after the hill visible from the house, *If* and *The Glory of the Garden*. For these he drew his material from the Kent and Sussex country-side, no longer looking east to the India of his childhood for inspiration. But the house also reflects his strong links with the sub-continent, with oriental rugs in many of the rooms and Kipling's large collection of Indian artefacts and works of art displayed in the parlour. His delightful bookplate shows a diminutive figure reading on top of an elephant.

The peaceful garden running down to the River Dudwell owes much to the Kiplings, who laid out paths and hedges and planted the rose garden. Kipling's sundial is engraved with the words 'It is later than you think'. As might be expected from the author of *Kim*, the pond was designed with young people in mind, shallow enough for his children and their friends to use it for boating and bathing. It is immortalised in the visitors' book, where the initials FIP stand for 'fell in pond'. The grounds also contain two oasthouses that were built in the late eight-eenth century and the mill on the river which Kipling harnessed for electricity when he first came to Bateman's. Now restored to working order, it is used for grinding flour.

Bateman's, hidden in a fold of the Sussex Weald, was the home of the writer Rudyard Kipling and is still much as he left it. In his book-lined study (left) is the long table where he wrote, sitting in the walnut armchair which is raised on blocks to make it the right height. Hanging on the stairs is John Collier's portrait of Kipling painted in 1900 (above) and several reliefs by his father, John Lockwood Kipling, include this illustration of a scene in *Kim* (top), in which Kipling presents a vivid portrait of India.

Diverse Landscapes

Britain is landscape-rich. Packed into a small island are rolling hills and lush pastoral valleys, craggy mountains, heather moor, grassy downland, oak woods and beech hangers, and open fen under huge skies. Sometimes the land meets the sea in towering cliffs, with islands offshore, sometimes sea and land mingle in a landscape of salt-marsh, tidal creeks and mud-flats, sometimes deep sea inlets penetrate far inland. All is on a small scale and nothing is very high, but these are landscapes to refresh and entrance. While man has made his mark almost everywhere, the character of the landscape owes much to Britain's complex geology and to the effects of the last Ice Age and other natural processes. Many upland landscapes are ice-sculpted, and the post-glacial rise in sea level drowned estuaries, flooded the East Anglian fen and created islands.

Looking at the big picture, the oldest and hardest rocks underlie the uplands of the far west, including the fastnesses of Wales, where the Snowdonia massif is the eroded stump of once mighty mountains; the dramatic scenery of the Lake District, where the lakes radiate out from the central hub like the spokes of a wheel; and the granite moors of the West Country, with their distinctive tors. These uplands are marked by extensive areas of igneous and metamorphic rock formed under high pressure deep beneath the earth's surface. The long wall of the Pennines, running 150 miles down the spine of England, offers high fell and moor cut by pastoral dales. Some is limestone country, with outcropping crags and cliffs where the strata are exposed on valley sides, deep-cut gorges and associated calcareous grassland and woodland. Some is a darker and more acidic landscape, underlain by the less permeable sandstone known as millstone grit, and marked by stretches of peat bog and cotton grass.

FARNE ISLANDS
146

Moving east and south, the countryside becomes lower and softer. There are still uplands, adding character to the local scene, but these are gentler hills, easily climbed in an afternoon. Limestone gives us the great escarpment of the Cotswolds, running 50 miles above the Severn Valley, while its near relation chalk, similarly calcareous in composition, arcs in a great belt from the Dorset coast to the Wash. Chalk underlies the Chilterns and Berkshire Downs, with their open grassland and beech woods, and, in two spurs running east through Kent and Sussex and holding the Weald in their embrace, forms the glorious walking country of the North and South Downs. More understated are Britain's lowland landscapes, many of them on fertile river flood plains or reclaimed wetland, and intensively farmed. These are landscapes of gravels, sands, silts and clays, with crumbling cliffs or mud-flats and saltings where they meet the sea, heathlands on less fertile deposits and, in the peaty country of East Anglia, some surviving pockets of the extensive wetlands, with their reed-beds, sedges and meres, which once characterised this area.

Some of Britain's most distinctive landscapes are underlain by igneous rocks. Formed by molten material from deep within the earth, these hard, resistant rocks can outcrop in dramatic sculptural shapes. On the coast of County Antrim in Northern Ireland is the Giant's Causeway, with columns of basalt like half-worked blocks in a huge abandoned quarry standing high above the sea. The basalt was formed from a lava flow, which solidified into a honeycomb of hexagonal columns as it cooled and has been further shaped by centuries of erosion. Similarly, the Great Whin Sill, which outcrops as a rocky wall across the far north of England, is formed from an intrusion of dolerite, a fine-grained igneous rock like basalt. At its eastern end, it forms the scatter of the Farne Islands off the coast of Northumberland. Here, the deeply fissured rock, some of it showing a hexagonal structure like that of the Giant's Causeway, rises in precipitous cliffs up to 24 metres

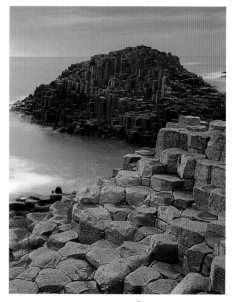

GIANT'S CAUSEWAY
275

(80 feet) high and is eroded into stacks, gullies and blow-holes. Isolated and unpopulated, the islands are a bird sanctuary and nature reserve, with populations of breeding seabirds and seals.

Some igneous rock does not get as far as the surface, but forms subterranean intrusions which cool as granite, a hard rock like basalt but with a much coarser texture. Later erosion may bring these bosses to the surface, as in the West Country, where both Bodmin Moor and Dartmoor are granite country. On the fringes of the moors, and along the valleys which cut into the massifs, the eroded and frost-shattered granite forms tors, great piles of tumbled blocks, spotted with lichen, as at Trowlesworthy Tors.

At the height of the last Ice Age, most of the British Isles was entombed in a carapace of ice, which was up to a mile thick in the north. The massive ice sheets melted and retreated over

10,000 years ago, but they have left their mark on the landscape. In Snowdonia and the Lake District ice moulded and gouged the ancient rocks, creating the dramatic landforms seen today. Higher ground was excavated by freeze-thaw effects to create knife-edged ridges and precipitous peaks, many of them now falling sharply to corrie lakes or tarns held in ice-deepened hollows. Elsewhere, as in the Skiddaw massif, the ice blanket smoothed the topography, and slow-moving glaciers scooped out valleys and excavated deep depressions – now filled with the lakes that are such a major feature of the Lake District.

Lower uplands such as the Shropshire Hills are similarly ice-moulded. Although now deeply incised by the winding valleys of post-glacial streams, the distinctive whale-backed plateau of the Long Mynd, running 10 miles down the Welsh Borders south of Shrewsbury, was smoothed and rounded by the ice. Lowlands, too, were marked by the great

CARNEDDAU
74

CATBELLS,
LAKE DISTRICT
212

TROWLESWORTHY TORS
308

LONG MYND
338

STRANGFORD LOUGH
376

MALHAM COVE
238

BOX HILL, NORTH
DOWNS
272

SEVEN SISTERS, SUSSEX
COAST
380

LYDFORD GORGE
232

sheets and glaciers, which left deposits of boulder clay over large areas. Some of the most intriguing are the elliptical rounded hillocks known as drumlins which formed beneath the ice, with their long axis parallel to the direction of flow. In Northern Ireland, the waters of Strangford Lough have drowned a drumlin landscape, with some of the hillocks now forming islands.

The North Yorkshire dales are limestone country, where the bare bones of the landscape show through in long white scars along the flanks of the valleys. Underground, as potholers know, there are stream-filled cave systems, the result of surface water draining away down enlarged fissures in the rock, which is both permeable and soluble. One of the most spectacular outcrops is the great cliff which encloses Malham Cove, and on the plateau above is this impressive stretch of limestone pavement. Fretted by solution and with a rectangular pattern that follows the joints in the rock, it is like a work of landscape art.

Chalk is calcareous like limestone, but is softer and more crumbly, forming gentler, more rounded landscapes. The rolling grasslands and woodlands of the North Downs rise to 193 metres (634 feet) at Box Hill in Surrey, where the chalk forms a prominent scarp overlooking the gap carved through the Downs by the River Mole. The steep south-facing cliff above the Mole, where the river has cut back into the escarpment, is covered by ancient box woodland that has been here since the end of the Ice Age and which thrives in the hot, dry conditions on this slope.

The South Downs, forming a mirror image ridge on the other side of the Weald, reach the sea in the gently swelling contours of the Seven Sisters, with flower-rich turf capping steep white cliffs. Constantly undercut by the sea, the cliffs are retreating and it is the falls of material which keep them looking so fresh and sheer.

On the west side of Dartmoor the River Lyd descends swiftly to the Tamar through the deep wooded ravine of Lydford Gorge. Boulders carried by the water and swirled round in the current gouge out potholes in the bed, carving it ever deeper. The sides are scalloped by the rounded shapes of old potholes, and mosses and ferns flourish in the constantly damp environment.

Much of East Anglia is low-lying, with coasts where land and sea merge in a fluid landscape of saltings and mud-flats, dunes and spits. Along the north Norfolk coast is one of the largest areas of salt-marsh in England, a lonely creek-cut wilderness built of sediments left by the sea. Nutrient-rich tidal inlets attract important populations of wading and overwintering birds, and drifts of purple sea lavender, part of a rich mosaic of coastal plants, colour the marshes in July. The marshes at Stiffkey in Norfolk are among the oldest and least disturbed, providing important winter feeding for Brent geese, widgeon and teal. Down the east coast of Suffolk, there is another haven for wildlife at Orford Ness, a long shingle spit stretching 10 miles south of Aldeburgh. Separated from the mainland by the River Ore, and with strips of grazing marsh, mud-flat and reed-bed on the inland side, this desolate, ever-shifting spit is a natural bird sanctuary, with the largest colony of lesser black-backed and herring gull in East Anglia.

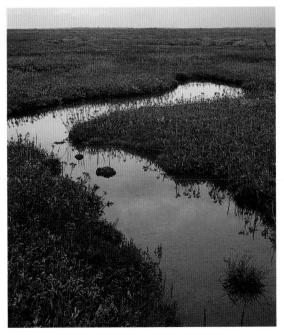

STIFFKEY
SALTMARSHES
277

Bath Assembly Rooms
BATH & NE SOMERSET

In Alfred Street, north of Milsom Street, east of the Circus
[442 F7]

This elegant place is straight from the world of Jane Austen, the setting for a thousand card parties and for the routs and masquerades with ices and claret cup that Emma Woodhouse would have revelled in. Although Bath had been known as a spa since Roman times, it was only under the influence of Beau Nash's forceful personality in the eighteenth century that what had been a provincial watering place was transformed into an international resort. By 1769, when work started on the Assembly Rooms – the third set to appear in the town – John Wood the Elder's showpieces, Queen Square and the Circus, were already completed, the start of the magnificent sequence of terraces and streets that was to culminate in his son's Royal Crescent.

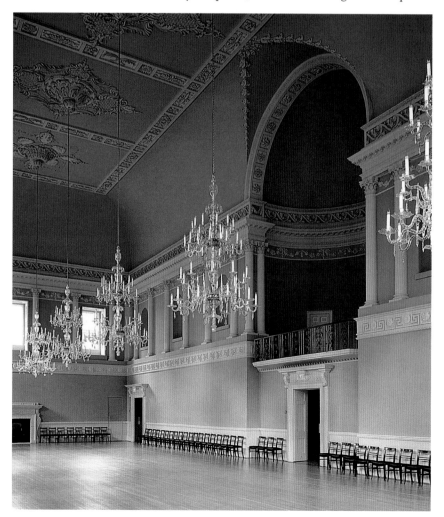

John Wood the Younger's Assembly Rooms echo the fashionable elegant world which created them, a place where the company could amuse themselves with dancing, drinking tea or playing cards, strolling from one pursuit to another as the fancy took them. Those who came here were expected to conform to certain standards of dress and behaviour, as laid down by the Master of Ceremonies. Captain William Wade, the Rooms' convivial and decorative host from their opening in 1771 until 1777, still scrutinises visitors from Gainsborough's full-length portrait. His published rules included instructions on where to sit, as well as exhortations such as 'no Lady dance country-dances in a hoop of any kind'.

Set impressively across a wide pavement, the Rooms dominate their surroundings, with two rather austere classical façades rising either side of the central pedimented entrance. This plain exterior gives no hint of the splendours within. The magnificent 30-metre (100-foot) ballroom, the largest eighteenth-century room in Bath, would once have been filled with 800–1,200 on ball nights, five great candlelit chandeliers illuminating the glittering company below and the orchestra housed in the apse on the south wall. Rising through two floors to a high coved ceiling, this superb classical interior is lit only at second-floor level, where Corinthian columns flanking the windows and lining the interior wall are picked out in white against the blue of the walls.

The lofty tea-room with a double screen of columns at one end is similarly splendid. Completing the original suite was the octagon, or card-room, where an organ was provided to entertain the company when card-playing was banned on Sundays, but in 1777 another card-room was added to cope with the numbers who flocked here. Concerts graced by such celebrities as Johann Strauss and Liszt continued to be popular, but the Assembly Rooms lost their attraction in the nineteenth century, closing at the start of the First World War. They were restored by the City of Bath after they had been presented to the Trust in 1931, only to be severely damaged by bombs in 1942. Reconstruction began in 1946, initially under the close supervision of Sir Albert Richardson, whose determination ensured the accurate reproduction of original features. Subsequent redecoration, and major restoration in the late 1980s, has been based on original colour samples found in the City Archives, thus re-creating the complete eighteenth-century scheme. A Museum of Costume (not owned by the Trust) is housed in the basement.

Bath Skyline BATH & NE SOMERSET

South-east and north-east of Bath [442 F5]

Bath's beauty owes a great deal to the way it sits among a bowl of hills. It is essential to this beauty that the skyline, largely wooded, should be preserved. The Trust plays its part in this preservation, holding over 202 hectares (500 acres) of the hills immediately south-east of the city. Rainbow Wood Farm on Claverton Down was the first acquisition in 1959, Smallcoombe Farm at Bathwick and farmland at Bushey Norwood nearby were added later, and in the early 1990s the Trust acquired both the 12 hectares (29 acres) of Fairy Wood and Klondyke Wood and the crucial 11.3 hectares (28 acres) of Prior Park (*see* p.316). Bushey Norwood is bounded on the north by the rampart of an Iron Age hill-fort on Bathampton Down, where a single bank and ditch enclosing an area of some 31.5 hectares (78 acres) overlie an earlier field system. Footpaths, in particular the Bath skyline circular walk, offer walking close to the centre of Bath.

Little Solsbury Hill, north-east of the city, rises to 190 metres (625 feet). The ramparts of its hill-fort, probably built in about 300BC, are faced with well-preserved dry-stone hedging. From the top of the hill there are wide views over Bath and the Avon valley.

Beatrix Potter Gallery CUMBRIA

In Hawkshead, next to the Red Lion inn [445 H4]

Like Hill Top, the little farm which she purchased in 1905 (*see* p.185), and the village of Sawrey, the nearby market town of Hawkshead was captured in several of Beatrix Potter's delicate illustrations for her children's books. The town still looks very much as she knew it in the late nineteenth and early twentieth centuries, a cluster of small limewashed houses ranged round three squares and two main streets. Next to the Red Lion inn overlooking one of the squares in the centre of town is the low, cream-coloured building where Beatrix Potter went to consult the local solicitor W.H. Heelis & Son on her property purchases in the district, all of which came to the Trust on her death. William Heelis, the junior partner she saw regularly over the years, not only gave advice on her acquisitions, but also kept an eye on her property when she was away and attended sales on her behalf. In 1912 he asked her to be his wife.

Four small rooms, two created out of the large upstairs office which William shared with his uncle and cousin,

are now the setting for a changing exhibition of Beatrix Potter's sketches and watercolours. There are also photographs of the Heelis and Potter families and of some of Beatrix's farms. Downstairs, what was the clerks' room has been refurnished as a nineteenth-century solicitor's office, using some of the original desks and furnishings.

Beesands Cliff DEVON

½ mile south of Torcross, 3 miles north of Start Point [442 D8]

Beesands Cliff is miles away from any other Trust property, but worth seeking out. The great sweep of Start Bay is best seen from Little Dartmouth (*see* p.124), and the A379 follows the beach for 2 miles between Slapton and Torcross, where it turns sharply west for Kingsbridge. A mile beyond, hidden by high ground, is the fishing hamlet of Beesands. In the cliff to the north, and south of the Limpet Rocks, a narrow cleft the width of a horse and cart is the entrance to a wildly picturesque quarry, where over a century ago roofing slates were dug for the houses of the South Hams, and carried there direct as they were needed.

Bellister NORTHUMBERLAND

¼ mile south of the A69, astride the Haltwhistle–Alston road [445 H3]

Just outside Haltwhistle, in the South Tyne Valley west of Hexham, the 445 hectares (1,100 acres) of Bellister are a rare survival of a small manorial estate which has escaped absorption by the large surrounding properties. The castle

Beatrix Potter showed artistic talent from an early age and she used her drawing and painting as an escape from an empty and isolated existence with her parents. She would depict her tame mice and rabbits and other creatures and plants and, on long summer holidays in the Lake District, would sketch a view over a lake, a path contouring round a hill, a flagstoned floor, the set of a dry-stone wall – all material for her animal fantasies and the watercolours which bring them alive. These illustrations are from *The Tale of Samuel Whiskers* (left, *1908*), *The Tale of Two Bad Mice* (above top, *1904*) and *Mrs Tiggy-Winkle* (above, *1905*), here seen removing an iron from the fire.

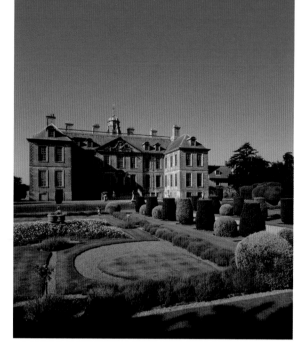

(not open to the public) originally stood on the north bank of the river, but in 1799, when the river changed its course, it was left well to the south. The former river banks lend character to the valley land, their gravelly hummocks showing all stages of colonisation, from herb-rich grassland to scrub woodland. The steep wooded cliffs above the river provide pleasant walks and run up to open moorland.

Belton House LINCOLNSHIRE

3 miles north-east of Grantham on the A607
Grantham—Lincoln road [443 I1 and 445 K8]

Belton is at peace with the world. Built in the last years of Charles II's reign to an H-shaped design by the gentleman-architect William Winde, its simple Anglo-Dutch style seems to express the confidence and optimism of Restoration England. Symmetrical honey-coloured façades crowned with a cupola look out over the tranquil, wooded park, the grandeur of the broad flight of steps leading up to the pedimented entrance front offset by domestic dormers in the steeply pitched roof.

The interiors reflect Belton's long association with the Brownlow and Cust families, descendants of the ambitious and wealthy Elizabethan lawyer who bought the estate in 1617. Family portraits hang in almost every room, from Reynolds's imposing study of Sir John Cust, Speaker of the House of Commons from 1761–70, which greets visitors in the coldly impressive marble hall, to Lord Leighton's magical portrait at the top of the stairs of the last Countess Brownlow as a young girl, the colour of the bouquet she holds against her long white dress echoed in the autumnal trees behind.

High-quality decorations and furnishings, including magnificent wall mirrors, a brilliant-blue Italian lapis lazuli cabinet and the remnants of an extensive collection of Old Masters, speak of wealth well spent. Glowing panelling lines the formal seventeenth-century saloon in the middle of the house, setting off delicate limewood carvings with beautifully detailed fruit and flowers that suggest the hand of Grinling Gibbons. Early eighteenth-century gilt wall mirrors between the three long windows looking onto the garden reflect two sets of Charles II walnut chairs arrayed on the pink and green Aubusson carpet, their seats and backs upholstered in faded crimson velvet and a host of cherubs adorning the frames. Two more cherubs, their grumpy expressions perhaps due to their rather precarious position, perch uncomfortably on the monumental reredos in the largely unaltered north-facing chapel, where an

The north front of Belton House (right) looks over the formal Dutch garden. Chinese wallpaper dating from the 18th century (above) in one of the bedrooms shows a very different kind of garden, filled with people enjoying a continuous party and with brightly coloured butterflies and birds darting amongst the trees.

exuberant baroque plaster ceiling by Edward Goudge contrasts with James Wyatt's classical compositions of the 1770s upstairs.

Apart from the silver awarded to Speaker Cust for his service to the House of Commons, some of the most prized pieces at Belton are the vast garden scenes by Melchior d'Hondecoeter acquired by the 3rd and last Earl. He and his wife presided over a golden age in the late nineteenth century, when Belton was sympathetically restored and redecorated. The last Earl also changed the garden, adding a final layer to the harmonious blend of styles and periods which characterises both the park and the grounds. To the north of the house is the last Earl's recreation of a baroque Dutch garden, a formal composition of clipped yew – golden globes alternating with green pillars – and gravel walks punctuated by ornamental urns and pieces of sculpture, among them an eighteenth-century sundial clasped by Father Time. Further from the house is the more extensive sunken Italian garden laid out onthe site of the kitchen garden. Dating from 1810 and designed by Jeffry Wyatville, this is overlooked by Wyatville's elegant orangery of 1820, and is another composition of clipped yew and urns, arranged round a central fountain pool.

The last Earl's Dutch garden was based on an engraving of the original elaborate baroque layout. A lime avenue sweeping east across the park to a tall prospect tower silhouetted against the sky is a remnant of this scheme, and a little Palladian temple facing across a short canal on the east side of the garden, and an unrestored picturesque wilderness to the west, are also survivals of earlier layouts, as depicted in a number of eighteenth-century paintings of the house and grounds in the breakfast room. Twentieth-century portraits hanging here include a painting of the 6th Lord Brownlow, Lord in Waiting to Edward VIII during his brief reign and a close friend of the King. Edward VIII stayed several times at Belton, perhaps deriving strength from the serenity of his surroundings.

Bembridge Windmill ISLE OF WIGHT

½ mile south of Bembridge on the B3395 [443 H7]

Set on a hill about a mile from the easternmost point of the Isle of Wight, this weathered four-storey stone mill with its great 9-metre (30-foot) sails is a familiar landmark and has inspired generations of artists, J. M. W. Turner among them. A fine example of an eighteenth-century tower mill, Bembridge was built in about 1700 and still contains original wooden machinery. The turning gear which rotated the wooden cap to bring the sweeps into the wind is still visible on the outside of the mill; the miller would originally have operated it by walking round the building hauling on a chain. For some two hundred years until the outbreak of the First World War the mill ground flour, meal and cattle feed for the village and surrounding countryside. Derelict by the 1950s, it has now been partly restored, the only windmill on the Isle of Wight to have survived.

Beningbrough Hall NORTH YORKSHIRE

8 miles north-west of York, 2 miles west of Shipton, 2 miles south-east of Linton-on-Ouse [445 J5]

Finished in 1716, dignified Beningbrough Hall is a product of the cultivated, secure decades of the early eighteenth century. The house is set on a slight rise above the water meadows of the Ouse, little pavilions crowned with cupolas framing the solid red-brick rectangle with stone dressings which stares confidently across the entrance court. A splayed flight of steps rises to the central front door, over which two lifelike stone horses struggle to escape the sculptured drapery which envelops them. Tiny attic casements one-third the size of the long sash windows in the two principal storeys are set just beneath the roof, sandwiched between massive console brackets supporting an overhanging cornice.

Built for John Bourchier, whose family had acquired the property by marriage in the previous century, the construction was supervised by the local carpenter-architect William Thornton, possibly with advice from Thomas Archer, although Thornton alone was responsible for the exceptional woodcarvings which are such a feature of the house. Mouldings and friezes usually executed in plaster are here realised in wood, such as the three-dimensional acanthus leaves which curl out of the deep ornamental frieze in the state bedroom. Beningbrough is also remarkable for the central corridor running the length of both floors, with a vista at ground level into the greenery of the conservatory at one end. Although the house has none of its original contents, it is furnished in period style and now also displays some hundred paintings from the National Portrait Gallery, including Kneller's portraits of members of the Kit-Kat club.

The formality of early eighteenth-century life is reflected in the suite of state rooms for honoured guests traditionally sited on the ground floor, and in the long saloon used for balls and large family gatherings. Rising through two storeys, the great hall which would have greeted all visitors is one of the most impressive baroque interiors in England. A flagged stone floor and soaring stone-coloured pilasters set against grey walls contribute to an overall effect of dignified elegance.

Another insight into the eighteenth century is provided by the intimate closets where important guests could receive their closest friends or relax in private. Always

Top: Beningbrough was built at a time when porcelain from China and Japan was highly prized. This closet is one of six rooms in the house with built-in shelves to display treasured pieces.

Above: Beningbrough's state bed, hung with crimson damask and elaborately fringed and braided, is one of the finest of its date to survive.

The fine panelling seen throughout Beningbrough is here used to set off two panels from a late 17th-century Chinese screen, a Kneller portrait and an 18th-century Chinese cabinet.

richly decorated, those at Beningbrough are crowded with oriental porcelain displayed on stepped ledges over the fireplaces. The contemporary taste for the exotic also shows in the sections of Chinese screen set into the panelling in one of the dressing rooms, with a Chinese lacquer cabinet standing below.

A door in the wall of the cobbled yard opposite the fully equipped nineteenth-century laundry leads into the garden spread along the south side of the house, where two formal layouts enclosed by yew hedges have been planted in contrasting colours, the plants in one flowering orange, yellow and red, those in the other cool-coloured and set round a pool with a fountain. Double borders are filled with peonies, irises, bush roses and climbers, and plants of North American extraction are featured in the area beyond the now grassy kitchen garden. The view south over the ha-ha to the water meadows has a feeling of the eighteenth-century landscaped park that once surrounded the house.

Benthall Hall SHROPSHIRE

1 mile north-west of Broseley on the B4375, 4 miles north-east of Much Wenlock, 6 miles south of Wellington [442 F2]

Although only a couple of miles from Coalbrookdale, the traumas of the Industrial Revolution passed Benthall by, precipitous wooded slopes successfully isolating the house on its plateau above the gorge of the River Severn. Seat of the ancient Benthall family whose origins stretch back to Anglo-Saxon times, the exterior has changed little since it was built in the late sixteenth century. Mullioned and transomed windows gleam in the south front looking towards the Shropshire Hills, its charming asymmetrical façade punctuated by two-storey bays on either side of the projecting porch. Five gables pierce the roofline and giant sixteenth-century brick chimneystacks rise from each end of the house. Five stone tablets set in a playing-card pattern above the door in the porch, perhaps alluding to the five wounds of Christ, were probably advertising the family's Catholic sympathies, also indicated by the hiding place in the little room above.

Early seventeenth-century interiors include a carved staircase of *c.*1618, with grotesque heads adorning the massive newel posts and the leopard of the Benthall crest proudly displayed on the panel at the turn of the stairs. In the sunny, welcoming drawing room, which is flooded with light from south- and west-facing windows, an elaborate white plaster ceiling and frieze merge with off-white oak panelling. Lions, horses, stags, griffins and other mythical creatures look down on the room from their plaster roundels. Rococo chimneypieces of *c.*1760 here and in the dining room were added by T.F. Pritchard, architect of the Iron Bridge spanning the River Severn just to the north, perhaps the most evocative symbol of the Industrial Revolution.

The intimate garden, sheltered and enclosed by trees, is largely the work of Robert Bateman, son of James Bateman who created the individual nineteenth-century layout at Biddulph Grange in Staffordshire (*see* opposite). During his tenancy (1890–1906), he laid out the terraces, rockeries and rose garden, built up the shrub banks and carried on the tradition of peopling the garden with unusual plants that had been established by the distinguished botanist George Maw and his brother in the mid-nineteenth century.

George Maw was responsible for the display of autumn and spring crocuses in the patch of woodland bordering the lawn, and with his care the Glory of the Snow (*Chionodoxa luciliae*) flowered at Benthall for the first time in Britain in 1877. The rich green leaves of the little mouse plant (*Arisarum proboscideum*) from the Pyrenees appear here and there, herbaceous geraniums, including *Geranium nodosum* and Mourning Widow (*G. phaeum*), have become naturalised under the trees, and there is much else of interest.

Berrington Hall
HEREFORD & WORCESTER

3 miles north of Leominster on west side of the A49 [442 E3]

Berrington is the creation of Thomas Harley, the 3rd Earl of Oxford's remarkable son, who made a fortune from supplying pay and clothing to the British army in America and became Lord Mayor of London in 1767 at the age of 37. The architect of his austere three-storey house, with its domestic quarters clustered round a courtyard behind, was the fashionable Henry Holland, who also decorated Claremont for Lord Clive and built Carlton House for the Prince Regent.

The house is beautifully set above the wide valley of a tributary of the River Lugg, with views west and south to the Black Mountains and Brecon Beacons and north-west to the Iron Age hill-fort of Croft Ambrey (*see* p.119). This was the site advised by 'Capability' Brown, whom Harley took to see the estate in 1775, shortly after he had acquired it, and who was to landscape the park, creating the lake with its artificial island (Berrington is one of the best examples of his work). Holland, Brown's son-in-law, started on the house three years later.

Approached through an entrance lodge built in the form of a triumphal arch, the rather plain Neo-classical exterior with a central portico and a wide flight of steps leading to the entrance gives no clue to the lavishness of the interior. Feminine plaster ceilings now decorated in muted pastel colours adorn the principal rooms. Holland is at his most fanciful in the drawing room, where a number of roundels thought to be by Biagio Rebecca are set off by white plaster cherubs leading seahorses by blue ribbons over a lavender background. Biagio Rebecca probably also executed the prominent grisaille panels in the library, deep shadows in those showing eminent Englishmen of letters on the ceiling giving them a three-dimensional quality, as if they were made of plaster. Bacon and Chaucer are easily recognisable; Pope is the only one of the eight to be shown in full profile.

Holland's masterpiece at Berrington is the staircase hall. Rising to a central dome, it shows an extraordinary ability to use perspective and space to dramatic effect, recalling the contemporary engravings of Piranesi. The rooms are set off with a collection of French furniture, including pieces which belonged to the Comte de Flahault, the natural son of Talleyrand, and Napoleon's step-daughter Hortense.

In the dining room, four panoramic paintings of battles at sea, three of them by Thomas Luny, are a tribute to the distinguished Admiral Rodney. Father-in-law of Harley's daughter Anne and one of the most eminent naval admirals of the eighteenth century, he played a prominent role in the American War of Independence. The paintings show important incidents in the war at sea, in which Rodney was in action against the French and Spanish, who had allied themselves with the rebellious Americans. Two large pictures at either end of the room are of the Battle of the Saints on 12 April 1782, an engagement which Luny, who served as a purser, may have witnessed. One is a morning scene showing Rodney breaking the French line, the other depicts the surrender of the French flagship in the evening of the same day.

More poignant reminders of members of the Cawley family, to whom the estate was sold in 1901, hang in Lady Cawley's room. One of the photographs shows the 1st Lord Cawley and his four sons on horseback in front of the house, ready for a day's hunting. A few years later three of the young men had lost their lives in the First World War.

Above: Among the service areas grouped round Henry Holland's elegant courtyard at the back of Berrington Hall is this delicious Georgian dairy, designed to be ornamental as well as practical.

Left: The dramatic Staircase Hall at Berrington, lit by a glass-domed lantern and with galleries set behind scagliola columns.

Biddulph Grange STAFFORDSHIRE

Off Grange Road on the A452, north of Biddulph town and 4 miles south of Congleton [445 |8]

The garden created over 20 years from 1842 on this cold, wet site at a height of 152–189 metres (500–600 feet) just below Biddulph Moor is one of the most exceptional in England. A wide range of trees, shrubs and other plants from all over the world reflects the many new species being brought back to England from the Far East and the Americas by David Douglas, Robert Fortune and others at this period. In this respect, Biddulph is no more than a garden of its time, although the links with collectors are particularly close. But the variety of picturesque settings providing diverse growing conditions suitable for a wide range of plants, the use of banks, rocks and tree-trunks to enclose and separate areas of the garden and planting schemes which aim for aesthetic effect as well as the display of individual species put this garden in a class of its own.

The genius of James Bateman, its creator, emerges most strongly away from the house, beyond the formal terraces falling to the lake below the south front. Huge boulders piled one on top of another, all of them laboriously brought to the garden from a quarry nearby, form the sides of a naturalistic glen with a collection of ferns thriving in the many nooks and crannies and semi-aquatic plants growing along the stream devised to flow down its length. At one end is the rhododendron ground, a brilliant display of colour at the right time of year, and from here a tunnel through more rockwork leads to the pinetum. Many tons of earth were moved to produce gentle slopes on either side of a winding path and a range of soils and situations was contrived to cater for all requirements. Impressive groups of monkey puzzles, deodars and pines are mixed with golden yew and hollies and a variety of oaks.

A second tunnel at the other end of the glen emerges in the enchanting Chinese Garden, a willow-pattern plate brought to life. A hump-backed bridge and a gaily painted temple hung with bells and decorated with dragons and grebes are reflected in the still waters of a pool. Completely enclosed with earth banks and walls of vegetation, this secluded heart of the garden once sheltered an impressive range of plants, including the first two golden larches to be cultivated in England, one of which still survives, a variety of tree peony and hostas, variegated bamboo and the Japanese anemone. Japanese maples set off an imitation of the Great Wall of China which partly bounds the garden. Even more remarkable, perhaps, is the Egyptian Court, with two pairs of stone sphinxes guarding a pyramid and obelisks of topiary yew. An ape-like god squats in an inner chamber, luridly lit through coloured glass in the roof above. At the back the pyramid is miraculously transformed into a half-timbered Cheshire cottage looking down the pinetum. More an architectural fantasy than a re-creation of the local vernacular, the cottage's decorative façade carries the date, 1856, when it was built, and the intertwined initials of James and Maria Bateman.

James Bateman's interest in plants began with a passion for orchids, his work on the species of Mexico and Guatemala – the first part of which was produced in 1837 when he was only 26 – earning him an international

Hidden away at the heart of Biddulph Grange is a Victorian vision of China, with a serene pool reflecting a brightly-painted temple and ornate hump-backed bridge. Here James Bateman planted a show of exotics from the Far East, many of them only recently introduced to England by the plant-hunter Robert Fortune.

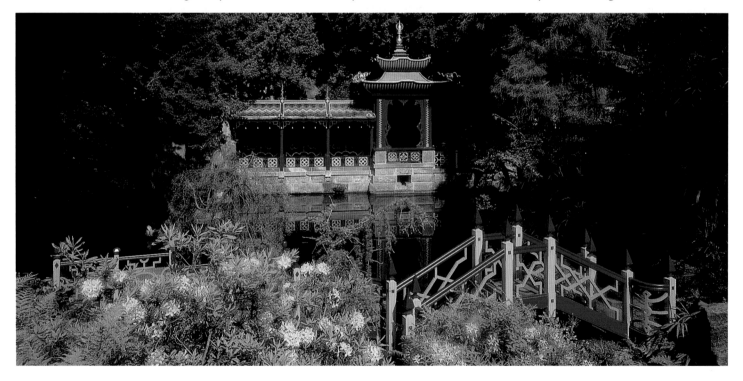

reputation and securing his election as a Fellow of the Royal Horticultural Society shortly afterwards. While absorbed in Biddulph he continued to cultivate orchids in the hot-houses of Knypersley Hall, his father's house only a short distance away. He was a frequent visitor to George Loddiges's nursery in Hackney and while there may have first met the man who was to help him with his creation, the marine artist and occasional garden designer Edward Cooke. Although Cooke was probably responsible for all the architectural features in the garden, the overall plan was conceived by Bateman, with the help of his wife Maria. Sadly, it seems this enterprise overstretched the small fortune James had inherited from his grandfather, a wealthy industrialist: although Maria's ill-health was a major reason for the couple's decision to leave Staffordshire in the late 1860s, it is also clear they could not afford to stay on there.

The Italianate mansion James designed to complement his garden was largely destroyed in a fire in 1895 and only the wings now remain, unhappily married to a late Victorian block built in Renaissance baronial style by Robert Heath, son of the successful industrialist who bought the property in 1872. For most of the twentieth century the house was a hospital, and although the garden continued to be well maintained there was no conservation or renewal and from the late 1960s it suffered enormously from vandalism.

Since Biddulph came to the Trust in 1988, a major restoration programme has returned the garden as closely as possible to Bateman's original scheme. On the two long terraces below the house, yew-framed nineteenth-century gardens have been recreated. A long dahlia walk flowers in a kaleidoscope of vivid colours; an ornamental orchard features Morello cherries and trained clematis; and a show of peonies, phlox, delphiniums and other hardy herbaceous plants marks the reinstatement of a collection of Mrs Bateman's favourite flowers. Throughout the garden, as well as restoring features such as the extraordinary stumpery, a mass of stumps and roots piled up to a height of 3–4 metres (10–12 feet) on either side of the tortuous path up from the Chinese Garden, the Trust has had an ongoing programme to return the planting more closely to Bateman's original scheme. The stone seat which terminates the lime avenue by the Italian garden is once again set off by a tiered rainbow arrangement of azaleas and rhododendrons, Bateman's great Wellingtonia avenue has been replanted and there have been extensive changes in the Chinese garden, to return plants to the positions in which Bateman had them.

Birmingham Back to Backs

On the corner of Inge Street and Hurst Street, opposite the Hippodrome Theatre [443 G2]

When Birmingham was growing rapidly as an industrial centre in the late eighteenth and early nineteenth centuries, developers threw up street after street of cheap, high-density, brick-built, back-to-back housing grouped around courtyards behind terrace frontages. Three storeys high, but with just one room on each floor, and with windows only at the front, these houses were home to sizeable families, and often to their relatives and a lodger as well, all of whom had to use the communal privy and wash-house in the court. Housing like this covered acres of Leeds, Liverpool and other industrial towns as well as Birmingham, but during the nineteenth century, as many became disease-ridden slums, increasing concern about public health led to controlling legislation. The 1858 Public Health Act, which allowed local councils to prohibit back-to-backs, was followed by the 1908 Housing Act, which made them illegal. Building back-to-backs was banned in Birmingham in 1876 but many existing courts survived until the slum-clearance programmes which followed the Second World War.

Today, court 15, Inge Street, in the heart of the city and lived in until 1966, is the only complete survival of a courtyard of early nineteenth-century back-to-backs. The housing forms an L-shape, with three pairs of back-to-backs on Inge Street adjoining a terrace of five blind-back houses on Hurst Street. These tenements form the north and west sides of the inner court: on the east is a tall brick wall once the blind back of housing in an adjacent yard and the south side is closed by a modern brick wall. During most of the nineteenth century the court was occupied by artisans – button makers, leather workers, locksmiths and the like – some of whom worked from home, using one room in the house as a workshop. On Hurst Street, the lower floors were all converted into shops by 1900.

A tunnel entrance from Inge Street leads into the brick-paved yard, which still has its privy and wash-house, where water was heated in coppers over a brick hearth. Four back-to-backs have been fitted out to show what life in Inge Court and Hurst Street was like at different times in their history: *c.*1840–50, *c.*1880–90, *c.*1930–40 and *c.*1960–70. Reconstructions have been based on what is known of the families and individuals who lived here, and provide authentic recreations of period furnishings and lifestyles. One is based on the life of a Jewish watchmaker and his family, whose well-kept house includes artefacts

such as a Seder plate for Passover and a nine-branched candlestick; another, with damp and peeling wallpaper, shabby clothes and little to be seen in the cupboards, reflects the day-to-day existence of the struggling Mitchell family, who were here during the recession and unemployment of the 1930s; while the most recent interior is based on the life of an immigrant from the West Indies who opened a tailor's shop in the court, using the upper floors as a workroom and for storage. A water pump has been reinstated in the courtyard and washing lines, a hoop and an old pram give it a lived-in atmosphere.

Blackdown Hills SOMERSET

2 miles south of Wellington on the A38, ½ mile east of the Wellington–Hemyock road [442 E6]

The Blackdown range runs east and west for 12 miles, south of the M4 and west of Taunton. The Trust owns 24 hectares (60 acres) of natural woodland on the ridge above the small town of Wellington. The visitor does not come here only for the views over the Taunton Vale to the Quantocks, and on a clear day right across the Bristol Channel to Wales, but also to see the extraordinary memorial to the Iron Duke (*see* p.422).

Black Down WEST SUSSEX

1 mile south-east of Haslemere, between the A286 and the B2131 [443 I6]

At 280 metres (918 feet) the summit of Black Down is the highest point in Sussex and the views are splendid. The down stands proud above the Weald (*see* p.359), and in Victorian times all the world knew that it was here, at Aldworth, that Alfred, Lord Tennyson had built his laureate's mansion.

The ridge is of sandstone, the dry acid soil supporting heather with bilberries, gorse, birch and pine. The latter is winning the battle for survival, having encroached steadily, as has *Rhododendron ponticum*. Roe deer live in the fringes for there is much private woodland adjoining. Steep clefts, wet bottoms with sphagnum moss and bog plants, and the occasional small landslip, provide some tough scrambling. This is a place for a proper walk, and on the north side is the contrasting Valewood Park, a mix of meadow and open parkland with a pattern of sunken tracks and field banks, bringing the Trust's holding here to over 283 hectares (700 acres).

Blackwater Estuary ESSEX

10 miles east of Chelmsford [443 K4]

The Blackwater estuary is a lonely place, a mosaic of windswept salt-marsh, mud-flat, creeks, rough grazing and arable, with each farm sheltering behind a sea wall. The Trust owns 404.5 hectares (1,000 acres) of this valuable estuarine habitat, with its important bird population. Copt Hall, purchased in 1989, is a mix of farmland and salt-marsh, where the Trust has planted new copses and sown grass to attract waders and geese in recent years. Northey Island at the head of the estuary, cut by a maze of tidal creeks, attracts wading and overwintering birds, and a causeway leads from here to South House Farm on the mainland, believed to be the site of the Battle of Maldon in 991, when the Anglo-Saxons were defeated by the invading Vikings. Ray Island, in the Strood Channel, is jointly managed with the Essex Wildlife Trust, which has a considerable presence in the estuary. The island's alluvial mud-flats and saltings are a haunt of waders and wildfowl, shelduck, teal, dunlin, grey plover and curlew among them.

Above: Looking south-east over the wooded landscape of the Weald from the summit of Black Down, the highest point in Sussex.

Opposite: The back-to-backs in Hurst Street as they were in the 1950s, with the Hippodrome Theatre to the right.

Blaise Hamlet BRISTOL

4 miles north of central Bristol, west of Henbury village, just north of the B4057 [442 E5]

John Nash, who designed these nine rustic cottages around a green outside Bristol, was once heard to say that no palace had ever given him as much pleasure as Blaise Hamlet. His tiny settlement is certainly individual. Built in 1810–11 for the Quaker banker and philanthropist John Harford, who had bought the Blaise Castle estate in 1789, it was one of the first Picturesque estate villages, an example of the growing appreciation of the intrinsic attractiveness of traditional vernacular architecture (*see also* Selworthy, p.334). In this vision of an idealised village each building is different. Some are thatched, some tiled, and all have varied rooflines, with gables and dormers at different levels. Porches, verandahs, sheds and lean-tos ensure no profile is the same and contribute to the deliberate asymmetry. Even the pump on the green is defiantly off-centre. But everything in the hamlet is to the same scale, and all the cottages have soaring brick Tudoresque chimneys, now seen against a backdrop of mature trees as Nash intended. And the aged retainers whom Harford housed here were all provided with a small garden and an outside seat where they could doze on summer afternoons.

The Blewcoat School LONDON

At 23 Caxton Street, near the junction of Buckingham Gate and Caxton Street, SW1 [443 I5]

A statue of a boy in a long blue tunic and yellow stockings in a niche over the front door represents the many children from desperately poor backgrounds who were given a start in life in this modest Georgian building. In the one airy pine-panelled room set over a semi-basement, children from the slums of Westminster were taught to read and write and then found positions suited to their station, the girls entering domestic service or apprenticed to seamstresses and fan-makers, the boys placed with joiners, tailors, watermen and a variety of other trades. Part of a nationwide charity school movement financed by subscriptions from local tradesmen, the Blewcoat School was built in 1709 at the expense of William Green, a local brewer. Although small, it is elegant and dignified, a pleasing mixture of red and yellow brick with stone dressings, decorative pilasters and a parapet concealing the hipped roof. The original oak double doors of the entrance front now lead into a Trust shop.

Blickling Hall NORFOLK

On north side of the B1354, 1½ miles north-west of Aylsham on the A140, 15 miles north of Norwich, 10 miles south of Cromer [443 K1]

A winding road from Aylsham leads to this serene Jacobean mansion set in some 1,942.5 hectares (4,800 acres) of gently undulating park and estate in a loop of the River Bure. Built of warm red brick with stone dressings, Blickling has curving Dutch gables, generous leaded windows, massive chimneystacks and corner turrets carrying gilded weather vanes. On the southern entrance front, long low service wings, their lines continued by yew hedges, frame the approach. The house was designed for Sir Henry Hobart, James I's distinguished Chief Justice of the Common Pleas, by Robert Lyminge, who transformed an existing medieval and Tudor manor. No traces of this manor can be seen, but its ghost lives on in the dry moat ringing the house, now planted with roses, hydrangeas and hostas, and in many features of the layout and dimensions of the new building, such as the double courtyard plan. Further remodelling in the eighteenth century by Thomas and William Ivory for John Hobart, the 2nd Earl of Buckinghamshire, resulted in a house which is a harmonious combination of Jacobean and Georgian, the later work, to the north and west ranges, blending beautifully with the earlier.

The most spectacular room is Sir Henry's long gallery, running 37.5 metres (123 feet) down the east front, adorned with Edward Stanyon's intricate plaster ceiling, on which heraldic motifs, including the Hobart bull, are intermingled with delightful depictions of the senses. In one panel a stag listens entranced to a man playing the mandolin, his lady following the music for him with her finger; in another, a woman lifts a brimming glass to her lips, her lap full of luscious fruit. In about 1745 the gallery was converted into a library to house the remarkable collection inherited from Sir Richard Ellys, a distinguished theologian and antiquary. The 12,000 volumes now housed here include a very rare Eliot Indian bible printed in Massachusetts in 1663 and a unique maritime atlas of the same period. J.H. Pollen's delicately painted frieze above the bookcases, full of timid rabbits and other wildlife of the Norfolk countryside, is part of the Pre-Raphaelite mural decoration commissioned by the 8th Marquis of Lothian shortly after he inherited the house in 1850.

A door from the gallery leads into one of the rooms fitted out in 1778–82 to display the works of art acquired by the 2nd Earl during his congenial three-year posting

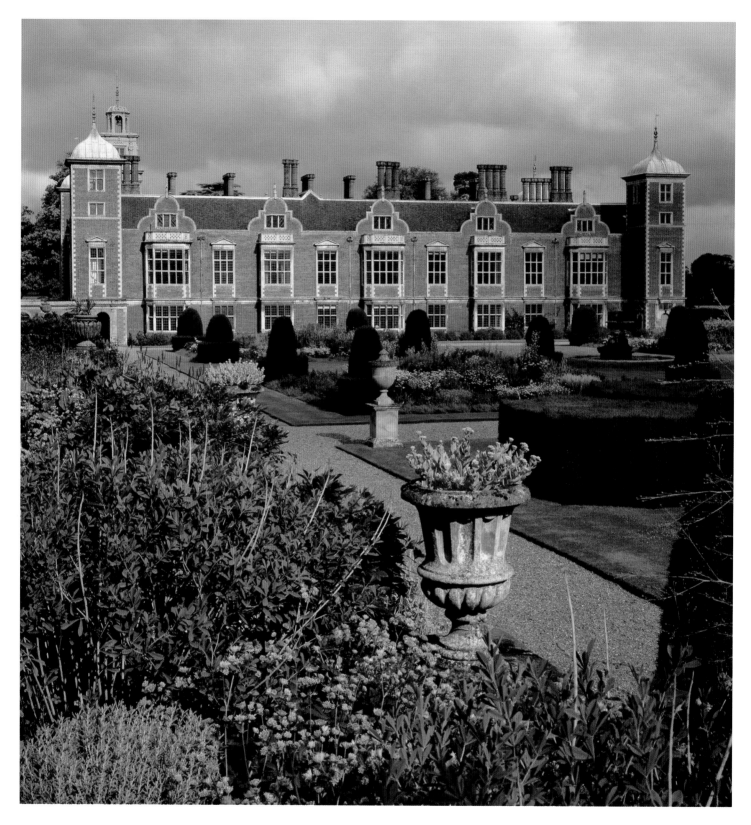

as Ambassador to the court of Catherine the Great. There are only three paintings here now, but the room still displays the magnificent tapestry, given to the 2nd Earl by the Empress as a parting present, which shows Peter the Great triumphing over the defeated Swedish army at Poltawa in 1709.

The main garden, bordering the Jacobean east front, is a long rectangle focused on a central path running east to a little pedimented and colonnaded early eighteenth-century temple set high on the massive terrace which overlooks the park. Immediately in front of the house, red brick edges a Victorian sunken garden, remodelled in the 1930s by Norah Lindsay, who filled the four parterre beds set round a seventeenth-century fountain with brightly flowering herbaceous plants, islands of yellow and orange, purple and blue. Clipped yews mark the corners of rose beds and yew grand pianos guard the steps leading up to the Temple Path. In the formal wilderness either side of this axis, two sets of radial walks meeting in circular clearings are lined by avenues of Turkey oak, lime and beech or cut through oak woodland. On the southern perimeter, half hidden in the trees and set with its back to

the garden looking out over the park, is the late eighteenth-century orangery, possibly by Samuel Wyatt. A secret garden with a summerhouse and a sundial in the northern wilderness is all that remains of an early eighteenth-century layout when the garden was first designed to an east-west plan. The earthwork defined by the brick Victorian bastion to the north of the parterre may be an even earlier survival, the only remnant of Sir Henry Hobart's formal Jacobean garden, laid out on a strong north-south axis.

Rolling wooded parkland landscaped in the eighteenth century stretches away to the north and west of the house, with beeches, sweet chestnuts and huge mature oaks framing a long sinuous lake. There are walks here and across the wider estate, a mix of arable farmland dotted with brick farmhouses and cottages, woodland and river meadow. A wide range of wildlife includes tufted duck and great crested grebe on the lake, the lesser spotted woodpecker, and kingfishers along the river, while archaeological remains include Bronze Age burial mounds, the remains of a Second World War airfield and a stretch of disused railway line.

Steps leading up from the parterre to the temple walk are guarded by 18th-century herms (above). Running the length of the east front is the Jacobean long gallery (left), with an original plaster ceiling. Used as a library since 1745, it still has the fine collection of books that was installed here in the 18th century.

Opposite: The Jacobean east front of Blickling Hall, with its curved Dutch gables and corner turrets, looks over the parterre garden remodelled in the 1930s by Norah Lindsay, who introduced the carefully-graded colour schemes of the central beds.

Boarstall Tower and Duck Decoy
BUCKINGHAMSHIRE

Midway between Bicester and Thame, 2 miles west of Brill
[443 H4]

This enchanting three-storey tower, with hexagonal turrets rising from each corner of the battlemented roofline, is all that remains of the fortified moated house built here in the early fourteenth century by John de Handlo. The only entrance to his carefully guarded property was through this gatehouse, its massive 3-foot limestone walls falling sheer to the waters of the moat and surviving arrow slits suggesting the grim prospect it must once have presented.

Today Boarstall seems charmingly domestic, an array of Tudor and Jacobean windows surveying the world, octagonal chimneystacks rising almost to the height of the turrets, and approached over a two-arched brick and cobble bridge. A beautiful room running 12 metres (40 feet) across the length of the third floor, now occasionally used for chamber concerts, was probably once a dormitory for the men of the establishment.

At the back of the tower, peacocks strut across romantic informal twentieth-century gardens. Just over the fields a tree-fringed lake marks Boarstall Duck Decoy, one of the few surviving working examples of a once-common feature of the English countryside, introduced from Holland by

Charles II. A trained dog entices the ducks into netted-over channels leading off the lake, each one ending in a narrow point. Once an important source of winter food, the birds are now ringed for scientific purposes.

Bodiam Castle EAST SUSSEX

3 miles south of Hawkhurst, 1 mile east of the A229 [443 J6]

By 1372, halfway through the Hundred Years War, England had lost control of the Channel and began to suffer devastating French raids. The Sussex ports of Winchelsea and Rye had both been destroyed a few years earlier; the manor of Bodiam, lying only some 10 miles from the coast and at the furthest navigable point of the River Rother, must have seemed similarly vulnerable. In 1385, Sir Edward Dalyngrigge, a veteran of the wars in France and an important figure in the defence of Sussex, asked Richard II for permission to fortify his house.

Rather than improving his manor, Dalyngrigge chose to build anew, on a site which gave a view of the river and a strategic bridge. Work started in 1385 and the fine, four-square castle which still stares south across the Sussex marshes was completed some three years later. Built just before siege artillery changed the approach to castle design, its strength lay in the height and might of its tower-studded circuit walls, which rise sheer from a broad moat. Three bridges connecting two islands lead from the north bank to the massive gateway, bristling with machicolations and gunports. Originally, to repel any attacker, this approach involved a dog-leg to the west bank, three draw-bridges and an outlying barbican, the remains of which stand on one of the islands. A ground-hugging pillbox by the path up from the car park shows how much things have changed since.

Although now in ruins, enough of the interior survives to give a vivid picture of the realities of castle life. The deep well and the remains of a pigeon loft suggest the preoccupations of a garrison expecting to be besieged, but in fact the French threat soon receded and the remnants of traceried windows and a number of fireplaces tell a different story. Like many contemporary buildings in France and England which Dalyngrigge must surely have seen, Bodiam combines domestic comfort with the trappings of defence and it is very likely the castle was built to be a status symbol as much as a fortress. The great courtyard beyond the gatehouse is surrounded by the outlines of domestic accommodation, including a traditional great hall with adjoining buttery, pantry and kitchen, such as

Bodiam Castle, with its wide moat and tower-studded perimeter wall, was built at a time when Sussex was being attacked by raiding parties from France.

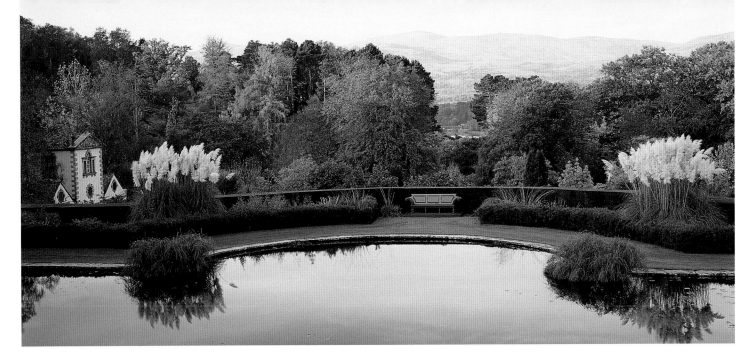

would have been found in any mansion of the period, and personal chambers for Dalyngrigge and his wife. Separate quarters, each suite with its own fireplaces and garderobe, were provided for his household, with additional provision for a military garrison. A chapel catered for the spiritual needs of the retinue and their lord. The emphasis on the castle as a grand residence also comes through in the recently identified remains of landscape gardens beyond the moat. Dips and hollows in the grass mark what was a series of ponds and there was a terrace on the hill above from which to admire the castle and its setting.

Bodnant Garden CONWY

8 miles south of Llandudno and Colwyn Bay on the A470
[444 F7]

This extensive, 32.5-hectare (80-acre) garden is alive with the sound of running water. It splashes over the worn baroque French fountain on one of the broad terraces which descend like a giant staircase into the valley of the River Hiraethlyn, trickles into the lily pond flanked by two majestic old cedars and feeds the long canal mirroring the classical façade of a stuccoed pedimented mill. In the ravine below, the Hiraethlyn tumbles several feet over a weir, water from the pool behind once being used to power a Tudor blast furnace. Minor streams and rivulets plunge precipitously to join the river on either side, helping to feed the Conwy only a short distance further downstream.

Whereas the gardens near the Victorian house are formal and open, with views across the Conwy to the mountains of northern Snowdonia, the depths of the valley are wild and enclosed. Conifers over a century old have thrived in the sheltered conditions, several of them, such as a fine *Abies grandis*, wellingtonias, redwoods and western hemlocks, now over 30 metres (100 feet) tall. Seen from the bridge crossing the weir, trees interlace in a green arch over the water downstream. A second mill, a functional building of granite and slate once used to grind flour, stands on the banks of the Hiraethlyn. Rhododendrons, azaleas and magnolias flourish beneath the trees, while hydrangeas among the herbaceous plants established along the river form unexpected splashes of blue in summer.

Apart from a number of fine beeches, cedars and oaks planted earlier in the nineteenth century, Bodnant has been created since 1874 by Mr Henry Pochin, his daughter Laura and her son and grandson, the 2nd and 3rd Lords Aberconway, ably assisted since 1920 by three generations of the Puddle family who have served as their managers and head gardeners. Now with all the beauty of a well-cared-for mature garden, Bodnant is notable for its collections of rhododendrons, magnolias and camellias among a wide range of trees, shrubs and other plants. The rhododendrons, ranging from dwarf alpines to trees 12 to 18 metres (40 to 60 feet) high, are particularly magnificent, and include many species from the Far East and Himalayas planted when they were first introduced into England in the early twentieth century by collectors such as George

From Bodnant's five great terraces there are panoramic views west towards Snowdonia. This is the Lily Terrace, with a glimpse of the little mill on the level below, which was brought to the garden from Gloucestershire.

Forrest, Frank Kingdon-Ward and Dr J.F. Rock. Most of the Chinese species grown from seed and sent back by Dr E.H. Wilson between 1900 and 1906 are represented here, and there are also examples of the many hybrids raised by the 2nd Lord Aberconway and the late F.C. Puddle, pioneers in this field, including *Rhododendron* 'Elizabeth', *R.* 'Winsome', *R.* 'Fabia Tangerine' and a hedge of *R.* 'Bluebird'. Some species particularly suited to the garden, such as *Eucryphia glutinosa* and *Camellia* 'J.C. Williams', are planted extensively, and many specimens of the Chilean fire tree, *Embothrium lanceolatum*, several of them a special form raised from seed brought back from the Andes by Harold Comber of Nymans (*see* p.280), dot the garden with patches of brilliant scarlet in late May.

Two of the five terraces are devoted to roses, with a rose-hung pergola framing the steps leading to the lower of the two. The Italianate theme is continued in the little open-air stage which closes one end of the Canal Terrace, facing down the water to the classical mill. Set several feet above the terrace, the stage is fronted by a curving hemispherical wall and bordered and backed by wings and hedges of clipped yew. Even more memorable is Henry Pochin's laburnum arch at the very top of the garden, transformed into a long feathery yellow tunnel in early summer, with thousands of strongly scented blossoms dangling only inches above visitors' heads. No wonder that Henry Pochin chose to be buried here. The sturdy granite tower which he built as a mausoleum on a bluff above the valley is now also the last resting-place of his daughter and her son and grandson, the 3rd Lord Aberconway, who died in 2003.

Bookham, Headley Heath, Holmwood and Limpsfield Commons SURREY

Running west to east along the North Downs [443 I5]

There are four sizeable Surrey commons, all different, all immensely valuable, on the fringes of London. The Bookham Commons, 2 miles west of Leatherhead, lie on clay, and are therefore different in character from the typical Surrey heath. Thickly wooded in the north, with open spaces to the south-west and ponds where all three species of newt breed, they have a good bird life. Four miles to the east lies Headley Heath, which was much churned up by tank training during the Second World War. The heathland, with scattered birch on the flatter, upper parts, has been extended by active habitat management, whilst

the steeper slopes carry mixed woodland and areas of chalk downland. At Holmwood Common, a mile south of Dorking, the land is clay again. Grazing ceased in 1960 and birch scrub is becoming established, followed by oak and beech, but the wide, grassy rides provide sunny clearings and glades and valuable remnants of the former open common. Four Wents Pond in the south-east corner is the honeypot. Limpsfield Common, on Surrey's boundary with Kent, lies on a greensand ridge at 152 metres (500 feet). Steep slopes combine with a well-varied vegetation, and the common has the classic ragged and irregular shape, funnelling out along numerous roads.

Bourne Mill ESSEX

1 mile south of centre of Colchester, in Bourne Road, off the Mersea road [443 K4]

This unusual little building with dormer windows in its steeply pitched roof and fanciful pinnacled Dutch-style gables was built by Sir Thomas Lucas as a fishing lodge in 1591. Constructed of rubble and brick from the ruins of the Abbey of St John in Colchester which had been dissolved some half a century before, the walls incorporate Roman remains and various medieval moulded stones, and the 1.6-hectare (4-acre) millpond may have been the monks' stewpond. A weather-boarded projecting sack hoist and the surviving machinery, including a 5.5-metre (18-foot) overshot water-wheel with 64 buckets, date from the mid-nineteenth century, when the mill was first used to grind corn. For the previous 200 years it had played a part in the East Anglian cloth industry, used to spin yarn and for fulling woven cloth. Golden-yellow butterworts and other water-loving plants along the mill stream and borders filled with herbs and medicinal plants contribute to the special appeal of this property.

Bradley Manor DEVON

On outskirts of Newton Abbot, on the A381 Totnes road [442 D7]

The panoramic view from the top of Wolborough Hill just outside Newton Abbot looks over rolling countryside to the barren heights of Dartmoor. Deep in the valley below, half hidden by a thick blanket of oak and beech, is this L-shaped medieval manor house, with glimpses of gables and tall chimneys through the trees. A long, low building, home of the Yarde family for over 300 years, it is

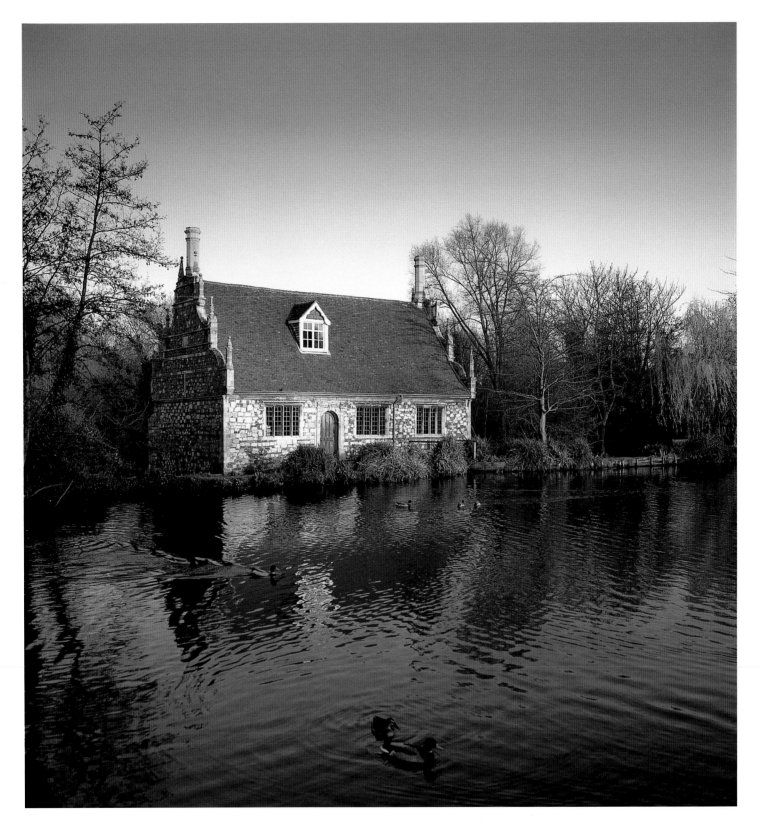

built of roughcast local limestone limewashed white, with granite doorways and fireplaces and a slate roof. Despite some intrusive nineteenth-century castellations, the striking east façade is almost entirely fifteenth century, from the projecting chapel with a magnificent Perpendicular window at one end to the original cusped Gothic lights in the gables.

The interior is medieval in plan, with the hall to one side of the screens passage running across the house. The rooms are mostly low-ceilinged and rough-walled, with a massive granite fireplace in the old kitchen. Only the hall, rising to the rafters, is spacious. There is a carved oak screen in the arch leading to the chapel and a brightly-painted Tudor coat of arms high on an end wall and, in an upstairs room, three-dimensional seventeenth-century plasterwork, with lifelike depictions of roses, tulips, primroses, acorns and beech husks echoing the flowers and trees in the woods around the house.

Bradnor Hill HEREFORD & WORCESTER

½ mile north-west of Kington, north of the A44 [442 E3]

The Welsh Marches provide some of the least-known but most wildly beautiful open country in Britain. Bradnor Hill, to the north of the hilly little market town of Kington, has a golf course laid out across its steep contours, but for once this use does not impair the hill's beauty, which

depends on its shape, the way it perches above the valley of the River Arrow, and the views from its 391-metre (1,284-foot) summit. From the top one can see for miles: east into the woods and meadows of fruitful Herefordshire, south down the great Wye Valley, west to Radnor Forest and the ramparts of Wales.

Braithwaite Hall NORTH YORKSHIRE

1½ miles south-west of Middleham, 2 miles west of East Witton on the A6108 [445 I5]

This remote seventeenth-century stone farmhouse is the centre of a hill farm in Coverdale on the eastern edge of the Pennines. Massive chimneystacks frame the gabled principal façade with mullioned windows looking north to Wensleydale. Original interior features include seventeenth-century fireplaces and panelling and the exceptional oak staircase with turned balusters which rises from the stone-flagged hall.

Bramber Castle WEST SUSSEX

In Bramber, south-east of Steyning, just north of the A283 [443 I6]

Like Cilgerran or Dunstanburgh (*see* pp.92 and 132), Bramber occupies a natural, defensive position, set high above the River Adur on a steep escarpment of the South Downs. This once-mighty Norman castle, the stronghold of William de Braose, was intended to guard the vulnerable route inland from the coast, and there are panoramic views eastwards over the river estuary and the low-lying land on either side.

Completed by about 1100, some 200 years before Dunstanburgh or Cilgerran, Bramber is one of England's earliest stone castles and is also one of the few mentioned in Domesday Book. Now only fragments remain, a stone finger 18 to 21 (60 to 70 feet) high marking the site of the massive square keep which once crowned the motte. The walls of flint, chalk and rubble have been continually mined for building materials but surviving portions are still 1.5 to 2 metres (5 to 6 feet) thick. There are also traces of the curtain wall and a deep ditch marks the site of the former moat.

Occupied into the fourteenth century, it seems Bramber was then abandoned by its owners, the Howards, later Dukes of Norfolk. By the sixteenth century the castle had already become part of history.

These charming cottages in Branscombe, a south Devon village set in a deep-cut valley leading down to the sea, date from the late 17th century. Many other thatched buildings in the village include the old smithy and a bakery.

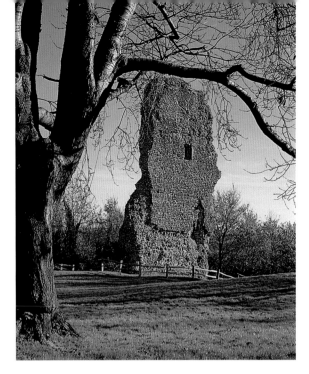

provide the particular stone needed for restoration work at Exeter Cathedral.

Rempstone Rocks, above the west side of Weston Mouth, rise to 158.5 metres (520 feet), the highest point on Devon's south coast, with views east to Portland and inland to Dartmoor. Because of the chalk and limestone on or under the soil, the flora is considerably varied, including several orchids and an abundance of blue gromwell, and while the more common seabirds nest here, as do jackdaws and kestrels, it is the smaller birds which find the scrubby thickets so attractive: chaffinch, chiff-chaff, dunnock, linnet, grasshopper warbler and wren.

The superb landscape surrounding the town of Sidmouth is protected by the Trust which owns Salcombe Hill to the east and Peak Hill to the west. Both hills offer marvellous panoramas stretching over 40 miles in either direction from Portland Bill to Start Point, and at a height of over 152.5 metres (500 feet) they are some of the finest cliffs on the south coast.

Left: Only a finger of stone remains of the once massive keep of Bramber Castle, built by the Normans to guard a vulnerable route from the south coast.

Below: Brean Down juts out dramatically into the Bristol Channel at the mouth of the River Axe. A naturally defensive site, this narrow promontory of hard, windswept limestone has many remains of prehistoric settlement and its seaward end is dominated by the fort which was built here in 1867 as part of the Channel defences.

Branscombe and Weston Mouth DEVON

On the south coast, stretching for 4 miles from Branscombe Mouth to Dunscombe Cliff, and overlooking Sidmouth [442 E7]

The south-east coast of Devon has a character all of its own. From the shingle beaches the ground rises steeply to 152.5 metres (500 feet) but the cliffs are not sheer; rather they are broken and tumbled. Only at Branscombe Mouth and Weston Mouth do valleys lead down to the coast. The geology is mixed, and worth sorting out, for it very clearly conditions what the visitor sees. Clay with flints covers the high ground; beneath it is cretaceous greensand and chalk, with red Triassic Keuper marl below.

The steep land, on the chalk and greensand, is scrubby, in some places wooded and excellent for exploring, but at Branscombe by no means all is owned by the Trust. Nearly all the farmed land between the village and the sea, the attractive wooded fringe of the escarpment and the beach itself belong to the Trust, but the cliffs, including Branscombe Humps, are in other hands.

At Weston Mouth to the west, south-east of the village of Salcombe Regis, the Trust owns a mile and a half of the cliffs and much of the wooded Dunscombe Valley leading down to the sea. Here are more Humps, as at Branscombe, where chalk was burnt to make lime and piles of discarded flints remain. In recent years a quarry was reopened to

Brean Down SOMERSET

2 miles south-west of Weston-super-Mare, the south arm of Weston Bay [442 E5]

The motorist driving west on the M5 from Bristol sweeps effortlessly over the spectacular Failand gorge. Running down the hill beyond, there is the glint of water ahead: the

Bristol Channel between Clevedon and Weston-super-Mare. Beyond Weston a great hump, like a submerging hippo, projects for three-quarters of a mile into the sea.

The peninsula, of hard carboniferous limestone, is 91.5 metres (300 feet) high, and was an island until the draining of the marshes of the Bleadon Levels, on the mainland at the mouth of the River Axe. Man has probably lived here since the Ice Age ended, 10,000 years ago. There are Bronze Age barrows and burial cairns, an Iron Age fort, Celtic field systems and, on the second highest point of Brean Down, the foundations of a Roman temple built between AD340 and AD367. It is possible to reconstruct in some detail the dignified design of this building, a square sanctuary within a tower, an entrance porch flanked by Tuscan pillars, an ambulatory, a vestibule and two annexes.

Much later, in the Middle Ages, the peninsula was used as a rabbit warren, easily enclosed from the mainland

and with an artificial mound to house breeding stock. In the nineteenth century a 'Palmerston' fort (now owned by the Trust) was built on the tip of the peninsula, and occupied as recently as the Second World War. The final development, an attempt to build a pier and construct an artificial harbour, failed when the works were swept away in a storm. There is a lot to see within a small compass and the vegetation of the western-facing slope is almost unique in Britain.

Brecon Beacons POWYS

5 miles south of Brecon, east of the A470 [442 D4]

The Brecon Beacons lie close to the industrial towns of South Wales: Merthyr Tydfil is only 10 miles to the south. They are much frequented, much written about and necessarily much organised by the admirable staff of the National Park. The immense views from the summits are superb.

At the west end of the dramatic cliffs above Cwm Sere and Cwm Cynwyn, carved out by the glaciers of the Ice Age and by erosion over thousands of years since, the Old Red sandstone reaches its highest point in Wales at Penyfan's 886 metres (2,906 feet). Penyfan and Corn Ddu, half a mile to the west, stand at the centre of the Trust's 3,642-hectare (9,000-acre) holding. From the latter the scramble along the ridges of Gwaun Taf and Fan Ddu is thrilling.

To the south and west, the grassy moors drop rather more easily down to the Merthyr reservoirs beside the A470, and the walker wanting something quite different in character can find it here by taking the track from the Storey Arms down Glyn Tarrell to the Trust's farm of Blaenglyn, and then back across the valley to the A470: a tumbling stream, little woods, shelter, peace.

Bredon Barn HEREFORD & WORCESTER

3 miles north-east of Tewkesbury, just north of the B4080 [442 F3]

Once slumbering peacefully on the banks of the River Avon, the rural tranquillity of this cathedral-like building has been destroyed by the ceaseless roar of traffic on the M5. Built in 1350 for the Bishops of Worcester, lords of the manor here for about 600 years, Bredon Barn is beautifully constructed of local Cotswold stone, with stone tiles on the steeply pitched roof. It is the only aisled barn in the

The Brecon Beacons: the view from the summit of Penyfan towards Corn Ddu, with the Black Mountains in the distance. These high, sheep-grazed moorlands cut by a series of deep, shadowy valleys are a dramatic, ice-sculpted landscape, home to the raven and buzzard and other upland birds and offering exhilarating walking and panoramic views.

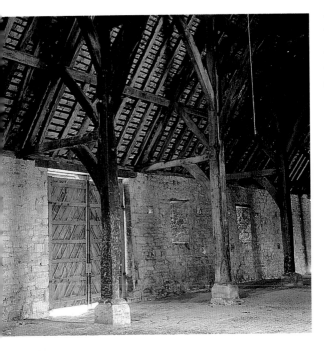

Bridestones Moor NORTH YORKSHIRE

12 miles south of Whitby, 7 miles north-east of Pickering, east of the A169 [445 K5]

Ten miles west of Scarborough, Staindale drains part of the enormous conifer forest of Dalby, eventually flowing into the River Derwent. Between the forest and the A169 lies the Trust's 485.5-hectare (1,200-acre) Bridestones property.

From the car park (not National Trust) beside the Staindale Beck, one can walk through an attractive open wood of oak and larch up the curiously named Dovedale Griff, with the hill farms of High and Low Pastures rising to the west. The valley forks and up Bridestones Griff becomes open moorland on either side, with the extraordinary Bridestones rising out of the heather, for all the world like the great rock figures of Easter Island. The stones, of Jurassic sandstone, are wider at the top than at the bottom, the lower strata of softer rock having weathered away more quickly than the harder rock above. The largest are named the Pepper Pot and the Salt Cellar, though it is not easy to see why. Nearby, hidden in the heather, are the remains of a number of prehistoric barrows which were excavated in the nineteenth century.

To the east, across Crosscliff Beck, is Thompson's Rigg, a substantial island of moorland in a sea of conifers. At its north end is Blakey Topping, a delightful pointed heathery knoll 267 metres (876 feet) high.

Left: The interior of Bredon Barn, showing the great timber posts which support the roof.

Below: Natural weathering has produced the extraordinary rock formations on Bridestones Moor: erosion of lower layers of softer rock has left sculptural stacks of hard Jurassic sandstone precariously balanced on slender supports.

old county of Worcestershire: eighteen great posts like the columns of a nave march down the interior, some blackened timbers being a salutary reminder of the fire which badly damaged the building in 1980.

External stone steps lead up to a room over one of the two porches on the east side, comfortably equipped with a fireplace and a garderobe. From here the bishop's reeve could look down into the barn to check the corn being brought in and the threshers at work.

Brent Knoll SOMERSET

3 miles east of Burnham-on-Sea, 1 mile north of exit 22 on the M5 [442 E5]

The 146.5-metre (480-foot) hill of Brent Knoll rises suddenly from the uninspiring scenery of the Somerset Levels, east of Burnham-on-Sea, and gives its name to a service station on the nearby M5.

The triangular hill-fort is particularly well preserved, perhaps because it is composed of a hard deposit of Midford Sand rising above the limestones and clays of the lower slopes. Re-used in late Roman times, it may have become a stronghold in the troubled period after the Romans withdrew.

The views are unimpeded in this flat landscape: north to South Wales, west to the Quantocks and Exmoor, with Glastonbury Tor (*see* p.162) prominent to the south.

The First Builders and Shapers

Although man has had most impact on the landscape in the last two thousand years, the process began very much earlier, in the long centuries when Britain and Ireland were peopled by our shadowy prehistoric ancestors. Over the millennia, prehistoric man produced a widely settled and farmed landscape. Much has been lost – ploughed out, built over, deliberately destroyed, or buried under later deposits – but much still remains, particularly in upland areas now too marginal and hostile for settlement. The hunting and gathering peoples of the earlier Stone Age, their numbers never more than a few thousand, have left few traces. It was the first farmers, from some time in the 4th millennium BC, who were responsible for the earliest enduring imprints on the landscape. Increasingly settled and territorial, they invested in the impressive communal tombs known as long barrows, dug the earthworks for sizeable enclosures and, as part of a lifestyle based primarily on livestock, began the parcelling up of the landscape.

Moving into the late Neolithic and Bronze Age, there is a sense of the growing importance of ritual and the sacred place, and of peoples with a sophisticated awareness of the heavens and geometry, who were able to create subtle alignments. This era, covering some two thousand years, has left us with the great henge monuments, with stone rows and circles, and with cemeteries of round barrows, each marking the grave of an honoured individual. Less obviously, but of equal importance, these peoples extended the farming landscape, establishing field patterns and trackways which endure. These farmers enjoyed a climate warmer than our own, allowing them to move into upland areas no longer cultivable. But the good times did not last. By *c.*700BC, when iron technology first appeared, Britain was colder

and wetter, and life seems to have become more stressful, with a need to mark and display territorial control. From this period date the spectacular banked and ditched forts that crown so many hilltops in the south of England, and mark sea-girt promontories in the south-west.

CHEDDAR GORGE
88

COLDRUM LONG BARROW
105

SUTTON HOO
380

In warmer inter-glacial periods during the Ice Age, and as the ice retreated, Britain was occupied by hunting bands, who camped in caves and rock shelters such as those which mark the dramatic limestone scenery of Cheddar Gorge in Somerset. Caverns here have yielded evidence of various periods of occupation, with finds that include flint tools, a necklace of fox's teeth, and the bones of horses, bears and wolves, conjuring up a picture of the animals that were roaming southern Britain at this period.

The impressive communal tombs known as long barrows seem to have been associated with early farming communities. Like many other such features, Coldrum Long Barrow in Kent is prominently placed high on the North Downs, suggesting that these monuments may have been territorial markers as well as burial places. After thousands of years of erosion, the barrow has almost lost its covering mound, and the stone walls of the internal chamber, which held the remains of at least 22 people, now stand proud of a gently swelling grassy terrace. The tradition of burying significant individuals in prominent

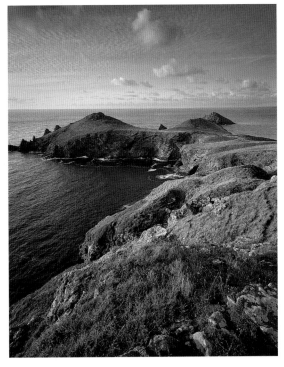

CASTLERIGG
76

EGGARDON HILL
142

TROWLESWORTHY
WARREN
308

THE RUMPS, PENTIRE
HEAD
267

AVEBURY
29

mounds was one that, with some changes in practice, was to endure a long time. Millennia later, in the late 6th and early 7th centuries AD, the local élite in one of the last pagan kingdoms in England were buried in a mound cemetery on the sandy Suffolk heath of Sutton Hoo.

Using only primitive tools of bone and flint and their own labour, Neolithic peoples built the enigmatic stone circles and rows which are a feature of upland and western Britain. The largest stone circle in Europe is Avebury, where the remains of a ring of sarsens, the biggest some 6 metres (20 feet) high, are surrounded by an immense bank, originally rising 15 metres (50 feet) from the ditch on its outer side. Over the centuries, Avebury village, which once stood outside the circle, has gradually encroached on the monument, leading to the unforgettable juxtaposition of pretty cottages and ancient stones. Avebury is part of a rich prehistoric landscape on the downlands of Wiltshire. Far to the north, on a fell-ringed plateau, Castlerigg stone circle in Cumbria stands alone. It is much smaller than Avebury, with 40 ice-smoothed boulders forming an enclosure with a maximum diameter of about

30.5 metres (100 feet), but is similarly elusive. Most probably these were sacred spaces, and focal points for festivities and trade.

Many hilltops in southern England carry the grassy banks of prehistoric defences dating from the late Bronze Age or Iron Age. Typified by the spectacular hill-fort on Eggardon Hill in Dorset, these were built on commanding sites with massive earth ramparts ringing a central enclosure. Although their function is disputed, these hill-forts seem to point to a period of rising tensions and insecurity, when local communities, perhaps under the leadership of a warlord, felt the need for a defended focal space. One explanation points to the gradually worsening climate after *c.*1300BC, when the long hot summer of the

Neolithic was followed by cooler, wetter conditions that would have forced a retreat from settled uplands and other marginal areas. The high moors of Dartmoor in Devon, for example, carry many remains of Bronze Age hut circles, such as at Trowlesworthy Warren. Some forts were built on defensible cliff-tops, like the promontory known as the Rumps on the north coast of Cornwall. Here, a series of ditches and ramparts was built across the narrow isthmus which is the only access to the promontory, and the area protected was large enough to hold flocks of sheep and wooden huts.

Bridge House CUMBRIA

On a bridge over the Stock Ghyll, in the middle of Ambleside
[445 H4]

This quaint two-storey building precariously poised over the Stock Ghyll in the middle of Ambleside, its rough stone walls and a slate-flagged roof typical of early Lakeland construction, has been immortalised by numerous artists, including Turner and Ruskin. Dating from the seventeenth century and consisting of just two rooms, one above the other, it was originally a summerhouse which also acted as a covered bridge for the Braithwaites of Ambleside Hall up the hill. Said to have housed a family of eight in the mid-nineteenth century, it has also served as a cobbler's shop and a tea-room and is now a Trust information centre and shop.

Brimham Moor NORTH YORKSHIRE

8 miles south-west of Ripon, 10 miles north-west of Harrogate [445 I5]

At Brimham Moor the Trust's 162 hectares (400 acres) of open moorland stand high above Nidderdale, with a profusion of millstone grit 'stacks' eroded by thousands of years of weathering. Many of the stacks are named in a rather pedestrian way: Mushroom, Flower Pot, Pulpit, Baboon's Head, Sphinx, Rhinoceros. The most imaginative is the Druid's Writing Desk.

Above: This weathered outcrop of millstone grit is one of the eye-catching rock formations on Brimham Moor, a windswept escarpment high above Nidderdale.

Right: The medieval manor house of Lower Brockhampton is reached through a little timber-framed gatehouse set over the moat. Both buildings were constructed of massive timbers from the surrounding estate and this is still a heavily wooded landscape, with some ancient oaks amongst more recent plantings.

Brockhampton Estate
HEREFORD & WORCESTER

1½ miles east of Bromyard, mostly on the north side of the A44 Worcester road [442 F3]

Due west of Worcester the A44 winds its way through gentle hills to the unassuming little town of Bromyard. At the top of the hill, 2 miles before the town, a tiny neo-Grecian lodge marks the gate into this substantial 680-hectare (1,680-acre) estate. Beyond, undulating, oak-studded parkland falls away steeply into a deep leafy valley; extensive woodlands are planted with oak, ash, Douglas fir and larch, all of which do well on the rich sandstone soil; and there is farmland, with pleasing groups of buildings. In the depths of the valley, reached by a private road that seems to descend for miles, is Lower Brockhampton, an enchanting timber-framed medieval manor house surrounded on three sides by a moat. A little gatehouse is set over the moat, its upper floor jettied out over the lower and the whole thing so warped and twisted that it lurches crazily. Set back 15 metres (50 feet) or so, and facing south across a grassy court, is the manor itself, an L-shaped building in which a great hall open to the rafters filling the stub of the L is attached to a two-storey wing. Red-brick chimneys rear up from the end walls.

When the manor was built, probably some time between 1380 and 1400, only a generation had passed since the population of England had been decimated by the Black Death. Crumbling walls on the fringes of the Malvern Hills to the east were typical of abandoned settlements on marginal land, and the economic depression of these years also saw the fragmentation of many great estates. But the middling landowners with modest holdings in well-endowed country were better placed to survive and prosper. John Domulton, a descendant of the Brockhampton family which was here from at least the twelfth century, may have been just such a man. His house is small and unpretentious, but it was comfortable for its day, with a great chamber, once filling the upper floor of the wing, for the family to distance themselves from their servants and retainers. The moat, which originally encircled the house, may well have been necesssary in the unsettled country of the Welsh Marches, but may also have been regarded as a status symbol, and the gatehouse is a later addition, dating from the fifteenth century.

Lower Brockhampton was constructed of massive timbers from the estate, the high quality of the woodwork particularly evident in the framework and roof of the hall. A ruined Norman chapel in the farmyard to the west of the house was probably built by the Brockhamptons in about 1180 and high in the parkland above, with panoramic views over a deeply rural landscape, is the mid-eighteenth-century red-brick Brockhampton Court (not open to the public), built to replace the old manor far below. The Court was left to the Trust with the rest of the property in 1946 by Colonel John Talbot Lutley, who wanted Brockhampton preserved as an example of a traditional agricultural estate. Waymarked walks lead across the park and through the woodland. There are buzzards, kestrels, woodpeckers and redstarts to be seen and views of the Georgian house and across the Teme Valley.

Brownsea Island DORSET

In Poole harbour, about 1½ miles south-east of Poole; boats run from Poole quay and Sandbanks [443 G7]

Since the Trust acquired Brownsea Island in 1962, great changes have taken place in Poole harbour and its surroundings. Poole is very much part of the prosperous south-east, and the boating industry, already well established there, has become a major business, with its full accompaniment of boat yards, chandlers, marinas and holiday flats. More than this, the large oilfield centred at Wych Farm, immediately to the west, has also brought new developments. The Trust's initiative in saving Brownsea Island from exploitation has therefore been tremendously worth the major effort involved, ensuring the preservation of an oasis for wildlife in a highly commercialised natural harbour.

One lands at the quay with a feeling of relief. At once peace envelops the visitor, for the island is remarkably inward-looking and self-contained. It is not the views that one remembers but what one finds within its 202.5 hectares (500 acres): reedy marshes, quiet beaches, heath and woodland, a place where one needs time to saunter.

The island belonged to the monks of Cerne Abbey and after the Dissolution of the Monasteries it was fortified by Henry VIII during his major revamping of coastal defences. Henry's castle was held for the Parliamentarians during the Civil War but had become a ruin by the Restoration. Thereafter the island passed through many ownerships until it was bought by a rich man, Charles van Raalte, in 1901. He lived here in great splendour and in 1907 invited General Baden-Powell to hold the first camp here from which sprang the Boy Scouts' Association.

The last private owner, Mrs Bonham Christie, lived in the property in seclusion from 1927 to 1961. She actively discouraged visitors and took no steps to control the encroaching undergrowth which, in the soft coastal climate, began to turn the island into a jungle, a paradise for wildlife during her time, but a problem for the Trust.

There is a little village at the quay, cottages formerly needed by the staff at the castle (now let as a holiday centre) and by the coastguards, and a little church. The cottages, strung out along the edge of the beach, add much to the island's character. Dating from the early nineteenth century, they are in a delightfully whimsical Gothick style, ornamented with battlements, armorial shields and even arrow slits. Marble steps and octagonal turrets flag the landing-stage for the castle, which was rebuilt in pseudo-medieval style after a fire in 1897. The rest of the island is wholly undeveloped. It is one of the few places where the red squirrel survives in Britain and is an important breeding site for terns, visiting waders and wildfowl. The Trust

The whimsical Gothick terrace at the eastern tip of Brownsea Island, embellished with castellations and the odd arrow slit, was built in the early 19th century for men of the coastguard service. Apart from this little village, the island is almost entirely undeveloped and is one of the last British haunts of the red squirrel.

has not opened it up in a ham-fisted way; rather, it has very gently cleared rides, modified the undergrowth and freed the rarer plants from being smothered. The process is continual but remarkably unobtrusive. The northern half of the island, including a freshwater lagoon, is let to the Dorset Trust for Nature Conservation and managed as a nature reserve. Tours of the reserve are available, and it is possible to see a wide variety of bird life. There are avocets in season, sandwich and common terns breed on gravel islets in the lagoon, and reed and sedge warblers are attracted to the vegetation along the water's edge.

Bruton Dovecote SOMERSET

½ mile south of Bruton across railway, ¼ mile west of the B3081 [442 F6]

Nothing remains of the Augustinian abbey which once dominated the little town of Bruton except a section of wall and this unusual dovecote standing alone on a hillock in what was the abbey's deer park. Adapted by the monks from a gabled Tudor tower with mullioned windows, it is now roofless.

Buckingham Chantry Chapel
BUCKINGHAMSHIRE

On Market Hill, Buckingham [443 H3]

The fine Norman south doorway, probably brought here from elsewhere and originally intended for somewhere grander, is the most memorable feature of this tiny, 11.5-metre (38-foot) rubble-built fifteenth-century chapel, the oldest building in Buckingham. It was used as a school from the Reformation until 1907 and was substantially restored by Sir George Gilbert Scott in 1875.

Buckland Abbey DEVON

6 miles south of Tavistock, 11 miles north of Plymouth [442 C7]

Francis Drake's tiny *Golden Hind* left Plymouth on a cold winter's day in December 1577 and did not return until nearly three years later, on 26 September 1580. This historic voyage was the first circumnavigation of the globe by an Englishman, involving what must have been a terrifying passage across the unknown expanses of the Pacific Ocean. A national hero on his return, Drake needed a house which reflected his newly acquired status, ironically choosing to purchase the abbey which had been so recently converted by his rival, Sir Richard Grenville. It was from here that he planned his assault on the Spanish Armada a few years later.

Set among sloping green lawns and exotic trees and shrubs on the edge of the sleepy Tavy Valley, Buckland Abbey is rich in associations with Drake and in echoes of the great monastery it once was, the last Cistercian foundation in England, established some 140 years after Fountains (*see* p.154) in 1273. Like Lord Sandys at Mottisfont (*see* p.254), Richard Grenville chose to form his house out of the thirteenth-century abbey church rather than using the domestic buildings of the community. The exterior of his mansion is dominated by the abbey's great crossing tower, the arch of the demolished south transept outlined clearly on the wall below, while the tracery of the chancel arch and ancient mouldings are visible inside.

Imaginative displays in the long gallery running the length of the top floor outline the history of the abbey from medieval times to the present day. Carved stones, pieces of tracery and floor tiles help recall the monastic community which lived here for some 300 years, growing gradually richer on an income derived from tin mines in the Tavy Valley as well as from the tenants on their estates. Drake's coat of arms over the fireplace, on which a fragile ship is guided by the divine hand of providence, heralds the displays on the floor below. Gorgeous flags – one showing the golden leopards of England on a red ground – may have flown on the *Golden Hind*. Other cases contain Elizabeth I's commission of 5 March 1587, giving Drake command of the fleet with which he 'singed the King of Spain's beard', Armada medals, the first ever struck to commemorate a historical event, and finds from Spanish ships that foundered off Ireland. A fascinating document details the Armada accounts from December 1587, early entries covering payments ('to drummers, carpenters, cooks, mariners, surgeons') concerned with preparations to meet the Spanish, later months including terse references to engagements. Marginal notes in Treasurer Lord Burghley's thin spidery hand record sums reimbursed, such as the payment in October 1588 to cover the loss of a fireship. Here, too, is Drake's drum, which was with him on his epic voyage and when he died of dysentery off Panama in 1596. It is said to beat if England is ever in danger.

The only complete interior surviving from these times is the fine sixteenth-century great hall. Dating from Sir Richard Grenville's conversion, it is warmly panelled in oak and decorated with an elaborate ceiling and a holly

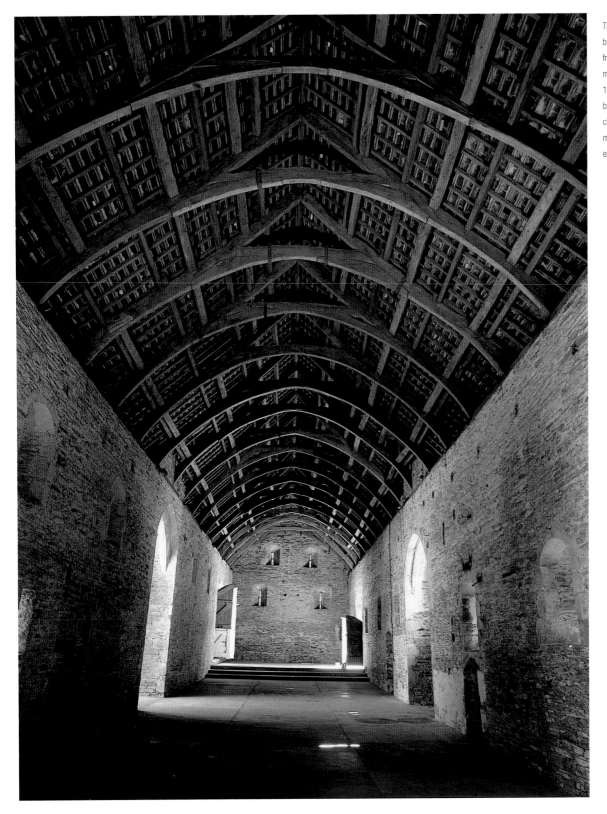

The Great Barn at Buckland Abbey, built to store crops, wool and hides from the estates of the Cistercian monastery that was founded here in 1278. The cathedral-like size of the barn, which was bigger than the abbey church, shows how successful the monks were with their farming enterprises.

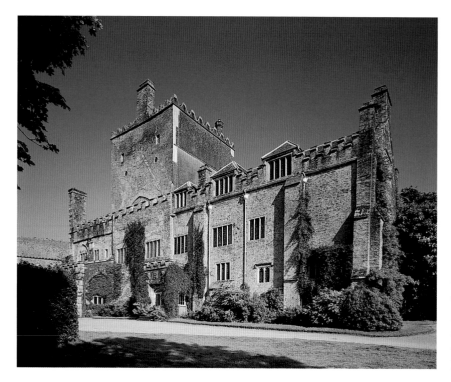

Buckland was one of several abbeys that were converted into great houses after the Dissolution of the Monasteries in 1539. Unusually, the abbey church was used as the basis of the house and three floors – a great hall with chambers above – were made out of the nave. The house is dominated by the former church tower on which the outline of a demolished transept can clearly be seen.

the River Tone joins the River Parrett which flows on to Bridgwater and the sea. The Mump, Triassic limestone with a cap of Keuper marl, stands at the rivers' confluence. It was an island before the levels were drained in the Middle Ages, and in a wet season when the levels flood it still gives the impression of being completely surrounded by water.

The most notable feature of the Mump is the shell of a late eighteenth-century church on its summit. In fact the building, on the site of an earlier church, was never completed but the ruin gives great character to the little hill. From it there are views in all directions.

Buscot Park OXFORDSHIRE

Between Lechlade and Faringdon, astride the A417 [443 G4]

This extensive estate straddling the River Thames in the fertile valley above Oxford was the scene of an extraordinary agricultural experiment in the nineteenth century, when a rich Australian, Robert Tertius Campbell, turned Buscot into the most progressive farm of its time. Largely given over to sugar beet, the grandiose schemes which eventually overwhelmed his resources included a distillery for converting the sugar into spirit and over 6 miles of narrow-gauge railway for bringing in the crop.

Two years after Campbell died in 1887, Buscot was sold to Alexander Henderson, later 1st Lord Faringdon, politician, financier of exceptional ability and connoisseur. The art collection acquired by this remarkable man was enriched by the 2nd Baron, a prominent socialist, who seems to have inherited many of his grandfather's talents.

The house itself is a rather severe late eighteenth-century Neo-classical building, probably designed by the then owner, Edward Loveden Townsend. Two pavilions set either side, and the imposing flight of steps flanked by bronze centaurs leading up to the pedimented entrance front, were added by Geddes Hyslop in the 1930s for the 2nd Baron, who also did much to reinstate the original character of the house. The interiors are both sensuous and cultivated, with extravagant chandeliers, inlaid and painted Regency and Empire furniture, richly coloured carpets and gleaming mahogany doors.

An original filigree ceiling looks down on the Italian paintings in the drawing room, including Pace's powerful *St Jerome*, and Palma Vecchio's strangely asymmetrical *Marriage of St Catherine*. Here, too, is the delightful *Rest on the Flight into Egypt*, attributed to Andrea Previtali, showing the Holy Family enjoying a substantial picnic of

and box frieze adorned with carved figures. Contemporary plasterwork on the end walls symbolising Grenville's retirement to Buckland shows his shield hanging on a tree and a large pile of discarded arms. A Georgian dining room and the elegant staircase curling up through four floors were added during late eighteenth-century improvements.

A picturesque group of granite outbuildings with lichen-stained roofs includes an ox-shed introduced by the agricultural improver William Marshall, who spent four years at Buckland in 1791–4. Only metres from the abbey is the huge, heavily buttressed monastic barn, built in about 1300. Almost 49 metres (160 feet) long, it is one of the largest in Britain, eloquently suggesting the wealth of the community. Sinuous box hedges like window tracery enclose a little herb garden, where it is easy to imagine white-robed figures moving silently from bed to bed collecting lovage, balm or sweet cicely. Close by is a recreation of an Elizabethan garden.

Burrow Mump SOMERSET

2½ miles south-west of Othery, just south of the A361 [442 E6]

At only 3.8 hectares (9½ acres), Burrow Mump is tiny. Pimple that it is, it rises boldly above the flat wastes of the Athelney marshes south of Sedgemoor. At Burrow Bridge bread and cheese, the food carefully set out on a white cloth on the ground. The Faringdons' catholic collection also embraces paintings by Gainsborough, Rembrandt and Reynolds, as well as some twentieth-century works, including two menacing bee pictures by Graham Sutherland. A number of canvases reflect the 1st Lord's interest in the Pre-Raphaelites, perhaps inspired by his neighbour, William Morris, whose house at Kelmscott lies close by over the fields. Works by Rossetti, Watts and Millais are overshadowed by Burne-Jones's cycle based on the Sleeping Beauty story, *Legend of the Briar Rose*, his richly coloured panels set in a gilt framework running round the walls of the saloon like a mural. The knight who has come to wake the beautiful princess faces her across the room, as if he has to fight his way through the rose forest on the walls to reach her, past the sleeping knights of the court entangled in thorny branches and the old king himself, slumbering on his throne, his grey beard reaching to his waist.

East of the house, wooded slopes fall to the large lake created when the park was landscaped in the eighteenth century. Cutting boldly through the trees, and linking house and lake, is a cool Italianate water garden, a chain of cascades, basins and canals fed by a dolphin fountain and crossed by a little hump-backed bridge. Box hedges frame the vista, which extends across the lake to a little classical temple on the further shore. This water garden, including the classical temple, was designed for the 1st Lord Faringdon by Harold Peto in the early twentieth century, reflecting period interest in the gardens of Renaissance Italy, where water was used to dramatic effect.

To the south, broad grassy avenues lead through the trees, with a series of circular clearings giving interest and contrast. One is ringed by variegated holly; a second is sunken and planted with low juniper round an Italian well-head; and a third has a marble vase containing the ashes of the 2nd Lord Faringdon, who devised this scheme in the 1930s.

Under the present Lord Faringdon, the garden is continuing to evolve. West of the house, reached by a dramatic switchback path, is the former kitchen garden with mellow brick walls tracing an irregular octagon. This is now a formal ornamental garden, quartered by alleys meeting at a central lily pond and fountain. The planting gives year-round interest, from the spring bulbs in the borders and early blossom of crab apples and cherries to a show of roses and laburnum in summer and autumn, and winter colour from rowans, maple and winter-flowering cherry.

Cadbury Camp BATH & NE SOMERSET

2½ miles east of Clevedon [442 E5]

Although it is not easy to find, Cadbury Camp stands high above the dramatic section of the M5 where the motorway carves its route through the high Failand ridge east of Clevedon. It has the inevitable Iron Age hill-fort and should not be confused with the very fine Cadbury Camp overlooking the Exe Valley north of Exeter, nor, nearer at hand, with the Cadbury Camps at South Cadbury or Congresbury.

Calke Abbey DERBYSHIRE

9 miles south of Derby, on the A514 at Ticknall between Swadlincote and Melbourne [443 G1]

However you approach it, this imposing three-storey baroque house is hidden in a fold of the landscape. Set some distance from any public road, Calke Abbey lies buried in its beautiful eighteenth-century park, the thousands of trees grouped in picturesque clumps and windbreaks and framing a chain of ornamental lakes seeming to provide insulation from the world outside.

Calke was built in 1701–4, but the symmetrical grey sandstone façades decorated with fluted pilasters and a balustraded roofline conceal the substantial remains of earlier buildings, some of the stonework perhaps recycled from the priory of Austin canons established here in the early twelfth century. Embellishments by William Wilkins the Elder in 1793–1811 include the pedimented entrance portico and the sophisticated suite of Georgian reception rooms on the first floor.

Like Kedleston only a few miles to the north (*see* p.200), Calke has been in the hands of the same family for hundreds of years, each generation of the Harpurs and Harpur Crewes contributing to the extraordinary individuality of the house. More remarkably, little has been changed since the mid-nineteenth century, providing a unique insight into mid-Victorian England.

William Wilkins's drawing room, with its yellow silk curtains and gilded wall mirrors by the fashionable Georgian cabinetmakers Tatham and Bailey, is still as cluttered as it appears in a photograph of 1886, a mélange of embroidered chairs and stools, numerous occasional tables and ornaments under glass domes. Display cases full of glistening polished stones are no preparation for the contents of the saloon next door, remodelled by Henry Isaac Stevens in 1841. Stevens's coffered ceiling decorated with the Harpur boar and his elegant panels hung with family portraits fade into insignificance beside the cases of stuffed birds and geological specimens and the stag trophies mounted on the walls. A noble head even looks down on Tilly Kettle's charming portrait of Lady Frances Harpur and her son.

These unusual exhibits reflect the interests of Sir Vauncey Harpur Crewe, the idiosyncratic recluse who inherited Calke in 1886 and filled the house with his collections. Increasingly unpredictable, Sir Vauncey took to communicating with his servants by letter, would make off into the woods when his wife entertained, and forbade his tenants to cut hedges so as to provide maximum cover for the birds. Carriages now displayed in the stable yard reflect his insistence that motor vehicles should not be allowed on the estate.

Sir Vauncey seems to have had nothing in common with the three Georgian baronets, two Sir Henrys and Sir Harry, whose keen interest in the turf is commemorated by paintings of racehorses by Sartorius and Sawrey Gilpin in the library and by three florid eighteenth-century racing cups. Lady Caroline, wife of the 5th Baronet, one of the Henrys, was given the sumptuous state bed, its beautiful Chinese silk hangings embroidered with dragons, birds, deer and other traditional motifs in rich blues, reds, greens and oranges still as fresh as when it arrived in the

eighteenth century. This treasure was found in a packing case, and many more gems also lay forgotten behind closed doors or languished in outhouses – Victorian dolls in mint condition, books full of dried flowers, a Georgian chamber organ and a harpsichord by Burckhardt Shudi. Household objects which would have been thrown away long ago in other establishments, such as the row of leather fire buckets and the antiquated kitchen equipment, have also survived here: a reflection of instincts that would drive the house-proud mad.

Several members of the family lie buried in Abbey's graveyard and vaults of the undistinguished early nineteenth-century church, a remodelling of an Elizabethan building which crowns a rise to the south of the house. Nearby, hidden by a screen of trees, is the large late eighteenth-century walled garden, a combination of the ornamental and the practical. Mixed borders against the walls and geometrical beds in the lawn of the flower garden echo Victorian planting schemes, and historical varieties of fruit and vegetables, many of them known in the 1770s when the garden was created, mark the site of the original physic garden. Of the 1.6-hectare (4-acre) kitchen garden, only some old fruit trees trained against the walls, the orangery and three ornamental ponds survive.

Specimen trees, including a wide variety of exotics, delicate shrubs and carpets of bulbs in spring adorn Sir Harry's pleasure ground round the house, separated from the park by a sunken wall. Red and fallow deer which were latterly allowed to wander here, causing considerable damage, are now restricted to the north-east corner of the park and varieties of trees and shrubs popular in the mid-nineteenth century are being planted. The park beyond is rich and varied, including patches of bracken woodland and stretches of closely cropped grassland grazed by a flock of rare Portland sheep. Gnarled old oaks, descended from the medieval woods out of which the park was created, harbour an unusually rich insect population, suggesting unbroken continuity with the primeval forest cover.

Canons Ashby NORTHAMPTONSHIRE

On the B525 Northampton–Banbury road [443 H3]

Set in the rolling, thinly populated country of south Northamptonshire, this ancient courtyard house seems lost in a time warp, summed up in the motto 'Antient as the Druids' which is set over the drawing room fireplace. A lime avenue from the garden leads to an unexpectedly grand church, all that remains of the Augustinian priory

Set low in a fold of an extensive wooded park, Calke Abbey is one of the most secluded of houses.

which gave Canons Ashby its name and which once dominated a thriving medieval village, now only bumps and furrows in the grass. Although reduced to a quarter of its former length, the church is impressive, with a striking red and white arcade on the west front and a massive pinnacled tower visible for miles.

John Dryden's modest H-shaped Tudor manor, built with material from the demolished east end of the church, now forms the great-hall range of the house, with its unusual squat tower like an echo of a Cumbrian pele rising over the south front. The wings to the east enclosing the cobbled internal courtyard were added by his son Sir Erasmus, the 1st Baronet. Unlike the finished stone and brickwork of the exterior, the courtyard walls are rough and irregular, patterned with lichen and moss and set with leaded windows.

Some recently uncovered murals painted in grey-blue monochrome date from Sir Erasmus's time, the most complete showing a great sailing ship at anchor in front of a walled city. Sir Erasmus was also responsible for the striking domed ceiling arching over the drawing room, every inch crowded with elaborate plasterwork, with thistles and pomegranates set on curving branches and grimacing Etruscan masks staring down. Three long sash windows lighting this room, added when Edward Dryden remodelled the south front in 1708–10, look out over a rare formal garden of the same date. A flight of terraces falls away from the house, stained stone steps linking one level to another. The character of the garden changes down the slope, the smoothly mown grass and topiary yew of the two upper terraces giving way on the third to an orchard planted with varieties of apples and pears known in sixteenth-century England, while the lowest level is a wild garden with meadow flowers in long grass. Florid baroque gate-posts pierce the enclosing walls. Edward was also responsible for Canons Ashby's dignified west front, now looking out over a grassy court but for centuries, from 1550 to c.1840, used as the main entrance to the house. Edward's imposing baroque doorway dominates the façade, and he probably commissioned the sculptor Jan Van Nost to supply the leadwork coat of arms above the entrance and figures for the garden, of which only a statue of a shepherd boy survives. The classical *trompe-l'oeil* decoration in the painted parlour also dates from Edward's time, executed by his cousin Mrs Creed, and it was he who purchased the exquisite needlework-covered furniture in the Tapestry Room, embroidered with flowers and pastoral scenes.

The present entrance to the house, across the cobbled courtyard and into the great hall, was arranged by Sir

Henry Dryden, the much-loved Victorian squire of Canons Ashby known as the Antiquary. Fired by a lifelong interest in medieval architecture, Sir Henry largely preserved the house as it was, his only major addition being the oak bookcases in the little library where he wrote his learned articles. Leather-bound volumes now filling the shelves include the works of the three important literary figures associated with the house: the poet Edmund Spenser (1552–99), author of *The Faerie Queene*, who was a cousin of Sir Erasmus Dryden's wife; the poet laureate John Dryden, who visited the house as a very young man in the 1650s to pay court to his cousin, daughter of the 3rd Baronet; and the playwright and novelist Samuel Richardson (1689–1761), who is said to have written much of *Sir Charles Grandison*, his improbable moral tale about a virtuous paragon, at Canons Ashby.

Carlyle's House LONDON

24 Cheyne Row, London SW3 – off Cheyne Walk, between Battersea and Albert Bridges on Chelsea Embankment
[443 I5]

When the historian and philosopher Thomas Carlyle and his wife Jane moved to London from Scotland in 1834, they decided to rent this unpretentious Queen Anne house in the then unfashionable area of Chelsea. Here they lived until their deaths, hers in 1866 and his fifteen years later, furnishing the house with good but unremarkable Victorian pieces and a wealth of books and pictures. Still filled with the Carlyles' possessions, the walls crowded with photographs, watercolours and drawings of themselves, their families and places they loved, this otherwise unexceptional house conveys a remarkable impression of the great man and his lively and intelligent wife.

The kitchen with its cast-iron range where Carlyle would smoke so as not to offend his wife, is very little

Above left: Once the main entrance to Canons Ashby, the Green Court is now a grassy sward presided over by a statue of a shepherd boy and his dog attributed to Jan Van Nost. The Court was turfed over in the mid-19th century by Sir Henry Dryden (above), who is shown standing on the steps of his preferred entrance, from the older and more romantic Pebble Court.

Opposite: The Winter Parlour at Canons Ashby, showing the intriguing painted decoration dating from the later 16th century. By that date, the family would have retired here to eat in privacy and comfort, using the Hall only on special occasions.

changed, and so too is the sitting room, with its *chaise-longue* covered in black horsehair and the cloth over the table brought from Mrs Carlyle's Scottish home. The book-lined drawing room upstairs is where Carlyle wrote *The French Revolution*, the work that was to establish his reputation, painstakingly recasting the first volume after it had been accidentally burned while on loan to John Stuart Mill. In the attic room, which the great man built on in 1853 in a vain attempt to provide himself with a soundproofed study, a scorched fragment of manuscript is all that remains of the original draft.

While Carlyle wrote with vision about the condition of mankind, his wife is remembered for her witty and caustic correspondence with family and friends and for the wide circle of eminent figures she received in Cheyne Row, including Dickens, Tennyson, Browning, Thackeray, Ruskin and Darwin. While Thomas Carlyle's reputation has since dimmed, Jane's stature has grown, and her observant letters are now regarded as among the best in the English language.

Carneddau and Glyderau
GWYNEDD AND CONWY

8 miles south-east of Bangor, astride the A5, near Capel Curig [444 F8]

The Carneddau and Glyderau are divided from the Snowdon massif by the Llanberis Pass. Here the Trust owns 7,053.5 hectares (17,430 acres) of superb hill country, the majority of which was acquired with Penrhyn Castle

(*see* p.298) and which offers exhilarating walking for the experienced and well equipped.

The area is divided by the A5, which crawls up the Nant Ffrancon Pass to Llyn Ogwen, and then gently descends to Capel Curig. To the south of the lake is a great semicircle of mountains, long beloved of climbers and geologists, but also of botanists, for here, miraculously preserved, is a prime example of the effect of the Ice Age on a volcanic landscape.

Beautiful Tryfan rises 610 metres (2,000 feet), from the shore of Llyn Ogwen to its peak of 3,010 feet, in little more than half a mile. Glyder Fach, to the south, is slightly higher, while Glyder Fawr, to the west, is tallest of all at 917.5 metres (3,278 feet). The range turns north to Y Garn and the semicircle is complete, enclosing the lake of Llyn Idwal, on the former site of a glacier. Here, and on the slopes of Cwm Idwal in which it lies, are alpine plants of the utmost rarity, such as the Snowdon lily. Travellers in the eighteenth century, on their last stage from London to Holyhead, thought the mountains were 'horrid'. Our twenty-first-century eyes can only find their screes and precipices magnificent.

On the north side of Llyn Ogwen rises the high Carneddau, much less frequented and accessible only to the stout walker. One can take in the peaks, the highest south of the Grampians – Carnedd Dafydd at 1,044 metres (3,426 feet), Yr Elen at 966 metres (3,169 feet) and Carnedd Llewelyn (just over the Trust's boundary) at 1,062 metres (3,484 feet) – or set one's course at a rather lower level. Perhaps the best approach is that taken in the Second World War by so many soldiers posted to Bangor to do their battle course, leaving the A55 coast road at Aber and winding up the beautiful valley of the Rhaeadr-fawr to Aber Falls, then up the Afon Goch with views over an upland landscape crossed by dry-stone walls and dotted with the occasional ancient sheepfold.

Cartmel Priory Gatehouse CUMBRIA

Cavendish Street, Cartmel [445 H5]

Although both the turret and battlements which once crowned this picturesque stone gatehouse-tower straddling Cavendish Street have been removed, it still rises imposingly above the roofs of the surrounding houses, a reminder of the need for protection against Scottish raids in the troubled border country of the Middle Ages. Apart from the church of St Mary, the gatehouse is all that remains of the Augustinian monastery founded here in

1189–90; a strengthening of the priory's defences with the construction of the tower in 1330–40 may have been prompted by Robert the Bruce's devastating raids in the neighbourhood a few years earlier. Despite the insertion of later windows and the slate roof, the gatehouse has a substantially medieval appearance and is the only secular pre-Reformation building in Cartmel. The large room over the archway was once used for manorial courts and from 1624–1790 as a school.

Castle Coole CO. FERMANAGH

1½ miles south-east of Enniskillen on the A4 Belfast–Enniskillen road [444 A4]

This austere white palace, James Wyatt's masterpiece, is one of the finest Neo-classical houses in the British Isles. Built between 1789 and 1795 for Armar Lowry Corry, the future 1st Earl of Belmore, it was designed to provide a suitably grand setting for a prospective member of the peerage and also to surpass Florence Court across Lough Erne to the south, the house which had recently been embellished by Lowry Corry's brother-in-law, Lord Enniskillen (*see* p.151).

The shady path up from the car park by the stables suddenly emerges on the grass in front of the house to give an oblique view of the dazzling entrance façade faced in creamy Portland stone, originally shipped from Dorset to a special quay built at Ballyshannon and brought by cart and barge up Lough Erne. A pedimented portico rising the height of the house is echoed in open colonnades linking the main block to pavilions on either side, a rather old-fashioned Palladian design reminiscent of Robert Adam's Kedleston (*see* p.200), which may reflect the fact that Wyatt had to work with the foundations for a scheme of *c.*1785 by the Irish architect Richard Johnston. This constraint clearly did not dim his enthusiasm. The quality of the interior detailing is superb, ceilings by Joseph Rose and chimneypieces by Richard Westmacott matched by the craftsmanship evident in the joinery of doors and floors. The unusual survival of a complete set of building accounts and many drawings show that Wyatt even designed furniture and curtains. But he never visited Castle Coole, leaving his plans to be realised by the builder-architect Alexander Stewart.

Sadly, Lord Belmore's ambitions far outstripped his purse, exhausting his funds before his new mansion was fully fitted out. Wyatt's chastely elegant interiors were furnished in an opulent Regency style between 1802 and 1825 by the 2nd Earl, whose relish for the job matched that of his father. Over £26,000 spent with the fashionable Dublin upholsterer John Preston, including the price of one of the few state beds in Ireland, exceeded even the cost of building the house.

Extensively restored by the Trust to reflect its early nineteenth-century appearance, Castle Coole is an intriguing blend of classical and Regency. The dignified entrance hall, with a screen of mock-marble columns and statues in niches, is painted a welcoming deep raspberry as it was by the 2nd Earl. In contrast, grey scagliola pilasters ringing the oval saloon beneath Joseph Rose's delicate ceiling echo the original colour scheme, while ceramic stoves set in niches and the curved doors following the line of the walls are again strongly reminiscent of designs for Kedleston.

The saloon is the centrepiece of the north front, dividing rooms of very different character. The dining room on one side, still lit only by candles, is pure Wyatt, with fan-like plaster tracery arching over the curtainless windows, family portraits set in plaster panels on the slate-green walls and a delicate classical frieze. Gleaming gold plate adorns Wyatt's sideboard, produced in eleven weeks by two joiners in 1797. The drawing room at the other end of the house is furnished with gilt couches and chairs upholstered in salmon pink and with a richly patterned nineteenth-century Aubusson carpet. The library across the hall is more comfortable, with plump tassels and a deep fringed pelmet adorning the crimson curtains, and a plentiful supply of cushions and bolsters lying casually on

One of the finest Neo-classical houses in the British Isles, Castle Coole was built by James Wyatt for the 1st Earl of Belmore, who wished for a house to match his status and to rival Florence Court (see *p.151*), where his brother-in-law lived.

the red velvet of the masculine Grecian sofas. The heavy folds of the drapes are immortalised in white marble on Westmacott's extraordinary chimneypiece, executed while Wyatt was employed on the house but not to the architect's surviving design.

Castle Coole looks out over a wooded park, landscaped in the naturalistic style in the late eighteenth century, which slopes gently down to Lough Coole, the site of a previous house. The double oak avenue along which Castle Coole has been approached since about 1730 is now being replanted and will reach maturity once again some time in the middle of the next century.

Castle Drogo DEVON

4 miles south of the A30 Exeter–Okehampton road via Crockernwell; or turn off the A382 Moretonhampstead–Whiddon Down road at Sandy Park [442 D7]

When Julius Drewe, the self-made millionaire, retired from his retailing business in 1889 aged only 33, he was determined to set himself up as a country gentleman. Fired with the belief that he was descended from a Norman baron, he resolved to build a castle on the acres that once belonged to his remote ancestor, apparently lord of the Dartmoor village of Drewsteignton. Although his initial grandiose plans were scaled down, Castle Drogo admirably fulfilled this ambition.

No medieval baron could have faulted the chosen site, a splendidly defensible moorland spur overlooking the gorge of the River Teign. A road runs along the top of the bluff but the castle is far more impressive if approached by the steep path leading up from the river hundreds of feet below. A jumble of granite walls and towers topped by battlements and pierced by mullioned windows suddenly rears up above the bracken-covered hillside ahead, gauntly forbidding even on the friendliest of summer days. A massive entrance tower with twin octagonal turrets on the west front sports a genuine portcullis and the heraldic Drewe lion is proudly displayed over the entrance arch.

This imposing fortress was commissioned in 1910 from Sir Edwin Lutyens, then at the height of his powers and with the transformation of Lindisfarne Castle already behind him (*see* p.224). The great architect's interiors initially seem as forbidding as the outside of the castle, with bare stone walls and unpainted woodwork suggesting cold discomfort. But Castle Drogo is a great country house masquerading as a fortress. In the airy, panelled drawing room, lit by windows on three sides, soft green walls and

chintz-covered sofas create a restful, luxuriant atmosphere and the agreeable bathrooms, one with an elaborate shower arrangement, were designed with pleasure in mind. Exotic Spanish furniture in several of the rooms was acquired as a result of the spectacular bankruptcy of the banker Adrian de Murrieta, friend of the Prince of Wales (the future Edward VII) and extravagant social butterfly, whose vast red-brick mansion in Sussex Drewe purchased in 1899.

Lutyens was also involved in the unexpectedly large formal garden to the north of the house, although the layout and planting probably owe more to the garden designer George Dillistone, who had worked for Julius Drewe at Culverden in Kent and was employed at Castle Drogo from 1922, than they do to Lutyens himself. Massive clipped yew hedges in geometric shapes and granite steps leading up a flight of terraces have much of the castle about them. A sunken lawn with rectangular rose beds at the lowest level is framed by Lutyens's intriguing raised walks, their sinuous curves based on patterns in Indian tilework, followed by the herbaceous borders on either side. At the top of the garden more yew rings a huge circular lawn, just under 305 metres (1,000 feet) above sea level. To the west, where the ground falls away into the valley, magnolias, camellias, maples and cherries are planted with species and hybrid rhododendrons in an informal shrub garden created in the 1950s.

Sadly, Julius Drewe died only a year after the castle was completed in 1930, but he must have been pleased with his progress in life. Whereas his similarly wealthy retailing rivals Lipton and Sainsbury were ignored by *Burke's Landed Gentry*, the acres he acquired with the fortune amassed from his Home and Colonial Stores gained his inclusion.

Castlerigg Stone Circle CUMBRIA

2 miles east of Keswick, just south of the old Penrith road [445 H4]

This impressive late Neolithic stone circle, also known as The Carles and Druids' Circle, is dwarfed by its magnificent surroundings. Although it is set on a 213.5-metre (700-foot) plateau, the fells rise all around, forming a vast natural amphitheatre. To the north, Skiddaw and Blencathra tower over the fertile valley followed by the Keswick to Penrith road, while Helvellyn dominates the view south.

The slightly flattened stone circle has a maximum diameter of about 30 metres (100 feet) and is formed of 40 ice-smoothed volcanic boulders, the largest of them over

1.5 metres (5 feet) tall. A subsidiary rectangular arrangement of stones jutting into the circle on the eastern side may be a much more recent addition to the monument.

Castle Ward CO. DOWN

7 miles north-east of Downpatrick, 1½ miles west of Strangford village on the A25, on south shore of Strangford Lough, entrance by Ballyculter Lodge [444 D4]

Castle Ward, crowning a gentle slope above Strangford Lough, is a very Irish house. Although built at one period, from 1762–70, it is classical on the east side, with a central pediment supported by four columns, and Gothick on the west, with battlements, pinnacles and ogival windows. This architectural curiosity is a result of the opposing tastes of Bernard Ward, later 1st Viscount Bangor, and his wife Lady Anne. Each favouring a particular style, they agreed to

differ. The interior also reflects the Wards' eccentric approach, with the rooms on his side of the house – the hall, dining room and library – decorated in a Palladian idiom, while those on the west – the saloon, morning room and boudoir – are in an ornate and opulent Gothick, with pointed doors and plaster vaulting. The versatile architect is unknown, although tradition has it that, like the stone of which the house is built, he may have come from Bath (the stone was brought from England in Lord Bangor's own ship and unloaded in Castle Bay below the house).

The stylistic division of Castle Ward was followed by the separation of Bernard and Anne, and by her departure for Bath. During the period of insanity of the 2nd Lord Bangor, his younger brother removed most of the contents of the house, but the elaborate decorative schemes have survived almost unaltered. Three-dimensional plaster motifs stand out white against the green walls of the hall; here a festoon of musical instruments, including drums

The dramatic setting of Castlerigg Stone Circle in Cumbria, with the fells rising all around.

and tambourines, across the room a cluster of agricultural implements, a harrow, axe and billhook. A pedimented door leads into the Gothick saloon, where ogival mirrors between the ecclesiastical traceried windows reflect a cluttered Victorian interior, with photographs on many surfaces, stuffed birds under a glass case, a gossip seat and feathery dried flowers. Next door is Lady Bangor's sitting room, transformed by the voluptuous curves of the Gothick ceiling into a large pink tent. There could hardly be a greater contrast with the restrained treatment of the elegant cantilevered staircase, with a Venetian window on the half-landing and a frieze of acanthus-leaf scrolls on the walls.

Steps lead down past an impressive array of bells to the kitchens, housekeeper's room and wine cellar in the basement, connected by a long whitewashed tunnel to the Victorian laundry, stables and servants' quarters set round a courtyard apart from the house, as was the fashion in eighteenth-century Ireland. A former billiard room in the basement is devoted to the exceptional Mary Ward (d.1869), scientist, painter and wife of the 5th Viscount Bangor. Delicate watercolours of wildlife vie for attention with atmospheric views of the house and estate and with cases of butterflies and insects. Most remarkable are the fruits of her pioneering work with the microscope – magnified images of the eye of a dragonfly, like a blue honeycomb, and of the silvery scales of the jewel beetle.

Castle Ward has one of the most beautiful settings of any house in Ulster, with an eighteenth-century landscape park, in the English style, sloping down to the lough and views over the water framed by mature oaks and beeches. Wildfowl glide over the water, now protected by the reserve established on the lough. Birds also enjoy the Temple Water north of the house, a serene artificial lake created in the early eighteenth century, fringed by palms and smoothly mown grass at its western end and overlooked by a little classical temple. The formal Victorian garden near the house is different in character, with grassy terraces planted with palms and roses rising from a sunken, brightly flowering parterre to a line of Irish yews and a pinetum beyond.

Corn- and saw-mills, a drying kiln and slaughterhouse round a yard near the Temple Water were once the centre of a thriving agricultural estate. Here, too, is the early seventeenth-century tower-house which the Wards built soon after they came to Ireland from England. Nearby is a row of slate-roofed late Victorian cottages constructed for workers on the estate. Only a few decades before, in 1852, the village of Audleystown had been destroyed and its inhabitants transported to America to improve the view from the house. As the accounts in the estate office reveal, some left still owing rent.

The Cerne Giant DORSET

On Giant Hill, north of Cerne Abbas, 8 miles north of Dorchester, just east of the A352 [442 F6]

The Trust owns two of the giant figures cut into Britain's chalk downland. Where the Uffington White Horse (*see* p.427) is unquestionably ancient, the origins of this huge, crudely drawn naked man set on a grassy hillside above Cerne Abbas are much more uncertain. While some believe he dates only from the seventeenth century, others argue that he represents a pagan fertility god, and is as much as two thousand years old. As befits a giant, he stands 55 metres (180 feet) high and the knobbly club he brandishes in his right hand is over 30 metres (100 feet) long. Scientific tests have suggested that a lion skin, now grassed over, may once have hung over his outstretched left arm, lending support to the theory that this is a depiction of Hercules, whose cult was at its height in the late second century.

On the downs above the giant's left arm is a rectangular earthwork known as the Trendle (not owned by the Trust), which may well have had a religious or social function connected with the huge virile figure.

This unspoilt downland is part of a wide belt of chalk country stretching across Dorset which is dotted with prehistoric remains, among them a number of Iron Age hill-forts in the care of the Trust (*see* p.128).

Right: These creamware pottery jugs in the scullery at Charlecote were used for bringing milk from the dairy outside. Each jug has two handles, so it could be carried more easily.

Below: Charlecote Park from across the River Avon, showing the formal garden bounded by a stone balustrade which was added to this side of the house in the mid-19th century.

Charlecote Park WARWICKSHIRE

1 mile west of Wellesbourne, 5 miles east of Stratford-upon-Avon, 6 miles south of Warwick on north side of the B4086 [443 G3]

Charlecote has been the home of the Lucy family for some 700 years. The present house, begun by Sir Thomas Lucy in the mid-sixteenth century, lies at the centre of an extensive wooded deer-park grazed by fallow deer and by a herd of rare Jacob sheep introduced by George Lucy in the eighteenth century. Standing on the banks of the River Avon within easy reach of Stratford, it is here that Shakespeare is said to have been caught poaching and to have been brought before Sir Thomas Lucy, the resident magistrate, in Charlecote's great hall. The young playwright may well have vaulted over the rough oak paling which still surrounds most of the park and which has been perpetuated since Elizabethan times. Shakespeare took his revenge some years later when he made fun of the knight in his portrayal of Justice Shallow in *The Merry Wives of Windsor*, with pointed reference to the Lucys' venerable coat of arms on which three silver pike rise for air.

The house itself is built of red brick to a pleasingly irregular E-shape. With great chimneys marching across the roofline and octagonal corner turrets crowned with gilded weathervanes, Charlecote seems to sum up the very

essence of Elizabethan England, especially when the brickwork is mellowed and burnished by the sun. Queen Elizabeth I spent two nights here in 1572, celebrated in the proud display of her arms over the two-storeyed porch. With the exception of the porch, however, most of the present building is the result of 'Elizabethan' restoration by George Hammond Lucy in the early nineteenth century. Apart from the family paintings, which hang in every room, he was also responsible for most of the furnishings, many of which came from the 1823 sale of the contents of William Beckford's Fonthill in Wiltshire. Most eye-catching is a sixteenth-century Italian marble table from the Borghese Palace, inlaid with brightly coloured birds and with a slab of onyx like a section through a fossilised tree in the centre. The general effect is rich and lush, reflecting advice from the designer and antiquarian Thomas Willement.

Two generations earlier, George Lucy, a cultivated and much travelled bachelor, had employed 'Capability' Brown to redesign the park, sweeping away the seventeenth-century water gardens (shown in the painting above Shakespeare's bust in the great hall) and altering the course of the River Hele (now the Dene) so that it cascaded into the Avon within sight of the house. The balustraded formal garden between house and river, with urns planted with geraniums and lobelia flowering pink and blue either side of the steps into the Avon, is a nineteenth-century addition. More steps lead up from the forecourt onto the Cedar Lawn, with a Victorian orangery and a rustic thatched summerhouse set across the grass. Beyond is the wild garden on a raised tongue of land extending north into the park, with wide views over the Avon to Hampton Lucy church. In deference to Shakespeare, a border close to the orangery has been planted with species mentioned in his plays, dog violets, columbine and cuckoo flower among them.

Some of the earliest parts of the house are in the extensive outbuildings, where the stable block includes a brew-house which was in operation until the 1890s, a wash-house, and a coach-house displaying a collection of vehicles used at Charlecote in the nineteenth century. But only the rose-pink gatehouse with its fretwork stone balustrade survives unaltered from Sir Thomas Lucy's original Tudor house – a tantalising taste of what must have been lost.

Chartwell KENT

2 miles south of Westerham [443 J5]

Several doors lead into the garden from Chartwell. From the windows of every room there are changing vistas down the little combe in which the house is built, up the wooded slope behind or over the soft Kentish countryside to the Weald. This serene setting, still breathtakingly beautiful, was to provide Winston Churchill with inspiration and strength for over 40 years, from 1922 until he left Chartwell for the last time in 1964.

The appeal of this unpretentious red-brick house, with its comfortable airy rooms created by Philip Tilden out of a gloomy Victorian mansion, lies in its powerful reflection of a great and complicated man, whose spirit still seems to linger on here. His bold, bright paintings hang throughout the house, some, such as the simple study of a magnolia on an upper landing, tranquil still-lifes, others recording landscapes he loved, in France, Italy and Morocco as well as around Chartwell. A half-finished canvas stands on the easel in his surprisingly large garden studio, paints laid ready nearby. Finished pictures hang five deep on the walls round about. In the airy, flower-filled drawing room, a card table is set for the bezique he so much enjoyed, and a painting over the fireplace records one of the finest colts from his racing stable. Velvet siren suits, his characteristic wide-brimmed hats and cigar boxes also suggest a man who relished life's pleasures.

But there are other mementoes too. In the lofty study, with its high roof open to the rafters, is the wide mahogany stand-up desk where Churchill wrote the sonorous prose of his *A History of the English-Speaking Peoples* and *The Second World War*. Here he reflected on the growing power of Germany during the 1930s, a threat which he felt was perceived by him alone. This room is still essentially as he left it, crowded with family photographs, a despatch box open on the table. A portrait of his father hangs by

This inviting oak bench, presented to Sir Winston Churchill on his eightieth birthday, stands against the walls of Chartwell, the great man's family home from 1922 until his death in 1965.

the fire and a drawing of his mother radiates her exceptional beauty. Medals, uniforms and other reminders of a life devoted to his country include Churchill's terse directive to Field Marshal Alexander, instructing him to expel the enemy from North Africa, and the Field Marshal's equally short reply, informing the Prime Minister that he had done so.

Chartwell is also very much a family house, with the warmth of a place which has nurtured children. The signatures of Lloyd George, Balfour and Field Marshal Montgomery in the visitors' book are interspersed with the more tentative efforts of less mature hands, friends and cousins of the four young Churchills. And it was the children who decided to mark Winston and Clemmie's 50th wedding anniversary by planting the glorious borders filled with 32 varieties of golden roses which run in a long corridor down the old kitchen garden, just metres from the wall which Churchill built when he was in the political wilderness before the Second World War.

The Churchills' spacious garden falling away to the lakes in the depths of the combe is divided by a loose framework of hedges and walls, with steps from one level to another. Stretches of trees and grass, such as the long terraced lawn in front of the house with wide-ranging views across the valley, are complemented by planting schemes reflecting Lady Churchill's love of cool colours and simple and direct effects. Her walled rose garden to the east of the house is full of pink and white blossom at the right time of year and buddleias bordering the path at the end of the terrace lawn are some of the species chosen to attract brimstones, tortoiseshells and other butterflies. Most evocative is the secluded pond, where an ample garden chair marks the spot where Churchill came daily to feed his golden orfe and ponder life.

Chastleton House, set in a well-wooded landscape on the fringes of the Cotswolds, has survived largely unaltered since Jacobean times.

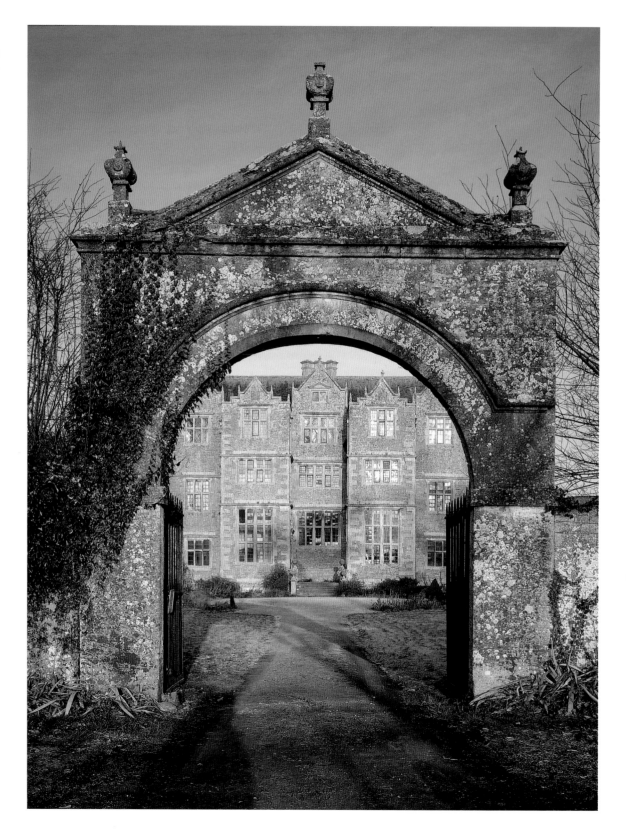

Chastleton House OXFORDSHIRE

At Chastleton off A44 4 miles south-east of Moreton-in-Marsh [443 G3]

On the fringes of the Cotswolds, westwards into Oxfordshire, is an unspoilt landscape of well-wooded farmland and limestone villages. Less than a mile off the main road from Oxford to Evesham, a leafy narrow lane runs steeply up through a straggle of cottages. At the top of the village, set back across a grassy court beside a stump-towered church, is a square, many-gabled Jacobean house. Of mellow local stone, with tall, three-storey ranges set round a tight internal court and mullioned windows, Chastleton is a charming and unaltered example of the kind of manor house which must have adorned a thousand English villages, lived in by families untouched by high office and national events. There are sophisticated touches, such as the arresting south front, with its show of glass and advancing bays, and some fine plaster ceilings, but much else, such as the rough and mossy dry-stone walls lining the entrance court, is rustic and *ad hoc*.

Until it came to the Trust in 1991, Chastleton had been in the hands of the same family for almost 400 years. Built *c.*1610–12 for Walter Jones, a successful wool merchant, who bought the estate from Robert Catesby, the future Gunpowder Plotter, it had been owned by Jones's descendants ever since, with tapestries and furniture identifiable on the inventory taken after his death in 1632. Early prosperity did not last. Although the family was staunchly royalist in the Civil War – when Arthur Jones is said to have evaded a Roundhead search party after the Battle of Worcester by hiding in a secret chamber – there were few rewards at the Restoration, and growing financial difficulties culminated in Henry Jones's imprisonment for bankruptcy in 1755. Chastleton's character comes from the slow accumulation of contents in a house that, like an old coat, was sometimes cut to fit but never drastically altered or updated. Preserving the house's atmosphere and unity was the cornerstone of the Trust's six-year restoration.

Above a substantial basement, where the smoke-blackened kitchen ceiling, said to ensure the family's luck, remains unwhitewashed, is a sequence of parlours and chambers, some tapestry-hung and the grander with carved chimneypieces of stone or wood and decorative plasterwork. Panelling, now dark with age and dirt, is used like wallpaper, and there are pegged plank doors, undulating floors and unfinished corners. The plan is conservative, centred on a traditional great hall, with an

A series of atmospheric interiors includes this bedchamber (left), hung with Flanders tapestries woven in *c.*1600 and with an original plaster ceiling. The bed was put together in the 19th century, but the beautiful crewelwork hangings are work of the 1720s or '30s.

oriel window lighting the high-table end and a carved strapwork screen, and with staircases in crenellated towers to either side of the house. The most ornate interior is the great chamber, where the overmantel, carved with the arms of Jones and his wife, still has traces of its rich red, blue and gold colour schemes and the ceiling is an extravaganza of trailing vines and hanging pendants; the most glorious is the bare and airy long gallery on the third floor, with its silvery panelling and plasterwork barrel ceiling. A glimpse of a more recent lifestyle is given by a spartan, unceilinged maid's bathroom open to the rafters of the roof. The long refectory table in the hall, leather chests in the gallery, and the blue and red flamestitch hangings lining a little closet are among the furnishings given on the 1633 inventory; a brief burst of refurbishment after 1697, when Walter Jones married the forceful Anne Whitmore, accounts for the James II walnut chairs and exquisite Queen Anne crewel-work; and the family's poverty ensured the survival of some seventeenth-century woollen hangings that were once commonplace and are now very rare. There is also an unbroken run of family portraits, including works by Kneller and Hudson.

It was Anne Whitmore who probably laid out the topiary garden to the east of the house, with a yew circle embracing 24 box figures. Including such unlikely arboreal sculptures as a galleon in full sail, these are slowly being coaxed back into shape by the Trust. To the north is a sequence of grassed terraces, the croquet lawn recalling the nineteenth-century Walter Jones Whitmore, who first codified the rules of the game. In a field beyond the garden, on a sightline from the house, is a mature oak, said to be grown from an acorn off the Boscobel tree, the oak in Staffordshire which Charles II hid under to avoid Cromwell's patrols during the Civil War. An eighteenth-century dovecote also stands in the parkland rising to the 241-metre (790-foot) summit of Chastleton Hill.

Man the Landscape Maker

The many generations that came after our prehistoric ancestors have continued the process of imprinting and taming the natural landscape. Where once there was forest or marsh, now there are fields and farm buildings, lanes and villages, while uplands which would naturally revert to scrub and trees are maintained as sheep-grazed grassland or heather moor. Nothing is static or unchanging, with each generation adding an overlay to what has gone before as needs and priorities shifted. Many traces of former landscapes have survived. Undulations in the turf mark the ridge and furrow of medieval farming, grassy mounds on a stretch of moor were once managed as rabbit warrens, and there are remnants of the great royal forests where kings hunted deer and wild boar, with ancient pollarded trees. In the same way, like a face which is etched with the experiences of a lifetime, many landscapes also carry traces of long-abandoned mines or of some other activity that is no longer economic. Sometimes, as with the roofless, rough-walled engine houses which stand high on the Cornish coast, these relics of the past have a haunting beauty of their own.

All these are in a sense fossil landscapes, preserved while the world has moved on. Elsewhere the past is embedded in the present, reflecting the slow and cumulative evolution of what seem like timeless landscapes. The familiar Lake District scene, with small walled fields on the valley floor and open fells above, has developed over centuries, from a medieval economy when vast areas of the fells were monastic sheepwalks and the cultivated land was in common fields to the present pattern of a series of individual farms, each with its own fields and with walled tracks leading out to the grazing on the hills. Although no longer viable, these upland farms are being supported by the National Trust in the interests of preserving one of the most beautiful landscapes in the country.

A characteristic of the Lake District, and of other historic countryside, is that buildings and field-walls are made of local materials, blending naturally into the view. Similarly, the traditional Cornish landscape has field-walls of slate, often built in an attractive herringbone design, with slate slab stiles leading from one field to the next, and the limestone of the Yorkshire dales was used for the dry-stone walls which fret the valleys and for the rough-walled barns, as big as houses, seen in many of the fields. Unlike the Cornish field systems, which are much older, this Yorkshire landscape was a product of late 18th- and early 19th-century enclosure. This was a period of agricultural revolution, when enterprising landowners sought to improve the farming on their estates, introducing crop rotation and other advances, and in some cases going so far as to build architect-designed model farms.

Tree-planting was another facet of improvement, but this was always an ongoing process. Over the centuries, landowners provided shelter belts, planted cover for pheasant and other game, or sought to enhance the scenic beauty of their parks in line with period views, so where one generation planted formal avenues, the next might soften outlines with artfully placed copses and clumps. The hand of man is perhaps most obvious where the landscape has to be artificially maintained, as in the great East Anglian fen. Now mostly under cultivation, with pumps and dykes controlling water levels, this was once a huge wetland, a place of fish and waterfowl, whose denizens lived on islands in the marsh and harvested sedges and reeds and dug the peat. Traditional crops are still taken on surviving pockets of fen in the Trust's care.

GLASTONBURY TOR
162

The distinctive stepped outline of Glastonbury Tor, Somerset, topped off by a 15th-century tower, rises high above the Somerset Levels. Now lapped by pastoral fields, the tor was once an island in an extensive area of fen and lake around the rivers flowing west to the Bristol Channel. A long process of drainage had started as far back as Anglo-Saxon times and was much advanced by the activities of Glastonbury and Muchelney abbeys, which organised the canalisation and control of the rivers. By the early Middle Ages, when local upland parishes had rights of pasture on the levels, they were integrated in a wider rural economy. Today, there are some 5,000 miles of ditches draining an area which is below sea level for up to $5^{1}/2$ miles from the coast.

The glorious medieval churches of Suffolk were built with wealth made from wool, which was exported to the Low Countries and elsewhere in an unprocessed state or woven into cloth. The flocks were grazed on the extensive coastal heaths, or sandlings, which bordered the sea for miles, giving these areas of poor sandy soil an economic importance they would

such as hornbeam, ash and hazel, were regularly coppiced or pollarded, to provide poles for fencing or the wood for tool handles and wheel rims, or to give a renewable supply of firewood. These hornbeams (**bottom**) are in one of the more open stretches of Hatfield Forest, a remnant of the once vast royal forest of Essex which covered the whole county in Norman times, and a

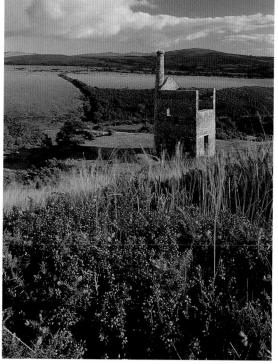

deep cleft in the cliffs forms Boscastle harbour, with a straggle of white-washed cottages above the quay. Two jetties help to shield the inlet from the Atlantic swell. The inner one, dating from 1584, was built at a time when Cornwall's defences were being strengthened against a possible Spanish invasion, the outer one was constructed in the 1820s when this little place was involved in a substantial coastal trade in slate, coal and wheat. Former stables at the head of the harbour housed carthorses for hauling slate and working capstans.

not otherwise have had and, through constantly manuring and treading the ground, helping to make it suitable for the arable farming which has now taken over. Dunwich Heath, a gently rolling extent of heather, tussocky purple moor grass, gorse and other heathland plants, is a remnant of these medieval sheepwalks. Towards the sea are crumbling cliffs of sand and gravel, part of an eroding coastline that gradually took the medieval town of Dunwich, to which the heath was attached, beneath the sea.

For centuries, woodland played as important a part in the rural economy as arable and pasture, and was managed and cropped in the same way. While oak was left to grow as standards, to provide timber for building and shipping, other trees,

mix of coppices and grassy parkland. The forest is divided into sections by ancient woodbanks and is still grazed by muntjac and fallow deer and cut through by the rides and chases followed by the king and his retinue.

The pastoral landscapes, sweeping moorland and pretty villages of the West Country contain the relics of a very different past, when mining and related activities played a major part in the local economy. Mineral-rich veins yielded tin, copper, lead and silver, and the extraction of slate and china clay, both of which continue to this day, has a long history. Both west Devon and Cornwall are dotted with the remains of the great engine houses constructed in

the late 18th and 19th century to drive pumps and winding gear in the mines, some of them set dramatically above the sea, others now romantically shrouded in ivy or half-buried in woodland, and one, the impressive remains of Wheal Betsy, acting as an eye-catcher on an open stretch of Dartmoor in Devon. Similarly, some peaceful villages, now primarily holiday locations, had a very different past. On the north coast of Cornwall, a

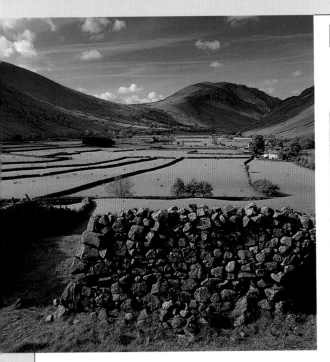

WASDALE
214

WETTON
295

patterned with dry-stone walls constructed from the local limestone, and this hard, grey-white rock was also used for the sizeable field barn, such as here at Wetton.

Trees formally planted in avenues are a notable feature of the country-house landscape. Although followers of the naturalistic landscaping style swept many away, by the early 19th century their aesthetic appeal, and the stamp of authority they give to an approach, was again recognised. This impressive avenue at Clumber Park in Nottinghamshire, over 2 miles long, dates from the 1830s, when it was part of the improvements to the park made by W.S. Gilpin, whose work blended formal and picturesque. Fittingly for an estate that was originally carved out of Sherwood Forest, the trees are lime, one of the native species of lowland England.

CLUMBER PARK
102

The glorious landscapes of the Lake District, with open fells rising steeply above pastoral valleys, have been shaped and moulded by farming practices, and shifts in population, over the centuries, a process which continues today. For a long time, this was a countryside of small farmers, each grazing cattle and sheep on the fells, and growing grain and hay, and keeping pigs, down in the valley. Incomes were supplemented by spinning, fulling and quarrying. From the late 18th century, as secondary occupations disappeared, and towns and cities seemed to offer brighter prospects, many smallholders sold out and moved away, leaving cottages and barns to crumble and decay. In 1578, there were eighteen holdings in the Wasdale Valley, each with its own arable, pasture and farm buildings, and this view down towards the lake (above), now so serene and sparsely peopled, would have seemed less deserted.

In recent times there have been other pressures. One is the growth of tourism, and a demand for second homes here. The other is continuing changes in land use, encouraged by government subsidies. In the Lake District as a whole, there has been a move away from mixed farming to a concentration on sheep, leading to overgrazing on the high fells and invasion of bracken on slopes that were formerly stocked with cattle. Ever-decreasing numbers working on the land mean that maintaining dry-stone walls, gates and stiles becomes increasingly burdensome. By supporting traditional regimes, the Trust is helping to preserve a landscape of great beauty that could be irrevocably changed within a generation.

Traditional farm buildings and other features built of local material blend naturally with the landscape, as if they have always been there. The pastoral dales of the southern Peak District are

The agricultural revolution of the late 18th century, which led to a new focus on the importance of soil quality, crop rotation, animal husbandry and other improvements, prompted some landowners to invest in redesigned farm buildings. At Wimpole Hall in Cambridgeshire, Philip Yorke, 3rd Earl of Hardwicke, commissioned the leading architect Sir John Soane to plan a model farm. Although better known for his work on grander projects, including the Bank of England, Soane's farm was practical and functional. The most important building in his scheme was the great 46-metre (150-foot) barn, completed in 1796. Designed in a vernacular style, with weather-boarded walls and a roof thatched with reed and sedge, it was used to store corn and straw, and for threshing in the winter months. Wicken Fen in Cambridgeshire is a

remnant of the great fen which once stretched across East Anglia to the Wash. Now an island standing above the surrounding farmland, which has shrunk through drainage, the fen's wetland character has to be artificially maintained, with water pumped in rather than out. Within the fen, too, the different habitats have long been man-managed. Beds of reed and sedge were harvested by the fen-landers and sold for thatch and other purposes; peat was dug for fuel; and fish and water birds were taken for food. If left alone, the more open fen would be slowly invaded by scrub and small trees and would gradually disappear. To maintain the wetland landscape, the Trust is continuing to cut reed and sedge, which is used for thatch (the roof of the great barn at Wimpole, for example, is thatched with materials from Wicken Fen).

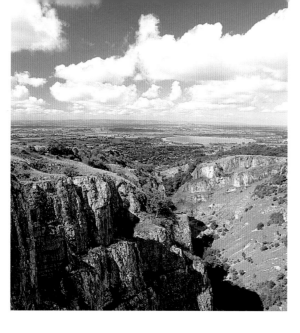

Cheddar Cliffs SOMERSET

8 miles north-west of Wells [442 E5]

On the north and west sides of the famous gorge are the Cheddar Cliffs, 152 hectatres (375 acres) of spectacular limestone cliffs and crags, acquired initially to prevent the spread of commercialisation which had begun at the gorge's lower end. Access is not for the faint-hearted. The Trust has recently devoted much effort to clearing scrub, opening up habitat for specialist limestone-loving plants such as the Cheddar pink, found nowhere else in Britain.

Chedworth Villa GLOUCESTERSHIRE

3 miles north-west of Fossebridge on the A429 Cirencester–Northleach road [443 G4]

Chedworth reveals a life of ease and luxury in Roman Britain. Consisting of low one-storey ranges fronted by verandahs set round a courtyard, with the north side extended in a long wing to the east, the villa strongly suggests the Roman equivalent of a Texan ranch. Although the walls now rise only a foot or two above the ground, exquisite mosaics and other details were preserved by a covering of silt until the remains were discovered in 1864. The impressive dining room, warmed by underfloor heating, is decorated with a fine pavement in red, white and blue, with drunken satyrs cavorting in Bacchic scenes and corner panels depicting the seasons, Winter warmly clad in a hooded cloak, Spring running with a basket of flowers.

Colourful mosaics also mark the two elaborate bath complexes fed from a nearby spring, one the equivalent of a modern sauna, the other providing the steamy heat of a Turkish bath.

This lovely site in a wooded valley in the depths of the Cotswolds was first occupied in the early second century. The villa, one of many in this area, was gradually improved and enlarged over the next 250 years, probably on the profits of a thriving agricultural estate serving the important Roman towns at Gloucester and Cirencester nearby, and perhaps also benefiting from proximity to the Fosse Way linking Exeter to the River Humber.

Early in the fifth century, Roman government in Britain collapsed and at some date after this Chedworth was abandoned.

Cherhill Down and Oldbury Castle
WILTSHIRE

On the A4, between Calne and Beckhampton [443 G5]

The Trust owns over 202.5 hectares (500 acres) of ancient downland overlooking the Vale of Pewsey. While the vale is given over to large-scale arable farming, this is prehistoric landscape, marked by tumuli, earthworks, long and bowl barrows, strip-field systems and ancient tracks, with the Iron Age hill-fort of Oldbury Castle at the down's summit. The Trust's acres are unimproved downland, untouched by plough or chemical spray. There are butterfly-attracting chalkland flowers on the steeper slopes, and a series of deep-cut sheltered combes, including possibly the finest example of a chalkland dry valley system in England, supports herb-rich grassland and clumps of beech.

Walkers clambering up from the A4 are rewarded with the recently restored Lansdowne Monument, built on the crest of the hill in 1845 by the 3rd Marquess of Lansdowne in memory of the economist Sir William Petty; by a fine white horse carved into the shoulder of the down (not owned by the Trust) and by exhilarating views from the 259-metre (850-foot) ridge. The air is like wine and from up here the cars on the A4 are reduced to toys. This is country to restore the soul.

Cherryburn NORTHUMBERLAND

Off A695 at Mickley, 11 miles west of Newcastle [445 I3]

A roughly built sandstone cottage set high above the deep green valley of the Tyne was the birthplace of the engraver and naturalist Thomas Bewick (1753–1828), known for his closely observed drawings, carved in box, of the creatures of the Northumbrian countryside. The cottage – now tiled but originally heather-thatched – looks over a sloping cobbled yard to the substantial farmhouse built in the late 1820s by Thomas's brother William, who took over the family smallholding.

Chiddingstone KENT

4 miles east of Edenbridge, 1½ miles north-west of Penshurst [443 J5]

This leafy single-street village is one of the most attractive of the Kentish Weald, built at a time when the Wealden iron industry was at its height and now all that remains of a much larger settlement destroyed when Chiddingstone Castle park was created. Opposite the largely seventeenth-century church of St Mary stands a perfect group of sixteenth- and seventeenth-century buildings, some half-timbered with black and white façades and overhanging upper storeys, some timber-framed with brick infilling, and all with lichen-stained red-tiled roofs. What is now the village shop and post office is mentioned in a deed of 1453, and most of the houses probably incorporate earlier material. The sandstone block known as the Chiding Stone, by which local men are supposed to have berated their nagging wives and from which the village is said to take its name, lies in the park, below the hill crowned with the Gothick castle (not owned by the Trust).

The Chilterns

Extending from Dunstable, in the north-east, to the River Thames, in the south-west [443 I4]

North-west of London runs the great chalk arc of the Chilterns, its ancient beech woods, heaths and downland offering splendid walking for Londoners with a day to spare. A number of Trust holdings are scattered along the ridge: some, like the 445 hectares (1,100 acres) of farmland and woodland based on the manor and village of Bradenham, are substantial estates; others, like the 45 hectares (112 acres) of Watlington Hill, or the 26.5 hectares (65 acres) of Pulpit Wood, protect prominent features of the landscape or important habitat. Altogether,

Top: The highest point of Cherhill Down is marked by the Lansdowne Monument (not NT), here seen silhouetted against the sky. To the left is the foreshortened outline of the white horse (not NT) carved into the shoulder of this ancient chalk downland.

Above: The small cottage at Cherryburn where the wood engraver Thomas Bewick was born in 1753. The love of the countryside and its creatures which comes through in his illustrations was first nurtured when he helped his father on the family farm.

including land attached to Hughenden (*see* p.195) and West Wycombe Park and village (*see* pp.425 and 427), the Trust owns some 2,833 hectares (7,000 acres) here.

From Coombe Hill, at 260 metres (852 feet) the highest viewpoint in the Chilterns, there are lovely views across the Vale of Aylesbury to the Berkshire Downs and the Cotswolds (*see* p.113). The handsome obelisk on the hilltop is a memorial to the men of Buckinghamshire who fell in the Boer War. On the chalk grow privet, juniper and whitebeam, with thyme, harebell, wild strawberry, bird's-foot trefoil, mullein and dog violet, but scrub would soon take over were it not for the grazing of sheep re-introduced by the Trust in recent years. At Low Scrubs, on the high ground to the east, there are woodland plants – yellow archangel, broad buckler-fern and enchanter's nightshade.

At the north-eastern end of the Chiltern arc is Ashridge. Formerly a monastic property, it was surrendered to the Crown in 1539, and then bequeathed by Henry VIII to his daughter Elizabeth, who spent much of her unhappy childhood here. In 1604 Sir Thomas Egerton bought the estate which remained in the Egerton family (successively Earls and Dukes of Bridgewater, and latterly Earls Brownlow, *see* p.42) until 1921.

The Egertons became enormously rich when the 3rd Duke (1737–1803) developed his coal mines in Lancashire.

This 'Canal Duke', whose splendid memorial column stands on the edge of Aldbury Common, took down the old monastic buildings; James Wyatt and his nephew, Sir Jeffry Wyatville, designed the new house in Gothic style – now Ashridge College – for the 3rd Duke's successor.

The estate, enlarged to some 6,070 hectares (15,000 acres), remained well managed, private and secure until the 3rd Earl Brownlow died in 1921, whereupon Ashridge – like so many other landed estates at that time – was put on to the market to be sold piecemeal for development. Stanley Baldwin, then Prime Minister, appealed to the Brownlow trustees, local people – including the children of the six village schools – worked valiantly to raise money, and help from generous outside donors was enlisted. It was a classic National Trust campaign of its day and 688 hectares (1,700 acres) were triumphantly bought.

The enthusiasm then generated was fully justified and has continued. The Trust's estate now covers over 1,619 hectares (4,000 acres) of wonderfully varied landscape running along the hills from Berkhamsted to Ivinghoe Beacon. There are 485.5 hectares (1,200 acres) of farmland; the rest is common, down and woodland.

To the north the chalk ridge of the Ivinghoe Hills compares with the best of the North Downs (*see* p.272), and has the same problems. When grazing by sheep became unprofitable in the 1930s, and even more after myxomatosis decimated the rabbit population in the 1950s, scrub encroached rapidly. Continual efforts to drive it back are gradually re-establishing the flora.

Crawley Wood, a mile to the south, rises to 244 metres (800 feet), and from there, west of the B4506 from Berkhamsted to Dunstable, is wonderful wooded country, with plenty of paths. Beech, oak, larch and pine predominate but the commons have self-sown silver birch, and Sallow Copse has mature sweet chestnut. Aldbury, Berkhamsted and Northchurch Commons continue the estate across the B4506 south to Frithsden Beeches, resplendent with ancient pollarded beech. View them on a winter's evening, their gnarled encircling branches like a drawing by Arthur Rackham.

Ashridge is the reward of a long campaign, and the extent of this is witnessed by the story of Dunstable Downs. Lying 4 miles to the north of Ashridge, this chalk ridge adjoining Whipsnade had lost its character due to encroachment by scrub. Since its acquisition in 1929–48, the whole plateau has been converted to arable land. The relict of chalk grassland has been cleared and fenced and is now grazed by sheep. Several interesting downland plants survive.

The sizeable Ashridge estate, which stretches along the north-eastern edge of the Chilterns, is known for its glorious woodland, criss-crossed by paths and rides and carpeted with bluebells in spring.

Chipping Campden Market Hall
GLOUCESTERSHIRE

Opposite the police station, Chipping Campden [443 G3]

This little gabled and pinnacled Jacobean building stands prominently in the centre of Chipping Campden, on one side of the wide high street. Like the medieval houses of wool merchants with which it is surrounded, the market hall is built of golden Cotswold stone and roofed with stone slabs. Open arcades on all four sides give access to the cobbled floor where farmers and traders gathered to sell and buy cheese, butter and poultry.

As the coat of arms in a gable at one end signifies, the market hall was built by Sir Baptist Hicks in 1627, only two years before his death. A financier who helped support the extravagances of the court of James I, Baptist Hicks was raised to the peerage at the end of his life and is commemorated by a restrained classical monument in the south chapel of the wool church down the street.

Chirk Castle WREXHAM

½ mile west of Chirk village off the A5 [442 E1]

Chirk Castle is an elegantly appointed house within the carapace of a medieval fortress. The long drive from the baroque entrance gates – a filigree of ironwork touched with gold – leads up through the undulating oak-studded park. The castle, appearing suddenly on the brow of the hill, is unexpectedly menacing, with drum towers projecting from battlemented fourteenth-century walls.

A pointed archway marked with the grooves of a portcullis leads into the internal courtyard. Here the west range still has the character of the stronghold Roger Mortimer started in *c.*1295 as part of Edward I's campaign to subdue the Welsh. Deep underground, reached by a spiral staircase in the thickness of the walls, is a dungeon hollowed out of the rock, only two narrow beams of light reaching those who were incarcerated here. In the courtyard outside a great shaft falls 28.5 metres (93 feet) to the castle well.

These reminders of the turbulent Middle Ages contrast with the domestic interiors produced by the Myddelton family who have lived at Chirk since 1595. The forbidding north range houses an elegant staircase and a suite of late eighteenth-century state apartments designed in the fashionable Neo-classical style by Joseph Turner of Chester, now stripped of the neo-Gothic decoration imposed by A.W. Pugin in the 1840s. A

brilliant-blue Adam-style coffered ceiling, inset with Greek mythological scenes by the Irish painter George Mullins, graces the sumptuous saloon, with gilded doors and dados, a red and white marble fireplace and Mortlake tapestries on the walls. Among the fine contemporary furniture, including a pair of stylish serpentine settees, is a rare signed harpsichord by Burckhardt Shudi, with eagles with outstretched wings depicted in the inlaid interior. These rooms are hung with seventeenth- and eighteenth-century family portraits, including two by the Flemish landscape painter Peter Tillemanns, and works by J.M. Wright, Michael Dahl and Allan Ramsay.

A door from the drawing room leads into the imposing 30-metre (100-foot) long gallery begun in 1670 when Sir Thomas Myddelton repaired extensive damage sustained in the Civil War. Filling the east range, and more than twice the size of the saloon, this room was conceived on the grand scale, perhaps by the gentleman-architect William Winde. Massive broken pediments crown the doors and a bold cornice of carved acanthus leaves runs above the portraits hanging on the richly panelled walls. Among the few pieces of seventeenth-century furniture is a delicate ebony Dutch cabinet inlaid with tortoiseshell and ivory and with a silver-encrusted interior decorated with scenes from the life of Christ, one showing Our Lord blessing children against the backdrop of the gabled façades of a Flemish town. Declining a peerage from Charles II, Sir Thomas accepted this cabinet instead.

Chirk lies in a mature oak-studded park, landscaped

Top: The oak panelling emblazoned with heraldic shields, massive stone fireplace and other 'medieval' fittings in the Cromwell Hall at Chirk Castle were introduced in Victorian times by A.W. Pugin, whose romantic vision is now the setting for a show of Cromwellian armour and muskets.

Above: Companionable figures carved on the handles of cutlery housed at Chirk Castle.

by William Emes in the late eighteenth century, in which the oldest trees date from replanting during the Restoration. On the east side of the castle the grim medieval walls are softened by roses, honeysuckle and other shrubs and plants bordering an expanse of grass and topiary yew, with a massive yew hedge cut to resemble a battlemented wall. A tiny sunken rose garden is focused on a sundial that was probably made for Chirk in the seventeenth century, and a long colourful mixed border nearby was established by Colonel and Lady Margaret Myddelton, who are largely responsible for the restoration of the garden since the Second World War. Two bronze nymphs stand guard over the steps leading down to the vine-entangled thatched hawk house on a lower lawn, picturesquely set against a rock bank planted with trees and shrubs. Other eye-catchers include the early eighteenth-century statue of Hercules, prominently placed at the top of the seventeenth-century lime avenue above the hawk house, and William Emes's delightful classical pavilion at one end of the long terrace fringing the lower lawn. This is the place to sit on a warm afternoon, gazing over the lush countryside of the Welsh borders.

Church House DEVON

Widecombe-in-the-Moor, in the centre of Dartmoor, north of Ashburton, west of Bovey Tracey [442 D7]

The medieval church in this over-visited Dartmoor village boasts a magnificent early sixteenth-century pinnacled tower, paid for by prosperous tin miners. The two-storey granite building known as the Church House in the tiny square by the lych gate is of much the same period, dating from 1537. One of the finest such houses in Devon, it is substantial and well proportioned, with round-headed two-light granite windows and a verandah supported on octagonal granite pillars running the length of the entrance front. Each pillar rests on a roughly hewn boulder. Originally a brew-house, it later became a school and is now partly leased as the village hall and partly used as a Trust information centre and shop.

Cilgerran Castle PEMBROKESHIRE

On rock above left bank of the Teifi, 3 miles south of Cardigan, 1½ miles east of the A478 [442 C3]

Like the great fortress at Durham, Cilgerran is so superbly sited that it seems a natural part of the landscape. Today

the ruins of this stronghold appear not so much formidable as romantic and picturesque, the inspiration of a number of artists including Turner, Richard Wilson and Pieter de Wint. Round towers linked by massive walls 1.2 metres (4 feet) wide in places stand on a rocky bluff above wooded slopes plunging precipitously to the gorge of the Teifi river and its tributary the Plysgog. Only a few miles from the sea, Cilgerran could be supplied by water, and also controlled the crossing point at the tidal limit of the Teifi.

Built by William Marshall, Earl of Pembroke, in about 1225 on the site of an earlier stronghold captured from the Welsh in the Norman conquest of Wales, Cilgerran was constructed only a few years after Skenfrith (*see* p.346), but already castle design had moved on. In place of a central keep, the stronghold's defensive strength is concentrated in the towers projecting from the curtain wall enclosing the tip of the promontory. The remains of a third, rectangular tower probably date from the late fourteenth century, when Edward III ordered the reinforcement of a number of Welsh castles against the threat of a French invasion. In the event, it was the south coast of England that suffered, with raids from Rye to Plymouth. A wide ditch separates this inner ward from the outer court, once crossed by a drawbridge to the gatehouse where the grooves for two portcullises still mark the walls. A second great ditch added further protection beyond the outer ward, where little of the original defences survives. Possibly ruined at the time of Owen Glendower's revolt in 1405, when the castle was briefly held by the Welsh, Cilgerran seems never to have been subsequently repaired.

Cissbury Ring WEST SUSSEX

1½ miles east of Findon, 3 miles north of Worthing [443 I6]

Often so conspicuously sited as to form local landmarks, prehistoric hill-forts would rarely receive planning permission today. Cissbury is no exception. Set 183 metres (600 feet) up on the South Downs behind Worthing, the views from this prominent site range east to Beachy Head and west to the Isle of Wight. The hill-fort itself is huge, one of the largest Iron Age examples in Britain, with a substantial ditch and earth rampart enclosing an area of about 26.5 hectares (65 acres). Built in 250BC but abandoned before the Romans arrived in AD43, the fort was apparently refortified in late Roman times, perhaps against coastal raids, and also shows traces of late Iron Age field systems.

Cissbury is notable too as one of the most important sites of Neolithic flint production. Used to make implements for land clearance and as the basis of formidable fighting and hunting weapons, flint was eagerly sought by prehistoric man, who sank 12-metre (40-foot) shafts into the chalk here, with galleries radiating into the rock following high-quality seams. Now marked by bumps and hollows on the west side of the hill, this early industrial site was worked from *c.*2500BC to 1600BC, when new sources of flint were discovered in Norfolk.

The City Mill HAMPSHIRE

At the foot of High Street in Winchester, beside Soke Bridge [443 H6]

This attractive brick corn-mill with tile-hung gables and a delightful island garden was built over the River Itchen by Soke Bridge in 1743 on a site that has been occupied by a succession of mills since Saxon times. The fast-flowing river which emerges in a spectacular mill race once powered several medieval mills in the city, a reflection of Winchester's early importance as capital of England and as a market for grain and wool. Already in decline by the late fourteenth century as a result of the ravages of the Black Death and the removal of the English wool staple to Calais, the city never recovered its former prosperity.

One of a number of Winchester mills recorded as being connected to the Church in Domesday Book, the Soke Bridge mill was then a property of the Benedictine nunnery of Wherwell a few miles north of the city, passing to the Crown when the monastery was dissolved in 1538–9. Some years later, in 1554, it was given to the city by Mary I in partial recompense for the expense of her marriage to Philip of Spain in Winchester Cathedral. The current mill is not in working order, but it is hoped to operate one of the undershot water-wheels and some of the mill machinery in the near future.

Clandon Park SURREY

At West Clandon on the A247, 3 miles east of Guildford on the A424 [443 I5]

Clandon looks as if it would be more at home on the corner of a piazza in Venice or Florence than set down in the Surrey countryside. It is a massive four-square block of a house, three storeys high and eleven windows wide on the long garden façade, built in the reddest of brick with stone dressings. On the entrance front, a central pedimented

Knyff's view of Clandon Park in 1708 shows the old Elizabethan house in a formal landscape. House and grounds were transformed later in the 18th century but West Clandon church, seen top right, survives.

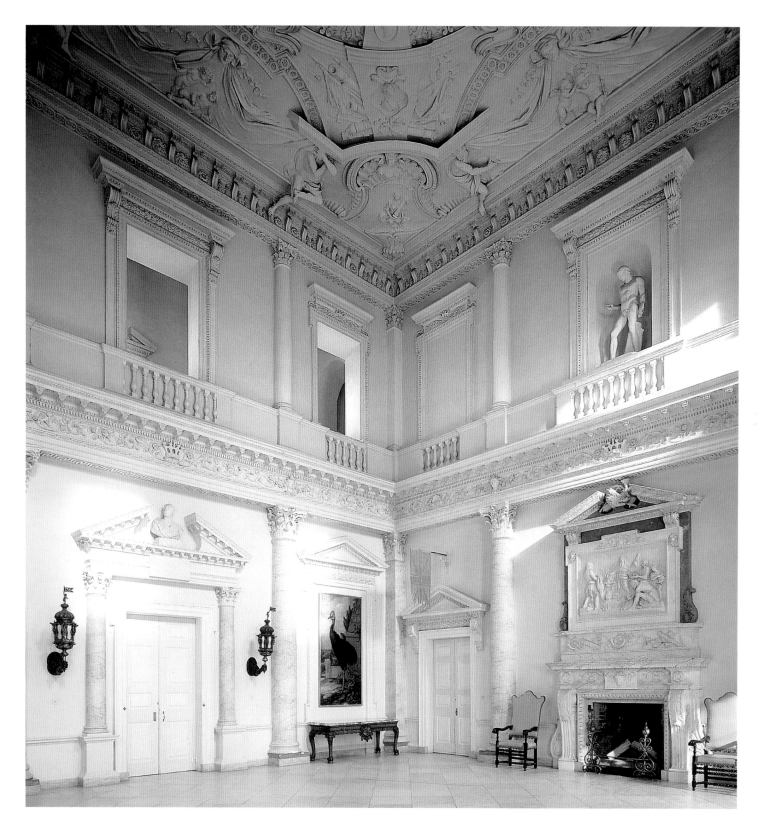

section of stone stands out starkly against the red on either side, as if somebody had forgotten to colour it in. No roof rises above the crowning balustrade to relieve the austere outlines of the building.

This individual Georgian country house, built in about 1731, owes its appearance to the Italian Giacomo Leoni and is one of only five surviving buildings by this Venetian architect in England (*see also* Lyme Park, p.323). The interior is as grand as the exterior, its most impressive feature being the richly decorated formal Marble Hall rising through two storeys with classical statues set in niches at first-floor level. Life-like slaves supporting the central relief of Artari and Bagutti's fine plasterwork ceiling have one leg over the edge of the cornice, as if they could leap down at any moment. The white walls and ceiling, the marble floor and intricately carved marble chimneypieces over the two fireplaces all contribute to the impression of light and space, refreshingly cool on a hot August afternoon. Leoni even extended the marble floor into the grand saloon next door, clearly forgetting the absence of a Mediterranean sun in an English summer.

Clandon was built for Thomas, 2nd Baron Onslow, to replace the Elizabethan house his great-grandfather had acquired in 1641, and it has remained in the family ever since. The Onslows have traditionally followed political careers; the three who served as Speakers of the House of Commons are commemorated in portraits in the Speaker's Parlour. Here too is the 'vinegar' bible which Arthur Onslow, Speaker from 1728–61 and the most famous of the three, presented to St Margaret's, Westminster, its name deriving from the misprint in the parable of the vineyard. The Maori meeting house in the grounds, its steeply pitched thatched roof reaching almost to the ground, is a memorial to another eminent Onslow, the 4th Earl, who was governor of New Zealand from 1888–92 and also rescued Clandon from half a century of neglect by his great-uncle.

Most of the original contents have been sold or re-moved over the years, but Clandon is now filled with magnificent furniture, porcelain, textiles and carpets acquired by the connoisseur Mrs David Gubbay in the 1920s and 1930s and brought here from Little Trent Park in Hertfordshire. Apart from the English eighteenth-century furniture, which includes fine satinwood and marquetry pieces, the jewels of the collection are the 50 or so seventeenth- and eighteenth-century Chinese birds. These exquisitely moulded, vividly plumaged creatures perch on baroque brackets and adorn tables and mantel-pieces, the many species represented including a pair of elegant fragile cranes in the Green Drawing Room and brilliantly blue parrots, red and green pheasants and plump ducks in the Hunting Room. A spectacular phoenix presides over the state bedroom, where the four-poster and accompanying chairs were probably made for Sir Richard Onslow, father of the builder of the house. Clandon now also houses the Queen's Royal Surrey Regimental Museum in the basement.

Claremont Landscape Garden SURREY

On south edge of Esher, on east side of the A307 [443 I5]

Claremont is the product of some of the greatest names in garden history – Charles Bridgeman, 'Capability' Brown and William Kent – and one of the first and finest gardens to be designed in the natural manner, predating Stourhead (*see* p.366) by some twenty years. Laid out round a lake on an undulating 20-hectare (50-acre) site falling away from the house (not owned by the Trust), Claremont is primarily a study in foliage, grass and water, where the overall effect is created by contrasts of light and shade, by the alternation of open glades with densely wooded serpentine paths and by little buildings and other features set as eye-catchers at strategic points.

Although visitors now come into the garden at the bottom of the hill, Claremont was designed to be seen from the top, looking down the broad grass path leading from Vanbrugh's dramatic castellated Belvedere (not owned by the Trust) to the yew-fringed bowling green, or out over the beeches, oaks, chestnuts and cedars to the ornamental lake with its little island crowned with a pavilion. Bordering the lake is an extraordinary turf amphi-theatre, one of only two on such a large scale in Europe. Five steep, giant-size terraces form a semicircle round an oval 'stage', three more spreading out in a descending fan below. Grass ramps on either side lead up to the top. More a piece of open-air sculpture than a setting for dramatic performances, the amphitheatre's curves are framed by a backdrop of trees and ornamented with strategically placed long white benches with high backs, copies of eighteenth-century garden furniture. Across the water, heaped-up boulders and a tangle of vegetation surround a naturalistic sandstone grotto.

The gardens at Claremont were established by the Duke of Newcastle between 1715 and 1750, initially with advice from Vanbrugh, who enlarged the house, but from 1716 with assistance from Charles Bridgeman. This talented landscape designer, who created the network of

Opposite: A carved ho-ho bird from the
virtuoso woodwork by Luke Lightfoot
which decorates the North Hall at
Claydon House.

avenues and paths, the grass amphitheatre and a circular
pond, was one of the first to break away from the formal
layouts epitomised by Le Nôtre's work at Versailles.
Bridgeman's naturalistic approach was taken further by
William Kent in the 1730s, who enlarged the pond into
a lake, planted trees to soften the lines of paths and
avenues and built a ha-ha, a section of which still exists,
to allow uninterrupted views from the garden into the
fields beyond. 'Capability' Brown, working for Lord Clive
on his acquisition of the estate in 1768, seems to have been
restrained from making his usual sweeping changes. Apart
from planting the amphitheatre with trees, now removed,
and building a new house (now used as a school), his main
contribution was to alter the line of the old Portsmouth
road to bring the prominent wooded viewpoint known as
The Mound within the bounds of the garden.

During the nineteenth century, when Claremont was
the home of Princess Charlotte, daughter of George IV,
and then acquired by Queen Victoria for her youngest son,
many exotic trees were planted throughout the estate.
A camellia house was established on the terrace below the
house, its site now marked by beds of tree-like specimens
enclosed by railings adorned with coronets and florid Ls
(for Leopold of Saxe-Coburg, Charlotte's husband).
Twenty years of neglect in the twentieth century almost
obscured Bridgeman and Kent's creation but, although
areas which were once open glades are now thickly covered
with laurel and rhododendrons, restoration has renewed
the vistas which gave Claremont its eighteenth-century
reputation as the most famous garden in Europe.

Claydon House BUCKINGHAMSHIRE

*In Middle Claydon, 13 miles north-west of Aylesbury,
3½ miles south-west of Winslow* [443 H4]

A combination of ambition and gullibility led Ralph,
2nd Lord Verney, to create one of the most extraordinary
houses in England. Inheriting the family estate in 1752,
Verney initially contented himself with reconstructing
and extending his father's old-fashioned Jacobean manor
house, but some ten years later he embarked on a far more
grandiose scheme for a great west front, partly, it seems,
to produce a house to rival that of his much richer neighbour, Earl Temple of Stowe (*see* p.374). The restrained
classical exterior of the surviving west wing conceals
extraordinary decoration by Luke Lightfoot, an eccentric
and difficult genius variously described as cabinetmaker,
master-builder and surveyor, but emerging at Claydon as
a carver of unique talent.

Lightfoot's work in the North Hall and Chinese Room
is in a class of its own. Ceilings, overmantels, doors and
alcoves are encrusted with lacy white woodwork. Herons,
swan-like birds and fantastic wyverns with barbed tails
perch on the tracery. Necks are coiled and snaky, wings
outstretched, claws extended. Tiny bells hang from the
roof of the built-in pagoda-like feature in the Chinese
Room, decorated when the fashion for chinoiserie in
eighteenth-century England was at its height. Carvings
resembling oriental summerhouses surround the doors,
with trelliswork connecting the supporting columns.
Bamboo furniture made in Canton in about 1800 completes the effect.

Lightfoot's extravagance and the failure of a speculative
housing project in which he had persuaded Lord Verney
to invest led to his dismissal before the house was completed. Exquisite plasterwork adorning the saloon and
staircase is by Joseph Rose, who was employed at Claydon
after 1768. Working in plaster where Lightfoot worked in
wood, Rose used conventional classical motifs but executed
them with skill and ingenuity to create two of the finest
Georgian interiors in England. The stairs themselves are
one of the marvels of Claydon, with delicate ears of corn
quivering in the ironwork scrolls that make up the
balustrade and a jigsaw of box, mahogany, ebony and ivory
forming the parquetry treads.

Growing financial difficulties, unrelieved by lawyers
employed to help manage mounting debts, led to the sale
of the contents of the house in 1783, and Verney's grandiose
ballroom and huge rotunda by the architect-squire Sir
Thomas Robinson were demolished by his niece when she

The grassy terraces of the
Amphitheatre at Claremont were
carved out of a natural hill. The lake
beyond was originally round and was
given its present form in the 1730s
by William Kent, who also had trees
planted along the edge of the water.

The alcove in the Chinese Room at Claydon, devised as a teahouse, is a froth of woodwork by Lightfoot, complete with bells, icicles and fantastic creatures.

succeeded to the estate. The Javanese musical instruments filling the museum room, an assortment of gongs and wood and bamboo xylophones collectively known as a Gamelan, were a present to Sir Harry Verney, 2nd Baronet, who inherited the property in 1827. Florence Nightingale would have seen this exotic gift from Sir Stamford Raffles, lieutenant governor of Java, when she came to visit her elder sister Frances Parthenope, Sir Harry's wife. Mementoes of the Lady of the Lamp are displayed in a room adjoining that where she always slept, including letters she wrote as a young girl as well as reminders of the privations she endured in the Crimea, two photographs showing how thin and frail she looked on her return. Unfortunately there is no record of what this most Victorian of ladies thought of the extravagant rococo decoration of her sister's home.

Clent Hills HEREFORD & WORCESTER

3 miles south of Stourbridge, south-east of Hagley, north and east of Clent [442 F2]

The Clent Hills, with the Walton Hill commons to the east, have long been the place where people from Stourbridge, Smethwick, Halesowen, Selly Oak and Bromsgrove have come to breathe clean air and to see a fairer countryside. The grassy hills, wooded in parts, are steep but easy to walk, and the views are superb. To the north-west lies the privately owned Hagley Park, with its

great eighteenth-century house and church lying snugly under the hill; beyond are Kinver Edge (*see* p.205), Wenlock Edge and the Shropshire Hills (*see* p.338). To the south, the rich farming landscape of Worcestershire stretches to the Cotswold ridge (*see* p.114), and west of that the unmistakable whaleback of the Malvern Hills (*see* p.239) rises starkly from the plain.

The view eastward is very different. Birmingham has generated much of the country's wealth, and continues to do so, but beauty is not its *raison d'être*. Far-sighted local authorities gave 178 hectares (440 acres) of the hills to the Trust in 1959, thereby securing their future. High Harcourt farm was added in 1986.

Clevedon Court SOMERSET

1½ miles east of Clevedon, on Bristol road [442 E5]

During the nineteenth century the little seaside village of Clevedon was transformed into a fashionable resort, with Italianate villas, a pier and a Royal Hotel, but the Eltons of Clevedon Court who had done so much to improve the town lived on in the remarkable medieval manor which Abraham Elton I, a wealthy Bristol merchant, had acquired in 1709.

Despite some later additions, Sir John de Clevedon's early fourteenth-century house has survived virtually unchanged, its buttressed walls and the portcullis groove on the projecting two-storey porch suggesting that he needed to build with defence in mind. Perhaps that is why he grafted his manor on to the even earlier massive four-storey tower which rises protectively from the north-east corner. Seen from the south, the low ranges and the steeply pitched roofs studded with tall chimneys are attractively set against the thick woods of Court Hill. Terraced gardens carved out of the hillside rise sharply behind the house, planted with tender shrubs and adorned with two eighteenth-century summerhouses.

Finely crafted fourteenth-century arches on the right of the traditional screens passage bisecting the house were openings to the medieval buttery, kitchen and pantry. To the left is the great hall, now embellished with an eighteenth-century coved ceiling and thickly hung with a mixed bag of Elton family portraits. Sir Abraham, the 1st Baronet, dressed in his scarlet robes as Mayor of Bristol, proudly surveys the descendants who were to enrich Clevedon with literary and artistic associations. A cartoon of William Makepeace Thackeray at the top of the stairs, a shock of white hair standing out from his head and pince-nez on his nose, recalls the novelist's friendship with Sir Charles, the 6th Baronet, a gifted poet whose elegy for his two drowned sons moved his contemporaries to tears. Sir Charles's youngest daughter Jane, with whom Thackeray fell hopelessly in love, was immortalised as Lady Castlewood in *Henry Esmond*, much of which was written in the house. The poet-baronet's circle also included Lamb and Coleridge, and his nephew Arthur Hallam was Tennyson's closest friend, for whom he composed 'In Memoriam'.

The family's artistic streak appeared again in Sir Edmund Elton, whose Eltonware pots and vases made of clay from the estate, mostly in rich, dark colours but including striking sea-blue pieces with metallic glazes, are displayed in the old kitchen and whose vivid portrait by Emmeline Deane hangs in the hall. This remarkable self-taught man began his career as a potter in about 1880, building up an international reputation for his work. Fragile glass walking sticks, some shot through with spirals and twists of colour, glass rolling pins and improbable pipes tinged rose-pink, crimson and blue are part of the collection of local Nailsea glass also shown in the house.

Another side of Victorian Britain emerges on the stairs, where boldly patterned wallpaper by G.F. Bodley shows off a number of prints and engravings illustrating triumphs of engineering in the late eighteenth and nineteenth centuries, from Abraham Darby's iron bridge at Coalbrookdale, constructed in the 1770s, to the Menai Strait, Severn and Clifton suspension bridges and a host of viaducts and aqueducts, their delicate arches carrying the railways and canals that were vital to the achievements of the age.

A tall red and green Eltonware candlestick, designed with Sir Edmund's characteristic flair and originality, stands in the tiny first-floor chapel of St Peter, originally consecrated in 1321. A net of stone tracery filling the south wall, with brilliantly coloured stained glass by Clayton and Bell, not only recalls the patron saint of fishermen to whom the chapel is dedicated but also the Bristol Channel only a mile or so to the west, where the little islands of Flat Holm and Steep Holm stand out black against the sea in the light of a setting sun.

Cleveland Hills NORTH YORKSHIRE

8 miles south-east of Middlesbrough [445 J4]

High above the Tees Valley at Great Ayton stands Roseberry Topping, a 322-metre (1,057-foot) landmark and

Left: Richly-coloured 19th-century stained glass warms the little chapel at Clevedon Court.

Below: The steep green humps of the Clent Hills offer some of the finest views in the Midlands.

viewpoint with the same pyramidal outline as Blakey Topping (*see* Bridestones Moor, p.61) and giving wide views over Cleveland to the North Sea. The Trust owns over 121.5 hectares (300 acres) here, including a brackeny expanse of common and the approach through an important pocket of natural oak woodland (Newton Wood and Cliff Ridge Wood) flanking the south-west slope of the hill, home to spotted woodpecker, pied flycatcher and tawny owl, and rich in woodland plants.

Ten miles to the south-west, above Osmotherley, Scarthwood Moor looks north-east, up the rim of the Cleveland range, and west to the Pennines. Half hidden in the heather are burial mounds from the Bronze Age and Mesolithic remains.

Cley Hill WILTSHIRE

3 miles west of Warminster, on the Somerset border, on north side of the A362 [442 F5]

As one drives west from Warminster on the A362, there are signs of a great estate on every hand. The country is well farmed, the woods well managed, the farms and cottages sturdy and well maintained. The estate is Longleat, to the south of the road, and its spreading woods were once part of the ancient Forest of Selwood.

To the north of the road a green hump appears, rising 91.5 metres (300 feet) out of the surrounding cornfields and dominating the placid Corsley Valley which lies between Warminster and Frome. While not exactly dramatic, it is certainly surprising and utterly fitting in this sylvan landscape. The history of the hill is written on its slopes for the enquiring eye to read. Its shape has been altered many times since the two bowl barrows were built in the Bronze Age. The men of the Iron Age followed by building one of their ubiquitous hill-forts on its summit. In the Middle Ages the hill formed the hub of the common arable field of the manor of Corsley, the village to the north. This Great Field of Cley covered 170 hectares (420 acres) when it was enclosed in 1783. In 1588 the hill was used as one of the chain of warning beacons lit to herald the arrival of the Spanish Armada. Finally, in 1807, substantial quarrying started, to provide lime for agricultural use, and this altered the north-west and south-west spurs of the hill.

From the top the views are east beyond Warminster to further hill-forts at Battlesbury and Scratchbury above the Wylye Valley, west across Frome into Somerset and south over Longleat.

The chalky downland of Cley Hill is known for its colonies of the delicately-tinted chalkhill blue butterfly.

Cliveden BUCKINGHAMSHIRE

3 miles upstream from Maidenhead, 2 miles north of Taplow on the B476 from the A4 [443 H4]

This three-storey Italianate palace floating on a chalk terrace high above the River Thames is the masterpiece of Sir Charles Barry, built in 1850–1 for the Duke and Duchess of Sutherland. An inscription in letters 46 centimetres (18 inches) high running below the urn-studded roofline parapet records the earlier building here which was destroyed by fire – a Restoration house by William Winde for the 2nd Duke of Buckingham, much of whose character Barry preserved – as well as the construction of the present mansion. Curved corridors link the main block to two eighteenth-century wings by Thomas Archer flanking a great sweep of gravel on the entrance front, from where the drive runs straight to a monumental marble fountain, its lines echoed in a mature avenue of limes. On the west side of the forecourt a rocket-like clock-tower rears up from the ornate stable court added in 1869.

From the south Cliveden is even more impressive. Here Barry's main block rises grandly over Winde's long arcaded terrace, 28 arches wide, which extends far beyond it on either side. In the centre a double staircase descends in elegant elbows of stone to the celebrated Borghese balustrade, brought here from the Villa Borghese in Rome in 1896, with elaborate pedestals framing the central opening. Beyond it is a closely mown grass terrace on which beds of cotton lavender and senecio fringed with box hedges and punctuated by clipped yews form a geometrical parterre.

This parterre, with its sweeping views over the beech woods framing the Thames, is a foretaste of one of the Trust's largest and most varied gardens. Some traces still remain of Charles Bridgeman's early eighteenth-century layout for Lord George Hamilton, 1st Earl of Orkney, who bought Cliveden in 1696, such as the yew walks which wind above the Thames to the west of the house, and the grass amphitheatre similar to the much larger example Bridgeman designed at Claremont (*see* p.95). Lord Orkney was also responsible for the two garden buildings by the Venetian Giacomo Leoni: a little temple with a green copper dome and the charming classical eye-catcher with an elaborate pedimented arched opening known as the Blenheim Pavilion.

The garden as it is today owes much to the 1st Viscount Astor, who bought the house in 1893. He introduced the Borghese balustrade, the Roman sarcophagi and the Italian sculpture which are such a feature of the grounds. He

laid out the Italianate long garden, with statuary set along grassy walks bordered with box hedges and topiary, and the informal water garden, with stepping stones leading to a brightly painted pagoda on an island and banks crowded with colourful, moisture-loving plants – golden king cups in spring, primulas, irises and day lilies – and with Japanese azaleas and rhododendrons. Lord Astor also commissioned J.L. Pearson to remodel the interior of the house, but of the three rooms shown (the house is now a hotel), the most seductive is the breakfast room, lined with mirrored, green and gold rococo panelling, brought from France.

The 2nd Viscount Astor and his wife Nancy, whose vivacious portrait by Sargent is a focal point of Pearson's low-ceilinged, oak-panelled hall, made Cliveden famous as a centre of literary and political society, entertaining Henry James, Rudyard Kipling, Curzon and Churchill here. Perhaps these distinguished guests liked to sit high above the Thames under the ancient tree known as Canning's Oak, drinking in the view of the river and its hanging woods which the statesman is said to have so much enjoyed.

The Cloud CHESHIRE

3 miles east of Congleton [445 I8]

The view from the terrace at Tatton (*see* p.384), looks south-east over gently sloping parkland and woodland to a peak rising in the distance. This miniature mountain might have

The grandeur of Cliveden's south front is enhanced by the immense arcaded terrace by William Winde on which it sits. In the foreground is a section of the 17th-century balustrade which once adorned the Villa Borghese in Rome and which was brought here in 1896.

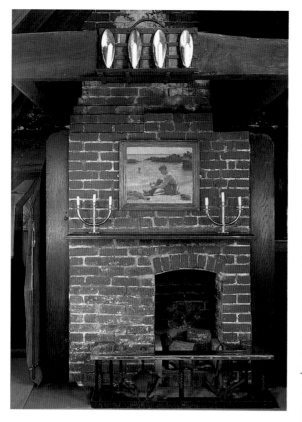

The fireplace in the upstairs room at Clouds Hill where Lawrence worked, read and listened to music. The candlesticks were a leaving present from friends in the RAF when Lawrence was discharged from the airforce in 1935 and the painting by Henry Scott Tuke, dated 1922, may be a portrait of Lawrence.

he used to play Mozart and Beethoven still dominates the music room in the roof and his cell-like bedroom, lit by a porthole window, is as it was.

Here Lawrence would come to read or write by the fire whenever he could get away from the camp, finding the peace and quiet he needed to work on his revision of *Seven Pillars of Wisdom*. Friends were served picnic meals washed down with water or Lawrence's own blend of China tea, but never with alcohol.

For Lawrence the cottage was an earthly paradise. Here he returned to live out his days on his discharge from the airforce in 1935 at the age of 46. Five days later he was dead, killed in a fatal crash when returning to the cottage from Bovington Camp on his motorcycle. The shed where he kept his machine is now used for an exhibition on Clouds Hill and Lawrence's life and times.

Clumber Park NOTTINGHAMSHIRE

4½ miles south-east of Worksop, 6½ miles south-west of Retford, 1 mile from the A1 and the A57, 1 mile from the M1, junction 30 [445 J7]

In the last 250 years Nottinghamshire has changed dramatically, much of its rural landscape scarred or obliterated by industrialisation and urban growth. This 1,619-hectare (4,000-acre) park, once surrounding the country seat of the Dukes of Newcastle, is an acute reminder of what has been lost, a mosaic of grassland, heath, farmland and wood, rich in butterflies and visited by some 130 species of birds.

At the heart of the park is an L-shaped serpentine ornamental lake, with wooded islands dotted down its length, part of Stephen Wright's landscaping scheme for the 2nd Duke in the mid-eighteenth century. The classical eye-catchers – a balustraded bridge across the lake and two temples on the north and south shores – are also his, as are the decorative lodges and gate piers at the park's many entrances. A long grassy terrace running along the north shore of the lake lies at one end of extensive pleasure grounds, with paths winding through glades of specimen trees underplanted with shrubs. The design probably owes something to William Sawrey Gilpin, who advised on the feature in the 1830s, and Gilpin was certainly responsible for the glorious lime avenue bordering the drive from the Apleyhead Lodge. Belts and clumps of broadleaved woodland are also nineteenth-century plantings.

With the exception of the Duke's Study, the grandiose Italianate mansion begun in 1767 to designs by Wright was demolished in 1938, its extent now outlined by paving

been placed there by 'Capability' Brown to give point to the view, and indeed it came to the Trust with Tatton. The Cloud rises sharply to 342.5 metres (1,124 feet) from the plain, its dark heather and screes of huge gritstone boulders making a sombre contrast with the fields and hedgerows below. The views – South Lancashire to the north, the rich farmland round Nantwich to the west, the Potteries to the south and the Pennine range to the east – are outstanding.

Clouds Hill DORSET

9 miles east of Dorchester, ½ mile east of Waddock crossroads on the B3390, 1 mile north of Bovington Camp [442 F7]

T.E. Lawrence – better known as Lawrence of Arabia, the legend of the First World War – bought this little brick and tile cottage on the slopes of Clouds Hill as a retreat from nearby Bovington Camp when he rejoined the RAF in 1925. Its tiny rooms with their simple, even austere furnishings are as Lawrence left them, a direct reflection of his monastic way of life and complex personality. His books have gone from the shelves lining the downstairs room, but the wind-up gramophone with a huge horn on which stones in the grass. The attractive stable block to the north, with a cupola crowning the clock-tower, predates the house by a couple of years. Along a cedar avenue from here, late nineteenth-century glasshouses overlook the walled kitchen garden, with a central palm house projecting in a fan of glass. The fig house and vineries occupying one of the long glassy wings have now been replanted, and fruit and vegetables have been re-established in the upper part of the garden, with a double herbaceous border dominating the ensemble.

Like Studley Royal to the north (*see* p.376), Clumber is crowned by a High Victorian Gothic chapel, built in 1886–9 by G.F. Bodley for the 7th Duke of Newcastle, who, like the 1st Marquess of Ripon at Studley, was a passionate Anglo-Catholic.

Heavily buttressed walls, tall Gothic windows and a soaring 55-metre (180-foot) spire give the chapel the look of a parish church. Inside, it seems like a miniature cathedral, the vaulted roof in shadow high above the nave. Six brass candlesticks stand conspicuously along the elaborately carved rood screen, and ornate Flemish-style chandeliers light the Rev. Ernest Geldart's walnut and oak choir stalls, with limewood musical angels looking down from crocketed canopies on either side. Stained glass by C.E. Kempe, rich tapestries and velvets and silk altar frontals, including an early work by J.N. Comper, complete a masterpiece of Gothic revival architecture.

Coggeshall Grange Barn ESSEX

South of Coggeshall, on B1024 to Kelvedon clock-tower
[443 J4]

This majestic building, with a sweeping tiled roof above weather-boarded walls, is one of the oldest timber-framed barns in Britain. Constructed for the Savigniac monks of Coggeshall Abbey, it dates from the thirteenth century. Although the barn was extensively rebuilt in the late fourteenth century, original posts still support the roof. Not far away is a thirteenth-century chapel which stood outside the abbey gate, and some other monastic buildings are now part of a nearby farm.

The Pearhouse in Clumber Park's kitchen garden.

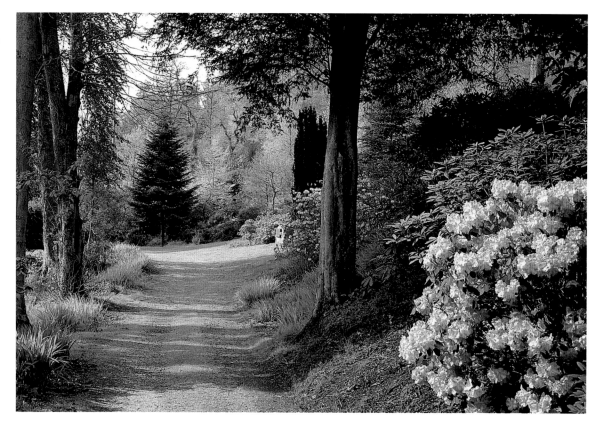

A shady path in Colby Woodland Garden, which is known for its displays of rhododendrons, azaleas and hydrangeas.

Colby Woodland Garden and Estate
PEMBROKESHIRE

1½ miles inland from Amroth, beside Carmarthen Bay
[442 B4]

The sheltered 9-hectare (22-acre) garden at the heart of this property lies in a deep and narrow valley running south to the sea. Steep wooded slopes rise to either side of a long stretch of meadow beside the stream, and a plain, cream-washed Regency house (not open) sits with its back against the hill, surveying the view down the combe. On the east side, the wood is largely composed of ancient oak trees and is more or less natural, but the western slopes have been planted and landscaped. A mixed canopy, which includes beeches and specimen trees, shades a show of rhododendrons, azaleas, hydrangeas and other plants while a network of paths and steps contour along the slope and plunge steeply up and down. Among the hundreds of species here are rhododendrons from China and Japan as well as the Himalayas, including *R. Yakushimanum*, from remote, windswept Yakushima Island, and the fine yellow *R. Macabeanum* from Assam.

In the nineteenth century this was mining country, with a string of pits yielding anthracite and iron ore; it was an industrial entrepreneur, John Colby, who built the lodge, to a design by John Nash, in 1803. The woodland garden was first planted at the end of the nineteenth century by Major Samuel Kay, whose brother had collected many rhododendrons on travels in the Himalayas, and it was then developed by Major Kay's daughter and son-in-law, Colonel and Mrs Crosland. It has been further enhanced by Mr and Mrs Peter Chance, who bought the house, the meadow and the east side of the valley in 1965 and looked after the woodland garden from 1979, when Major Kay's granddaughter left it to the Trust, until Peter Chance died in 1984. The Chances introduced a number of eye-catchers and other features and Peter Chance replaced many rhododendrons and other ornamental shrubs after extensive storm damage.

Visiting the garden is like entering a private world. Below the car park set high on the eastern slope, a gate opens into the meadow and a path crosses the combe, skirting the lodge and a huge clump of bamboo and leading onto the hill opposite. A classical urn punctuates the view down valley, and high in the wood, with a magical view of a strip of blue through the leaf canopy, is a little rustic summerhouse. A vista across the valley focuses on the obelisk in the eastern wood which was erected to the memory of Peter Chance, and there are changing views of the little walled garden laid out on a slope above the lodge, with an octagonal gazebo set in the north-eastern corner, above a glistening rill.

Beyond the garden, a shady path leads down to Amroth, where a cluster of cottages looks out to sea. Other paths offer walking over the 394-hectare (973-acre) Colby estate, which surrounds the garden and stretches from the sea 1½ miles inland to a limestone ridge. A landscape of cliffs, tranquil farmland, steep wooded valleys, and overgrown quarries and mine workings, the estate is rich in wildlife, with wood warblers and pied flycatchers among the many birds breeding here. There are panoramic views over Carmarthen Bay to Caldy Island and the Gower, and to the distant hills of Somerset across the Bristol Channel.

Coldrum Long Barrow KENT

Between the Pilgrims' Way and the A20 Folkestone road, 1 mile east of Trottiscliffe [443 J5]

This impressive prehistoric burial mound is crowned by a 'U' of standing stones and surrounded by a ditch. Like many similar features in the west of England, it is prominently placed, lying near the prehistoric track following the crest of the North Downs, later the pilgrim route from Winchester to Canterbury. A mile to the east is Trottiscliffe church, where a cabinet displays some of the human bones found when Coldrum was excavated in 1910 and 1922.

Coleridge Cottage SOMERSET

At west end of Nether Stowey, on south side of the A39, 8 miles west of Bridgwater [442 E5]

The Ancient Mariner pub at the end of Lime Street flags the rather unprepossessing cottage across the road where the young Samuel Taylor Coleridge lived for three years from 1797 with his wife Sara and infant son Hartley. Once a pretty, low, thatched building, it was substantially altered at the end of the nineteenth century and only the four front rooms are relatively unchanged. Coleridge wrote some of his best poems here, including 'Fears in Solitude', 'This Lime Tree Bower My Prison', 'The Nightingale',

'Frost at Midnight', the first part of 'Christabel' and 'The Rime of the Ancient Mariner', with its many references to places in the neighbourhood. Here, too, he eagerly started to set down the opium-inspired 'Kubla Khan', the visionary epic which came to him in his sleep and which he was prevented from completing while it was still fresh in his mind by the interruption of 'a person … from Porlock'.

Mementoes of the poet now displayed here include his massive boulle inkstand, locks of his hair and letters in his distinctive hand. There are pictures of the Devonshire village where he was born, the church where he was married, the room at No.3 The Grove, Highgate, where he died, and also of friends and acquaintances, such as Dorothy and William Wordsworth. In the little garden at the back of the house the lime-tree bower of the poem has disappeared, but the bay tree still stands as it did when Coleridge dug this plot.

Coleton Fishacre DEVON

2 miles from Kingswear; take Lower Ferry road, turn off at tollhouse [442 D8]

One of the most delightful stretches of the South Devon coastal path follows the headlands fringing the Dart estuary, looking down over wooded slopes plunging precipitously to the sea. Just beyond Kingswear, near the mouth of the estuary, the path skirts this individual property lying in a deep combe running steeply down to the cliffs above Pudcombe cove. At the head of the valley,

This little cottage in a Somerset village on the edge of the Quantocks was the home of Samuel Taylor Coleridge in the late 1790s. It was the setting for a growing intimacy between the poet and William Wordsworth and his sister Dorothy, who for a year or so were settled nearby.

The scagliola top of the table in the dining room at Coleton Fishacre echoes the blue of the sea below the house.

Built of Dartmouth shale quarried from the combe, and roofed with Delabole slates, the house is an attractive and unobtrusive backdrop to the planting, its walls now softened by climbers and shrubs such as wintersweet, the chocolate vine and Chilean jasmine. Designed by Oswald Milne, it reflects the arts and crafts influence of Milne's mentor, Sir Edwin Lutyens, in the attention to craftsmanship and materials. Inside, the impression is of a comfortable, unpretentious family house but also of a kind of spare modernism, relieved by strong splashes of colour and Art Deco light-fittings and other details. Rooms are low-ceilinged, walls are often roughly plastered, and there are deep window sills and much use of limed oak and pine. Not many original furnishings remain, but the house, intended for outdoor pursuits and weekend parties, was only ever sparsely fitted out. Long passages on both floors with smooth coves joining walls and ceiling are bland and impersonal but the main rooms have individuality and character. At the west end of the house, angled out from the main building so as to give clear views over the garden, is the saloon. Entered down a theatrical flight of steps, and almost 12 metres (39.5 feet) long, the room is dramatically furnished in yellow and green, including original carpets made in the 1930s by the designer Marion Dorn. A little library filling the bay on the entrance front is fitted out with sweet-smelling pine shelves and is dominated by George Spencer Hoffman's delightfully rose-tinted view of Coleton Fishacre, setting the house and combe in an enchanting blue-green patchwork of fields and lanes bounded by the sea. At the east end of the house, opening off the dining room where a scagliola table top and lapis lazuli bell push provide strong blue accents, is an airy vine-hung loggia, designed for dining and lounging *al fresco* and with views deep into the combe. Upstairs, the rooms are largely unfurnished, but original features include splashes of colour from blue-green tiles round the basins in every room and the period bathrooms with their sunken baths. A glitter of gold on the stairs comes from the gleaming cupolas and crosses in a painting of St Marks, Venice by W.R. Sickert.

Even before the house was completed, Rupert and Lady Dorothy were planting shelter belts of holm oaks and Monterrey pine to protect the valley from the prevailing wind, and together they planned every detail of the garden, capitalising on the drama of the site, with its panoramic views, and on the presence of a little stream rushing headlong to the sea. Close to the house is the walled Rill Garden, where semi-tender plants flowering in pastel pinks, blues and purples, and alive with bees and

with its back against the slope, is a long low house, with mullioned windows, tall chimneys and steep tiled roofs. Below, filling the vast natural amphitheatre of the combe, is a richly planted garden. Architectural near the house, with terraces, steps and walls continuing the lines of the building, the garden becomes wilder and more jungle-like as it nears the sea, with many rare and exotic trees and shrubs flourishing in the mild climate. Both house and garden have been created since 1925, when the site was acquired by Rupert and Lady Dorothy d'Oyly Carte. Son of the impresario who promoted Gilbert and Sullivan, Rupert took over the company which produced their operettas and also took over his father's other enterprise, the Savoy Hotel. While Lady Dorothy lived at Coleton Fishacre, Rupert came down from London for weekends, often bringing guests such as Sir Malcolm Sargent.

butterflies in high summer, set off a silver thread of water in a stone channel. Water enhances the terraces too, where still pools, one shaded by clumps of Arum lilies, are a counterfoil to a new generaton of tender sun-loving plants, such as the banana-scented *Michelia* and the fragrant *Camellia Sasanqua*, and two more pools interrupt the course of the stream. Paths contour round the sides of the combe, follow the stream, or zig-zag steeply up and down, with steps linking different levels. An upper path from the lawn by the loggia leads along the north side of the valley to the vine-hung gazebo, perched high above the quarry from which stone was taken for the house. The lower garden is spread out below, filled with colour in spring from a display of rhododendrons, azaleas, magnolias, dogwoods, camellias and Chilean fire trees. Beyond lies the sea, with views to the glistening humps of the Blackstone rocks and the Mewstone just offshore. And immediately below a fig tree spreads itself against the quarry face and clumps of agapanthus flower blue against the cliff.

Throughout the garden there are mature specimen trees, such as the massive tulip tree and the dawn redwood and swamp cypress flanking the terrace path, or the tree of heaven, handkerchief trees and snowdrop tree below the gazebo. Above the dramatic rock outcrop known as Newfoundland in the lower valley is a graceful Kashmir cypress, too tender for most British gardens, a sweet gum and the golden rain tree, notable for its long yellow spires in late summer. Autumn is spectacular here, with scarlet Japanese maples along the stream leading a memorable display of coloured foliage and purple and red berries. And for those drawn to the sea, a gate leads from the lower garden out onto the cliffs above Pudcombe Cove.

Combe Martin and the Hangman Hills
DEVON

On the north coast, between Combe Martin and Heddon's Mouth [442 C5]

Exmoor National Park, nearly 20 miles across at its widest point, narrows westward, with a boundary which runs into the sea just before the resort of Combe Martin. This western extremity has some of the most dramatic coast in Devon. The windswept, humpbacked ridge which follows all this coast here approaches closest to the sea, with long, steepening slopes above some of the highest cliffs in England.

The Trust owns some 162 hectares (400 acres) east of

Combe Martin, dominated by the brooding mass of the Great Hangman, 318 metres (1,044 feet) above the sea. Stand on its summit on a rough day and the sea, far below, looks scarcely ruffled. The old miners' track leading towards Blackstone Point below is not for anyone who suffers from vertigo. Silver, copper, lead and manganese have been dug here since the Middle Ages. The remains of former works are all around Combe Martin, and silver mining may account for the medieval grandeur of the Trust's West Challacombe farmhouse (now a holiday let).

The walk to the top is strenuous, and for the less adventurous the pull up to the Little Hangman, to the west and closer to Combe Martin, will suffice. The views from both are very fine, not so much seaward – for the coast runs due east and west here – as inland into the heart of the moor. These sandstone hills are covered in heather, with patches of low-growing western gorse and bracken, and grassy areas grazed by sheep. Skylarks, wheatears and stonechats abound; ravens, crows and jackdaws tease each other endlessly as they wheel about.

Across Combe Martin Bay, and therefore just outside the boundary of the Exmoor National Park, is the beautiful Golden Cove, no longer accessible since the path to it fell away a few years ago. A viewpoint above enables one to look down to what is now a wholly sequestered beach. (*See also* the Heddon Valley, Trentishoe and Woody Bay; Lynmouth; Holnicote Estate.)

Compton Castle DEVON

At Compton, 4 miles west of Torquay, 1 mile north of Marldon [442 D7]

A delight of towers, battlements and buttresses, this fairy-tale castle hidden in a deep lush south Devon Valley 2 miles from the sea seems to have strayed from the set of a remake of *Camelot*. A heavy wooden door in the north front leads into a stone-flagged rectangular courtyard, where the long south side is filled by a reconstructed medieval great hall rising two storeys to the roof. A spiral staircase gives access to a minstrels' gallery at one end. A little chapel running north and south closes the courtyard on the west. Five towers, all provided with garderobes, rear up from the house itself, and a sixth, the watch-tower, is set into the south-east corner of the 6-metre (20-foot-) high curtain wall which extends the defences of the entrance front.

This magical fortified house, one of very few to survive so unaltered, was built between the fourteenth and sixteenth centuries. The fortifications date from the reign of Henry VIII, when the Gilbert family who had lived here from the mid-fourteenth century probably felt threatened by the French raids on Teignmouth a few miles north along the coast and on Plymouth to the west. Although the new defences did not make the manor impregnable, they would have deterred attack from a roving shore party.

The three Gilbert boys born in the mid-sixteenth century, half-brothers to Walter Raleigh, were among the small group of Westcountrymen who earned a place in the history of Elizabethan England. John, the eldest, who became Vice Admiral of the Western Coast, played a major part in the defences against the Armada, providing for a possible landing in Torbay. And it was he who reported to Sir Francis Walsingham that Francis Drake had captured the Spanish galleon *Rosario*, which was brought into harbour here by Walter Raleigh.

His younger brother Humphrey was one of the brave men who crossed the Atlantic in fragile ships in a wave of colonisation and expansion. Armed with the first Letters Patent granted by the Crown for the 'planting' of an English colony, he claimed Newfoundland for his queen on 5 August 1583, sadly drowning when his tiny ship *Squirrel* foundered on the return voyage (*see also* Trengwainton, p.399). His torch was picked up by his younger brother Adrian, who formed a group of adventurers which included Philip Sidney, Francis Drake, John Hawkyns and Martin Frobisher as well as his half-brother. Although the colony established by Sir Walter Raleigh in Virginia in 1585 foundered, it marked the birth of English-speaking America, 35 years before the Pilgrim Fathers set sail.

The confidence of the age, which elsewhere led to the building of prodigy houses such as Hardwick (*see* p.175), or Wollaton Hall in Nottinghamshire, here led men to risk their lives in a quest for new lands, preserving Compton Castle as an unaltered medieval manor. Sold by the Gilbert family in 1800, and neglected for about another century, the house was bought back in 1930 and meticulously restored by Commander and Mrs Walter Raleigh Gilbert, who refurnished it as a family home.

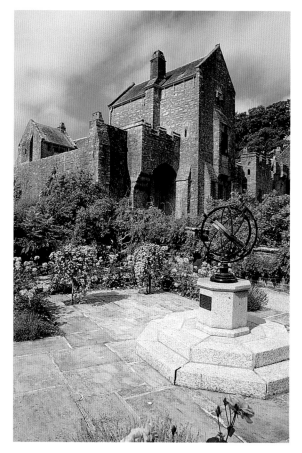

Compton Castle's rose garden. Sir Humphrey Gilbert's 'colonisation' of Newfoundland, which he claimed for the Crown in 1583, is commemorated by the armillary sphere in the centre. This was made in 1983, on the 400th anniversary of Sir Humphrey's ill-fated voyage.

Coney Island CO. ARMAGH

In Lough Neagh close to the southern (Armagh) shore [444 C4]

The little wooded Coney Island, at the south end of Lough Neagh, is about a mile from Maghery, from which it can easily be reached by boat. It was once joined to the mainland by a causeway, parts of which may still be seen, and was inhabited in very early times. Recent excavations have revealed traces of Neolithic settlements. St Patrick is believed to have used it as a retreat, and the shape of an ancient round tower still stands. It was used as a stronghold by the O'Neills of Tyrone during the sixteenth century and possibly earlier. The thick belt of reeds which surrounds the island provides an ideal resting place for large numbers of waterfowl.

Conwy Suspension Bridge CONWY

100 metres from Conwy town centre, adjacent to Conwy Castle [444 F7]

Increasing trade with Ireland in the late seventeenth and early eighteenth centuries meant that goods had to be carried to and from Holyhead along the appalling roads of North Wales, with the added hazards of ferries across the wide estuary of the Conwy as well as the Menai Strait, the only alternative being a journey 15 miles or so upriver

Corfe Castle DORSET

On the A351 Wareham–Swanage road [442 F7]

Corfe's ruins rise like jagged teeth from the summit of a steep chalk hill, a splendid strategic site guarding the only natural route through the Purbeck Hills. Although now reduced to broken towers and walls, this monument to the power of medieval kings is still architecturally striking and still dominates the little village huddled below. Even today it is easy to understand why this most defensible of all English castles was eventually reduced not by might but by treachery.

Although there may have been a royal hunting lodge at Corfe in Saxon times and King Edward is traditionally said to have been murdered here in 978, the castle was begun by William the Conqueror, whose fortifications formed part of the network of carefully placed strongholds with which he consolidated his hold on his new kingdom. These early Norman defences were gradually strengthened, with wooden features such as the original timber palisade being slowly replaced in stone. The massive keep

to the first bridge at Llanrwst. In 1811 the great engineer Thomas Telford, 54 years old and much in demand, was asked to survey a road to Holyhead. Now followed by the A5, this route through Snowdonia is a triumph, never exceeding the gradient of 1 in 50 over which a stagecoach could make a steady 10 miles an hour.

Six years later Telford designed a suspension bridge to carry the road across the Menai Strait, only the third to be built in the British Isles and closely following the pioneering Union Bridge over the Tweed. His scheme for Conwy came shortly afterwards, his early plan for conventional arches soon abandoned in favour of another suspension bridge. The site of the crossing is magnificent. On the wooded left bank of the river the bridge seems to spring from the rocky crag crowned with Conwy Castle, the masterpiece of Edward I's great castle-builder, Master James of St George, completed in 1288. With their battlements and machicolations, the 13-metre- (42-foot-) high turrets supporting the road look like extensions of the castle itself. Between them stretches the 100-metre (327-foot) span of the bridge, suspended from the graceful curve of Telford's chains, probably the only original ones still surviving on such an early bridge.

The bridge was opened in 1826, the same year that the Menai Bridge was badly damaged in a storm, convincing the old engineer that a length of 183 metres (600 feet) was the limit (although young Brunel's design for the Clifton Bridge over the Avon was to exceed this span in Telford's lifetime). The bridge and toll house have been restored to their nineteenth-century glory, with a contemporary specification used to reconstruct the road surface.

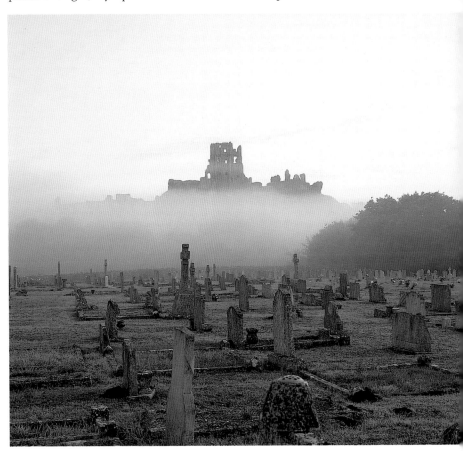

crowning the hilltop, still rising 21.5 metres (70 feet) in dramatic fingers of stone, was completed during the reign of Henry I, who imprisoned his elder brother Robert, Duke of Normandy here in 1106. The tower-studded curtain wall looping round the crest of the hill was a later addition, dating from the early years of the reign of King John (1199–1216), when Corfe's position so close to the south coast became of considerable importance in the renewed war with France. After the loss of Normandy in 1204, the castle was in the first line of the king's defences should Philip II try to cross the Channel.

In a time when kings would travel round their kingdoms administering justice and enforcing loyalty by their presence, Corfe was a centre for government and administration as well as a stronghold. Part of the huge sum of £1,400 spent on building operations at Corfe during John's reign went to construct the king's 'Gloriette', a tower-house arranged round a courtyard in the topmost inner ward. The quality of the surviving masonry shows that this was a building of distinction, a compactly planned domestic residence fit for a monarch, with a great hall, chapel and parlour, and chambers for the queen overlooking a garden.

Apart from a brief period in the mid-sixteenth century, Corfe remained in royal hands until it was sold by Elizabeth I to Sir Christopher Hatton. Some 50 years later the castle and estate were bought by Sir John Bankes, a staunch Royalist, who also purchased the neighbouring property of Kingston Lacy (see p.204). Of major strategic importance to both sides in the Civil War, Corfe was twice besieged. In 1643 Lady Bankes, who must have been a woman of strong character, held the castle against a force of local Parliamentarians in her husband's absence, but in the winter of 1645–6 Corfe was again attacked and fell through the treachery of one of the defenders. The victorious Roundhead colonel, impressed by Lady Bankes's courage, not only allowed the garrison to depart but permitted his spirited opponent to take the keys of the castle with her, now to be seen hanging in the library at Kingston Lacy. Corfe's defences were destroyed, leaving only the romantic remnants immortalised in Turner's evocative watercolour.

Cornish Coast

See North Cornish Coast, p.263, *and* South Cornish Coast, p.349. [442 A8–C6 and A8–C7]

Cornish Mines and Engines

At Pool, 2 miles west of Redruth on either side of the A3047, on the west coast near St Just and other locations [442 A8]

The tall outlines of ruined engine houses standing high on windswept moorland or perched on lonely cliff-top sites are romantic reminders of the great days of the Cornish mining industry in the mid-nineteenth century. At the height of the boom the population of the county almost doubled as newcomers flooded in to provide the manpower needed for the extraction of rich sources of tin, copper and china clay. Now only the china-clay quarries remain open, but the technology refined here was exported all over the world, from South America to Australia.

The key to the growth of the Cornish mining industry was the expiry of the patent on the Boulton and Watt steam engine in 1800. Developed in the coal-rich areas of the north, where fuel efficiency was not the prime consideration, this engine was expensive to run in the south-west where all coal had to be brought over the sea from Wales. The moment restrictions were removed, Cornish engineers – in particular Richard Trevithick (1771–1833), the first to realise the potential of high-pressure steam – set about producing more efficient engines, leading to the establishment of a number of great engine-building firms, such as Holman's of Camborne and Harvey's of Hayle. Necessity was the mother of invention, giving Cornwall the lead in mining technology that it was to hold for half a century.

The Trust owns several survivals from this great chapter in Cornish history. At the East Pool and Agar mine, straddling the A3047, is the largest of the great beam engines left in Cornwall, commissioned from Harvey's in 1891 and put to work here in 1925. With a gleaming cylinder 2 metres (7 feet) in diameter and a huge beam weighing some 52 tons, this monster could lift 450 gallons of water a minute from a depth of 518 metres (1,700 feet). The 1853 engine, designed by a pupil of Trevithick at South Crofty tin and arsenic mine about a mile to the south-west, could operate at even greater depths, raising 340 gallons a minute from 609.5 metres (2,000 feet). A working example of the rotative engines normally used for lifting men and materials survives at the East Pool mine, where F.W. Michell's 1887 engine made by Holman's is now powered by electricity. Also at East Pool is the Industrial Discovery Centre, which gives an overview of Cornish mining and sets it in context.

Further west, where the Penwith peninsula runs south to Land's End, a rich mining coast is centred on St Just.

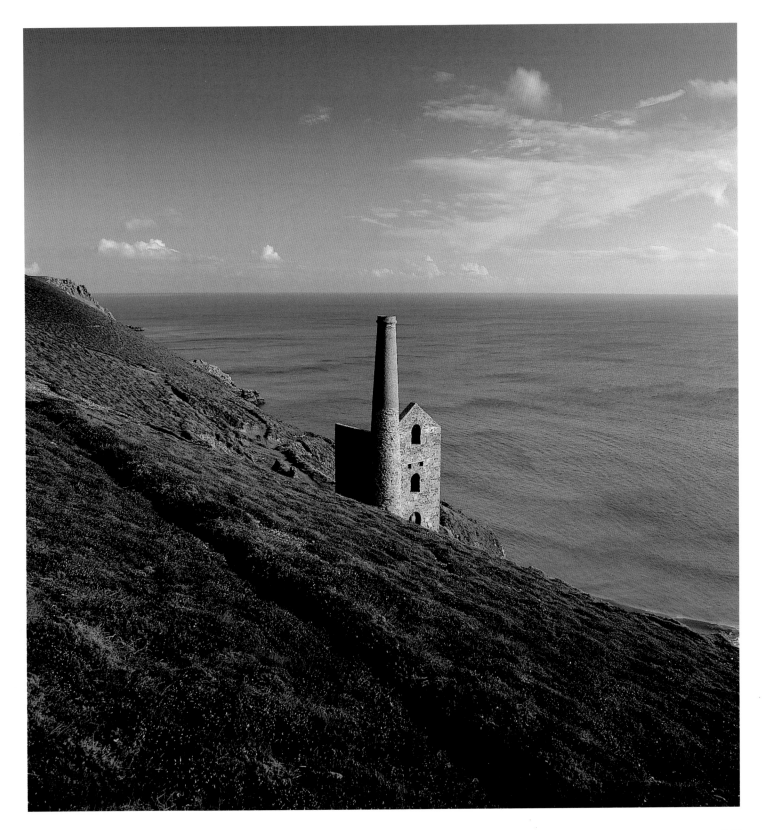

At the Levant mine to the north is the oldest surviving beam engine in Cornwall, memorably sited in a tiny engine house right on the cliff edge. Once again being worked by steam, this machinery was designed by Francis Michell, another member of the engineering Michell family, and was built by Harvey's in 1840. Even more spectacular are the engine houses at Botallack, which cling to the rocks just a few feet above the pounding Atlantic. This whole mining coast, with Botallack and Kenidjack at its heart, has been the focus of considerable restoration and stabilisation by the National Trust in recent years.

A number of other empty engine houses in the Trust's care stand in similarly dramatic situations. Wheal Prosper dominates the cliff above Porthcew Cove, while Towanroath engine house at Chapel Porth is perched on a ledge several hundred feet above the sea. Equally romantic is Wheal Betsy, set on lonely Black Down on the west edge of Dartmoor, its tall chimney a conspicuous sight from the A386 to Okehampton. Richard Trevithick's whitewashed thatched cottage at Lower Penponds, Camborne, from where he departed for the silver mines of Peru in 1816, is also Trust property.

Cotehele, an ancient manor house tucked away in the valley of the Tamar, has a fine collection of period textiles. Dutch and Flemish tapestries set off this four-poster bed in Queen Anne's Room (right) and there are examples of crewelwork, such as the 18th-century bedspread in the South Room (detail, above), knotted wool and stumpwork.

Cotehele CORNWALL

On west bank of the Tamar, 1 mile west of Calstock by footpath (6 miles by road), 8 miles south-west of Tavistock
[442 C7]

The River Tamar which divides Devon and Cornwall has proved the most effective natural boundary in England. Until the opening of the suspension bridge between Plymouth and Saltash at the mouth of the river in 1962, there was no road link below Gunnislake, 15 miles upstream as the crow flies but almost double that distance following the twists and turns of the river. For the villages and hamlets along its banks, the Tamar was for centuries the only effective route to the outside world. So it was for this Tudor courtyard house built by Sir Richard Edgcumbe and his son Sir Piers between 1485 and c.1540.

Low granite ranges set round three courtyards lie at the head of a steep valley running down to the river, woodland on either side sheltering a luxuriant garden where palms, rhododendrons, azaleas, ferns and the umbrella-like *Gunnera manicata* thrive in the exceptionally mild climate. A domed dovecote and a stewpond near the house provided meat and fish for what was a largely self-sufficient community.

Cotehele quay, an example of the many which once lined the river, lies a quarter of a mile downstream. Described in 1819 as 'a very large and commodious quay with a most desirable situation on the river', the old grey stone buildings restored by the Trust are still impressive. A sign advertises the Edgcumbe Arms, now a tea-room, and Shamrock, one of the last surviving Tamar sailing barges, is berthed here (*see* p.336). The quays saw some of their busiest years at the end of the nineteenth century, when strawberries and other soft fruit from growers in the valley were taken over the river to Bere Alston station on the new Plymouth-Tavistock line. During the previous decade there had been shipments of ore from mines in the steep-sided wooded Danescombe Valley upstream, among over a hundred workings which exploited rich sources of copper and arsenic along the Tamar Valley, their sites now marked by grassy humps and some old mine buildings. The mining industry was already declining when the Danescombe mines were at their peak of production in 1844–70, and by the early years of the twentieth century many miners were seeking work overseas, some of them setting out for America as steerage passengers on the ill-fated *RMS Titanic*.

The buildings of Cotehele quay seem too tranquil for this industrial past, but hidden in the woodland across a reedy inlet to one side are the remains of a row of huge lime kilns, now romantically shrouded in greenery but once a source of lethal fumes. A path from here leads through woodland up the tributary valley of the River Morden to another picturesque group of estate buildings, including a three-storey eighteenth-century mill powered by an overshot wheel. This is now in working order and produces stoneground wholemeal flour which is sold in the Trust shop. Here, too, are a wheelwright's shop, with a lathe driven by a huge flywheel, a forge where charcoal smoulders gently in the hearth, a saddler's shop filled with harness, lengths of chain and stirrups, and a sawpit and carpenter's shop.

A steep wooded ride takes visitors back to the house, past Sir Richard's massively buttressed barn flanking the route to the battlemented gateway tower. This medieval approach, the arch of the gateway just wide enough to admit a loaded packhorse, signals the character of the house, left largely undisturbed for over 200 years from the end of the seventeenth century, when the family chose to live at Mount Edgcumbe, their grander seat overlooking Plymouth Sound. The rooms are small and mostly dark, reached by flights of worn stone steps and through massive wooden doors in granite archways. Three Tudor windows light the dais end of Sir Richard's medieval great hall, with an oak refectory table marooned in the middle of the rough lime-ash floor and whitewashed walls rising the height of the house to a decorative timber roof. Adam and Eve are carved on one of the early seventeenth-century chairs at either end of the table, and the walls are hung with a collection of arms and armour which includes Elizabethan matchlocks, Civil War breastplates and lobster-tail helmets, and some exotic pieces, such as long Indian swords and an Arab musket.

The family chambers, with their large Tudor fireplaces and richly coloured hangings used like wallpaper, are far more inviting. On the late seventeenth-century bacchic tapestries adorning the little Punch Room, naked figures treading huge vats of grapes as if indulging in a communal bubble bath are clearly preparing a vintage to fill the arched niches in the cupboard-like wine cellar in one corner. In the Red Room upstairs, rich crimson drapery on the huge four-poster is set off by faded seventeenth-century arras on the walls, children at play with marbles and hoops on three of the panels contrasting with the scene of nightmarish violence by the bed illustrating the death of Remus. Across the landing a steeply winding stair leads to two bedrooms at the top of the three-storey battlemented tower added in 1627.

Although the east front was rebuilt in 1862, the new work blends harmoniously with the Tudor ranges behind. Three formal stone terraces below this front, and dating from the same period, are softened by informal planting and, since January 1990, when winter gales blasted the shielding woods and opened up the vista down the valley, there is a view from here across a bend in the Tamar to Calstock village and the railway viaduct which crosses the river. Above the house is the walled upper garden, with lawns and specimen trees round a lily pond and a sloping meadow where hundreds of daffodils flower. Collected here as part of Cotehele's daffodil project, they include both local and traditional varieties. Across a field from the upper garden granite pinnacles and dummy Gothic windows mask a triangular prospect tower, perhaps built to celebrate the visit of King George III and Queen Charlotte in August 1789. The panorama from the top looks west to Kit Hill and east to Dartmoor, beyond the graceful arches of the Calstock viaduct in the valley below, part of a new railway opened in 1908 whose advent killed the river traffic.

Cotswolds GLOUCESTERSHIRE

Between Stratford-upon-Avon, to the north, and Wotton-under-Edge, to the south [442 F4–443 G3]

Travelling south down the M5, or on the A46 from Stratford-upon-Avon, the Cotswold scarp closes the view eastward for 50 miles to Wotton-under-Edge. The Trust's flag flies at Hidcote (*see* p.182), Snowshill (*see* p.348) and at several other places.

Dover's Hill rises above Weston-sub-Edge on the A46. Steep pasture with a woodland fringe, it forms a natural amphitheatre, but it would be no more than an incident in the escarpment if it did not commemorate Captain Robert Dover (1575–1641). A jolly, sporting lawyer, who thought life ought to be fun, he was licensed by James I to found the 'Cotswold Olimpicks'. When they started in 1612, the Games were a great success. Events included cudgel-play, wrestling, jumping, pitching the hammer, balloon (a mixture of football and handball), hare-hunting, horse racing, virgins dancing for prizes and much feasting and drinking. Banned by the Puritans when they came to power, the Games were brought back with the Restoration of 1660, and continued until 1852. They have been revived in recent years and are now re-enacted on the Friday following the spring bank holiday. Dover's Hill is a good place to walk, if steep, with views over the Vale of Evesham.

Forming a spur north of Birdlip, below the B4070, is Crickley Hill, where the Trust has joined its 27 hectares (67 acres) with 31 hectares (78 acres) belonging to the County Council to make a country park. Trails illustrate archaeology (Neolithic, Iron Age and post-Roman settlements), geology (oolitic limestone with outcrops of pea grit) and ecology (beech woodland and lime-rich grassland). There are spectacular views over the Severn Vale to the Malvern and the Welsh Hills. About three miles southwest, near the village of Sheepscombe, stretches of fine beech woodland, one of which overlooks the village, and some 243 hectares (600 acres) of Cotswold farmland make up the Ebworth estate.

Near Stroud, the Trust owns two properties on the crest of the scarp. To the north-west is Haresfield Beacon, standing proud above the headwaters of the Severn estuary. The Cotswold Way follows the line of the ridge, with panoramic views over the Severn estuary to Wales, and there are miles of other paths running down through the beech and mixed woodland and open pasture of Standish Wood and Shortwood on the steep slopes of the scarp. The smaller Coaley Peak is a high point to the south-west, off the road from Stroud to Dursley, with similarly breathtaking views.

Quite different are the secluded acres of Woodchester Park (*see* p.434), buried in a deep valley, and the expanses of Rodborough and Minchinhampton Commons, on

the plateau above the escarpment between Stroud and Nailsworth. The Trust first acquired land here in 1913 when the large commons were threatened by quarrying. There was a local uproar, a committee was set up, money raised and land bought and vested in the Trust. Substantial additions totalling nearly 405 hectares (1,000 acres) have been made since, much of it high and windswept land forming an invaluable series of open spaces close to the industrial towns.

Nine miles west of Gloucester, May Hill rises to 295.5 metres (969 feet), though the clump of trees at its summit does not belong to the Trust. The wooded and heathy skirts of the hill are attractive, there are plenty of paths, and the view from the top stretches for miles around.

Coughton Court WARWICKSHIRE

2 miles north of Alcester on east side of the A435 [443 G3]

Only an expanse of meadow separates Coughton Court from the main Studley to Alcester road, giving passing motorists a memorable view of the great Tudor gatehouse dominating the entrance façade. Dating from the early years of Henry VIII's reign, when even in remote countryside on the southern fringes of the Forest of Arden men could at last build to please themselves rather than to protect their property, the gatehouse is a glittering glass lantern, the gleaming panes of a two-storeyed oriel window stretching the width of the two upper floors. Though Sir George Throckmorton thought it prudent to surround his new house with a moat, this may also have been regarded as a status symbol rather than as a purely defensive device. Late Tudor ranges flank the grassy lavender-fringed courtyard reached through the gatehouse passage, their domestic gabled façades covered with roses and other climbers and their half-timbered upper storeys a direct contrast with the stone splendour of the gatehouse. Yew-framed lawns at the back of the house lead down to the little River Arrow and peaceful wooded countryside beyond.

The Throckmortons first came to Coughton Court in 1409 and much of the fascination of the house derives from its continued association with this prominent Roman Catholic family. Increasingly prosperous during the fifteenth and sixteenth centuries, they were to pay a high price for their faith during the reign of Elizabeth I and the years that followed. Sir Nicholas Throckmorton, previously Ambassador to France, was imprisoned by the queen for his friendship with Mary Queen of

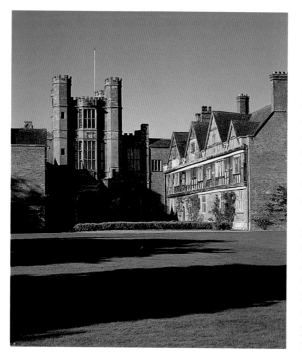

The garden front of Coughton Court, showing the gatehouse with its double-storeyed oriel and the half-timbered 16th-century north wing.

Scots and his nephew executed for plotting to replace Elizabeth with her cousin. Another nephew, Thomas, was more circumspect. Although he lent Coughton to the conspirators in the Gunpowder Plot, he took care to be absent on the night of 5 November 1605 when an anxious group waited in one of the gatehouse rooms to hear news of the venture.

Like Baddesley Clinton only a few miles to the north-east (*see* p.31), Coughton was a refuge for recusants. The mass continued to be celebrated here and priests were concealed in ingenious hiding places, such as that discovered in the north-east turret, furnished with a bed and a folding leather altar. Another reminder of these times is the painted canvas hanging in the Tower Room displaying the arms of all the Catholic gentry imprisoned for recusancy during Elizabeth's reign.

Staunchly Royalist during the Civil War, the Throckmortons' loyalty was tested when the house was besieged and occupied by Parliamentary troops in 1643, the rising ground where the Roundhead army placed their guns only too visible in the view west from the top of the gatehouse tower. Two generations later the entire east side of the courtyard was destroyed when Coughton was sacked by a Protestant mob running wild after the flight of James II and it was never subsequently rebuilt. A number of mementoes in the house, including the shift in which Mary Queen of Scots was beheaded as well as locks of hair from the Old and Young Pretenders, recall the Throckmortons' allegiance to the Stuart cause.

In later years the family fortunes revived, partly through prudent marriages. The stone-built Gothick wings on either side of the gatehouse were added in the 1780s and the moat was filled in shortly afterwards. A mid-Victorian Roman Catholic chapel a few metres away from the house is one of the family's last and most interesting additions. Standing cheek by jowl with the ancient parish church just to the south, these three buildings are an enduring reminder of the divisions bred by religion.

The Courts WILTSHIRE

In the middle of Holt village, 2½ miles east of Bradford-on-Avon, on south side of the B3107 [442 F5]

Like many of the Trust's gardens, The Courts was created in the twentieth century. The skeleton of the garden, a largely formal layout with hedged compartments in the style of Hidcote or Sissinghurst (*see* pp.182 and 341), was partly established by the architect Sir George Hastings in the early years of the century. He planned backdrops of clipped yew to show off the stone statues which are now such a feature of The Courts, and he was also responsible for the little stone temple and the pretty eighteenth-century conservatory.

The large rectangular pool at The Courts, set in a leafy framework of trees and shrubs and with rafts of water lilies on the water.

Right: Cragside, built for the
industrialist William Armstrong,
is romantically set on a wooded
hillside sloping steeply to a little
Northumberland burn. These idyllic
surroundings were combined with up-
to-the-minute technology introduced by
Sir William. Cragside was the first
house in the world to be lit by electricity
derived from waterpower and the
service areas, such as the cavernous
kitchen (opposite), were fitted with
recent inventions, among them a
primitive form of dishwasher, a water-
powered spit, an internal telephone and
a hydraulic lift.

Lady Cecilie Goff, who came here with her husband in 1920, created the present 2.8-hectare (7-acre) garden around the structure left by Sir George. Her lavish and varied planting schemes with subtly blended colours and textures fill long herbaceous borders in the style of Gertrude Jekyll. Beds of floribunda roses hedged with clipped yew set off a rectangular lily pond, and more water-loving plants thrive round a small lake. There are yew- and holly-hedged vistas, fine trees, and spacious lawns, and as a backdrop the eighteenth-century stone house on which the garden is centred.

The Mexican red-ink plant seen throughout the garden, its maroon-black fruits yielding a dark and potent crimson dye, is one of several reminders of The Courts's close connections with the West Country wool trade. As its name suggests, weavers brought disputes for arbitration here until the end of the eighteenth century; although the water-mill which stood by the house has been demolished, the dyeing pond and the stone pillars between which wool was once hung on chains to dry have been incorporated in the garden.

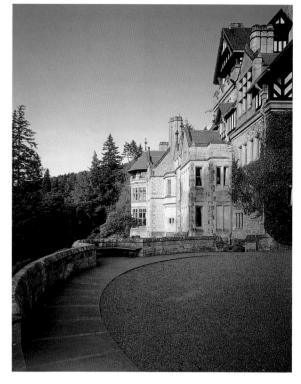

Craflwyn GWYNEDD

One mile north-east of Beddgelert on A498 [444 F8 and 442 C1]

This 100-hectare (247-acre) miniature Victorian estate was once the home of minor Welsh nobility. Developed as a Victorian gentleman's retreat in the 1870s and 1880s, the house, which is currently being restored as a volunteering and educational centre, is surrounded by overgrown gardens featuring rhododendrons and exotic conifers, parkland and plantations. There are woodland walks with viewpoints and paths leading up the Nantgwynant Valley through Hafod y Porth farm to Dinas Emrys, a Dark Age site associated with early legends featuring the Welsh dragon, and over to the Hafod y Llan estate (*see* p.171) and the routes up Snowdon.

Cragside NORTHUMBERLAND

13 miles south-west of Alnwick on the B6341 and 15 miles north-west of the Morpeth–Wooler road [445 I2]

When the inventor and industrialist William Armstrong made a nostalgic visit to Rothbury in 1863 as a break from the unrelenting pressures of his factory on the River Tyne, he determined to purchase what he could of the secluded Debdon Valley where he had so often wandered as a boy.

Four years earlier he had seen the army adopt the new gun he had developed after the poor British performance in the Crimean War, initiating the transformation of his works from a prosperous engineering firm to a vast industrial concern. Once primarily concerned with hydraulic machines, by the late nineteenth century Armstrong's was an international arms manufacturer, rivalled only by Krupps of Germany.

A couple of watercolours showing tall chimneys belching smoke over factory buildings ranged along the Tyne are the only direct reminders of the works which financed the rambling house set high above a ravine on the Debdon burn, with a jumble of gables, soaring chimneys, mullioned windows and half-timbering framed against a wooded hillside. But there are other pointers to the inventive mind of the man who built it. This was the earliest house in the world to be lit by hydroelectricity and water was also used to power a saw-mill, a revolutionary hydraulic lift and even a kitchen spit.

Armstrong's activities are reflected too in the gradual transformation of the modest weekend retreat he had built in 1864–6. Shortly afterwards he engaged the distinguished architect Richard Norman Shaw, who over the next fifteen years turned Cragside into a country mansion and enriched it with some of his most original work. Shaw's grandest rooms were designed for important overseas clients. The King of Siam, the Shah of Persia and the Crown Prince of Afghanistan all slept in the monumental black walnut bed with solemn owls carved on the end posts and a massive half-tester which Shaw created for the guest chambers. No doubt they appreciated the plumbed-in washstand and the sunken bath in an alcove in the dressing room next door. A long top-lit gallery, with a wooden barrel ceiling and portraits and sculpture set against deep-red walls, leads from the Owl Suite to Shaw's *tour de force*, the drawing room completed for a royal visit in 1884. The top-lit cavernous interior is dominated by W.R. Lethaby's monumental, Renaissance-style carved marble chimney-piece, with sinuous veining in the stone round the fireplace suggesting running water. Inglenooks with cosy red leather settees are set incongruously on either side and fragile white lamps hang in clusters from the ceiling like bunches of snowdrops.

The little rooms of the original lodge and Shaw's early additions for the family are quite different in character. His beautiful and unusual library with magnificent views of the glen is perhaps the most harmonious room in the house, the warm reds and browns of the furnishings setting off brilliant-blue tiles framing the fireplace and glowing enamelled lamps along the low bookcases.

Armstrong alone seems to have been responsible for Cragside's wildly romantic setting, blasting the hillside to expose craggy rock formations and creating over 688 hectares (1,700 acres) of pleasure grounds by planting millions of conifers, rhododendrons and alpines on what were originally bare slopes. A pinetum was established in the valley, the mature trees here now including a western hemlock, a white Colorado fir and other conifers from western North America which are among the largest in Britain, as well as outstanding specimens of oriental and tiger-tail spruces and Caucasian, Spanish and Grecian firs. Badly overgrown when the Trust took over Cragside, the grounds have now been renovated and the 3-acre rock garden on the steep slope below the house, like a giant scree above the burn, has been cleared and replanted with heathers, alpines and shrubs. Before the trees grew up, the views westward from the house took in the terraced garden laid out on a south-facing slope on the other side of the valley. Reached along a steep path up from the stream, this ordered space points up the wild romanticism of the glen. Formal and contained, it includes ferneries, a fruit house and an Italian garden, and looks out over gently undulating parkland. An intricate network of paths snakes across the estate, the higher routes along the summit of the crags

above the house giving dramatic views to the Cheviots, and a scenic drive of some 6 miles follows the perimeter of the landscaped grounds, taking in the lakes 103.5 metres (340 feet) above the house which were used to feed the hydroelectric turbine.

Cregennan GWYNEDD

1 mile east of Arthog on the A493 [442 D2]

The impressive landscape of the Cadair Idris massif, lying between the A487 and the A493 running along the south side of the Mawddach estuary, is more accessible than Snowdon. It is classic mountain terrain, a mix of crags, scree, lakes, heath and grassland. The Trust owns two substantial holdings here: Bryn Rhug, adjoining the Tan y Gadair sheepwalk on the north side of Cadair Idris, and, below the Chair of Idris, Llyn y Gadair itself. To the west, along the mountain road which rises to 228.5 metres (750 feet) above the estuary, is Cregennan, with two hill farms marked by a patchwork of dry-stone walls, two lakes fed by streams running off the tops, and an expanse of open mountain. The views – up to Cadair, down to Barmouth and across Cardigan Bay – are superb and this is a perfect place for those whose scrambling days are over.

Looking across to the summit of Cadair Idris over the clear waters of Llynau Cregennan. This is a classic mountain landscape of open grassland, scree, crags and lakes.

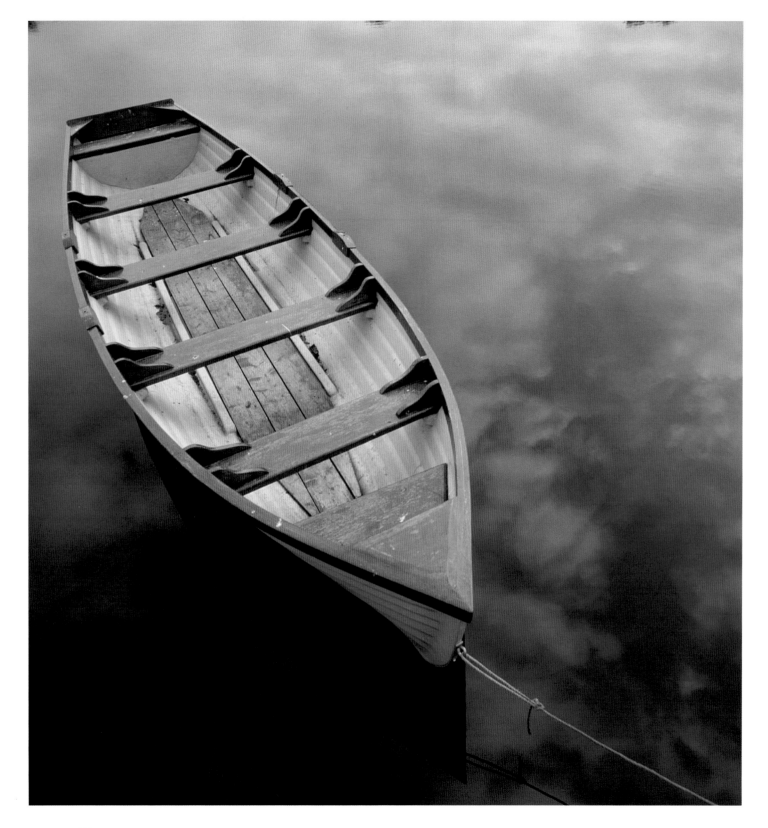

Croft Ambrey HEREFORD & WORCESTER

Above Croft Castle, 6½ miles south-west of Ludlow, 2¼ miles north-east of Mortimer's Cross, 1 mile east of the A4110 and Yatton [442 E3]

A path from Croft Castle (*see below*) leads up through a conifer plantation to this spectacularly sited Iron Age hill-fort at a height of 305 metres (1,000 feet) on the hill above. A triple ring of banks and ditches encloses a roughly triangular area of 13 hectares (32 acres), with some additional defences on the most vulnerable southern side. Granaries and storage pits and a quantity of ironwork and decorated bronze have been found within the ramparts, evidence of occupation from about the fourth century BC until *c*.AD50, when the Romans finally conquered Wales. The views from the fort are stunning: south over the wooded border country and west into Wales, where the hills fade ridge behind ridge into the distance.

Croft Castle HEREFORD & WORCESTER

5 miles north-west of Leominster, 9 miles south-west of Ludlow [442 E3]

This engaging house, with slender corner towers and rough stone walls, has a long history. Dating back to a time when this glorious country on the Welsh borders was insecure and torn by rebellion, the shell of the house is the four-square castle round a central courtyard which the Croft family, who came here from Normandy some years before the Conquest, built to defend their rights and property. Much modified since, Croft was massively remodelled in the eighteenth century, with features from various periods contributing to its present picturesque appearance. On the entrance front, the corner towers frame Georgian sash windows and delightful Gothick bays either side of a mock-Jacobean castellated porch. The approach is through what appears to be a medieval archway, but this too was a more recent addition, probably built in the 1790s.

The country house takes over inside. Thomas Farnolls Pritchard, the Shrewsbury architect who designed the world's first iron bridge at Coalbrookdale, was responsible for the delightful Gothick interiors introduced in 1765, his pointed arches in white plaster on a coffee background on the stairs strongly reminiscent of a row of church windows. Even the stair balustrade looks ecclesiastical: column clusters forming the newel posts are miniature versions of those which might support the vaulting of a nave. Rare and valuable furniture in the same style includes a set of Gothick chairs in dark oak in the long gallery, suitable props for a dramatisation of Mary Shelley's *Frankenstein* or Horace Walpole's *The Castle of Otranto*. T.F. Pritchard also had a hand in the similarly striking but quite different decoration of the Blue Room, where *trompe-l'oeil* gold rosettes stud blue Jacobean panelling. Family portraits hang in almost every room, including a beautiful study by Gainsborough of Elizabeth Cowper, wife of Sir Archer Croft, the colours all brown and red, and works by Lawrence and Philip de Laszlo. Crofts also dominate the little church of rough local stone only a few metres from the house, where the many family memorials are crowned by a splendid early sixteenth-century altar tomb to Sir Richard and Dame Eleanor Croft, with realistic effigies showing the couple in extreme old age.

Thickly wooded parkland surrounds the castle, as it has done for centuries, the great avenues for which Croft is famous including a line of Spanish chestnuts stretching about half a mile to the west, in which some of the trees are perhaps 350 years old, and oaks and beeches flanking the long entrance drive. The ancient lime avenue which once shadowed the chestnuts has now been replanted. While most of the park escaped the attentions of an improver of the 'Capability' Brown school, the late eighteenth-century landscaping of Fish Pool Valley in the Picturesque mode was a direct reaction to his ideas. This little steep-sided glen planted with mixed deciduous and evergreen trees has a dramatic wilderness quality that Brown would have hated but which is in perfect accord with the castle's Gothick interiors. Another notable feature of the 607-hectare (1,500-acre) estate is the Iron Age hill-fort of Croft Ambrey, set on a ridge a mile north of the house (*see above*).

Crom Estate CO. FERMANAGH

3 miles west of Newtownbutler on the Newtownbutler–Crom road [444 A5]

The 769-hectare (1,900-acre) Crom estate is a patchwork of land and water, an intricate pattern of amoeba-like islands and peninsulas separated by fingers of upper Lough Erne. Patches of cultivated land and pasture come down to the water, but the shores are mostly wooded, the varied outlines and contrasting foliage of oak, ash, beech, alder, willow, spruce and pine mirrored in the tranquil waters. Yellow and white water lilies flower profusely in summer and the rare marsh pea can be seen in the extensive banks of reeds. Wood and water birds thrive here, including a flock of the whooper swan, while feral roe deer and the red Irish hare bound away from approaching visitors.

At the centre of the estate lies the massive limestone pile of Crom Castle (not owned by the Trust), built in 1832–8 for the 3rd Earl of Erne by Edward Blore, whose assemblage of turrets, bay windows, oriels and gables fully justifies Mark Girouard's description of his work as 'gently Picturesque and gently Elizabethan'. Crowning a slight prominence in the park, the castle looks magnificent from a distance, seeming to rise out of the trees which surround it. Just below the house are a charming gabled boathouse, also designed by Blore, with a slipway into the lough, and

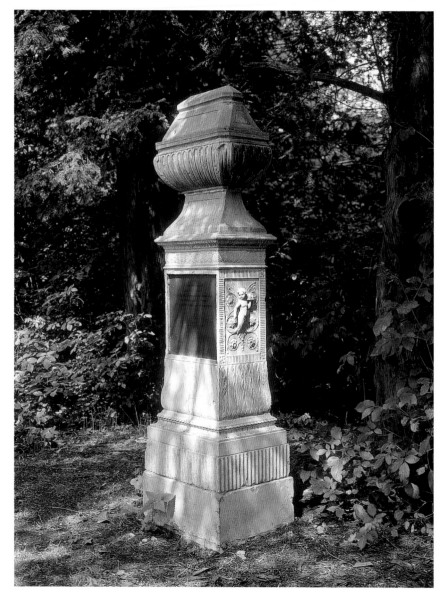

a small Gothic teahouse placed to look over the water.

A number of other eye-catchers were added in the 1840s, most notably the round battlemented Crichton Tower like a dark finger on the tiny patch of Gad Island. A schoolhouse nestles against the trees on the Corlatt peninsula, the children who came by boat to the landing places on the shore below perhaps being ferried in a traditional Fermanagh cott. (One of these boats now waits to transport passengers from the cobbled causeway on Inisherk Island over the lough to the mid-nineteenth-century church on the Derryvore peninsula.) Nearer Crom Castle itself, the remains of a once-formidable façade stretching skywards mark the defended tower-house built here in 1610, said to have been destroyed by fire in 1764 and developed as a Picturesque folly in the nineteenth century.

This romantic landscape with its varied woodland may reflect the influence of the painter and garden designer William Sawrey Gilpin, whose uncle the Rev. William Gilpin was one of the great pioneers of the Picturesque movement. As at Scotney (see p.332), where he was employed some five years after Castle Crom was begun, Gilpin may have advised on the siting of the house and the vistas leading to it, and may have suggested the mixed planting which now contributes so much to the appeal of the place. He may also have had a hand in embellishing the seventeenth-century formal gardens laid out near the tower-house, although not much of these remain apart from two ancient yews, their tangled stems and branches supporting a vast tent of foliage. Like the rest of the estate, these ruined gardens are a haven for wildlife, many of the woodland and water species found at Crom, such as the purple-hairstreak butterfly or the silver-washed fritillary, rarely seen elsewhere in the British Isles.

Crook's Peak, Wavering Down and Shute Shelve Hill SOMERSET

West of Axbridge, off the A38 [442 E5]

The Trust owns 293.5 hectares (725 acres) of steep southern slopes at the western end of the Mendips, where the hills form an extensive area of rolling downland above the Somerset Levels. A landscape of combes and spurs with some craggy outcrops, much is sheep-grazed grassland, rich with butterfly-attracting flowers and herbs. There is some ancient woodland, marked by old pollards and boundary banks and including an unusual stand of yew, and pockets of heath. Rising to 191 metres (626 feet) at

Winscombe Hill, this is a place for a brisk walk and for extensive views over Somerset and the Bristol Channel, with the M5 plunging dramatically through the ridge at Loxton Gap below.

Croome Park WORCESTERSHIRE

8 miles south of Worcester and east of A38 and M5, 6 miles west of Pershore [442 F3]

In 1751 Lancelot 'Capability' Brown, then in his mid-thirties and relatively untried, was given the commission which would make his name and establish the naturalistic style of the English landscape garden. Brown was working for the 6th Earl of Coventry who had recently inherited the Croome estate and was determined to remodel both house and grounds. Out of an unpromising site, a stretch of marshy ground between the Avon and Severn, Brown created pleasure grounds and parkland bearing all the hall-marks of his later work: curving outlines and artfully spaced clumps of trees; a stretch of crystal-clear water mirroring planting and a variety of ornamental features; a play of light and shade; vistas to distant eye-catchers and the borrowing of the wider landscape, with which the park seems to merge. Equally revolutionary was Brown's scheme for using the parkland and its surrounding shelter belts productively, to pasture cattle and sheep and for timber.

As well as being his first complete landscape design, Croome also gave Brown an opportunity to practise as an architect. With advice from Sanderson Miller, he remodelled Croome Court (not a Trust property) as a fashionable Palladian mansion, with a portico on the entrance front looking south over the park, and he was also responsible for several of the estate buildings and other features. The new design continued to evolve for the next 60 years, with the involvement of Robert Adam in the 1770s and of James Wyatt in the 1790s. Although Brown left to pursue other commissions, he returned to Croome regularly and the 6th Earl became a close friend.

The park was a fashionable place to visit in the early nineteenth century and was maintained by the Coventry family until 1949 but, by the end of the twentieth century, when it had passed through several hands, the lake was weed-choked and the surrounding landscape had been ploughed, replanted for commercial forestry or invaded by brambles. In 1996, with the help of a large grant from the Heritage Lottery Fund and a donation from Royal and Sun Alliance, the Trust bought 270 hectares (670 acres) of the pleasure grounds and inner park and is now involved in an ongoing restoration programme to return Croome to its eighteenth-century appearance.

Brown's design is centred on the pleasingly irregular lake to the south of the house, with an artificial river winding away across the park to the south-east. A long walk, originally shaded by carefully tiered trees and shrubs and perfumed by scented plants, curves down towards the water. Originally, too, the shrubberies were punctuated with a clearing with statues of the four seasons and a number of artfully placed seats gave views over the park. Near the house, the walk passes the church of St Mary Magdalen (not National Trust) which Brown designed in Gothic style to replace an existing building; Robert Adam contributed the half-gothic, half-classical interior and also created the greenhouse in the form of a temple further down the path. There are more features along the route circling the lake, among them a grotto with a statue of Sabrina, goddess of the River Severn, a monument to Brown and, on one of the three islands, a classical pavilion by Adam with Coade stone reliefs. Wyatt was responsible for the iron bridges, early examples of wrought-iron work, which lead on to this island and for the bridge which raises the drive over the long walk from the church: as approaching visitors topped the crest of the arch, they were treated to a sudden panoramic vista of the Court across the park. From the pleasure grounds there are uninter-rupted views back towards the mansion and church over Brown's ha-ha, which also served to stop stock from wandering into the ornamental plantings. Further foot-paths lead across the wider estate and there are vistas to more distant eye-catchers – a tower and two purpose-built ruins – and to the long ridge of the Malverns closing the western horizon.

Of the original diverse plantings, which included a flower garden and an arboretum, only remnants survive, among them some massive yews, holm oaks and a Manna Ash in the shrubberies framing the approach walk and some mixed groups of trees around the lake. In the wider estate, which once boasted hot-houses, orchards and a menagerie of exotic birds, most of the fields have their eighteenth-century boundaries and there are a number of ancient oak trees and the massive brick culverts of Brown's drainage scheme, still in use today. The Trust's restoration, which has got to a stage where Brown's vision is reappear-ing, includes replanting over 5½ hectares (14 acres) of shrubberies according to the original plans and several thousand parkland trees, restoring buildings, statues and other features, clearing the lake and river and returning arable land to pasture.

which once ground to a halt nearby. With the door shut against the noisy crowd outside, the snugs become private drinking compartments, each one guarded by crouching heraldic beasts carrying shields with Latin mottoes. Mellow gaslights, bar staff in waistcoats and bow ties and a menu board offering Irish broth and oysters in season all contribute to the Crown's individual atmosphere, a jewel of a pub in a city which boasts places of refreshment on almost every corner.

Above: The theatrical exterior of the Crown Liquor Saloon in Belfast, one of the most flamboyant of High Victorian public houses.

Right: The little late Georgian terrace at Cwmdu boasts a pub and a shop, and has a chapel at one end.

Crown Liquor Saloon BELFAST

Great Victoria Street, Belfast [444 C4]

The Crown Liquor Saloon glitters and gleams. Coloured glass in bright blues, oranges and reds sparkles behind the bar, mirrors reflect tilework and polished wood, and the shiny finish on the moulded ceiling is a kaleidoscope of changing patterns set up by the lively clientele below. Originally the Railway Tavern, designed to serve thirsty travellers disgorged from the terminus of the Great Northern railway across the street, the Crown was renamed in 1885 and remodelled in 1898 to produce this High Victorian fantasy, one of the greatest late nineteenth-century public houses in the British Isles.

Classical pilasters, a parapet topped with urns and a portico crowned with finials and supported by cast-iron columns add theatrical touches to the exterior, suggesting an affinity with Frank 'Matchless' Matcham's opera house only a few metres away. Inside, the Crown offers opportunities for general conviviality and secluded intimacy. A long bar runs down one side of the room, its inward curve designed for the comfort of those perched on stools along its length. Facing the bar is a row of snugs enclosed by screens of wood and coloured glass, their upholstered benches and fitted tables an echo of the railway carriages

Cwmdu CARMARTHENSHIRE

7 miles north of Llandeilo, off B4302 [442 C3]

Deep in Welsh-speaking Wales, in a countryside of green hills, steep narrow lanes and scattered farms and dwellings, is the small hamlet of Cwmdu. In 1991 the Trust acquired the little late Georgian terrace beside the youthful River Dulais which forms the focal point of the community. Of rough stone and slate in the Welsh vernacular tradition, and washed a warm rich yellow, the terrace consists of two tiny one-up, one-downs, originally intended for agricultural workers, a village shop and a small inn that was once a farmhouse, with a lean-to stable. A riverside garden across the street still has the original stone-built lavatory range, with two 'two-holers', and the terrace is flanked, at one end, by an eighteenth-century chapel and graveyard, at the other by the chapel vestry. Here, in this small cluster of buildings, are all the elements – non-conformist chapel, vestry, pub and shop – which have fostered the distinctive Welsh identity and sense of community.

After a break of over ten years, both shop and inn are once again going concerns with the latter being run on traditional informal lines. There is a small bar and beers are served to customers sitting on settles and benches in what was the farmhouse parlour.

Danbury and Lingwood Commons
ESSEX

5 miles east of Chelmsford, astride the A414 [443 J4]

The large villages of Danbury and Little Baddow are now virtually a suburb of Chelmsford. To the west of Little Baddow the 44.5 hectares (110 acres) of Blake's Wood, a chestnut and hornbeam coppice with plenty of footpaths, provide good walking, despite the damage of the Great Storm of 1987. Close at hand is Lingwood Common, at the north end of the sandy, gravelly ridge between Chelmsford and Maldon, one of the few pieces of higher ground in this part of Essex. Grazing of the common died out in the early 1920s and oak and silver birch, with pleasant grassy glades, now cover much of it.

The larger Danbury Common, at the south end of the ridge, is more open, but even here the bracken, broom and gorse are giving way to self-seeded birch and oak. The heather areas are now being reinstated by careful management. Danbury is only 5 miles from the head of the Blackwater estuary (*see* p.49), and just 12 miles from the sea. During the Napoleonic Wars when Boney was expected to invade at any moment, the east side of the common became a military camp. The site survives as a grassy open space.

Dartmouth and its approaches DEVON

On the south coast, between Brixham, to the east, and Little Dartmouth, to the south-west [442 D7–D8]

While Dartmouth and the coast on either side of its estuary are very beautiful, the National Trust owned nothing here for most of its existence. As a deliberate act of policy, following the initial success of Enterprise Neptune, the Regional Committee decided to seek to acquire the approaches from the sea on either side of the harbour. Between 1970 and 1987 this major project was virtually completed.

The Trust now owns not only some 6 miles of this coast but also substantial areas of farmland behind it, particularly east of the River Dart, thus enabling the way to the coast to be made beautiful by the removal of eyesores, the planting of trees and the replacement of hedges, which in places were ruthlessly grubbed up in the agrarian revolution of the 1960s. Five miles to the east of the estuary the ancient town of Brixham, wedged into a narrow cleft above its harbour inside Berry Head, straggles up the hill on the road to Kingswear. A mile to

the south, beyond an untidy fringe of holiday camps, the coast is almost wholly unspoilt.

On the west side of Sharkham Point, which is not the Trust's property, the Trust owns a short stretch of cliff and the land behind it. Sharkham is a geological muddle of sandstone, limestone, tuffs and mineralised rocks, the strata tilting sharply. These cliffs are especially good for seabirds, best seen from a boat in the breeding season between mid-March and mid-June. This stretch is followed by the broken cliffs of Southdown and Woodhuish Farms, which the Trust owns, on either side of Man Sands. Here the formations are Meadfoot slates and Staddon grits, the latter rock the reason for the unstable cliffs, where the broken slopes are covered with scrubby vegetation.

The attractive group of Victorian coastguard cottages at Man Sands does not belong to the Trust, nor does part of Scabbacombe Head, but beyond this all the land to the mouth of the Dart has now been acquired, and a most lovely length of coast it is. Scabbacombe Head is a nesting site for seabirds, fulmars, guillemots, razorbills and, especially, kittiwakes, who imitate their name endlessly in April, May and early June.

A mile to the west lies the Coleton Fishacre valley above Pudcombe Cove. In this valley Rupert d'Oyly Carte, the son of Richard d'Oyly Carte who produced all the

The tranquil estuary of the Dart winds far inland, with steep wooded slopes rising from the water and flotillas of small boats at every anchorage. This view is at Kingswear, near the mouth of the river.

operas of Gilbert and Sullivan, built a remarkable house in 1925 and laid out a substantial tree and shrub garden sloping towards the sea (*see* p.105).

Off Outer Froward Point is the Mew Stone, one of several off this coast. Mew is the old name for gull. Herring gulls and black-backs, cormorants and shags breed in noisy intimacy on the more sheltered faces of the rock. Here we are on a kinder soil, over the Dartmouth slates, and at once the coast becomes gentler. At Inner Froward Point pines have been planted, Monterey, maritime and Corsican, which can withstand the salt-laden gales and flourish on an inhospitable site. Hidden among the trees, and sprawling down the cliff below, are the substantial remains of a gun battery, with its attendant searchlights, built to defend Dartmouth in the Second World War. It is served by a military road from the Coleton to Kingswear lane high above. Halfway along this road is the portentous Daymark, a stone obelisk 24.5 metres (80 feet) high and mounted on tall lancet arches, erected by the Dart Harbour Commissioners in 1864 to mark the mouth of the Dart for seamen, before the days of radar beacons.

On the Dartmouth side of the harbour Dyer's Hill, high above the south end of the town, is a pleasant little wood which hides within it the old Rope Walk of the town.

Every shipbuilding harbour needed to make its own ropes, and here the long terrace which the operation required was built on the contour.

Immediately to the south, across Warfleet Cove, rises the wooded hill of Gallant's Bower, the derivation of its name uncertain. During the Civil War Royalist troops raised earthworks to fortify the hill, and its ramparts and bastions are still impressive. The wood is delightful, while from the top, which is more open, there are views south and north, with the great buildings of the Britannia Royal Naval College in the middle distance.

Below, at the water's edge, Dartmouth Castle defends the narrow harbour entrance, its counterpart of Kingswear Castle on the further side. From the Bower a path leads out to Blackstone Point which shelters the west side of the harbour, and then past Compass Cove out to Little Dartmouth. This farm stretches for a mile and a half to the south-west, lovely cliffs below well-farmed fields, beyond Coombe Point to Warren Point, one of the numerous rabbit warrens on the Devon and Cornwall coast, where rabbits were bred both for their fur and their meat until comparatively recent times.

Dinefwr CARMARTHENSHIRE

On the western edge of Llandeilo, off A40(T) [442 C4]

At the western end of the Black Mountains, in the broad green valley of the River Tywi, is an extensive and beautiful eighteenth-century landscape surrounding an arresting Victorian mansion. Newton House, former seat of the Rice family, Barons Dynevor, dates from the mid-seventeenth century but was remodelled between 1760 and 1780, when the angle towers and crenellated parapet were added, and again in 1852, when the 4th Baron Dynevor commissioned the local architect Richard Kyrke Penson to redesign the house and face it in limestone. Penson's main façade suggests a cross between a Venetian palazzo and a French château, with an array of Gothic windows, an Italianate *porte-cochère*, and tall pyramidal roofs crowning the angle turrets.

The ruins of a former castle (owned by the Dyfed Wildlife Trust) overlooking the valley reflect Dinefwr's and the Rice family's involvement in the early history of Wales. This stronghold, rebuilt in stone some time in the twelfth century, was the capital of Deheubarth, one of the three ancient kingdoms of Wales and seat of the great Rhys ap Gruffydd, ancestor of Henry Tudor and sponsor of the first recorded eisteddfod, held in 1176. Rhys was anglicised

The fanciful mid-Victorian mansion at the heart of the Dinefwr estate. Parkland dating back to the Middle Ages was once attached to a castle on the hill above, the ruins of which still look down on the valley.

to Rice in 1547, following the return of family lands confiscated sixteen years earlier because of a trumped-up charge of conspiracy against Henry VIII.

The naturalistic landscaping of the park was the work of George Rice (1724–79) and his wife Cecil Talbot, with some advice from 'Capability' Brown, who visited Dinefwr in 1775 and is said to be responsible for some clumps of trees and a path. The 194-hectare (480-acre) park stretches down to the banks of the Tywi, with water-meadows and abandoned meanders along the river attracting waders and overwintering birds and panoramic views over the valley from the higher ground. Mature oak woodland includes trees up to 300 years old, descendants of the ancient wildwood that was enclosed for a medieval deer-park. There are still fallow deer beneath the trees and the Trust has reintroduced Dinefwr's distinctive white cattle, a feature of the park for at least 700 years until the herd was dispersed in 1976, at the same time as financial difficulties forced the sale of the house and the home farm. With the help of local authorities and other organisations, the Trust acquired the park in the 1980s, Newton House in 1990, and is now involved in an extensive programme of restoration.

Dolaucothi Gold Mines
CARMARTHENSHIRE

At Pumpsaint, between Lampeter and Llanwrda on the A482 [442 D3]

One of the attractions of Britain for the Romans was as a source of minerals – lead and silver from the Mendips, tin from Cornwall, iron from the Weald and the Forest of Dean. The Roman army also secured these open-cast gold workings on a remote hillside above the valley of the River Cothi, now blanketed with birch and oak woodland. Still in a remarkable state of preservation despite mining activity in the last hundred years, the Roman workings include at least five open-cast sites and a number of adits, horizontal tunnels dug into the hillside for drainage and access. Pick-marks in the rock recall those who laboured here nearly 2,000 years ago, and there are also faint traces of the leats which brought water from the River Cothi and a neigh-bouring valley. Stored in large tanks above the workings, the water was used to wash away debris and topsoil concealing the ore-bearing rock. A trail through the woodland with views over the valley leads to the main features of the Roman and more recent workings, and there is also a collection of 1930s mining equipment.

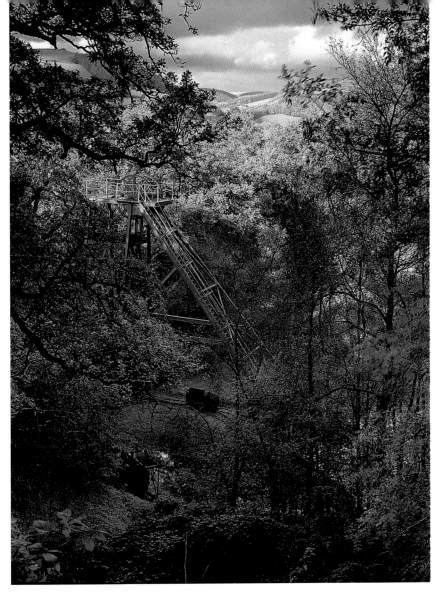

Dolebury Warren BATH & NE SOMERSET

12 miles south of Bristol, east of the A38 above Churchill [442 E5]

Dolebury Warren forms the western bastion of the Mendip range, giving views across the mouth of the Severn estuary to Newport and Cardiff, the hills above Ebbw Vale and the Rhondda rising behind. There is a fine Iron Age fort, the remains of a Celtic field system and traces of a medieval rabbit warren. Although, like the rest of the Mendips, the underlying rock is limestone, there is heather representing an unusual limestone heath as well as herb-rich grassland which is a good site for butterflies.

Gold has been mined in the remote Cothi valley since Roman times. Wooded trails lead past features associated with mining and across the wider estate, where the red kite, which breeds here, may be seen hovering over the trees.

Dolmelynllyn GWYNEDD

5 miles by road north-west of Dolgellau, on the west side of the A470 [442 D1]

Dolmelynllyn, on the west bank of the River Mawddach, came to the Trust in 1936. Nearly half its 546.5 hectares (1,350 acres) are wooded: ancient oak predominates and, although there are some beeches and conifers, they are planted with sensitivity. High above the valley is Rhaiadr Ddu, where the little Gamlan river rushes over the black rock ledges which give the waterfall its name. Visited for its romantic beauty since the mid-eighteenth century, its damp shade encourages an abundance of mosses, as well as a wonderful growth of ferns – the filmy-fern, the hay-scented buckler-fern, the mountain male-fern and the lemon-scented fern.

Above the woods lies open hill crossed by dry-stone walls and with substantial remains of the Cefn Coch gold mine, worked until 1914. Three miles to the north-east, across the Dolmelynllyn sheepwalks, rises the grassy 754.5-metre (2,475-foot) summit of Y Llethr, source of the Gamlan. This is the highest mountain of the rocky Rhinogau range and has a wonderful out-of-this-world character, with vast lonely views. To the east, the heather moor of Derlwyn completes the Trust's vital holding here.

Dorset Coast

[442 E7–F7, 443 G7]

Ballard Down forms the eastern tip of the great chalk ridge of the Purbeck Hills. The sheer cliffs drop 152.5 metres (500 feet) to the sea below, with what remains of the chalk stacks called the Old Harry Rocks gradually crumbling away offshore. As well as Bronze Age barrows, there is a great view: eastward to the Isle of Wight, north over Poole Harbour with Brownsea Island (*see* pp.65) in the foreground, south-west over Purbeck with Portland Bill in the far distance.

To the north, hidden from view round the wooded Handfast Point, the coast drops sharply to Studland Bay, where the Trust owns 4 miles of coast with the farms, heathland and woods behind it, over 1,214 hectares (3,000 acres) of countryside, some of which is a National Nature Reserve. It is a place precious for its flora and fauna, particularly on the heaths where reptiles and lizards thrive and unusual plants, such as the beautiful blue heath milkwort, can be found. These sandy southern heaths are under great pressure from development, and it is fortuitous that the Trust owns this large area acquired with the bequest of the Corfe Castle and Kingston Lacy estates (*see* pp.109 and 204). Active steps have now been taken to protect these rare habitats. The same bequest included 2 miles of the exposed and rocky coast at Langton Matravers west of Swanage, where the Trust has since acquired Spyway Farm and the old cliff quarry known as Dancing Ledge, and cliffs and undercliffs at Blacker's Hole, noted for the Early Spider Orchid.

The Trust has 182 hectares (450 acres) at Southdown and Seabarn Farms, including the beautiful Burning and Whitenothe Cliffs. Although the Purbeck Hills finish at Lulworth, the great chalk downs continue westward to end dramatically at Ringstead Bay, where the land falls away towards Weymouth. From Ringstead to Whitenothe makes an exhilarating walk. The chalk runs into greensand, and where these have slipped over the underlying gault clay there is an exciting undercliff – dangerous for all but experienced walkers, but providing good sites for nesting seabirds. This is the country of J. Meade Falkner's romantic smuggling novel *Moonfleet*.

From Portland Bill the great shingle beach of the Chesil Bank runs north-west for 15 miles. At West Bexington, just beyond Abbotsbury, are the 91.5 hectares (225 acres) of Labour in Vain Farm and, on the crest of the ridge behind, Tulks Hill and Lime Kiln Hill, an area of rough grazing and old stone workings with views over

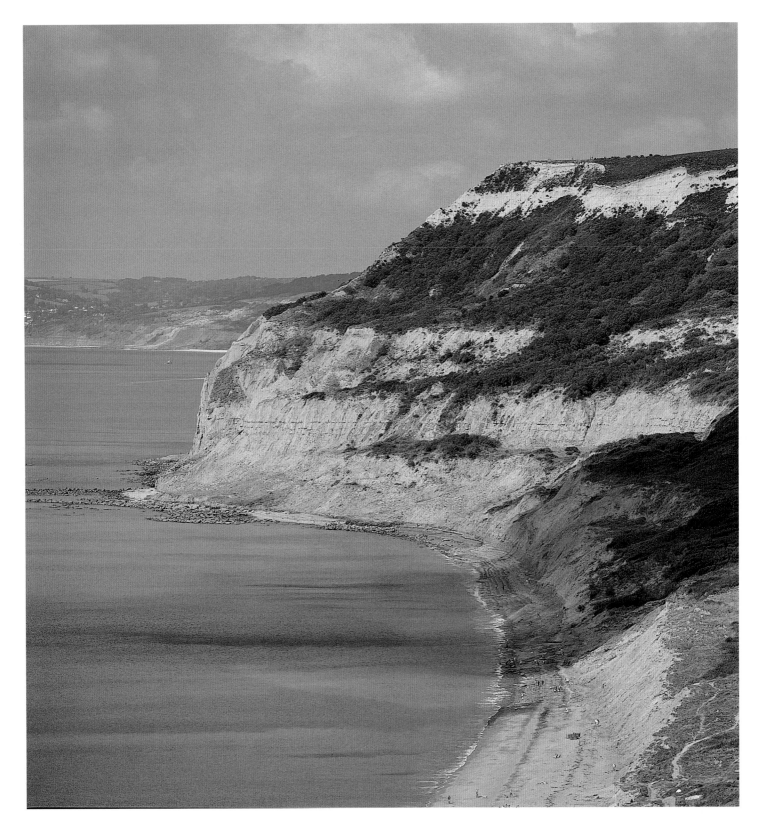

Chesil Bank to the south and the Bride Valley to the north. A mile or so further west, at Cogden, a 105-hectare (260-acre) segment of coast, including a stretch of the shingle ridge and Burton Mere reed-bed, came to the Trust in 1994, and seaward of the unattractive village of Burton Bradstock is the glorious expanse of Burton Cliff, rising steeply from the River Bride to a windy open bluff 30.5 metres (100 feet) above the sea.

Golden Cap is one of the Trust's great successes. When Enterprise Neptune was being planned, it was decided to build on previous experience in Devon and Cornwall and concentrate on acquiring one substantial coastal estate in Dorset, to include the essential hinterland as well as the immediate coastal strip, rather than to dissipate the available funds in small and unconnected purchases along the country's beautiful coast. In twelve years, from 1966 to 1978, the scheme was brought to fruition, both literally and metaphorically crowned by the purchase in the latter year of Golden Cap itself, 188.5 metres (618 feet) above the sea. The orange-coloured sandstone indeed shines golden above the grey cliffs on a sunny day, and from this great landmark there are panoramic views along miles of unspoilt coast, between Portland Bill in the east and Start Point, in South Devon, in the west.

The coastal walks are lovely but equally good are those in the hinterland: gentle rolling hills and valleys with seemly farm buildings, woodland, clumps of trees planted as landmarks, and views inland as well as seaward. Below the cliffs are rocky coves and little beaches reached by scrambly paths. The whole area is rich botanically, with a considerable acreage of unimproved grassland in which rare species of plants have survived. There is an intricate system of footpaths and bridleways and a good walker will need a week to get to know this magical place.

Dorset Hills DORSET

North of the A35 between Dorchester and Charmouth, and between Shaftesbury and Blandford [442 F6–F7]

The A35 from Dorchester sweeps boldly west through Bridport and Charmouth. To the south, the high ground behind the coast allows occasional views of the sea beyond. To the north lies the pastoral Vale of Marshwood and, overlooking it, a delightful series of steep hills, some chalk, others greensand, and each with its Iron Age hill-fort, built most probably by the Durotriges, the local tribe, whose capital was at Maiden Castle near Dorchester, 20 miles to the east. Each hill provides a good walk and lovely views.

Pilsdon Pen is one of Dorset's best-known landmarks and, at 277 metres (905 feet), its second-highest hill. As well as the grassy outlines of the prehistoric defences ringing the summit, there are the banks of medieval pillow mounds denoting rabbit warrens within the ramparts of the fort and the panoramas from the top are superb, particularly southwards across the vale to Golden Cap, with the sea sparkling to either side.

Lambert's Castle, 842 feet high, is a larger, whale-backed hill, with gorse and bracken on its flanks and scrub woodland to the north. An annual summer fair was held here from 1709 to 1947 when horses were raced on a hilltop track outside the ramparts of the fort. Coney's Castle is on the spur of a ridge only a mile away and both forts may have been border posts between the territory of the Durotriges and their neighbours, the Dumnonii, who occupied what is now Devon and Cornwall.

At 256.5 metres (894 feet), Lewesdon Hill commands the north side of the vale, with sweeping views over Devon, Dorset and Somerset. The most dramatic of these hills is Eggardon Hill to the east (*see* p.142), only half of which belongs to the Trust. It is bonier, more muscular, feels incredibly ancient, and the hill-fort is wonderfully preserved.

Three hills of a different character lie in the east of the county and, although each has considerable archaeological remains, they were acquired for their combination of natural history, landscape and archaeology. Fontmell Down, on the chalk between Blandford and Shaftesbury, has superb views: south-west over the rich country of Blackmore Vale, north over Cranborne Chase and south towards the coast. It was bought by public subscription in 1977 as a memorial to Thomas Hardy, whose spirit hovers over so much of Dorset, and is now part leased to the Dorset Wildlife Trust. Since 1977 the Trust has acquired further land, over 162 hectares (400 acres) in all, including Compton Down and Melbury Beacon, a major piece of preservation of what was once commonplace and is now rare. On a summer's day the down is alive with blue butterflies: the small blue, common blue and chalk-hill blue.

At Turnworth Down, in the wooded hills west of Blandford, there is more of this very special downland, and here the woods surround a Romano-British settlement on the Ridgeway. Hod Hill, standing between the two downs, has the largest Iron Age hill-fort in Dorset. Re-used as a military base by the invading Romans, it has earthworks from both periods as well as an exceptional, butterfly-attracting downland flora.

Downhill House and Mussenden Temple CO. LONDONDERRY

1 mile west of Castlerock and 5 miles west of Coleraine on the A2 Coleraine–Downhill coast road [444 B2]

The wild and beautiful Ulster coast, with broom, ling and blaeberry heath clothing cliffs of limestone and basalt falling hundreds of feet to the Atlantic, was where the remarkable Frederick Augustus Hervey, Bishop of Derry and later 4th Earl of Bristol, chose to site his house. The construction of this mansion began in about 1775, and the bleak headland round about was transformed into a landscape park, with moorland converted into 'a green carpet sprinkled with white clover' – as the Bishop described it in an invitation to his friend, the agriculturalist and travel writer Arthur Young – and thousands of deciduous and evergreen trees were planted to tame the wilderness.

The Bishop's obsession with circular buildings, which reached its full flowering at Ickworth in Suffolk (*see* p.196), was heralded at Downhill. Perched right on the edge of the cliffs to the north of the house is the little Mussenden Temple, a domed rotunda crowned with a huge urn and with twelve Corinthian columns adorning the façade. The design, which was based on the Temple of Vesta at Tivoli, had been suggested to the Earl-Bishop by James Wyatt, although the long-suffering Irish architect Michael Shanahan, who had overseen the construction of the house, again executed the plans for his difficult client. The little building was named after the Bishop's attractive cousin, Mrs Frideswide Mussenden, who died shortly before it was completed in 1785, and it was fitted out as a library. Here Frederick could study undisturbed, the silence broken only by the screaming of the gulls, by the ceaseless roar of the waves breaking on the rocks below and by the Atlantic gales, which sometimes threaten to tear the building from its roots. In recent years, the temple has been increasingly threatened by cliff erosion, and in 1997 the Trust carried out a major stabilisation programme to prevent the building being lost to the sea.

Downhill itself is now only a shell, a bleak ruin in the middle of the estate, but the eighteenth-century landscape park still survives. From the grand triumphal arch forming the Bishop's Gate on the Coleraine road, a path leads north to the coast along the steep wooded valley known as Black Glen, emerging on the edge of the cliffs. The Mussenden Temple stands a few metres to the west and there are glorious views beyond over Lough Foyle to the coast of Donegal. On the edge of the woods framing the view south from the house, another triumphal arch on a pedestal is the remains of the mausoleum Frederick erected in memory of his brilliant eldest brother George, Ambassador to Madrid and Turin, Lord Lieutenant of Ireland and Lord Privy Seal.

Downs Banks STAFFORDSHIRE

1 mile south-east of Barlaston, 1½ miles north of Stone, between the A34 and the A520 [442 F1]

On the edge of the Potteries, only 6 miles south of the parish church at the centre of Stoke-on-Trent, lies Downs Banks. Industry is close at hand, but the hilly landscape encloses an oasis: a peaty valley in 69 hectares (170 acres) of moorland covered with bracken, gorse and broom; marshy bottoms with snipe; and water-loving plants along the stream.

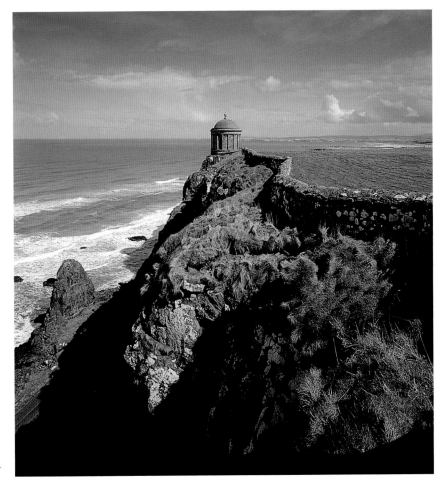

When the eccentric Frederick Hervey, Bishop of Derry and later 4th Earl of Bristol, was looking for a site for his new house in the 1770s, he chose a wild and dramatic spot on the north coast of Ulster. Only ruins survive of the great house that was once here, but Mussenden Temple, the most original of a number of eye-catchers built to enliven the estate, still stands precariously poised above the Atlantic.

The late 18th-century stables at Dudmaston. The clock-tower, with two stone clock faces, was added slightly later, but a clock mechanism was only installed for the first time in 1981, to mark the gift of Dudmaston to the Trust.

Dudmaston SHROPSHIRE

At Quatt, 4 miles south-east of Bridgnorth on the A442
[442 F2]

Dudmaston lies close to some of the most beautiful countryside Britain has to offer, looking west over the River Severn to the Clee Hills. An unpretentious four-square, late seventeenth-century house attributed to Francis Smith of Warwick, with some later alterations, its small-scale intimate family rooms are the ideal setting for an unusual assemblage of paintings and sculpture. This individual collection was built up by Sir George Labouchere and his wife, Rachel Hamilton-Russell, who inherited the property in 1966, the last of an unbroken line stretching back 850 years.

Lady Labouchere's interest in botanical art, continuing a long family tradition, is shown in the collection of works by such great exponents as P.-J. Redouté (1759–1840), P. Reinagle (1749–1833), G.D. Ehret (1708–70) and W.H. Fitch (1817–92). Formal studies by these masters and glowing flower canvases by Jan Van Os in the library contrast with the fresh, fluid approach adopted by Mary Grierson (b.1912), official botanical artist at Kew for twelve years. A similar love of nature is revealed in the displays of photographs and drawings by the naturalist Frances Pitt (1888–1964), who lived in this area all her life and was a close friend of the Wolryche-Whitmore family. A notebook in her neat writing meticulously records her finds.

Two rooms devoted to twentieth-century painting and sculpture, including abstracts by Ben Nicholson, sculptures by Henry Moore and Barbara Hepworth, and some rather forbidding Spanish paintings acquired by Sir George while he was Ambassador in Madrid, set a more sombre tone. Apart from flashes of red and yellow from two Poliakoffs and A. Davie's still-life in red, green and orange, colours are muted: grey and black, green and brown. Chinese porcelain and French furniture are also fruits of years in the diplomatic service, as are some of Lady Labouchere's delightful topographic watercolours, including pictures of Barcelona, Bruges, India and China – such as Edward Lear's tiny study of the gardens of Government House, Calcutta, or William Alexander's cameo of a smoking Chinaman – as well as atmospheric English landscapes and local views of Bridgnorth and Shrewsbury.

Associations of a different kind are reflected in the gallery devoted to the connection between Lady Labouchere and the Darbys of Coalbrookdale, cradle of the Industrial Revolution. By a strange coincidence, Dudmaston is also linked with the twentieth-century

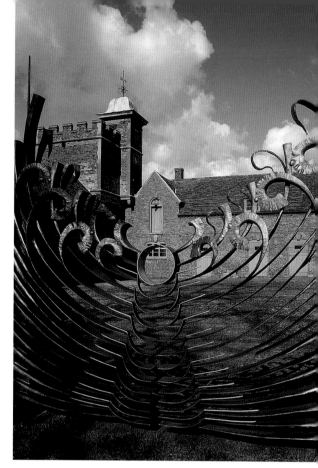

microchip revolution, as Charles Babbage, the father of the computer, married a daughter of the house in 1814 and spent much time here.

The magnificent oaks and cedars on the terraced lawns stretching down to the lake known as the Big Pool on the garden side of the house are reminders of another pioneer, Geoffrey Wolryche-Whitmore, who spent the first half of the twentieth century building up a national reputation for enlightened forestry on the estate. The giant cuckoo flower or ladies' smock (*Cardamine raphanifolia*) by the stream which runs into the pool was brought back from Norway by Mary Wolryche-Whitmore.

A memorable display of spring and summer colour comes from mature magnolias, rhododendrons, azaleas, Japanese cherries and other shrubs, and heaths, thymes and lavenders flourish on the sunny ledges contrived on one of the sandstone outcrops which are a feature of the grounds. The wilderness garden created in the eighteenth century in the little valley known as the Dingle, with rustic bridges, ornamental waterfalls and serpentine paths leading to artful vistas, is now being restored, a rare surviving example of this gardening style.

Dunham Massey CHESHIRE

3 miles south-west of Altrincham, off the A56 [445 H7]

A beautifully made mechanical model of the solar system, showing how the six known planets moved round the Sun (Neptune, Pluto and Uranus were yet to be discovered), is the centrepiece of the early eighteenth-century library, dating from the time of the obscure John Norris's changes to the house for George Booth, 2nd Earl of Warrington, whose cipher can be seen on many of the faded bindings in the fitted oak bookcases. Over the fireplace is a dramatic, in-depth carving of the Crucifixion by the young Grinling Gibbons, who based it on a painting by Tintoretto and set his agonised figures in a tranquil floral border.

Apart from the south front, with its sash windows and Edwardian dormers, the exterior of Dunham Massey is much as George Booth left it, an attractive red-brick building, long and low, set round two courtyards and still protected by the medieval moat that embraced the earlier house. The sombre, low-ceilinged, oak-lined chapel and the magnificent collection of Huguenot silver are both reflections of the Booth family's ardent Protestantism. The glittering display now set out in the Rose Room includes a superb wine cistern made by Philip Rollos in 1701, with the wild boars of the Booth crest formed into handles, eternally glowering at each other over the bowl.

Dunham Massey's exceptional Edwardian interiors were commissioned by William Grey, 9th Earl of Stamford, whose family acquired the estate through the marriage of George Booth's daughter, Mary, to the 4th Earl. With advice from the connoisseur and furniture historian Percy Macquoid, and the outstanding firm of Morant & Co., decorators to Edward VII, the 9th Earl and his wife created rooms which rival the appeal of those from 200 years earlier. In their long saloon with a bay window arching out into the garden, Grey family portraits hang against deep-green walls suggested by Macquoid, who also advised dyeing the two mossy Donegal carpets lying on the polished boards and re-upholstering the set of early eighteenth-century walnut chairs to match the room. Yellow damask curtains hanging at the long sash windows give the final touch in a colour scheme which could well have been created for Bunthorne in Gilbert and Sullivan's *Patience*. The 9th Earl also commissioned J. Compton Hall to create an elaborate neo-Jacobean entrance front loosely based on Sudbury (*see p.377*).

A remarkable series of early views of Dunham Massey, recording its gradual transformation, hang in the great gallery and here, too, is Guercino's early seventeenth-

century *Mars, Venus and Cupid, with Saturn as Time*, possibly purchased by the 2nd Earl of Warrington. The young 5th Earl of Stamford, when on his Grand Tour, arranged for the two huge caricatures of his travels by Thomas Patch, which hang in the early eighteenth-century tea-room. Commissioned as light relief from the serious study of Italian art and culture, they are an irreverent look at the earl and his friends.

An ancient deer-park surrounds the house, enclosed by George Booth's high brick wall and still shaded by trees he established, some forming a series of radiating avenues. Yews and oaks on the lawns to the east of the house were part of an informal Victorian and Edwardian layout which has now been re-established and enhanced, with beds of rhododendrons and late-flowering azaleas, a water garden along the stream feeding the moat and a collection of skimmias. A curious mound at the north-west corner of the house, smothered with acacia, laburnums and Irish ivy, may be the remains of a Norman motte, and a gabled brick mill dates from Elizabethan times (*see below*).

Dunham Massey Saw-mill CHESHIRE

In grounds of Dunham Massey (see above) [445 H7]

An attractive gabled building of warm red brick with mullioned windows, Dunham Massey mill is the only visible survivor of the Tudor hall built by Sir George Booth, 1st Baronet, most of which was reconstructed in

Top: Dunham Massey is largely the creation of George Booth, 2nd Earl of Warrington (1675–1758), whose portrait by Michael Dahl shows him with his daughter Mary, who was also his heir. Above: Great avenues in the deer-stocked park perpetuate the 2nd Earl's late 17th-century layout.

the early eighteenth century (*see above*). Powered by a
4.7-metre (15½-foot) -diameter overshot water-wheel fed
from a continuation of the lake in front of the house, the
mill was originally used for grinding corn, but in *c.*1860
was refitted as a saw-mill and estate workshop. It retains
its Victorian machinery, including the Dunham Ripper, a
big frame saw for cutting up trees, a power-fed circular
saw and a crane for handling the timber, all now restored
to working order.

Above: The mill at Dunham Massey
is a remnant of the earlier estate, which
was built in 1616. With its warm red
brick, mullioned windows and gabled
roofline it conveys something of what
the old hall would have looked like.

Below: The ruins of Dunstanburgh
Castle form a romantic eye-catcher
on a lonely stretch of Northumberland
coast. The castle was once reached by
a paved causeway from inland and was
also served by a harbour in a deep
narrow inlet, which is now blocked
with shingle.

Dunstanburgh Castle
NORTHUMBERLAND

9 miles north-east of Alnwick [445 J2]

There are no roads to Dunstanburgh. This magnificent
ruin stands lonely and isolated on the Northumbrian coast,
approached only by shore from Craster to the south or
Embleton to the north. Built where the Great Whin Sill
reaches the sea in a bold outcrop of basalt, the castle
occupies a natural defensive site. To the north, cliffs a
hundred feet high fall sheer to the waves breaking on the
rocks below; to the west the ground drops almost as
precipitously to the patchwork of fields stretching away to
the Cheviots; and to the south the castle overlooks a deep
ravine-like inlet. Only on the east does the land slope
gently away into the sea.

Like Cilgerran some 250 miles away looking west over
the Irish Sea (*see* p.92), Dunstanburgh's might is concentrated in the massive towers which punctuate the walls
enclosing the 4.5-hectare (11-acre) site. Approached from
the south, where the strongest defences were needed, a
substantial curtain wall with two projecting towers ends in
an impressive gatehouse-keep guarding the castle's south-
west corner. The two D-shaped towers bulging out round
the entrance passage look formidable even today. On the
north the long finger of the Lilburn Tower, its three storeys
still largely intact, stands on the highest point of the bluff,
often seen silhouetted against an angry sky.

Dunstanburgh was built between 1313 and 1316, the
stronghold of Thomas, 2nd Earl of Lancaster, grandson
of Henry III. But the Earl had little time to enjoy his castle,
for he was executed only six years after it was completed,
following his defeat by his cousin Edward II at the Battle
of Boroughbridge. Strengthened by John of Gaunt in the
late fourteenth century against the Scots, Dunstanburgh's
defences were put to the test in the Wars of the Roses,
when the Yorkists besieged Lancastrian forces here in 1462
and 1464. Severely damaged in these engagements, the
castle was barely repaired; too remote to be useful, it was
quarried for building materials and gradually decayed into
an empty shell. It is now a hauntingly beautiful place, the
restless murmur of the sea and the plaintive cries of seabirds
wheeling overhead adding to its enchantment.

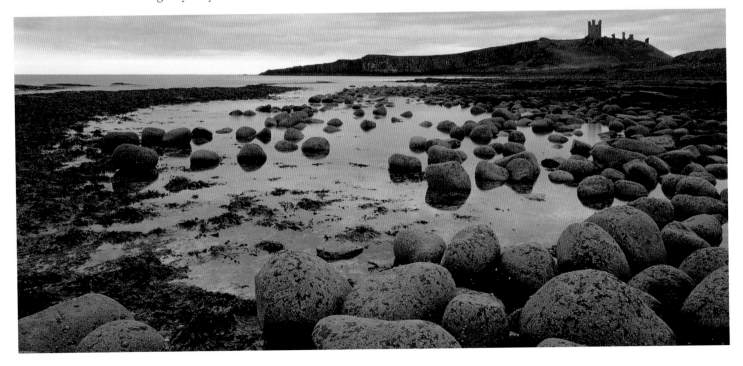

Dunster Castle SOMERSET

In Dunster, 3 miles south-east of Minehead on the A396, just off the A39 [442 D5]

A few miles east of Minehead a ridge of the Brendon Hills reaches almost to the Bristol Channel, ending in a steep-sided outlier. This spectacular natural defensive site was chosen by the Norman William de Mohun for his castle.

Although no trace of the original defences survives, Dunster still looks like a castle, with a tangle of towers and battlements rising romantically from the thickly wooded hill. This medieval fantasy was created by Anthony Salvin in 1868–72 for George Fownes Luttrell, whose family had lived here since 1405. It was grafted on to an earlier Jacobean house built within the original stronghold by the local stonemason William Arnold, the architect of Montacute (*see* p.245). Besieged for 160 days by Cromwell's troops in the Civil War, Dunster was considered a major threat to the Commonwealth and the regime ordered its complete destruction, miraculously issuing a reprieve when the curtain wall alone had been razed.

Struggling up the hill from the village clustered below the tor, it is easy to appreciate the defensive advantages of the castle's position. A steep slope leads up to the fifteenth-century gatehouse, and a second thirteenth-century gateway, the oldest surviving feature of the castle, gives access to what was once the lower ward. The north façade is dominated by Salvin's great four-storey tower on the left, bordered by an octagonal staircase turret complete with authentic medieval arrow loops. The nineteenth-century work blends so well with the Jacobean wing to the right that only details in the New Red sandstone masonry show where one ends and the other begins.

Two of the finest features of the interior were commissioned by Colonel Francis Luttrell during the late seventeenth century. He was responsible for the magnificent oak staircase with naked cherubs and dogs racing through a thick acanthus undergrowth carved on the panels of the balustrade, one of the beasts leaping over a clutch of Charles II silver shillings from the 1683–4 issue which cunningly dates the work. Of a standard comparable with the staircase at Sudbury Hall (*see* p.377), this may also reflect the skill of the distinguished Edward Pearce.

Craftsmanship of similar quality is displayed in the three-dimensional plasterwork ceiling in the dining room, thickly encrusted with flowers and foliage which almost conceal the creatures hidden in the design. Here a cherub shoots a deer with a bow and arrow; there a winged horse bursts from a blossom. A spider's web of plaster in the hall

was the only original Jacobean ceiling to escape remodelling, looks down on the famous allegorical portrait of Sir John Luttrell, dated 1550, in which he is shown emerging half naked from a stormy sea while sailors abandon a foundering ship behind him. Less enigmatic but equally striking is the set of seventeenth-century painted leather hangings illustrating the story of Antony and Cleopatra which fills Salvin's gallery, the curiously expressionless faces and wooden horses redeemed by the brilliant, glittering colours produced by painting on silver foil.

A deliciously cool Victorian conservatory, like a leafy extension of the airy, pale-green drawing room, leads out on to a sheltered south-facing terrace. Although the tor is exposed to westerly winds, the mild maritime climate allows some remarkably tender plants and shrubs to grow here, including an olive, palms and a now famous lemon, laden with fruit in midsummer. Steep paths curling round the hill below the castle are lined with fuchsias and hydrangeas, there is a grove of strawberry trees and huge conifers tower above willows, camellias and rhododendrons, the giant rhubarb-like leaves of *Gunnera manicata* and other moisture-loving plants along the River Avill in the depths of the valley.

The grassy platform which was the site of the keep and many rooms in the castle have magnificent views over the countryside around, a patchwork of small hedged fields rolling away to the hills of Exmoor which still looks very much as it is depicted in a set of early eighteenth-century scenes. To the north the tower of the village church is echoed in the folly on Conigar Hill, with the blue of the Bristol Channel beyond.

Below: The main staircase at Dunster has a richly-carved elm balustrade dating from the 1680s. In the panel from which this detail is taken, dogs race through acanthus leaf foliage in pursuit of a stag.

Above left: The leather hangings in the gallery at Dunster Castle show Octavius pursuing Antony and Cleopatra as they flee from the battle of Alexandria. The process used to produce the hangings was developed in Moorish Spain. Involving oil paint on top of silver foil, the technique gives a gleaming richness to the colours and allowed highlights such as Antony's helmet to be hand-tooled.

The Portrait Phenomenon

HARDWICK
HALL
175

Whatever else the country house offers, portraits are almost certainly going to be on the agenda. For centuries men of any standing or pretension immortalised themselves and their families in paint, in compositions which affirmed and proclaimed their sense of social superiority. Often, too, the family would own one or more copies of royal portraits, whose presence would lend lustre and authority to the ensemble. Although there are earlier royal images, portraiture as an art took off in the sixteenth century. Partly this was a response to Renaissance ideas about the worth of the individual, partly a reflection of more peaceable times, and partly a way of dealing with the great expanses of wall in the newly fashionable long galleries.

Some portraits were little more than wallpaper, purchased in sets, and with quality to match. Others had more to offer but, despite the example of Holbein, who produced penetrating images of Henry VIII and his court, and some exquisite miniatures by Nicholas Hilliard, Isaac Oliver and others, portraits of this period tended to be about propaganda rather than realism, relying on costume and the trappings of authority to make their mark. Those of Elizabeth I reached an almost iconic quality, showing a doll-like figure clothed in the most sumptuous garments. The queen wanted it so. In later centuries, too, the court tended to lead the way at the top end of the market, forming taste and image with its patronage and introducing foreign talent to the British scene. Charles I, one of the most discerning of art lovers, had himself and his family immortalised by Van Dyck, whose distinctive style – mixing elegance and dignity with informality and glamour – has been a reference point for portrait painters aiming for the grand effect ever since.

Image-creation is still important, as the ranks of sober-suited gentlemen in the boardrooms and dining halls of today affirm. And while there were always production-line artists, such as Kneller, whose prodigious output, involving as many as fourteen sittings a day, was achieved only by adopting some formulaic approaches, others moved the genre on. Where once foreigners tended to overshadow native artists, by the later eighteenth century, English painters such as Gainsborough, Reynolds, Lawrence and Romney were among the best in the field, producing works which, although often dramatic and romantic, were also psychologically and emotionally charged.

Alongside the grand society portrait have run other strands. Where the élite went for the top names with a national or international reputation, local artists established followings among the county gentry, who passed them on from one house to another. Children have been captured through the centuries, often with a spontaneity and freshness which sets their portraits apart. And there has been a long tradition of the self-portrait. Sometimes artists produced paintings of themselves as a form of advertisement, sometimes to experiment with pose and mood, sometimes as an exercise in self-revelation. Intimacy and charm are the mark of a raft of less showy portraits produced from the later nineteenth century onwards, a reflection of increasing social informality and the tastes of a prosperous middle class, and also of groups, such as the Pre-Raphaelites, who painted each other. These are portraits to be savoured by those close to the sitter, not to shout at the world.

HARDWICK
HALL
175

This iconic portrait of Elizabeth I, combining formulaic face painting with sumptuous and richly-detailed costume, hangs in the long gallery at Hardwick Hall in Derbyshire. Painted in the 1590s, it is typical of the impersonal and rigid images of the queen from this period in her reign and a reflection of the rarefied climate of the late-Elizabethan court. Possibly, this painting is from the workshop of the leading miniaturist Nicholas Hilliard, whose training as a goldsmith and jeweller gave him an exquisite sense of detail and decoration.

A more certain example of the miniaturist's art, and showing the period love of allegory and symbolism, is the little portrait of Edward Herbert by Isaac Oliver at Powis Castle (**opposite, above left**). Edward Herbert was a Renaissance man, poet, courtier, soldier and philosopher, friend of John Donne and Ben Jonson. Here, alluding to some of his poetry, he is shown as the melancholy knight or lover, as indicated by the burning heart on his shield. This painting is only

23 centimetres (9 inches) wide, but even so it is large for a miniature, most of which were of a size which could be worn in a locket or set as a cameo.

Van Dyck's paintings of the court of Charles I introduced a new and distinctive approach to the grand portrait. Helped by the period taste for richly-coloured silks and loose curls, he produced pictures which combined elegance with sensuous-ness, glamour with dignity. The copy of his portrait of Henrietta Maria, from *c*.1633, shows the queen with her favourite dwarf, Jeffery Hudson (**right**). Henrietta Maria is portrayed with sensitive, elongated Van Dyck hands and loose hair, and is set off by sumptuous drapery and a classical column. The orange tree behind alludes to her love of Italianate gardens. Van Dyck's portrait of Sir Robert Shirley (**above right**) in Persian dress is even more theatrical. It was painted in Rome in 1622 when Shirley was serving as Persian ambassador to Pope Gregory XV, and is one of several Van Dyck portraits of sitters in flamboyant exotic dress.

In the 18th century, poses became more informal and psychologically telling, and trappings and props were often direct reflections of the life rather than symbolic. Yet the Van Dyck approach, with low sight lines to enhance the authority of the sitter, continued to exert a strong influence. The portrait of Sir Walter Calverley

POWIS CASTLE
314

PETWORTH
302

PETWORTH
302

WALLINGTON
414

Blackett of Wallington by Reynolds (**left**), probably painted between 1759 and 1761, suggests a country gentle-man of means and endeavour, while setting him against a stormy sky gives him a romantic air. Sir Walter was a man of significance. He was High Sheriff of Northumberland in 1732 and five times Mayor of Newcastle, and he transformed the Wallington estate, building bridges and cottages, planting woods and enclosing new fields. He was also, as Reynolds suggests, deeply attached to his dogs. Gainsborough's portrait of Augustus John Hervey (**overleaf**), 3rd Earl of Bristol and Vice Admiral of the Blue, was painted in 1768, when Gainsborough was in Bath.

ICKWORTH
196

CLIVEDEN
101

Again it is a grand statement, with the trappings of an anchor and a marine background which Van Dyck himself used, but the pose is almost casual, reflecting Gainsborough's preference for informality and sensitivity to personality. Into the late 19th and early 20th centuries, the very rich still lived in large houses and there remained a demand for portraits in the grand manner. John Singer Sargent's portrait of Nancy, Lady Astor (right), who presided over the Cliveden Set, is much in the Van Dyck tradition: self-consciously grand, with a strong vertical emphasis to exaggerate the elegance and slenderness of the subject. This is a painting of the social mask, effortlessly suggesting the confidence of huge wealth.

Mirrors have always been used in artists' studios and from the 15th century, when they were first good enough to reflect an undistorted image, they allowed painters to produce portraits of themselves. Usually, the mirror was set at an angle to the canvas, resulting in the typical sideways glance, as if the artist is being disturbed at work. From the start, these paintings were used to advertise skill, but the rising status of artists in the 17th century, coupled with a growing interest in personality and individuality, increased their appeal. In particular there was a demand for self-portraits by women, which had scarcity value. One of the very few who managed to pursue painting professionally was Elisabeth Vigée le Brun (1745–1842), whose twenty or so self-portraits, which projected her attractiveness as much as her painterly skills, were marketing tools, used to sell herself to potential clients. This charming example (**right**) was commissioned in Naples in 1791 by the eccentric Frederick Augustus Hervey, the Earl Bishop, brother of the 3rd Earl who was painted by Gainsborough.

Elisabeth's contemporary, Angelica Kauffmann (1741–1807), was made to choose at an early age between her painting and her passion for music. Later in life, when she was in her fifties, Angelica turned this pivotal moment into an allegorical painting (**right**). In it she shows herself as a young girl regretfully parting from Music, whose hand she is clasping, and choosing Painting, who is urging her along the hard road this choice will give her to the temple of glory in the distance.

When photography was invented, artists could work from images of themselves without the aid of a mirror. The self-portrait by John Everett Millais (1829–96), dating from 1878 (**above right**), suggests his prosperous later career as a portrait painter, when, in contrast to his youthful Pre-Raphaelite phase, he became an establishment figure and was rewarded with a baronetcy.

Quite different from the grand formal portrait is the rich seam of private and more intimate compositions, many of them produced for the prosperous middle classes, which are a feature of the later 19th and 20th centuries. In these the sitter may be shown in their daily surroundings, or at some characteristic occupation. William Nicholson's portrait of Margaret Beale (**right**), who was an expert needle-woman, shows her knitting. Painted in 1905, it is a pair to Nicholson's more sober and formal picture of her husband, the prosperous London solicitor James Beale who com-missioned Standen in West Sussex. Similarly, Pauline Dower's portrait of Mary, Lady Trevelyan (**far right**) shows her working on the needlework panel that illustrates a family legend, and

STANDEN
362

WALLINGTON
414

which can be seen at Wallington in Northumberland. Begun in 1910, the piece took her until 1923 to complete. Although more colourful, and with a freer use of paint, Vanessa Bell's impressionistic watercolour of her sister Virginia Woolf (**below left**) has the same sense of a window onto a private world. Painted in 1935 as a study for a larger, more finished piece, it shows Virginia relaxing in the comfortable book-lined sitting room of the Woolfs' London house, 52 Tavistock Square. Edmund Fairfax Lucy's delightful Suffolk interior (**below**), painted in 1977 and shown as part of an exhibition by the artist at Mompesson House in Wiltshire in the early 1990s, is in the same idiom. With its open door, play with perspec-tive and inclusion of a mundane mop and bucket, and of the family cats, it recalls the intimate Dutch interiors of the 17th century.

This portrait of Winston Churchill (**opposite**, **above left**), one of several at Chartwell in Kent, was painted in 1942, in the middle of the Second World War. In depicting the great man at his desk in one of his signature siren suits, Frank Salisbury, who was an official painter, has injected informality and realism into what is a carefully posed composition, suggesting authority and application.

Child portraits have an appeal all of their own. Lady Arabella Stuart (**right**), painted in 1577 when she was only two, is dressed as a miniature adult, and the doll she clutches is also in full Elizabethan dress. This charming little girl, granddaughter of Bess of Hardwick, had a claim on the throne through her father, Charles Stuart, Earl of Lennox, and became something of a political pawn, bandied about as

MONK'S HOUSE
244

CHARTWELL

HARDWICK HALL

WADDESDON MANOR

a possible successor to Elizabeth I and posing a threat to the insecure James I. Arabella's fate was sealed by a secret marriage to William Seymour, later 2nd Duke of Somerset; she was imprisoned in the Tower, where she died in 1615. Gainsborough's portrait of Master Nicholls (*The Pink Boy*, **above**) was painted in the last years of the artist's life, after he settled in London in 1774. It shows the child, then eight years old, in a Van Dyck pose and wearing shimmering Van Dyck costume, as Gainsborough often used for his pictures of the young.

Dunwich Heath SUFFOLK

*South off the Westleton–Dunwich road, ½ mile before
reaching Dunwich* [443 L3]

South of the now vanished Saxon capital of East Anglia,
the once-prosperous town of Dunwich which was overwhelmed by the sea in the fourteenth century, lies the
Trust's outpost at Dunwich Heath, between Aldeburgh
and Southwold.

At first sight the heath seems unprepossessing: an
oblong block of dry sandy soil covered with heather,
bracken, gorse and some silver birch, the half mile of low
crumbling cliffs being constantly gnawed away by the sea.
Nightjars breed here in small numbers and there is a rare
butterfly: the silver-studded blue. The Dunwich Rose is
rare too; it is said to have been planted in the Saxon town
by medieval monks.

Dunwich Heath acts as a buffer to the RSPB's much
larger Minsmere Reserve which adjoins to the south, the
two holdings separated by Docwra's Ditch, dug to provide
both a firebreak and a reservoir, these dry heaths being
much at risk from fire. The views looking down into this
beautiful reserve are lovely and, half a mile to the south of
the Trust's cliff-top car park, the RSPB provides hides
from which the birds may be observed.

Dyrham Park GLOUCESTERSHIRE

8 miles north of Bath, 12 miles east of Bristol [442 F5]

After recording the burial of John Wynter in 1688, the local
rector drew a thick line across the page. He knew it was
the end of an era. Two years previously John's only
surviving child, his 36-year-old daughter Mary, had
married William Blathwayt, a rising civil servant, and by
the end of the century this energetic, self-made man had
totally transformed the Tudor manor his wife inherited,
creating this great mansion set beneath a spur of the
Cotswolds. Despite his loyalty to James II in the Glorious
Revolution, a rare fluency in Dutch coupled with an
unusual gift for administration recommended Blathwayt
to William III, for whom he acted as Secretary of State
from 1692–1702.

Although built over only ten years, Dyrham shows two
faces to the world, reflecting Blathwayt's rising fortunes.
The west front, with glorious views over the countryside
towards Bristol, is an attractive building crowned with a
balustrade, and with a courtyard terrace flanked by
projecting one-storey wings, one of which leads to the
medieval village church. An Italianate double stairway
descends from the terrace to a great sweep of grass, and the
façade as a whole has continental overtones, as if its

architect, the shadowy Frenchman S. Hauduroy, was planning a grand Parisian town house.

By the time Blathwayt constructed the east front with its state apartments, he was important enough to command the services of William Talman, Wren's second-in-command, whose grand baroque façade is proudly surmounted by the Blathwayt eagle. The monumental orangery extending the range to the south, successfully obscuring the service quarters in the view from the hill above the house, is also Talman's.

An extensive formal Dutch water garden which once surrounded this palatial mansion has long disappeared, replaced by Charles Harcourt-Master's beautiful late eighteenth-century park, with groves and clumps of beeches, chestnuts and cedars spilling down the hillsides. But the interior still reflects the taste for Dutch fashions inspired by the new king, which Blathwayt would have had ample opportunity to see at first hand. In Talman's entrance hall bird paintings by Melchior d'Hondecoeter hang against embossed leather bought in The Hague. Door locks and hinges are engraved with tulips and daffodils in the Balcony Room and characteristic blue and white delftware is seen throughout the house, including two impressive pyramidal flower vases intended for the display of prize blooms. Sumptuous crimson and yellow velvet hangings adorning the state bed in the Queen Anne Room are typical of the rich fabrics and textiles with which Dyrham was once furnished. And then there are the paintings – cool, Dutch interiors, soft land- and seascapes and serene still-lifes, including works by Abraham Storck, David Teniers the Younger and Samuel van Hoogstraeten. One of Hoogstraeten's perspective paintings shows a view through an unmistakably Dutch interior, stretching invitingly across tiled floors to a chair with a red cushion by a glowing fire in a distant room.

Eastbury Manor House LONDON

In Eastbury Square, Barking, ¼ mile south of Upney station [443 J4]

This arresting, three-storey, red-brick building, now surrounded by a municipal housing estate, is a fine example of an Elizabethan manor house. Dating from *c*.1572, it has mullioned windows, finialled Dutch-style gables and huge chimneystacks. With the exception of some sixteenth-century wall painting, few original interior features remain. West of the house a Tudor-style kitchen garden has recently been created, and the walled garden to the east survives.

The garden front of intriguing East Riddlesden Hall, with the ruined Starkie wing on the left and a rose window and pinnacled battlements marking the flamboyant two-storey porch which is the most striking feature of the house.

East Riddlesden Hall WEST YORKSHIRE

1 mile north-east of Keighley on south side of the A650, on north bank of River Aire and close to Leeds and Liverpool Canal [445 I6]

Although W.S. Gilbert is said to have based the Bad Baronets in *Ruddigore* on the Murgatroyds of East Riddlesden, it seems the family does not entirely deserve its dubious reputation. Certainly the rich clothier James Murgatroyd who bought the estate in the 1630s was a respected local figure, and it is he who was largely responsible for the present house, set on a bluff above the River Aire. The impressive entrance front is dominated by a striking two-storey porch with a doorway flanked by classical columns and an ecclesiastical rose window set beneath battlements and Gothic pinnacles. To the left stretch the mullioned windows and gabled façades of the square main block of the house, while to the right a one-storey great hall forms a link to the remains of another substantial wing. Pedimented windows and other classical details on the one surviving façade of this part of the house are the work of Edmund Starkie, James Murgatroyd's great-grandson, although he may have simply refaced an older building rather than reconstructing it.

Absentee owners from the beginning of the nineteenth century ensured that this fine example of a seventeenth-century Yorkshire manor survived unaltered, although most of the 'Starkie' wing was demolished in 1905 and none of the original contents remains. Virtually empty when it was saved from dereliction by the Briggs brothers of Keighley in the early 1930s, East Riddlesden has been refurnished by the Trust. The locally made period oak pieces which now fill the panelled family rooms include a carved and canopied early seventeenth-century cupboard in the dining room, described by Emily Brontë in

Wuthering Heights, and a magnificent oak settle in the drawing room. A late sixteenth-century copper curfew for keeping in the embers of a fire overnight, a grain chest and a shepherd's chair designed with a hutch for a lamb or a dog under the seat are among a number of rare and intriguing objects in the house, and there are also displays of pewter and Dutch and oriental porcelain.

Old stone walls round a small formal garden created by the Trust at the back of the house enclose lawns bordered by pyramid apples and pears and a sunken paved rose garden defined by low box hedges. Umbrella-like Robinia trees decorate the grass on the site of the demolished Starkie wing and there is also a herb garden.

The great stone barn in front of the house, one of two shielding the hall from the sprawl of Keighley, is said to be the finest in the north of England. Tradition has it that this is a medieval barn incorporating later masonry from either nearby Kirkstall Abbey or Dalton Priory, and that the present external stone cladding was added by James Murgatroyd when he rebuilt the house, but it is more likely that the whole building was constructed in the seventeenth century. The ancient fish-pond, across which visitors get their first view of the house, has more certain monastic origins. This little pool is also associated with the ghost of a woman in white, a lady of the manor who drowned here when she was thrown from her horse. Among several other apparitions said to be connected with East Riddlesden is the Grey Lady, reputed to have been shut up in her room to starve to death by her sadistic husband after she had been discovered with her lover.

Emmetts, laid out on a Kentish ridge, merges into the countryside around. Beyond the informal plantings of rare shrubs and specimen trees on the higher ground, a path leads steeply downwards, across slopes carpeted with bluebells in spring, into a deep wooded valley.

Ebbor Gorge SOMERSET

3 miles north-west of Wells [442 E5]

Cheddar Gorge is only too well known, beautiful Burrington Coombe much less so, but the most lovely and least-known of these steep ravines which plunge down from the Mendip plateau to the Somerset plain is Ebbor, most of which is leased to English Nature. There is no road up the valley, only a path which snakes through the limestone cliffs for a mile, arched over by trees. The gorge has caves and rock shelters which were inhabited from the early Stone Age until after the Roman occupation.

Eggardon Hill DORSET

2 miles north of Askerswell, 10 miles west of Dorchester [442 E7]

The boundary between the parishes of Askerswell and Powerstock runs through the centre of this spectacular shield-shaped hill-fort, the smooth cultivated contours of the privately owned northern half in Powerstock contrasting with the pock-marked, ridged terrain of the Trust's holding to the south: this has never been ploughed and preserves a wealth of untouched prehistoric features. Eggardon is one of Britain's most impressive late Iron Age hill-forts, superbly sited overlooking the Vale of Marshwood on the most westerly chalk scarp in England and ringed by three massive ramparts. Causeways snake through the defences on the north-west and south-east, their sinuous paths ensuring they could be properly defended. The remains of a late Bronze Age barrow within the ramparts were respected by the Iron Age inhabitants. There are also traces of occupation here and the banks of a probably earlier enclosure.

Emmetts Garden KENT

1½ miles south of the A25 on Sundridge–Ide Hill road,
1½ miles north of Ide Hill off the B2042 [443 J5]

This little 2.5-hectare (6-acre) garden and arboretum stands at the highest point of Kent, on top of a 213-metre (700-foot) ridge. Once it was thickly screened with trees to create an inward, intimate atmosphere, but the character of the garden was transformed by the freak storm in the autumn of 1987, which felled the 25-metre (80-foot) beeches and oaks crowning the ridge and opened up superb vistas over the Weald as far as Crowborough Beacon to the south and north to the North Downs.

Emmetts is principally the creation of the banker Frederick Lubbock, who bought the estate in the late nineteenth century and whose love of trees and shrubs was inspired by his friendship with William Robinson. This great gardener could well have been responsible for the layout of the arboretum planted on the shoulder of the ridge, with beautifully placed mature trees and shrubs, including a wide variety of rhododendrons and camellias as well as such exotics as the Japanese maple, the dove or handkerchief tree from China, the North American sweet-pepper bush and the Chinese ginkgo. The grassy glades are full of daffodils in spring.

A deep wooded valley, part of the Trust's 121.5-hectare (300-acre) estate here, falls precipitously away from the arboretum, a contoured path leading down from the garden into the upper wood which is carpeted with bluebells in spring. Summer interest is provided by the formal rose garden beside the gaunt Victorian house, cultivars of old-fashioned varieties flowering white, pink and crimson around a central fountain. The rock garden is more intimate, with slabs of Cumbrian limestone planted with maples, dwarf pines and rhododendrons and tree heathers, and with a waterfall cascading gently into a lily pond.

Erddig WREXHAM

2 miles south of Wrexham [445 H8]

Visitors to Erddig are made aware of the country house as a functioning community. Instead of being welcomed at the front door, they are taken through the estate yards, an extensive and atmospheric complex of eighteenth- and nineteenth-century brick outbuildings which present a unique picture of how these empires were nurtured day by day. Saws hang on the walls of the pit where timber was cut into manageable widths, the tools in the blacksmith's shop are the very ones that were used to repair the fine eighteenth-century ironwork screen in the formal garden, and the dry laundry sports a mangle in which clothes were pressed using the weight of a box of stones. Similarly, the tour of the house includes the attic floor, with the spacious, airy rooms where the servants slept.

Judging by the staff portraits in the servants' hall, life was agreeable here. One of the housemaids is depicted at the age of 87 and the 75-year-old estate carpenter looks spry enough to wield the axe he carries over his shoulder. In contrast to the negro coachboy who starts this unique series, they at least would have been used to the gales and

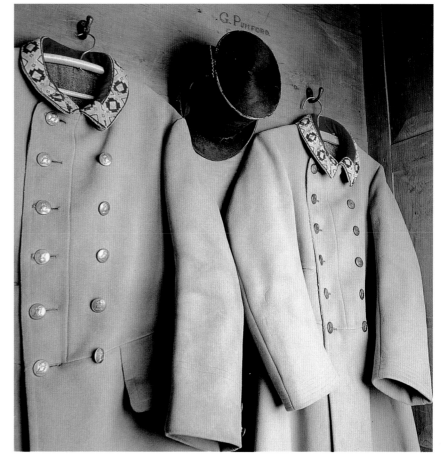

driving rain which regularly sweep across Wales to batter the house.

It was weather damage which led Philip Yorke I to re-face the west front of the house which his great-uncle, the successful London lawyer John Meller, had acquired in 1716. James Wyatt's rather severe Neo-classical composition of the 1770s contrasts with the warm brickwork of the garden front, where a pronounced change in the colour of the materials marks the wings added in 1721-4 on either side of the late seventeenth-century central block. The length of the façades and their uniform sash windows suggest nothing so much as a row of town houses.

After the architecturally modest exterior, Meller's superb furniture and rich textiles are a surprise, his sets of silvered and walnut chairs and ornate looking-glasses all obtained from leading London cabinetmakers. Goblin-like masks smiling wickedly at each other across the head of the pier glass in the saloon are by the same hand as the carved and gilded birds on the tester of the sumptuous state bed, their exotic plumage echoed by a flock of

The butler's pantry at Erddig displays livery worn by footmen here in the 19th century.

diminutive painted companions, flashes of brilliant peacock-blue suggesting kingfishers on the wing. More birds perch in the borders of the summery Soho tapestries made for the principal bedroom.

Philip I created the library which now displays his passionate antiquarianism as well as his great-uncle's legal tomes, and he was also responsible for the delightful Chinese wallpaper in the room next to the chapel, with handpainted cameos showing orientals at work. His concern for the past also led him to preserve the then old-fashioned garden. Although William Emes was employed to landscape the park between 1767–89, contributing the original circular waterfall known as the Cup and Saucer, the hanging beech woods and picturesque walks, Philip deliberately retained the formal layout near the house, the essential features of which, such as the enclosing walls, date from 1718–32. Much decayed when Erddig came to the Trust in 1973, the garden has been reconstructed as it was in the early eighteenth century with the aid of a bird's-eye view engraved by Thomas Badeslade in 1740, and is now a rare example of a design of the period.

A long gravel path stretching away from the east front, its line emphasised by a double avenue of young pleached limes, provides a strong central focus which is continued by a canal. A decorative wrought-iron screen closes the vista at the far end and the water is shaded by magnificent mature limes on either side. To the north, apple trees

planted in blocks mirror the orderly rows shown on the engraving. Plums, pears, peaches and apricots are trained on the walls, most of them varieties listed as growing here in 1718, and a range of flowering plants in the borders below includes old varieties of daffodils and narcissus. Immediately in front of the house, walls topped with exotically curling gables frame a Victorian parterre, its stalagmitic fountains, L-shaped beds and clipped box perfectly in tune with the formal eighteenth-century layout.

Exmoor DEVON AND SOMERSET

See Combe Martin and the Hangman Hills; the Heddon Valley, Trentishoe and Woody Bay; Lynmouth; Holnicote Estate [442 D5–6]

Falkland Memorial BERKSHIRE

1 mile south-west of Newbury, on the Andover road [443 H5]

A nineteenth-century obelisk beside the road from Newbury to Andover commemorates Lucius Carey, 2nd Viscount Falkland, and other Royalists who fell at the inconclusive 1st Battle of Newbury on 20 September 1643 during the Civil War.

Farnborough Hall WARWICKSHIRE

6 miles north of Banbury, ½ mile west of the A423 [443 G3]

Buried in the wooded Warwickshire countryside, this honey-coloured two-storey stone house looks out over a patchwork of fields and hedgerows to the scarp of Edgehill and the Malvern Hills beyond. It is still largely as created between 1745 and 1750 by William Holbech, who remodelled the old manor house acquired by his grandfather as a setting for the sculpture and art he had collected on a protracted Grand Tour, perhaps on the basis of designs by his close friend, the architect Sanderson Miller, who lived only a few miles away. Long façades with sash windows, pedimented doorways and a roofline balustrade reminiscent of a Palladian villa were added to the earlier classical west front commissioned by William's father.

The front door opens straight into the Italianate hall. Busts of Roman emperors and of goddesses from classical mythology look down on visitors from their niches high up in the walls, apparently ignoring the magnificent rococo decoration on the ceiling by the Yorkshireman William

Opposite: Erddig's state bed, exquisitely decorated with birds, survived being transported from London to Wales in 1720. It is hung with embroidered Chinese silk and set off by 18th-century Chinese wallpaper and other harmonious period pieces, such as the Chinese lacquer screen.

Below: The servants' hall at Erddig is hung with portraits of staff who worked here in the 18th and early 19th centuries, providing a rare record of figures in the household who were usually faceless. Edward Prince, a carpenter portrayed at the age of 75, was one of those painted between 1791 and 1796 by John Walters of Denbigh.

The richly-decorated staircase at Farnborough is a mix of work from two periods. The chunky plaster wreath ringing the skylight dates from the years around 1700, while the plaster-work of the walls and skylight dome, by the leading rococo plasterer William Perritt, is half a century later. Perritt was paid £83 8s 9d for his work.

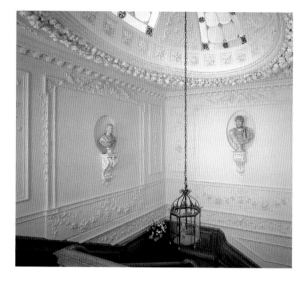

Perritt. The plasterwork and the copy of a view of Rome by Panini over the fireplace are a prelude to the sunny former saloon, now a family-sized dining room, which was designed to take four large canvases of Venice by Canaletto and two of Rome by Panini. Although copies now fill the plasterwork frames set into the walls, the original scheme survives intact.

But it is the sinuous plasterwork which clamours for attention, the three-dimensional motifs white against the blue walls. A cornucopia bursts with fruit and flowers over the wall mirror between the windows, a fully stringed violin and guns, bows and arrows reflect William's musical and sporting interests, and little dogs with upturned noses are profiled on the picture frames. Although probably also by Perritt, some of the detailing, such as the foliage curling over the mirror as if embracing it, suggests the work of Roberts of Oxford, or even the hand of an Italian crafts-man. The late seventeenth-century garland of fruit and flowers ringing the domed skylight above the stairs is similarly fine, each plaster blossom, grape and pomegranate fashioned individually.

The south front surveys a stretch of grass and trees bordering a long ornamental lake below the house, one of two in the eighteenth-century landscaped park. To the south-east William's unique grass terrace stretches three-quarters of a mile along a ridge high above the valley, its smooth sward wide enough for two carriages to pass with ease and adorned with what are probably Sanderson Miller's eye-catchers. Screened by beeches and other hardwoods to the east, the panoramic views west are seen across a bushy laurel hedge which weaves around bastion-like observation points. A little pedimented temple, its

Ionic columns pleasingly weathered, is almost hidden by trees. Further along the terrace, a curving stone staircase gives access to the upper room in a two-storey domed pavilion, the rococo plasterwork picked out in white against blue echoing the craftsmanship in the house. Perhaps the Italian prisoners treated at the military hospital set up here during the Second World War, who inscribed their names on the obelisk at the end of the terrace, appreciated the many reminders of their own country. Not so those who have promoted the route of the M40 through the Warmington Valley below the house, the advent of which has detracted from Farnborough's peace and individual charm.

Farne Islands NORTHUMBERLAND

2 miles off the coast, opposite Bamburgh, reached by motorboat from Seahouses harbour [445 I1]

Three names should be remembered when visiting the Farne Islands. For nearly eight centuries monks lived on the Inner Farne, and it was here that St Cuthbert, worker of miracles and revered throughout Northumbria, died in AD687. His body remained whole for many years and was finally transferred to Durham Cathedral in 1104 (*see* p.328). In 1838 the 22-year-old Grace Darling, daughter of the keeper of the Longstone lighthouse, rowed with her father in the teeth of a northerly gale to rescue the survivors from the wrecked steamship *Forfarshire*. In 1848 Charles Thorp, who as Archdeacon of Durham ranked next below the Bishop in this great diocese, leased the inner islands and employed watchers to safeguard the seabird colonies during the breeding season. He bought these islands a year before his death in 1862, and his descendants continued to own them. His initiative led to the Trust acquiring all the islands in 1925. The Farnes are a National Nature Reserve and the Trust seeks to ensure that the birds and the seals flourish while visitors are shown as much as is possible without endangering the habitat.

The approach is by boat from Seahouses. Although visitors may land only on the Inner Farne and on Staple Island, the teeming bird life can be seen from the boat. Sea campion covers much of the islands and fifteen species of bird nest here regularly, including four species of tern, guillemots, razorbills, puffins and the eider duck, beloved of St Cuthbert who laid down rules for its welfare.

Atlantic grey seals have been recorded in the Farnes for over 800 years. They give birth on the outer islands in late autumn, each cow producing a single pup.

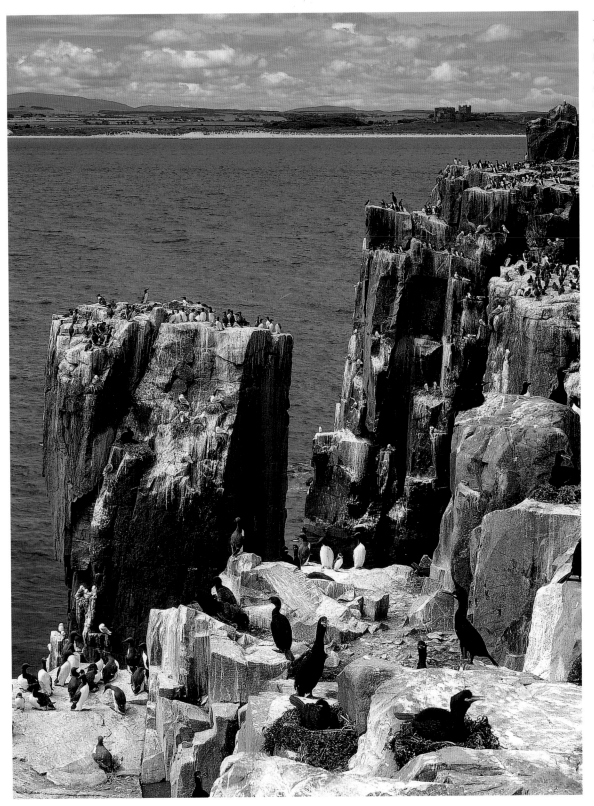

The cliffs, stacks and rocky pavements of the Farne islands attract a huge population of seabirds, each with their own distinctive habits. Fulmars and guillemots lay a single egg, on open ground, cormorants build nests of seaweed, while kittiwakes colonise the cliff faces, using the tiniest projection to support a nest. Terns are summer visitors, flying away to winter off the African coast. Most numerous of the nesting birds are the puffins, whose burrows are found anywhere where the soil is deep enough.

Felbrigg Hall NORFOLK

Near Felbrigg village, 2 miles south-west of Cromer, off the A148 [443 K1]

In 1738 William Windham II, accompanied by his multi-talented tutor Benjamin Stillingfleet, whose sartorial habits are the origin of the term 'blue stocking', set off on a protracted five-year Grand Tour. As soon as William succeeded to Felbrigg in 1749, he asked James Paine to remodel some of the rooms to provide a suitable setting for the picture collection he had acquired, the cream of which now adorns the intimate Cabinet in the west wing. Here small Dutch and Italian canvases, including 26 delightful gouaches by Giovanni Battista Busiri, hang three deep on crimson damask, displayed in frames which William commissioned and in a carefully balanced arrangement which he worked out.

Paine's sumptuous and beautiful eighteenth-century interiors, with some flowing rococo plasterwork by Joseph Rose the Elder, lie within a largely seventeenth-century building, the work of Thomas Windham, a descendant of the wealthy merchant who had purchased the estate in 1459, and his son William Windham I. Thomas was responsible for Felbrigg's south entrance front, a perfect unaltered Jacobean exterior, almost certainly by Robert Lyminge of Blickling (*see* p.50). Built of plaster-covered brick and flint with stone dressings, the weathered façade with its octagonal brick chimneys is now pleasingly encrusted with lichen. Two bays filled with glass and the projecting central porch are crowned with the inscription *Gloria Deo in Excelsis*, unusually pierced through the stone parapet along the roof. Paine's Gothick library, with pinnacled cluster columns between the bookcases, was intended to complement this Jacobean façade. The exceptional collection now housed here, started by William Windham II, was greatly extended by his politician son, whose friendship with Dr Johnson is commemorated in books once owned by the learned lexicographer.

Although William Windham I was building only 50 years later than his father, a mid-century revolution in architectural styles resulted in an extraordinary contrast between their work. Walking round the house, there is an abrupt transition from the romantic Jacobean front to the ordered classicism of William Samwell's late seventeenth-century west wing, with its sash windows and hipped roof. This austere exterior hides contemporary ornate plaster-work that is probably by the celebrated Edward Goudge, best known for his work at Belton (*see* p.42). Peaches, pears, grapes, apricots, lemons and other fruits moulded in sharp relief on the drawing-room ceiling are accompanied by lovingly detailed depictions of pheasants, partridges, woodcock and plover. More birds dart and perch amidst lotuses and peonies on the eighteenth-century Chinese wallpaper adorning a bedroom, the relatively sombre plumage of a couple of ducks floating companionably on a pond contrasting with the brilliant-red tail feathers of a bird of paradise.

Birds also feature in the delightful walled garden to the north of the drive, where a peacock weathervane crowns the octagonal brick dovecote at one end. Set on a gentle south-facing slope and divided by box-edged gravel paths, it is both productive and ornamental. Pears, vines, figs and other fruits are espaliered against the high brick walls and there are apple and plum orchards; a kitchen garden growing vegetables and soft fruit is marked by cloches and pea and bean tents; and two huge herb borders flank the dovecote. In spring there are bulbs and wild flowers under the orchard trees, summer brings colour from borders growing phlox, asters, roses, dahlias and other cutting plants, and in early autumn there is a show of lilacs, whites and deep reds from the collection of colchicums.

Felbrigg's undulating park coming right up to the front of the house is studded with stands of now mature woodland. Thousands of trees – beeches, sycamores, oaks and maples – date from the time of William Windham I, who laid the foundations of the Great Wood which shelters the house from biting winds off the North Sea only 2 miles away. His work was continued by his son with advice from the improver Nathaniel Kent and possibly also from Humphry Repton, and was taken up again by the last squire of Felbrigg, who planted some 200,000 trees and formed the V-shaped rides commemorating VE day in Victory Wood. Memorials of a different kind, monuments to generations of Windhams, including some particularly fine brasses, fill the little flint church isolated in the park, the only remains of the village that once stood here.

Fenton House LONDON

In Hampstead, on west side of Hampstead Grove [443 I4]

Hidden away in a leafy road just off busy Heath Street, this charming William and Mary house with its secluded walled garden is an oasis of peace and tranquillity in the heart of London. Standing at one of the attic windows looking out over the surrounding gardens, it is easy to imagine that Hampstead is still no more than a rural settlement on the heights above the city. Of the many mellow brick houses built here in the late seventeenth century, when mineral springs on the slopes of the hill attracted London merchants and lesser gentry to this village in the country, Fenton House is both one of the earliest and one of the best architecturally: a square two-storey building with dormers in the steeply pitched roof and tall chimneystacks. A pediment crowning the south façade marks what was once the entrance front, from which a gravel path leads to an elaborate iron gate on Holly Hill. The house was called after the Baltic merchant who owned the property by 1793, neither the builder nor the family who commissioned it being recorded.

The home of Lady Binning from 1936 to 1952, many of the rooms in Fenton House now display the furniture, pictures and outstanding eighteenth-century porcelain which she inherited from her uncle, the connoisseur and collector George Salting, who also donated magnificent oriental porcelain to the Victoria and Albert Museum. There are two sets of seasons among the figures from the short-lived Bristol and Plymouth factories, Winter in one being represented as an old bearded man leaning on a stick, a bundle of faggots under his arm. Two billing doves, their beaks locked together, are among the pieces from four German works, while a wall of one of the sunny first-floor

Left and above: All three floors of Fenton House are used to display a collection of early keyboard and other instruments in a domestic setting. The two-manual harpsichord is by Burkat Shudi, one of the best-known makers of the 18th century, and on the mantelpiece beyond is some of the porcelain for which the house is also known.

rooms is filled with the blue and white Chinese porcelain which was to inspire the colouring of Delft pottery.

Much of the individuality of the house also comes from the early keyboard instruments standing in nearly every room and filling the little attics, brass hinges gleaming on the richly polished cases. Originally formed by the late Major Benton Fletcher, the collection includes harpsichords by the two most prominent makers in London in the later eighteenth century, Jacob Kirckman and Burkat Shudi, as well as earlier Continental and English harpsichords and spinets. A virginals dated 1664 by Robert Hatley of London could have been the instrument Pepys saw being rescued by boat from the Great Fire on 2 September 1666. Most of the instruments are kept in working order and are used by students of early music; visitors may have the enjoyable experience of wandering through the rooms to the sound of distant playing.

Terrace walks flanked by mop-head laurels in tubs and beds of lavender frame the lawn and sunken rose garden to the north of the house, a layout which may date back to the original seventeenth-century garden. Magnolias thrive on the high retaining wall, the mature trees in the orchard are laden with apples in good years and there is a well-stocked vegetable garden. Three diminutive headstones in a border near the house mark the graves of Lady Binning's beloved dogs.

Figsbury Ring WILTSHIRE

4 miles north-east of Salisbury, ½ mile north of the A30 [443 G6]

The defences of this sizeable early Iron Age hill-fort follow the contours of a prominent, 152.5-metre (500-foot) chalk ridge. A roughly circular bank and ditch breached by two entrances enclose an area of about 6 hectares (15 acres), an inner ditch forming the second 'ring' probably dug to provide material to strengthen the outer defences. A fine Bronze Age leaf-shaped sword was ploughed up here in 1704, but little evidence of permanent occupation has been found and it seems the rings may have been an occasional refuge for the local population. A rich variety of downland flowers thrives on the south-facing banks.

Finch Foundry DEVON

At Sticklepath, 4 miles east of Okehampton, off A30 [442 C7]

Now bypassed by the busy A30, Sticklepath stands on the old route from Exeter to Okehampton, where the youthful River Taw has carved a deep valley into the northern flank of the Dartmoor massif. The nineteenth-century Finch Foundry, housed in rugged buildings of granite and cob, is the only survivor of the village's once flourishing water-powered industry. Used to produce agricultural implements and tools for the local mining and china clay industries, the foundry is still in working order, its three overshot wheels driving huge tilt hammers, a grindstone, metal-cutting shears and a polishing wheel. In business from 1814 to 1960, the foundry was always a Finch family affair, and there was much *ad hoc* patching-up of machinery and buildings.

Flatford SUFFOLK

On north bank of River Stour, 1 mile east of East Bergholt [443 K3]

This gentle countryside on the banks of the lower Stour, with its meadows, ponds and pollarded willows, and a cluster of half-timbered houses and cottages, is where the artist John Constable (1776–1837) spent his boyhood and where he painted some of his most evocative work. The Trust's holding of some 201 hectares (496.5 acres) includes the eighteenth-century water-mill which was owned by Constable's father and which the artist painted, and also the substantial Suffolk farmhouse known as Willy Lott's House which appears in the *Haywain*. These and other buildings are let to the Field Studies Council and are not open, but there is a small permanent exhibition on John Constable and his links to Flatford at Bridge Cottage and visitors to the area can experience Constable's viewpoints for themselves. There are gentle walks along the valley towards Dedham, where wetland plants such as yellow flag and purple loosestrife on the rivers, ponds and ditches in the meadows attract dragonflies and butterflies in summer.

The Fleece Inn HEREFORD & WORCESTER

In Bretforton, 4 miles east of Evesham, on the B4035 [443 G3]

The delightfully irregular black and white half-timbered façades of this little village pub with a partly tiled, partly thatched roof date back to *c.*1400, when the inn started life as a one-storey long house, which sheltered a farmer and his stock under the same roof. Owned by the same family from the Middle Ages until it was bequeathed to the Trust in 1978, the inn's rooms are crammed with furniture, crockery and farming implements handed down through the generations. An inn since 1848, when Henry Byrd Taplin decided to become a publican rather than a farmer, what was once the byre for the animals is now the beer cellar at the south end of the building and beer was still being brewed for sale in the back kitchen well into the twentieth century.

Florence Court CO. FERMANAGH

8 miles south-west of Enniskillen, via the A4 and the A32 Swanlinbar road [444 A4]

South of Lough Erne, the border between the Republic and Northern Ireland runs across the wild and dramatic Cuilcagh mountains. These lonely hills were the backdrop chosen by Sir John Cole for his new house, built on a site 8 miles from Enniskillen where the family had been established since 1607. Sir John's early eighteenth-century building, probably little more than a hunting lodge, has long been replaced, but the name he gave it, that of his wife, lives on. And it was Florence Cole's considerable fortune that enabled their son John, 1st Lord Mount Florence, to build much more grandly than his father.

The 1st Lord's dignified house, constructed in about 1750, now forms the heart of Florence Court. Seven bays wide and three storeys high, it is built of rendered brick with stone dressings and crowned by a parapet. Delightful baroque details adorn the entrance front, giving the house an archaic touch. On the garden façade, a projecting bay window lighting the staircase stretches the height of the building, ornamented with three massive scallop shells at the top. Open colonnades with round-headed arches leading to one-storey pavilions on either side of the central block were added in 1771 by William Willoughby Cole, later 1st Earl of Enniskillen, probably to designs by Davis Ducart, the Sardinian-born architect.

The main feature of the interior is the riotous rococo plasterwork attributed to Robert West, the talented Dublin

stuccadore. In the dining room thick encrustations of acanthus foliage swirl round the central motif, where an eagle with outstretched wings is surrounded by puffing cherubs representing the four winds. Tendrils of foliage hang over the border of the design, as if new young fronds are outgrowing the frame. The acanthus theme is repeated on the staircase, where three panels filled with fluid foliage are set either side of the well. Fine examples of Irish furniture, such as the marquetry desk prominently decorated with scallop shells in the study, and recently acquired family portraits and other pieces belonging to the Enniskillen family, such as an eighteenth-century Italian specimen table, help to re-create the atmosphere of a great Irish country house.

The service rooms in the basement, including a stone-flagged kitchen with a fire-proof ceiling like a huge umbrella, look out on to cobbled courtyards on either side of the house, one a coach yard, the other housing a dairy, laundry, drying rooms and other essential facilities. A saw-mill down the lane to the south is powered by an

Above: The welcoming interior of the Fleece Inn.

Below: The elegant Hall at Florence Court, with a bust of the 3rd Earl of Enniskillen in the niche on the right.

Above: This fine rococo plasterwork in the dining room at Florence Court is one of the ceilings in the house which survived a fire in 1955. The ceiling still has two of the holes which were drilled through from the room above to drain away water used to douse the flames.

Right: The coastline of Formby Point is being constantly moulded by wind and tide. Currents running parallel with the shore sweep the sand into ridges which are exposed as the tide ebbs.

overshot Victorian waterwheel. To the north is a 1.6-hectare (4-acre) walled garden with an extensive clematis- and wistaria-hung pergola.

The surrounding park, first laid out in the eighteenth century, was improved by the celebrated Irish landscape gardener John Sutherland, for the 2nd Earl, who planted many of the mature beeches, oaks and sycamores, and the rhododendrons and magnolias growing in impressive clumps in the valley below the house. Here, too, there are superb examples of the graceful Florence Court weeping beech and several fine specimens of the Irish yew (*Taxus baccata* 'Fastigiata'), a freak plant discovered at Florence Court in 1767 which can only be reproduced from cuttings, but which now adorns numerous gardens and churchyards.

Formby Point MERSEYSIDE

6 miles south-west of Southport, via the A565 [445 G7]

The proximity of the urban sprawl of Liverpool is what gives this stretch of unspoilt coast its unique value. It comprises 202.5 metres (500 acres) of sand dunes, backed by attractive pine woods, the dunes built up as the Crosby Channel silted up and the sea receded. Unusual plants

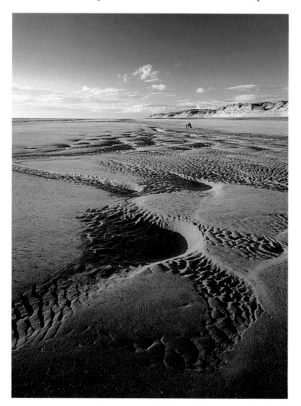

grow here, due to the sweepings from grain cargoes discharged at Liverpool and washed here by the tide. The hills of Wales shape the horizon to the south-west; waders feed at the tideline. This uncommon place is highly unexpected.

20 Forthlin Road LIVERPOOL

Allerton, off A561 [445 H7]

The sound that helped define the 1960s was born in this unremarkable terraced house in Liverpool. The childhood home of Paul McCartney, this is where Paul and John Lennon worked out their first songs and where the newly formed Beatles met to rehearse. Places nearby, such as Penny Lane, became immortalised in their lyrics.

Forthlin Road is part of the Mather Avenue estate, built between 1949 and 1952 by Liverpool council and one of several developments following the Second World War, when heavy bombing destroyed or damaged much of the city's housing stock. A two-storey, mid-terrace, brick-built house, with three rooms on each floor, there is nothing special about No. 20, although the city architect, Sir Lancelot Keay, planned the estate well, specifying good materials and such modern conveniences as an inside toilet, which the McCartneys' previous house had not had.

The McCartney family moved here in 1955, when Paul was thirteen and his brother Michael twelve. Little more than a year later their mother died, and Jim, their father, was left to bring up the boys alone. Music was always part of their lives. Jim played popular show tunes on the upright piano which dominated the living room and which he had bought from Harry Epstein, father of the Beatles' future manager, who ran a music shop; he rigged up extensions from the radio so the boys could listen to Elvis, Fats Domino and other current idols while they were in bed; and, inspired by seeing Lonnie Donnegan at the Liverpool Empire in 1956, Paul bought an acoustic guitar on which he practised for hours.

A meeting with the seventeen-year-old John Lennon at a church fête in 1957, where Lennon was appearing with his skiffle group, led to Paul joining the band and soon both teenagers were playing truant, Paul from the Liverpool Institute, the city's top grammar school, John from art college, to spend the afternoons composing at Forthlin Road, scribbling the lyrics down in a school exercise book. 'Love Me Do' and 'I Saw Her Standing There' came out of these afternoon sessions, when the boys knew Jim would be safely out at work. Paul's friend George

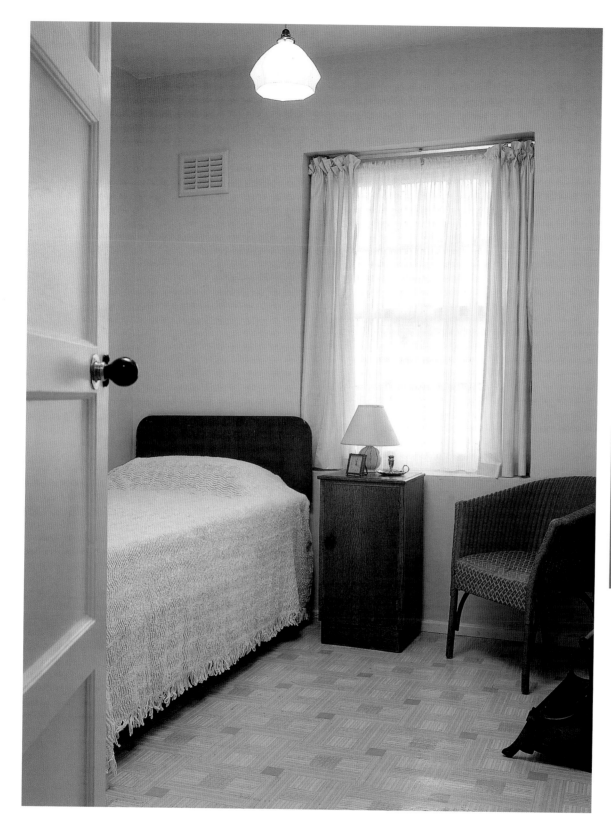

Left: Paul McCartney's bedroom at 20 Forthlin Road. This unexceptional mid-terrace house on a post-war Liverpool estate is where he and John Lennon first worked out the sound which came to define the 1960s.

Below: The kitchen at Forthlin Road with its original Belfast sink and sycamore draining boards: all the interiors are being returned to how they would have looked when the McCartneys were here.

Harrison, whom he had got to know on the bus to school, joined the band in 1958 and in 1960, with Pete Best on drums, the name Beatles emerged and the group got their first big break, in Hamburg. A year later they had their debut at Liverpool's Cavern Club and their new manager, Brian Epstein, had got them an EMI recording contract; in 1962 Ringo Starr replaced Pete; and in 1963 the boys took off, with concerts all over the country and recording sessions and television and radio appearances.

At Forthlin Road, Jim and Michael were increasingly besieged by fans, and in 1964 Paul bought his father a new house 5 miles from Liverpool. No. 20 was sold to the Jones family, who lived here for 30 years and made a number of changes, such as replacing the sash windows. The Trust acquired the house in 1995, and is gradually returning it to what it would have looked like when the McCartneys were here. The back garden still has its original coal shed and outside WC, there are displays of Beatles' memorabilia loaned by Hunter Davies and evocative photographs of the family and the early years of the group by Michael McCartney.

Fountains Abbey NORTH YORKSHIRE

2 miles west of Ripon, off the B6265 to Pateley Bridge [445 J5]

Fountains lies hidden away in the valley of the River Skell, with steep wooded slopes framing the long vista upstream from Studley Royal (*see* p.376). Approaching the abbey from the west, as medieval visitors would have done, is just as memorable. A narrow lane past the Elizabethan Fountains Hall, partly built with stone from the abbey ruins, suddenly opens out into the grassy court in front of the monastery. Ahead the towering west end of the nave is dwarfed by Abbot Marmaduke Huby's tower, 52.5 metres (172 feet) high, so tall that it can be seen from far away peering over the rim of the valley. To the right stretches the west range, as impressively long as Huby's tower is tall and extending over the Skell at one end. All is built of the greyish sandstone which outcrops just beside the abbey.

Fountains is not only the largest abbey in England, but has survived remarkably complete, too remote to be turned into a country house or extensively plundered for building stone after its dissolution in 1539. These impressive remains

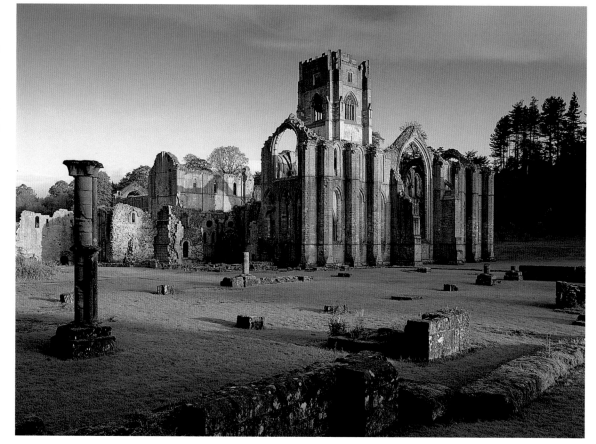

The east end of the abbey church at Fountains, showing the great east window which was inserted in the reign of Henry VII, some three hundred years after this part of the church was originally built. In the foreground are the fragmentary remains of the monks' infirmary, which was built on a platform over the River Skell.

illuminate the religious community which lived here for 400 years. The cloister at the heart of the abbey, the nerve centre of monastic life, still has the arched recess for the towel cupboard which the monks used when washing their hands before meals. The stone supports for the tables in the refectory itself still protrude from the grassy floor, and a flight of steps built into the thickness of the wall leads up to the pulpit where devotional works were read to the brothers while they ate.

St Mary of Fountains was established in the twelfth century as a pioneering Cistercian community, founded in 1132 by a group of idealistic monks who had rebelled against the relaxed atmosphere of their parent Benedictine house. The first Cistercians' austere and simple lifestyle is reflected in the unadorned architecture of the earliest parts of the abbey, such as the huge tree-trunk pillars supporting the cathedral-like nave. But the very success of the community was to lead to the relaxation of principles which had made it great. With the aid of lay brothers, who vastly outnumbered the monks themselves, the abbey controlled huge estates stretching west into the Lake District and north to Teesside, the source of the wealth which made it one of the richest religious houses in Britain by the mid-thirteenth century. Wool merchants who came to Yorkshire from Flanders and Italy were accommodated in self-contained suites in the guest houses still standing on Abbey Green.

This prosperity financed later building, such as the early thirteenth-century Chapel of the Nine Altars at the east end of the church, with its soaring Perpendicular window. But the greatest monument to earthly concerns, Marmaduke Huby's tower, was added in the community's final decades. A prodigy tower in the spirit of Sissinghurst or Tattershall (*see* pp.341 and 383), Huby's creation was in direct contravention of early Cistercian practice, erected to his personal glory. A magnificent example of the strength of religious faith, Fountains is also a monument to lost ideals.

Fox Talbot Museum WILTSHIRE

In the village of Lacock, at entrance gates to Lacock Abbey, 3 miles south of Chippenham, just east of the A350 [442 F5]

A sixteenth-century barn at the gates of Lacock Abbey (*see* p.209) houses this museum commemorating the pioneer photographer, scientist and classicist William Henry Fox Talbot, who inherited the estate as a baby in 1800, although his family did not come to live here until

1827. A grainy, indistinct image of the latticed panes of an oriel window in the abbey is a copy of the print Fox Talbot made in August 1835 from the world's earliest negative, a scrap of paper measuring only ⅞ by ⅞ inches. Nearby is the 'mousetrap' camera commissioned from a village carpenter which was used to capture the image. Although the very first photograph was produced by Joseph Niepce in 1826, Fox Talbot was responsible for inventing the negative-positive process which paved the way for the development of modern photography.

The ground floor of the converted barn is devoted to this exceptional man's life and work, displaying the skeletal forms of leaves and flowers captured in early experiments as well as portraits of his family and life at Lacock. Fox Talbot's achievements in other areas are also recorded, from his translation of the cuneiform inscriptions discovered in 1847 at the palaces of the Assyrian kings in what is now Iraq, to his work on microscopy, demonstrated by magnified insect wings and plant sections. Also a prominent mathematician and astronomer and a Fellow of the Royal Society, Fox Talbot's scientific interests were accompanied by an appreciation of the artistic possibilities of photography, illustrated clearly by his plates in *The Pencil of Nature* (1844–6), the first book to include photographs. The museum also exhibits examples of the work of other pioneers in this field, such as Daguerre, Niepce and Wedgwood, and early photographic equipment.

Frensham Common SURREY

Astride the A287 Hindhead–Farnham road [443 H5]

The principal features of the 394.5 hectares (975 acres) of Frensham Common are the Stony Jump – a heathery hill – and the two ponds, visited by many migrant birds. The first of many rarities recorded here was a party of black-winged stilts seen by Gilbert White of Selborne (*see* p.334). The common is large and includes places to get away from one's fellows; perfect for solitary walks.

Gawthorpe Hall LANCASHIRE

On east outskirts of Padiham; ¾-mile drive to house on north of the A671 [445 I6]

Set on the edge of the Pennines, with peaceful views to distant hills, Gawthorpe seems magically detached from the urban sprawl along the Burnley road out of Padiham by which it is approached. A compact three-storey

Frensham Common is one of the largest expanses of open heathland in the Weald. Sand lizards can be seen here and there is an important population of heathland birds such as the nightjar, whinchat and stonechat.

Elizabethan house crowned with a prospect tower and with close-set tiers of mullioned windows, it is like a huge lantern. Very possibly the work of the talented Elizabethan architect, Robert Smythson, Gawthorpe is strongly reminiscent of his prodigy houses at Hardwick (*see* p.175) and Wollaton in Nottinghamshire.

Gawthorpe had been the home of the Shuttleworth family for some 200 years before the present house was started in 1600, financed by the fortunes of the Elizabethan barrister, Sir Richard Shuttleworth. Inside, original Jacobean ceilings and woodwork set off the nineteenth-century restoration by Sir Charles Barry, architect of the Houses of Parliament, who also made some changes to the exterior. He and his collaborators, A.W.N. Pugin and J.G. Crace, were employed in 1850–2 by Sir James Kay-Shuttleworth, the great Victorian reformer who had married the heiress to the property. Barry also laid out an Elizabethan-style formal garden, part of which still overlooks the River Calder on the north.

The interior has an atmosphere of crowded opulence. In the richly furnished drawing room startling green curtains and velvet upholstered settees are combined with a striking carpet strongly coloured in blue and red. Photographs in ornate silver frames clutter the rare octagonal table made by Pugin and Crace. Potted ferns on pedestals, fringed table covers and a florid pink and blue Italian glass chandelier complete the effect. With the addition of a few cobwebs, it would be a perfect setting for Miss Havisham. The Jacobean frieze, with ornate three-dimensional

plasterwork in which mermaids and other half-human creatures are entwined amongst writhing foliage, seems perfectly in tune with the Victorian furnishings.

The long gallery running the length of the south front on the second floor is equally evocative and still has the feel of a place where people came for exercise in inclement weather. Decorated with original plasterwork, it is hung with portraits of early seventeenth-century society figures. These pictures and many others in the house are on loan from the National Portrait Gallery, including a rather unflattering depiction of Charles II's mistress, the Duchess of Cleveland. Several rooms on the first floor contain an exhibition of needlework, embroideries and costumes assembled by the Hon. Rachel Kay-Shuttleworth, the last of the family to live here. This unparalleled collection displays a wide range of needlework techniques: beautifully embroidered waistcoats, smocks, christening robes, quilts and many other pieces, largely of the eighteenth and nineteenth centuries but also including some charming modern samplers. This delightful verse, dated 1961, is embroidered with a border of seashells and mischievous fish: 'I wish I were a fish/In the Aegean Sea/Instead of which, here is my niche/In London, being me.'

The George Inn LONDON

In Southwark, on east side of Borough High Street, near London Bridge station [443 l5]

Looking down into the courtyard from the wooden galleries fronting the first and second storeys of this seventeenth-century inn, it is possible to ignore the rather unattractive surroundings and to imagine the noise and excitement when the George was a major terminus for stagecoaches to all parts of England in the eighteenth and nineteenth centuries. Now the last galleried inn in London, several similar staging-posts once stood nearby, including the Tabard where Chaucer set the beginning of his *Canterbury Tales*.

The George was built in 1677 on the site of a much older hostelry which had been destroyed by fire the year before. Originally it enclosed three sides of the yard reached through the rather uninviting arch off Borough High Street, but two wings were pulled down in 1889. A strong period atmosphere survives inside, the coffee room lined with private drinking compartments, the bar with an open fireplace and the panelled dining room all conjuring up the kind of establishment described by Dickens, who certainly knew the George as he mentions

Above: Gawthorpe's Elizabethan entrance is marked by dramatic bays with a glittering grid of windows. Original stonework on the plainer façade to the left is laid in a characteristic Pennine fashion.

Below: The George Inn's open galleries give an impresssion of what many hostelries would once have been like.

it in *Little Dorrit*. Even today the open galleries are the only way to reach rooms on the first and second floors.

Although it is no longer possible to stay here overnight, the George is still very much an inn. Occasional performances of Shakespeare plays foster the legend that the bard himself once acted in the courtyard.

George Stephenson's Birthplace
NORTHUMBERLAND

8 miles west of Newcastle, 1½ miles south of the A69, at Wylam [445 I3]

George Stephenson, the engineer whose revolutionary *Rocket* of 1829 paved the way for the development of the modern locomotive, was born in this little eighteenth-century stone tenement beside the River Tyne in 1781. At the time the now green valley was an industrial slum, despoiled with coal pits, ironworks and slag heaps. George's father was an impoverished colliery worker, and the Stephensons lived in just two rooms, sharing the tenement with three other families. George himself started work at the age of ten. Lying half a mile east of Wylam village, the cottage is still accessible only on foot or by bicycle. Immediately in front of the house is the track of the old Wylam colliery wagonway, now a riverside walk, for which the Cornish engineer Richard Trevithick (1771–1833) had produced an earlier, less successful steam engine (*see also* p.110).

Gibside TYNE & WEAR

6 miles south-west of Gateshead, 20 miles west of Durham between Rowlands Gill and Burnopfield [445 I3]

This atmospheric property in the leafy Derwent Valley is at its best at dusk, when the urns set along the roof of the chapel and the central dome are silhouetted dramatically against the dying sun. From the chapel a great avenue of ancient oaks runs over half a mile along the side of the valley, focusing on a column which rises 42.5 metres (140 feet) from the wooded hill at the far end. These features are the surviving remnants of what was once one of the greatest examples of eighteenth-century landscape design.

The Gibside estate came into the Bowes family in the early eighteenth century and it was George Bowes, who inherited it in 1722, who was responsible for the transformation of the grounds around Gibside Hall. Until his death in 1760, he pursued an imaginative landscaping scheme which involved radiating avenues, a series of connected buildings and wooded ravines and slopes. Although it seems he was his own landscape designer, he was probably influenced by Stephen Switzer, whose ideas form a link between the formal layouts of the eighteenth century and the 'natural' landscapes of 'Capability' Brown. Gibside is a rare survivor from this transitional period.

George Bowes commissioned the chapel to be built within six years of his death. It was begun to the design of James Paine in 1760, but the interior was not completed until 1812. In the shape of a cross with a portico reached by a double staircase, the exterior strongly resembles an Italian villa.

Inside, the chapel is dominated by a three-tier mahogany pulpit which rears up behind the central altar, the umbrella-like sounding board ensuring that the preacher's message reached his flock seated below. On either side elliptical cherrywood pews for servants and visitors fill the semicircular apses in the arms of the cross. There are few other examples of such superb early nineteenth-century furnishings.

Apart from the chapel, the stables and banqueting hall by Daniel Garrett also survive, but the orangery is now a ruin and Gibside Hall itself was abandoned early this century. A circular walk takes visitors down the avenue, past the remains of house and orangery, to the column, topped by a statue to British Liberty, and then back through woodland and along the Derwent.

Below left: Gibside Chapel is part of an extensive 18th-century landscape in the Derwent Valley, standing at one end of an avenue which extends over half a mile along a terrace above the river. Below: The interior has a rare, three-tier mahogany pulpit and pews made out of the finest cherrywood.

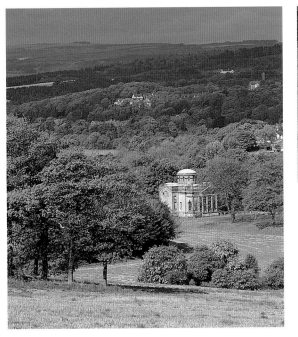

Dutch Art

For Holland, the seventeenth century was a golden age. The yoke of Spanish domination had been thrown off, the country was at peace, and trade, fishing and financial activities underlay a new prosperity. For art, too, this was a high point, with giants such as Rembrandt and Vermeer heading up a long list of talented and now sought-after painters. Unlike the situation in the rest of western Europe, where artistic patronage was principally in the hands of the aristocracy, in Holland it was the merchants and their like who bought art, and their tastes are reflected in the range of subject matter.

Although there was an interest in Italianate and other foreign landscapes, art of this period tends to focus on the familiar and domestic, showing everyday activities such as reading a letter or sweeping the floor, portraying the kind of interiors which the burghers could identify with, or capturing a distant town view. Sea paintings reflected the nation's maritime and naval activities. Style was original too. There was a new realism, and a new sense of perspective and atmosphere. Some artists, such as Samuel van Hoogstraten, took realism to the limit, producing paintings which gave the illusion of a vista extending through the house, and there was a new genre of social situation paintings. Realism and detail also marked the still-lifes which are such a feature of this period. Here, artistic ingenuity was taxed by the faithful rendering of the bloom on a flower, or by the mixing of textures and materials such as glass, porcelain, pewter, wood and cloth.

Already in the mid-seventeenth century some of these paintings were being bought by English connoisseurs, such as Thomas Povey, Treasurer to the Duke of York. In the 1690s, several of Povey's canvases were acquired by his nephew, William Blathwayt, who was busy fitting out his new house at Dyrham in Gloucestershire in the latest Dutch style. Blathwayt, Secretary at War to William of Orange and previously a diplomat in the Hague, had been steeped in Dutch taste, but it was not until well on into the eighteenth century that the particular qualities of Dutch art, which lacked the classical allusions and grander approach of painters such as Claude, were widely appreciated by English collectors. Gradually, though, the paintings of Holland found their way to many an English country house. Young aristocrats on the one- or two-year Grand Tour which was designed to turn them into men of taste and discernment generally started their travels in the Netherlands, while their elders and betters back home used agents in Antwerp, Rome or Venice to purchase art for them, or were customers of the new breed of speculative dealers who bought paintings on the Continent for sale by auction in London.

Following the long upheavals of the Industrial Revolution, new patrons appeared. Now the collectors were industrialists, tycoons, financiers and others, many of whom, such as the Rothschild banking dynasty, were hugely wealthy. Rothschild money financed the collections at Ascott and Waddesdon in Buckinghamshire, while Upton House in Warwickshire, a picture gallery in all but name, was created with the fortune of the 1st Viscount Bearsted, who founded the oil giant Shell. While new money flourished, landed wealth faded, particularly after the ravages of the Second World War. Many paintings passed from one to the other in the stream of country-house sales which marked the first half of the twentieth century.

This portrait of Catrina Hooghsaet by Rembrandt van Rijn is a painting of the 50-year-old wife of a prosperous dyer. Catrina is soberly dressed, as was appropriate for a woman of the Netherlandish merchant class of the mid-17th century, and she wears the hair-covering headdress which Protestant custom demanded. Dated 1657, it is a late work, and shows all Rembrandt's skill at conveying character and personality. It is part of the collection at Penrhyn, created in the 19th century by the 1st Baron, who relied heavily on the advice and expertise of the Belgian dealer C.J. Nieuwenhuys.

When landscape painting emerged
as a major art form in the 17th century,
Dutch painters made a significant
contribution. A new realistic approach
involved lower horizons, a new sense of
perspective and appreciation of light
and colour in the landscape. In his
View of Dordrecht (left), Aelbert Cuyp
is depicting the town where he was
born and died. Like most of his best
pictures, it is lit with a low sun, in this
case the warm glow of a summer
evening. The panoramic composition
and focus on sky and water fore-
shadows later masters of the distant
view such as Canaletto and Turner.

Pieter J. Saenredam's church portraits
were similarly innovative, moving away
from the imaginary buildings which had
dominated architectural painting before
his time. In *The Interior of the Church
of St Catherine, Utrecht* (far left), he
shows his sensitivity to light and feeling
for the vast spaces of these great
buildings. Jan van der Heyden, who
recorded towns with great attention to
detail, also contributed to the development of architectural painting. His
Square in a Dutch Town (left) has an
apothecary's shop on the left carrying
the date 1491 and the warm
harmonious colouring of the painting
is typical of his approach.

DYRHAM PARK
140

This illusionist view through a serene Dutch interior by Samuel van Hoogstraten, entitled *A View Down a Corridor* (above), is at Dyrham Park in Gloucestershire, where it is hung so as to continue the long vista through the open doorways of the enfilade on the east front. Dated 1662 and painted when the artist was in London, it is one of the canvases acquired by William Blathwayt's uncle, Thomas Povey, for his house in Lincoln's Inn Fields. Here, it was much admired by Pepys, who was a frequent guest at Povey's dinner parties.

ASCOTT
26

UPTON HOUSE
408

A major strand of Dutch art in the 17th century was concerned with scenes of daily life, a kind of social history of the present, rich in detail on period interiors and everyday objects and often with a telling sense of social mores. *A Lady Receiving a Letter* by Ludolph de Jongh (above), warmly lit from the window on the left, and Gabriel Metsu's *The Duet (Le Corset Bleu)*, showing a woman singing accompanied by a man on a guitar (left), are simple scenes of middle-class life, packed with detail and nuance.

Other painters became known for their interest in low life. The tavern scenes of the artist and innkeeper Jan Steen are painted with humour and vitality. His picture of a peasant singing, *The Sense of Hearing* (opposite, above left) is from a set of paintings of the five senses, of which four now hang at Upton.

Almost every painting of a Dutch interior contains an element of the still-life, and this genre was much valued in its own right. The work of Jan van Huysum, whose career stretched on into the 18th century, reflects the Dutch passion for flowers and flower paintings, and the increasingly elaborate approach to portraying them. His *Still Life of Fruit and Flowers* (above right) from Dudmaston in Cheshire mixes fruit and blooms, including the exotic pineapple, of idealised perfection, and is painted with exacting detail, showing the bloom on every grape and giving a precise rendering of the butterfly and other insects in the composition. Often,

flower painters would accumulate watercolour sketches of favoured flowers so they could mix blooms from different seasons in the final work. Another class of still-life painting focused on tableaux of sea foods or the prizes of the chase and some painters, such as Melchior d'Hondecoeter, specialised in bird painting. Most of his pictures showed birds in some kind of naturalistic setting. The birds in this detail from *View of a Park with Swans and Ducks* (right) are set in a formal park with an avenue stretching away behind, and are taken from one of the three vast canvases by this artist that are now at Belton House in Lincolnshire.

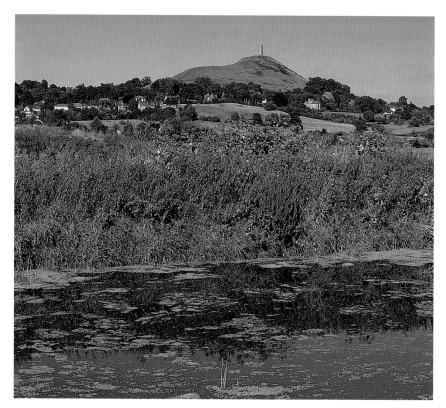

The conical outline of Glastonbury Tor dominates views across the Somerset Levels. Now drained, this area was once a watery landscape of lake and marsh surrounding the tor.

could be grown. Strip lynchets – narrow fields of unequal width – were terraced on the contours, just as one sees in a Himalayan village today, and it is the shadows cast by the supporting banks which add to the dramatic outline of the hill.

Man has occupied the tor certainly since the sixth century AD. In Anglo-Saxon and medieval times a church, possibly monastic, was founded here. At least two substantial churches were built, the latest – of which only the tower survives – probably after an earthquake had toppled its predecessor in 1275. This church was a large and sophisticated building, closely associated with the great abbey in the town at the foot of the tor, both buildings being dedicated to St Michael. After the Dissolution of the Monasteries in 1539, the church became a ruin, though the tower was restored as a historic landmark in the late eighteenth century.

Glendurgan CORNWALL

4 miles south-west of Falmouth, ½ mile south-west of Mawnan Smith, on road to Helford Passage [442 B8]

The glorious Lizard peninsula is almost severed from the rest of Cornwall by the deep estuary of the Helford river, a tidal inlet extending more than 5 miles inland. Glendurgan is situated on the north side of the river, laid out in one of the secluded steep-sided valleys that are such a feature of Cornwall. Warm, wet and sheltered, this is a paradise for plants, with many tender species, such as the prickly, grey-green American aloe, flourishing in the open.

It is no accident that Glendurgan lies only a few miles from the Fal estuary, the great deep-water harbour that was once the first port of call for shipping returning from the Americas, Africa, the Far East and the Antipodes. In the little town of Falmouth at the mouth of the river, a thriving shipping company established by the Fox family in the eighteenth century provided an ideal vehicle for importing plants from all over the world, and many species were to find their way to the garden Alfred Fox planted in the 1820s and 1830s.

Fox also built the unpretentious Victorian house at the top of the valley, looking over a sweep of grass to a foliage-framed view of the Helford. Some of the oldest trees in the garden today are probably his, such as the two magnificent tulip trees below the house. And he was responsible for the laurel maze laid out on a slope, its gently curving silvery-green hedges looking like a glistening serpent coiled up on the grass.

Glastonbury Tor SOMERSET

East of Glastonbury, on north side of the A361 [442 E5]

The unmistakable outline of Glastonbury Tor is visible from much of south-west England, often from many miles away. Most visitors to Somerset take in both Wells and Glastonbury, only 6 miles apart, for the cathedral and the abbey. Yet how many make the steep climb up the tor? From its summit, at 160 metres (525 feet), there is a wide prospect: Brean Down and the island of Steep Holm, the Quantocks, Exmoor, much of Dorset and the distant finger of Alfred's Tower at Stourhead (*see* p.366).

The hill is conical and in certain lights appears to have been sculpted, almost terraced. This is partly due to its geological structure which is like that of Brent Knoll (*see* p.61), horizontal beds of Lower Lias clays and limestone at the base rising through the Middle Lias to a cap of hard Midford Sand, locally known as Tor Burrs. This material resists erosion better than the clays and the limestone which have gradually fretted away. A second factor which has modified the shape of the tor is its agricultural use in medieval times. When the surrounding levels were undrained it was only here, above flood level, that crops

Alfred's son and grandson enhanced and enriched his creation, introducing some of the species which now contribute so much to the garden's character. Conifers thrive here, cedars, cypresses, pines and the weeping spruce giving a variety of colour and texture. Rhododendrons, many of them sweetly scented, flower pink, cream, white, yellow and deep crimson, their thickly covered branches matched by the profuse blossoms of magnolias and camellias. There are delightful cameos here too: primroses, bluebells, naturalised primulas and columbines growing beneath the trees in spring, orchids and lantern lilies in quiet corners, ferns on mossy banks, and the Holy Corner planted with trees and shrubs associated with the Bible, including a yew, a tree of heaven, a Judas tree, an olive and a tree of thorns. In the deep cleft of the valley, tree ferns, bamboo and the umbrella-like *Gunnera manicata* thrive in tropical luxuriance.

Serpentine paths wind through the garden, slowly descending the valley to the little fishing hamlet of Durgan, where boats are usually clustered on the shore and the air smells of seaweed. Like Trelissick only a few miles to the north (*see* p.398), this is a place where time seems to stand still, caught in the somnolence of a perpetual afternoon.

The Godolphin Estate CORNWALL

Between Hayle and Helston, off zig-zag road from Godolphin Cross to Townshend [442 A8]

This 222-hectare (550-acre) estate lies deep in Cornwall, in a well-wooded landscape of small fields, scattered settlements and twisting lanes, and with a sense of the sea near at hand. At its heart, shielded by woodland along the Hayle river, is a magical seventeenth-century courtyard house (not National Trust owned). Behind the house rises the gentle cone of Godolphin Hill, with fields and copses on the lower slopes giving way to open heath with bracken, heather and gorse towards the summit. A few wind-sculpted trees are a reminder of the gales that regularly batter this peninsula. Occasional outcrops and bedrock showing through the thin soil reveal that this is granite country, an outlier of the chain of massifs and bosses which runs down the West Country, underlying Bodmin moor and Dartmoor. Granite is the key to the estate. Intruded in a molten state from the depths of the earth millions of years ago, as it cooled mineral-rich vapours and gases forced themselves into cracks and fissures in the boss and the surrounding rocks. With further cooling, these crystallised into veins of mineral ores. Godolphin and the neighbouring Tregonning Hill were richly seamed with copper and tin and it was this mineral wealth, worked from medieval times to the nineteenth century, which founded the family fortunes, enabling the Godolphins to become one of the leading families of Cornwall, and to display their importance in their family seat.

To walk across the estate today is a many-layered experience. Some massive stone walls once bounded a deer-park on the hill and sycamore avenues flanking the paths behind the house were planted when these trees had only recently been introduced from Europe and were regarded as a status symbol. Mining remains, mostly dating from intense activity in the nineteenth century, mark both the hill and the woodland along the Hayle. A substantial engine house and three-tiered stack of granite and brick on the shoulder between Godolphin Hill and Tregonning Hill marks the Leeds shaft of the Great Work mine, which was operating into the 1890s, and also for a brief period in the 1930s. This was a tin mine, but down in the woods the miners were after copper. Here, seen in the half-light filtering through a mixed canopy of oak, sycamore and conifer, the ground is broken and scarred by the pits, shafts and gullies of the extensive Godolphin mine. Nearly 500 men were working here at its height. Deep in the trees is the grand three-storey Count House, once the administrative heart of the mine, and now partially converted to an education base, bookable by schools and other community users. Rare mosses and liverworts have colonised abandoned spoil heaps, and the woods are still threaded by old mining paths. Superimposed on all this is a gentle farming landscape, with a droving lane leading from the house to the hill, and traditional granite stiles and cattle-grids between fields. Those who climb the hill are rewarded with panoramic views: south-west to the pinnacled outline of St Michael's Mount rising from Mount's Bay, north-west to the long line of gently swelling sand dunes at Hayle on Cornwall's other coast, and east to Goonhilly Downs, where the dark shapes of the huge listening dishes stalk the far horizon.

Goodameavy DEVON

6 miles north-east of Plymouth, 2 miles south of Yelverton [442 C7]

The rivers Meavy and Plym tumble off Dartmoor to meet here at Shaugh Bridge. High above stands the Dewerstone, one of a group of granite crags which provide first-class rock climbing; the longest climb of 50 metres (165 feet) is on the Devil's Rock towering above the trees high over the Plym.

Wigford Down above rises to 259 metres (850 feet), full of the relics of prehistoric and medieval man, as is so much of Dartmoor, but as well as evidence of early man the wooded slopes of Goodameavy hide a mass of industrial remains of much later periods, all now softened by time and covered with the moss and lichen which grow so well in the damp and unpolluted Atlantic air.

Platforms made by charcoal burners for their fires are dug into the hillsides. There are abandoned granite quarries, served by a tramway the stone sleepers of which still remain, though the rails have long gone. Stone was brought down a cable-operated incline, the full trucks in descent hauling up the empty trucks from below. The quarries had their own blacksmith's cottage and smithy, now a Boy Scout basecamp. All this activity came to an end before 1914.

Gower Peninsula SWANSEA

Immediately to the west of Swansea [442 C4]

Wedged between Swansea, to the east, and Llanelli, to the north, is the Gower peninsula, where the Trust has played a major part in the preservation of its beauty.

Just clear of Swansea's suburbs, the delightful Bishopston Valley runs down to the sea, a mixture of old coppice woodland and limestone crags. From Pwlldu Bay, a sandy beach below a shingle ridge, the Trust's coast runs westward for 5 miles, round Pwlldu Head. Long-abandoned quarries make this a highly picturesque walk, but at Three Cliffs Bay there is a change. To the west of Pennard Pill is Penmaen Burrows, with the crag of Great Tor standing proud above the dunes and where sand has been blown on to 61-metre (200-foot) limestone cliffs in places nearby.

The Trust owns the coast either side of Oxwich Point, with a short gap at Port Eynon, and then for a glorious 6 miles westward, to Worms Head, where there are more limestone cliffs, their strata wildly contorted and wonderfully cut about with crags and caves. The best known is the Paviland Cave, where the 'Red Lady' skeleton (later found to be male and now in the University Museum at Oxford) was ceremonially buried in prehistoric times. The cliff flora is especially good, early summer being the best time to appreciate it.

At Worms Head the coast turns north, with Rhossili

The great sweep of Rhossili Bay on the Gower peninsula is backed by the grassy whaleback ridge of Rhossili Down. There are many prehistoric remains here, including stone circles and ancient field boundaries.

Down rising 193 metres (633 foot) above the great sandy sweep of Rhossili Beach. One looks south to the Devon coast, with Lundy (*see* p.231) rising sharply before it, and west to the Pembrokeshire coast (*see* p.296) fading away into the distance.

The north coast is very different, there being no more cliffs but miles of sand dunes and salt-marsh on the south shore of the Loughor estuary, 4 miles across at this point. Whiteford Burrows, like virtually all the Gower coast, is a very special place for bird watchers. Waders find rich feeding grounds on the tidal flats and in Landimore Marsh and Llanrhidian Marsh, which run for a further 5 miles east from Whiteford Point.

Grange Arch DORSET

At Creech, 3 miles west of Corfe Castle, 4 miles east of Worbarrow Bay [442 F7]

This simple early eighteenth-century folly, a pierced wall of lichen-stained grey Portland stone, stands on a crest of the Purbeck Hills, with magnificent views south to the sea and north over the unspoilt wooded Dorset countryside. Battlements and obelisks crown the stepped profile rising to a central round-headed arch, two smaller rectangular openings forming subsidiary features either side. Also known as Bond's Folly after its creator Denis Bond, the arch was specifically designed to be silhouetted against the skyline as seen from Creech Grange, the family house nestling in the woods below.

Grantham House LINCOLNSHIRE

Immediately east of Grantham church [445 K8 and 443 H1]

Those using the footpath through Sedgwick meadows by the River Witham can look across willow-lined banks to the garden front of Grantham House. The long two-storey stone façade attractively smothered in creeper, with its elegant sash windows, central pedimented doorway and dormers peeping over the parapet of the roof, suggests a modest country estate rather than a house set in the middle of a market town. To the left, only a stone's throw away across a road, is Grantham's cathedral-like parish church, St Wulfram's, with its soaring fourteenth-century tower and spire.

The earliest part of Grantham House, the central hall, dates from the same period, built in about 1380, but most of the building is Elizabethan or later. Sixteenth-century mullioned windows inserted by the wealthy Hall family, wool merchants of the Staple of Calais, look over the church and the entrance court on the north, while the garden façade, apart from two early windows in the central bay, was part of the eighteenth-century alterations carried out by Anne, Lady Cust, soon after 1734 when her husband bought the house. She was probably also responsible for panelling the drawing room and for introducing the three large still-lifes attributed to G.B. Ruoppolo in the hall, thought to have come from Belton House just to the north of Grantham which she subsequently inherited (*see* p.42). A walled garden leads down to the River Witham.

Gray's Monument BUCKINGHAMSHIRE

At Stoke Poges, off the B473, east of the churchyard [443 I4]

James Wyatt's massive monument – a classical sarcophagus on a square plinth inset with inscribed panels – stands on the edge of a field just east of the churchyard which Thomas Gray immortalised in his 'Elegy' and where he chose to be laid to rest next to his mother. It was erected in 1799, 28 years after the poet's death in Cambridge from 'severe internal gout', and was commissioned by John Penn, who lived nearby.

Gray's Printing Press CO. TYRONE

49 Main Street, Strabane [444 B3]

The words 'GRAY PRINTER' set above an early nineteenth-century shop front in the main street of this little border town advertise the only survivor of the printing concerns which flourished here when Strabane was an important publishing centre in the late eighteenth century. At one time there were no fewer than ten printing businesses here and Strabane had both the *Strabane Journal* and the *Strabane Newsletter* before Londonderry began producing its own newspaper.

The works were housed on the upper floor of the long, whitewashed building over a yard at the back of the shop, now used to display nineteenth-century printing machinery and a fine collection of wood and metal type. John Dunlap, who printed the American Declaration of Independence in 1776 and introduced the first daily newspaper in the United States, is said to have served his apprenticeship here, one of the many who learnt their trade on Strabane's two newspapers and ten presses before emigrating to America and the colonies to set up successful printing and publishing businesses.

Great Chalfield Manor WILTSHIRE

3 miles south-west of Melksham, via Broughton Gifford Common [442 F5]

When Thomas Tropnell rebuilt his house between 1465 and 1480, England was still torn apart by the Wars of the Roses and no one could feel secure. The domestic yellow-stone building around a central courtyard was approached through a defensible gatehouse, and encircled by a curtain wall and a moat. Visitors coming to the porch could be assessed through the squint from the dining room, and a little wicket in the front door admits only one at a time.

Seeing the house today, so peacefully set in the countryside only a few miles from Bath, it is difficult to connect it with the troubled times in which it was built. The honey-coloured stone, gabled façades and mullioned windows give it the look of a Cotswold manor, as if it has strayed from the hills to the north. Griffins holding the Tropnell arms face each other on the gables either side of the porch, while others are crowned with figures of soldiers in fifteenth-century armour, giving the house a light-hearted air.

Inside, Tropnell kept the traditional great hall rising to the rafters, lit by windows high in the walls and with a screens passage at one end. Arched openings lead to the fine first-floor rooms in the two gabled blocks flanking the hall. Both are dominated by their charming oriel windows, the beautiful semicircular example in the family's solar marked by a crown of decorative tracery on the exterior. From this window there is an excellent view of the little fourteenth-century church across the outer courtyard, which Tropnell enhanced with a bellcote and spire. From here, too, ladies could look down on proceedings in the hall through two of the curious stone masks with cut-away eyes which hang in the room below – one a king with ass's ears, another a bishop in his mitre, the third a laughing face. Another curiosity of the house is the mural painting in the dining room, showing a man with five fingers on each hand. This painting may depict Thomas Tropnell himself, a 'perilous, covetous man'.

The house as it is seen today reflects Sir Harold Brakspear's restoration in 1905–12 for the Fuller family after about two centuries of neglect and disrepair, during which the east wing flanking the courtyard was demolished (the south wing, now marked only by foundations in the garden, has also disappeared). Sir Harold's sensitive and scholarly reconstruction used drawings made by Pugin's pupil Thomas Larkin Walker in 1836, when the house was already in a ruinous state. The medieval brewhouse, the former mill and the moat – created out of mill- and fish-ponds – are all reflections of an earlier self-sufficiency. Since its restoration Great Chalfield has taken on a new lease of life, now once again the hub of a rural estate including home farms, woodland, labourers' cottages and its own parish church. Few changes have marked the passing of the years on the land, with field names and boundaries still as they are shown on a map of 1794.

Great Coxwell Barn OXFORDSHIRE

2 miles south-west of Faringdon between the A420 and the B4019 [443 G4]

On the edge of Great Coxwell village is a mid-thirteenth-century 46.5-metre (152-foot) monastic barn which once belonged to the Cistercian abbey of Beaulieu. Built of Cotswold stone and oak, it has buttressed walls and a stone-tiled roof soaring to more than double the height of the building. Inside, 2-metre (7-foot) stone piers carry the oak posts supporting the roof timbers. Projecting porches either side of the barn, one graced with a dovecote, house the original doors, those at each end of the building being insertions of the eighteenth century designed to accommodate the larger wagons of the day.

Greenway DEVONSHIRE

Greenway Road, Galmpton, on east bank of Dart off A3022 [442 D7]

The most romantic approach to Greenway is by water. Set on the winding estuary of the Dart, some 4 miles upstream from Coleton Fishacre (*see* p.105), this richly planted 13-hectare (30-acre) woodland garden rises steeply from the river on a jutting promontory. Across the water, the little village of Dittisham climbs the opposite bank, with ferries from here, and from Dartmouth downstream, to Greenway Quay. The garden is individual. Where Coleton Fishacre is mature, in recent years Greenway has passed from maturity into semi-wildness. Specimen trees and tender plants well-suited to this sheltered south-facing site have been left to flourish and have grown luxuriantly: redwoods, beeches, monkey puzzles, chestnuts and many other trees soar overhead; a cluster of figs, clumps of black bamboo, tree ferns and magnolias spread and sprawl; at the same time, some garden buildings, such as the vinery and peach house, are slowly crumbling. The result, like finding ancient ruins invaded by the jungle, is a heady

Massive buttresses support the end wall of Great Coxwell Barn, which dates from the mid-13th century.

mixture of luxuriance and decay. The plants are taking over, but underneath the bones of the garden are still visible. The Trust, which has been involved in Greenway only since 2000, has embarked on a ten-year plan of restoration and conservation, but always with the goal of preserving the spirit of the place.

Greenway has benefited from a series of knowledgeable and involved owners. Some elements may date from the garden developed by the adventuring Gilberts of Compton Castle (*see* p.107), who built a new house here in the sixteenth century and are reputed to have used Spanish prisoners of war to landscape the site. Similarly, a merchant adventurer who built the core of the present house (not open to the public) in *c*.1790 may have introduced seeds from the New World. More certain are the contributions of the last 200 years. The former park, landscaped in the early nineteenth century in the spirit of Humphry Repton, underlays much of the garden, and the shelter belts and drive date from this era. Over the next hundred years, until the late 1930s, a series of owners gradually extended the garden beyond the area round the house and enriched it with new features, such as the glasshouses, and with specimen trees and rare and tender plants, including new introductions by plant hunters such as George Forrest. In 1938, Greenway was acquired by Agatha Christie and her husband, the archaeologist Max Mallowan, as a holiday home. Both became deeply attached to the place and bought much for the garden, ordering plants from nurseries such as Veitch, Treseder and Hillier. Requisitioned by the Admiralty in 1943, Greenway played a part in the lead-up to D-Day, when the 10th US Patrol Boat Flotilla was based in the Dart estuary and the Officers' Mess was in the house. In 1959 Agatha

Bridget McCrum's *Mother and Child*, one of several pieces of modern sculpture in the garden at Greenway, lies on a grassy slope amongst a carpet of narcissi and cyclamen.

all-weather tennis court, one of the earliest of its kind. Away from the house, the garden stretches across former park along the river bank, descending steeply to the water. Some paths follow the contours, some plunge downwards, with spectacular views over the Dart where the foliage thins. There are specimen trees – the tree of heaven, handkerchief tree, Turkey oak, tulip tree and Foxglove tree – magnolias, rhododendrons, camellias and eucryphias, sun-soaked borders bright with crinums, agapanthus and anemones and, where the garden opens out, banks of primroses, bluebells, cyclamen and narcissi. Garden sculpture, including a mother and child in the spirit of Henry Moore and an elegant long-legged bird, both by Bridget McCrum, gives added interest. On the river is an eighteenth-century bastion, possibly part of Napoleonic defences, and a substantial two-storey, late Georgian boathouse. The lower level is a bathing room, which would fill with salt water at high tide, while above, with a balcony onto the water, is a roomy saloon, complete with fireplace. This is the place where Agatha Christie set the murder of Marlene Tucker in *Dead Man's Folly*.

The Greyfriars HEREFORD & WORCESTER

Friar Street, Worcester [442 F3]

Thomas Grene, a wealthy Worcester brewer, built himself this fine town house on a site next to a Franciscan monastery in 1480, recording his initials on the jetties either side of the entrance. Although one of the two ranges running back from the street is Elizabethan and the present casement windows were probably inserted in the early seventeenth century, the Greyfriars is none the less a very good example of the medieval timber-framed buildings that must once have housed Worcester's wealthier citizens, the upper floor jettied out over the lower and the timbers on the long street façade set expensively close together. A double gateway large enough to take a coach gives access to a cobbled passage leading to a little courtyard.

None of the original furnishings has survived, the appearance of the house today being the work of Mr Matley Moore and his sister Elsie, who took on the derelict building from the Worcester Archaeological Society in 1943 and gradually restored it. Seventeenth-century furniture and sixteenth-century tapestries in the great hall contrast with the eighteenth-century atmosphere of the parlour, with its rare Georgian hunting wallpaper. Upstairs, a fine frieze of carved dragons is a reminder that we are now in the Welsh borders.

Christie sold Greenway to her daughter Rosalind Hicks who, with her husband Anthony, contributed most to the garden planting as it is today. Anthony ran a commercial nursery here, and this led to the specialised collection of plants from the Southern Hemisphere, such as eucryphias and *nothofagus*. Rosalind Hicks also bought Lower Greenway Farm, whose fields surround the property.

The long nineteenth-century drive, shaded by oaks, rhododendrons and other trees and shrubs, and with tantalising glimpses of the river, winds down through the park. Around the house are walled gardens and more intimate areas in various stages of decline. In the south walled garden, the beds around the central lawn are planted with some rare species and there are remnants of espaliered apples, an ancient wistaria and the collapsing vinery; enticing openings in the wall lead to the nineteenth-century fernery, with paths winding through artificial outcrops of limestone and quartz and a central fountain, and to a stretch of grass where clock golf was played. In summer, a border here still has a show of dahlias planted for Agatha Christie. Another compartment is filled by an

Greys Court OXFORDSHIRE

3 miles west of Henley-on-Thames, east of B481 [443 H4]

This tranquil, picturesque assemblage of trees, grass and old buildings was caught up in one of the most notorious murders of the seventeenth century. When the poet Sir Thomas Overbury died in the Tower of London in 1613 in mysterious circumstances, James I's favourite, Robert Carr, Earl of Somerset, and his beautiful wife, Frances Howard, were found guilty of poisoning him. Reprieved by the king, the two were confined at Greys Court, the home of William Knollys, whose wife was Frances's sister.

There could be few more enchanting prisons. The modest brick and flint Tudor house of the Knollyses, with some eighteenth-century improvements, is set within the courtyard of the medieval manor of the de Greys, who gave the property its name. The romantic remains of the fourteenth-century fortifications are all around, in sections of wall now festooned with climbing plants, in the lines of foundations in the grass and in the two towers across the lawn from the house, one now ruined, but the other, the Great Tower, still looking as it did when Edward III granted the 1st Lord de Grey a licence to crenellate in 1347. Its massive corner buttresses now rear up from the walled White Garden, where magnolias, Californian poppies and other white-flowering plants are set against old stone.

Other walled areas include a rose garden planted with old-fashioned species and the garden of Japanese cherries within the remains of the old tithe barn. A wistaria arbour, flowering profusely from craggy and monstrous stems, leads to the ornamental kitchen garden, with a central fountain and organic fruit and vegetables growing between a matrix of paths. An unusual feature added to the garden in 1981 is the 'Archbishop's maze'. Conceived as brick paving in the grass and centred on an armillary sphere, this intriguing feature is symbolic of the path through life. These enclosed areas contrast with the sweep of grass to the north of the house, from where there is an uninterrupted view across the ha-ha to fields and woodland. A Chinese bridge over the ha-ha strikes a strangely exotic note.

Early Tudor brick outbuildings grouped around the former courtyard include a wheelhouse, where water was raised from an ancient 61-metre- (200-foot-) deep well by a donkey wheel, the largest still surviving in Britain. In the house itself, intimate family rooms are furnished with a number of late seventeenth- and early eighteenth-century pieces. Exceptional plasterwork on the walls and ceiling of the elegant classical drawing room, added in about 1750, may be by Roberts of Oxford.

Gunby Hall LINCOLNSHIRE

2½ miles north-west of Burgh-le-Marsh, 7 miles west of Skegness on south side of the A158 [445 L8]

Gunby lies at the southern tip of the Lincolnshire Wolds, only 10 miles from the North Sea. This is one of the most remote corners of England, a countryside of scattered villages and hamlets and of great vistas across rich arable land, criss-crossed by a network of drainage dykes in the fen country around the Wash. Gunby is out of place in these surroundings. Built of a warm rose-red brick with stone dressings, this elegant oblong with a flat roofline and a broad flight of steps rising to a pedimented front door should face an identical façade across the leafy centre of a London square. It is a town house stranded in the country.

As the keystone over the front door proclaims, Gunby was built in 1700. It was commissioned by Sir William Massingberd, whose ancient Lincolnshire family had risen from the ranks of the yeomanry in the early Middle Ages to a baronetcy by the time of Sir Henry Massingberd in the seventeenth century, helped on their way by judicious marriages. When the last baronet died only twenty years after the house was built, the property and the name descended through the female line.

The warm panelled rooms are filled with fine old paintings, furniture and china, most of which have been in the family for generations. Among the treasures is Sir

This old pigeon house, with the domed canopy of a garden seat in front of it, is a feature of the walled gardens at Gunby Hall. The pigeon-house wall is covered with the huge trusses of the Seven Sisters rose, one of many rose varieties planted in the gardens.

Joshua Reynolds's portrait of Bennet Langton, whose son Peregrine married the heiress to the estate in 1784 and who was a lifelong friend of Dr Johnson. This association brought Gunby a very rare autographed copy of the first edition of Boswell's biography, one of only six known to have survived and the only one in England. Bennet was also on close terms with Reynolds, who shows his friend to have been curiously effeminate, his long unpowdered hair falling in curls over his shoulders.

The gardens are another of Gunby's attractions, the present layout dating largely from the turn of the century. The old red-brick walled gardens to the north-east of the house are planted with traditional English vegetables, fruit and flowers, with rose-hung pergolas, espaliered apples and pears and a dovecote which predates the house. Sitting on the seat against the brick wall of the dovecote and listening to the hum of insects in summer, time slips gently by. Perhaps Tennyson, born at Somersby only a few miles north, was thinking of just such moments when he wrote the autographed poem that now hangs in the front hall. Gunby, slumbering far from the nearest motorway or large town, is indeed 'a haunt of ancient peace'.

The extensive wooded estate, crossed by a network of paths, incorporates some fifteen farms and a stretch of disused railway line. The property also includes the remote Monksthorpe Chapel, near the little place of the same name. Dating from the late seventeenth century, and still looking like the barn it once was, the chapel was used by local baptists who needed a secluded place of worship during the years when dissenters were persecuted. It has its original baptismal pool.

Hadrian's Wall and Housesteads Fort
NORTHUMBERLAND

6 miles north-east of Haltwhistle, 4 miles north of Bardon Mill railway station, ½ mile north of the B6318 [445 H3]

When the Emperor Hadrian ordered the construction of a wall from Tynemouth to the Solway Firth in AD122, 80 years after the Roman conquest of Britain, the Empire was at its height, stretching east to what is now Iraq and south to the Sahara Desert. Few other frontiers can have matched the natural grandeur of much of this northern boundary, running for mile after sinuous mile along the wave-like cliffs and ridges of the doleritic Whin Sill, its steep, craggy northern face set against the barbarians, its gentle southern slopes leading towards the civilised world. Over 5 miles of the most dramatic section of the wall, where it rises over Hotbank Crags and Steel Rigg, are in Trust ownership, set in a landscape of vast distances, sun and shade chasing each other across huge fields bordered by dry-stone walls and turning the waters of a chain of little loughs from brilliant-blue to steel-grey.

Originally standing 4.5 metres (15 feet) high and 2.5 to 3 metres (8 to 10 feet) broad, the wall is still impressive in places, although the stone watch-tower turrets which once studded it every third of a mile have entirely disappeared. Turf-capped walls forming rectangular enclosures mark the remains of three mile-castles, each once manned by some 30 Roman soldiers who monitored all traffic through the border at these points. The much more substantial fort at Housesteads, only one of thirteen permanent bases along the wall, conjures up an evocative picture of Roman life. Inside the standard card-shaped perimeter set right on the crest of the Whin Sill there are considerable remains of the commanding officer's house, with ranges set round an open courtyard, and of barracks for the ranks. A forest of pillars marks the site of the granary, its wooden floor raised to allow air to circulate underneath. An ingenious latrine system in the south-east corner of the compound could accommodate up to 30 men at a time on the wooden seats set over deep sewers. A hospital building and the site of the baths complex outside the fort also reflect the Roman concern with hygiene and health, although the lack of an adequate permanent water supply must have restricted the bathing facilities.

Housesteads Fort on Hadrian's Wall is set in the huge rolling landscapes of Northumbria. Like all Roman forts, it was laid out to a standard pattern which included a hospital and a regimental shrine. Baths were also provided, but these were away from the main area of the fort.

The B6318 from Greenhead to Chollerford runs half a mile south of the dolerite ridge along which the wall strides, with the Trust's farms of Housesteads, Hotbank, Bradley, High Shield, East Bog, Shield on the Wall and Cawfields extending from the road up and over the ridge and down to the valley beyond. The homesteads, modest farmhouses with clusters of low stone buildings, fit the landscape perfectly, as do the remains of forts, mile-castles and other military works. These features survive in greater or lesser degree along the whole of the Trust's property, but the landscape is not as the Romans knew it. Then it must have been much more wooded. Centuries of enclosure have made it what it is today: a wonderful expanse of hill-farming country. The in-bye fields close to the homesteads are green and well cared for, the grassy moorland – wet in places – is grazed by sheep and cattle, small woods and shelter belts of windswept trees dot the landscape, and away to the north looms the dark bulk of Kielder Forest, the largest man-made woodland in Britain.

An exhilarating walk west from Housesteads leads over Cuddy's Crags, Hotbank Crags and Peel Crags to the 375-metre (1,230-foot) crest of Winshields, the highest point on the wall. Galloway cattle and Swaledale sheep graze the windswept fields far below and wildfowl bob on the waters of Crag Lough. To the south, the great ditch marking off the military zone, once 6 metres (20 feet) deep in places, still parallels the wall for long stretches.

Hadrian's Wall faded quietly away. By the mid-fourth century troops were being withdrawn from Britain to defend Rome, and 50 years later, in AD410, the Emperor Honorius unceremoniously instructed the Britons to fend for themselves. Like Roman civilisation itself, the wall gradually decayed, its stone plundered for building material and gentler sections ploughed out, melting into history.

Hafod y Llan and Hafod y Porth
GWYNEDD

3 miles north-east of Beddgelert on either side of A498 [444 F8]

In 1998, after a major public appeal, the Trust was able to buy the 1,666.5-hectare (4,118-acre) Hafod y Llan estate set in the magnificent Nantgwynant Valley in the heart of the Snowdonia National Park. It is made up of three hill farms, two of which, Hafod y Llan and Bwlch, form a block of land rising north and west from the valley floor and the Afon Glaslyn to the summits of Snowdon and Y Lliwedd. The third farm, the more remote Gelli Iago, lies a mile to the south, on the other side of the Glaslyn. This is classic mountain scenery. Dry-stone walls enclosing

Opposite: The extravagance with which Ham House was fitted out in the 17th century comes through in the tapestry-hung drawing room, with its set of rare Parisian chairs, a reflection of the influence of the court of Louis XIV, and its carved and gilded chimney-piece (bottom); in the overblown ceiling paintings by Verrio (top left) which adorn the little rooms that were used as private inner sanctums and filled with precious things; and in the silver bellows (middle right) in the bedroom that was prepared for a visit by Catherine of Braganza. The gilded X-frame chair in the style of William Kent (top right) is from the elegant 1740s drawing room.

pastoral fields on the lower ground give way to long slopes of sheep- and cattle-grazed mountain pasture rising steeply to the ice-sculpted crags, with their corries, knife-edge ridges and cascades of scree. There are five lakes, areas of blanket bog, oak and ash woods and an important occurrence of the rare prostrate Juniper.

The Watkin path, built in the 1890s by Sir Edward Watkin and one of the major routes up Snowdon, climbs steeply across Hafod y Llan. Following Cwm Llan up the mountain, it takes walkers past the spoil tips and ruined buildings of the South Snowdon slate quarry, in operation for 40 years in the later nineteenth century. Slate was carried by packhorses from here down to Porthmadog. Elsewhere on the mountain are the remains of the copper-mining industry which ceased here at the end of the nineteenth century.

This is magnificent walking country, with waymarked paths on the lower slopes, one of which runs along the banks of the Glaslyn, for the less energetic, and tougher hill walking for the experienced, with the chance of seeing peregrine falcon and chough. There is a route over a spur of Snowdon westwards to Craflwyn (*see* p.116) through the adjoining property of Hafod y Porth, a 385-hectare (951.5-acre) mountain farm acquired in 1993 and notable for an impressive network of dry-stone walls dating from the first half of the nineteenth century when the land was enclosed.

Hailes Abbey GLOUCESTERSHIRE

2 miles north-east of Winchcombe, 1 mile east of the A46 Broadway road [443 G3]

Apart from seventeen cloister arches and parts of the chapter house, this great abbey with its 103.5-metre (340-foot) church is now no more than outlines in the grass. But at one time pilgrims from all over Europe flocked to this secluded spot under the wooded western edge of the Cotswolds to worship at the shrine of the Holy Blood. Authenticated by no less a person than the Patriarch of Jerusalem, this precious relic was given to the community in 1270 by Edward of Cornwall, whose father had founded the abbey twenty years before to fulfil a vow he had made on escaping shipwreck off the Scilly Isles.

Although the abbey did not always prosper, its income fluctuating with the price of wool from its huge flocks of sheep, this gift considerably enhanced the fortunes of the struggling community, who rebuilt and extended the east end of their church to create a shrine worthy of their relic and to accommodate the throng of visitors. The found-

ations of five radiating chapels enclosing the ambulatory where the phial was displayed form a five-lobed leaf on the grass, the shrine itself marked by a heap of stones. Further evidence of secular concerns can be seen in the little museum, where tiles which once floored the church display the arms of the community's rich patrons, Earl Edward and his father and the principal magnate families with whom the Earls of Cornwall were associated. Intricately carved bosses housed here, including a sculpture of Jesus wrestling with a lion, also suggest how splendid the monastery once was. And the little stream which provided the monks with water still flows across the site in a deep, stone-lined channel.

One of the last Cistercian houses to be founded in England, Hailes came at the end of a great reforming wave which had started in the late eleventh century and was typified by the teaching of St Bernard of Clairvaux, who rejected all worldly values for a life of austerity and prayer. But at Hailes, as in so many other communities, the ideals faded. The early Cistercians would never have condoned the relic cult or have approved the fine fifteenth-century cloisters built partly on the profits of pilgrim donations. As at Fountains Abbey (*see* p.154), Hailes enjoyed years of prosperity at the end of its existence, but this Indian summer was terminated abruptly in 1538. In the autumn of that year Henry VIII's commissioners removed the Holy Blood to London, declaring it 'honey clarified and coloured with saffron'.

Ham House SURREY

On south bank of River Thames, west of the A307, at Petersham [443 I5]

Ruthless ambition created this red-brick palace beside the River Thames, with its principal rooms still furnished in the style of Charles II's court. Elizabeth, Countess of Dysart, was not content with the Jacobean house she inherited from her father, William Murray, 1st Earl of Dysart, despite the improvements he made in 1637-9. A second marriage gave her the opportunity to spend lavishly on remodelling. Even before the death of her first husband, the countess's name was being linked to the high-flying Earl of Lauderdale, a member of Charles II's cabal ministry. When his wife conveniently died, the two were married. In the same year, 1672, the Earl received a dukedom, and the couple set out to mark their position with new building. He was at the height of his power; she, it was said, with complete ascendancy over him. The haughty, rather unattractive couple confidently surveying the world from Lely's portrait in the round gallery clearly deserved each other – and together they produced one of the most lavishly appointed houses of their day.

Externally, Ham is sober enough, a three-storey U-shaped building with shallow wings flanked by colonnades projecting from the entrance front. Sixteen busts set in niches at first-floor level are companions to those in the brick wall enclosing the forecourt. Wings once also extended to the south, but these were engulfed when the Lauderdales doubled the size of the house by building new apartments along this front. The rooms were given sash windows, which had only recently been invented, but these were designed to blend with the Jacobean casements.

Inside, there are few traces of the interiors created in 1610 for Sir Thomas Vavasour, Knight Marshal to James I, but several rooms still display the taste of Elizabeth's father, which reflects the period love of rich effect. Bronzing picks out martial details – a drum, armour, a cannon with a pile of shot – on the carved and pierced panels of his great staircase and on the baskets of fruit crowning the newel posts. The stairs lead to the sequence of first-floor state rooms created by William Murray along the north front. His great dining room is now the gallery above the hall. Beyond lie his tapestry-hung drawing room and his refurbished long gallery, the first with original plasterwork, woodwork and marble chimneypiece, the second lined with gilded panelling divided by Ionic pilasters, which the Earl added to the Jacobean room.

Portraits in sumptuous gold frames line the gallery, among them several works by Lely and the portrait which Charles I gave to William Murray, who was one of his most loyal supporters. A rare survival is the intimate Green Closet off the gallery, where some 60 miniatures and small paintings framed in ebony and gilt are hung closely on brilliant green damask. Many of the pictures, which include miniatures by Nicholas Hilliard and Isaac Oliver, are original. The ceiling paintings of cupids, nymphs and satyrs, in tempera, are by Franz Cleyn, principal designer for the Mortlake tapestry works.

Along the south front, arranged over two floors, are the apartments created by the Lauderdales. On the first floor, the long gallery leads into a suite of three rooms fitted out for Charles II's queen, Catherine of Braganza, in 1673. Although partly refurnished in the eighteenth century by the duchess's great-great-grandson, the 4th Earl of Dysart, many of the extravagant original fittings remain. There are hangings of silk damask and velvet, fire-irons ornamented with silver, intricate parquet floors and a carved wooden

garland of subtle craftsmanship. Most of the seventeenth-century decor survives in the intimate closet at the end of the suite, which is still hung with winter hangings of 'crimson and gould stuff bordered with green and gould stuff' and has a baroque ceiling painting by Antonio Verrio, who had worked extensively for Charles II. More paintings by Verrio in the overblown style favoured at the time, such as a group of maidens representing the arts, also adorn the private closets in the two suites of rooms which the Lauderdales created for themselves on the ground floor of the south front. Here the flavour is more mixed. The Duchess's closet, where she would have retired for privacy, or to talk to her closest friends, shows the white crackled teapot which brewed her precious tea; and survivals of the original decorative scheme include inset sea paintings by William van der Velde (in his rooms) and bird paintings by Francis Barlow (in hers). But her bedroom has had to be re-created as it might have appeared. Recently returned to its eighteenth-century splendour as a drawing room is the former Volury Room, which now shows the 1740s furnishing scheme of the 4th Earl. Flemish tapestries have an elegant French flavour, gilded chairs and sofas upholstered in gold silk have X-frames in the style of William Kent, and a new carpet woven for the room, based on archive material, has been designed to pick up the strong blues and pinks in the tapestries.

The spirit of the house extends into the garden, where the formal seventeenth-century layout, in which the garden was devised as a series of contrasting compartments, has been re-created. The south front looks over a broad terrace to a lawn divided into eight uniform square plats and beyond to the wilderness. Looking from a distance like a well-ordered wood, this too has an architectural plan. Grassy walks lined by hornbeam hedges radiate from a central clearing, dividing the wilderness into a series of small enclosures filled with mixed trees and shrubs and some scented plants. Little summerhouses secreted in four of the compartments are flagged by the golden balls which crown their conical roofs, just visible over the hedges. In the seventeenth century, as a painting attributed to Henry Danckerts in the house shows, the central clearing was ringed with statues. The white pedestals to carry them are in position, and the Trust will restore the sculpture as funds allow.

In the secluded knot garden to the east of the house, box-edged beds punctuated by cones of box are filled with silvery Dutch and cotton lavender. Hornbeam alleys either side form restful green tunnels, cool even on the hottest summer's day. Also from the seventeenth century is a long wistaria-hung orangery west of the house, where tender plants were overwintered. A period kitchen garden has been restored in front of it, with four compartments growing orderly rows of vegetables and cutting flowers for the house. Outhouses round the kitchen court include the eighteenth-century dairy, with marble shelves carried on cast-iron cow's legs, and the late seventeenth-century slate-floored still house, where soaps, sweet scented waters and ointments were prepared. Close by, down one of the avenues which lead the eye beyond the garden, is the Thames and the little ferry from Twickenham which has for centuries brought visitors across the water.

Hanbury Hall HEREFORD & WORCESTER

4½ miles east of Droitwich, 1 mile north of the B4090, 6 miles south of Bromsgrove, 1½ miles west of the B4091
[442 F3]

James Thornhill was at the height of his career when Thomas Vernon, a successful barrister, commissioned him to decorate the staircase of his new house in 1710. Although his work for St Paul's Cathedral was still in the future, Thornhill had completed the Sabine Room at Chatsworth in Derbyshire and was halfway through his magnificent Painted Hall at Greenwich. Like this masterpiece, the Hanbury staircase is exuberantly Baroque, with mythological scenes framed between classical columns on the walls and a host of deities set among clouds looking down from above. The subtle monochrome ceiling in the long hall below, probably by one of Thornhill's assistants, matches the quality of the master's work, with musical instruments and agricultural tools representing the seasons of the year separated by *trompe-l'oeil* domes and shells.

Remarkably, Thornhill's preliminary drawings were changed to include an allusion to the notorious Dr Sacheverell, who had been brought to trial earlier in the year by the Whig government for preaching a seditious pro-Tory sermon from the pulpit of St Paul's. Although he was personally unattractive, the doctor's trial made him a popular hero and Queen Anne responded to this political blunder by gradually replacing her Whig ministers with Tories. At Hanbury, Mercury leaps away from his fellow deities above the staircase, his head still on the ceiling but his feet on the walls. A portrait of the infamous doctor in his upraised right hand is just about to be set alight. Vernon could not have stated his political sympathies more plainly.

The painted hall and staircase are the highlights of Vernon's square red-brick house, a typical example of Restoration domestic architecture in the style of Belton and Uppark (*see* pp.42 and 405), with a central cupola and dormer windows in the hipped roof. But Hanbury is individual too. Unusual French- or Dutch-style pavilions project from all four corners, and the striking pedimented entrance façade, set between Corinthian columns, has flowing carving framing the central window. Although the builder is unknown, these sophisticated details suggest the influence of William Talman, Wren's assistant, and Robert Hooke, architect of Ragley only 8 miles away. Hanbury is also unusual for its detached long gallery, where some Jacobean panelling may survive from the house purchased by Vernon's grandfather in 1631. Little domed gazebos at the corners of the entrance court are Victorian.

George London's formal Dutch garden, of which only one long path remained, has been reinstated, though with enclosing hedges rather than the original brick walls. Recently the eighteenth-century bowling green, too, has been restored and is available for visitors to play on. A handsome orangery to one side was a mid-eighteenth-century addition to the design. Of the early eighteenth-century layout of the park, with formal avenues, only remnants survive, although a knoll on the site of the original amphitheatre still gives views to Kinver Edge, the Malvern and Clent Hills and several church steeples. Hanbury's original contents have also mostly disappeared, having been sold in 1790 after the dissipation of the family fortunes during the disastrous marriage between Emma Vernon and Henry Cecil, later Lord Exeter. Some family pieces and all the portraits have recently returned, but the English furniture and porcelain and seventeenth-century Dutch, Flemish and English flower paintings seen in the house are largely from the collection of Mr R.S. Watney.

Hardcastle Crags WEST YORKSHIRE

5 miles north-east of Todmorden, 1 mile north of Hebden Bridge [445 I6]

Six miles west of Halifax, Hebden Water, which drains the great Heptonstall and Wadsworth Moors to the north-west, tumbles down to join the River Calder at Hebden Bridge, an archetypal woollen town, its long grey mills wedged beside the river and railway.

A mile up Hebden Water is New Bridge, where the Trust's property begins. To the north the Trust owns a mile of the west bank of Crimsworth Dean, with its steep woods and the little farm of Hollin Hall. To the west, Hebden Dale runs up into Wadsworth Moor, the Trust owning one or both banks for nearly 3 miles. Halfway up the steep wooded valley loom the Hardcastle Crags, 'stacks' of millstone grit, for generations a place for Sunday school and chapel outings. Red squirrels can be found in the oak, larch and pine woods, planted and given to the Trust by the Savile family, grandee landowners whose shooting box of Walshaw stands at the head of the dale.

The west bank was the gift of the Gibson family, whose fine late eighteenth-century cotton-spinning mill, subsequently turned over to wool, stands peacefully beside the river below the Crags. High Greenwood continues the Trust land on the west bank, with three small hill farms above it. It is a most beautiful place, close to a decayed industrial area which is now being brought back to vigorous life.

Hardwick Hall DERBYSHIRE

6½ miles west of Mansfield, 9½ miles south-east of Chesterfield [445 J8]

This cathedral of a house stands tall and proud on the top of a windswept hill, its distinctive many-towered outline lifting the spirits of those hurtling past on the M1. As the huge stone initials set along the roofline proclaim, this is

Above: The flower parterre at Hanbury Hall has been created by the Trust in recent years. In the style of 1700, it is based on the original designs for the formal garden which once existed here. Nearby are recreations of a topiary fruit garden and formal Wilderness.

Below: The gritstone stacks of Hardcastle Crags overlook mixed woodland – oak, birch, beech and rowan – along the banks of Hebden Water.

Top: Hardwick's magnificent High Great Chamber, on the top floor of the house, is an undiluted Elizabethan interior. When guests dined in state here, the food was carried in a formal procession up the great stone staircase from the kitchens, floors below. The indomitable Bess, Countess of Shrewsbury, who created the house, had her initials carved on the openwork balustrade of the roof. Her monogram and arms appear on much of Hardwick's outstanding collection of embroidery, such as this velvet panel appliquéd with cloth of gold and silver (above).

the house of Elizabeth Shrewsbury, better known as Bess of Hardwick, the formidable and ambitious squire's daughter who rose from relatively humble beginnings to become one of the richest and best-connected people in Elizabethan England.

By the time Hardwick was begun, Bess was already approaching 70 and had four marriages behind her, each of which had advanced her social position and increased her wealth. Estranged from her last husband, George Talbot, 6th Earl of Shrewsbury, the head of the oldest, grandest and richest family in England, his death in 1590 transformed her situation, providing her with the funds to finance her magnificent house. The foundations were laid just a few months before he died on a plot only metres from the site of the manor house where Bess had been born and which she had started to remodel a decade earlier. But whereas, in seeking to transform Hardwick Old Hall, Bess had to struggle with an awkward and cramped site, her new house rose on virgin land and was designed all of a piece by Robert Smythson, the most original of Elizabethan architects. It is a prodigy house, in a class of its own.

The strong vertical thrust of the six towers is enhanced by windows that become progressively larger up the house, giving Hardwick the appearance of a glittering glass lantern. Inside, a broad, tapestry-hung stone staircase weaves its way majestically to the state apartments lit by the huge windows on the third floor. These rooms are still very much as Bess left them. Her High Great Chamber

for the reception and entertainment of important guests was designed round the tapestries which still hang here, purchased new in 1587. The goddess Diana with her court on the three-dimensional plaster frieze above was intended as a tribute to Elizabeth I, whom Bess always hoped would visit Hardwick (she never did).

A tapestry-hung door leads into the atmospheric long gallery crammed with over 80 pictures, many of them here in Bess's time. Portraying royalty, family, friends and patrons – evidence of her good connections – they include three of Bess's husbands and a glittering representation of the queen herself, her famous red hair piled high and her dress decorated with sea creatures and birds and studded with pearls. Here, too, is a memorable painting of the philosopher Thomas Hobbes, tutor to Bess's grandson, the 2nd Earl of Devonshire. Hobbes is shown just a few years before he died at Hardwick, toothless in extreme old age.

Elizabethan tapestries, needlework and paintings are complemented by original furniture, such as the eglantine table in the High Great Chamber, probably made to celebrate Bess's marriage to the Earl of Shrewsbury in 1568. Its elaborate inlay is a mosaic of musical instruments, playing cards and board games, even including the setting of a four-part motet. Hardwick's unique character owes much to the 6th Duke of Devonshire, who inherited in 1811 and deliberately enhanced the antiquarian atmosphere of the house, promoting the legend that Mary Queen of Scots stayed here and filling it with additional furniture, paintings and tapestries from his other properties, particularly from Chatsworth some 15 miles to the west.

The formal gardens to the south, laid out in the late nineteenth century, are partitioned by long walks edged with yew and hornbeam. One section has been planted as a herb garden, with a wide variety of culinary and medicinal plants known in Tudor England; another is a pear orchard, the long grass bright with bulbs in spring. Colourful herbaceous borders line some of the walls and a row of black mulberries heralds the little Elizabethan banqueting house in the south-east corner of the garden, used as a smoking room by the 6th Duke's private orchestra who were forbidden to smoke in the Hall itself. The surrounding 805.5-hectare (1,990-acre) estate embraces two different landscapes. At the back of the house a formal stretch of grass focused on a central basin looks out across the flat, partly cultivated land on the limestone plateau east of the house. To the west is the oak-wooded, hillier terrain of the former deer-park, with a series of fishponds and a partly restored duck decoy. Now a country park, it is grazed by rare breeds of cattle and sheep.

Hardy Monument DORSET

*6 miles south-west of Dorchester, on the Martinstown–
Portisham road* [442 F7]

What from a distance might appear to be the chimney of
a factory desecrating the South Dorset Downs is in fact a
monument to Vice Admiral Sir Thomas Masterman
Hardy, Flag Captain of *Victory* at Trafalgar, who was
immortalised by Nelson's dying words. Designed by A.D.
Troyte and erected by public subscription in 1846, it stands
boldly on the crest of Black Down, from where there are
glorious views over Weymouth Bay.

Hardy's Cottage DORSET

*At Higher Bockhampton, 3 miles north-east of Dorchester,
½ mile south of the A35* [442 F7]

The main bedroom at the top of the stairs, with a window
looking east towards Egdon Heath, is where the novelist
and poet was born in 1840, his hold on life so tenuous
that he was at first thought to be dead. Here Hardy grew
up, walking 6 miles to school in Dorchester every day.
Although he set off for London in 1862 to work as an
architect, he returned five years later to practise locally,
continuing to write in the little upstairs room with a
window looking west to the monument on Black Down
10 miles away (*see above*). With the success of *Far from the
Madding Crowd*, published in 1874, Hardy devoted himself
totally to writing and this was also the year in which he
finally left the cottage for his troubled marriage to Emma
Gifford, a time of deep unhappiness but also the inspiration for some of his most moving poems.

 Although only a short distance from the busy main
road into Dorchester, the cottage is still as quiet and
secluded as it was in Hardy's day, the sheltered old-
fashioned garden crowded with pansies, lupins, lavender,
day lilies, pinks, marigolds and a host of other plants, just
as he knew it and still rich with butterflies in summer.
Dating from 1800 when the family settled here, it is
everybody's idea of what a cottage should look like, with
casement windows peering from beneath the overhanging
thatch and roses, honeysuckle and japonica smothering
the walls.

 Many of the settings Hardy describes so vividly are
drawn from the south Dorset countryside round about.
The cottage itself appears in *Under the Greenwood Tree*, in
which the villagers' dance is set in the parlour, left of the
porch. And the musicians ousted by the new-fangled organ

in Mellstock church echo what happened in Stinsford
church, where Hardy's grandfather, father and uncle used
to play the violin and cello for services and where Hardy's
heart is buried. In *The Return of the Native*, wild and
desolate Egdon Heath is used to symbolise the darker note
which runs through so much of his writing, Hardy's
concern with man's desperate struggle against the hand of
an indifferent fate perhaps reflecting his own lost faith.

Hardy's Cottage is much enhanced by
the richly-planted little garden which
borders the path to the front door, here
seen bright with lupins and Jacob's
Ladder.

Hatchlands Park SURREY

*East of East Clandon, north of the A246 Guildford–
Leatherhead road* [443 I5]

Edward Boscawen, second son of the 1st Viscount
Falmouth and Admiral of the Blue, financed his new house
built in the late 1750s out of prize money from victories
over the French in the long struggle to control trading
waters which culminated in the Seven Years War. The
architect of his square red-brick Georgian mansion,
probably Stiff Leadbetter, ingeniously designed it with
seven different floor levels. Looking at the house from the
south-west, three storeys on the west front change
mysteriously into two on the south. Sadly, the Admiral
did not live to enjoy his new mansion, dying only a year
or so after he and his wife moved in.

 Hatchlands contains the earliest-recorded decoration
in an English country house by Robert Adam, who was
engaged in 1758, just after he had returned from his Grand

Above: In 1903, this large music room designed by Sir Reginald Blomfield was added on to the 18th-century house at Hatchlands. The organ is original.

Opposite: Most of Hatfield Forest is a mix of traditional woodland trees, but the area round the lake, where 18th-century owners built a rustic grotto, has the remnants of some purely ornamental planting. There is a stone pine, a swamp cypress and this ornamental plane.

by this maker. The collection is maintained for concert performance and visitors to Hatchlands may be lucky enough to hear the distant sound of music by Mozart, Couperin or Schubert.

Hatfield Forest ESSEX

3 miles east of Bishop's Stortford, on the south side of the A120 Bishop's Stortford–Colchester road [443 J4]

This 404.5-hectare (1,000-acre) mosaic of ancient woodland and grassland is a rare survival of a medieval royal hunting forest, where kings and their retinues pursued deer and wild boar. It is a remnant of the once enormous Forest of Essex, which covered the whole county in Norman times. Hatfield Forest has been privately owned since the thirteenth century – the Crown finally relinquished all rights in 1446 – and in 1729 it was bought by the Houblon family, who created the attractive lake and built the rustic Shell House on its banks.

This medieval survival is divided into sections separated by permanent wood banks and is broken up with chases – wide grassy rides – and areas of woodland pasture, marsh and open water, all offering a variety of habitats for bird, animal and plant life. Thirty-six species of native trees and shrub have been found here, reflecting the forest's long continuity, as do plants such as herb Paris, oxlip and purple helleborine. In the forest core are great pollarded hornbeams and oaks which support a variety of rare insects associated particularly with ancient trees. Woodland flowers thrive in the glades and rides and there are nightingales, owls, woodpeckers, blackcaps and fallow deer among the trees.

Hawford Dovecote
HEREFORD & WORCESTER

3 miles north of Worcester, ½ mile east of the A449 [442 F3]

Like Kinwarton 15 miles or so to the east (*see* p.206), Hawford was once a monastic grange, the property of the Abbey of Evesham. The dovecote itself, a three-storey half-timbered square building standing on a sandstone plinth, with four gables pierced by mullioned windows, probably dates back to the sixteenth century. Unusually large doors on the ground floor gave access to a storage area, the birds being accommodated in the two upper storeys, where only a few of the wooden nesting boxes now survive.

Tour. Appropriately, his ceilings in the saloon and library feature nautical motifs, ranging from mermaids, dolphins and seahorses to drums, cannon and anchors. At the end of the century Joseph Bonomi made alterations to the staircase and the garden entrance and a hundred years later Sir Reginald Blomfield added the music room in seventeenth-century style for Stuart Rendel, one-time managing partner in London of Sir William Armstrong's engineering firm (*see* p.116) and created Lord Rendel of Hatchlands.

Apart from a few pieces from the Rendel collection, such as the eighteenth-century gilt pier tables in the saloon, Adam's interiors are now complemented by pictures, furniture and keyboard instruments lent by Mr Alec Cobbe, a collector and musician who is the Trust's tenant at Hatchlands. Red silk panels in the saloon set off works by Carlo Dolci, Rubens, Frederick de Moucheron and a rare sixteenth-century altarpiece by the Florentine Alessandro Allori, and a number of portraits in the house include canvases by Gainsborough, Wright of Derby, Angelica Kauffmann and Hoppner. Among the exceptional collection of harpsichords, fortepianos and other keyboard instruments by European makers from the period *c.*1750–1840 are an Erard pianoforte reputedly made for Marie Antoinette, one of the few French harpsichords to escape destruction for firewood in the years after the Revolution, and a very rare quadruple-strung piano by Conrad Graf, one of only three known such instruments

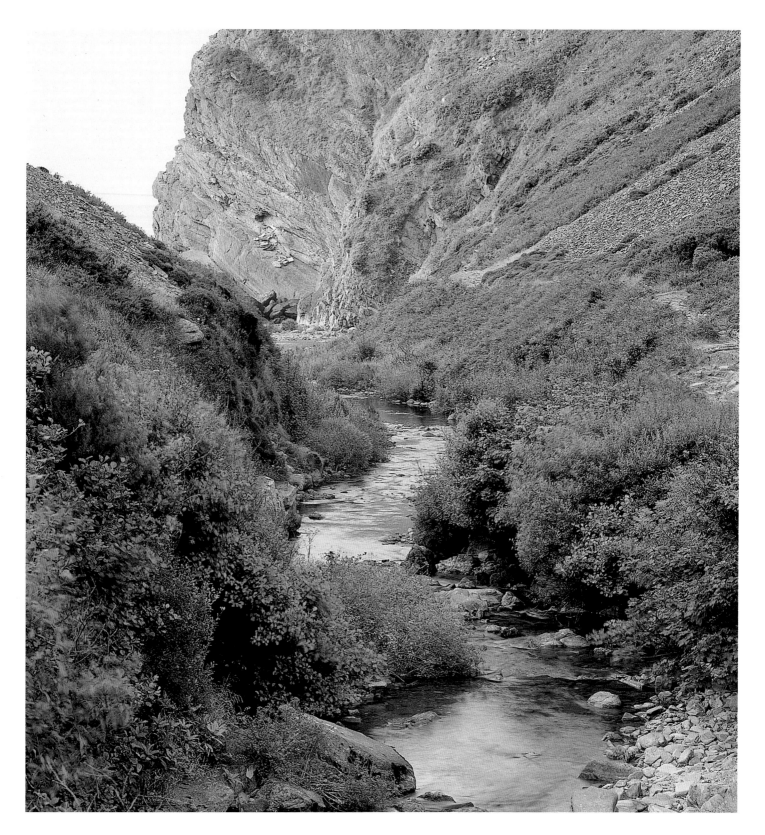

THE HEDDON VALLEY, TRENTISHOE AND WOODY BAY

Hawkshead Courthouse CUMBRIA

At junction of Ambleside and Coniston roads, ½ mile north of Hawkshead on the B5286 [445 H4]

This modest two-storey gatehouse, set back from the road just outside Hawkshead, where the Ambleside and Coniston roads meet, is all that remains of the medieval grange from which the monks of Furness Abbey, found some 20 miles to the south of the site, once administered their extensive estates between Lake Windermere and Coniston Water. For the most part dating from the fifteenth century, Hawkshead Courthouse is a plain rectangular building of rough slate rubble. Carved sandstone forms the central archway, the large traceried window in the south gable and the trefoil-headed windows on the east façade. Manorial courts are traditionally said to have been held in the large upper room reached by an exterior flight of slate steps at the north end of the building.

Hawksmoor STAFFORDSHIRE

1½ miles north-east of Cheadle on the B5417 [445 I8 and 443 G1]

To the north-east of the little town of Cheadle, the River Churnet starts its circuitous descent to the River Trent. On its right bank the Trust owns 121.5 hectares (300 acres) at Hawksmoor which has long been run as a nature reserve and bird sanctuary. It is a secretive place, providing habitats for redstarts, nightjars and warblers. Lodgepole pines and red oaks do well on the sandy soil, as, unfortunately, does *Rhododendron ponticum*.

The Heddon Valley, Trentishoe and Woody Bay DEVON

On the north coast, between Heddon's Mouth and Lynton [442 C5]

The most exciting approach to this superb stretch of coast forming the seaward boundary of the Exmoor National Park for nearly 4 miles is via the by-road from Combe Martin to Parracombe, turning north-east at Stony Corner and then over the saddle between Holdstone and Trentishoe Downs, both over 305 metres (1,000 feet). The views from this road are superb: across the Bristol Channel to the hills of South Wales, along the coast to east and west, inland over much of the moor.

In August the heather is in bloom but at any time of the year, and perhaps especially in winter, a gleam of sun can bring out wonderful colour in the varied vegetation and, if late in the day, show up the bones of the country which are invisible in summer.

The road crosses Trentishoe Down, with Bronze Age barrows to the right, and then forks. The branch to the left runs through enclosed farmland down to the little Trentishoe church, hidden at the head of its combe which falls south to the valley of the Blackmoor Brook below. The road down the combe is steep and difficult, but the alternative route from Trentishoe Down takes the branch to the right. This is a well-graded road, built as late as the 1890s, and curls down through beautiful hanging oak woods to Hunter's Inn, far below, where the Blackmoor Brook joins the River Heddon.

The Trust protects a good 2 miles of the Heddon Valley, with opportunities for quiet woodland walks upstream from Hunter's Inn towards Mill Farm. Below the inn, which is an information point, the walk to Heddon's Mouth provides an easy stroll along either side of the river, with a footbridge at two places. The steep slope on the west side of the valley is covered with sandstone scree. Limestone and coal were brought from Wales in small vessels which ran up on to the beach, and were then burnt in the long-disused lime kiln at Heddon's Mouth, the resulting lime being carted to farms nearby to counter the acidity in the soil.

On the east side of the beach Highveer Point soars steeply up, too steeply to scramble in comfort, and the way to it, and from there to Woody Bay, is by one of the two paths which leave the Heddon Valley to strike eastwards along the contours, one from Hunter's Inn itself, the other from the upper footbridge. This is the North Devon coast at its best. By setting out at one level and returning by the other one can make a superb circular walk. Kittiwakes and fulmars swoop and call below the lower path; buzzards, ravens and jackdaws soar above the higher one, from which access can be gained to the Martinhoe Roman signal station.

Two-thirds of the way to Woody Bay both paths cross the Hollow Brook Combe, the brook dropping 244 metres (800 feet) in half a mile to tumble over the cliff edge. At Woody Bay the hanging oak woods, now cleared of strangling rhododendrons, curve to enclose the bay, which was once a port of call for Bristol Channel paddle steamers. The stump of the pier still stands, the walkway itself long since swept away in a storm. (*See also* Combe Martin and the Hangman Hills; Lynmouth; Holnicote Estate.)

Opposite: Heddon Valley, surrounded by some of the finest scenery on Exmoor, runs down to a beach which can only be reached on foot. There are gentle walks down the valley from the nearest road and more demanding routes leading along the cliffs or up on to the open moorland which backs much of this coast.

Hembury and Holne Woods DEVON

On west bank of River Dart, west of Newton Abbot [442 D7]

The foothills of Dartmoor provide lovely walking country and the Trust owns two wooded properties in the middle reaches of the River Dart where the river runs off the moor.

At Hembury, on the river's west bank, where it begins to curve eastward above Buckfast Abbey, is the Iron Age hill-fort of Hembury Castle, with the later motte and bailey of Dane's Castle within its substantial earthworks. The castle stands at 152.5 metres (500 feet) and surrounding it are 141.5 hectares (350 acres) of oak woodland, much of it coppiced in the past, with an open heath of gorse and bracken on its west flank.

Since coppicing became uneconomic two generations ago, the Trust has pursued the forestry practice of converting the coppice into an oak wood, ultimately of tall timber, by selecting the best coppice stems and removing the others. During the course of the work viewpoints down to the river below, and to the woods on the east bank, have been opened up and will be kept open, thus making walks along the system of rides much more interesting.

North of Hembury the river turns west, north again and then in a spectacular loop round Holne Chase, where it is joined by the Webburn river which rises on the east side of Dartmoor. It then goes south, round again to the north-west and back towards the confluence of the East and West Dart rivers at Dartmeet. It is on this higher ground, 3 miles below Dartmeet, that the Trust owns the Holne Woods, running for a mile on the west bank upstream of New Bridge. The trees, mainly oak, grow among the granite boulders swept off the moor during the Ice Age, and up the steep slopes to the hill farms at the edge of Holne Moor.

Hezlett House CO. LONDONDERRY

5½ miles west of Coleraine on the A2 Coleraine–Downhill coast road [444 B2]

This long, low, one-storey cottage, with Georgian sash windows half hidden by fronds of creeper and a trim thatched roof, is one of the few buildings in Ireland dating from before the eighteenth century. Probably built as a parsonage for the rector of Dunboe in 1691, it was acquired by Isaac Hezlett, a prosperous Presbyterian farmer, a century later and his descendants continued to live here for another 200 years.

Apart from its age, Hezlett House is also unusual for its cruck construction, involving a frame of curved lengths of wood stretching from the floor to the ridge of the roof. Relatively common in buildings of the same date in Cumbria, this technique is rare in Northern Ireland. The tiny cottage rooms, including a womb-like kitchen painted deep red, are furnished with some eighteenth-century pieces, and one has been left open to the roof to display the carpenters' work.

Hidcote Manor Garden
GLOUCESTERSHIRE

At Hidcote Bartrim, 4 miles north-east of Chipping Campden, 1 mile east of the B4632 off the B4081 [443 G3]

Lawrence Johnston, the creator of Hidcote, was always very close to his mother and it was she who bought her only son this property at the northern end of the Cotswolds, with its pleasant eighteenth-century manor house, 113.5 hectares (280 acres) of farmland and a lovely view west over the Vale of Evesham to Bredon Hill. There was no

A peat fire burns in one of the intimate cottage rooms of Hezlett House, which is furnished as it might have been in the 19th century.

garden. The bones of what is now one of Europe's most famous layouts emerged over several years of relentlessly hard work from 1907, a unique vision that was to inspire many imitations. Like Charles Wade at Snowshill, just a few miles away (*see* p.348), Lawrence Johnston was influenced by the Arts and Crafts movement, combining a formal framework with the apparent artlessness of a cottage garden. During the 1920s and 1930s, the garden benefited from the interest and advice of Mrs Norah Lindsay and from the contributions of Frank Adams, the talented head gardener.

Hedges are the skeleton and arteries of Hidcote. The varied greens of box, yew, holly, hornbeam and beech both contain and connect the outdoor rooms into which the garden is divided, and give vital protection against the winds on this 183-metre- (600-foot-) high site. Some hedges are low, mere borders to planted beds, others form solid walls of green too tall to look over. Many are clipped into comfortable topiary shapes – well-fed peacocks, plump hens and contented doves – with patches of the flame flower adding brilliant red plumage here and there.

The garden is only 4 hectares (10 acres) in all, but the effect of the numerous compartments, as at Nymans or Sissinghurst (*see* pp.280 and 341), is to make it seem larger. The major part lies to the south of the house, sloping down to a little stream and then rising up the other side in a long tongue of land. Here a formal long walk leading to a magnificent view framed by iron gates fringes the informal Wilderness area, with acres of trees and shrubs planted for spring, summer and autumn colour surrounding open glades. Another long grass walk runs from east to west, rising up a flight of brick steps flanked by two charming brick gazebos topped with stone balls to the distinctive Stilt Garden, named after the tall clipped hornbeam hedges on stems which may have reminded Lawrence Johnston of features he had seen as a child in France.

Some of the garden rooms, like the Theatre Lawn, are simple arrangements of grass and hedges; others contain an abundance of plants, with species scattered as if they had sown themselves, an apparently artless but carefully contrived confusion which means that Hidcote never displays barren clumps devoid of interest. And each compartment has a character of its own. Clipped English yews form the distinctive elongated cones framing the Pillar Garden, their smooth outlines like the pieces in a giant board game emphasising the rougher textures of yuccas, herbaceous and tree peonies and decorative onions. In the White Garden, predating the more famous example at Sissinghurst, pale-blossomed species like tobacco plant,

phlox and the old rose '*Grüss an Aachen*', create a languorous effect, a direct contrast to the flames of orange and scarlet and the purple foliage seen in the red borders from July to October. From the Bathing-pool Garden, where the still water is closely shielded by a high hedge as if to avoid a southern sun, a path leads along a stream planted to give subtle changes of mood down the water, white magnolias threaded with blue *Brunnera macrophylla* and periwinkles giving way to orange and yellow azaleas and lilies. A hint of the Mediterranean reappears in Madame Winthrop's Garden, named after Lawrence Johnston's mother, with its strong blue and yellow colour scheme and pots of the purple cabbage palm and the variegated agave put out on the brick paving adding to the exotic effect created by yuccas and the Chusan palm.

Everywhere there are rare and unusual plants from all over the world, some of them, such as *Mahonia siamensis* and *M. lomariifolia*, and the delectable *Jasminium polyanthum*, the fruits of Lawrence Johnston's plant-gathering expeditions to South Africa in 1927 and to China in 1931. And there are several examples of the varieties he raised and selected, such as Hidcote lavender, Hidcote hypericum and the deep-yellow rose 'Lawrence Johnston'. The latter was grown at Serre de la Madonne, Lawrence Johnston's property in the south of France where he cultivated subtropical plants too tender for the Cotswolds. Here he lived until his death in 1958 after making Hidcote over to the National Trust.

Hedges and walls divide Hidcote into a patchwork of individual gardens, each with a different layout and imaginative planting. In the Pillar Garden, columns of clipped yew set off the shapes and colours of old peonies, alliums and other decorative plants.

The cottage garden at Hill Top is a rich profusion of flowers and vegetables, with an arrangement and planting loosely based on old photographs and on Beatrix Potter's watercolours of the garden, used as a backdrop in many of her illustrations, and surviving notes.

Highdown Hill WEST SUSSEX

1 mile north of Ferring, 3 miles north-west of Worthing, 1 mile south of the A27, between the South Downs and the sea [443 I6]

This wooded chalky hill between the South Downs and the sea, a mile or two from the sprawl of Worthing, is crowned by the single ditch and rampart of an early Iron Age hill-fort. It is a site of great archaeological importance. The Iron Age defences were built on top of the earthworks of a late Bronze Age settlement, there is evidence of Romano-British occupation in the third century AD and a rich Saxon cemetery has been excavated within the ramparts. Finds from the site are in Worthing Museum.

High Ham Mill SOMERSET

2 miles north of Langport, ½ mile east of High Ham [442 E6]

This stately stone tower set high above Sedgemoor is the last thatched windmill in England, the reed-covered peaked cap supporting the sails perched rather incongruously on a substantial four-storey building. Dating from about 1822, the mill continued to work until the early years of the twentieth century, although its wind power was being augmented with steam by the 1890s. The miller could grind 300lbs of meal an hour in an average wind.

A pulley system, used to turn the cap, has not survived, nor has most of the milling machinery. A bake-house and miller's cottage stand near the earth platform supporting the mill – intended to stop livestock or people wandering too close to the sails – and there is a little privy, used until modern conveniences were installed in 1970.

Hill Top CUMBRIA

At Near Sawrey, behind the Tower Bank Arms [445 H4]

The young Beatrix Potter met virtually nobody and went almost nowhere. The one bright spot in a stifling existence with her domineering parents in London was the annual family holiday, in her early years to houses in Scotland, but from 1882, when she was sixteen, to the Lake District. These brief episodes and the freedom they brought fuelled a longing for the country which emerged in meticulously observed watercolours of wild creatures and plants and in the beginnings of the animal fantasies which have delighted children and adults for over 70 years.

Beatrix's purchase of this small hill farm in 1905 was a momentous step. Presented to her parents as nothing more than a good investment (which it was), to their lonely 39-year-old daughter the little rough stone, largely seventeenth-century house with a view over Sawrey to the fells beyond represented the possibility of escape from an increasingly dreary and unchanging regime. Although she was able only to snatch weeks here in the eight years that followed, this period was to see her best work, with the production of thirteen of the stories in which rabbits, mice, squirrels, hedgehogs and other creatures become humans in miniature, all of them illustrated with Beatrix's charming and individual paintings.

Anyone who has read these nursery classics will recognise Hill Top and its well-furnished, homely rooms, filled with accumulated clutter. The long sloping garden flanking the steep path to the house, with rows of vegetables on one side and sweet peas, phlox and hollyhocks among a medley of traditional flowers on the other, is still as it appears in *The Tale of Tom Kitten* and *Pigling Bland*. The old-fashioned kitchen range with a black kettle bubbling away strikes a reassuring note in several animal holes and burrows, the nineteenth-century dresser is featured in *The Tale of Samuel Whiskers*, and the grandfather clock with a cheerful sun on its face was the model for the one in *The Tailor of Gloucester*. Peter Rabbit's red-spotted handkerchief and the doll's house food stolen by Hunca Munca and Tom Thumb – dishes of oranges and pears and a large ham – are in one of the tiny upstairs rooms. Some grander pieces of furniture, striking an unexpected note, were acquired after Beatrix's mother died, and one of the bedrooms is hung with her brother Bertram's landscape paintings.

For the last 30 years of her life, during which she was contentedly married to William Heelis, a local solicitor, Beatrix lived as a prosperous farmer in the nearby, but much larger, Castle Cottage (not open), reserving Hill Top for those times when she wished to be alone with her memories. This period saw her love of the countryside turned outwards rather than inwards. The affection for the Lake District which is evident in her illustrations of dry-stone walls, stone stiles, oak woods and sweeping hillsides was now channelled into an increasing concern for the conservation of the fells and into the deliberate accumulation of land to save it from being broken up or developed. Perfectly in sympathy with the aims of the young National Trust founded by her friend Canon Rawnsley in 1895, she began to see that her own land purchases could preserve property in perpetuity if given to the new organisation. In 1930 she acquired the substantial Monk Coniston estate covering a key area of the central Lake District, half of which she immediately re-sold to the Trust, and another fourteen farms and many cottages, together totalling 1,619 hectares (4,000 acres), went to her husband on her death in 1943, and the Trust on his death two years later. Hill Top itself was kept exactly as it was, as if Beatrix Potter could not bear to disturb the place where she found peace and fulfilment. (*See also* Beatrix Potter Gallery, p.41.)

Hindhead Commons SURREY

12 miles south-west of Guildford, on both sides of the A3 [443 H6]

Covering 566.5 hectares (1,400 acres) on either side of the Portsmouth road is a classic Trust property, built up by gifts and bequests since 1906 when the Hindhead Preservation Committee, alarmed by the rash of newly built rich men's houses, raised funds and bought over 283 hectares (700 acres) for the Trust.

The main feature is the large natural amphitheatre of the Devil's Punch Bowl, formed by springs cutting down and back from their sources. The great curve of the bowl is dry heathland, a mix of heather, gorse, bracken and grasses, with active reclamation or areas where the heather has been invaded by birch and pine. The Smallbrook stream runs east to drain the valley, providing a wetter habitat in the bottom. As recently as 1918 squatters who had settled in the Bowl were making birch brooms for a living. The Broom Squires – or broom squarers – made brooms of birch twigs for sale on the London market.

From the car park, on the edge of the town of Hindhead, there are glorious walks round and down the Bowl, or up to the sandstone summit of Gibbet Hill,

Hinton Ampner HAMPSHIRE

On the A272, 1 mile west of Bramdean village, 8 miles east of Winchester [443 H6]

Ralph Dutton, the 8th and last Lord Sherborne, was a man born long after his time. A true connoisseur with a wide-ranging knowledge of architecture, interior decoration and gardening, and with the income to indulge his tastes, he would have been in his element 200 years ago. Given the very different world of the twentieth century, his achievements were remarkable. The large Victorian mansion he inherited at Hinton Ampner was remodelled in 1936–9 to create a pleasing neo-Georgian house in warm red brick, a suitable setting for a distinguished collection of furniture, *objets* and paintings. The framework of his individual formal garden was also established at this time, to be filled in and embellished after the Second World War, and a wooded landscape park, its features composed as carefully as a work of art, gradually emerged from a former muddle of hedgerows and scattered trees to form the foreground to the unspoilt chalk countryside beyond.

The house is built near the top of a rise with the ground falling away gently to the south, a magnificent site which Ralph Dutton used to full advantage, mellow brick steps linking frequent changes of level. Much of the charm of the garden lies in the way it seems to embrace the surrounding countryside, with grassy walks leading to vistas looking north and west, and with a great sweep of Hampshire stretching away from the broad terrace on the south front. Strategically placed eye-catchers, such as the large urn centred on the north vista or the sundial lined up with an oak in the park, are all exactly right for their settings. A statue of Diana faces the sundial down the length of the 183-metre- (600-foot-) long walk flanked with pairs of Irish yews, and a little classical temple about halfway down marks another grassy corridor aligned on the remains of an old lime avenue crossing the park. These outward-looking compositions contrast with the more inward eastern side of the garden, where steps lead down to a yew-enclosed garden room and where the deep hollow of an old chalk pit, once the village dump and now known as the Dell, is walled by sloping beds planted with hostas, paulownias, rheums and giant hogweed. High box hedges frame the curving philadelphus walk flanking the Dell, and the site of the Tudor manor beside the house is now marked by a peaceful orchard, a mass of daffodils in spring. Throughout the garden restful colour schemes seen against a background of evergreens reflect Ralph Dutton's belief in tranquillity and harmony. There are few signs that the

Above: The east front of Hinton Ampner looks out over the yew garden, where blended bedding plants contrast with dark hedges; falling ground to the south of the house gives magnificent views.

Below: A snakeshead fritillary flowering at Hinton Ampner in the spring.

272.5 metres (894 feet) high, where a stone commemorates the hanging of three miscreants who murdered a sailor walking to Portsmouth (when the London to Portsmouth road crossed the common). From Hurt Hill, to the southeast, there are splendid views over the Weald (*see* p.416).

One and a half miles west of Hindhead lies Ludshott Common and Waggoners' Wells. Parts of the common were enclosed in the nineteenth century. Local efforts raised funds to vest over 202.5 hectares (500 acres) in the Trust in 1908, now increased to 283.5 metres (700 acres). A very severe fire burnt out 162 hectares (400 acres) of heath and pine wood in 1980 but subsequent clearance of scrub and careful management of the regenerating heather has restored one of the best expanses of open heath in the Weald. The 'wells', man-made ponds fed by springs which form one source for the River Wey, provided waterpower for hammering wrought iron during the sixteenth century, and now provide a home for swans, and in high summer for dragonflies and small hot boys. Marley, south of Haslemere, is a hilltop common with steep wooded slopes split into five separate pieces. At Shottermill there are two hammerponds like those at Ludshott. It pays to explore quiet corners here with the Ordnance Survey map.

soil is generally very thin, with solid chalk just below the surface, but a magnificent display of magnolias and hydrangeas marks a rare patch of deep loam.

In the house, too, everything has been chosen and placed to fulfil an overall vision. The elegant drawing room facing east and south, with a classical screen partitioning the northern end, is particularly pleasing, the opulent gold and sea-green of the walls and curtains echoed in the more subdued tones of the carpet. The furnishings are indicative of Ralph Dutton's taste, an inlaid English cabinet of about 1800 and a giltwood side table with a top of white marble and bluejohn (once in Lord Curzon's house in Carlton House Terrace) revealing his love of hardstones. A landscape by Locatelli hanging above the cabinet and canvases by Pellegrini in the hall show Lord Sherborne's appreciation of Italian seventeenth-century painting and of Venetian art in particular. Some pieces were purchased on his travels abroad, others acquired at auction, from dealers, or from houses that had been or were being demolished.

It is difficult to believe that a disastrous fire on 3 April 1960 almost completely destroyed the house and most of its contents. Lesser men would have been defeated by this tragedy, but Ralph Dutton immediately set about rebuilding and refurnishing as beautifully as before.

Holnicote Estate SOMERSET

Astride the A3, between Minehead and Porlock [442 D5]

Exmoor, the smallest of Britain's National Parks, is perhaps the most appealing of them all. Only in the most extreme weather does it appear grim, like the Peak District or Dartmoor can so easily do. Its small compass allows the visitor to absorb its character more easily, yet within it are many very different places, each quite distinct from the rest.

The Trust owns a handsome slice of the moor, a large part in Devon (*see* pp.107, 181 and 234). In Somerset the 4,856-hectare (12,000-acre) Holnicote estate takes pride of place. It extends from Porlock Bay, where Trust land includes an important area of salt-marsh, eastward for 4 miles, with steep cliffs running up to Selworthy Beacon at over 305 metres (1,000 feet), and inland over the rich farms of Porlock Vale and the beautiful villages of Allerford, Bossington, Horner, Luccombe and Selworthy (*see* p.334). The houses, cottages and farm buildings are of cob and thatch, red sandstone and slate. Each one is seemly, fits its purpose and almost appears to have grown there rather than having been built by man. The valley farms are mixed

sheep and cattle holdings while the hill farms, with steep combes running up the thin pastures next to the open moor, are much harder to work. They fit into the landscape just as the buildings do.

There are lovely walks, some of them scrambles in part, based around Selworthy. Perhaps the best is up the wooded combe above the church, where there are oak, birch, some conifers, bracken and tumbling streams. As the trees tail off one reaches open moorland, heather and bilberry, bracken and gorse, with the hill-fort of Bury Castle to the west. The path leads up to the Beacon, passing the Memorial Hut, a stone shelter facing four ways to enable the walker to sit and rest in comfort whichever way the wind is blowing. The view from here is immense in every direction and, while the energetic can walk west – to Bossington Hill and Hurlstone Point above Porlock Bay – or east to North Hill and the Trust's Greenaleigh Point, above Minehead, those with less stamina can track a little west and then down the wooded Holnicote Coombe and past Catherine's Well.

To the south of the vale the moor is approached through the wooded fringe as the land rises sharply. Here is the Exmoor of the travel posters. Open oak woodland, heavily exploited for coppice in the past and including an ancient wood in Horner Vale, clothes the steep slopes

The Holnicote estate includes much of the Vale of Porlock (below), where the Horner River runs out to the sea at Bossington Beach. The vale's charm is enhanced by the farms and cottages in traditional style, with thatched roofs, circular chimneys and local-stone walls or cream rendering. Many date from the 17th century, others are restorations. Particularly picturesque is Luccombe (above), where the cottages cluster round the 15th-century St Mary's church.

which run up to the open country above. It is spectacularly beautiful and so, in places near the road, such as Webber's Post, sometimes uncomfortably crowded, but one has to walk only half a mile to reach complete seclusion. Paths stretch from every direction up to the heathery slopes of Dunkery Beacon, 519.5 metres (1,705 feet) above sea level and Exmoor's highest point, marked by a summit cairn. On a clear day, there are views across the Bristol Channel and south-west to Dartmoor, and, in the foreground, across this border country's characteristic mix of farmland, wooded combe and open moorland. These diverse habitats support rare and locally specialised plants and animals, including 170 species of lichen in the Horner oak woods and the largest British colony of the rare heath fritillary butterfly on the heather moorland.

At Winsford Hill, six miles to the south, and South Hill which adjoins it, the Trust leases a further 396 metres (1,300 acres) of glorious moorland, an outlier of the main moor and, except beside the B3223 which crosses it to connect Simonsbath and Dulverton, rarely a soul to be seen upon it.

The Homewood SURREY

Portsmouth Road, Esher [443 I5]

Just outside Esher, set in a 2.8-hectare (7-acre) landscaped garden, is this striking and unusual country house. From the garden, it appears as a long white box on stilts, with an almost unbroken wall of glass lighting the first floor and open terraces either end. Inside, it is airy and spacious, with panoramic views of the garden and sliding glass doors leading onto a balcony. Completed in 1938, when the Modern Movement in Britain was still very much in its infancy, it is an early and important example of a house built under the influence of the Continental avant-garde, in particular Le Corbusier and Mies van der Rohe. It was designed, for his parents, by the young Patrick Gwynne (1913–2003), who started working on the house when he was only 24. Gwynne had begun his architectural training with John Coleridge, a former assistant of Sir Edwin Lutyens, but, inspired by what was happening on the Continent, he had joined the practice of the pioneering Modernist Wells Coates, where he was introduced to new construction techniques, using reinforced concrete, and cutting-edge design. By the time he started on The Homewood he had also seen key Modernist buildings abroad and had studied Le Corbusier's iconic Villa Savoie, outside Paris, which was a major influence on his thinking.

For his parents, who took the courageous decision to entrust the building of the new house to their son, Gwynne combined Modernist architecture with a concern for living that was to be a hallmark of all his residential work. The house is built of reinforced concrete with a flat roof and two unequal wings joining a central block. One wing holds the bedrooms; the other, staff quarters and service areas. The wings are joined by a dramatic spiral staircase, lit from below by a sunken spotlight. As at the Villa Savoie, the main living area is on the first floor, carried by slender columns faced with brick and lit by huge windows looking onto the garden. Although uncompromisingly modern, the house is based on a classical system of proportions and has a pleasing sense of order and harmony.

The sophisticated interior shows Gwynne's attention to detail and materials. The living room is a multi-purpose space for relaxation and entertaining. The maple floor is sprung for dancing and doors to the dining room and balcony beyond can be pushed back to create one huge room. Sliding doors in an interior wall hide a drinks cabinet and gramophone; a drop-leg table swivels out to serve as a bar; and food can be passed through a hatch from the kitchen. For more private living there is a cosy arrangement round the fireplace and a pair of loungers placed by the window to give views over the garden. Stylish finishes include a wall of Levanto marble and tiny Murano glass wall tiles lining the hall.

Much of the furniture, such as a writing desk doubling as a drawing board and the Chinese lacquered book table, was designed by Gwynne and there are many imaginative and witty touches. The round table in the dining room has a central well for holding flowers or a low light. The house owes much to its setting, which was initially landscaped by Gwynne's father, and there is an oval pool designed by the young Denys Lasdun whom Gwynne worked with at Wells Coates.

The Homewood was Gwynne's first independent commission. Returning to Esher after service with the RAF in the Second World War, Gwynne went on to design a series of private houses for distinguished clients, among them Charles Forte and Laurence Harvey, as well as a number of larger projects, such as the glass and concrete extension to the gothic Theatre Royal in York and the Serpentine Restaurant in London's Hyde Park, where he used glass lavishly to give the impression that diners were eating *al fresco*. He continued to live at The Homewood after his parents died and in 1999 gave the house with the majority of its collection and the garden to the National Trust.

Financing the House

The country house conjures up an image of a great mansion at the heart of its estate, with an income from the rents of tenant farmers and the felling and coppicing of woodland. Near the house would be the home farm and a walled kitchen garden, together keeping the family supplied with fresh milk and other produce and, during the London season, the source of hampers sent up to town, packed with individually wrapped fruit or some other delicacy.

Few families, though, relied on land alone for their wealth, and most estates were acquired and houses built or remodelled with money from other sources, even if there was a substantial agricultural estate attached. The Brownlows of Belton and the Hobarts of Blickling owed their fortunes originally to the rise of the legal profession in the sixteenth century, the Hoares of Stourhead and Sir Francis Child, who employed Robert Adam to remodel Osterley, were bankers, and many ambitious men, such as William Sharington of Lacock, or Curzon of Kedleston, were players at court or in the wider political arena. Commerce and industry were also important sources of funds, particularly in the nineteenth century, when there were rich pickings for the entrepreneur and inventor, but also in earlier times, when mineral wealth could make a substantial difference to estate income.

CRAGSIDE
116

This romantic gabled house, set on a craggy hillside high above a Northumbrian burn, was the creation of the inventor and industrialist William Armstrong, who financed it from the profits of his Tyneside works. A lifelong innovator, Armstrong experimented with the possible uses of waterpower and, after the Crimean War had shown up the weaknesses of existing big guns, his firm became involved in armaments.

Cragside was started in 1863, when Armstrong's career was at its height. In later years, he withdrew from the day-to-day business, concentrating instead on his house and estate, where many of his ideas were put into practice. Harnessing the burn and the fall from a series of reservoir lakes, Armstrong lit the house with water-generated electricity, for which existing fittings, such as the *cloisonée* lamps in the library (**right**), were adapted; he installed a hydraulic lift to take heavy pots and pans from the basement scullery to the kitchen; and developed water-powered threshing and winnowing machines for his estate farms.

Below the house, the deep cleft of the Debdon burn is spanned by Armstrong's steel footbridge, over 46 metres (150 feet) long. At the end of the century, when his firm was a key player on the international armaments scene, Cragside was used to entertain foreign VIPs, such as the Shah of Persia. The Prince and Princess of Wales visited in 1884. In the picture (**above**), the Prince is relaxing on the entrance terrace on the south side of the house, with Armstrong opposite him in a frock coat and top hat.

Castle Drogo, crowning a moorland spur in rural Devon, was financed from a fortune made in the retail trade. Its builder, Julius Drewe, was a late-Victorian entrepreneur. After a few years' experience buying tea in the Far East and running a tea store in Liverpool, he joined forces with another enterprising young man, borrowed £10,000, and, in 1883, opened a shop in London. This was the first of what was to become a chain of Home and Colonial Stores. Six years later, when only 33, Drewe was rich. Retiring from day-to-day business, he set out to turn himself into a country gentleman.

CASTLE DROGO
76

Encouraged by a genealogist who came up with connections with the medieval baron Drogo de Teigne, he turned his sights on Devon, buying land just outside the village. The renowned Edwin Lutyens was commissioned to design the castle, only one wing of which was ever built. On the stately main staircase is Charles Hardie's portrait of Drewe as a country gent – dressed in a Burberry and out fishing in Scotland. The 39lb salmon behind him is now in a glass case in the castle tea-rooms.

In the property game, court connections have been a mixed blessing. Royal favour could bring great estates, but monarchs were omnipotent, able to take way as easily as they could give. Knole, the great Tudor house set in a wooded park just outside Sevenoaks in Kent, is connected with two high-fliers, one a loser, the other a survivor. The first, Thomas Cranmer, inherited Knole as one of the perks of his office when he became Archbishop of Canterbury, but was forced to yield it to the covetous Henry VIII. Thirty years later Elizabeth I presented it to her cousin, the diplomat Thomas Sackville, lst Earl of Dorset, but by then it had sitting tenants and Sackville had to wait until 1603 to buy them out.

In the next six years he made up for lost time. Drawing on a huge fortune, Sackville remodelled and redecorated the place, putting in the panelling, rhythmic plaster ceilings and carved chimneypieces which can still be seen in the principal rooms and creating the airy great staircase, with its painted decoration. Sackville leopards sit on the gables with which the earl softened the Tudor entrance front, and his initials and arms adorn the leadwork of the drainpipes and rainwater heads.

Some of the finest work he commissioned is in the Ballroom, where the marble and alabaster chimneypiece is an outstanding example of virtuoso Renaissance carving. His portrait, attributed to de Critz, presides over the Great Hall, where the Earl's private orchestra entertained from the gallery above his carved screen.

KNOLE
207

PENRHYN CASTLE

298

Fortunes could be made overseas as well as at home. The Pennant family of Penrhyn were able to draw on income from sugar plantations in the West Indies and on the profits from slate workings on their estates in north Wales. An enterprising ancestor, who emigrated to Jamaica in 1658, was one of the first to grow sugar as a cash crop, using African slaves to work the fields, and reaping the rewards from rising demand in Europe, fuelled by the need for something to sweeten the newly-fashionable drinks of tea and coffee. The Georgian Richard Pennant used the wealth which sugar generated to consolidate and develop the estate, planting trees, introducing crop rotation, and, most importantly, developing the embryonic slate workings. A road was built to take the slates to the coast, a new port created, and an agreement made with the Wyatt brothers, fashionable London architects, to use Penrhyn slates – which they did with gusto.

Richard Pennant's portrait by Henry Thomson shows him with a map of his new road, later to be adopted by Telford for his route to Holyhead.

George Dawkins-Pennant, who inherited in 1816, poured the family wealth into this fantasy castle. His architect was the little-known Thomas Hopper. The castle, for which Hopper and his patron used Welsh materials and local craftsmen, is a combination of genuine medieval detail and up-to-the-minute luxuries, such as fitted carpets, piped hot water, and lavish provision of water closets. Castle and slate workings fuelled the local economy, and the quarry, now owned by Sir Alfred McAlpine, today accounts for about one-sixth of world slate production. The painting by Henry Hawkins shows it in 1832, when it was visited by Princess Victoria.

A good marriage could make a dramatic difference to wealth and position. Bess of Hardwick started life in 1527 with £26 13s 4d, left to her by her father. At the end of her life, in her eighties, she was one of the wealthiest people in England, possessed of vast estates, and mistress of one of the most spectacular Elizabethan houses in England, which she had built.

In between came four marriages, each of which brought greater wealth and, with the exception of the first, enhanced status. Bess's short-lived first marriage, when she was sixteen, was to a cousin, who died very soon afterwards, leaving her with a respectable income of £66 a year. Four years later she caught the eye of the elderly, twice-married and extremely rich Sir William Cavendish, one of a breed of Tudor new men who had profited from government business. Sir William set out to please his new young wife, buying property in her home county of Derbyshire, including Chatsworth. At his death ten years later Bess was left significantly richer. Not long afterwards she married the similarly wealthy but socially more elevated Sir William St Loe, and when he died, after only five years, he likewise left much of his property to Bess. Her fourth marriage was to George Talbot, 6th Earl of Shrewsbury. He too was extremely rich and he came from one of the oldest and most exalted families in England, but disputes over Chatsworth, which Bess had started to remodel, and other difficulties meant the marriage was soon in trouble, and by 1584 it had broken down. At this point Bess turned her attention to Hardwick, which was undisputedly hers.

Initially, she concentrated on remodelling the now-ruined Old Hall, but in 1590, when the death of the Earl left her one of the richest people in the country, she started on the prodigy house with which she is so firmly connected. A status symbol as much as a home, Hardwick Hall glitters with glass, and at the top of the house, reached by a processional stone staircase which weaves its way from floor to floor, are Bess's showy state rooms. A portrait of her painted in the 1590s gives an impression of the tough and formidable woman she must have been, but not of the qualities which must have entranced her husbands.

HARDWICK HALL
175

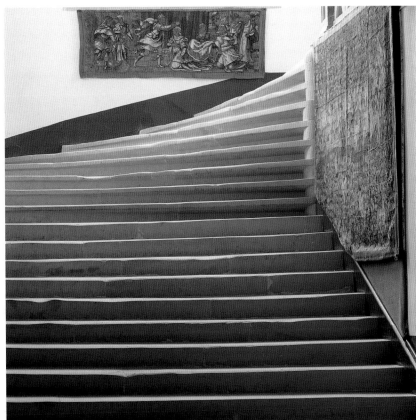

Horsey NORFOLK

2½ miles north-east of Potter Heigham, 11 miles north of Yarmouth astride the B1159 [443 L1]

In 1948 the Trust acquired what had been the private nature reserve of a branch of the Buxton family (ubiquitous in East Anglia), Horsey Hall with its 518 hectares (1,700 acres) of farmland running down to the coast, and surrounding Horsey Mere with its 'marshes and marrams'. It is satisfactory that a Buxton still lives here and will arrange limited access to the mere. The area includes the farm of Heigham Holmes above the marshes of Heigham Sound which form the east end of Hickling Broad. Lovers of Arthur Ransome's *Peter Duck*, for children of all ages up to 102, will not fail to recall that Mr Duck's married daughter, Rose, lived at Potter Heigham, a mile to the south.

The Horsey windmill is not for grinding corn but is a drainage mill pumping water from the low-level system to the high, which then reaches the sea 23 miles away at Yarmouth. A south-east wind allows the water to escape from the mere naturally. A north-west wind, in particular during spring tides, holds up the natural flow, and pumping is necessary if flooding is to be avoided. The mill was working until 1943, when it was severely damaged by lightning. It was repaired in 1958, and may be seen by visitors.

Horton Court SOUTH GLOUCESTERSHIRE

3 miles north-east of Chipping Sodbury, ¾ mile north of Horton, 1 mile west of the A46 Bath–Stroud road [442 F4]

When Robert de Beaufeu was a prebend at Salisbury Cathedral in the early twelfth century, he would have travelled from his living at Horton, snuggled in the lee of the southern Cotswolds, to Old Sarum, built within Iron Age and Norman defences high on a hill above the River Avon, and worshipped in the church which is now no more than outlines in the grass. It was this worldly ecclesiastic – who wrote a poem in praise of beer – or his successor who built the Norman hall at Horton. This remarkable one-storey building, now attached to a Cotswold manor house, stands only a few metres from the church for which the prebends were responsible, two carved Gothic doorways and Norman windows set high in the buttressed walls giving the hall itself the look of a simple chapel. Probably the oldest rectory in England, it looks back to the single-storeyed manor halls of the Anglo-Saxons.

Just as remarkable is the 15-metre (50-foot) detached loggia in the garden of the manor, built some 400 years after the hall, when the prebend, William Knight, combined his ecclesiastical responsibilities with a high-flying career in the king's service. Appointed chaplain and then private secretary to Henry VIII, Knight was employed on several diplomatic missions, culminating in a visit to Pope Clement VII in 1527 in an attempt to negotiate the king's divorce from Catherine of Aragon. Knight's first-hand knowledge of Italian culture undoubtedly inspired the charming Renaissance features which he added to his manor at Horton. The open arcade of his Italian-style loggia is decorated with stucco caricatures of classical worthies, including a portrait of a bearded Hannibal, and the doorway of the manor house is carved with helmets, weapons and foliage. Although Knight seems to have had a particular affection for Horton, one of several rich livings he enjoyed, he must have had little time to visit the magnificent thirteenth-century cathedral at Salisbury, laid out on a virgin site by the Avon as the centrepiece of the new town.

Houghton Mill CAMBRIDGESHIRE

In village of Houghton, signposted off the A1123 to St Ives [443 I2]

One of a handful of surviving mills along the River Great Ouse, this unusually large four-storey brick and timber

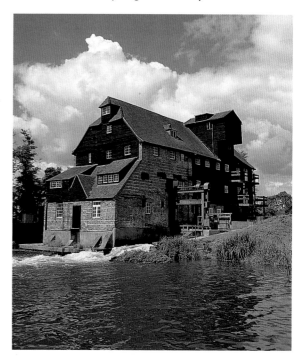

Houghton Mill, built on an island in the River Ouse, is one of several watermills owned by the Trust. Once common elements of the English countryside, these picturesque buildings were also the forerunners of the first great mills of the Industrial Revolution, which were similarly sited in deeply rural locations.

building rises from an artificial island 2 miles downstream of Huntingdon, the tarred weather-boarding of the upper storeys easily recognisable across the flat water meadows bordering the river. Once a property of Ramsey Abbey 10 miles to the north (*see* p.319), there has been a corn-mill on or near this site for at least 1,000 years, although the present building dates only from the seventeenth century. Three breastshot wheels – removed when the mill ceased working in the 1930s – powered the ten impressive pairs of millstones on the first floor and the hoists in the projecting gables which raised sacks of grain for storage at the top of the building. On open days the restored machinery is operated by electricity.

Hudswell NORTH YORKSHIRE

2 miles west of Richmond [445 I4]

Richmond, on the River Swale, is one of the most seemly towns in the north of England, emphatically a place to be walked round. In the valley below, on the south bank, lie the Hudswell Woods – Calfhall, Round House, Billybank and Hag Wood – which are all delightfully cool on a summer's day.

Hughenden Manor BUCKINGHAMSHIRE

1½ miles north of High Wycombe; on west side of the Great Missenden road [443 H4]

The six years of Tory government from 1874 saw some of the greatest successes enjoyed by any ministry of Queen Victoria's reign, including progressive social reforms and an imperialist foreign policy which gained the queen the title of Empress of India. These achievements owed much to the personal skills of the Prime Minister, Benjamin Disraeli, already 70 when the new parliament began. His radical policies had been foreshadowed some 30 years earlier in his political novels – *Coningsby* and *Sybil* – concerned with the condition of the rural and urban poor.

But this forward-looking politician still adhered to some traditional values, his strong belief that landed property was essential to support the status of a leading public figure perhaps reflecting the insecurity generated by his Italian-Jewish descent. With no great financial resources at his command, the Hughenden estate was acquired in 1847 – on the eve of his possible appointment as leader of the Conservative Party – only with the generous assistance of Lord George Bentinck and his

brothers, who lent Disraeli two-thirds of the purchase price. Here he and his wife Mary Anne lived until their deaths in 1881 and 1872 respectively, entertaining many of the great political and society figures of the day and leaving an indelible mark on the house and its beautiful setting.

Hughenden stands high up surrounded by trees, with a sweeping view over lawns to the hills beyond High Wycombe. Disraeli's writings show how he loved this place, the primroses he enjoyed still sprinkling the park in spring, and the cuckoo and wood pigeons still calling in the woods. On the long terrace where he paced back and forth are the Florentine vases acquired by Mary Anne, although his peacocks have gone, and conifers replanted by the Trust on the entrance lawn echo those Disraeli established here, as shown in an early photograph.

Inside, every room of this gothicised three-storey Georgian house includes some reminder of the Disraelis and their friends. The staircase and hall are lined with the Gallery of Friendship, portraits of those the statesman held most dear. The library contains an autographed copy of Queen Victoria's only published work, and Disraeli's novels appear among a notable collection of 'Theology, the Classics, and History'. Upstairs, his study is largely as he left it, portraits of his parents hanging over the mantelpiece and the black-edged notepaper that he always used after his wife's death lying ready on the table.

The obelisk crowning a far hillside in the view from the windows, erected by his wife in 1862 in memory of his father, would have reminded him of the two people who influenced him most. Disraeli never let political ambition destroy his very evident humanity and he was the only premier other than Melbourne to be honoured with a visit from the Queen. As Bismarck observed at the Congress of Vienna in 1878, 'Der alte Jude, das ist der Mann'.

Top: At a time when leading politicians were expected to be men of property, Disraeli felt it necessary to bolster his position with a country estate. He acquired Hughenden, then a plain Georgian building, in 1847 and had it embellished with romantic, vaguely Jacobean details. Above: His portrait by Sir Francis Grant, painted in 1852, is part of a collection of his pictures, furniture and books in the house.

Right: The 4th Earl of Bristol's passion for round and oval buildings led to the design of Ickworth, which is centred on a monumental rotunda. Still unfinished when the Earl died, Ickworth was completed by his son who made the decision to live in one of the flanking wings and to use the rotunda for entertaining and to display family treasures. Below: Included in a fine collection of art now on show here is the painting of Don Balthasar Carlos by Velázquez.

Ickworth SUFFOLK

In Horringer, 3 miles south-west of Bury St Edmunds on west side of the A143 [443 J3]

Frederick Augustus Hervey, 4th Earl of Bristol, must rank as one of the Church's more remarkable bishops. Appointed to the see of Derry, the richest in Ireland, in 1768 when only 38, his sympathy with both Roman Catholics and Presbyterians made him enormously popular, despite a sometimes light-hearted approach to his duties which once led him to organise a curates' race along the sands at Downhill (*see* p.129), rewarding the winners with vacant benefices. A large income coupled with an inherited fortune allowed the 4th Earl to embark on extensive foreign tours, now commemorated in Hotels Bristol all over the Continent, during which he amassed the works of art which he intended to display in his new house on the family's Suffolk estate.

Ickworth is as grandiose and flamboyant as its creator, a larger version of his earlier house at Ballyscullion and inspired by the circular Belle Isle on an island in Windermere (as was the little Mussenden Temple at Downhill). A huge domed rotunda decorated with classical columns and terracotta friezes is linked by curving corridors to rectangular wings, the whole building some 183 metres (600 feet) from end to end. But Frederick was never to see his house completed. Started in 1795 to the designs of the Italian architect Mario Asprucci the Younger, building came to a halt on the 4th Earl's death from gout in an outhouse in Italy in 1803 (from where his body was shipped back to England labelled as an antique statue). Even more tragically, the Bishop's magnificent collection had been appropriated by Napoleon's armies in 1798.

The 4th Earl's ambitious plans were realised by his son, created 1st Marquess of Bristol in 1826. The superb paintings, porcelain and furniture now displayed here largely represent the slow accumulation of several generations of Herveys, who have owned the estate since the mid-fifteenth century and most of whom have followed brilliant political careers, but much was acquired by Frederick's gifted eldest brother, the 2nd Earl, Ambassador in Madrid and Turin. It was their grandfather, the 1st Earl, who bought the early eighteenth-century Huguenot pieces among the silver displayed in the Museum Room, the relatively restrained hand of Paul de Lamerie contrasting with more ornate rococo Italian work. One case is devoted to a shoal of silver fishes, some designed as ornamental pendants, others as scent containers, their realistic, scaly forms including a whale and a swordfish as well as more mundane species.

The 1st Marquess housed the bulk of the collection in the grand state rooms in the rotunda rather than in the wings as his father had intended. The largest room in the house is the hemispherical library across the south front, notable for its rare late seventeenth- and early eighteenth-century political periodicals and ornamented with busts of Pitt, Canning, Fox and Liverpool. Hogarth's *Holland House Group in the Smoking Room*, showing John, Lord Hervey, in the centre of a group of friends including the 3rd Duke of Marlborough, is one of a number of outstanding portraits in the house, rivalled by Velázquez's study of the Infante Balthasar Carlos, son of Philip IV, a grave little boy with two greyhounds and a huge mastiff at his feet, and by Gainsborough's full-length canvas of the colourful Augustus John Hervey, Vice Admiral of the Blue, who briefly succeeded as 3rd Earl between his two brothers. It seems this philanderer deserved his wife, Elizabeth Chudleigh, whose bigamous marriage with the Duke of Kingston in 1769 gave rise to one of the most famous scandals of the eighteenth century. Quite different in character is the charming self-portrait by Madame Vigée Lebrun, commissioned by the Earl-Bishop in Naples in 1791, the artist's severe black dress setting off her vivacious face crowned with a mop of curly hair loosely caught up in a white handkerchief. The most extraordinary exhibit is undoubtedly Flaxman's marble group, *The Fury of Athamas*, based on a scene from Ovid's *Metamorphoses*, which dominates the staircase hall. Commissioned by the 4th Earl, Athamas is here shown holding his young son over his shoulder by an ankle, about to dash him to death. A second child clings to their mother, terrified.

From the 1st Marquess's orangery, the only part of the west wing to be completed, floor-length windows lead out onto a terrace looking south over the heavily wooded garden, where tall cypresses, yews, evergreen oak and box create the illusion of an Italian landscape. Artfully contrived vistas give enticing glimpses of the rotunda. In spring bluebells in the Silver Garden hidden in the trees form a sea lapping at hexagonal columns brought from the Giant's Causeway (*see* p.275). Subtle colours here are a direct contrast to the brassy yellow, salmon-pink and purple stripes in the Edwardian-style border fronting the nineteenth-century east wing. From the long raised terrace walk beyond the trees, created in *c.*1870 to shield the garden, there is a sweeping panorama over clumps of mature beeches and oaks in the park, many of them probably planted by 'Capability' Brown for the 2nd Earl. In the foreground, partly hidden in a dip, is Ickworth church, while an obelisk just visible above a wooded ridge on the far horizon was erected by the people of Derry in affectionate memory of their bishop.

Ightham Mote KENT

6 miles east of Sevenoaks, off the A25, and 2½ miles south of Ightham, off the A227 [443 J5]

Descending the steep path from the car park, Ightham Mote suddenly appears hidden in the deep, wooded valley below, its walls rising sheer from a surrounding moat. Half-timbered upper storeys project from the façade here and there, as if peering down at the little hump-backed stone bridge which crosses the water to an old wooden door. The

Bottom: The romantic medieval manor of Ightham Mote appears all of a piece but in fact is the result of gradual extension from the 1340s, when the oldest part was built, to the 1530s, which is about the date of the range, carried on wall-brackets over the moat. Below: The heart of the 14th-century house was the Great Hall, set at one side of the interior courtyard. The arching timber roof is original, but the central hearth that was once here, and which would have filled the room with smoke, was replaced with a fireplace later in the Middle Ages.

Opposite: Looking down into
Scratchell's Bay, on the western tip of
the Isle of Wight. The magnificent chalk
cliffs of the island, rising sheer from the
water, are home to many nesting birds,
among them cormorant, shag and
guillemot.

Below: Between Ilfracombe and
Woolacombe is a glorious stretch
of unspoilt coast, most of it in Trust
ownership, with a dramatic headland
at Morte Point.

roofline is a medley of steeply pitched gables, massive brick chimneys and moss-stained tiles. Ducks paddle about beneath the walls.

Built round three courtyards and dating originally from the fourteenth century, this beautiful manor house has retained its medieval appearance, despite many later alterations, largely because additions were always made using local oak and Kentish ragstone and were sympathetic to the ancient building. Some traces of the early house still remain. On the oak bargeboards in the cobbled courtyard, twining branches carry the Tudor rose of England, the fleur-de-lis of France and the pomegranate of Granada, the badge of Catherine of Aragon. The window of the great hall still has its original early sixteenth-century glass, in which the Tudor rose and Aragon pomegranate glow brilliantly on a sunny day. This armorial decoration is the work of Richard Clement, the great courtier who bought Ightham in 1521 and who was anxious to display his allegiance to the house of Tudor. Less than a decade later Catherine was to be cast aside by Henry VIII, thus securely dating the period when her arms could have been added to the house.

Sir Richard Clement was also responsible for decorating the long, half-timbered room on the first floor. Now a chapel but originally intended as a gallery, its arched wagon roof is exuberantly painted to imitate a tournament tent with vividly coloured badges and emblems in red, orange, green and white representing the royal houses of England, Spain and France. The colours have faded now, but it is easy to imagine how glowing they must once have been. An elaborately decorated pulpit with Gothic tracery and choir stalls carved with grotesque faces was installed when the room was converted into a chapel, possibly in the mid-seventeenth century. There is also some fine linenfold panelling, sixteenth-century stained glass in the windows and a remarkable oak door at the west end.

Across a landing from the chapel is the drawing room, a startling change in atmosphere and style. One end is filled with a monumental Jacobean fireplace decorated with carved Saracen heads and painted in black and gold. The walls are covered in eighteenth-century hand-painted Chinese wallpaper and the room as a whole has a distinctly exotic flavour, although, as in the rest of the house, the furniture has been added since the 1950s when the original contents were sold.

An extensive lawn stretches up the combe north of the house, framed by woods on the steep valley sides, its regular outlines marking the site of a medieval stewpond that was once fed by the stream which now tumbles over a cascade

and crosses the grass to fill the moat. A raised walk fringing the east side leads to a lake hidden in the trees beyond the lawn and to a network of woodland paths through mixed native and exotic trees underplanted with evergreens. Near the house a long border is crowded with traditional English flowers such as pinks, sweet williams, lilies and roses, but the clematis and rose pergola that once shaded the path above the west side of the lawn has disappeared.

This consciously old-fashioned garden, based on a medieval layout, reflects the late nineteenth-century's romantic view of the Middle Ages (see also Oxburgh, p.285) and also the influence of William Morris's Arts and Crafts movement (see also Snowshill, p.348). Although the garden was severely damaged by the Great Storm of 1987, which felled several fine cedars, Scots pine and yew, these are now being replanted and the paved Fountain Garden with pinks and rock roses in the crevices between the flags is being restored. Part of the charm of this unusual place derives from the constant sound of running water, like soothing background music.

Ilfracombe to Baggy Point DEVON

On the north coast, between Ilfracombe and Morte Bay
[442 C5]

At Morte Point the coast of North Devon, which has run due west since the Somerset border, turns south into the great sweep of Bideford Bay. It is different in character from the Exmoor coast, for here the hinterland, though it runs up to 244 metres (800 feet), is all farmed. The farms extend to the cliffs and sheep graze wherever the walker can go, and in many places where he cannot.

The Trust owns nearly all of this coast, both east and west of Morte, some 9 miles of very varied terrain. Ilfracombe still retains the charm of an early Victorian watering place, seemly stucco terraces ranked up the slopes above the harbour which is tucked under the steep cliff of Hillsborough on its east side. Immediately west of the town, the cliffs rise sharply to a series of rocky outcrops and this land, known as Torrs Walks, is well provided with paths cut into the slatey rock known as the Ilfracombe Beds. These lead on westward along the slopes of the Seven Hills and the Runnacleaves. Beyond Brandy Cove Point a former carriage road runs as far as Lee. The views are to the west; the air exhilarating.

The old road drops down to Lee Bay, the village in the combe behind it, and then on to the Trust's land again up Flagstaff Hill to the cliffs of Damage Barton. The Trust has made a staircase here to Sandy Cove, access to which was previously vertiginous. The cliff is particularly attractive, gorse thickets separated by humpy pasture, good for spring and summer flowers. Bennett's Water runs down to rocky reefs at Bennett's Mouth, its valley giving shelter to wintering birds.

The lighthouse on Bull Point was rebuilt in 1972 after its predecessor had become unsafe due to rockfalls. From the point the coast runs south past the sandy Rockham Beach and then curves westward to Morte. This is one of the great headlands of the West Country. Sailing ships beating up to Bristol had to weather Morte or stand offshore, for the reefs, and the Morte Stone beyond them, are perilous. In the churchyard at Mortehoe many drowned sailors are buried. The cliffs are low, still formed of slate, here called by geologists the Morte slate, but the slopes above them are grazed by sheep which keep the bracken, gorse and bramble at bay. To the west, Lundy (*see* p.231) looms on the horizon, and on the mainland Hartland Point at about the same distance, 11 miles south of the island.

The village of Mortehoe stands above the cliffs, followed by the hotels of Woolacombe behind Barricane Beach. Behind them the little Combesgate Valley runs up to Twitchen, giving a sheltered walk on a blustery day. The Trust owns much of the farmland behind Woolacombe and this ownership has stopped the town spreading except up the hill towards the former railway station, for the line from Barnstaple to Mortehoe and Ilfracombe was a casualty of the Beeching era.

The 2 miles of Woolacombe Beach are all firm golden sand. Above rise the high dunes of Woolacombe Warren and, behind the dunes, the Marine Drive, a speculative venture made before 1914 in an attempt to develop this coast which thankfully never came off. It serves a most useful purpose as a car park, not only for users of the beach but also for the elderly and disabled who can sit by their cars and absorb the atmosphere of this splendid place. Above the Drive the bold outline of Woolacombe Down forms a backdrop to the great beach.

The south end of the beach at Vention does not belong to the Trust. Its land starts at Ramson Cliff (ramson is the West Country name for the broad-leaved garlic, *Allium ursinum*), and from here the cliff path runs for a mile to Baggy Point which closes Morte Bay. Baggy is very different from Morte. Its rock is sandstone and it juts into the sea, high and bold, the house and buildings of Croyde Hoe Farm near its tip, the fields reaching out to the cliff edge. Shags and cormorants, fulmars and gulls nest on the point, with ravens, jackdaws and kestrels breeding here as well.

Isle of Wight

[443 G7–H7]

Although the island is small – 13 miles from Cowes south to St Catherine's Point and 17 miles from the Needles east to Bembridge – a great deal is packed into it, and the Trust has been active here since 1922, its estate largely built up by the efforts of a devoted Local Committee.

Much of the Trust's holding lies on the chalk hills which run right across the island. Bembridge and Culver Downs at its east end rise to 104.5 metres (343 feet), with sheer cliffs providing safe nesting sites for seabirds (for the early eighteenth-century Bembridge windmill, *see* p.43).

At Ventnor, to the south-west, there are panoramic views from Littleton and Luccombe Downs, both seaward and north over the island to the Solent and the New Forest.

At 233 metres (764 feet) St Boniface Down above Ventnor is the highest point on the island. At its southernmost tip, however, the geology changes. St Catherine's Hill, with a fine view over West Wight, is chalk, while St Catherine's Down is greensand, but Knowles Farm, which runs down from there to the foreshore, is on blue lias clay, known locally as Blue Slipper. The clay is unstable and landslips are comparatively common; hence the scrubby slopes and hollows with an interesting flora. St Catherine's Point is a place where migratory birds assemble, and records have been kept by ornithologists for many years.

Westward again, beyond Brighstone, the Trust protects by ownership or covenant over 7 miles of coast and downland from Chilton Chine to the Needles, offering a spectacular coastal walk and at Compton Bay some of the island's best bathing beaches. Much of the land is chalk down, the thin soil covered with short downland grasses and lime-loving plants, with thickets of hawthorn and gorse and the typical downland birds: wheatears, larks and pipits. Walking is exhilarating: the chain of downs, Mottistone, Brook, Compton and Afton, the prehistoric ridgeway along the crest of the hills, the barrows from the Bronze Age and the views along the coast make this a very special place. At Mottistone there is an additional bonus as the Trust's estate includes much of the village grouped round the church and manor house (*see* p.255), framed by the woodland behind.

To the west, beyond Freshwater, Tennyson Down is held in memory of the poet who walked there daily when living at Farringford nearby. West High Down provides the final link which connects the westerly tip of the island to the Needles, the best known and most spectacular of all chalk cliffs.

The tallest pinnacle, known as Lot's Wife, collapsed in 1764 and erosion still continues, but the three which remain, with the lighthouse crouched protectively at their outer end, live in the mind's eye of anyone who has seen them. Built into the cliff is the nineteenth-century Old Battery (*see* p.260), part of the defences of the Solent against the French, now restored and with an exhibition telling its history.

Newtown is something utterly different. The Newtown river, now a sequestered wooded estuary, was in the thirteenth century a flourishing harbour. What remains of the town mostly belongs to the Trust and is of great interest (*see* p.263), but it is the estuary, with its seven miles of creeks and four miles of the Solent foreshore, which is especially good: oyster beds, yacht moorings, saltings and bird life, copses rich in butterflies, quietness, beauty.

Kedleston Hall DERBYSHIRE

3 miles north of Derby, easily reached and signposted from the A38 Derby bypass [445 J8 and 443 G1]

No one could describe this grand Neo-classical palace as homely. But then, it was always intended as a showpiece. On the impressive entrance front, looking north over a sweep of open pasture, a massive pedimented portico adorned with classical sculpture rises the full height of a three-storey central block. To either side are substantial rectangular pavilions, linked to the main block by curved corridors. A tower seen peeping above the west pavilion is part of a little medieval church, all that remains of the village swept away when the landscape park was created.

Sir Nathaniel Curzon, later 1st Lord Scarsdale, began the house in 1759, only a year after he had inherited the estate. A cultivated man who was interested in the arts, he saw it as a setting for his collection of paintings and sculpture – on view to visitors from the day the house was built. The formal reception rooms and guest suite filling the central block were never intended to be used except for the entertainment of important visitors. The family lived in one pavilion, with the kitchen and domestic offices in the other.

Although work began under the direction of Matthew Brettingham and James Paine, by 1760 these two architects had been superseded by the young Robert Adam, recently returned from Rome, who transformed his predecessors' rather conventional designs. Adam's monumental Marble Hall, with ten alabaster columns like tree-trunks on either

The builder of Kedleston was Sir Nathaniel Curzon, seen here with his wife Lady Caroline Colyear in a portrait by Nathaniel Hone. The picture was painted in 1761, the year Curzon was created 1st Lord Scarsdale.

side and classical statues in niches along the walls, is top-lit to suggest the open courtyard of a Roman villa. The adjoining rotunda known as the Saloon, its coffered dome rising to a height of 19 metres (62 feet), was based on the Pantheon in Rome, one of the most admired buildings of classical antiquity. To either side lie formal reception rooms, Adam's hand evident in virtually every detail of their decoration. Delicate plaster ceilings were executed by the Yorkshireman Joseph Rose, paintings were grouped and hung according to Adam's schemes – plaster frames built into the walls in some rooms ensure his arrangements have survived – and the furniture, some of it by Adam, some designed by the London cabinetmaker John Linnell, some with inputs from both men, picks up on decorative themes. In the State Withdrawing Room, carved and gilded dolphins, merfolk and sea nymphs on the four great sofas echo nautical touches in the ceiling. Made by Linnell, they are based on an Adam design, but one that Linnell radically altered.

The paintings hanging double-banked in all the principal rooms, including a number of epic canvases such as Benedetto Luti's *Cain and Abel* or Salomon Koninck's *Daniel before Nebuchadnezzar*, illustrate Lord Curzon's taste for seventeenth-century Italian and Dutch art. Family portraits dating back to the sixteenth century adorn guest apartments, a charming study by Nathaniel Hone showing the 1st Lord Scarsdale walking in the grounds with his wife. Thomas Barber's portrayal of the elderly Mrs Garnett, the housekeeper who took Boswell and Dr Johnson round Kedleston in 1777, is also memorable.

Bluejohn vases and ornaments are part of a notable collection of this prized Derbyshire stone, and Kedleston was further enriched in the early twentieth century by Marquess Curzon of Kedleston, who acquired Indian and oriental artefacts during travels in Asia and while he was Viceroy of India from 1899–1905.

The long drive from the great arched gateway of Adam's north lodge runs through his idealised landscape park, with its carefully placed clumps of trees and a chain of serpentine lakes crossed by a three-arched stone bridge. Adam also designed the fishing pavilion on the upper lake, a Venetian window facing north over the water enabling ladies to cast a line into the water while being shielded from the sun.

To the south of the house, a broad open lawn bounded by a ha-ha marks the eighteenth-century informal garden, with uninterrupted views across the park beyond as it rises gently to a belt of trees. An hexagonal summerhouse and orangery were both designed by George Richardson in the

Left: The Marble Hall at Kedleston is one of the grandest 18th-century interiors in England. Designed by Adam to imitate the central courtyard of a villa in ancient Rome, it is lit from above and is ringed with niches holding copies of antique statues. Above: Adam was also responsible for much of the furniture, including the four great sofas in the drawing room, decorated with gilded merfolk, tritons and sea-nymphs, although his designs were altered by the maker, John Linnell.

late eighteenth century and a pair of gates leads into the Long Walk, a winding 3-mile circuit of the park with views back towards the house from the section following the wooded skyline.

Keld Chapel CUMBRIA

1 mile south-west of Shap village, by River Lowther [445 H4]

The little hamlet of Keld, on the eastern edge of the Cumbrian fells, was once part of the estates of Shap Abbey, now an isolated ruin about a mile away, and this modest stone and slate building by the River Lowther was probably built by the abbey in the late fifteenth or early sixteenth century for the people of the village. Occasional services are once again held in the chapel, which was long used for other purposes.

The North Downs meet the sea at the spectacular white cliffs which frame Dover harbour, the wall of which can just be seen in the distance. The cliffs were once continuous with the similar chalk formations of northern France, but ever since the end of the last Ice Age, when the Straits of Dover were formed, they have been retreating, and global warming may cause them to retreat more quickly.

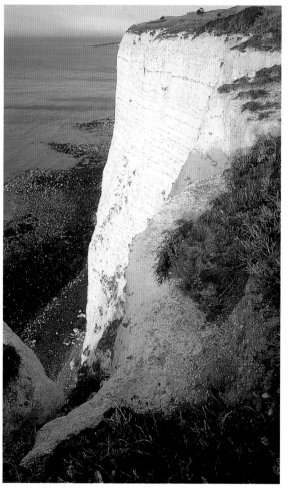

Kent Coast: The White Cliffs

[443 L5]

At the south-east corner of England, the rounded outlines of the North Downs meet the sea in spectacular chalk cliffs, where the advent of the Channel Tunnel has emphasised the importance of the Trust's protective role. The string of properties held here, amounting to some 226.5 hectares (560 acres) and over 5½ miles of the famous White Cliffs, lies either side of Dover: a mile of farmland and cliff at Great Farthingloe, to the west, close to the tunnel approaches; undulating, orchid-rich chalk grassland and farmland at Langdon Cliffs and Langdon Hill, behind Dover, with stunning views over the port and, on a clear day, across the Channel to France; and a number of holdings at St Margaret's Bay to the north-east, including a lighthouse (*see* p.360). Butterflies and birds abound, and there are fossils in the chalk, remains of Second World War defences and exhilarating walking.

About 12 miles up the coast, the Trust protects some 222.5 hectares (550 acres) of saltings, sand-dunes and mud-flats at Pegwell Bay, where the River Stour winds lazily to the sea. Managed by the Kent Wildlife Trust as a nature reserve, this estuarine coast attracts migrant waders and native sea and shore birds.

Killerton DEVON

On west side of the B3181, formerly the A38, Exeter−Cullompton road [442 D6]

Sir Thomas Dyke Acland's decision to engage the Scottish gardener John Veitch to lay out the grounds round his new house at Killerton in the 1770s was an inspired choice. Then a very young man − not yet 21 − who had walked from Edinburgh to seek his fortune with only ten shillings to his name, John Veitch was about to become one of the greatest nurserymen and landscape designers of his day. The firm he founded was the first to send plant-hunters to little-known parts of the world, from where they brought back exotic specimens that had never before been seen in England.

Killerton reflects Veitch's lifetime association with the estate. His garden − more accurately an arboretum − is laid out on the slopes of the steep volcanic outcrop known as Killerton Clump, the highest point for miles around. Paths climb ever upwards through the trees, with views down over a sea of foliage and across the flat fertile landscape of the valley of the River Clyst. Veitch's beech walk follows the contours of the hill, a cool green arch meeting overhead. Mature wellingtonias, redwoods, spruces and cedars, introduced from the Veitch nursery, tower over a varied collection of rhododendrons, some of them Veitch introductions, others grown from seed brought back from the Himalayas in the 1920s, when Sir Francis Acland supported Captain Kingdon-Ward's plant-hunting expeditions, all of them flourishing in the acid soil. May and June here are magnificent, with hummocks of scarlet, crimson, yellow and white against young foliage. Earlier in the year there are daffodils between the trees and the white blossoms of magnolia, and there is autumn colour too. The more formal garden near the house – a long terrace planted with dwarf shrubs, from which Lloyd George once addressed 19,000 people in the park, and a broad herbaceous border – was created on the advice of the great Edwardian gardener William Robinson, and the rock garden by the ice-house was also added at this time.

At the edge of the arboretum, tracks continue through woodland planted on the clump to an Iron Age hill-fort on the southern edge of the outcrop, from where there are panoramic views south and east over the busy M5 to the wooded Clyst Valley. To the north of the prehistoric earthworks trees give way to the open parkland of The Plain on the highest point of the hill, with views to north and west over the Culm Valley and through or over the woods to the main railway line from London to Penzance far below. Deer walls on the western slopes of the hill are relics of the herd that was kept here until c.1920.

The house does not compete with its surroundings. It is a straggling buff building at the foot of the hill, and later additions to it almost conceal the unpretentious square block built in 1778 by Essex architect John Johnson. Originally the intention was to replace it with a grandiose mansion by James Wyatt on the hill. Johnson's magnificent stables at the foot of the drive, with an elegant cupola rising over the impressive pedimented archway leading into the courtyard, are a much better monument to his talent. Another Sir Thomas – the 10th Baronet – was responsible for the Victorian chapel by C.R. Cockerell to the north of the stables, built to supersede the tiny Elizabethan building on the other side of the hill, almost all that remains of the former Acland house at Columbjohn.

Killerton's interiors, much altered over the years, recall country living between the First and Second World Wars, when weekend parties sat down to eat off the family silver laid out in the dining room, the most privileged female guests nearest the fire. The masculine library next door now houses the collection of the Rev. Sabine Baring-Gould (1834–1924), the larger-than-life parson of the Devonshire village of Lewtrenchard, best known for his hymn 'Onward Christian Soldiers', who is unlikely to have approved of the set of false book-backs with fanciful titles in a corner of the room. Music by Samuel Sebastian Wesley on the chamber organ dominating the music room is dedicated to the wife of the 10th Baronet, who took lessons from Wesley when he was organist of Exeter Cathedral.

Some of the rooms at Killerton are now devoted to the Paulise de Bush collection of costume, displayed on dummies in carefully composed tableaux to show the life and society of the day, flimsy floral chiffon evening gowns of the 1930s contrasting with high-necked, full-skirted Victorian gowns.

Killerton sits at the centre of an extensive estate in the fertile valleys of the Clyst and Culm. A mix of farmland and sizeable areas of woodland, much of which was planted by the 10th Baronet to provide timber for the estate, it also includes the villages of Broadclyst and Budlake and many traditional buildings and is crossed by a network of footpaths and waymarked trails. East of the M5 is the sizeable Ashclyst Forest, with some ancient oak pollards among mixed plantings of broadleafed trees and conifers. Butterflies are attracted to the sunny forest glades and there are roe deer and woodland birds to be seen. About half a mile north is the smaller White Down Copse, planted in the nineteenth century. Notable buildings on the estate include Marker's Cottage, a small cob and thatch house dating back to the fifteenth century in the village of

Top: Killerton House, an unpretentious building at the heart of a substantial estate, was intended as a temporary residence while something much grander was built nearby. But the new house, a palace by James Wyatt, never got further than the drawing board. Above: Much of Killerton's first floor is now used to display the Paulise de Bush costume collection, which includes such treasures as these early 18th-century brocade shoes resting on a pink quilted petticoat dating from the same period.

Broadclyst. It has some mid sixteenth-century paintings on a wooden screen and a stair turret leads to the upper floor created in the seventeenth century. A few minutes' walk away, on the River Clyst, is the working Clyston Mill, probably built in the early nineteenth century but occupying an ancient site, and half a mile north up the B3181 is Budlake village, with a surviving 1950s Post Office Room.

King John's Hunting Lodge SOMERSET

In the Square at Axbridge, on corner of High Street [442 E5]

Like contemporary towns in East Anglia (*see* Paycocke's, p.293), Axbridge, Trowbridge, Bradford-on-Avon and other centres of the medieval wool trade in the West Country were once filled with prosperous merchants' houses such as this misleadingly named example of *c.*1500. A three-storey timber-framed building on the corner of Axbridge's market place, it is jettied out over the street in a double overhang. A small museum of local history and archaeology run by the Axbridge and District Museum Trust is now housed here.

The King's Head BUCKINGHAMSHIRE

At north-west corner of Market Square in Aylesbury [443 H4]

A narrow passage from Aylesbury's busy market square leads to this lovely old coaching inn dating back to 1450. A large cobbled stable yard has its original mounting block, there is a priest's hole and the large mullioned and transomed window which lights the bar, once the hall of a medieval house, has fragments of fifteenth-century glass.

Kingston Lacy DORSET

On the B3082 Wimborne–Blandford road, 1½ miles west of Wimborne [442 F6]

Home of the Bankes family from 1663 when Sir Ralph Bankes built a house here to replace the earlier seat at Corfe Castle (*see* p.109), ruined in the Civil War, Kingston Lacy is a monument to the eccentric and original William John Bankes (1786–1855), friend of Byron. With the aid of Sir Charles Barry, architect of the Houses of Parliament, William transformed the house into an Italianate palazzo,

Right: A pair of Japanese bronze cranes greets visitors in Kingston Lacy's basement-level entrance hall.

Top: The supposed portrait of Marchesa Maria Grimaldi with her dwarf by Rubens is one of many fine paintings on view in the imposing Saloon on the principal floor.

Above: a pair of Paris porcelain stands decorated with Egyptian motifs from *c.*1805 is one of a number of treasures from the Near East in the house.

filled with pictures and other works of art he had acquired during his extensive travels in the Mediterranean. But he had little opportunity to enjoy what he had created. In 1841 he was accused of behaving indecently with a soldier in a London park and he fled to Italy, where he spent the rest of his life. Nevertheless, although unlikely ever to see his house again, this extraordinary man continued to concern himself with its furnishing and decoration.

Still retaining the shape of the original Restoration mansion by Sir Roger Pratt, Kingston Lacy is a symmetrical three-storey oblong with a balustrade and central cupola crowning the hipped roof. Tall chimneys give the house the look of an upturned footstool. On the grand south front a broad Italianate terrace sweeps right across the façade, with central steps flanked by urns and guarded by lions descending on to a lawn dotted with Venetian well-heads. The impressive marble staircase leading visitors up to the principal rooms on the first floor is also of Italian inspiration, provided with an airy loggia on the half-landing as if to give protection from a Mediterranean sun. One of three bronze figures set in niches here depicts brave Lady Mary Bankes, still holding the key of Corfe Castle which she twice defended for King Charles in the Civil War (the actual keys hang in the library upstairs).

No traces of Roger Pratt's house survive inside, but some rooms still remain from R.F. Brettingham's remodelling in the 1780s for Henry Bankes. The painted ceiling by Cornelius Dixon in the saloon arches over the room like elaborate wrapping paper, delicate curves and spirals of foliage echoing the rich floral borders on the opulent Savonnerie carpet. The paintings hanging two and three deep include Rubens's portraits of the Grimaldi sisters acquired by William, one encased in her gleaming wedding-dress like an exotic beetle, the other pictured with her dwarf.

Next door is the Spanish Room, where works William procured during his travels in Spain at the time of the Peninsular War against Napoleon are set against gilded leather hangings and seen beneath a sumptuous coffered ceiling, thought to be one of those Scamozzi added to the Palazzo Contarini on the Grand Canal in Venice. Papal power and splendour shine through Velázquez's portrait of Cardinal Massimi, clothed here in peacock blue. Another arresting painting, Sebastiano del Piombo's unfinished *The Judgement of Solomon*, dominates the dining room.

The centre of an extensive estate (*see* pp.31 and 427), Kingston Lacy is also surrounded by a naturalistic 101.5-hectare (250-acre) park landscaped in the late eighteenth century, dotted with mature trees and now grazed by a

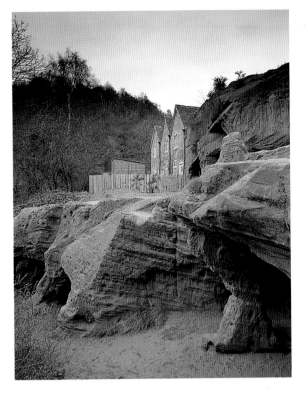

Almost at the top of the red sandstone escarpment of Kinver Edge, a terrace of gabled cottages, recently restored by the Trust, is built into the cliff.

herd of North Devon cattle. The Edwardian garden restored by the Trust includes a brightly coloured parterre to the west of the house, where beds of forget-me-nots and crimson and yellow wallflowers in the spring are replaced by begonias and heliotrope later in the year, and a Victorian fernery to the east. A cedar walk lined with trees planted by visiting notables, including the Duke of Wellington, leads to the lime avenue and the arboretum known as the Nursery Wood beyond, where a number of young specimen trees includes cedars, a swamp cypress, a wellingtonia and Brewer's weeping spruce. A pink granite obelisk, one of four in the garden, was brought here by William Bankes from a temple on the Nile which he saw on his journeys.

Kinver Edge STAFFORDSHIRE

4 miles west of Stourbridge, 4 miles north of Kidderminster, west of the A449, adjoining Kingsford Country Park [442 F2]

The Trust has had a foothold on this prominent sandstone escarpment above the village of Kinver since 1917, and continues to add to its holding, part of which is designated as an SSSI, as opportunity allows. Once forested, the Edge is now acid heathland with some oak-birch woodland and pockets of scrub. It is rich in butterflies and birds, such as the wood warbler, tree pipit and redstart, and the Trust's 133 hectares (330 acres) also include a rare area of sandy grassland, which attracts adders, slowworms and lizards. A grassy bank bounded by a ditch at the northern end of the Edge traces out the defences of an Iron Age hill-fort and there are wide views to the Clent Hills (*see* p.98), Wenlock Edge (*see* p.339) and the Clee Hills, but it is the remains of the extraordinary rock dwellings honeycombed into the soft, crumbly rock which have made the place famous. At Holy Austin Rock to the north of the Edge, where the cave houses were occupied from before the eighteenth century into the 1950s, some houses have been restored and are furnished as they would have been in 1900.

Kinwarton Dovecote WARWICKSHIRE

1½ miles north-east of Alcester, just south of the B4089 [443 G3]

This substantial fourteenth-century circular dovecote sitting proudly in a field at the end of a muddy lane probably once belonged to the Abbey of Evesham some 12 miles away to the south, the only survivor of a former monastic grange. Doves are still housed in some of the 580 nesting holes built into the limestone walls, filling the air with their cooing and perching picturesquely on the red-tiled conical roof. Those who dare can climb the original potence, the ingenious manoeuvrable ladder supported on a pivoting central post which gives access to all the nesting boxes. Apart from this rare survival, Kinwarton Dovecote is also notable for its fine ogee doorway.

Knightshayes Court DEVON

2 miles north of Tiverton [442 D6]

The drunken mob who destroyed his Leicestershire factory on 28 June 1816 prompted the young John Heathcoat to move his revolutionary new lace-making machines to the safety of Devonshire, where he set up in one of the Tiverton mills left empty by the decline of the wool industry. The profits from what was to become the largest lace factory in the world enabled his grandson, John Heathcoat-Amory, the 1st Baronet, to purchase the Knightshayes estate and to build the idiosyncratic Gothic house that overlooks the little town in the valley below.

Dating from 1869 to 1874, it is a singular place. Built of

The yew hedge enclosing one of the formal gardens at Knightshayes is clipped to form a topiary fox and hounds. These lively beasts were first cut in the 1920s.

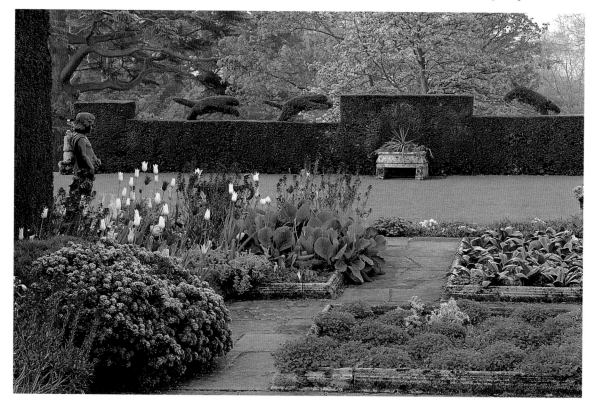

dark-red Hensley stone, the house rises forbiddingly from the terraces to the right of the drive in a frontage of pointed gables, large mullioned windows and prominent gargoyles. A rare example of the domestic architecture of William Burges, the High Victorian medievalist who is much better known for his churches, such as the masterpiece at Studley Royal (*see* p.376), this rather dour exterior was planned to conceal interiors of exceptional richness. Although Burges's designs were never executed, the schemes produced by his more conventional replacement, John Diblee Crace, were by no means subdued. Quotations from Robert Burns in gold letters several inches high run round the frieze in the dining room, set off by dark panelling and a rich red and green wallpaper and vying for attention with the brightly painted ceiling, one of several in the house. The corbels of the principal beams are carved with creatures from the Devon countryside: a badger, a fox and an otter with a fish. The medievalism of the hall, the only room to be completed largely as Burges planned, is even more striking, with its Gothic arches, gallery, timber vault and whimsical carvings. In addition Burges designed the painted bookcase with panels by Burne-Jones and Rossetti that stands here. Burges's intentions can also be seen in a newly created room that has been based on original drawings that were never executed and fitted out with furnishings on loan from the Victoria and Albert Museum.

The Old Masters in the drawing room and morning room, the nucleus of the collection acquired by the 3rd Baronet (1894–1972), provide a show of a different kind, including Constable's vivid red poppies like a scarlet splash on the wall by the fireplace, a misty Turner seascape, a Rembrandt self-portrait with fleshy face and thickly curling hair and Holbein's delicate *A Lady in a White Cap*, her high unmarked forehead suggesting extreme youth.

Although based on a nineteenth-century design by Edward Kemp, the garden owes much to the 3rd Baronet and his wife, who greatly enlarged it and made it one of the finest in the county. A formal layout near the house includes a water-lily pool in a battlemented yew enclosure and a topiary hunt on the hedges framing the lawn to the south, one of the pursuing hounds shown gathering itself to leap a leafy obstacle. To the east, grassy walks and glades cross 12 hectares (30 acres) of rare trees and shrubs, a place of dappled shade and varied foliage. A tongue of land thickly covered with large-leaved rhododendrons contrasts with a majestic stand of Douglas fir and with the elegant, soaring trunks in the larch wood. West of the house, a little valley has been planted with a wide variety of willows and

has a show of daffodils in spring, and most recently the large walled kitchen garden, with its unique stepped walls, has been restored and is open to visitors.

Knole KENT

At south end of Sevenoaks, just east of the A225 [443 J5]

The gateway to Knole lies off the main A225 through Sevenoaks, a sudden opening between the buildings lining the road. The drive from this modest entrance emerges unexpectedly into the glorious 404.5-hectare (1,000-acre) park surrounding the house, scored with deep valleys, planted with ancient oaks, beeches and chestnuts, and grazed by herds of fallow and Sika deer. As the road breasts a rise, there is a view of what looks like a compact hilltop town, with rabbit-cropped turf running almost up to the walls and a jumble of chimneys, gables, battlements and red-tiled roofs rising behind.

Sprawled round courtyards like an Oxford college, Knole could house the retinue of a medieval prince. The main ranges are of rough Kentish ragstone, but hidden away in some of the minor courts are half-timbered façades, like those that can be seen in a hundred villages

Below: In the late 17th century, the 5th Earl of Dorset helped to restore Knole's fortunes by marrying Frances Cranfield, whose portrait by Van Dyck hangs in the Ballroom.

Bottom: The Spangle Bedroom at Knole is called after the bed-hangings, which are appliquéd with silver sequins.

Right: The battlemented banqueting
house which crowns The Kymin, a
prominent hill to the east of Monmouth.

Below: Silver furniture was made in
England in the late 17th and early 18th
century in imitation of the splendour of
Louis XIV's Versailles. Much was later
melted down, but Knole contains some
rare survivals: these pieces are shown
to visitors in a warm half-light which
makes them glow.

round about. Inside, in contrast to the rather plain and
rugged exterior, are furnishings and decoration of great
richness and rarity.

The core of Knole was built by Thomas Bourchier,
Archbishop of Canterbury, between 1456 and his death
in 1486, when he bequeathed it to the see of Canterbury.
Four more archbishops enjoyed the splendid residence
Bourchier had created before Archbishop Cranmer was
forced to give it to Henry VIII. The covetous king
considerably enlarged his new palace, but it seems that he
spent little or no time here. It was later held briefly by
Elizabeth I's favourite, the Earl of Leicester, but in 1566
the queen granted the house and estate to her cousin
Thomas Sackville, whose descendants, the Earls and
later Dukes of Dorset, and then Lords Sackville, have
lived here ever since. Largely due to the cultivated 3rd
Duke of Dorset, who treasured Knole's sense of age, the
house was not remodelled in the classical style during the
eighteenth century. It is this lack of alteration which makes
Knole such a precious survival amongst the great houses
of England.

Knole's collection of seventeenth-century furniture
and textiles was mostly acquired by the 6th Earl some half
a century after the original contents of the house had been
dispersed in the Civil War. As Lord Chamberlain to
William III, the Earl was entitled to take away discarded
furnishings from the royal palaces and he also enriched
Knole with the furniture acquired by his grandfather, the
Earl of Middlesex, who was Master of the Great Wardrobe
to James I. As a result, Knole's galleries and bedchambers
are filled with state beds, tapestries, chairs and stools that
would once have adorned the palaces of Whitehall,
Hampton Court and Kensington. For many the culmination of a visit to the house is the King's Room, where
some of the rarest and finest pieces are displayed. The
famous silver looking-glass, table and candlestands shine
brilliantly in the simulated candlelight, drawing the eye
away from the magnificent great bed with its cloth of silver
and gold and matching chairs and stools.

The furniture, the embroidered fabrics and tapestries,
the ornate plaster ceilings and carved marble chimneypieces are all a reflection of the painstaking craftsmanship
which created this house. Even the drainpipes have ornate
leadwork heads, some in the form of a tiny castle, each one
subtly individual. And each gable on the entrance front is
carved with a proud, beautifully carved Sackville leopard.
Knole is a tribute to the genius of an unsung army of men
and women as well as a memorial to wealth and power.

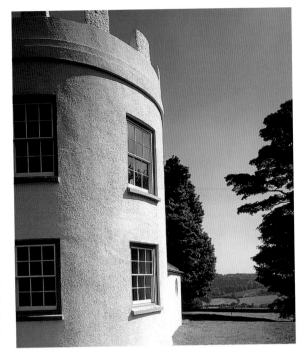

The Kymin MONMOUTHSHIRE

1 mile east of Monmouth between the A466 and the A4136
[442 E4]

The prominent 244-metre (800-foot) hill known as The
Kymin is renowned for its wide-ranging views over the
Wye and Monnow valleys, said to embrace nine counties.
The Trust owns 3.5 hectares (9 acres) of the high ground
and the two structures which crown it. In the late eighteenth century members of a local dining club formed the
habit of meeting here on summer evenings for a cold
supper and in 1794 built the round battlemented banqueting house on the brow of the hill for use in bad weather,
each of its windows placed so as to enjoy a spectacular
panorama. Nelson's celebrated victory over the French in
the Battle of the Nile four years later inspired the construction of the little temple in honour of the British navy
which stands nearby. Its pyramidal stepped roof suggests
an Egyptian summerhouse, despite the prominent statue
of Britannia which crowns the structure and the medallions
recording the names and principal achievements of sixteen
great eighteenth-century admirals. When Nelson himself
visited this spot in 1802, he thought it was one of the most
beautiful places he had ever seen. History does not record
the feelings of Emma Hamilton and her husband who
were accompanying him on his journey down the Wye.

Lacock Abbey WILTSHIRE

3 miles south of Chippenham, just east of the A350 [442 F5]

Seen across the River Avon when the sun is low, the abbey is a golden building floating in a sea of grass, its roofline punctuated by twisted chimneystacks and a prominent octagonal tower. This unusual and romantic place has a history going back over 700 years, with many echoes of the nunnery for Augustinian canonesses founded in 1232 by the redoubtable Ela, Countess of Salisbury, in memory of her husband William Longespee. At its suppression by Henry VIII's commissioners in 1539, the nunnery was granted to the duplicitous and self-seeking William Sharington, a rather unattractive man who seems to have behaved with more than the usual dishonesty in his public life but who showed both sensitivity and imagination in converting his purchase into a house, retaining much of its medieval character while also incorporating innovative Renaissance features that were rare in England at this date. Beautiful fifteenth-century cloisters still frame a grassy court at the heart of the house, with carved bosses adorning the vaulted passages. The daughters of well-to-do families who formed the community sunned themselves on the stone seats set into the walls or stretched out their hands to the blaze in the great fireplace preserved in the warming room on the east side. The ghost of the nunnery is also evident in the long gallery which Sharington created out of the refectory: in corbels which once supported a timber roof, in a worn section of original floor and in the 'pulpit' niche from which improving works were read at mealtimes.

The Stone Gallery on the site of the dormitory is still much as Sharington left it, furnished with a set of sixteenth-century shell-back painted chairs and with a delicately carved classical chimneypiece by John Chapman, who had also worked for the king. Renaissance features also adorn Sir William's three-storey octagonal tower. A narrow angled passage leads to the high-ceilinged chamber on the first floor where he kept valuables and important papers. This tiny cupboard of a room is almost filled by John Chapman's elaborate octagonal stone table supported

Left: Surrounding a tranquil grassy square at the heart of Lacock Abbey are the glorious cloisters of the Augustinian nunnery that was once here, with traceried openings and fine rib vaulting studded with carved bosses. When William Sharington transformed Lacock into a house, he used much of the existing building but he also added a three-storey octagonal tower, the first floor of which was designed as a strong room. Books and other precious things stored on the shelves and in the recesses would have been studied and admired on the finely-carved stone table which half fills the room, its octagonal top matching the shape of the walls (above).

on the shoulders of four satyrs and carved with the scorpions of the Sharington crest, their vicious tails and matchstick legs also recognisable in Chapman's pendants studding the vaulted ceiling. Here Sharington entertained his guests, Sir John Thynne of Longleat among them.

The newest architectural fashions were again introduced to Lacock in the middle of the eighteenth century, when John Ivory Talbot, a descendant of Sharington's niece, made extensive changes to the house and grounds. Sanderson Miller's Gothick hall, commissioned in 1753, is the first room that visitors see, entered by a prominent double flight of steps on the west front. Decorative niches with pinnacled canopies are filled with terracotta figures by the Austrian sculptor Victor Alexander Sederbach, a mixed company including two nuns, a bishop, a knight and a grisly skeleton dominated by Ela in heroic pose over the fireplace, a bird perching on her outstretched left arm.

In the lovely south gallery hung with family portraits, including a painting of Sir William dressed in black with a long, red beard, a brown indistinct photograph placed by one of the oriel windows shows the bare outlines of the lattice panes. This blurred print was produced from a tiny negative made in 1835 by the pioneer photographer William Henry Fox Talbot, whose work is commemorated in a museum at the abbey gates (*see* p.155).

Only a low wall separates the smoothly mown lawns around the house from the rough grassland of the park, giving the illusion of an uninterrupted green sward stretching away from the abbey. Masses of *Crocus vernus* in early spring are followed by a spectacular display of daffodils and there are several mature specimen trees, including black walnuts, a tulip tree and a swamp cypress.

Lacock Village WILTSHIRE

3 miles south of Chippenham, just east of the A350 [442 F5]

This charming village filled with unspoilt medieval buildings lying at the gates of Lacock Abbey (*see above*) seems to have been blessed with good fortune. Although there were people living here permanently in Saxon times and probably earlier, Lacock first became important in the Middle Ages following the establishment of a planned village for those working the abbey estates in the thirteenth century. Its inhabitants grew rich on the medieval wool industry and the weekly market initiated by Ela, Countess of Salisbury, the founder of the abbey. Lacock was ideally placed for both, being within a day's journey of prime grazing lands on the Cotswolds and Marlborough Downs, a staging-post on the road linking centres of the wool trade in the West Country and having access to the sea via the River Avon, which meanders past to the east. At its height in the late Middle Ages, Lacock's continued prosperity after the decline of the wool trade owed much to its position on a through route between Marlborough and Bristol, which brought wealth to the village and travellers to fill its many inns until the mid-eighteenth century. From then onwards Lacock stood still. Lack of development in the nineteenth century, when many nearby settlements expanded rapidly, was largely due to the Talbot family (*see above*), who ensured no railway lines came near the village. Lacock fossilised, resulting in one of the most pleasing and individual places in England.

The village is laid out around four main streets forming a square, the irregular terraces that line the roads being built on narrow medieval house plots running back from the frontages. Houses dating from the fourteenth to the late eighteenth century include timber-framed buildings with mullioned windows and jettied upper storeys, seventeenth-century stone cottages and elegant Georgian brick mansions, such as the two examples dated 1719 and 1779 in East Street, but recent surveys have shown that many of the apparently later buildings are older than they look and were originally timber-framed. Lichen and moss

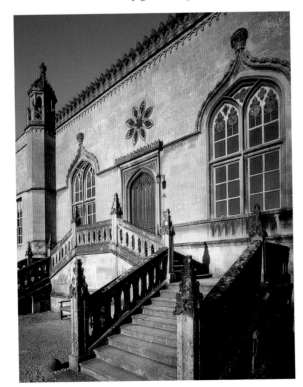

The entrance front, with its rose window, cupolas and cresting, is among a number of Gothick touches that were added to Lacock in the mid-18th century.

encrust stone-slated roofs and gables, and dormers add to the pleasingly varied street façades.

Of the numerous inns, the timber-framed Angel in Church Street retains its medieval layout and the passage through which horses would be led to the yard behind, while the George in West Street has an original dog-powered spit. A magnificent fourteenth-century tithe barn would once have stored rent paid to the abbey in kind: corn, hides and fleeces. Standing slightly apart is the battlemented and pinnacled church of St Cyriac, largely rebuilt when the village was at its most prosperous in the fifteenth century and filled with stone carvings of every kind. It also contains the grandiose Renaissance tomb of Sir William Sharington, who converted the abbey into a private house. A narrow lane leads from the church to the eighteenth-century packhorse bridge over the Bide Brook and beyond to the Avon, crossed by a medieval bridge. (*See also* Fox Talbot Museum, p.155.)

Lady's Well NORTHUMBERLAND

At Holystone, 7 miles west of Rothbury [445 I2]

Lying amid farmland on the western side of the Coquet Valley, just to the north-west of Holystone village, Lady's Well is as simple as can be. A farm track leads up a slight hill to the site, a small wooded area enclosed by a low wall. The entrance is a small porched gateway from which the path runs down the embankment to the rectangular pool, rounded at one end, which lies in the base of the hollow. A stone cross stands in the shallow water, and at the western end there is a weathered statue away from the water's edge. The slopes surrounding the pool are vegetated with broadleaved trees, rhododendrons and holly, providing a secluded corner in an otherwise open farming landscape.

Lake District CUMBRIA

[445 G4–H4]

The dramatic landscapes of the Lake District, with open fells and rocky crags rising steeply from peaceful lakes and green valleys with stone-walled fields, are among the most beautiful and varied in the country. Packed into a compact 30 square miles, this area is also among the most pressured of the national parks, visited by thousands in the summer months. The Trust has a major presence here, with estates that make up about a quarter of the national park and

roughly the same proportion of the Trust's total land holding. Acquired piece by piece over the century or more since the purchase of Brandelhow Park on the shores of Derwentwater in 1902, the Trust's holdings now include England's highest mountain, Scafell Pike, the deepest lake, Wastwater, and over 90 farms.

The Trust's work encompasses protecting lake shores against development, maintaining traditional farming practices and the buildings and landscapes that go with them, and safeguarding historic features and classic views. To the north, just a few miles from tourist-thronged Keswick, Borrowdale runs down 609.5 metres (2,000 feet) from the stark grandeur of Scafell, Glaramara and the fells to the wooded shores of Derwentwater. Almost entirely obscured now are the remains of the graphite workings at Seathwaite which brought the pencil industry to Keswick and wealth to the landowners. In the late seventeenth century the statesmen, or yeoman farmers, of Borrowdale rebuilt their farmhouses which are so good to look at today. By far the greater part of the valley now belongs to the Trust, and virtually all the high ground.

At 977 metres (3,206 feet), Scafell Pike is for the stout walker, but for the less agile the popular route from Seathwaite up Sty Head Gill, past the three tarns – Sty Head Tarn, Sprinkling Tarn below Great End and Angle

Ashness Farm, set below the fells on the east side of Derwentwater. There are spectacular views over the lake from the crags above.

Tarn – and down to Great Langdale is wholly satisfying. Rather less frequented is the delightful path from Stonethwaite up the Langstrath Beck and over the Stake Pass to Great Langdale.

Rain Gauge Cottage at Seathwaite has a good claim to be the wettest house in England, with an average annual rainfall of 317.5 centimetres (125 inches). Below the hamlet the valley drops down to Derwentwater, through a mixture of well-tended fields, whitewashed farmhouses, numerous little woods and old mine workings now grown over, and with the famous Bowder Stone looming over the Jaws of Borrowdale. As in so many places, the Trust has provided footpaths to help walkers avoid cars. Some stay close to the road, others climb away from it, and it is perhaps the middle-height walks which are the most exciting.

To the east, tucked away behind Grange Fell, is the Watendlath Valley, with the two farms of Stepps End and Fold Head and a café making up the hamlet. Here several old packhorse tracks meet: from Keswick, from Thirlmere, from Langdale across Stake Pass, and from Honister via Rosthwaite. A considerable mess when the Trust acquired the farms in the 1960s, the hamlet has now recovered its calm and simplicity.

Two places are particularly good for middle-ground walking. Ashness Farm, running from High Seat down to the lake shore, with the Ashness Woods beside the road from Barrow Beck to Lodore, forms the backdrop to the south-east end of Derwentwater. At Ashness Bridge, half a mile up the Watendlath road from Ashness Gate, is the superb view north to Skiddaw. Another half mile further up the road, the Surprise View suddenly opens on to Borrowdale and to Derwentwater 152.5 metres (500 feet) below. The counterpart height south-west of the lake is beautiful Catbells above Brandelhow, where generations of children searching for Mrs Tiggy-Winkle's home have

been tempted, like Lucy, to drop a pebble down the chimney of the farmhouse at Little Town. Far below is the lake, a long blue finger with four wooded islands, all owned by the Trust, rising like grassy hummocks from the water. St Herbert's Island, out in the middle, is the home of Old Mr Brown, the sinister owl in *The Tale of Squirrel Nutkin*. The northernmost is Derwent Island, the largest of the four, where a sizeable Italianate house, a late eighteenth-century villa extended by Anthony Salvin in the 1840s, is set off by landscaped grounds and fine trees. The few rooms on show include Salvin's dining room and staircase hall, the former with mahogany and oak furniture of the 1850s, the latter hung with English and Dutch paintings. The drawing room, designed to command spectacular views of Derwentwater, illustrates how the beauty of the Lake District, for so long unappreciated, was already beginning to be an attraction in the late eighteenth century.

West from Borrowdale over the Honister Pass, or over the Newlands Pass from Keswick, the Trust either owns or protects some 4,856 hectares (12,000 acres) of the beautiful and vulnerable valley which includes Buttermere, Crummock Water and Loweswater. All three lakes are in Trust ownership as is the whole of Buttermere Commons, four farms, one of which has been brought back to life by the Trust, and pockets of woodland. From the bare rugged heights of the Honister Pass, where the Trust owns only the roadside strips (and can thus prevent road-widening), with protective covenants over Buttermere Fell and Fleetwith Pike on either side, the visitor pauses at Gatesgarth for the superb view over Lake Buttermere, with the great ridge of High Stile and Red Pike to the south providing a dramatic backdrop. Crummock Water lies a mile further down the valley, the great bulk of Brackenthwaite Fell and the 850.5-metre (2,791-foot) summit of Grasmoor rising above it. Completing the picture is little Loweswater, in gentle farming country, with Holme Wood on its far side. In only 8 miles harsh wilderness has become pastoral beauty.

South over the craggy ridge rising to Red Pike is the remote Ennerdale Valley, where, after the massive felling of mature woodland during the First World War, the Forestry Commission sought to restore the national stock of timber. In 1925 it bought most of the valley, from Ennerdale Water up to Great Gable, and filled every corner that was plantable with Sitka spruce, a species which was dark, impenetrable and utterly alien to these hills. After an outcry led by the Council for the Protection of Rural England and the Friends of the Lake District, the Commission reluctantly agreed not to afforest the central

300 square miles of the Lake District. The Trust took a 500-year lease of plantable land at the valley head, and of the unplantable tops and screes from Great Gable to High Stile on the north, and from Great Gable to Haycock on the south. The Commission's planting was thus boxed in, but it was the warning note sounded by the amenity societies which saved the central Lake District from blanket forestry.

Later the Trust acquired the farms of How Hall, Howside and Beckfoot at the west end of the lake, Mireside on the north bank, and most of the south shore, including The Side and Angler's Crag, running up to the wild and remote tracts of Kinniside Common and Stockdale Moor.

Similarly off the beaten track, and accessed by minor roads, is neighbouring Wasdale to the south. This little valley, only 4 miles long, has the deepest lake in England and a stark and dramatic beauty – a 'horrid' place in the eighteenth-century sense. Great screes plunge down to the water's edge on the south side of Wastwater and high peaks form a majestic horseshoe round the head of the dale. Towering over all is Scafell Pike, the highest point in England at 977 metres (3,206 feet).

The Trust acquired the farms of Wasdale Head Hall, Middle Row, Row Head and later Burnthwaite under Kirk Fell at a time when forestry syndicates, formed to take advantage of tax concessions, were actively seeking land for planting. It was of the utmost importance to keep the farms and their great sheepwalks – High Fell, Eskdale Fell, the head of Mosedale, the south side of Pillar to the Black Sail Pass and Yewbarrow running down to the head of the lake – clear of blanket forestry.

By 1979 the Trust had acquired virtually the whole of Upper Wasdale, and none too soon, for a new threat was at hand. British Nuclear Fuels Ltd, needing more water for their works at Sellafield, sought to take it from Wastwater by building a massive weir which would facilitate the raising or lowering of the level of the lake at will. At the same time similar proposals were made for Ennerdale Water by the North West Water Authority. A great battle ensued and the trump card turned out to be the Trust's statement that, even if planning consent were granted, it would rely on its legal right to ask Parliament to protect its inalienable land as a matter of national importance. The battle was won and the beauty of Wasdale was preserved.

Across the Lake District, on the eastern side of the Trust's empire, are important holdings around Ullswater and running south along the A592 that leads to Windermere and Ambleside.

In 1911, because of the threat of building development, the Trust's first acquisition in this area was Gowbarrow Park on the west bank of Ullswater, a medieval deer-park with the waterfall of Aira Force which had long attracted visitors. Glencoyne Wood, fine oak woodland to the south, was added in 1928, and twenty years later the magnificent gift of Glencoyne Park joined the two together so that the Trust now owns the whole of the south-western quarter of the shores of Ullswater. Glencoyne is one of the Trust's largest sheep farms, running up its own valley to Hartside at 756 metres (2,481 feet) on the north, and on the south along the Glenridding Screes to Raise at 880.5 metres (2,889 feet). This high ground is part of the Helvellyn ridge between Thirlmere and Ullswater, the Glencoyne Beck being the boundary between Cumberland and Westmorland. In 1984 Matterdale and Watermillock Commons were added, making over 2,832.5 hectares (7,000 acres) of particular beauty, with thickly wooded slopes above the lake thinning out to open fells on the heights. To the south, above the village of Patterdale and the narrow valley leading to the Kirkstone Pass, is the 69-hectare (170.5-acre) Glenamara Park. A sixteenth-century deer-park, Glenamara is still ringed by substantial deer walls and is dotted with ancient trees. Above it rises St Sunday Crag, with fine views over Ullswater from the popular route to the summit which skirts the park.

Snaking down the valley below is the A592, which bypasses the village of Hartsop and the 691 hectares

(1,708 acres) of Grove Farm, which runs up into the Hayswater and Pasture Beck valleys as it climbs to the Kirkstone Pass. The farm of Hartsop Hall, which includes the delightful small lake of Brotherswater, and the adjoining farm of Caudale Beck border the road on both sides, and as it ascends it is squeezed between the 631.5-metre (2,072-foot) summit of Hart Crag to the east and the 642-metre (2,106- foot) Middle Dodd to the west. On the other side of the pass, the A592 runs down into the Troutbeck Valley where is one of the most famous farms in the Lake District, the 809.5-hectare (2,000-acre) Troutbeck Park, left to the Trust by Beatrix Potter in 1943, and standing mercifully clear of the hurly-burly of Ambleside, Windermere and Bowness. The Trust owns other fine farms here: The Howe, Long Green Head, Stonethwaite and Townend (*see* p.389).

In the southern lakes, the Trust has substantial holdings in the more open country flanking Lake Windermere and runs up the valleys leading to the central fells.

Windermere is the largest of the lakes, stretching for 10 miles from Ambleside to Newby Bridge. It is also the most accessible, and was reached by rail in 1847 when the line from Oxenholme, near Kendal, was extended to Birthwaite and the town of Windermere sprang up there. Wordsworth was horrified when substantial villas, the summer homes of Manchester businessmen, suddenly appeared on the east shore: 'Persons of pure taste throughout the island, by their oft-repeated visits to the lakes, testify they deem the district as a sort of national property, in which every man has a right and interest who has an eye to perceive and a heart to enjoy.' It took another 50 years before his views began to be heeded, and the Trust's early efforts were not at Windermere but at wholly unspoilt Derwentwater and Ullswater.

The Trust's first purchase in the valley, in 1913, was on the east shore at Queen Adelaide's Hill, west of the town of Windermere, and even today it owns little of the east side of the lake, where development still proceeds. Nevertheless, acquisitions have been made over the years, and some of the viewpoints, such as Jenkin Crag, Post Knott, Cockshott Point and the Trust's country park at Fell Foot, provide magnificent panoramas across the lake to the Langdale Pikes and Coniston Fells. Below Jenkin Crag, half a mile south of Ambleside on the A591, is Stagshaw Garden. Created by the late Tubby Acland, former Regional Agent for the Trust, this steep wooded site is planted with a collection of rhododendrons, azaleas, camellias and other shrubs. Paths through the adjacent Skelghyll Woods lead on to the fells above.

On the west side the entire shore has been acquired, from Bee Holme and Wray Castle near the head of the lake down to the ferry which crosses over to Bowness. Mostly covered by the extensive Claife woodlands, this is a secluded, unspoilt shoreline accessed by a network of paths and with the Trust's first basecamp for volunteers at Low Wray. Prominent on the hill above the ferry crossing is the castellated Claife Station, dating from 1799 and much visited in Victorian times for its magnificent views over the lake.

Wild Wasdale, with scree slopes rising dramatically from the lake.

At the head of the lake, dales lead north and west into the high fells. Beyond Ambleside, and followed by the A591, is the tranquil valley of the River Rothay, which runs past Rydal Water and Grasmere. The Trust has considerable property here, much of it acquired in the early days. There are miles of gentle walking country, with views across to the high tops, small lakes and tarns and a number of fascinating old houses. Buildings and countryside have associations with such literary names as the Wordsworths, Coleridge, de Quincey, and at Hawkshead and Sawrey with Beatrix Potter (Mrs William Heelis), greatest of all the Trust's benefactors in the Lakes (*see* pp.21, 231 and 233).

A few miles west of Ambleside, in the heart of the Lake District and overlooked by the majestic Langdale Pikes, is the wilder country of the Langdale valleys. This is an ancient landscape which includes a Viking site, a thirteenth-century stone wall at the head of Great Langdale, and slate farmhouses with bank barns dating from the seventeenth and eighteenth centuries. Little

Langdale to the south is smaller and gentler, with isolated tarns, meadows and patches of woodland. Most of the valley is easily accessible on foot or by bicycle, and it is good walking country; the valley road, a scenic link to the west coast over the Wrynose and Hardknott passes, is also attractive but can be very congested in high season. The Trust owns much of the valley, including three of the four remaining farms and Little Langdale Tarn, given in 1985 by the invaluable Friends of the Lake District to mark their 50th birthday.

Heading west beyond the tarn the road forks: to the left it leads up to Wrynose Pass; to the right it runs up to Blea Tarn on the saddle between the two valleys, and then plunges down into Great Langdale, where there is a classic view of the great semicircle of rock and fell. To the left are Pike o'Blisco, Crinkle Crags, Bow Fell and The Band; across the valley, the beetling Langdale Pikes. The valley rises steeply to the surrounding fells from a wide, ice-scoured floor at the foot of the Pikes and the farms here –

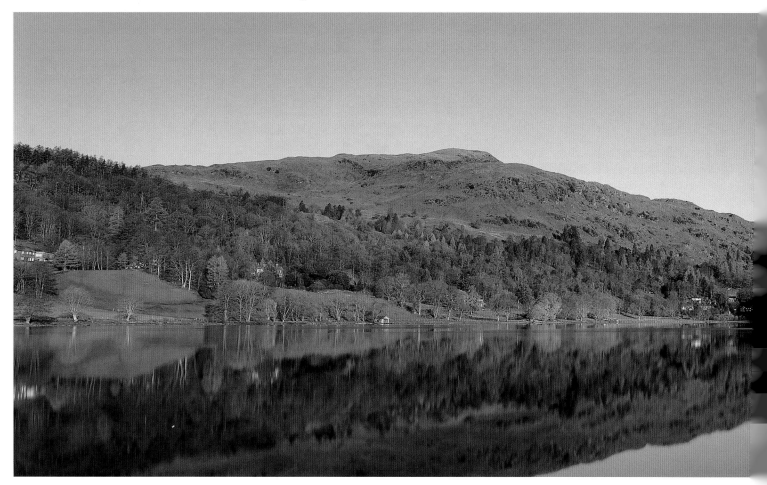

Stool End, Wall End, Harry Place, Millbeek, Middlefell Place and Robinson Place – are larger than those in Little Langdale, their fields divided by well-maintained dry-stone walls. A careful eye will notice much unobtrusive National Trust care: new farm buildings nestling by the old, a screened camping site, eroded tracks repaired. The pressure of visitors here is very great, as this is the principal approach to the most popular walks and climbs.

At the foot of Great Langdale, between Elterwater and Loughrigg Fell, is something very different. The High Close estate comprises a large house, now a youth hostel, one farm, a dozen cottages and the delightful Loughrigg Tarn below the fell. It is perfect territory for family exploration: up and down country which rises to no great height, beautifully wooded, and well provided with paths.

Over the Wrynose Pass from Little Langdale are the isolated Eskdale and Duddon valleys running west and south-west to the coast, the Duddon to a great estuary where the Trust acquired the dune and marsh reserve of Sandscale Haws in 1984. The Duddon Valley is a very special place indeed and has retained its beauty primarily because of the work of one man. The Rev. H.H. Symonds helped to found the Friends of the Lake District in 1934 and was its Secretary until his death in 1950. Over a period he bought five farms in the valley, carefully chosen for their key positions: Browside and Thrang on the left bank above Seathwaite, and on the right, above Ulpha, Brighouse, Pike Side and Hazel Head, the last being on both sides of the beautiful road running over Birker Moor to Eskdale. In buying them himself, and because of his formidable reputation as a conservationist, he was able single-handedly to frighten off public authorities who wanted to make reservoirs and build power stations in the valley. Like Beatrix Potter seven years before, on his death he left his beloved farms to the Trust.

The Hardknott Pass, which links the valleys, runs through the Trust's farms of Black Hall in the Duddon Valley and Butterilket in Eskdale. A great battle had to be

Gondola, the Trust's elegant steam yacht, on a trip down Coniston Water, with the distinctive cone of the Old Man of Coniston rising up behind.

fought in the 1930s to keep out the Forestry Commission, which had already bought land for planting (which it proposed to transform into the Hardknott Forest Park) and only reluctantly held its fire. It took 30 years before the Commission was persuaded to sell its land to the Trust which, with other gifts and purchases, now owns all the valley head from the river's source at Eskhause to the farm of Penny Hill opposite the Woolpack Inn in Eskdale. This vast area includes the 902-metre (2,960-foot) summit of Bow Fell, and from Crinkle Crags to Pike o'Blisco and Three Shires Stone on Wrynose Pass, including Wrynose Bottom, Mosedale and Hardknott Pass. North of the village of Boot, the Trust's land runs up Hardrigg Gill, over the shoulder of Eskdale Fell and then up to the Scafell massif. The valley head of the River Duddon has been secured by these manoeuvres, and by the gift in 1929 of Cockley Beck and Dale Head farms.

This area of the Lake District is rich in history as well as natural beauty. A medieval wall is a survival of the extensive monastic sheep walks which fed the wealth of Furness and Fountains abbeys, a Roman military road ran through Eskdale, from Ravenglass to Ambleside, and the Ravenglass and Eskdale railway, now a tourist attraction, was opened in 1875 to ship out iron ore.

East of the Duddon Valley, across the ridge that rises to the Old Man of Coniston, is the Coniston Valley, a serene landscape with grassy meadows and beech and oak woods sweeping gently up from the shores of the lake. Island-studded Coniston Water is *Swallows and Amazons* country, with many tiny creeks and bays for the little boats which powerfully evoke childhood dreams. From Coniston Pier at the head of the lake, the Trust runs cruises in the 25.5-metre (84-foot) *Gondola*. An elegant steam yacht dating from the mid-nineteenth century, when the company which constructed the first rail link to the valley operated it as an added attraction, *Gondola* was rebuilt by the Trust to original designs. With room for over 80 passengers, it has opulent Victorian saloons fitted out with plush red seats and steam heating, and the long black hull carries a gilded serpent at the prow.

On the east shore of the lake the Trust owns two substantial outposts: Park-a-Moor Fell, enclosed as a sheep run by Furness Abbey in 1339, the woods along the water's edge planted much later, and Nibthwaite Woods to the south, with the tiny Peel and Fir Islands offshore, the latter marked by magnificent stands of Scots pine. The oak woods, so peaceful now, and supporting a wide range of mosses and lichens, were busy places until this century, playing their part in local industry. Coppiced at regular intervals, they provided not only wood for fuel but bark for tanning leather and charcoal for smelting iron ore.

On the west bank, the Old Man of Coniston stretching away upward in the background, stands Coniston Hall, with a mile of lake shore. The Elizabethan farmhouse, with traditional Westmorland cylindrical chimneys, is but a fragment of a mansion built by the Fleming family, who moved to greater grandeur at Rydal a century later. Its attractive park-like meadows were disfigured by a large camping and caravanning site when the Trust acquired the farm in 1971. The tents and caravans are now hidden in Park Coppice Wood close by.

At the head of the lake is the glorious Monk Coniston estate. Partly bequeathed to the Trust by Beatrix Potter, it comprises 1,618.5 hectares (4,000 acres) of farmland, woodland and fell on a more intimate scale than many of the Trust's holdings. Although the Tilberthwaite Fells run up 762.5 metres (2,502 feet) to Wetherlam, north of the Old Man, the estate includes Yewdale, the south side of Little Langdale, excellent woodland, gentle walks and the beautiful honeypot of Tarn Hows. This artificial lake, made and planted in the nineteenth century to enhance the landscape, has become the most-visited spot in the Lake District. It is a place for picnics and gentle strolls. Heathery mounds, stretches of short turf and a light scattering of trees make it a perfect setting for a family outing.

Lamb House EAST SUSSEX

In West Street, Rye, facing west end of church [443 K6]

In 1726 a fearful storm drove the ship carrying George I from Hanover to England ashore on the sands fringing the estuary of the River Rother 2 miles from Rye. James Lamb, mayor of the prosperous little town, escorted the king to his house where he entertained him for three days, apparently taking in his stride the fact that his wife gave birth to a son on the first night and that the king's lack of English was fully matched by his own ignorance of German. The modest brick-fronted house which bears this exceptional man's name, one of the many delightful buildings lining Rye's cobbled streets, had been completed just two years earlier.

Some 200 years later the house was connected with another outstanding character, in this case the American novelist and critic Henry James, who bought it for £2,000 in 1900. Already in late middle age and well established in both Europe and America, James was to reach the height of his powers here. It was at Rye that he wrote his three greatest novels, *The Ambassadors*, *The Wings of the Dove* and *The Golden Bowl*, dictating them in a sonorous voice to his secretary in a garden pavilion in the summer and in a small, sunny study in winter. Here, too, he entertained a stream of other established figures, including H.G. Wells, Ford Maddox Ford, Rudyard Kipling, Max Beerbohm and Edith Wharton.

Remarkably, after James's death in 1916, Lamb House became the home of three other novelists, the brothers A.C. and E.F. Benson, and later Rumer Godden. They too found the tranquil atmosphere conducive, with the neighbourhood and society of Rye clearly inspiring E.F. Benson's *Lucia and Mapp* novels. The books now shown in the morning room are a more tangible memento of Henry James.

The tiny, ¾-acre walled garden, much loved by those who have lived here, contains a rich variety of plants, including a sweet gum on the central lawn, roses of many varieties and a trumpet creeper on a sunny wall.

Lanhydrock House CORNWALL

2½ miles south-east of Bodmin, overlooking valley of River Fowey [442 B7]

Lanhydrock is lost in a long Victorian afternoon. No one is at work in the cool, tiled dairy, or in the huge stone-flagged kitchen, and buckets and brushes are lined up in the housemaids' closet ready for the next day. No sound comes from the extensive servants' quarters, where a pair of black boots stands neatly by a bed and the footman's livery lies ready to wear, while in the nursery wing all is still. Pipes lie waiting in the masculine confines of the smoking room and the dining-room table is laid for ten, the menu already handwritten in French. The period feeling is so strong that it would be no surprise to meet a scurrying maid with a tray or to hear the Robartes family and their guests, or their nine children, coming in from the garden.

Lanhydrock's interiors vividly evoke gracious living in the 1890s. The house itself was largely rebuilt at the end of the nineteenth century after a disastrous fire in 1881, the designs by the London-trained local architect Richard Coad incorporating the latest comforts and conveniences, such as the massive radiators featured in almost every room, and also a full range of service rooms. The well-equipped kitchen area includes steam jets for scouring greasy pots in the scullery and a dairy cooled by spring water from the hill above the house, which is chanelled

along runnels in the slate and marble slabs where jellies and custards were stood. At the same time Coad's exterior faithfully reflects the old-fashioned house built by Sir Richard Robartes and his son between 1630 and 1642, merging beautifully with the one wing which was not consumed in the flames. With their battlemented silver-grey granite walls and mullioned windows, Lanhydrock's three ranges set round a courtyard seem typical of the conservatism of mid-seventeenth-century Cornwall. An enchanting detached gatehouse still stands at the head of a beech and sycamore avenue leading away across the park as it has done since the seventeenth century, and obelisks crowning this little architectural conceit are echoed by more on the main building and on the low wall enclosing formal gardens around the house.

Only the north wing, which survived the fire, gives a flavour of the original interiors. A sunny 35.5-metre (116-foot) gallery running the length of the second floor and lit by windows on either side suggests what might have been lost. The barrel ceiling arching overhead is covered with magical plasterwork dating from just before the outbreak of the Civil War. Although the 24 panels illustrating incidents from the Old Testament take centre stage, the delightful creatures surrounding them are far more memorable, furry porcupines, bears, armadillos and peacocks rubbing shoulders with mythical beasts, such as dragons and centaurs.

Like Coad's interiors, Lanhydrock's nineteenth-century garden is a mirror to Victorian taste. In front of the house clipped yew marks the corners of six geometric shapes planted with roses in George Gilbert Scott's formal

Top: Lanhydrock's enchanting 17th-century gatehouse and the main house behind appear all of a piece, but most of the house was rebuilt in the late 19th century after a disastrous fire. Above: Victorian interiors include up-to-the-minute comforts and conveniences and a full range of service rooms, among them the kitchen. The copper *batterie de cuisine* hanging above the range was very much for best cooking; iron pots in the scullery were used for vegetables and preparation.

layout of 1857 and more yew studs his intricate parterre beside the north wing, bedded out twice a year. Beyond the obelisks and castellations of the surrounding parapet, a large informal garden dating from the 1860s covers the steep slopes rising above the house. Winding paths through shrubs and trees, including exceptional displays of large Himalayan magnolias, rhododendrons and camellias, lead ever upwards, past the well used by the monks of St Petroc's Priory at Bodmin, who held Lanhydrock before the Dissolution, and the strong spring feeding the stream which runs down the slope, its course marked by a strip of primulas, astilbes, arums, rodgersias and other water-loving plants. A long flowering season from early spring to July is extended into October in the herbaceous circle, where there is spectacular coloured foliage in autumn.

Vistas over the house and the wooded valley of the River Fowey culminate in magnificent views from the broad terrace walk at the top of the garden. From here the gatehouse appears set against the valley of the Fowey, with Bodmin Moor behind. More extensive walks follow the network of paths crossing the 900-acre estate, a mix of park and woodland running down to the Fowey. Patches of bird-rich ancient woodland looking over the river are within the medieval deer-park that surrounds the house.

Lanyon Quoit CORNWALL

4 miles north-west of Penzance, via the B3312 [442 A8]

Lanyon Quoit stands on an open stretch of moorland in the far west of Cornwall like a giant's three-legged stool, with a trio of granite uprights supporting a fourth huge slab 5.5 metres (18 feet) across. The remains of a Neolithic chambered tomb dating from *c*.3500BC, the boulders were reconstructed in 1824 after collapsing a few years earlier and their original form has been lost. The chamber was probably built as a rectangular box and was designed to be seen, with the huge capstone protruding from any covering mound and possibly serving as a territorial marker.

Larkton and Bickerton Hills CHESHIRE

4 miles north of Malpas, 12 miles south-east of Chester, east of the A41 Whitchurch road [445 H8]

The Peckforton Hills rise from the Cheshire plain rather like Alderley Edge (*see* p.19). At their southern tip, the 113.5 hectares (280 acres) of Bickerton and Larkton Hills,

with the Iron Age earthwork of Maiden Castle on one flank, are an attractive mixture of heath, woodland and little fields. This is a good place for a walk, with a network of paths and spectacular views from the long-distance Sandstone Trail following the scarp of the hills.

Lavenham: The Guildhall of Corpus Christi SUFFOLK

Market Place, Lavenham [443 K3]

The medieval town of Lavenham, with streets of crooked half-timbered houses and a glorious late fifteenth-century church, is a monument to the prosperity brought by the Suffolk cloth industry, at its height in the fifteenth and early sixteenth centuries. Apart from the church, one of the finest buildings is the guildhall, prominently sited in the little market square. Traditional timber-framing, its exuberant carving now heavily weathered, is limewashed to a pleasing silvery-grey, the upper floor is jettied out over the lower and both are lit with oriel windows. An ornate two-storey porch projects into the square and the building as a whole rests on a brick plinth, which deepens over the cellar as the ground slopes away behind.

The hall was built in about 1510 by the Guild of Corpus Christi, one of four religious and social guilds in the town. Less than twenty years later, when Henry VIII turned against the Roman Catholic Church, the guild was dissolved, and the guildhall was subsequently used as a town hall, prison and workhouse before being restored in 1887. The former meeting rooms of the guild, with moulded ceiling timbers and an ancient oak floor, are on the ground floor. The warren of small rooms above (probably let as storage to cloth merchants) now houses a local history museum. Mostly devoted to the cloth industry which made Lavenham so rich, displays here include, for example, the range of colours – from pale blue to black – which can be obtained from woad and a model of the tenter frames on which cloth was stretched to dry. The most unusual exhibit is a mummified cat, found in the roof where it had been placed to ward off evil spirits. Despite the guild's close association with the Church and its prominence in the great annual procession on the Feast of Corpus Christi, heavenly protection was clearly considered insufficient.

At the back is a walled garden with dye plants used in the production of medieval cloth. There is also a restored nineteenth-century lock-up and mortuary and a Newsham fire engine, thought to be the oldest in East Anglia.

Lanyon Quoit, set prominently on a stretch of open moorland, may have been a ceremonial tomb for the local community in prehistoric times.

Lawrence House CORNWALL

9 Castle Street, Launceston [442 C7]

This modest Georgian brick house in the shadow of the remains of Launceston's great Norman castle was built in 1753 by the wealthy local lawyer Humphrey Lawrence and is typical of houses of the period seen in small country towns throughout England. Once the home of Caroline Pearse, a prolific Victorian author, it is now leased to the Town Council as a local museum and civic centre.

Leigh Woods SOMERSET

On left bank of the Avon, by Clifton Suspension Bridge, north-east of the A369 [442 E5]

Few people nowadays approach the city of Bristol as our ancestors did, up the River Avon from the Bristol Channel, but the motorist can enjoy the same dramatic view of the Trust's Leigh Woods, leased to English Nature, by leaving the M5 at junction 18 and following the A4 as it snakes along beside the river towards the old docks. The road swings round a bend to reveal one of Brunel's greatest works, the Clifton Suspension Bridge, poised 76 metres (250 feet) above the river. On the far bank, to the west, the woods plunge steeply down the limestone escarpment, framing the bridge. The woods formed part of the estate of Ashton Court, now the property of the city, and are the remains of a semi-natural forest of great age, with wych elm, ash, oak, small-leaved lime and two species of whitebeam that grow only here. There are plenty of footpaths and the Nightingale Valley provides a less steep approach from the riverside walk.

Leith Hill Tower and Rhododendron Wood SURREY

1 mile south-west of Coldharbour, on the A29 and B2126 roads [443 I5]

This battlemented Gothic folly rises from a sea of heather and bilberries clothing the highest point in south-east England. The monkey puzzles and Scots pine which until recently also crowned the sandstone ridge were decimated by the storms of 1987 and 1990, opening up magnificent views over the wooded landscape of the Weald to the South Downs and glimpses of the Channel beyond. First built by Richard Hull of Leith Hill Place in 1766, as a tablet over the door records, the tower was subsequently

heightened and now rises to 313.5 metres (1,029 feet) above sea level. Over 1,000 years ago, in 851, this strategic site was secured by a Saxon army under cover of darkness, giving them the advantage in a great battle with Danish forces who had camped across the valley on Anstiebury Hill.

The slopes of the hill are wooded, with some ancient stands of oak and hazel among much replanting. On the southern slopes, just above Leith Hill Place, the childhood home of Ralph Vaughan Williams, is the rhododendron wood planted by Josiah Wedgwood, grandson of the famous potter. The collection of rhododendrons, which includes an enormous clump of *Rhododendron falconeri*, *R. arboreum*, *R. edgeworthii* and many early-flowering species and hybrids, survived the great storms but the sheltering oaks and conifers were severely depleted. Numerous azaleas and *Magnolia obovata* are among other flowering shrubs planted here.

Leith Hill, the highest point in south-east England, is crowned by a delightful castellated folly. The hill's wooded slopes attract birds such as the nuthatch and wood warbler, and the white admiral butterfly may also be seen here.

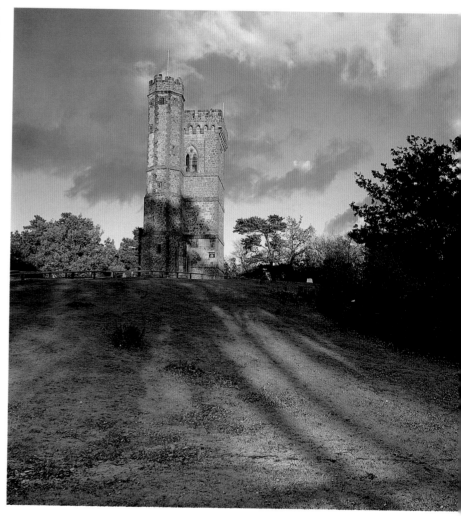

Using Local Materials

Until recent times, people drew on what was around them for the materials of everyday life. Buildings great and small were literally rooted in the landscape, reflecting the colours and textures of soil and rock. Because of its varied geology, with transitions from one rock type to another over quite short distances, Britain has a particularly rich legacy of building types, with local practice adding an additional gloss to regional variation. The major contrast is between the stone-rich and geologically older north and west and the stone-poor and younger east and south. Stone is king, for example, in the grey granite country of the south-west, among the dry-stone walls and field barns of the Pennines and Lake District, and in the seductive villages strung along the belt of limestone which arcs across England from Dorset to Yorkshire, the colour of the stone sometimes creamy white, sometimes tinged with iron to a warm brown or honey. Where building stone was scarce, or where there was a plentiful supply of suitable timber, people used the materials of fields and woods. The beech hangers of the Chilterns and oaks of the Weald were the raw material for the many enticing half-timbered houses which survive in these areas, and in the oak-rich Welsh borders timber framing was employed into the eighteenth century, long after it had been abandoned in the rest of the country because of shortage of wood. Poverty meant cottagers everywhere built their homes of mud mixed with straw, sand or gravel, thatching them with reed, straw or heather. Brick was used for important buildings from the late Middle Ages onwards, but rarely for cottages until the eighteenth century.

The red sandstone Powis Castle in Powys, built of the same rock as the outcrop on which it stands, overlooks the valley of the infant Severn in the Border country of Wales. Formed of the cemented sands of an ancient desert, sandstone is coarse-grained and crumbly, lending itself to bold and blocky treatment, as here. Over the centuries the outlines of the originally Medieval keep have been made less forbidding, and the rock below softened with garden terraces.

POWIS CASTLE
314

Slate is everywhere in Cornwall, used for stiles, walls, floors as well as roofs and, as here, to give added protection against the salty air and driving damp of this peninsula. This five-sided building, known as the Birdcage, is in the fishing village of Port Isaac, just a couple of miles down the north coast from the slate quarries of Delabole.

Cornwall is a grey county, with traditional buildings and field walls of lichen-spotted granite and slate. Hard, compact and crystalline, granite is an uncompromising and difficult stone to work, but it weathers pleasingly, and is very durable. At Lanhydrock, in the wooded valley of the Fowey, it was used both for the two-storey Jacobean gatehouse, crowned with stumpy obelisks, and the main house. When this was largely rebuilt in the late 19th century, after a disastrous fire, the architect Richard Coad, in tune with a period sensitivity to local traditions, used granite from an adjoining parish and slate from the still-operating quarry at Delabole, near the north coast.

The pastoral landscape of Upper Wharfedale is in the Yorkshire Dales where the Trust has an estate in the valley of the River Wharfe. This is limestone country, with stone-built farms and bridges, and a patchwork of fields edged with dry-stone walls.

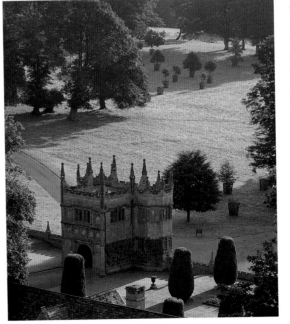

LANHYDROCK
219

Many fields still have their barns, as big as houses, which were used to shelter cattle and their fodder over the winter. The great abbeys, Fountains among them, started sheep farming in the dales, but the pattern of fields here largely dates from 18th- and 19th-century enclosure.

Although it has a granite core, Devon is generally softer, more rounded and more fertile than Cornwall. Cottages here have traditionally been of cob and thatch, using the materials – mud, straw, sand and gravel – that were to hand. The whitewashed example below, with delightful eyebrow dormers, is on the Killerton estate near Exeter.

The limestone plateau of the Cotswolds, dropping gently eastwards from the scarp overlooking the Severn Valley, is a country of stone-built villages and barns and of fields edged

UPPER WHARFEDALE
408

CHASTLETON HOUSE
83

KILLERTON
202

PAYCOCKE'S
293

with dry-stone walls. The Jacobean Chastleton House, tucked away in north Oxfordshire, is built of warm, iron-rich stone from the nearby Hornton quarry, now freckled and spotted with lichen. Like all limestones, it catches every change of light, and it is a stone which can be cut and carved to give crisp finishes and fine detail, such as the carved obelisks and crest above the main entrance and the string courses above the windows.

Ightham Mote lies in a deep, wooded cleft of the Kentish Weald, one of the geologically youngest parts of England and lacking in good building stone. Typically, this moated courtyard house, from the 14th century, is built partly of ragstone, a brittle form of limestone, and partly half-timbered, reflecting the dense oak forests which blanketed the region into the late Middle Ages. The decorative brick chimneys were 17th-century improvements.

East Anglia is distinctive. Formed of geologically-recent deposits, with

rich farmland reclaimed from former marsh and fen, it is a region of wide horizons and huge skies, with little in the way of building stone, while almost every village has a rich legacy of buildings financed by the medieval cloth trade. While stone was obtained for the great wool churches, prosperous clothiers used local oak with wattle and daub infilling to build substantial half-timbered houses, thatching them with reed from the fens, or straw from the fields. Thomas Paycocke, leading clothier of Coggeshall in Essex, finished his house by 1505. Although much restored in

the early 20th century, and now with a tiled roof, Paycocke's still has many original features, including the over-hanging second storey and the carved decorative frieze. Much of the brick nogging is also original and reflects another corner of this area's history. The art of brick-making, lost after the Romans left, was probably first re-introduced in East Anglia in medieval times through close contacts with the Low Countries.

IGHTHAM MOTE
197

Letocetum STAFFORDSHIRE

In Wall, 2 miles south-west of Lichfield, on north side of the A5 [443 G2]

The little Romano-British town of Letocetum grew up round a posting station on Watling Street, the main imperial route to Chester and North Wales, becoming sufficiently important to be included in a list of the 28 cities of Britain produced by Nennius in the eighth century. Of the remains visible at Wall, the communal bathhouse is the most complete example of its kind in Britain, the extensive facilities on offer showing a full appreciation of the good life. The Roman equivalents of a Turkish bath and a sauna were part of a suite which also included cold baths, an undressing room and an exercise hall. Here the men of the community and tired imperial messengers journeying along Watling Street would spend long, indulgent afternoons (the women were allowed to bathe only in the mornings), with slaves on hand to massage scented oils into their bodies.

A courtyard building nearby, destroyed by fire in 160–170, was probably an inn. Finds from these excavations and from another Roman site, at Shenstone, a short distance to the south-east, are exhibited in a small museum.

Lindisfarne Castle NORTHUMBERLAND

On Holy Island, 6 miles east of the A1, across causeway [445 I1]

Lindisfarne's stark outline rises from the dolerite crag on which it is built as if it were part of the rock itself. The castle is accessible only by the causeway to Holy Island which is submerged for several hours at high tide; a visit here still feels like an adventure into the unknown. A cobbled approach curves steeply up the face of the crag to the entrance high above, a precipitous drop on one side, a cliff-like stone wall on the other. With spectacular views south to Bamburgh Castle and east over the water to the Farne Islands (*see* p.146), this is an entrancingly romantic place, even when lashed by the gales that come sweeping in from the North Sea.

Created in 1903 by the young Edwin Lutyens out of the shell of an originally Tudor fort, Lindisfarne's small rooms look backwards rather than forwards, with Norman-style pillars, huge fireplaces, deeply recessed mullioned windows and rounded stone arches. Varied materials and floor levels characteristic of Lutyens add to a very individual charm. Herringbone brick floors are juxtaposed with stone and timber. Some rooms are austerely whitewashed, others left bare, such as the dark drawing room in the bowels of the building where massively thick vaults arching overhead once protected the castle's magazine. With the exception of the kitchen, where a high-backed settle and armchairs are grouped round the leaded range, none of the rooms could be described as cosy, although carved English and Flemish oak furniture, blue and white delftware and richly coloured carpets give a feel of seventeenth-century Dutch interiors.

The old fort would probably have been left to quiet decay if Edward Hudson, the founder of *Country Life*, had not happened upon it on a visit to the island and employed Lutyens to turn it into a summer retreat. He was a hospitable man who loved to entertain; a cello and music stand in the long upper gallery recall the many house parties he hosted at the castle, when the celebrated cellist Madame Suggia used to play for her fellow guests.

The castle's enchanting little walled garden, designed by Gertrude Jekyll on a south-facing slope to the north of the crag, is easily overlooked. Sheltered from the worst of the weather, it is a mass of purple, grey, pink and burnt-orange in high summer, a faithful re-creation of Miss Jekyll's original planting scheme.

Little Clarendon WILTSHIRE

In Dinton, ½ mile east of church, close to post office [442 F6]

Stone built, with a projecting porch, mullioned windows and a stone-tiled roof, Little Clarendon dates back to the late fifteenth century, when it was built for a family of some local importance. There were alterations in the seventeenth century, and then, in the late nineteenth century, it was

Below: The timber framing of Little Moreton Hall, with square panels holding a variety of patterns, is one of the most exuberant examples of the virtuoso decorative effects developed in Lancashire and Cheshire. Right: At the top of the house, running the length of the south range, is the atmospheric long gallery, its oak timbers twisted and warped out of shape by the weight of the stone-tiled roof and the lack of an adequate supporting framework. In the 1580s, when it was built, it was used for exercise and games and was largely unfurnished, as it is today.

divided into two, probably to house local farm labourers. In a state of decay, and with many of its original features obscured, the house was rescued by the Reverend George Engleheart and his wife Mary, who bought the property in 1901 and set about reopening blocked fireplaces, taking down room partitions, re-exposing beamed ceilings and generally restoring it. A brick-built cart shed close by was converted into a little Roman Catholic chapel and George Engleheart, who was fascinated by daffodils, experimented with new strains of narcissi here, raising them in greenhouses and long numbered beds separated by grassy walks.

The three rooms on show, hall, dining room and parlour, are crammed with the Englehearts' collection of oak furniture, in particular a fine array of corner cupboards. The greenhouses and daffodil field have gone, but in spring the pretty triangle of grass behind the house, viewable from the footpath beside the garden wall, is covered with the Reverend Engleheart's narcissi hybrids, and more of his daffodils flower along the woodland walk to the north.

Little Moreton Hall CHESHIRE

4 miles south-west of Congleton, on east side of the A34
[445 l8]

The prosperous Moretons of Little Moreton Hall were gentleman farmers, profiting like many others from the opportunities to acquire land following the Black Death and the Dissolution of the Monasteries. Their timber-framed, moated manor house was begun in the mid-fifteenth century and was extended and modernised as the family grew richer, doubling the size of their estates between then and c.1580. Most striking is the south wing,

built in the 1560s. This was intended to be two storeys high, but, before it was completed, a long gallery was added on top. It is this that has given the house its curiously top-heavy appearance, like a stranded Noah's Ark, and has pulled the supporting timbers out of shape, so that the building lurches drunkenly. A charming projecting gatehouse links the range to the bridge over the moat.

Apart from three pieces, all the original furniture has disappeared and rooms are shown unfurnished. As a result nothing distracts from the remarkable building. Built in an age when wood was plentiful and half-timbered houses common in the West Midlands and Welsh Marches, Little Moreton Hall is still exceptional. It seems to have been devised to display the full range of the joiner's and carpenter's art, with timbers arranged in a huge variety of patterns to glorious effect. The confidence and pride of the carpenter who carried out work in 1559 is proclaimed in the inscription he left on one of the prominent bay windows built for William Moreton II: 'Rycharde Dale Carpeder made thies windovs by the grac of god.' The leaded windows are similarly unusual, with glazing patterns varying from room to room and even window to window. Wood and glass together give Little Moreton Hall its unique, complete sixteenth-century character.

The interior is a corridor-less warren, with one room leading into another and four staircases linking different levels. Some rooms are little more than cupboards and simply decorated; others are much grander with fine chimneypieces and panelling. A simple chapel, to which worshippers are still summoned on Sundays by a bell in the courtyard, is decorated with texts from the Bible. The Moretons' religious sympathies are also evident in the house. A frieze crowning the elaborate painted panelling in the parlour – the whole composition a rare example of sixteenth-century painted decoration – illustrates the story of Susannah and the Elders, a favourite Protestant theme. Characters are shown in contemporary Elizabethan dress, the blues and reds of their costumes still fresh and bright. In the long gallery, where the massive weight of the roof is taken by huge curved beams morticed and tenoned into the rafters, plasterwork picked out in orange and green at either end of the room depicts the virtues of hard work and the power of knowledge over superstition.

A hedge of hornbeam, holly, thorn and honeysuckle edges the moat, enclosing a lawn planted with fruit trees and a reconstruction of an Elizabethan knot garden, with box-edged compartments filled with gravel. Two prominent mounds – one across the moat – were probably vantage points for surveying the surrounding countryside.

Llanerchaeron CEREDIGION

Off A482, 2½ miles east of Aberaeron [442 C3]

Just inland from Cardigan Bay and the sea, in the pastoral valley of the Afon Aeron, is a rare survival of the small gentry estates which were such a mainstay of the economy of rural Wales in the eighteenth and nineteenth centuries. By 1700, it had passed to the Lewis family and it was William Lewis who commissioned the young John Nash to replace an existing house. Dating from 1794, when Nash was only 26, Llanerchaeron is a charming mix of the conservative and the unexpected. The plain, well-proportioned late Georgian exterior is unexceptional, but Nash included decorative oval dressing rooms and a dramatic top-lit staircase, and his elegant service courtyard is surrounded by a verandah-shaded, slate-slabbed walkway.

The surrounding park was landscaped in the spirit of the Picturesque, with gothicised cottages and a church beside the drive used as an eye-catcher in the view from the house. The family's sporting lifestyle comes through in the home farm, where the buildings round the yard, mostly contemporary with the house, include kennels for otter hounds and elegant stables. Their importance in the local economy is seen in the little church, where 40 of the 60 seats were once occupied by estate employees. Although embedded in rural life, the Lewises were not unworldly. Running through the park is the now abandoned track of the railway to Aberaeron, which the family encouraged.

House, gardens and grounds have recently been restored by the Trust. Vegetables, fruit and herbs are grown in the two walled gardens and the estate is run as an organic farm. There are extensive walks across the park and estate.

Llŷn Peninsula GWYNEDD

In the north-west corner of Wales [442 B1–C1]

Dividing Caernarfon Bay from Cardigan Bay is the Llŷn peninsula, in shape remarkably like a quarter-scale Cornwall, and with a coast equally as fine. It was the stamping ground of the three remarkable Keating sisters of Plas-yn-Rhiw (*see* p.306). A mile to the south-west of Plas-yn-Rhiw, Mynydd-y-Graig rises to 244 metres (800 feet), covered with bracken and heather and with a panoramic view south over Cardigan Bay. Beyond lies the headland of Mynydd Penarfynydd, and here the view opens to the west. The Gwylan Islands, a mile offshore, have a large colony of puffins and, beyond them, Aberdaron Bay is closed by the sheep-cropped turf of

Pen-y-Cil, while just west of the little town a footpath leads south along the cliffs to Porth Meudwy, frequented by the rare and distinctive chough and with colonies of seals and seabirds on offshore islands. This sheltered cove was the traditional landing place for pilgrims coming back from the monastery on Bardsey Island, 2 miles away across the tidal race of the Sound.

Round the headland of Braich-y-Pwll the coast turns north. The views are now across to Ireland and, from the 191.5-metre (628-foot)-high Myndd Anelog, the Wicklow Hills rise clear to the west. Below is the cove of Porth Llanllawen, where seals breed, and, beyond, the Trust's two tiny islands of Dinas Fawr and Dinas Bach and the curious Whistling Sands at Porthor, where 29.5 hectares (73 acres) are now protected by the Trust.

This is an exposed, wind-clipped coastline. Where the land turns briefly east again, low cliffs back a sheltered sandy bay and the Trust-owned village of Porthdinllaen: a huddle of cottages, the Ty Coch Inn and a Lifeboat Station looking across the bay to the triple-peaked Yr Eifl, falling almost 609.5 metres (2,000 feet) to the sea. To the north of these hills, near the granite-quarrying village of Trefor, the Trust owns Morfar and Nantbach, a dramatic,

Above: The herb garden in the East Walled Garden at Llanerchaeron, with fennel in the foreground.

Below: The wild, beautiful Braich-y-Pwll juts into the sea at the Llŷn peninsula's tip. In the Middle Ages pilgrims set out from here for Bardsey Island, beyond the headland.

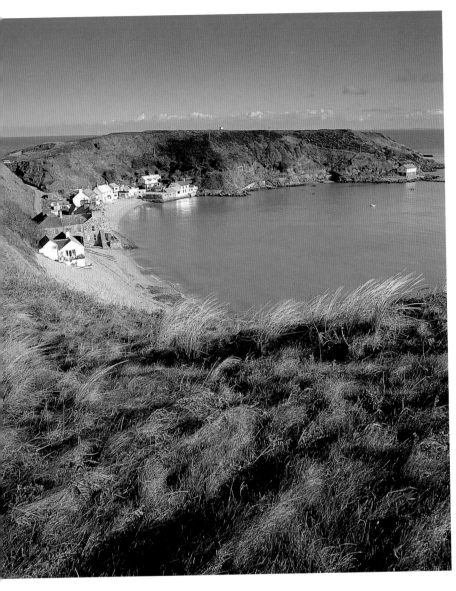

extraordinary Grey Wethers. These are sarsen stones, a hard sandstone which when on the surface is eroded by wind and rain to every sort of shape. Here they lie, as they have done since the Ice Age, although vast numbers have been taken away, both to build prehistoric circles, as at Avebury (*see* p.29), and to build churches, houses, walls and farm buildings.

The Trust owns two clusters of these peculiarly attractive stones. Lockeridge Dene, close to the village of Lockeridge south of the A4, can be seen without leaving the car. The more extensive Piggledene, to the north of the main road, needs to be walked through. Although it is entered directly from the tarmac, the dene curves westward and the bustle of traffic is soon left behind. The time for a wander here is late on a summer's evening.

Lode Mill CAMBRIDGESHIRE

In grounds of Anglesey Abbey, 6 miles north-east of Cambridge [443 J3]

Lode Mill and the village which it once served are called after Bottisham Lode, an ancient man-made waterway linking with the River Cam which enabled supplies to be brought here by boat. There has probably been a mill at the junction of Bottisham Lode and Quy Water since the time of Domesday Book, but the present distinctive white weather-boarded building with a projecting lucam on the fourth floor dates from the eighteenth century. Four pairs of millstones driven by a 4.5-metre (14-foot) breastshot wheel were used to grind corn until 1900, when the mill was converted to produce cement, ceasing operations altogether twenty years later. Now incorporated in the grounds of Anglesey Abbey (*see* p.20), where it provides an attractive focus for a number of leafy vistas, the mill is once again a working water-mill, used for grinding flour.

windswept coast, with a pebble beach and chough feeding sites. On the other side of the peninsula, facing south-east across Cardigan Bay, the Trust has recently acquired the sheltered sandy beach at Llanbedrog.

Lockeridge Dene and Piggledene
WILTSHIRE

3 miles west of Marlborough, on south and north sides of the A4 Bath road respectively [443 G5]

On Clatford and Fyfield Downs, west of Marlborough, and on nearby Overton Down stand thousands of the

Lodge Park GLOUCESTERSHIRE

3 miles east of Northleach, across the A40 from Sherborne village [443 G4]

On the open Cotswold plateau west of Cheltenham is a unique survival of a finely wrought building set in a sporting landscape. Commanding sweeping views south and east towards the Thames Valley is an exquisite Jacobean hunting lodge, its main façade positively crammed with architectural detail. Pedimented windows set shoulder to shoulder across the first floor carry bearded and moustachioed heads, there are exaggerated quoins, shell-headed niches and a columned portico supporting a wide balcony, and a massive classical chimneystack breaks the balustraded roofline.

This compact architectural caprice, more box than house, was built to overlook a broad grassy track edged with dry-stone walls which still runs over a mile south from the A40. From the roof and balcony of the lodge, the well-to-do would watch and bet on dogs chasing fallow deer along the course, with a finishing line marked by a ditch in front of the house. Originally consisting of just two large rooms, with a grand staircase leading to a 13.5-metre (44-foot) banqueting hall opening on to the balcony, and the roof beyond, the lodge was built in the 1630s for Sir John Dutton, a characterful hunchback who was known as Crump and who seems to have weathered the Civil War by keeping a foot in both camps. The designer is uncertain, but may have been the local mason-architect Valentine Strong, perhaps working with the help of pattern books which illustrated the kind of Italianate detail favoured by Inigo Jones. Crump had created a deer-park too, but in the early eighteenth century the lodge was made the focus of a 81-hectare (200-acre) landscape by Charles Bridgeman, who planted wooded enclosures for the deer, artful clumps of trees and a double lime avenue leading away behind the house.

About the same time as Bridgeman's landscaping, the lodge was refurbished and furnished to a scheme devised by William Kent. In later years, it was converted into estate cottages, and, in the nineteenth century, when the gate lodges were added, turned into a house. The Trust has returned it, as far as possible, to its original configuration, with a reconstructed, Jacobean-style oak staircase leading to the banqueting hall and a copy – in plaster and wood imitating stone in the seventeenth-century manner – of the great hooded fireplace that was once here. The Kent furniture has been dispersed, although some pieces may find their way back, but there is a selection of family portraits and an atmospheric landscape by George Lambert showing the open, well-wooded countryside of the 1740s, without the regular stone-walled fields that now dominate the view from the roof. The Bridgeman setting, similarly, is being clarified, with replanting of the double lime avenue.

Lodge Park is part of the 1,677-hectare (4,144-acre) Sherborne estate which came to the Trust in 1987. Straddling the A40 and the serene Windrush Valley, this largely agricultural holding includes much former parkland and most of Sherborne village. Strung out along the valley,

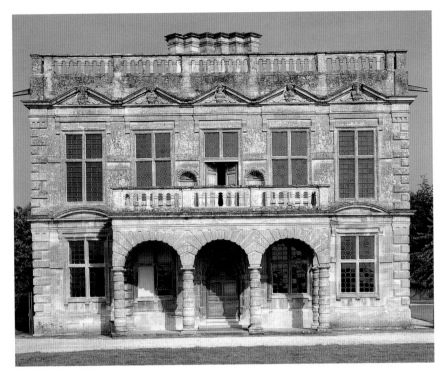

this is a charming collection of nineteenth-century, estate-built cottages in a Cotswold vernacular style, with gabled stone-tiled roofs and stone-mullioned windows. All are south-facing, with gardens separating them from the road. The big house, seat of the family since the sixteenth century, was sold away in 1970, and the 7th Lord Sherborne (the peerage dates from 1784 and died with the 7th Lord's cousin, Ralph Dutton of Hinton Ampner, *see* p.186) lived at the lodge. Lady Sherborne used the deer course as a runway for her aeroplane, and the short avenue of rowans now breaking the track in front of the house was planted by the 7th Lord in her memory.

Set high and exposed on the Cotswold plateau above the Windrush Valley is this delicious Jacobean hunting lodge, built to provide a grandstand from which the local elite could watch deer coursing along a track in front of the lodge.

Long Crendon Courthouse
BUCKINGHAMSHIRE

2 miles north of Thame, via the B4011, close to the church
[443 H4]

Long Crendon courthouse lies in one of the most attractive and unspoilt villages in Buckinghamshire, its long timber-framed façade with a jettied upper storey blending perfectly with the sixteenth- and seventeenth-century thatched cottages which line the street winding down to St Mary's church. Red handmade tiles form a warm streak of colour above the whitewashed walls. Steep wooden stairs lead

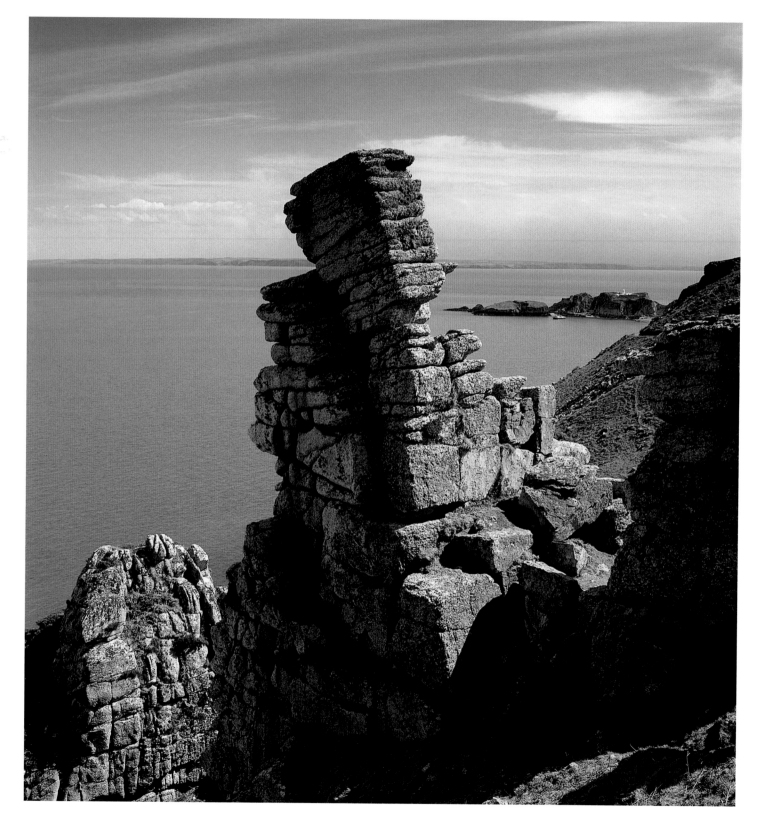

directly from the street to the large room, open to the roof and floored with undulating oak boards, which runs most of the length of the upper storey.

Dating from the early fifteenth century or even the end of the fourteenth, the courthouse seems originally to have been built for the cloth trade, to store wool from Oxfordshire destined for the weavers of East Anglia. The first floor was being used to hold manorial courts in the first half of the fifteenth century, and manorial business continued to be conducted here into Victorian times, while the ground floor was often used to accommodate the village poor.

Loughwood Meeting House DEVON

4 miles west of Axminster, 1 mile south of Dalwood, 1 mile north-west of Kilmington [442 E6]

In the seventeenth century people walked miles to attend Baptist meetings in this little flint and sandstone building dug into the hillside. For their troubles they risked imprisonment, transportation or even death, until the Toleration Act of 1688 legalised nonconformist forms of worship. Built as a refuge from persecution in 1653 by Baptists from the nearby village of Kilmington, Loughwood was originally buried in dense woodland and approached only along narrow footpaths. Even today it is remotely sited in rural Devonshire.

A homely thatched roof and round-headed clear-glass windows give this unassuming chapel the appearance of a cottage rather than a church, despite the surrounding burial ground and the buttressed walls. Inside, it is cheerful and airy, dominated by the preacher's raised pulpit set above the baptismal pool. Unvarnished pine box pews fill the body of the chapel and the whitewashed walls and barrel roof are undecorated. Those who came from a long way away passed the time between services on Sundays in the retiring rooms underneath the musicians' gallery at the back of the building; those lucky enough to have horses quartered them in the detached stone and cob stable.

Lundy DEVON

11 miles north of Hartland Point [442 B5]

Lundy rises boldly out of the Bristol Channel 11 miles north of Hartland Point. The island is in fact the top of an undersea mountain, the water offshore deep and wonderfully clean. A little over 3 miles from north to south, the island, largely made of granite, is only a quarter of a mile wide. The cliffs on its west coast rise to 122 metres (400 feet), and although the east coast is still formidable it is gentler, with little valleys running down to rocky beaches, patches of scrubby wood and *Rhododendron ponticum*. Above the cliffs the island is flat and very exposed. The main landing-place is from a jetty at the south-east corner of the island.

The thirteenth-century Marisco Castle, on a precipice overlooking the South Light, commands the landing place. Nearby is the small village, a farm, a shop, an inn, one or two larger houses, cottages and a large Victorian church. At Millcombe, where the road runs down to the landing place, is the seemly manor house of the island, built in 1835. At the highest point, 142 metres (466 feet), stands the Old Light, a magnificent stone tower designed by Daniel Asher Alexander, architect of Dartmoor Prison. Completed in 1820, it was found to be of little use, for the fogs of the Bristol Channel obscured its beam far above the water and ships continued to drive onto Lundy's reefs. It was replaced by the North and South Lights, built at the foot of the cliffs at either end of the island and still in use, although now automated.

The island is leased to the Landmark Trust, which has done a superb job in restoring the many dilapidated buildings, removing eyesores and fostering an island community which keeps the place alive. The Landmark Trust also provides a good deal of accommodation for visitors, who come here in search of solitude, the absence of traffic, noise, people, to walk and, in particular, to watch the bird life.

The island lies on a north-south migratory route and at the right time of year there are many migrant species passing by. Kittiwakes, fulmars and Manx shearwaters nest here. There is a now very small colony of puffins, while peregrines have long nested in inaccessible eyries.

There are important heathlands and grasslands, where the flora includes the rare fern *Ophioglossum*; rabbits abound and inbreeding has led to distinctive black and brown varieties. There is a type of pigmy shrew which is found only here. The Lundy ponies, originally New Forest ponies crossed with Welsh Mountain mares, are now recognised as a distinct breed.

The Landmark Trust's own handsome ship, *M.S. Oldenburg*, runs throughout the year from Bideford and during the summer from Ilfracombe, and a weekend helicopter service operates in the winter. Arrangements for visitors are distinctly well organised. For a first visit to this very special place the inside of a week is ideal.

Opposite: Sea-battered Lundy, a slim fastness of granite twelve miles off the coast of north Devon, has rocky stacks and outcrops similar to the tors of Dartmoor and Bodmin Moor and is home to thousands of sea-birds, among them the puffin, the emblem of the island.

Lydford Gorge DEVON

Halfway between Okehampton and Tavistock, 1 mile west of the A386, at west end of Lydford village [442 C7]

Lydford Gorge is a geological curiosity. Some 450,000 years ago the River Lyd flowed southwards along the western edge of Dartmoor, via the course of the present little River Burn, to join the River Tavy. Some disturbance of the earth's crust diverted its flow into the valley of the River West Lyd, close at hand, which then carried it away westwards from the moor, ultimately to join the Tamar east of Launceston. The phenomenon is known as river capture and its result has been the carving out of the spectacular gorge we see today, where the greatly increased volume of water from the two rivers flows over the 228.5-metre (750-foot) contour near Lydford village to drop to 91.5 metres (300 feet) at the lower end of the gorge. Its walls are now 18 metres (60 feet) high in places, the river bed marked with the remains of rounded basins or potholes scoured out of the Upper Devonian slates of which the gorge is formed by boulders carried down from the moor by storm water, a process which still continues.

The gorge is one and a half miles long, and near its foot a tributary stream plunges down the 27.5-metre (90-foot) White Lady waterfall to join it. The steep sides of the gorge are thickly wooded, though a severe storm in 1977 did much damage. The trunks of the trees are covered with lichens, mosses and ferns, for the place can be like a greenhouse on a humid day. It is the potholes which the visitor remembers most vividly, the most awesome being the Devil's Cauldron below Lydford Castle.

A circular walk takes visitors down the gorge on a high-level path through the fringing oak woods, and back along the river by a much narrower, often rock-cut route, with a final precipitous descent to view the Devil's Cauldron.

Lyme Park CHESHIRE

On south side of the A6; 6½ miles south-east of Stockport, entrance on western outskirts of Disley [445 I7]

Used to the blinding sun and hard shadows of his homeland, the Venetian architect Giacomo Leoni must have found it hard to contend with the lowering grey skies and misty distances of the bleak Peak moors at Lyme when Peter Legh engaged him to remodel his largely Elizabethan mansion in 1725. As at Clandon (*see* p.93), Leoni responded by bringing a touch of Italy to the English countryside.

The courtyard of the Tudor house was transformed into an imitation of the *cortile* of a grand *palazzo*, ringed by shady arcades and with a double flight of steps rising to the pedimented entrance. The Mediterranean effect was later enhanced by the addition of a marble pavement and an Italian Renaissance well-head. On the long south front built of rose-tinted stone, Leoni's great classical portico rises the full height of the house, crowned by lead figures of Venus, Neptune and Pan staring at their reflection in the lake below. Six bays separated by pilasters stretch away on either side. Something of the grand Elizabethan house survives on the north, where a towering Tudor gateway leads into Leoni's courtyard.

Eighteenth-, nineteenth- and twentieth-century decorative schemes are accompanied by two surviving Elizabethan interiors: a light and airy panelled long gallery hung with seventeenth- and early eighteenth-century portraits and a richly panelled Tudor drawing room. Leoni's saloon looking over the park through the columns of his portico has all the elegance of the eighteenth century,

with a gilded rococo ceiling and oak panelling. The pale three-dimensional limewood carvings were introduced to the room from elsewhere in the house by Lewis Wyatt in the early nineteenth century. Traditionally attributed to Grinling Gibbons, one of these lifelike compositions cunningly intertwines an artist's palette and brushes, a partly folded chart and navigation instruments. In another, a beautifully embroidered lace handkerchief falls in naturalistic folds.

The full-length portrait of the Black Prince in the entrance hall is a vivid reminder that the land of Lyme was won for the Legh family in 1346 on the battlefields of France. Lyme was to remain the home of the Leghs for 600 years, its contents intriguingly alluding to episodes in the family's history. A copy of Velázquez's *Las Meninas* portrays the celebrated mastiffs bred here until the twentieth century and traditionally presented as royal gifts to the courts of Europe. The ancient Greek sculptures in the library were excavated in the early nineteenth century by the intrepid Thomas Legh, whose portrait in oriental

Opposite: The White Lady Waterfall, where a stream cascades 27 metres (90 feet) into the deep wooded gorge of the River Lyd on the western edge of Dartmoor.

Below: Brooding over the approaches to Lyme is this square stone box known as 'the Cage', set high on a moorland ridge. Originally an Elizabethan hunting tower, it was refaced in 1733–5 by Leoni and there was an 18th-century plan to make it the focus of meandering walks.

Right: The south front of Lyme is dominated by Leoni's great three-storey portico, which is topped off by lead figures of Neptune, Venus and Pan.

Below: Windows looking out between the columns light the Saloon, one of the grandest interiors in the house, where exquisite festoons of carved limewood on the panelling are attributed to Grinling Gibbons.

of the house is called after the horticulturalist who was a friend of the family. Currently being restored, this sunken area will feature various trees and shrubs raised by Gibbs in his Hertfordshire garden, including *Sorbus hybrida* 'Gibbsii', *Berberis aldenhamensis* and *Malus aldenhamensis*.

From the terrace on the south front there are views across the lake to Lyme's medieval deer-park, 9 miles in circumference and already walled in Elizabethan times. Set dramatically on a windswept ridge high above the grazing herds broods Lyme Cage, an eighteenth-century hunting tower modified in the early nineteenth century by Lewis Wyatt, its forbidding outline crowned by domed turrets greeting approaching visitors.

Lynmouth DEVON

On the north coast, east of Lynmouth, on both sides of the A39 [442 D5]

East of Lynmouth the Trust has built up a very beautiful estate of over 647.5 hectares (1,600 acres) since its first purchase in 1934. The area seems much larger, for the steep wooded valleys of the East Lyn river and the Hoar Oak Water curve deeply back into Exmoor, and their headwaters 404.5 metres (1,000 feet) above are only 4 miles from the sea as the crow flies.

Twenty-three centimetres (9 inches) of rain fell on the high ground in 24 hours. The great sponge of the peaty moorland could absorb no more and some 90 million tons of water surged down the valleys which converge on Lynmouth. Thirty-four people lost their lives in the tragedy, nearly all the bridges were swept away, as were a number of houses, the valley bottoms were scoured and much other damage was done. The sad memory of this dramatic event will abide but the scars to the landscape have virtually healed.

The Trust's property, though all contiguous, falls into two parts, the inland valleys centred on Watersmeet and the high cliffs and moorland running out to Foreland Point beyond Countisbury and east to the cliffs of Glenthorne. Although the Trust has acquired its land in many different parcels, it was originally nearly all one estate. In the first quarter of the nineteenth century a young man named Halliday, heir to a merchant's fortune, fell in love with the wild beauty of this north-western corner of Exmoor and began buying land. Halliday and his wife were philanthropists and planned to set up an ideal – if patriarchal – estate, peopled with tenants for whom they laid out farms and provided employment. The young

costume enlivens the staircase. His grandest find, a stele of Melisto and Epigenes of *c.*350BC, has pride of place over the fireplace, but the little tombstone of the same date in the window bay, commemorating a mother and her newborn babe, is far more memorable. A tragedy of a different kind is recalled in the Stag Parlour, where faded red covers on the Chippendale chairs were reputedly made from the cloak Charles I wore on the scaffold. Much more recently the house has been enriched by the magnificent collection of seventeenth- and eighteenth-century bracket and longcase clocks acquired by Sir Francis Legh, born at Lyme in 1919. The earliest is an instrument by Ahasuerus Fromanteel, dated 1658, one of the first pendulum mechanisms ever produced, and there are also examples of the work of masters such as Thomas Tompion and Joseph Knibbs.

The late nineteenth-century garden was laid out by William John Legh, 1st Lord Newton, who inherited the estate in 1857. Lewis Wyatt's orangery to the east of the house is fronted by a formal Victorian design, its garish colours echoed in the brightly coloured beds surrounding an ornamental pond in the sunken Dutch garden on the other side of the house. The planting along the deep ravine carved by the stream feeding the lake is quite different in character, primulas, hostas, irises and other moisture-loving plants creating an informal semi-wild area through which a path leads to a rhododendron garden on the slopes above. The similarly secluded Vicary Gibbs garden to the west

Lytes Cary is one of several small late-medieval manor houses in the care of the Trust. This is the east front, with a stone-paved path leading to the porch and a glimpse of the little detached chapel on the left.

couple built a romantic mansion beside the sea at Glenthorne, 2 miles east of Countisbury, with a drive plunging ever more steeply down from County Gate 404.5 metres (1,000 feet) above, at the border of Devon with Somerset. In 1832 they constructed Watersmeet House, in an equally romantic setting, at the confluence of the East Lyn and Hoar Oak Water, to provide a base for fishing and shooting parties. It now accommodates the Trust's restaurant, shop and information point.

From Watersmeet paths run in every direction, many of them originally donkey tracks made by men working in the woods burning charcoal. Every 25 years or so the trees were coppiced; the bark was stipped for leather tanning and poles were shipped over the Bristol Channel to be used as pit-props in the Welsh coal mines. There are also signs of the mining of iron ore and a restored lime kiln. The high-level walks give the best views; those at a lower level the best peeps of rock pools and waterfalls.

The woods are largely of sessile oak, with two rare whitebeams (*Sorbus devoniensis* and *S. subcuneata*), while Watersmeet is one of two places in Britain where the Irish spurge (*Euphorbia hibernica*) is found. Revelling in the damp clean air so close to the sea, lichens, ferns and mosses abound, creating a site of national importance for ancient woodland flora. The two birds most characteristic of the rivers are the grey wagtail and the dipper, always bobbing in and out of the water.

The coast is wholly different from these wooded valleys. The Foreland is all that a great headland should be, bare, sheep-grazed, facing west into the Atlantic gales. A steep path from Countisbury Hill leads down to its beach at Sillery Sands. Half a mile west of Countisbury village, with its church, pub, and a handful of cottages, is Wind Hill, with the massive earthworks of an Iron Age promontory fort. Some 2,000 years old, it was probably the site of a battle in AD878 when the Danish raider Hubba was defeated by the men of Devon.

Above the church a path leads over Butter Hill, where the roofless stone building was once a Lloyd's signal station. It now houses a television relay station which ensures that viewers at Lynmouth can receive the West Country's television services. Before it was provided they had to use the services from Wales.

The Great Red landslip on the way to the Foreland marks the point where sandstone grits meet the slates comprising the rest of this coast. The path then runs steeply down into Caddow Combe to the east, finishing at the Foreland lighthouse, tucked into the slope above Foreland Point. The keepers' cottages are now owned by the Trust.

At Warmersturt, a rocky knoll to the east of the combe, is a view eastwards along the Glenthorne Cliffs. This stretch of coast provides miles of walking, for more than 2 miles on or alongside the Trust's land, and from there for a further 4½ miles, as the crow flies, to Porlock Weir, with no road reaching the sea for its entire length. The landscape here is very different, for not only is the soil on these Lynton slates more kindly but the cliffs are sheltered from the south-west gales. Oak woodland is a prominent feature, some of it pollarded in the past, with ash, beech, rowan, sycamore and holly, and rather too much *Rhododendron ponticum*, which tends to smother the flora which would otherwise flourish here. (*See also* Combe Martin and the Hangman Hills; the Heddon Valley, Trentishoe and Woody Bay; Holnicote Estate.)

Lytes Cary Manor SOMERSET

1 mile north of Ilchester bypass on the A303 [442 E6]

This enchanting manor house built round a courtyard in the depths of rural Somerset bears the name of the family who lived here for 500 years, from the thirteenth to the eighteenth century. A flagged path across smoothly mown grass leads to the projecting entrance porch, crowned by the swan of the Lyte family, wings half raised as if to defend the house. Rounded topiary yews lining the path look like crinolined ladies stepping over the grass. To the left is the oldest feature of Lytes Cary, the simple little chapel built by Peter Lyte in *c.*1343, attached to the house but only accessible from the outside. Family coats of arms in red, white and yellow stand out prominently on the painted frieze added in the reign of Henry VII which decorates the whitewashed interior.

Although the north and west ranges are eighteenth century and later, Lytes Cary has a feeling of great age, of a place that has grown out of its surroundings. The Tudor great hall between the porch and the chapel, with a little oriel off it where the family would eat in privacy away from their servants and retainers, rises the full height of the house to a magnificent timber roof, the ends of the rafters adorned with carved angels. Here, too, is a copy of Henry Lyte's *Niewe Herball*, first published in 1578, which was translated from the work of the famous Flemish herbalist Dodoens and dedicated to Queen Elizabeth I. Subsequently known as the *Lytes Herbal*, it was still being reprinted in 1678. Henry would have enjoyed the splendid plaster ceiling in the great chamber on the floor above which his father commissioned in 1533, interlaced hexagons and diamonds studded with armorial bosses heralding Elizabethan plasterwork of a generation later. This room is also notable for a fine interior porch, covered in linenfold panelling and with a crest of trefoils.

Neglected after the departure of the Lytes in about 1748, the house was rescued in this century by Sir Walter Jenner, who refurnished it with high-quality seventeenth- and early eighteenth-century oak pieces and with fabrics in authentically medieval browns, olives and muted reds. Sir Walter was also responsible for the beautiful Elizabethan-style garden, with clipped yew hedges enclosing a series of outdoor rooms. A vivid herbaceous border punctuated with urns set between buttresses of yew leads to a long raised walk overlooking an orchard planted with the crab apples, medlars and quinces that the Elizabethans loved, graceful arches of weeping ash marking paths across the grass. Other yew compartments frame smoothly mown lawns and a pool ornamented with statues of Flora and Diana. An urn placed at the end of a hornbeam tunnel is set off by the green and white foliage of variegated weigela and a border along the south front has been stocked with species cultivated when Henry Lyte published his herbal.

Lyveden New Bield NORTHAMPTONSHIRE

4 miles south-west of Oundle via the A427, 3 miles east of Brigstock [443 I2]

Like Staunton Harold in Leicestershire to the north (*see* p.364), Lyveden New Bield is a moving testament to the strength of religious faith. This strangely compelling, roofless architectural shell, with its mullioned and transomed windows staring sightless over an empty rolling landscape of woods and cornfields, stands half a mile or so from a minor road, far from any other house. It was started in 1594 by the exceptional and talented Sir Thomas Tresham as a garden lodge to his new manor house at Lyveden, but work proceeded very slowly. Although staunchly loyal to Queen Elizabeth, who knighted him in 1575, Sir Thomas converted to the Catholic faith in 1580 and spent fifteen years of the twenty-five left to him either in prison or under house arrest for his religious beliefs, while fines for recusancy made heavy and continuing demands on his pocket. In the circumstances it is extraordinary that he built anything at all.

Two storeys high and devised in the shape of an equal-armed cross, Lyveden New Bield's design and decoration

Lyveden New Bield is a fantasy building, devised in the shape of a cross and as a play on numbers with religious symbolism. It was probably left unfinished when its creator, Sir Thomas Tresham, died in 1605.

both illustrate the Elizabethan love of symbolism and devices and unequivocally declare where Sir Thomas's religious sympathies lay. Allusions to the numbers five and seven in the design of the faces on the end of each wing are references to salvation and the Godhead. Carved emblems of the passion again refer to the mystical number seven and the 81 letters which made up the inscriptions running below the roof, of which only fragments remain, hinted at the nine leaves in the trefoils on the Tresham coat of arms. Extending over some 6 hectares (15 acres) beside the house are the remains of the canals, terraces and mounds which made up Sir Thomas's ambitious formal garden. A recently created orchard has been planted with Elizabethan varieties of fruit trees.

The garden lodge was probably incomplete when Sir Thomas Tresham died, just months before his son was arrested and imprisoned for complicity in the Gunpowder Plot. This intriguing ghost is a memorial to a brave but foolhardy man.

Maister House HUMBERSIDE

160 High Street, Hull [445 K6]

Until the building of the first commercial dock on the River Humber in 1770 heralded its gradual decline, Hull's old harbour was the focus of the town's considerable trading interests, with grand merchants' houses lining the narrow, winding thoroughfares along the river. This fine Palladian house on the High Street is one of the few surviving from this era. Rebuilt for the merchant Henry Maister after a fire in 1743, it is still substantially as it was when finished a year later on, a plain three-storey classical building fronted by railings and with a stone parapet concealing the roof. The only sign of ostentation is the fine pedimented doorcase in the centre of the façade.

This severe and dignified exterior and the sober pine-panelled counting house on the ground floor act as a foil for the staircase, richly decorated with plasterwork by Joseph Page, leading to what would have been the Maister family apartments. A statue of Ceres by John Cheere in a niche above the first flight surveys swags of drapery suspended from lion masks, festoons of shells and acanthus-leaf medallions and scrolls. The coved ceiling above the gallery on the second floor is similarly richly stuccoed and a fine ironwork balustrade was supplied by Robert Bakewell. The work of a highly competent architect, Maister House was probably influenced by Lord Burlington, who knew Henry Maister and whose Yorkshire home was 25 miles away.

Malham Tarn NORTH YORKSHIRE

6 miles north-east of Settle [445 I5]

Malham Tarn, high up on the moors between Ribblesdale and Wharfedale, lies at the centre of 1,740 hectares (4,300 acres) of dramatic limestone country which is farmed by the Trust's tenants with Swaledale sheep and crossbred cattle. The rock is deeply fissured, and water vanishes suddenly and reappears miles away. This is why the approach from Malham village, past the spectacular limestone cliff of Malham Cove, and up the valley to the tarn, is such an eerie landscape: humps and bumps, holes and hollows, huge boulders and outcrops of rock. Having disappeared underground, the River Aire emerges at the base of the cove. Before the Ice Age it filled the valley above and careered over the cliff in a great waterfall.

The tarn, however, sits in a saucer of Silurian slate which is impervious, dammed by glacial waste left here when the ice retreated. The mixture of limestone cliffs, known as scars, the acid 'raised bog', the alkaline fen and the nutrient-rich shallow lake make it a wonderful place for plants and an internationally important site for nature conservation and geological interests. It is worth a visit in early summer to see myriads of heart's-ease starring the sward as one approaches the tarn from the south. The mountain pansy flourishes here too, while the bird's-eye primrose (largely confined to the northern Pennines, Lake District and southern Scotland) grows in the wetter places.

Great-crested grebe, common sandpiper and coot breed on the shores of the tarn, which is stocked with brown trout. One is bound also to record that Malham Tarn inspired the social reformer Charles Kingsley to write his book *The Water Babies* (1863).

Dramatic scars, where beds of bare rock form cliffs and steps above the valleys, are typical of the classic limestone scenery of the Malham Tarn estate.

The woods, mainly broadleaved species with Scots pine and larch, provide shelter and give point to the landscape. Sycamore flourishes particularly well, as it roots firmly into the fissured limestone.

The Smelt Mill, the remains of which stand south-west of the tarn, was used to roast lead and zinc ores from Pikedaw to the south. The smelted metal was then carted down to the Leeds and Liverpool canal at Gargrave.

The Pennine Way skirts the east end of the tarn, and then continues over the high ground to the north, where Great Hill, Green Hill Scar and Little Fell are all part of the Trust's estate. The Abbot Hills, in the south-east corner, remind us that this property, like Brimham (*see* p.64), was once part of the great possessions of Fountains Abbey (*see* p.154), providing it with the wool on which its fortunes were based for centuries.

Malvern Hills HEREFORD & WORCESTER

4–8 miles south of Great Malvern, along the A449 [442 F3]

This is the landscape captured by Elgar, whose music seems to conjure up the wooded slopes and grassy summits of the hills rising above a patchwork of fields and villages and stretching away into the distance. The northern part of this fine range has long been vested in a local body of conservators, and the Trust has protective covenants over the gentler southern half. To the west, Eastnor Park drops down into Herefordshire: brackeny slopes flanking a great deer-park dominated by the early nineteenth-century castle of the Hervey Bathurst/Somers Cocks family. Above the park, Midsummer Hill (*see* p.243) is held as a memorial to a Somers Cocks relation killed in the First World War.

Manor of Cookham and Maidenhead
BERKSHIRE

North of Maidenhead [443 H4]

This string of commons and greens to the south of the Thames provides more than 323.5 hectares (800 acres) of open land and walking country between Maidenhead and Cookham. Crown property from before the Conquest until 1818, they were under threat when acquired by the Trust in 1934. A mix of woodland, grassland, thicket and riverside meadow, and crossed by paths and bridleways, the commons extend 5 miles north and east from Maidenhead Thicket at the southern end, with a steep chalk scarp

Exhilarating walking country in the Malverns, where grassy ridges stretch into the distance.

running down to meadows along the Thames at Cock Marsh. Commoners' cattle still graze here, and areas of pond and marsh support many rare and local plants.

Market House DERBYSHIRE

4 miles west of Matlock, on south side of the B5057, in main street of Winster [445 J8]

This ruggedly attractive two-storey building is one of the few clues to Winster's former importance as a market town. Built in the late seventeenth or early eighteenth century, the Market House is a pleasing mixture of brick and stone, with thick sandstone slabs covering the steeply pitched roof and mullioned and transomed windows lighting the first floor. As was traditional with such buildings, the ground floor was originally open, but its five pointed arches are now filled in. Still the dominant feature of Winster's long main street, it was bought in 1906, as the Trust's first acquisition in the Peak District. It is now a Trust information centre.

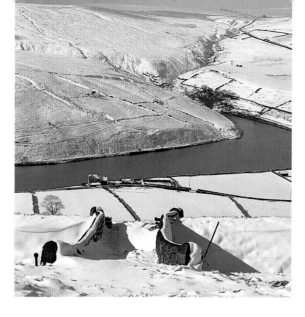

The bleak expanses of Marsden Moor on the northern fringes of the Peak District are an important stretch of open country between Huddersfield and the Manchester conurbation. This is a view over Butterley reservoir towards Standedge ridge.

Marsden Moor WEST YORKSHIRE

7–8 miles south-west of Huddersfield, astride the A62 [445 I6]

Marsden Moor and its outliers, Holme and Binn Moors, rise steeply on three sides of the mills and houses of Marsden, south-west of Huddersfield. This is a great sweep – some 2,306.5 hectares (5,700 acres) – of bleak dramatic moorland, much of it over 305 metres (1,000 feet) above sea level and reaching 476 metres (1,561 feet) on Wessenden Moor. The peat blanket, habitat for mosses and moorland grasses, and for curlew, golden plover and lapwing, feeds streams tumbling down the steep-sided cloughs or valleys which dissect the upland. The Pennine Way crosses Marsden Moor, while a line of airshafts marks an older crossing far beneath, the 8-mile-long Standedge Tunnel on the railway from Ashton under Lyne to Huddersfield, one of the great monuments of nineteenth-century engineering.

Max Gate DORSET

1 mile east of Dorchester on A352 [442 F7]

Thomas Hardy designed this tree-shrouded red-brick villa for himself and lived here from 1885 until his death, in 1928. The Hardy associations are strong, this being the place where he wrote *Tess of the d'Urbervilles*, *Jude the Obscure*, *The Mayor of Casterbridge*, and the moving poetry rooted in the disintegration of his marriage to Emma Gifford (after Emma's death, in 1912, he lived with Florence Dugdale, marrying her in 1914). Here, too, in his last years he received a stream of literary visitors, among them T.E. Lawrence, whose Clouds Hill (*see* p.102) was nearby, W.B. Yeats, Robert Louis Stevenson and Virginia Woolf. It is strange that a man so sensitive to buildings should have designed such an unexceptional place for himself, but it seems Hardy wanted convenience and privacy, and there is a fine view. Sadly, none of his furniture remains (his study is re-created in Dorchester County Museum).

Melford Hall SUFFOLK

In Long Melford on east side of the A134, 14 miles south of Bury St Edmunds, 3 miles north of Sudbury [443 K3]

Set into the high brick wall bordering Long Melford's village green is a delicious octagonal Tudor banqueting house, with finials rising like brick fingers at every angle and from all eight gables. This giant doll's house faces along a grassy terrace – the former bowling-green – to one of the most satisfying Elizabethan houses in East Anglia.

As the great wall suggests, Melford faces west over the park, as if turning away from the village. Massive chimney-stacks and fanciful turrets crowned with onion domes rise dramatically from the U-shaped red-brick mansion, with two long wings flanking the courtyard on the entrance front. The house dates from some time in the mid-sixteenth century, after the shrewd Tudor lawyer who built it, Sir William Cordell, was granted the manor that had belonged to the great Benedictine abbey of Bury St Edmunds. Despite subsequent alterations, such as the removal of the gatehouse range that once enclosed the courtyard, and the disappearance of part of the moat, the exterior is still very much as Queen Elizabeth I must have seen it when she was entertained lavishly here in 1578.

Although the house was ransacked during the Civil War and suffered a disastrous fire in 1942, there are still many associations with the Cordells and with the seafaring Parker family, notable for producing no fewer than three admirals, who bought the hall in 1786. The Tudor great hall rising through two storeys is hung with both Cordell and Parker portraits and here too is the survey of the estate which Sir William commissioned in 1580; every field is named and the long strip of the village green with the church at one end is clearly shown. The panelling and Jacobean furniture in this room contrast with classical touches added by Thomas Hopper, much better known as the architect of Penrhyn Castle (*see* p.298), and with his Regency Library with its curved oak bookshelves, florid Greek couches and armchairs appropriately decorated with owls. Paintings of historic naval engagements fought by the 5th Baronet, Vice Admiral Sir Hyde Parker, and his second son, also an admiral, line the library walls, one of the most memorable showing fireships drifting on the tide towards a British fleet on the Hudson river.

The 5th Baronet himself, who ran away from school to join the merchant navy and worked his way up through the ranks to become the most technically skilled admiral of his day, appears as a larger-than-life figure in a portrait by Romney in the little octagon off the main library. His grandson Harry, aged only fourteen, was lost at sea with his grandfather when the Admiral was on his way to the East Indies in 1783 to take up his last post. The ivory figure in the great hall and much of the Chinese porcelain seen throughout the house were taken from a Spanish galleon laden with presents from the Emperor of Peking to the King of Spain which the 5th Baronet captured in 1762. The house also has connections with Beatrix Potter, whose cousin married the 10th Baronet. Mementoes of the author include the model for Jemima Puddleduck, neatly dressed in a blue poke bonnet.

The small garden has lawns studded with domes of box and planted with specimen trees, including a Judas tree, a tree of heaven, a black mulberry and a huge copper beech. An undulating crinkle-crankle wall frames one side. The north arm of the moat is now a sunken garden by the bowling-green terrace but the west arm still runs along the village green, past some intriguing topiary figures outside the garden wall.

Mendips LIVERPOOL

251 Menlove Avenue, Liverpool [445 H7]

The distinctive musical voice which defined the Beatles was forged by the partnership between John Lennon and Paul McCartney. Less than a mile away from the brick terrace on a council estate where Paul grew up (*see* Forthlin Road, p.152) is this 1930s pebble-dashed semi, where the young John Lennon was raised by his Aunt Mimi. With its bay windows, leaded panes, Art Nouveau-style stained glass and other tasteful features, such as Art Deco fireplaces, Mendips is typical of thousands of similar suburban houses of the period aimed at the aspiring middle classes.

John came to live here in 1945 at the age of five, after his parents' marriage, undermined by his father's long absences at sea, had fallen apart. His mother Julia's sister Mimi and her husband George, childless themselves, gave John the stable and loving home he needed and, particularly after George's sudden death in 1955, it was the rock-like Mimi who kept John's teenage rebelliousness within bounds. Early experiences and interests fed through

into John's later writing, among them his love of nonsense verse, which was a continuation of his childhood enthusiasm for the fantasy world of Lewis Carroll, and his use of lyrics inspired by newspaper headlines, which was rooted in Uncle George's habit of teaching him to read from the *Liverpool Echo*. The teenage Lennon would sit writing poetry and songs in the front room, encouraging Mimi to keep what he threw aside because he would be 'famous one day'.

John would sit in the small front room and practise the guitar (which he had badgered Julia into getting him) until his fingers were raw. He soon formed his own skiffle group, and it was while performing at St Peter's Church Fete, in Woolton, that he met the 15-year-old Paul, who impressed John with his musical skills. Mimi warmed to John's new friend and the two of them first started to compose songs at Mendips, among them 'Please, Please Me', but the noise they made did not go down well. First taking refuge in the glazed porch, which has just the right bathroom acoustic for their sound, the boys then retreated to Forthlin Road. Paul was still at school, John at art college, but they would both skive off in the afternoons to compose and practise undisturbed while Paul's father was out at work.

Mimi lived on at Mendips after John and the Beatles became famous, but in 1965, when she retired to a bungalow which John bought her in Dorset, the house was sold. John's wife, Yoko Ono, generously gave the house to the Trust. Mendips is presented as a 1950s interior with echoes of the young Lennon, such as the posters in his former bedroom.

Middle Littleton Barn HEREFORD & WORCESTER

3 miles north-east of Evesham, east of the B4085 [443 G3]

Produce from the fertile Vale of Evesham once filled this coursed lias barn in market-gardening country on the banks of the River Avon. Some 96.5 metres (316 feet) long and buttressed like a church, it is both one of the largest and one of the finest in the country, although not all its wagon porches have survived.

Inside, oak framing forms an aisled bay at either end and eight base-cruck trusses divide the nine intermediate bays. The barn was built by the Benedictine monks of Evesham Abbey and may date from *c*.1300 or even earlier. Like Ashleworth (*see* p.28), the barn is part of a picturesque group of buildings which includes an Elizabethan manor.

Right: The small front bedroom at Mendips where John Lennon and Paul McCartney sat for hours, picking out chords and listening to records. Both this room and the lounge (above), where John wrote poetry and lyrics, have touches of Art Nouveau-style stained glass, among several details in the house designed to appeal to aspiring purchasers.

Glen, past Lisnabreeny, leads to a gorse-covered 122-metre (400-foot) hill with views over the city to Belfast Lough, east to Strangford Lough (*see* p.376) and south to the Mournes. At Newtownards, the beech woods of Killynether creep up the south side of Scrabo Hill, with a vast view over Strangford Lough to the Ards peninsula on its further shore.

To the west of Belfast, the stream tumbling down to wooded Collin Glen runs up the cleft between Black Mountain and Collin Mountain, a quick way out of the urban fringe to the hills above. At Glenoe, south of Larne, in a pocket handkerchief of a glen, the Glynn river plunges over a waterfall, surrounded by beeches and ferns, past the pretty village of limewashed cottages terraced along the steep hillsides.

Mompesson House WILTSHIRE

In Salisbury, on north side of Choristers' Green in the Cathedral Close, near High Street Gate [443 G6]

Salisbury seems the perfect setting for Anthony Trollope's Barsetshire novels. It takes no effort of the imagination to see Mrs Proudie, the bishop's domineering wife in *Barchester Towers*, lifting her skirt as she crosses the smoothly mown grass of the close, or the Rev. Septimus Harding, the mild-mannered hero of *The Warden*, ending his days here quietly snoozing in the sun.

Mrs Proudie would certainly have been at home in Mompesson House, with its beautiful eighteenth-century plasterwork and marble chimneypieces and its elegant airy rooms looking over the close towards the cathedral spire soaring above the rooftops. In early summer a white magnolia softens the two-storey limestone façade. A central front door is placed symmetrically between three sash windows on either side and dormers peer down from the hipped roof.

The house was built in 1701 by Charles Mompesson, MP for Old Sarum, but the sumptuous, high-quality decoration by an unknown hand was commissioned by his brother-in-law and heir Charles Longueville, son of the patron and literary executor of the poet Samuel Butler. The most spectacular plasterwork is in the staircase hall, where the bold florid designs include flowers, fruit, satyrs' masks and the head of King Midas with ass's ears. In the Green Room an eagle with outspread wings crouches in the middle of the ceiling, ready to pounce.

Later residents have also left their mark. Cool seascapes in an upstairs corridor and a scene of peaceful

Midsummer Hill
HEREFORD & WORCESTER

4 miles east of Ledbury, ¼ mile north of the A438 Tewkesbury road [442 F3]

The impressive ramparts ringing this 7.5-hectare (19-acre) Iron Age hill-fort at the southern end of the Malvern Hills enclose both the 285.5-hectare (937-foot) summit of Midsummer Hill and the lower Hollybush Hill. A huge bank and ditch form the principal defences, but there are also traces of a second bank on the outer, counterscarp slope of the ditch. Scoop-shaped hollows inside the fort mark the remains of a considerable settlement which apparently included rectangular wooden houses arranged in tidy rows.

Minnowburn Beeches, Killynether and Collin Glen CO. DOWN

At south end of Shaw's Bridge, Lagan river; 1 mile south-west of Newtownards; from the B38 Glen road to the foot of Collin mountain respectively [444 D4]

Three much-valued places lie on the outskirts of Belfast. At the south end of Shaw's Bridge, over the Lagan river, the Minnowburn Beeches clothe the steep slopes as the river makes a horseshoe bend. The path up the Cregagh domesticity hanging on the stairs are two of several water-colours by Barbara Townsend, one of the three daughters of George Barnard Townsend, a local solicitor who came to Mompesson in the mid-nineteenth century. Living on here until her death at the age of 96 in 1939, Barbara became a legend in the close, continuing to sketch and paint right up to the end of her life, a tiny figure wrapped in layers of shawls, scarves and veils. Mompesson is also notable for the Turnbull collection of over 370 English eighteenth-century glasses, some delicately poised on slender twisted stems shot through with spirals of colour, some engraved with foliage, flowers or ears of corn.

A secluded garden at the back of the house, with a fine specimen magnolia and a wistaria- and honeysuckle-covered pergola providing welcome shade on hot summer afternoons, is bounded by the high wall of the close, partly built with material from Old Sarum. The old privy hides behind a tree in one corner.

Monk's House EAST SUSSEX

4 miles south-east of Lewes, off the former A275 (now the C7) in Rodmell village, near the church [443 J6]

This modest weather-boarded house at the far end of Rodmell village was the home of one of the most innovative novelists of the twentieth century. By 1919, when Virginia Woolf and her husband Leonard bought the property as a retreat from London life, Virginia's first two novels had been completed, but the experimental work which was to establish her reputation, in particular *To the Lighthouse*, *The Waves* and *Mrs Dalloway*, was still in the future. Two years earlier she and Leonard had founded the Hogarth Press at their house in Richmond, whose outstanding list, including the first published works of T.S. Eliot, was to make a major contribution to literary life. Ten miles or so across the South Downs stood Charleston, where Virginia's sister Vanessa, the gifted painter, had set up house with her art-critic husband Clive Bell and the artist Duncan Grant.

Although there are only echoes of Virginia at Monk's House, the house is full of reminders of the talented circle in which she moved. Painted furniture by her sister and Duncan Grant in a post-Impressionist style includes a table and chairs in the sitting room: muted abstract designs in brown, blue and olive-green are relieved by a panel of peaches on the back of each chair. Books are piled on one of Duncan's tile-topped tables and a formidable portrait of Einstein in old age, his face only half-lit, is one of a number of telling photographs. China on the mantelpiece was decorated by Duncan Grant, Vanessa Bell and her son Quentin, and their work also fills the top half of the dresser in the tiny kitchen.

Every room is hung with paintings by the family circle, including Italian and Sussex landscapes and tranquil still-lifes – apples or a jug of flowers – by Vanessa, as well as some of her distinctive portraits, one of them a haunting likeness of her sister. Flowering potted plants might have come from the heated greenhouses where Leonard nurtured the begonias, lilies and gloxinias with which he filled the house. A gurgling fish tank behind the sitting room door recalls his habit of looking after ailing fish from the garden ponds, and the dogs' blue pottery water bowl is still in its place.

During the years the Woolfs lived at Monk's House, these modest simple rooms were used to entertain some of the best-known literary and artistic figures of the day, among them Vita Sackville-West, Maynard Keynes, Lytton Strachey, E.M. Forster, David Garnett and Roger Fry. A black Chinese silk shawl embroidered in pink and green, casually thrown over a chair in Virginia's sunny bedroom at the east end of the house, was a present from Lady Ottoline Morrell. Many visitors were members of the Bloomsbury Group which Virginia and Vanessa had founded with their brother Thoby and which was to give the sisters an influence far beyond their own work.

Near the house, where low flint walls are the remains of a piggery, informal cottagey plantings spill over brick paths and there is a paved area with sculpture. The garden

The eclectic mix of furniture at Monk's House includes these painted chairs in the dining room. On the mantelpiece behind is some 18th- and 19th-century porcelain and the picture above is one of three primitive paintings which Leonard Woolf bought when the possessions of the previous occupants were auctioned.

continues into grass and trees; there is a dewpond and orchard and the large open lawn where the Woolfs played bowls. Here the view opens out and from the weather-boarded garden house where Virginia wrote there is a wide panorama east towards the River Ouse and a spur of the South Downs beyond. The huge battered table at which she sat and her distinctive blue paper are still here and there is also a display of her photographs accompanied by quotations from her diaries and letters.

Montacute House SOMERSET

In Montacute village, 4 miles west of Yeovil, on south side of the A3088, 3 miles east of the A303 [442 E6]

Montacute invites the kind of elaborate compliment paid by one sixteenth-century visitor, who thought the fronting stone terrace superior to St Mark's Square in Venice. Probably finished by 1601, it is an H-shaped building of local honey-brown Ham stone. Like Hardwick Hall in Derbyshire (*see* p.175), Montacute is every inch an Elizabethan house, a product of a confident and enquiring age. It was designed by a local stonemason, the gifted William Arnold (*see also* Dunster Castle, p.133), for the successful lawyer Sir Edward Phelips, later Master of the Rolls and Chancellor to the Household of Prince Henry.

Montacute's long east and west façades rise three storeys to a roofline fretted with delicate chimneys, parapets and pinnacles, and adorned with curved Flemish gables. Unlike a medieval house, turned inwards to a central courtyard, Montacute looks boldly out at the world through a huge display of glittering glass. Classical details on the entrance front, such as the nine curiously lumpy statues in Roman dress, betray the influence of the Renaissance, slowly filtering north from its beginnings in Italy.

The other side of the house is even more engaging. Here stonework from nearby Clifton Maybank, a splendid sixteenth-century mansion partly dismantled in 1786, ornaments the two-storey front grafted on between the existing wings in the late eighteenth century. The crowning parapet is crowded with heraldic beasts on pedestals, while shadows cast by the fluted stone pillars decorating the façade give the house a sculptural quality. Montacute's fantasy outline is continued in the spiky balustrade and the two delightful Elizabethan pavilions topped with obelisks which border the entrance court.

Although hardly any of the original contents survived the decline in the Phelipses' fortunes, leading to

Montacute's sale in 1929, fine furniture and tapestries from the Sir Malcolm Stewart bequest give the rooms an authentic atmosphere. In the medieval-style great hall the early-morning sun casts richly coloured pools through the heraldic glass in the east-facing windows. Phelips portraits hang above the original panelling and an elaborate stone screen with rusticated arches set between three pairs of columns runs across one end, extravagant horns curling back from the rams' heads carved on the decorative capitals. Two rare early seventeenth-century plaster panels illustrate village life, one showing a hen-pecked husband being berated by his wife as he draws beer from a barrel rather than attending to the baby he clasps in his left arm.

At the top of the house a magnificent long gallery, the largest surviving Elizabethan example in Britain, runs 52.5 metres (172 feet) down the length of the building. Used for entertaining important guests and for exercise in inclement weather, the gallery has panoramic views from the two great oriel windows framed by orange trees in pots at either end. Tudor and Jacobean paintings from the National Portrait Gallery echo the portraits of family and notables which would once have hung here, a set of stiff kings and queens like a pack of playing cards contrasting with more realistic works, such as the delightful picture showing Robert Carey, 1st Earl of Monmouth, with his

Top: The east front of Montacute as seen from one of the raised gravel walks in the formal garden. This beautiful Elizabethan house, of warm Ham stone, was built by Sir Edward Phelips (above), who made a fortune at the bar and moved on to play a prominent role in public life.

family, the five adults posed as if in a photograph, or the portraits of the handsome, curly-headed Robert Sidney, 1st Earl of Leicester (1563–1626), and of little Henry, Prince of Wales (1594–1612), the child's creamy pallor emphasised by his rich crimson dress.

Although now incorporating both nineteenth- and twentieth-century features and planting schemes, the extensive garden still follows the outlines of the original layout. The oriel window at the north end of the long gallery looks down on a formal rectangle of trees and grass which lies on the site of the Elizabethan garden, the raised walks framing the sunken lawn with its bracelet of clipped yew and thorn and a nineteenth-century balustraded pond in the centre probably dating from when the house was built. A border of shrub roses under the retaining wall, planted with the advice of Vita Sackville-West (see p.341) and Graham Stuart Thomas, includes species in cultivation in the sixteenth century, such as *Rosa gallica* 'Officinalis', the Red Rose of Lancaster, and the double white Yorkist *R. alba* 'Maxima'.

Mrs Reiss of Tintinhull (see p.389) was responsible for the strong colour schemes surrounding the lawn filling the entrance court, with roses, delphiniums, lupins and dahlias forming vivid splashes of red, orange, yellow and blue against dark foliage, the ideal foil for the warm yellow stone of the house. The cedar lawn, with an arcaded garden house to which Lord Curzon, who leased Montacute in the early twentieth century, added an Elizabethan façade, lies on the site of an old orchard and the car park fills what was the walled kitchen garden. A mature avenue of cedars, beeches and limes, fronted by clipped Irish yew, frames the west drive created in 1851–2, its lines continued in the wide grassy ride edged with limes which stretches away across the park to the east.

Moseley Old Hall STAFFORDSHIRE

4 miles north of Wolverhampton; south of the M54 between the A449 and the A460 [442 F2]

In the early hours of 8 September 1651, five days after the Royalist defeat at the Battle of Worcester, Charles II disguised as a woodcutter came through the gate at the end of the Nut Alley and moved silently up the flagged path leading to the back of the house. Waiting anxiously in the dark outside were Thomas Whitgreave, the owner of Moseley, and his chaplain, John Huddlestone. Together they escorted the king through the heavily studded back door and by the light of a flickering candle he was shown

up the narrow stairs into the priest's room, now known as the King's Room.

Here he sat sipping a glass of wine while his sore feet were soothed, watching the firelight playing over the hangings of the four-poster bed where he was to spend his first night in comfort since the battle. Here, too, he was shown the hiding place barely 4 feet high concealed under a trapdoor in the cupboard to the right of the fireplace, the cavity where Charles was to crouch when the Parliamentarians came to the house two days later. The night after this unwelcome visit, the king mounted a horse brought to the orchard stile and rode away disguised as a serving man on the first leg of his long and hazardous journey to safety on the Continent.

Visitors to Moseley Old Hall retrace Charles's route on that fateful night 350 years ago when the Stuart cause was nearly lost. Although the façades of the Elizabethan house were faced in brick in the nineteenth century and the mullioned windows have been replaced by casements, much of the original panelling and timber framing inside the house survives and heavy oak seventeenth-century furniture, including the bed on which Charles slept, and contemporary portraits of the king and those who helped him, all contribute to an authentic atmosphere, miraculously not destroyed by noise from the M54 only metres away. Standing at the window of Whitgreave's study over the front porch, as he and the king did, it is possible to imagine that the remnants of the defeated army will shortly appear straggling up the lane on their long walk back to Scotland. Mementoes of these perilous days include a proclamation of 10 September 1651, offering a £1,000 reward for the capture of the king, and Charles II's letter of thanks to Jane Lane, who helped him to escape.

The house is now surrounded by a reconstructed seventeenth-century garden, based on a design of 1640. In the elaborate knot garden, box hedges outline a geometrical pattern like a horizontal wrought-iron screen, with each compartment filled with coloured gravels and stones. The orchard has been planted with old varieties of fruit trees; quinces, mulberries and medlars frame the path from the Nut Alley and a little herb garden now shelters beneath more box hedges. Perhaps the king saw a similar garden from the chapel windows when John Huddlestone took him to visit the oratory in the attic, now adorned with an eighteenth-century painted barrel ceiling. Charles was certainly to remember Moseley, giving Thomas Whitgreave a pension of £200 a year on his restoration in 1660 and summoning Huddlestone to administer the last rites of the Catholic Church when he lay dying in 1685.

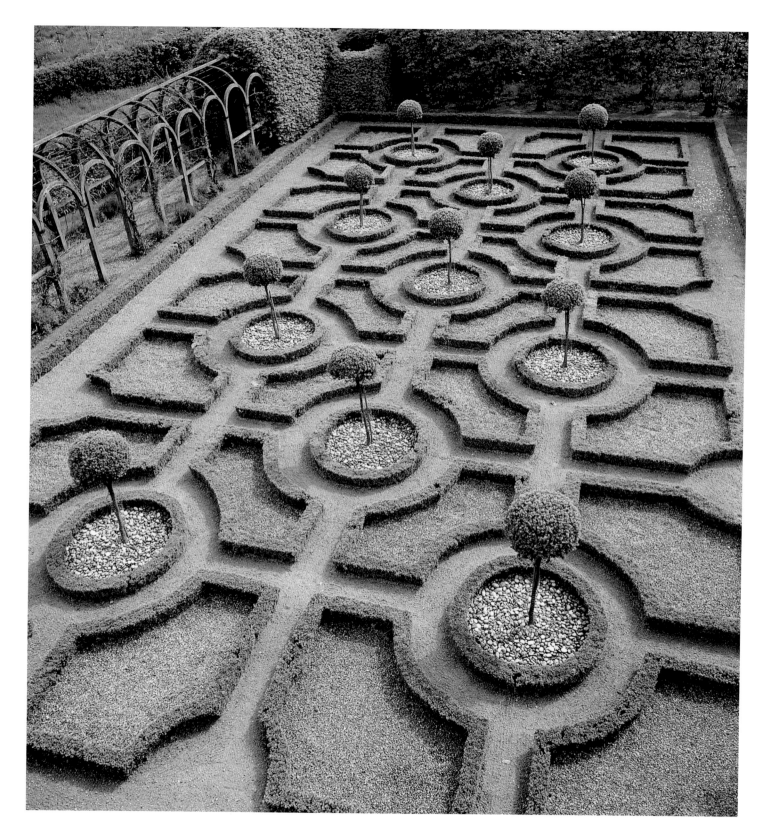

Adventuring

The European world map, for so long centred on the Mediterranean, was redrawn in the sixteenth and seventeenth centuries. To the west was the New World of the Americas, south lay Africa, and beyond, round the Cape of Good Hope, the vast sub-continent of India, the Spice Islands of the East Indies, and the still-mysterious Pacific. In England, the reign of Elizabeth I kickstarted a long period of colonial conquest, new trading ventures and the pursuit of traditional hostilities in settings far from the usual European arena. Intrepid privateers, often sailing with the queen's blessing, but pursuing personal wealth and advancement, planted infant colonies in North America, harried and attacked Spanish ships and settlements in the vast new empire which England's old enemy had seized in the Americas, and searched for the fabled north-west passage, which, some believed, offered a safe route round the top of North America. And it was Elizabeth who chartered the East India Company, first seen as a way to get a foothold on the lucrative Spice Islands, but increasingly involved in trade with India and in establishing a sphere of influence in the sub-continent.

By the eighteenth century, although the navy had largely taken over the aggressive role of the privateer, much remained the same. Spain was still a key enemy, and squadrons were sent to harry her possessions in the Pacific and to pursue the richly-laden galleons which sailed between Acapulco and Manila, and which brought South American silver back to Europe. The value of a captured cargo was still shared out among the crew, and squadron commanders could found family fortunes with a rich prize. There were similar pickings in India. Here, the East India Company now fielded private armies and was dramatically extending its power and territories, with opportunities

for some company men to make huge fortunes. By the twentieth century, the challenges and rewards had shifted. Now men in the adventuring mould made their mark in the globe's most inhospitable and remote places, climbing unscaled mountains or, attracted by the spartan lifestyles of those living in extreme environments, going native in the desert or the Amazonian jungle. Some found themselves playing a role on the wider stage, championing the causes of the peoples they encountered.

COMPTON CASTLE
107

The West Country, half-islanded by the Atlantic and with a long maritime tradition, produced some of the greatest seafarers of Elizabethan times. The Gilberts of Compton Castle, an ancient fortified manor just 2 miles inland from the Devon coast, were among the foremost. Of the three sons of Otho Gilbert, two, John and Adrian, provided ships for the Armada, and Sir John, who once presented the queen with a parrot, made preparations against a possible Spanish landing nearby.

Their brother Humphrey (1539–83, **left**) was the true adventurer of the three. His promotion of the north-west passage to Asia, round the top of Canada, came to nothing, although a sound in Greenland is now called after him. His other dream was to establish an English colony in America, and in 1578 the queen gave him her backing for the scheme. A first expedition only got as far as the Cape Verde Islands, but in 1583 Sir Humphrey fitted out another fleet and sailed to Newfoundland, already an important landfall for whaling and fishing boats, and annexed it for the Crown. But he left no permanent settlement, and on the return voyage, sailing in the tiny 10-ton *Squirrel*, he went down with the ship in a storm off the Azores.

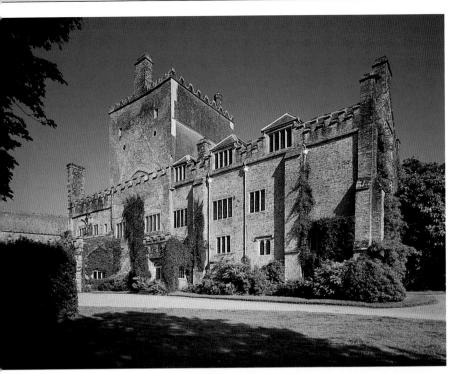

late 16th-century side-drum (**below left**) which may be one of those taken on Drake's last voyage, in 1595, when he died of dysentery in the Caribbean. Legend has it that the drum will start beating to wake Drake from the dead if England is ever in danger. Thirty years later, Drake's nephew, another Sir Francis, burnished his uncle's reputation by publishing gilded accounts (**below**) of the circumnavigation and of Drake's equally piratical voyages to the West Indies in the early 1570s.

As English naval strength grew, the kind of expeditions that were once led by free agents like Drake were now openly sanctioned and carried out by ships of the line. But seized treasure and prize money still provided rich pickings. The fortunes of the Anson

Across Devon, in the wooded country running down to the Tamar, lived Sir Francis Drake, one of the greatest adventurers of them all and a pirate by any other name. Secretly given sanction by Elizabeth I to attack Spain, in 1577 Drake set out on the voyage that would see him return to Plymouth three years later, having sailed round the world and seized a fortune from a Spanish treasure ship. Now a very rich man and, as an aspiring *nouveau riche*, anxious to match his wealth with respectability and position, Drake paid the enormous sum of £3,400 for Buckland Abbey (**above**), a former Cistercian monastery that had been converted into a house by Sir Richard Grenville, another adventurer in the same mould as Drake but without his luck. An overmantel in the house carries Drake's coat of arms (**above, right**), which features a ship guided by the divine hand of Providence, and these arms are also painted on a rare family of Shugborough were made by Admiral George Anson, seen here at the pinnacle of his career in a portrait by Reynolds (**above**). In 1739, when Britain was once again at war with Spain, Anson, then still a captain, was sent with a squadron to harass Spanish shipping in the Pacific and to cut off the supply of treasure from the mines of Peru which fuelled the Spanish war machine. In an epic voyage that lasted from 1740 to 1744, Anson followed in the footsteps of Drake, becoming the second Englishman to circumnavigate the world. In pursuit of his aims, he sacked a Spanish town on the South American coast and, still hoping to engage the treasure galleon which sailed annually from Acapulco to Manila in the Spanish-held Philippines, set out across the Pacific. On 20 June 1743, in an engagement immortalised by John Cleveley (**above, right**), he at last intercepted and captured the *Nuestra Señora de Covadonga*, which carried treasure worth £400,000. The fortune earned from this prize financed the building of Shugborough in Staffordshire.

With Anson on his voyage round the world was a young lieutenant, Hyde Parker, later 5th Baronet and Vice-Admiral of the Blue, who had run away from school and joined the navy as a child. Some twenty years later, in October 1762, when he had his own command, Hyde Parker also captured a Spanish galleon, the *Santissima Trinidad*, off Manila. Fine Chinese porcelain from the ship is on show at Melford Hall in Suffolk, which was bought by Hyde Parker's son, and here too is the bluff admiral in a portrait by George Romney (**right**).

Starting from small beginnings in 1600, with a few trading posts in the Bay of Bengal, by the mid-18th century the East India Company had its own army and was a power to be reckoned with on the Indian sub-continent, offering lucrative careers for the sons of impoverished gentry. One such was Robert Clive, who joined the company at the age of sixteen and arrived in India in 1744, destined, it was hoped, to restore the family fortunes. Astutely transferring to the military arm of the company, Clive was a major player in a series of actions against the French, who were also trying to carve out an area of influence, and their allies among the Indian princes. A dramatic expansion of British influence was made possible by Clive's defeat of the Nawab of Bengal at Plassey in 1757.

Each time he returned to England he had amassed more loot and a larger fortune, some of which he used to bribe the electorates who gave him a Parliamentary seat, some of which he invested in property and art, thus matching his wealth with social position. His status was confirmed when he was made a lord. General unease at the huge wealth of returning nabobs, as the *nouveaux riches* of the company were known, rebounded on Clive. Faced with a parliamentary inquiry into his activities, he committed suicide.

His son, the 2nd Lord Clive, following in his father's footsteps, arrived in India in 1798 to serve as governor of Madras. Almost immediately he was involved in a campaign against the anti-British Tipu Sahib, Sultan of Mysore, whose capital Seringapatam,

POWIS CASTLE
314

the wealthiest city in south India, was comprehensively looted by the victorious army. Some of the richest pickings were acquired by Lord Clive and are now part of the collection of Indian loot on show at Powis Castle in Powys, which was inherited by the 2nd Lord's son. Among them is a gold tiger's head from the sultan's throne (**left**), his state tent of painted chintz (**below**), and many pieces acquired by the lst Lord Clive, including painted ivory playing cards (**right**) and a bejewelled dagger with a jade hilt fashioned as a goat's head with ruby eyes (**below, left**). Nathaniel Dance's dignified portrait of the 1st Lord (**previous page**), painted *c.*1770, not long after he came back to England for the last time, hangs in the castle.

POWIS CASTLE
314

The loners and men of action who once assuaged their restlessness and need to live apart by sailing uncharted waters or engaging in far-flung military campaigns found other outlets in the shrinking and ever more complex world of the 20th century. Among them was the enigmatic and romantic figure of T.E. Lawrence, seen here in a portrait by Augustus John. Drawn to the Middle East by his twin passions for archaeology and travel, the young Lawrence spent four years excavating Carcemish in Syria, where he learned Arabic and increasingly identified with the peoples of the desert, then under the yoke of the failing Turkish empire. When the First World War began, and Turkey threw in its lot with Germany, Lawrence, working for British intelligence, joined and aided the Arab revolt against the Turks, eventually leading the rebel advance into Damascus in 1918.

A few years after the war, in search of a haven of his own where he could write and lead a simple, uncluttered life, he rented and later bought a tiny, workman's cottage in Dorset known as Clouds Hill. Here he read, wrote and listened to music, sometimes entertaining friends from the army camp where he had enlisted as a

private. While the cottage fed a need for a retreat, Lawrence was no recluse. In his speedboat *Biscuit*, shown here as a model, he took part in the Schneider trophy races in 1929 and explored the south Devon coast. His alterations to the cottage included a thatched garage for his motorcycle, which he was riding when he was involved in an accident on 13 May 1935. He died six days later; he was 46. Fittingly, the effigy on his tomb, shown here in the maquette by Eric Kennington, portrays him in Arab dress.

CLOUDS HILL
102

Top: The Georgian south front of Mottisfont, as seen in a contemporary lithograph by G.F. Prosser, gives no hint of the medieval abbey buildings which are incorporated in the house.

Above: A delicately-coloured Petite Lisette rose from the outstanding display of old roses in Mottisfont's two walled gardens.

Mottisfont Abbey HAMPSHIRE

4½ miles north-west of Romsey, ¾ mile west of the A3057 [443 G6]

Those lucky enough to acquire monastic houses during the time of the Dissolution were then faced with the problem of transforming them into domestic residences. Most chose to adapt the monks' living quarters, but a few ambitious men sought to incorporate the church itself into their conversions. One such was William Lord Sandys, Lord Chamberlain to Henry VIII, who was granted the priory of Mottisfont in exchange for the villages of Chelsea and Paddington and whose descendants were to move here from The Vyne (*see* p.410) after the Civil War. The silvery stone north front of his Tudor house runs the full length of what was the nave of the church and ends in the truncated tower, where the arch leading to the north transept is outlined on the façade. The medieval buttresses are now crowned with eighteenth-century stone balls, transforming them into ornamental pilasters. Original mullions survive on the ground floor, but sash windows were inserted above as part of extensive Georgian alterations.

The cultured world of the 1740s is far more pronounced on the south, where an elegant red-brick Georgian façade with a central pediment is framed by two shallow bayed wings stepped out from the main body of the house. Three storeys here, in contrast to two on the north, reflect the sloping site.

Few traces of the Tudor interior escaped the Georgian remodelling, but the ghost of the priory emerges in the atmospheric early thirteenth-century cellarium, with columns of Caen stone, now partly buried, supporting a vaulted roof. The main glory of the house, the Whistler Room over the cellarium, is a much later addition. This enchanting drawing room takes its name from Rex Whistler's elaborate *trompe-l'oeil* murals imitating Gothic plasterwork, executed in 1938–9 after the completion of his mammoth work at Plas Newydd (*see* p.305). At Mottisfont Whistler had also been commissioned to design the furniture, but he never returned from the Second World War to complete his assignment.

The Abbey lies low on green lawns by the River Test, the centrepiece of beautiful wooded gardens. Many of the mature walnuts, sycamores, Spanish chestnuts, beeches and cedars for which the property is now famous were part of the eighteenth-century grounds, but some are even older. A London plane by the river is said to be the largest in the country, its spreading branches covering some 1,254 square metres (1,500 square yards). A little Gothick summerhouse, almost surrounded by trees on the lawns to the north-west of the house, also dates from the eighteenth century and incorporates medieval floor tiles and a corbel from the priory.

The garden as it is today also owes much to Mr and Mrs Gilbert Russell, who came to Mottisfont in 1934. The north lawn bordered by a pleached lime walk and the paved octagon surrounded by clipped yew were designed by Geoffrey Jellicoe in 1936–7 and a few years later Norah Lindsay laid out the box- and lavender-edged parterre on the south front and planted wistaria, clematis and other climbers on the house. A magnolia garden and a beech circle are other notable features of the grounds, but most visitors now come to see the two walled gardens containing Mottisfont's collection of old roses. What was the kitchen garden holds the national collection of pre-1900 shrub roses. Box-edged beds round a fountain pool contain over 300 varieties, many of them cultivars developed in nineteenth-century France, such as those collected by the Empress Joséphine, but including species from all over the world. Ancient hybrids flowering white, purple, carmine and maroon mix with the tomato-red and brilliant yellow of Persian roses and the clear lemon and deep crimson of Chinese varieties. In 1982, ten years after the kitchen garden was laid out, the collection was extended into an adjacent walled garden to the north, which was planted with roses from the German National Rose Garden at Sangerhausen. On the far side of the grounds crystal-clear water still gushes from the spring which attracted the Austin canons to this sheltered spot nearly 800 years ago.

Mottistone Manor Garden ISLE OF WIGHT

In the village of Mottistone [443 H7]

This young garden largely created by Lady Nicholson and her family over the last twenty years lies in a beautiful sheltered valley sloping down to the medieval and sixteenth-century manor and to the sea beyond. A flight of steps behind the house leads up to grassy terraces formally planted with roses and fruit trees. An avenue of cherries, plums and apples marks the site of the old orchard, and a broad stretch of grass sweeps up to Shern Place, an idyllic secondary valley, planted with beech and ash and carpeted with bluebells in spring, which runs up to the Long Stone on the downs above. This impressive Neolithic long barrow was probably also the site of a Saxon moot. Most of the trees in the garden are still young, but some more mature specimens, including a tulip tree, a magnolia, a liquid amber and a mulberry, date from John Seeley's restoration of the house in the late 1920s. The garden is circled by a grassy walk following the steeply sloping valley sides, with views east to St Catherine's Point and west to the spire and golden weathervane of Mottistone church.

Moulton Hall NORTH YORKSHIRE

5 miles east of Richmond [445 J4]

This compact stone house of 1650, about a mile east of the A1, is adorned with large Dutch gables and boasts a very fine carved wood staircase.

Mount Grace Priory NORTH YORKSHIRE

6 miles north-east of Northallerton, ½ mile east of the A19 and ½ mile south of its junction with the A172 [445 J4]

The simplicity and austerity of this little Carthusian community on the edge of the wooded Cleveland Hills is far removed from the splendours of Fountains, which is some 20 miles to the south (*see* p.154). Whereas the remains of the Cistercian house speak of a life lived in common and of an increasing relaxation of the principles on which it was founded, Mount Grace reflects the pursuit of asceticism, untouched by the attractions of the world. The Carthusians were more hermits than monks, living apart from each other as well as in isolation from the world. Whereas other orders ate, prayed and slept together, each Carthusian lived largely in isolation in his own cell, to which meals were brought.

The main feature of Mount Grace is an extensive grass cloister, measuring 82 hectares (270 feet) on its longest side. Ranged around it, and along one side of an outer court, are the remains of the stone-built, four-roomed cells where the little community – there is provision for only 21 monks – spent long hours in prayer and contemplation and in copying out devotional works. Most of the cells still show the hatch through which food was served from the cloister, the right-angled bend ensuring that monk and server did not see one another. And each monk had his own walled garden, about 6 metres (20 feet) square, with his own garderobe at the far end. Perhaps some allowed themselves to sit here and doze in the sun on warm summer afternoons. On the north side of the cloister is the diminutive 36-metre (118-foot) church, a plain simple building that was rarely used except on Sundays and feast days, its little battlemented, pinnacled tower a telling contrast to Marmaduke Huby's soaring monument at Fountains Abbey.

But although Mount Grace turned its back on the world, sheltering behind the high precinct wall which still encloses much of the site, the community was not averse to modern conveniences. Arched recesses still visible in the cloister walls of some cells once held taps fed from a spring just outside the priory walls. Another spring was channelled to flush the drain serving the garderobes, some of which still project from the garden walls on the north side of the precinct.

Mount Grace was founded in 1398 by Thomas de Holland, Duke of Surrey and Earl of Kent, and is one of only nine Charterhouses established in England, most of them part of the great Carthusian expansion between 1343 and 1414. It was surrendered quietly to Henry VIII's commissioners in December 1539, and more than a century passed before the range housing the priory's guest accommodation and kitchens was converted into the long gabled house with a projecting two-storey porch which is now such a feature of the site. On the north side of the cloister the reconstructed cell like a tiny two-storeyed cottage dates from the early twentieth century, the fireplace in its living room suggesting a degree of comfort in winter. For those who chose to live like hermits here, physical privation was probably not the major burden of the regime. The cells outlined on the grass would have been a spiritual sanctuary for the strong and resolute, but a prison for those who found they could not live with themselves or began to doubt their faith.

Above: Lord Castlereagh, the 2nd Marquess of Londonderry, seen here in a painting by an unknown artist, is the most significant of the many political figures associated with Mount Stewart. Castlereagh was largely reponsible for the unification of Great Britain and Ireland in 1801 and played an important role in the Congress which sealed the end of the Napoleonic wars in 1815.

Opposite, above: The staircase hall at Mount Stewart, one of the finest interiors created by George Dance when he rebuilt the house in the early 19th century. On the half landing is George Stubbs's painting of the racehorse Hambletonian.

Opposite, below: This grinning dinosaur on the Dodo Terrace at Mount Stewart is one of many creatures and other statuary adorning the luxuriant and exotic gardens, which are full of imagery and allusions.

Mount Stewart CO. DOWN

15 miles east of Belfast on the A20 Newtownards–Portaferry road, 5 miles south-east of Newtownards [444 D4]

This long, low, grey house beautifully situated looking south over Strangford Lough is associated with two exceptional men, the architect James 'Athenian' Stuart and the politician Viscount Castlereagh, but it is alive with the spirit of vivacious, brilliant Edith, Lady Londonderry, wife of the 7th Marquess, who redecorated and furnished most of the house between the First and Second World Wars.

The main block, with a huge classical portico fronting the balustraded entrance court, was designed in the mid-1830s by the renowned Irish architect William Vitruvius Morrison for the 3rd Marquess of Londonderry. Morrison's grandiose octagonal hall, with a black-and-white chequered floor and classical statues framed by Ionic pillars, fills the centre of the house, lit from above by a huge dome. A bust immortalises the linen merchant Alexander Stewart, the 3rd Marquess's grandfather, who acquired the estate in 1744, while the outstanding rust-coloured early eighteenth-century Chinese dinner service displayed here was inherited by Stewart's wife, whose brother was Governor of Bombay. Morrison's vast drawing room divided by screens of green Ionic columns is similarly imposing, giving Lady Londonderry just the setting she needed for her lavish entertaining.

George Dance's west wing, created for the 1st Marquess in the early nineteenth century, has a lighter and more intimate touch. The delightful music room, the least changed of his interiors, has an inlaid floor by John Ferguson, with a scalloped octagon of oak and mahogany surrounded by radiating boards of mellow bog fir enclosing a central motif like a Catherine wheel. Delicate plaster-work on the ceiling reflects the design. Double doors lead into Dance's elegant domed staircase hall, dominated by George Stubbs's intriguing painting of the racehorse Hambletonian. Stubbs' painting shows the horse after his win at Newmarket in 1799, a race in which Stubbs felt he had been driven too hard. Hambletonian is depicted in an impossible pose, standing on his two left legs, his groom's right arm stretched like elastic over his neck.

The principal bedrooms called after European cities (Rome, Moscow, even Sebastopol), the mementoes in the Castlereagh Room and Empire chairs used by delegates to the Congress of Vienna in 1815 (including those occupied by Wellington and Talleyrand) recall the proud and austere 2nd Marquess, Foreign Secretary for ten years, who died so tragically by his own hand in 1822, misunderstood by

the nation to which he had devoted his life. The main architect of the act of 1801 which united Great Britain and Ireland until the creation of Eire in 1922, Castlereagh went on to play a major role in the war against Napoleon and in the Congress which concluded it, rightly regarded as the world's first summit. It is a measure of Castlereagh's achievement that the boundaries established at this time were to endure until the start of the First World War.

The 6th and 7th Marquesses also followed prominent political careers, and both Edward VII and the future George VI were entertained at Mount Stewart. As Secretary of State for Air, the 7th Marquess promoted the Hurricane and Spitfire fighter planes which were to prove so crucial in the Battle of Britain and introduced legislation establishing air corridors. Perhaps a premonition led him to make several private visits to Germany in the late 1930s to meet Hitler and other Nazi leaders in an effort to promote Anglo-German understanding.

Leading politicians, among them Sir Arthur Balfour, Harold Macmillan and Ramsay MacDonald, featured at the celebrated house parties which Lady Edith, wife of the 7th Marquess, gave in the interwar years. Her flamboyant 1920s decor, the backdrop for these glittering occasions, survives in most of the principal rooms. Salmon-pink walls in Morrison's drawing room set off a green grand piano and comfortable chairs and sofas are spread invitingly on the pink Aubusson carpets. Subdued low-level lighting comes from lamps of every description, some made out of classical urns, others once altar candle-sticks. Chinese tea caddies converted into lamp stands, chinoiserie screens and other oriental pieces were brought back from a trip to China in 1912.

Two chairs in this room and the friendly stone animals adorning a terrace on the south front – four plump dodos, a grinning dinosaur, a hedgehog and a frog among them – recall the famous Ark Club, formed at the family's house in London where Lady Londonderry held Wednesday gatherings for political and military figures during the First World War. Members of the club were known by the names of a wide variety of creatures, including the albatross (Sir Arthur Balfour), the warlock (Winston Churchill), and the wild boar (Lord Hailsham). Appropriately, Lady Londonderry was Circe the Sorceress.

This legendary beauty, whose charm is if anything enhanced by the drab khaki uniform in the portrait showing her as head of the Women's Legion, was also largely responsible for Mount Stewart's enchanting 31.5-hectare (78-acre) garden, which flourishes with sub-tropical luxuriance in the temperate climate of the Ards peninsula.

Notable for its evergreens and species from the Southern Hemisphere, many tender trees and shrubs cultivated here are rarely seen elsewhere in the British Isles.

The formal garden around the house is laid out as a series of varied outdoor rooms reminiscent of Hidcote or Sissinghurst (*see* pp.182 and 341). A majestic flight of steps sweeps down into the Italian garden on the south front, created with the help of twenty ex-servicemen after the First World War, where two parterres set around fountain pools either side of a palm-fringed broad grass walk are planted to give contrasting effects, one flowering strongly orange and red against violet and purple foliage, the other in softer pinks, blues, mauves and white with silver foliage. Imaginative statuary, including mischievous monkeys and winged dragons perched on columns, was all designed by Lady Londonderry. Mature trees form a continuous backdrop, casting ribbons of shade across the grass.

In the more intimate sunk garden to the west of the house, based on a design by Gertrude Jekyll, tall cypress hedges shield rose-hung pergolas and four scalloped beds round the central lawn, particularly spectacular when the vivid orange azaleas, blue delphiniums and yellow lupins are all in flower. In contrast, only blue and white flowers, such as forget-me-nots, blue and white African lilies, white roses and buddleia, are allowed in the secluded, shady Mairi Garden laid out in the shape of a Tudor rose, some creeping over the stone flags of the paths. Cockleshells round the central fountain pool, 'silver bells' (various campanulas) and 'pretty maids' (*Saxifraga granulata*) illustrate the nursery rhyme, here a play on the name of Lady Mairi Stewart, the 7th Marquess's daughter, who gave Mount Stewart and many of its contents, together with an endowment, to the Trust in 1976.

Away from the house the planting is informal, with magnificent trees, shrubs and herbaceous plants along the drive, in the Lily Wood and lining the walks round the lake created by the 3rd Marquess, part of a nineteenth-century layout which Lady Londonderry embellished. There are rhododendrons of each and every variety, many sweetly scented, and species from the Mediterranean and Far East, such as the Chinese birch. Several Southern Hemisphere plants include New Zealand tree ferns, the Tasmanian cedar, eucalyptus and the rare evergreen *Gevuina avellana* from Southern Chile.

A network of paths explores the slopes of the hill beyond the lake, planted with unusual specimens such as the Kashmir cypress, the Tatarian maple, the calico bush and the fragrant South African *Buddleia auriculata*. Conical roofs glimpsed above the trees mark the

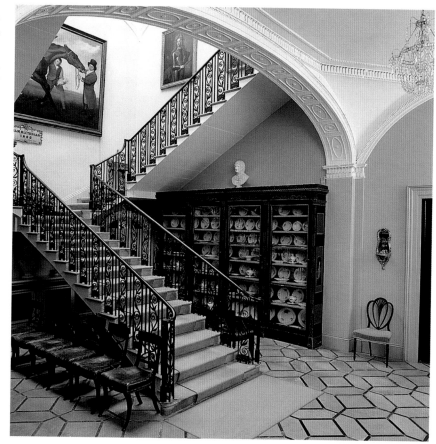

Londonderrys' burial ground, Tir Nan Og, on the summit, guarded by statues of Irish saints and with a fruiting olive, believed to have been grown from seed brought back from the Mount of Olives, spreading along the high enclosing wall. The 7th Marquess and his wife rest here.

The octagonal Temple of the Winds, on a prominent knoll in the woods to the south of the house, is from another age, a replica, like its counterpart at Shugborough (*see* p.339), of the Tower of the Winds in ancient Athens and the only building in Ireland by the pioneering Neo-classical architect James 'Athenian' Stuart. Erected by the 1st Marquess between 1782 and 1785, it was designed as an eye-catcher and banqueting house. The sumptuously decorated upper room has another star-like marquetry floor by John Ferguson, the design again echoed in plaster on the ceiling, and a dew-drop chandelier hangs from the central medallion. On the floor below, long sash windows can be lowered into the basement to give an uninterrupted view over the island-studded waters of Strangford Lough to the prominent silhouette of Scrabo Tower on the north shore, built in memory of the 3rd Marquess.

The Mournes CO. DOWN

South of Newcastle [444 D5]

The granite humps of the mountains of Mourne dominate the landscape of this south-east corner of Northern Ireland. Mostly smooth and rounded, with slopes of purple heather and mossy summit heaths, the hills are cleft by deep valleys and occasionally erupt into crags and cliffs. At the northern end of the range, where the mountains stand high above the coastal resort of Newcastle, the Trust has acquired 526 hectares (1,300 acres) of prime walking and climbing country, including the 852-metre (2,796-foot) Slieve Donard, the highest peak, Slieve Commedagh and the whole of the upper Glen River Valley, where the jagged Eagle Rock cliffs were the last northern Irish home of the sea eagle. A number of paths lead up into the mountains, including a track along the Bloody River which links with the Trust's coastal path (*see* p.273). Those who make the climb – effectively from sea level – are rewarded by spectacular views to the Isle of Man and the Lake District.

Above: The ridge of Mow Cop, crowned by an 18th-century folly, rises high over the Cheshire plain.

Below: Looking across Murlough Bay to the rain-shrouded Mountains of Mourne.

Mow Cop CHESHIRE

5 miles south of Congleton, 2 miles south-east of Little Moreton Hall [445 I8]

From a distance Mow Cop looks like a ruined medieval fortress, with a roofless round tower and what appear to be remnants of a curtain wall picturesquely silhouetted against the sky on the western edge of the Pennines. In fact this castle is a romantic sham, built as a summerhouse and eye-catcher in 1754 by Randle Wilbraham of nearby Rode Hall and placed exactly on the boundary between Cheshire and Staffordshire. It is worth braving the steep approaches for the views from the top of the 305-metre (1,000-foot) ridge, west over the Cheshire plain to the Welsh hills and east over the Peak District, where long tentacles reach up the valleys from the Potteries to the south. To the north, over the trees which shield Little Moreton Hall (*see* p.226), looms the futuristic dish of the radio telescope at Jodrell Bank. As an inscribed stone by the path to the summit records, in 1807 this spectacular but windswept spot was the site of a historic open-air meeting led by Hugh Bourne and William Clowes which resulted in the birth of Primitive Methodism.

Mr Straw's House NOTTINGHAMSHIRE

7 Blyth Grove, Worksop [445 J7]

This bay-fronted, three-storey Edwardian villa is like a thousand other red-brick suburban semis built for well-to-do tradesmen and professionals at the turn of the century. But the Straw brothers – William and Walter – who lived here for 50 years were anything but ordinary. Perhaps never quite recovering from the deaths of their parents, William and Florence, in the 1930s, perhaps naturally reclusive and conservative, they preserved the house as it was when their father and mother were alive, ignoring modern conveniences, such as central heating and the telephone, and the advent of radio and television.

Today, 7 Blyth Grove is partly a shrine to William and Florence, partly a uniquely well-preserved example of interwar middle-class living. Completely refurbished before the family moved in, in 1923, the house boasts dark 1920s wallpapers with decorative Sanderson borders, doors and other woodwork painted to simulate oak, and period carpets and lino. Furnishings are heavy, the rooms cluttered, with the parents' belongings still in their customary places. William senior's coats and hats still hang in the hall, and in William and Florence's bedroom, where the

Bottled jam made from fruit from the garden, a foot-operated vacuum cleaner and Second World War ARP wardens' helmets are among the many things that were squirreled away in the lumber room of Mr Straw's House.

brass bedstead is covered with newspaper to keep off the dust, the dressing-table still has the box for William's detachable collars and drawers of personal belongings, such as the blue sunglasses Florence wore on her annual holiday in Scarborough. The period detail even includes trade calendars advertising the grocery business which William built up, and an unheated, starkly functional 1920s bathroom. The kitchen, where bread was baked every Saturday night, is similarly uninviting, although the brothers did put in a 1950s gas stove.

The boys seem to have fitted in round their parents' space, living largely in the south-facing dining room, one of only two rooms where a fire was regularly lit in cold weather and, in William junior's case, sleeping in a small atticky bedroom at the top of the house. An ordered routine, unchanged for 40 years, included the Sunday outing to church, where the brothers always sat in the same pew, and the Sunday afternoon walk into town to inspect their grocery store and other property, while every weekday, after the shop closed, Walter would call in at his cousin's house over the road to listen to the 6 o'clock news on the radio. Both brothers liked to work in the little garden, which still has its outside privy. It seems William, who read English at university and taught for some years in London, was the dominant personality, resisting innovation and refusing to let Walter bring the car he bought in the 1960s to the house. It was William, too, who became the custodian of Blyth Grove, leaving notes around the place to record details about the family and its possessions. But he was by no means unworldly. Savings from his teacher's salary were invested in Marks & Spencer shares, worth over £150,000 at his death.

The Needles Old Battery ISLE OF WIGHT

West of Freshwater Bay and Alum Bay [443 G7]

The threat of a French invasion in 1858, fuelled by Lord Palmerston's aggressively nationalistic foreign policy, threw Britain into a panic, not least because the coastal defences, little changed since Trafalgar in 1805, were clearly inadequate. This magnificently sited little fort, set 76 metres (250 feet) above the sea on the far western point of the Isle of Wight, was one of the new artillery works built to guard the approaches to the Solent and the major naval base at Portsmouth.

The dagger-shaped headland with precipitous chalk cliffs falling to the jagged outlines of the Needles is reached by a walk of about a mile across the downs. On the other side of a ditch cut to protect the landward approaches is the only entrance, a massive archway dated 1862. A tunnel-like passage emerges in the parade ground where five semicircular gun emplacements, two of them now mounted with guns rescued from the sea by the Trust in 1983, face west and north. Built into the rock are underground chambers for storing gunpowder, shells and cartridges, still showing the ingenious arrangements which allowed candles or oil-burning lanterns to be used without danger of igniting the powder and the system of ventilation ducts to keep the ammunition dry. From the parade ground another tunnel leads out to the look-out point positioned on the very tip of the headland where a searchlight was set up in 1899. The views are breathtaking – down on to the points of the Needles, with their wheeling colonies of cormorants and seagulls, and across the bay to the mainland, where the outline of Hurst Castle marks the western arm of the Solent. Just up the hill, on the site of the original Needles lighthouse, are the remains of the Needles New Battery, built in 1893–5 and finally closed in 1954 when the guns were scrapped.

Although the Needles batteries saw little active service, they have played an important role in military history. A massive iron ring in the parade ground of the Old Battery marks the site of the world's first anti-aircraft gun, set up here in 1913. And in 1956 the headland was the engine-testing site for the Black Knight rocket, subsequently launched at Woomera in Australia.

Nether Alderley Mill CHESHIRE

1½ miles south of Alderley Edge, on east side of the A34 [445 I7]

Nether Alderley is a most unusual water-mill. On one side a long sweeping stone-tiled roof reaches almost to the ground, giving just a glimpse of warm sandstone walls. On the other the mill is wedged right up against a wooded bank, the dam of the little reservoir which provides the water to turn the wheels. The stream on which the mill was sited was too small and irregular to power the machinery effectively and this ingenious solution – with the later addition of three more reservoirs – was devised when Nether Alderley was first built, in the sixteenth century. The mill is noteworthy, too, for having a pair of water-wheels, set one below the other, a short trough leading from the first to the second. Both are 3.5 metres (12 feet) in diameter and, like all the mill machinery, date from the nineteenth century.

Four dormer windows in the sloping roof light the interior, the most remarkable feature of which is the Elizabethan oak woodwork which supports the roof. Wooden pins hold the timbers together, and some display the numbers used by the carpenters when assembling the frame. A floor of finely perforated tiles is the remains of a kiln for drying wet grain, a feature more usually seen in Scotland.

Remarkably, Nether Alderley was operating as late as 1939, over 600 years after the earliest mention of a mill here in 1290. The machinery and the culvert from the reservoir have been restored and further restoration work is planned over the next few years.

The Needles Old Battery, set high above the sea at the westernmost tip of the Isle of Wight, was built to guard the approaches to the Solent in the mid-19th century.

sophisticated world of the court rather than local building styles, and suggests something of the Elizabethan prodigy houses that were to follow at the end of the century (*see* p.175). A prominent three-light oriel projects from the centre of the building and a pedimented doorway flanked by Doric columns is a remarkably pure Renaissance feature for its date. The two top floors were originally banqueting rooms, from which Sir Nicholas and his guests would have enjoyed wide views over the deer-park around the house and the wooded countryside beyond.

Internally, Wyatt left the lodge more or less as it was, and Tudor fireplaces still warm some of the rooms in this part of the house, but he remodelled a second block added in the late seventeenth century, introducing Neo-classical interiors. More Doric columns divide the unusual hall he inserted between the two buildings, his frieze of sheep's skulls perhaps intended to recall the wool trade which brought wealth to this area in the Middle Ages.

Formal axial gardens to the north and east were laid out by Mr Robert Parsons, the tenant from 1970 to 1994, who began to restore the property, but there are still remnants of the wild bulb garden and rock gardens created in the late nineteenth century on the slopes below the house.

Newark Park GLOUCESTERSHIRE

1½ miles north-east of Wotton-under-Edge, 1½ miles south of junction of the A4135 and the B4058 [442 F4]

This unusual, atmospheric house stands high on a spur of the Cotswolds looking south over steep, wooded slopes plunging to the valley of the River Severn. Buttresses, battlements and Georgian sash windows added by James Wyatt in the 1790s only partly disguise the modest four-storey Elizabethan hunting lodge built by Sir Nicholas Poyntz in *c.*1550, still surmounted by the romantic dragon weathervane with which he crowned his new property, a proud beast with a long coiled tail silhouetted against the sky. Like his father and grandfather before him, Sir Nicholas was prominent at court, becoming Groom of the Bedchamber to Henry VIII after 1539. His hunting lodge was built on monastic land granted by the king after the Dissolution of the Monasteries, formerly the property of the Abbey of Kingswood in the vale below, some materials from which were incorporated in Newark.

The Tudor building emerges most strongly on the east, where Wyatt's sympathetic hand did not destroy original features. Although Sir Nicholas's architect is unknown, this tall, symmetrical façade, with huge mullioned and transomed windows lighting the third floor, reflects the

New Forest HAMPSHIRE

Extends from Bournemouth, to the west, to Southampton, to the east [443 G6]

The Trust owns three areas of common on the edge of the New Forest. The largest, at Bramshaw to the north, covers 566.5 hectares (1,400 acres) and consists of Cadnam and Stocks Cross Greens, together with the commons of Cadnam, Furzley, Half Moon and Black Hill, Penn and Plaitford. North-east of Fordingbridge lie Millersford Plantation and Hale Purlieu, over 202.5 hectares (500 acres) in extent. Purlieu means land on the border of a forest, not within its boundaries but subject to forest laws controlling the hunting of game. Finally, 2 miles east of Ringwood, there is the small Hightown Common.

Since 1964 these commons have been included 'within the perambulation' of the New Forest. Grazing keeps the land largely as open heath, with heather and gorse interspersed with areas of woodland and with some wet places covering the gravelly peat soil. It makes good walking terrain. There is a sense of remoteness and solitude here and a rich flora and fauna which includes the Dartford warbler and woodlark and heathland butterflies such as the green hairstreak and silver-studded blue.

Newtown ISLE OF WIGHT

Midway between Newport and Yarmouth, 1 mile north of the A3054 [443 G7]

Despite its name, this shadow of a place on an arm of the Newtown estuary dates back over 700 years. Founded by the Bishop of Winchester in 1256 and laid out to a grid plan, much like a French bastide, it was at its height in the mid-fourteenth century when a community of some 300 prospered on the revenue from oyster beds, salt works and the ships using the magnificent natural harbour of the estuary, regarded as the best in the Isle of Wight. Now shrunk to a handful of scattered buildings, grassy lanes mark the lines of the town's former streets and cattle graze on what were medieval house plots, their outlines still visible in the turf. It seems Newtown never recovered from a disastrous French raid in 1377, gradually losing its trade and importance to Newport.

Surrounded by fields, oddly isolated from the rest of the village, is the little brick Town Hall of 1699, a relic of the days when Newtown elected two Members of Parliament despite its tiny population, the franchise granted in 1584 perhaps an attempt to stem the community's decline. Lit by four long round-headed windows down each side and crowned by a steeply pitched hipped roof, this simple building on an earlier stone basement was dignified by the addition of a classical portico in the late eighteenth century. During the eighteenth century, elections were increasingly controlled by two families and Newtown's political life came to an end with the Reform Act of 1832, under which it was declared a 'rotten borough' and disenfranchised.

Another of the Trust's properties initially rescued from dereliction by Ferguson's Gang (*see* p.336), the building's interior has now been refurnished and is used to display documents relating to local history and a replica of Newtown's Tudor silver mace. Not far away is Noah's Ark, a stone house of *c.*1700 that was once an inn and is now the oldest building in the village, most of the others having been rebuilt in the nineteenth century.

North Cornish Coast

[442 A8–C6]

Much of this coast is wild, sometimes grim. Except in the valleys the country is austere, windswept and treeless but grandly beautiful. There has of course been some holiday development, but it is minor, and substantial acquisitions by the Trust mean that the best of this coast is now preserved.

The spirit of Parson Hawker will always haunt Morwenstow. The Rev. Stephen Hawker (1835–74) was the subject of Baring-Gould's bestseller *The Vicar of Morwenstow* (1876) which is still in print today. A considerable poet, eccentric to a degree, Hawker loved his people dearly. The Trust owns what was once his glebe and other land surrounding his beautiful Norman church. On the very lip of the 137-metre (450-foot) Vicarage Cliff is perched Hawker's Hut, made of driftwood dragged up from the rocks below. Here, clad in the fisherman's jersey he habitually wore, he wrote his ballads. This coast was a nightmare for seamen in the days of sail, for there was no harbour in which ships could take refuge in a northerly gale. Hawker attended every wreck, insisting on Christian burial for every corpse was washed ashore.

In the face of the cliff is the holy well of Morwenna, virgin and saint, with a tiny well house built by Hawker, but it is dangerous to go down there. St John's Well, the ancient holy well of the parish, in the garden of the former vicarage, also belongs to the Trust. Church, farm, vicarage, holy wells, a few cottages, the wild cliff and the sea boiling on the wicked reefs far below all make this an atmospheric place.

A lane leads towards Duckpool, passing the immense saucer aerials of the Ministry of Defence's communications system, built in the 1970s to receive messages from orbiting satellites which keep an eye on the rest of the world. Far from being an eyesore on the high cliffs, these great constructions are beautiful as they turn gravely on their axes to perform their secret duties.

Beyond them is the Trust's 91.5-metre (300-foot) Steeple Point; below it the narrow valley leading from Coombe down to the sea at Duckpool. Here there are green meadows, a bustling stream and a single cottage.

The hamlet of Coombe is a happy example of co-operation between the Landmark Trust, which owns the delightful cottages and the water-mill, and the National Trust, which owns the farmland and woods for a mile inland. Above Coombe stand the handsome house and farm buildings of Stowe Barton, its fields running out to the cliffs. Stowe belonged to the great West Country family of Grenville and it was from the old Tudor house, long since demolished, that Sir Richard Grenville set out in 1591 to perform his last service for Queen Elizabeth I 'at Flores in the Azores'.

It is a stiff climb up the cliffs from Duckpool and it can be a bracing walk for the mile and a half to Sandy Mouth.

Opposite: The cliffs above Sandy Mouth on the north Cornish coast, topped with sheep-grazed turf.

At Warren Gutter a valley drops steeply to the rocky beach where the sea has eroded away the softer bands of rock, leaving the hard bands in sharp ridges. Nearing Sandy Mouth the path crosses a sheltered valley where gatekeeper, speckled-wood and meadow-brown butterflies flourish on the kinder herbage. At Sandy Mouth a long valley opens on to a great beach of yellow sand. When the Trust bought the place in 1978 it was a mess, with cars and caravans parked everywhere, a seedy café and overhead wires. All has been swept away, the scars made good, a car park hidden in the landscape, a café built in local stone.

The cliffs here are unstable. At Houndapit Cliff, south of Sandy Mouth, the sandstone and shale rock has been buckled into a massive fold, visible on the cliff face. At its foot is a clutter of great sea-smoothed boulders which have been falling here over many thousands of years.

Dunsmouth Farm, with Menachurch Point, does not belong to the Trust but is crossed by the coastal path. The Trust's land starts again at Northcott Mouth. From here for ¾ mile to Bude is the much lower Maen Cliff, sheep-grazed pasture with a massive landslip at Furzey Cove making a new access to the sea.

At Crackington the rock is a particular type of shale, known to geologists as the 'Crackington formation'. Wildly contorted by movement of the earth's crust millions of years ago, it is easily fractured, landslips are common and the cliffs are layered with ledges and hollows from slips in the past.

On Dizzard Point, a mile to the north, is something very rare, an extraordinary witch's wood of dwarf trees, stunted and clipped by salt spray and high winds. Mainly of sessile oak, the wood is no more than 4.5 to 6 metres (15 to 20 feet) high, the trees straining to follow the contours of the cliff slope.

Tucked behind the beetling Penkenna Point, north of Crackington Haven, the church of St Gennys stands in a hollow behind the cliffs, some 122 metres (400 feet) above the sea. Grouped around a green, the church, the farm and the former school comprise the whole churchtown with not even a row of cottages. The view northward from the churchyard across the steep valley of the Coxford Water is very lovely, an Iron Age promontory fort in the foreground, the broken coast stretching away beyond. The slopes of the fort, covered with western maritime heath, are a brilliant purple colour in high summer. The stunted thickets on sheltered parts of the cliff provide nesting cover for dunnocks, linnets, whitethroats and stonechats. The latter species are rarely missing from any part of the Cornish coast.

From Crackington Haven the long proboscis of Cambeak stretches westward for a mile with a wart on the end of its nose. Here the coast turns south and the next 2 miles are the wildest in Cornwall. The Northern Door, a spectacular rock arch, its strata bent through 90 degrees, dominates the beach of Little Strand. Beyond it the Strangles, a beach with a fearsome reputation, is backed by screes leading up to a weird middle cliff of humps and bumps, perfect for a picnicking out of the wind, and then up to High Cliff, at 223 metres (731 feet) the highest in the county. The path to the beach is a scramble for the sure-footed but the walk to the cliff-top is easy and gives much of the flavour of this awesome place. Trevigue huddles in a fold behind the cliffs, its handsome Tudor farmhouse forming two sides of a picturesque enclosed court.

In the 40 miles of iron-bound coast between Hartland and Padstow the picturesque Boscastle harbour is the only natural haven. It is a terrifying place to enter in anything but the calmest seas, but many sailors have sought it thankfully with this cruel coast on their lee. Penally, to the north, and Willapark, to the south, guard a gorge-like entrance which turns through two right-angles before funnelling into the mouth of the harbour. Sailing vessels could not enter unassisted. They were towed in by 'hobblers', boats with eight oars, men on either shore using guide ropes to keep them in mid-channel.

The slightest swell builds up at the narrow entrance and from early times there has been a breakwater. The present curving jetty was rebuilt by Sir Richard Grenville in 1584, deliberately made with a hollow in its centre to absorb the force of the seas, the slate stones set upright in courses allowing the water to drain out between each wave. During the heyday of the harbour, when slate was exported in quantity, an outer breakwater was built in about 1820. More than a dozen ketches and schooners traded from here, bringing coal, iron and limestone from South Wales, timber and general merchandise from Bristol. In 1941 the outer breakwater was blown up by a drifting sea-mine. No repairs could be carried out and storms quickly began to damage the quay walls. Until 1962 when the Trust rebuilt the breakwater.

Beyond the outer breakwater is a good example of a 'blowing-hole'. At the right combination of sea and tide the thump of the swell entering the hole, the snort as the compressed air forces it back and the spurt of spume it throws across the harbour entrance is an enthralling sight.

The Palace stables at the harbour head belong to the Trust. Now a youth hostel, they once housed the carthorses which worked the capstans and hauled goods from quays to warehouses. The harbour is still used by fishermen, most of whom work the rich shell-fishing grounds south of Hartland, only accessible for small boats.

The Trust owns only a handful of the buildings round the harbour but virtually all the surrounding land, including the headland of Willapark, with an Iron Age cliff castle, and a lookout, recently refurbished by the National Coastwatch Institute. Inland from the headland is Forrabury Common, which preserves a remarkable survival of the Celtic tenure of 'stitchmeal' and provides a habitat for a rich and interesting flora. There are 42 rectangular plots, all of which now belong to the Trust, divided by low banks. The tenants may crop their stitches individually from Lady Day to Michaelmas (25 March to 29 September), usually with hay, corn or potatoes, but during the winter the land is grazed 'in common'. The views from Willapark are superb, both up and down the coast and inland up to the plateau which runs parallel with it.

The Valency river, which runs into the harbour, is only 6 miles long but drops over 183 metres (600 feet). In this area of high rainfall, 152 centimetres (60 inches) and more each year, it runs brim full after a storm. The Trust owns much of the valley as far as Newmills: steep scrubby slopes, oak woodland and a good path (there is no road) up to the delightful church of St Juliot where Thomas Hardy, as a young architect sent to restore the church, courted and married Emma Gifford, sister of the rector's wife. In February the churchyard, standing high above the river, is white with snowdrops. In 1997 the Trust's holdings here were increased by the purchase of Home Farm, set on the hill behind Boscastle and including Minster Wood in the Valency Valley. New paths lead through the wood and across farmland to the Minster church and Jordan Valley, and there are fine views of the harbour, of Forrabury Common and out to sea.

About 2 miles further west is the magical Rocky Valley, a mini gorge where a stream tumbles to the sea through gullies, cauldrons and cataracts and of national importance for the over 150 species of mosses found here. The Trust owns the western half, and the stretch of coast from here to the rugged peninsula of Willapark (not the Boscastle Willapark). Sheltering below is the sandy beach of Bossiney Cove, whose name John Galsworthy took for Irene Forsyte's lover in *Man of Property* (1906). Like its namesake at Boscastle, Willapark has an Iron Age cliff castle protected by a ditch and rampart across its narrow neck. Here the local tribe would take refuge in times of strife some 2,000 years ago.

Strangles Beach to the south of Crackington Haven is part of one of the more remote stretches of the north Cornish coast.

Barras Nose, to the west, was the Trust's first coastal property, bought after a local appeal in 1897, two years after the Trust was founded. There was widespread concern at the number of houses and hotels springing up to cater for the growing popularity of Tintagel, symbolised by the monumental King Arthur's Castle Hotel built by the London and South Western Railway, whose new line to Wadebridge passed only 6 miles away.

The massive 'island' at Tintagel, crowned by the remains of a twelfth-century castle, belongs to the Duchy of Cornwall. Beyond it the Trust's cliffs stretch for 2 miles to Trebarwith Strand. For centuries these cliffs were quarried for slate. At sea level the cliff face was cut back to the vertical to allow small sailing vessels to lie at its foot. The slate was lowered directly into the vessels' holds from 'whims', capstans worked by horses or donkeys. This trade survived until 1937 and a close inspection of the cliffs will pinpoint many relics of what must have been a hazardous livelihood. On these steep cliff faces are nesting sites of guillemots, fulmars, razorbills and shags, and the edible rock samphire grows near the water's edge.

Two miles to the south of Trebarwith is Tregardock, a sombre and menacing place. The approach is down a track from the farm above which curls round The Mountain, past the ruined engine house of an abandoned silver-lead mine, to enter the beach below crumbling cliffs. Together with the adjoining property of Dannonchapel, the Trust owns 1½ miles of lonely coastline here.

To lovers of Cornwall the 6 miles of coast from Port Quin to Polzeath is holy ground. The cliffs, which have been wild and often grim all the way from the Devon border, suddenly become kinder. They are still high but the country begins to smile and has a settled look about it. In the large parish of St Minver, farms have been occupied by the same families for generations. The hedges, made of small stones laid dry in a herringbone pattern and filled with earth, are covered with flowers in spring and summer. May and early June are the best months. On the cliffs the vernal squill is overtaken by violets, sea-pinks, thyme, bladder campion, kidney vetch and stonecrop. In the lanes primroses are followed by a glorious mixture of bluebells, pink campion and stitchwort. Later, miles of hedges are covered by valerian in its three colours of white, pink and purple. Poppies have not been sprayed out of existence. The land has a bloom.

Port Quin can be a frightening place in a north-west

Fractured and contorted rock formations around Crackington Haven. This wild and unstable coast, where landslips are common, has given its name to a type of shale, the Crackington formation.

gale in March, great rollers sweeping in and breaking over the road and battering the buildings at the head of the inlet. But most people see it in its summer dress, children playing in the rock pools, the little stone cottages smiling in the sun. It was a busy place in the middle of the nineteenth century. Small vessels landed coal and timber on the beach and at the two little quays, then loaded lead and antimony ores (used in ceramic glazes and in hardening other metals) from the small mines nearby. In good years large catches of pilchards were landed. The approach lanes are narrow and these are Port Quin's best defence. There is no factual evidence for the legend of the lost fishing fleet, the men of the village drowned, the cottages abandoned. It seems rather that the antimony mine closed, the pilchards failed to arrive for several seasons, and the men of the hamlet were persuaded by an agent of the Canadian government to emigrate *en bloc*.

From Doyden Point there are wonderful views over Lundy Bay to the Rumps, the rocky peninsula 2 miles to the west over the wide sweep of Port Quin Bay, and this whole coast, much more than 2 miles to walk, is now the Trust's property. The three-storeyed miniature castle on Doyden Point was built by Samuel Symons, merchant of Wadebridge, soon after his purchase of the farm of Trevigo in 1827. He used it to entertain his friends, as the ample wine bins on the ground floor bear witness. The Gothic folly is built of the pockmarked stone dug on the site, a near relation of the pillow lava found at Pentire across the bay. Winter gales have scoured the soft parts of the stones into whorls and ridges. Doyden House also belongs to the Trust, now, like the castle, used for holiday lets. The square open shaft on the cliff in front of it, fenced with slate posts, connects to a sea cave below. It once formed part of the workings of the Doyden antimony mine.

The path runs over Trevan Head and steeply down into Lundy Bay, with its two coves of Lundy and Epphaven all that Cornish coves should be. The astonishing Lundy Hole in the cliff-top, with an arched entrance from the sea, was once a sea cave invisible from above. The rock overhead collapsed into it centuries ago. To the west Markham's Quay lies below a vertical cliff up which sand and seaweed were hauled to counteract soil acidity and provide a fertilising mulch for the farms of the parish. They were loaded into carts and driven up the 'sanding road', which some people say was a smugglers' lane. Now wholly overgrown, it still runs up the valley to the road above.

There are dense thickets in the Lundy Valley, the home of goldfinch, whitethroat and stonechat. In the cliff-top fields corn bunting, skylark and meadow pipit are common.

The north-facing cliffs provide perches for predators and nesting sites for seabirds. The fulmars glide effortlessly about their business just below the cliff edge, quite unworried by walkers.

Beyond Carnweather Point are the overgrown burrows, or waste tips, of the Pentireglaze silver-lead mine, active from Elizabethan times until a century ago. Pentireglaze Farm is the scene of Baring-Gould's thriller *In the Roar of the Sea* (1892). His picture of this countryside early in the nineteenth century still rings true.

From Pentireglaze the coast sweeps on to Pentire Farm, 360 acres (145.5 hectares) bought by public appeal in 1936 when the whole farm, incredible as it may now seem, was divided up into desirable building plots. There was an immediate outcry, a committee was formed to save the farm, the *Times* published a photograph and a benefactor underwrote the appeal until the money was raised. It was this sort of event which inspired the Trust's great Enterprise Neptune Appeal nearly 30 years later.

The walk out to the Rumps, with its very well-preserved Iron Age cliff castle, is one of the classic walks of the Cornish coast. The path continues at about 91.5 metres (300 feet) outside the field hedge to Pentire Point and here the greenstone and shale give way to the pumice-like pillow lava, the product of volcanic action many millions of years ago. The views are westward across the mouth of the Camel estuary to Stepper Point with Trevose Head beyond, and up the sandy estuary to Padstow (hidden by high ground) with the dreaded Doom Bar at the entrance to the channel, covered with breakers at

The picturesque fishing village of Port Quin lies at the head of a sheltered inlet, with fine walking along the cliffs to either side.

Bedruthan Beach with the headland of Park Head beyond. At low tide there is a great stretch of sand here, studded with wave-sculpted stacks and with deep pools round the rocks.

low water. Along the coast to the south-east is the great sandy beach of Polzeath, with some of the best surfing in Cornwall.

Bedruthan Beach, at Carnewas, became a popular venue for carriage drives from Newquay when the town was developed as a holiday resort in the 1880s. The famous view on a fine summer's day must have appeared on more postcards than anywhere else in Cornwall: yellow sands, cotton-wool clouds, a sparkling blue sea, rocks of every colour clothed in lichen, drifts of sea-pinks. Yet in a winter gale it can be an awesome sight, yellow spume scudding inland for miles. And bathing here is never advisable. The beach is covered at high tide, there are strong currents offshore and there is no lifeguard.

The name Bedruthan Steps was first recorded in 1847, in the local newspaper *The West Briton*, and appears to refer to the precipitous cliff staircase which leads down to the south end of the beach, as does Pentire Steps at its north end. The name has since been applied to the several isolated stacks along the beach, the hard rock still standing after the softer rock surrounding it has been eroded away. The cliff staircase was probably originally made by miners to give access to the Carnewas iron mine dug beneath the cliff-top, the remaining buildings of which house the Trust's café, shop and information point. After the mine closed in the 1870s the staircase was kept open. The cliffs are tortured, the strata writhing in all directions, the rock friable. The Trust has had to rebuild the staircase twice (it reopened in 1995, after being closed for some years), and techniques developed for motorway construction have been used to stabilise loose rock. As well as the staircase, the Trust owns the cliffs to north and south of the beach, but the middle section of beach and most of the stacks are privately owned.

Across the great beach Park Head stretches out to close the view to the north. Here is another Pentire Farm, one of four owned by the Trust in Cornwall (the word means headland), and the walk runs right round it. A narrow, deliberately unsignposted lane leads off the coast road. From the car park a path runs down the valley to the sea at Porth Mear, sand and rock pools, and then round to west and south, with eight tiny coves, some accessible with great care. At the tip of the headland is a fine arch where the sea has gouged out a vein of softer rock. On a clear day the view south-west stretches for 26 miles down the coast to St Ives.

Shut off from the razzmatazz of Newquay by the estuary of the River Gannel, the great sandy beaches of Crantock and Holywell are both excellent for family outings and safe, providing the advice of the lifeguards is followed precisely. They attract large numbers of visitors and give enormous pleasure. But there is very much more to see, for the landscape is exceptionally diverse. As well as the beaches and sand dunes, there is a tightly grazed common, a boggy valley running down to the sea with a paradisal cove, a tidal estuary with mud-flats, woodland, farmland and rocky headlands.

The River Gannel rises near the village of Mitchell, on Cornwall's spine road, the A30. Although only a small stream, it has a sizeable estuary, and until Newquay harbour was built it had a considerable trade in small sailing vessels, while wooden ships were constructed on its north bank. Most of the estuary dries out at low water and for much of the year the mud-flats are alive with waders. In its lower reaches the mud becomes sand and by the time Crantock is reached it is hard and yellow. The dunes of the Rushy Green rise steeply behind the beach, always changing in shape on their seaward side but achieving stability further inland. They are held in place by the long roots of marram grass, and when too many people use the same track through the dunes the grass is killed and wind starts shifting the sand.

West Pentire closes Crantock Beach to the west, with a collapsed sea cave at its tip. The cliff turns south and opens into Polly Joke (more properly known as Porth Joke). Here the Trust fought a famous battle in the 1950s, to prevent cars driving down the valley behind the cave on to the sand; ironically, after victory had been achieved the track collapsed and is now impassable! Polly Joke is a narrow inlet of the most perfect hard sand, with low rock cliffs to sit on or under, rock pools, and not a building or a vehicle in sight. At low water cattle pastured on the farmland to the south come down to the beach to drink from the stream before it enters the sea, a beautiful sight.

The track, now only a footpath, leads up the valley to the Trust's car park at Treago Mill. The stream runs through a boggy bottom and the mixture of wet habitat with the blown calcareous sand gives rise to quite different plants and insects. High above the car park is Cubert Common. Although its underlying soil is acid, blown sand from the Holywell dunes has created a lime-rich tilth, for the sand is composed of the crushed shells of myriads of small sea creatures and is rich in calcium carbonate. So in spring the common is covered with cowslips, only found in Cornwall where there is blown sea sand. It is grazed by horses, not the best use, but while the Trust owns the freehold of the land the commoners are assured of their longstanding right to graze it.

The Kelseys, 121.5 hectares (300 acres) of open headland between Polly Joke and Holywell Beach, has been farmed for centuries, the field boundaries the same now as shown on a map of 1694. Under the blown sand on its surface there is good soil: in years when the harsh salt winds and low rainfall allow, hay and corn are grown here for a farmer based several miles inland. Cattle are grazed after the respective harvests until ploughing begins. The walk round Kelsey Head is bracing, with sea on three sides, springy turf and offshore the rocky islet of The Chick, where seals breed. In spring and early summer the flowers are similar to those on the chalk downs of southern England, with some extras such as dwarf centaury and the deep blue vernal squill.

The modern village of Holywell has little to commend it, for what was once reasonably seemly is no longer so. A cave at the north end of the beach, accessible only at low water, hides the holy well which gives the place its name. The cave is slippery and one needs to climb up towards its inner end to find the well, fed by a freshwater spring in the rock behind.

At St Agnes the landscape changes markedly for, although almost every parish in Cornwall has been worked over for its minerals in the past, here we meet the relics of mining carried out on a larger scale and until comparatively recently. The cliffs are still high, between 91.5 to 122 metres (300 to 400 feet). From the village of St Agnes, above Trevaunance Cove, and for 2½ miles to Porthtowan the landscape is scarred by old workings for copper and tin. St Agnes was one of the great mining parishes of the eighteenth and nineteenth centuries and Seal Hole, a mine close to the village, is said to have paid vast dividends to 'Guinea-a-Minute Daniell' who, from his princely mineral income, rebuilt Trelissick House overlooking Falmouth harbour (see p.398) and planted the park and woods there. The scarred landscape, the burrows (heaps of waste rock) and the ruined engine houses with their attendant stacks have a melancholy beauty in their decay.

The Trust owns over 162 hectares (400 acres) here, dominated by St Agnes Beacon, rising up to 192 metres (629 feet) above St Agnes Head. Beneath the Beacon is a boss of granite, pushed up red hot from the earth's core about 225 million years ago. The great heat and pressure affected the overlying rock, while gases and liquid forced up through fissures altered its chemical composition to give veins of silver, lead, zinc, tin and copper. This mineralisation, eons ago, is the reason for the rich mining country all about the beacon. From the top there are views right across the county to the south coast, on a clear day, and

for 26 miles of this coast, from Trevose Head to the north, to Carn Naun, near St Ives, to the south-west. The beacon is covered with heather, ling and the prickly dwarf gorse which grows on all this mineralised soil, so it pays to keep to the paths. When these plants flower together in August the hill is a sheet of purple and gold.

The Trust owns Newdowns Head, north of St Agnes Beacon and near the village, but not St Agnes Head which is owned by the local authority as far as Tubby's Head where the Trust's coast starts again. The mines here were worked until the steady fall in the price of tin forced their closure in the 1920s. On a ledge below the top of the cliff is the most photogenic of all the abandoned mine buildings in Cornwall, the roofless engine house and stack of the Towanroath Shaft of Wheal Coates, spectacularly sited high above the great sandy beach 91.5 metres (300 feet) below (see p.112). The miners' track from Towanroath runs down into the narrow cleft of Chapel Porth. Here a small subsidiary valley joins the path and this is the site of the chapel, possibly of the tenth century, which stood for centuries but was ruined by 1750. At high tide the sea thunders to the base of the cliff but retreats at half-tide to open up a flat sandy beach 2 miles long. There is good surf but it is essential to follow the lifeguard's instructions. All the way up Chapel Coombe the land is scarred by mine workings. The cliff path climbs steeply towards the vestigial ruins of Wheal Charlotte high above the sea. Beyond is the seedy holiday village of Porthtowan where developers have been active.

Between Carvannel Farm, to the east, and Godrevy Farm, to the west, the flat-topped cliffs, high and often sheer, are tidily farmed almost to their edge. All this coast was part of the great Tehidy estate of the Basset family, who prospered mightily on their mineral dues in the

Natural sculpture among the rocks and pebbles of a north Cornish beach.

Looking north towards Godrevy Island, where the lighthouse was built in 1859 to warn sailors of a submerged reef. Virginia Woolf, who used to holiday at St Ives nearby, called her novel *To the Lighthouse* after Godrevy.

eighteenth and nineteenth centuries and became Lords de Dunstanville.

From Portreath the path runs steeply up Tregea Hill and along the cliff to the narrow and precipitous cleft known as Ralph's Cupboard. The sun never reaches the base of the cliffs here. Further on is Samphire Island, one of many on this coast where the edible samphire (*Crithmum maritimum*) grows profusely.

At Porthcadjack Cove, at the foot of the narrow valley below Carvannel, there is good bathing off the rocks. The next place where the beach can be reached is Basset's Cove, with a track down to the sea through former mine workings. Above it lie the remains of the earthwork of Crane Castle. From here the path follows the cliff edge, nearly sheer and at a height of 76 metres (250 feet), the walk exhilarating, the view magnificent. In 2 miles the coast road and the cliff converge at the yawning chasm of Hell's Mouth. This is a 'horrible' place, in the eighteenth-century meaning of the word, and the walk from here round Navax and Godrevy Points is even more so. The coast provides a good habitat for flowers, for the dwarf gorse and heather provide some shelter. The royal fern (*Osmunda regalis*) grows in damp places and the sea spleenwort (*Asplenium marinum*) can also be found. Seals breed in the caverns on the east side of Navax Point and can be seen playing on the beach at Fishing Cove which is sheltered from the west. These caves can now only be entered from the sea, though one great cavern was connected to the North Cliff Mine, the workings of which honeycomb the area.

Strong currents swirl round Godrevy Point. On the day of Charles I's execution a ship containing his wardrobe and household possessions was sunk here. Its dangers are now advertised by the little white lighthouse on Godrevy Island offshore. Virginia Woolf's novel *To the Lighthouse* (1927) was entitled in affectionate memory of childhood days spent here, and lovers of that best of diaries kept by a Victorian clergyman, *Kilvert's Diary*, will remember the author's description of a fight he witnessed here between a seal and a conger eel.

Between St Ives and Land's End is granite country. The slates, shales and limestones which have run down the north coast from the Devon border have finished. Granite is everywhere, protruding on the skyline, vast blocks tumbled about the little farms, gathered into the great hedges of the tiny fields, outcropping wherever cultivation is attempted. The houses and buildings are of granite, even the gateposts. Yet the black soil to which this intractable stone gives rise is productive, and patient clearance over many generations has made the farms of the Penwith peninsula into excellent dairy holdings, some still with the traditional herds of Channel Island cattle which look so beautiful on their rich green pastures.

Beneath the farms and crofts, or enclosed moorland, on the higher ground lies a series of earlier landscapes going back over the centuries to the first men who lived here. Historical circumstance has preserved in this peninsula the richest large-scale prehistoric landscape in Britain. This has only become widely recognised in recent years, and is now the subject of exhaustive investigation, scheduling and, very fairly, subsidy to the farmers, who are encouraged to farm in a way which is sensitive to the needs of the archaeologist. Haunted by the ghosts of early man, grey and lonely, sparsely populated except in the mining villages near St Just, this is in many ways the most fascinating of all the differing coasts of Cornwall.

Hor Point, 2 miles west of St Ives, is a modest 9.5 hectares (24 acres) of rocky cliff. It hit the local headlines in 1957 when the borough council proposed to tip its rubbish here. The Trust moved fast and bought the land in the afternoon before the council met in the evening. Its members were not pleased. Hor Point remained as an isolated Trust outpost until 30 years later when it was possible to add to it the cliffs running westward to Pen Enys Point, making a mile of excellent walking.

At Zennor the Trust has built up a patchwork of ownership and protective covenants which cover virtually all the land east of the village, from Zennor Quoit, the rocky hill south of the coast road, over the lower farms and down to the cliffs. The approach is by the track through the churchtown, past Treveglos Farm (the homestead, *tre*, beside the church, *eglos*) and out to the wild grandeur of Zennor Head. Below the headland is Pendour Cove, where the celebrated Mermaid of Zennor lured the squire's son to her watery home. The legend is depicted on a bench end (now a seat) in the church. To the east are 3½ miles of cliffs running past Porthzennor Cove and Wicca Pool to Treveal Cliff, which overlooks The Carracks rocks and Carn Naun Point beyond.

Gorse and heather on the cliffs, with many different plants in the sheltered or wetter places, is backed by neat granite-hedged fields and inland of the point are the wild uncultivated hills of Rosewall and Little Trevalgan, with the road from St Ives to Zennor rising to a pass between them. Footpaths take in both summits, there are spectacular views and, on Little Trevalgan, a granite boulder carrying a plaque to the Cornish painter Peter Lanyon, a leading figure of the St Ives school, who died in a gliding accident in 1964.

Like many other artists, Lanyon was attracted by the special qualities of the light in Penwith. It is constantly changing and seems alive. This is the coast on which to see the phenomenon known as the 'green flash'. As the sun sinks into the sea on a summer's evening, a green light suddenly suffuses the western sky. One of the best places to see the flash is from Zennor Head.

West of Zennor the Boswednack Cliffs overlook the narrow coves of Porthglaze and Rose-an-Hales. Beyond, the bony whaleback of Gurnard's Head juts northwards,

outcrops of granite at its tip. It is presumably now named after the ugly gurnard fish, found in these waters, but its old name was Treryn Dinas, referring to the cliff castle (*dinas* means fortress), outside the ditch of which lie the remains of a medieval chapel.

At Bosigran, as at Zennor, the Trust has achieved protection of a whole landscape, this time largely by ownership, partly by protective covenants. Its 243 hectares (600 acres) run from the summits of Watchcroft and Carn Galver, looming high over the coast road, down over farmland and out to the cliffs, taking in a remarkable early landscape, farmed for some 2,000 years, many of the field boundaries unaltered in this immense span of time.

The Trust has two farms in the valley running down to Porthmeor Cove, the third is privately owned. Their fields are mixed up in an apparently random way which makes sense when one understands how such a jigsaw happened. Each little farm needed access to water, a share of the better land as of the poorer, of the sheltered fields as well as the exposed. Overlying this ancient pattern are much later relics of small-scale tin mining, which occur almost everywhere along this coast.

The cliffs run south-west past the Great Zawn to the sheer granite precipice of Bosigran, an awesome sight but a place of pilgrimage for rock climbers who flock here from far afield. Beside the road are the ruined engine houses of the Carn Galver mine, which came to grief in 1871. Below lies Porthmoina Cove, and south of the cove the attractive Rosemergy Cliff, boulder-strewn, bracken-covered land stretching for a mile between the road and the sea. The three Brandys Rocks awash in the broken water below the cliffs are so called because, seen from above, they are in the triangular shape of a *brandis*, the Cornish word for a three-legged trivet.

The unmistakable humped outline of Cape Cornwall thrusts westward below the mining town of St Just. To north and south of the Cape, from Botallack Down to Aire Point, stretch 4 continuous miles of Trust coastline, with high cliffs cut by parallel valleys. This is an ancient landscape, with prehistoric field systems, cliff castles and burial mounds overlain by extensive remains of some two thousand years of tin mining, including several ruined engine houses, and it is also a site of great ecological interest, with wind-sculpted coastal heath and grassland. South down the coast, the headland of Pedn-men-du, above Sennen Cove, hides Land's End from view. From here the mile of Mayon Cliff curves round Gamper, the bay north of Land's End and the Trust's furthest western outpost in Britain. (*See also* South Cornish Coast, p.349.)

North Downs SURREY

Between Farnham and Canterbury [443 I5–K5]

The Pilgrims Way, the views over the Weald (*see* p.416), proximity to London and good bus and train services mean that the North Downs have long been Londoners' country and many stretches are publicly owned. The North Downs Way links all these, including the Trust's considerable holdings. All are important for their wildlife, especially butterflies and orchids. Management of the downland grass requires grazing with sheep and cattle at certain times of year.

Overlooking the beautiful Tillingbourne Valley, the wooded slopes of Abinger Roughs, Hackhurst Down and Netley Park rise to the escarpment. On either side of the Dorking Gap stand Denbies Hill and Box Hill while, above Reigate, Colley Hill and the woods of Gatton provide good walking. Furthest east is Oxted Downs, the most recent of many individual acquisitions, but the jewel in the Trust's North Downs crown is surely Box Hill. It takes its name from the steep chalk slopes, clothed in places with box, which John Evelyn noted in 1655. The shrub box (*Buxus sempervirens*), most commonly seen in gardens and planted as game cover in southern chalky woods, is native here – one of only a handful of places where it grows wild in Britain. Like the yew, common here, especially on steeper slope, it dominates small sections over thin soils, almost to the exclusion of other plants.

It is the dramatic beauty of the 122-metre (400-foot) escarpment of the downs, where the River Mole has cut through the hills on its way to the Thames, which has brought visitors here ever since an eye for landscape began to be cultivated in the eighteenth century. Including Mickleham Downs nearby, the Trust owns over 404.5 hectares (1,000 acres) here, with wonderful walks through beech woods. The Zig-Zag road runs from the Roman Stane Street steeply up the grassy slope to the summit, giving superb views over the thickly wooded Weald, with Chanctonbury Ring prominent on the South Downs 20 miles away (*see* p.359).

Stane Street ran from London to Chichester, and the Romans used the Dorking Gap as the only practicable way through the North Downs. This strategic point had been forgotten when in 1871 General Sir George Chesney alarmed the military establishment with his essay 'The Battle of Dorking', showing how an enemy force could land on the south coast and threaten London in a matter of days. Chesney's warning was acted upon and forts were built along the downs. One survives at Box Hill, another at the Trust's Colley Hill above Reigate.

The woods and gentle valleys on the north side of the hill are much less frequented, and the indigenous plant and animal life here and throughout the whole property is extremely rich. Naturalists have been coming to Box Hill for many decades, and it probably has one of the longest insect lists of any Trust property as a result. Juniper Hall is now let by the Trust to the Field Studies Council, which uses the area as an outdoor laboratory.

North-East Coast

[445 I1–J3]

Between the spread of Tyneside and the Teeside conurbation to the south, undeveloped coast is especially precious. The Trust has three footholds, all of them on the Permian magnesian limestone, which is good for both geologists and plants.

To the north of Easington lies Beacon Hill, at 85 metres (279 feet) the highest point on Durham's coastline, and the beach below. To the south, at Horden, there are wooded denes behind the mile of cliff where streams run down to the shore. Near South Shields there is a larger foothold at The Leas, where some 121.5 hectares (300 acres) of attractive grassy land lie behind 3 miles of limestone cliffs, with good sandy beaches. Erosion of the limestone has produced a much-indented coast, with caves, rock arches and detached 'stacks', the principal feature being the mighty arch through Marsden Rock. A large colony of kittiwakes can be found here from late winter to late summer, spending the rest of the year at sea.

North of Blyth the coast has been much less developed and, 5 miles south of Seahouses, the little village of Low Newton-by-the-Sea lies at the centre of a 4-mile stretch owned by the Trust. Running from Long Nanny Burn in the middle of Beadnell Bay south round Newton Point, it encompasses the whole sweep of Embleton Bay where the view is dominated by the dramatic ruin of Dunstanburgh Castle (see p.132). Most of Low Newton, including the Ship Inn in the village square, belongs to the Trust. The sturdy houses nestle into this low-lying coast at the eastern tip of the Great Whin Sill. Wind-cropped turf, with some wet hollows, runs down to the beach, and there are sand dunes in places. Oystercatchers, eider duck and rock pipits breed there and can be seen feeding among the rock pools in spring and summer, while turnstones and purple sandpipers frequent them in winter. There is a considerable kittiwake colony on the low cliff at Dunstanburgh.

The inland side of the dunes is somewhat disfigured near Low Newton by chalets, built on plots let on long leases before the Trust's acquisition, but these are forgotten at the reed-fringed 6.5 hectares (16 acres) of Newton Pool, bought as a nature reserve. Sedge warblers and reed buntings nest here, as do many common freshwater species. Ruffs, redshanks, water rail, snipe and other waders are found, and in winter tufted duck, pochard and goldeneye.

Northern Ireland Coast

[444 B2, C2, D3–5]

The Mourne Coastal Path is a good example of how ownership of land is much fragmented in Northern Ireland. At Bloody Bridge, just south of Newcastle, the Mountains of Mourne sweep literally down to the sea, with Slieve Donard towering above at 850 metres (2,788 feet). By a series of small purchases the Trust has acquired 2 miles of coastal footpath along geologically interesting cliffs and boulder beaches where the yellow-horned poppy and the rare oyster plant grow. The narrow valley of the Bloody River runs up the mountains to the Saddle, and to the remarkable Mourne Wall, a high granite boundary wall which runs from summit to summit for over 20 miles. The Bloody Bridge River Path provides a point of access to the high Mournes, and from the wall the views are superb: east to Dundrum, the Murlough dunes and beyond to Strangford Lough; south to the Annalong Valley below the peaks of Slieve Lamagan, Cove Mountain and Slieve Beg; north to the brooding Slieve Donard.

Dundrum Bay is of particular interest to the geographer, the archaeologist and the naturalist because much of the great range of sand dunes, which has developed across it and forms the Murlough Nature Reserve, is at least 5,000 years old.

Above: Tidal mud-flats on the shores of Strangford Lough, one of the varied habitats around this great sea lough which support rich marine fauna and attract a wide and diverse population of birds.

Left: The smooth sands of Embleton Bay, with Dunstanburgh Castle in the far distance. Some pillboxes along the beach are the remains of Second World War defences, when this coast was seen as a potential landing area for invading forces.

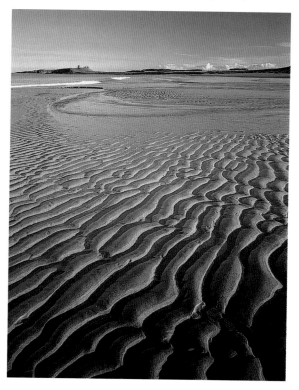

The Trust manages its 283.5 hectares (700 acres) of dune as a nature reserve, but the area is big enough to allow visitors ample space and to carry on a substantial programme of research and education. The dunes support a wide range of plants, some uncommon like the carline thistle, the Portland spurge and the pyramidal orchid, and there are valuable areas of dune heath. Sea buckthorn, planted before the First World War to stabilise blowing sand, does only too well and has had to be controlled since myxomatosis reduced the rabbit population.

There is evidence of habitation in the dunes since the earlier Neolithic period. Traces of dwellings, pottery, weapons and implements from this and later ages, as well as from early Christian and medieval times, turn up regularly as the wind removes overlying sand.

The Ards peninsula forms the east side of Strangford Lough (*see* p.376). Its sea coast is low, and here the Trust has gathered together 2 miles of foreshore, beach and adjoining land, from the cove with the insalubrious name of Stinking Port south round Kearney Point to Knockinelder. North of Kearney Point stands what remains of the once-flourishing village of Kearney. In 1900, 75 people lived here but fishing failed, farms were mechanised and many of the inhabitants emigrated. The place became virtually deserted. Thirteen cottages survive, a cluster of whitewashed buildings on the furthest point of the peninsula.

East of Bangor, at the mouth of Belfast Lough, the little village of Groomsport lies between Ballymacormick Point and Orlock Point, rocky gorsy places which have not been subjected to the municipal tidiness of the cliff walks nearer Belfast. They are places from which to watch ships entering or leaving the lough, and to see oyster-catchers, stonechats, rock pipits, reed buntings, willow warblers and linnets, all of which breed here. In winter dunlin, redshank, purple sandpiper, curlew and ringed plover feed on the shore. Ballymacormick Point is also an important botanical site.

Four miles offshore Lighthouse Island is now a misnomer, for the lighthouse has moved to nearby Mew Island. A landing permit is needed, for the island is a bird observatory where eider duck, red-breasted merganser, shelduck, fulmar and black guillemot breed, and there is an exciting colony of Manx shearwaters, which breed in rabbit burrows and emerge only at night to avoid attack by predatory gulls.

To the north and west there are three places in County Londonderry not to be missed. The estuary of the River Bann opens below Coleraine to run west to the sea at Bar Mouth. The Trust owns some 75 hectares (185 acres) of tidal mud-flats, saltings and dunes here and has established a refuge for migratory birds, where divers and auks, great-crested grebes, eiders, mergansers and kittiwakes feed offshore in autumn. Waders rest and feed here before going

Golden sands backed by dunes and chalk cliffs at Whitepark Bay. Both the dunes and the grassland behind are rich in plants, the former sheltering uncommon species such as sea sandwort and fragrant agrimony, the latter containing orchids, lady's mantle, bird's foot trefoil and other wild flowers.

further south: knots, sanderlings, little stints, curlews, sandpipers, whimbrels. Later on ringed, golden and green plover, dunlin and redshank arrive, while resident duck species – mallard, teal, shelduck and goldeneye – are always about.

Across the river lie the 3 miles of beach and dunes of Portstewart Strand. A popular family beach, overlooked at one end by houses and hotels, with a golf course behind the dunes, it seems an unlikely candidate for preservation by the Trust, yet the Trust was the one body able to act decisively to save it.

Increased mobility had meant a growing number of visitors. The dunes were being eroded away by motor-cyclists and users of the beach, and many interesting and uncommon plants and insects were being threatened. In 1981 the Trust bought the whole and took on the unpopular job of stopping this destruction. While cars can still park on the hard sand of the beach, the dunes are slowly recovering.

West of the estuary, the ground rises and the B69 runs out to the cliff edge with a wonderful view over Magilligan Strand to the mouth of Lough Foyle. Between the road and the sea lies the extraordinary demesne of Downhill (*see* p.129), with the beautiful circular shell of the Mussenden Temple on the cliff edge.

The Giant's Causeway has been a mecca for tourists since the eighteenth century and, like Land's End and John o'Groats, had become rather tacky, with huts selling foodstuffs, drinks and souvenirs, a wishing well, a gated entrance and an admission fee. When the Trust was given the property in 1961, there was prolonged discussion as to how it should be presented, some people taking the view that the tackiness had historic interest. Fortunately wiser counsels prevailed; the gates, huts and much else were removed, the admission fee given up. There is now an information centre, educational facilities, the Trust's own brand of souvenir shop and a tea-room. All is in good taste but another generation may question whether such a place cannot speak for itself.

In the Tertiary era, 60 million years ago, lava poured out through fissures in the earth's surface to flow over the chalk and solidify into basalt, much of it polygonal in section. Most of the columns are six-sided but columns with four, five, seven and ten sides are found. The Causeway itself is fascinating, and should be fully explored, but the coast to which it leads is truly spectacular. It was the Trust's involvement in the Causeway which led to the acquisition of land, or rights of way, to make a 12-mile walk along, above and below these wonderful cliffs, a remarkable

Volcanic eruptions millions of years ago cooled to form the sculptural columns of basalt which make up the extraordinary coastal landscape of the Giant's Causeway.

feat of construction, some of it vertiginous and not for the faint-hearted, though this does not deter the ravens, peregrines and choughs.

The most memorable features are the bays between the series of great headlands which run out to Benbane Head, with its view of Inishowen 16 miles out to sea. Each bay forms an amphitheatre with its own particular features: man-made, like the Shepherd's Path, where 149 steps join the upper and lower paths; or natural, like the Organ, its basalt pipes 12 metres (40 feet) high; the Harp; the Spanish Organ; Horse Back; Lover's Leap; Giant's Gate. This imposing landscape has now been designated a World Heritage Site.

East of Benbane Head, the path runs along the cliff, over Bengore Head at 114 metres (374 feet), past Portfad and Port Moon to the wildly romantic and now vestigial ruin of Dunseverick Castle, the oldest and once the most strongly fortified place in Ireland. Its building was probably begun during the early Celtic period, 2,000 years ago, and Conal Cearnach, leader of the Red Branch Knights, Ulster's ancient order of chivalry, lived here. Stormed by the Vikings in 870, and again in 924, Dunseverick was held by the clan McDonnell, whose fief covered both North Antrim and Argyllshire. The last owner, Giladuff O'Cahan, was subdued by the Great O'Neill in the 1641 rebellion, and the castle, the remains of which are of the sixteenth century, was slighted by Cromwellian troops.

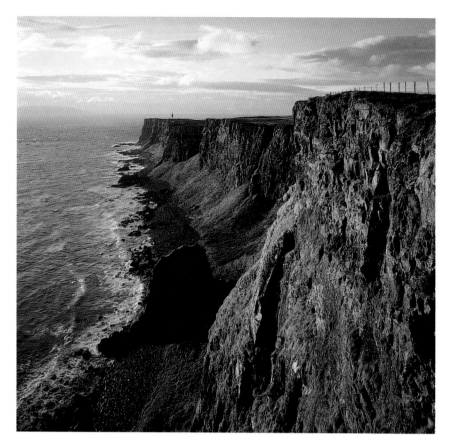

Wild, unspoilt Rathlin Island has some of the richest seabird colonies in Ireland.

coastal scenery in Northern Ireland. The great headland of Fair Head is a landmark from the sea, from the air and from many miles along the adjoining coast. The dolerite cliffs rise for nearly 183 metres (600 feet) above the sea. The brow of the headland is heathery, wild and rocky, frequented by buzzards, ravens, peregrine falcons and quantities of choughs. A herd of wild goats lives here, moving in winter to the woods of birch, hazel and rowan on the slopes above Murlough Bay. The bay is very different: cliffs of white chalk over red Triassic sandstone in its centre, the great basalt columns of Fair Head to the north, crumbling mica-schist to the south, a little farm perched between the woods and the sea. Among the rarer plants is Grass of Parnassus, with pure-white buttercup-like flowers in September.

Out to sea is the low, 8-mile-long bulk of Rathlin Island, accessible by ferry from Ballycastle. Wild and unspoilt and only a mile wide, so the sound and smell of the sea are everywhere, the island is rich in seabirds and other wildlife, and there are waymarked trails for walkers across the Trust's land. To the south, the beautiful coastal farm of Benvan is held as a memorial to the Earl of Antrim, Chairman of the Trust from 1965 until his death in 1977, whose home was at Glenarm nearby.

Cushendun lies snugly at the foot of Glendun, one of the famous Nine Glens. The River Dun rises on Orra Mountain, picks up the streams from Aggangorive Hill as the beautiful glen widens, and plunges under the fine viaduct (built by the Belfast architect Charles Lanyon in 1839) to reach the curving bay at its mouth.

The Trust owns 24.5 hectares (60 acres) here, and much of the seemly village. This is partly nineteenth century, but the whitewashed terraced cottages in the square, with their mansard roofs and small-paned windows, were built in 1912 by the Welsh architect Clough Williams-Ellis.

North Norfolk Coast

[443 J1–K1]

The Trust has been established since 1912 on the north Norfolk coast and its initiative has brought in a number of most welcome partners, so that by far the greater part of the coast between Hunstanton and Sheringham (*see* p.338) is now managed for the preservation of its exceptional scientific interest. The Norfolk Naturalists' Trust was the National Trust's first partner; English Nature, the Norfolk Ornithologists' Association and the RSPB have also acquired reserves.

At Port Braddon, a tiny fishing village, the basalt finishes and white limestone begins. Here is lovely White-park Bay, acquired by the Trust in 1938 and one of the few properties gained before the Second World War. The low limestone cliffs jut out of green turf above a mile of golden sand; beyond is the little harbour of Ballintoy, and offshore are the islands of Long Gilbert, Carricknafurd, Sheep Island and Island Lean, breeding places for seabirds.

The path ends at the rock island of Carrick-a-Rede, 'the rock on the road', the road being the path of the salmon as they make their way to the rivers Bann and Bush. During the visiting season, March to September, the 18-metre (60-foot) chasm between the island and the cliff is spanned by a rope bridge. The salmon do not swim through the narrows below it but go north round the island where fishermen have set their nets for centuries. The Trust owns a stretch of unspoilt and dramatic coatline at Larrybane, next to the rope bridge and fishery, and has blown up unattractive quarry buildings masking a former limeworks here.

The 404.5 hectares (1,000 acres) comprising Fair Head, Murlough Bay and Benvan are without question the finest

The 20 miles between the chalk cliffs at Hunstanton and Sheringham are of exceptional interest to naturalists of all disciplines, and also to geographers, for there are classic sites illustrating the phenomenon of longshore drift, the action of waves in shifting shingle and sand along a coastline, giving a completely different shape to a system of spits and creeks in only a few years. Scientists may also observe the formation of sand dunes, the build-up of mud-flats and saltings, the zonation of plants and animals on the salt-marshes according to their height above mean tide level, and the richness and variety of the bird life for which this ever-changing coast is deservedly famous. And the coast is very beautiful in a way peculiar to itself. It can be bleak, raw and very lonely but he would be a dull man whose heart strings were not touched by it.

Brancaster Staithe is the centre of the western section, and from there one may embark for Scolt Head Island, 655.6 hectares (1,620 acres) of sand dune, salt-marsh, ever-changing shingle ridge and foreshore, with a ternery (in which sandwich terns are particularly abundant) at its west end, to which there is no access during the breeding season in May, June and July. The island can be reached over the mud-flats at low water, but only by those who really know the route. The beach is little frequented and makes an exhilarating walk for the beachcomber, for as well as offering every sort of flotsam it is one of the best places for picking up complete razor shells. The island was acquired in 1923, but it was not until 40 years later that the 898.5 hectares (2,220 acres) of Brancaster Marshes, on the mainland opposite, were bought, adding greatly to the value of this lovely place. There is an information point at Brancaster Staithe.

One embarks at Morston or Blakeney Quay for claw-shaped Blakeney Point, 526 hectares (1,300 acres) of shingle spit creeping ever westward and creating more creeks and mud-flats as it goes. There is a large ternery and many migrant birds, including occasional rarities, which can be seen in spring and autumn. The Lifeboat House has a display which shows how Blakeney Point has been built up and describes the flora and fauna to be found here.

The 404.5 hectares (1,000 acres) of salt-marsh at Stiffkey and Morston complement Blakeney Point, as the Brancaster Marshes act as a foil for Scolt Head Island. The Stiffkey Marsh, with plenty of sea aster and sea lavender, provides winter feeding ground for brent geese, widgeon and teal. The Morston Marsh, cut up by tidal creeks, has a population of redshank and shelduck as well as brent geese in winter. Little and common terns breed on the shingle banks. East of Blakeney, the grazing marshland of the Freshes attracts overwintering wildfowl and many other species, and the salty lagoons of Arnold's Marsh, along the coast at Salthouse, are visited by migrant waders, bearded tit and avocet. Gramborough Hill, above the marsh, also belongs to the Trust.

North Yorkshire Coast

[445 K4–5]

On the fine stretch of coastline between Scarborough and Whitby is Hayburn Wyke, 6 miles north of Scarborough. High cliffs overlook a little bay with a wooded stream and waterfall, traversed – as is the whole length of the North Yorkshire coast – by the Cleveland Way footpath. After a short gap the cliffland of four farms – Rigg Hall, White Hall, Prospect House and Bent Rigg – rises up to over 152.5 metres (500 feet), with the broken faces of Bent and Common Cliffs below.

On the south shore of Robin Hood's Bay the Trust has built up a patchwork of cliffs, farmland, disused alum and silica quarries and an abandoned brickworks, all lying behind the great peak of Ravenscar, a spectacular headland rising 183 metres (600 feet) above the sea. The Ravenscar Trail, starting from the Trust's centre in the village, illustrates the extraordinary geology of this unusual landscape, where pink and grey shale is capped with a thin layer of ironstone, with bands of orange-coloured sandstone called dogger and massive beds of deltaic sandstone intermixed. At the base of the cliffs are the so-called Mermaids' Tables, circular platforms of hard limestone left where the softer shale has eroded away.

Beyond the picturesque village of Robin Hood's Bay, Ness Point closes the bay to the north, with the Boggle Hole, a precipitous inlet, in the middle. As a new venture, the Trust has recently acquired the north side of the bay which surrounds the little harbour of Port Mulgrave near Staithes, north of Whitby.

Nostell Priory WEST YORKSHIRE

On the A638 out of Wakefield towards Doncaster [445 J6]

Sir Rowland Winn, 4th Baronet, commissioned two houses at Nostell in the mid-eighteenth century. The second, a classical building only a few feet high, stands at the foot of the south staircase of the priory. Like the similarly fine dolls' house at Uppark, it is fully furnished in period style, and was built to delight an adult as much as enchant a child. Marble chimneypieces are copied from plates in James Gibbs's *Book of Architecture* of 1728, carved mouldings and cornices in the principal rooms are picked out in gilt, and the furnishings are accurate in every detail. Little figures representing the family are looked after by servants in the Winn livery of grey and yellow and there is even a glass mouse under the kitchen table. If family tradition is correct, this minor masterpiece was the work of two young men closely associated with Rowland Winn's new mansion: James Paine, responsible for executing and modifying the plans of the gentleman-architect Colonel James Moyser, and Thomas Chippendale, both then still in their teens.

The estate had been acquired by the Winns, a family of London merchants, in 1650, ten years before the 1st Baronet was created, and has been held by the family ever since. The present house, built to the north of an earlier building formed out of the old priory, was created over 50 years, beginning in 1735, with a strong contrast between James Paine's rococo decoration for Sir Rowland and the severer classical designs of his successor, Robert Adam (later to oust Paine again at Kedleston, *see* p.200), for Sir Rowland's son. Fine interiors include paintings by Antonio Zucchi, among his earliest work in England, plasterwork by Joseph Rose the Younger and furniture by Chippendale.

Because only one of Adam's planned extensions to Paine's pedimented classical house was ever completed, the exterior of the priory is pleasingly asymmetrical. Adam was also responsible for the terrace fronting the entrance reached by two flights of curving steps which lifts the main façade. Inside, however, it is Paine's rooms which are the more flamboyant. Adam's beautiful hall is a serenely graceful room, with Rose's delicate plasterwork picked out against a subtly darker background. The library, with its pedimented bookcases and Zucchi's stylised classical paintings, is sombre and studious, dominated by Chippendale's superb desk in the centre of the room.

These intellectual treatments only serve to heighten the opulent over-ripeness of Paine's rooms. Zucchi's playful cherubs in the elaborate panels over the doors in the dining room and the plaster frieze of vines and satyrs' masks suggest an appreciation of the good things in life. Paine also carried out the splendid ceiling in what is now the state bedchamber, with its trio of music-making cherubs, but the exquisite Chinese paper, with brightly coloured birds of all sizes and varieties perching on branches laden with flowers and foliage, was the choice of Chippendale, chosen to complement his rich green and gold lacquer furniture, among his most unusual work.

The 4th Baronet set his house in a park designed by Stephen Switzer, but few traces of this innovative gardener's layout survive. The main view from the house is across a sweep of grass to a natural lake and the little three-arched hump-backed bridge built in 1761 to carry the main Wakefield to Doncaster road. Adam's Gothick menagerie still stands in a clearing west of the lake.

The attention to detail in the architecture and fitting out of Nostell Priory's 18th-century doll's house (above) suggest this was intended for adults rather than as a plaything for children. The interiors include a first-floor drawing room (above left) where every item has been made with exact precision.

Nunnington Hall NORTH YORKSHIRE

In Ryedale, 4½ miles south-east of Helmsley on the A170 Helmsley–Pickering road; 1½ miles north of the B1257 Malton–Helmsley road [445 J5]

Only a brave man could have told Elizabeth I that she would never have children. The bearer of this unwelcome message was Robert Huicke, physician to Henry VIII and Edward VI as well as the queen. Traces of the Elizabethan range he built while renting Nunnington from the Crown are perhaps still evident in the west front. Badly damaged by Parliamentary troops garrisoned in the house during the Civil War, Nunnington was restored by Richard Graham, 1st Viscount Preston, who inherited it in 1685.

A convert to Rome, Lord Preston was Master of the Wardrobe to James II and one of five peers entrusted with the government of the country when James fled in 1688. Apprehended on the fishing boat which he had hoped would bear James triumphantly back to England, Preston was taken to the Tower of London and saved from execution only by the pleadings of his youngest daughter Susannah. Stripped of his offices and disgraced, he returned to Yorkshire, where he died a few years later.

Preston's south front is Nunnington's finest architectural feature: the long, two-storeys with projecting gables at either end are both welcoming and refined. Unusually, two central doors stand one above the other, with a charming wrought-iron balcony round the upper one.

Inside, the house is cosily elegant, its warmly panelled rooms filled with period furniture, tapestries and porcelain collected by the last owner. The grandest room is Preston's oak hall, with its elaborate chimneypiece supporting his coat of arms joined with those of his wife and a three-arched classical screen leading to the great oak and

Arches of delicately coloured climbing roses frame an Italianate fountain at Nymans in Sussex.

Nymans WEST SUSSEX

On the B2114 at Handcross, 4½ miles south of Crawley, just off the M23/A23 London–Brighton road [443 |6]

Set 152.5 metres (500 feet) high and surrounded by the woods of the Sussex Weald, this enchanting 12-metre (30-acre) garden was created over more than half a century from 1890 by Ludwig Messel and his son Leonard, and was subsequently nurtured and enriched by the Earl and Countess of Rosse. Laid out on the side of a valley, the garden is designed as a series of open-air rooms, with lichen-stained stone steps or grassy slopes connecting one levelled area with another. Trees, walls and hedges surround the rooms, sheltering the remarkable collection of rare and choice plants for which the garden is now so well known, including magnificent rhododendrons, magnolias, azaleas and camellias. Many species reflect the Messels' sponsorship of plant-collecting expeditions to the Far East, Burma, South America and Tasmania. Several plants, such as *Populus lasiocarpa*, *Picea likiangensis purpurea* and *Magnolia sargentiana*, were raised from seeds collected by George Forrest, Colonel Kingdon-Ward and others, while Chilean shrubs and trees, including *Sophora macrocarpa* and *Asteranthera ovata*, were introduced by Leonard Messel's head gardener's son, Harold Comber, who made several plant-gathering trips to this part of the world. Now much healed since the freak storm in the autumn of 1987, which completely destroyed the pinetum and felled many trees elsewhere in the garden, Nymans displays an unusually rich collection of plants and also specimens of the many that were hybridised here, including the now widespread *Eucryphia nymanensis*, *Magnolia* 'Leonard Messel', *M.* 'Anne Rosse' and *Camellia* 'Maud Messel'.

The heart of the garden lies in what was a walled orchard. Entered through decorative brick arches, one crowned with pinnacles, another covered with romantically tangled roses and clematis, two peaceful walks planted for spring and summer display – a medley of red, yellow, orange, blue and scarlet – converge on an Italian fountain guarded by formally clipped yews. A prominent *Eucryphia nymanensis* is a mass of white in July and August. A hint of a Tuscan hillside is echoed in the sunken garden, where a huge grey stone Byzantine urn and a classical loggia adorned with grinning heads set off brightly planted beds flowering red, pink and mauve. Four Lawsons cypress stand sentinel on the edge of the grass.

Other features of this varied garden include beds of old-fashioned roses and the heather and rock garden

pine staircase climbing round three sides of a well. Preston emerges again in the two large ceiling canvases he commissioned in a small upstairs room, curiously depicting various family coats of arms against a cloudy sky, and in the little oratory adjoining a bedroom in the west wing, a reminder of his adopted faith and of the family's continued recusancy in the eighteenth century. Part of the attic above now houses the Carlisle Collection of Miniature Rooms, fully furnished in different period styles.

The delightful walled garden to the south of the house is a rare survival from the seventeenth century which still bears traces of the original formal layout. A rusticated stone gateway inserted in the south wall in the 1920s marks the site of the *clair-voyée*, a railing on a low wall which extended the view beyond the garden, shown in Samuel Buck's sketch of *c.*1720. A lawn cut to suggest the formal pattern of the parterre also shown in Buck's sketch is flanked by orchard plots. These have recently been replanted with old varieties of fruit trees, including pears and culinary and dessert apples only found in Ryedale. Clematis and roses grow against the walls. Eccentrically individual arches and gates through which the garden is approached may have helped Lord Preston recall happier times when he was Ambassador to France for Charles II.

created on a series of hillocks, heavy with the scent of lavender and cistus in summer and crowned by a weeping hornbeam on the highest point. The pinetum has been replanted and the magnificent wistaria pergola, knocked sideways by the storm, has been rebuilt so that visitors can again enjoy the pendant blooms in May and June. There is something of interest all year round, from carpets of daffodils in spring to the brilliant scarlet and gold of the Japanese maples in autumn. The mullions and Tudor chimneys of Ludwig Messel's pastiche fourteenth-century manor, now largely a picturesque shell after it was gutted by fire in 1947, provide a charming and romantic backdrop to the planting and to spacious lawns shaded by cedars and fringed with topiary beasts.

Much of the pleasure of the garden lies in its intimacy, and the feeling of a place secure from the world, but there are also glorious views to the heights of the Weald and to the South Downs from the balustraded terrace overlooking the park and from the perimeter walk past the little classical summerhouse and up the lime avenue. In April cuckoos calling in the woods herald the approach of summer.

Oakhurst Cottage SURREY

In the village of Hambledon, 5 miles south of Godalming
[443 I6]

Furnished as a labourer's cottage of the mid-nineteenth century, this little timber-framed building on the fringes of London's affluent commuter belt is a rare survival illustrating a now vanished way of life. Unlike so many other cottages of this type dating from the prosperous fifteenth and sixteenth centuries, Oakhurst has not been modernised and gentrified in the last hundred years.

Rows of onions, cabbages and beans mingled with traditional flowers, such as hollyhocks, sweet peas and roses, crowd the little garden which lines the path leading to the front door. This opens straight into the main room, a quarry-tiled kitchen dominated by a dresser set with Wedgwood willow-pattern china. A huge pot hangs over the hearth and samplers adorn the walls. A steep staircase leads directly into one of the bedrooms in the roof, which is lit by dormer windows. In the little back kitchen, where clothes were once washed and ironed, a low bench known as a hog-form is where the hair was scraped from the family pig after it had been slaughtered, a prelude to the annual pork feast enjoyed by wealthier cottagers and so vividly described by Flora Thompson in her book *Lark Rise to Candleford*.

Oldbury Hill KENT

On north side of the A25, 3 miles south-west of Wrotham
[443 J5]

The Iron Age hill-fort built on this prominent sandy ridge enjoyed a magnificent defensive position, protected by exceptionally steep slopes on all sides except the north. First fortified in about 100BC, the original bank and ditch enclosing an area of 50 hectares (123 acres) seem to have been strengthened at a later date, perhaps at the time of the Roman invasion in AD43. Natural caves in the slopes on the north-east side of the hill-fort were occupied by Neanderthal huntsmen during the last Ice Age.

The Old Manor DERBYSHIRE

At Norbury, 6 miles south-west of Ashbourne
[445 I8 and 443 G1]

At the north end of the seventeenth-century red-brick manor house in this leafy village on the River Dove is a low medieval building with rough buttressed stone walls dating from the thirteenth to the fifteenth centuries. The airy first-floor hall built over an undercroft and cellars has a rare king-post roof, perhaps installed here in the seventeenth century when the Tudor manor was demolished, and original Gothic two-light windows in the west wall, with stone window seats. From the little knot garden below, there is a good view of the tower of the fine fourteenth-century church only a stone's throw away, packed with monuments to the Fitzherbert family who held the manor of Norbury for over 650 years from 1125.

The Old Post Office CORNWALL

In centre of village of Tintagel [442 B7]

The considerable increase in postal traffic resulting from the introduction of the penny post in 1844 led to a much-improved service in remote parts of the country. Tintagel, then a little-known village called Trevena on the wild north Cornish coast, was blessed with its first post office, set up to receive incoming mail, in a room in this ancient cottage.

The Old Post Office is traditionally built of slate, now weathered to a uniform grey. Nothing about it is symmetrical, from the placing of the sturdy two- and three-tier chimneys to the off-centre projecting porch and the undulating roof. Dating in parts from the fourteenth century and a rare survival of local domestic architecture,

The hall of the Old Post Office, with a large slate overmantel above the hearth, rises the height of the house to smoke-blackened rafters. Like the other rooms here, it is furnished with pieces from local farmhouses and cottages.

it is also now one of the few remaining picturesque buildings in Tintagel, most of the others having been ruthlessly torn down in the late nineteenth century to be replaced with a rash of boarding houses and hotels catering for Victorian romantics in search of King Arthur.

The interior suggests a very small manor house, with a diminutive hall rising to the roof in the middle of the building and a passage running through the house to the little split-level garden. The rooms are furnished with local oak pieces such as would have been found in farmhouses and cottages in this part of the world.

Old Soar Manor KENT

2 miles south of Borough Green on the A25; approached via the A227 and Plaxtol [443 J5]

The rectangular solar block attached to a red-brick early Georgian farmhouse is all that remains of the manor house of *c.*1290 which stood here until the eighteenth century. The 8.5-metre (28-foot) solar over a barrel-vaulted undercroft was once the apartment of a medieval knight, a private retreat away from the noise and community of the great hall. Rough walls of Kentish ragstone rising to an open timber roof, a bare flagged floor and an absence of furniture underline the spartan nature of life in the Middle Ages, although the remains of a fireplace suggest some degree of comfort. Openings at the corners of the room lead to two projecting chambers, a chapel and a garderobe.

Orford Ness SUFFOLK

On coast between Aldeburgh and Orford [443 L3]

Stretching 10 miles south of Aldeburgh, with a gentle curve westwards opposite Orford, this long shingle spit is one of the most desolate and lonely places along an often wild and inhospitable coastline. Separated from the mainland by the River Ore, which it forces ever further south, the bank is still fluid and impermanent, changing shape in the winter storms which sweep in from the North Sea. Sea kale, sea pea, yellow vetch and horned poppy colonise the shingle, there is a thin strip of grazing marsh, mud-flat and reed-bed on the inland side, and this rare habitat is an overwintering and breeding ground for seabirds, waders and wildfowl, including the largest colony of lesser black-backed and herring gull in East Anglia.

In 1993 the Trust acquired 5 miles, or some 627 hectares (1,550 acres), of the northern end of the spit. Apart from its great natural history interest, this stretch of shingle bank includes the remains of a one-time military research station, now reduced to rotting timber and concrete. First occupied in the First World War, when there was a staff of 600 and a prisoner-of-war camp here, Orford Ness was used for 60 years for testing guns, sights, explosives and aerial combat techniques. It was here, in a timber hut, that Robert Watson-Watt and his team did pioneering work on the development of radar in 1935–6, and in its last years, from 1959–71, the station was used to develop the atomic bomb. Eerily futuristic concrete pagodas were built to absorb the blast should a test carried out in the cavernous pits beneath them go wrong. Some structures have now been demolished, others are being allowed to gently decay, a symbol of the futility of war and man's destructiveness.

Ormesby Hall MIDDLESBROUGH

3 miles south-east of Middlesbrough, west of the A171 [445 J4]

Sir James Pennyman, 6th Baronet, and his aunt Dorothy were clearly people of taste. Although 'Wicked Sir James', a spendthrift in the best eighteenth-century manner, ran through the fortune he inherited in 1770 in eight years, he spent his wealth on enlarging the Ormesby estate and enriching the house his aunt had built some 30 years earlier. Unfortunately, he was then obliged to surrender the property to the bailiffs.

Probably completed by 1743, Ormesby was designed by an unknown architect in a characteristically plain Palladian style then popular in North Yorkshire. The rather

The house is now filled with Regency and Victorian furniture and a number of family portraits reflect the generations of Pennymans who continued to live at Ormesby despite the 6th Baronet's extravagance. Sir James's dignified stables crowned with a cupola, probably also designed by Carr of York, are now let to the mounted police.

A small rose garden and mixed flower beds and borders, some planted in cottage-garden style with delphiniums, phlox and lupins, set off the house. A holly walk shows off fancy-leaved varieties, and naturalised spring bulbs carpet the woodland towards the church, where William Lawson, author of several gardening books, was vicar in the early seventeenth century.

Osterley Park MIDDLESEX

Just north of Osterley station, on the western outskirts of London (Piccadilly tube line) [443 I5]

This grand Neo-classical villa was created in the mid-eighteenth century out of a Tudor mansion built by Sir Thomas Gresham, Chancellor of the Exchequer to Elizabeth I. The ghost of the sixteenth-century courtyard house still lingers on. Delightful corner turrets crowned with cupolas, somewhat reminiscent of those at Blickling (*see* p.50), rise either side of the wide flight of steps and pedimented portico which give access to the raised courtyard. Also like Blickling, Osterley is built of warm red brick, with windows and decorative stone dressings standing out in white.

Gresham's mansion was principally transformed from 1761 by Robert Adam, who spent the next 20 years creating this superb house with its beautifully unified interiors. Statues of Greek deities standing in niches and 'antique' vases on pedestals in Adam's cool grey and white entrance hall introduce the classical theme of the house. In the airy library, paintings depicting the world of ancient Greece and Rome by Antonio Zucchi crown the pilastered and pedimented bookcases. Marquetry furniture attributed to John Linnell includes a pedestal desk inlaid with trophies representing the arts, and there is a delicate Adam ceiling. Close by is an eating room arranged in the eighteenth-century way, with the chairs against the walls and no large central table.

Adam's plasterwork also graces the three rooms which form the state apartment, and one of his most ambitious pieces of furniture, a domed eight-poster bed, can be seen in the state bedroom. The most original decorative scheme

severe outlines of the high three-storey main block rising to a hipped roof are relieved only by a heavy cornice and pediments on the two main façades. Projecting porches were Victorian additions. A two-storey service wing on the east was formed out of the earlier Jacobean house, thought to have been built in about 1600, its low façades an interesting contrast to the later building. Although most of the original features of the service wing have been lost, one fine ornamented Jacobean doorway has survived, with the crest granted to James Pennyman in 1599 proudly displayed on the coat of arms above.

The interior of the main block is a complete contrast. Ormesby is not at all grand but the most talented of local craftsmen were employed to create the rich plaster decoration and woodwork which are now such a feature of the house. Ionic columns screening both ends of the hall and Palladian motifs here and in the library are of Dorothy's time, but Sir James introduced the delicate Adamesque ceilings attributed to Carr of York in the drawing room and dining room, where the silver cup he presented to Northallerton racecourse now stands proudly on the sideboard. Plain family rooms on the first floor contrast with some decorated guest rooms on the north side, one adorned with carved festoons of fruit and foliage. A notable panelled gallery runs across the house at the top of the staircase, the five pedimented doorways echoing the Palladian emphasis on symmetry and balance evident in the hall.

The elegant eating room was one of the first interiors remodelled by Adam at Osterley. It is shown with all the furniture against the walls, as it would have been in the 18th century.

prematurely, perhaps partly as a result of anxiety about his only child Sarah Anne, who eloped with the 10th Earl of Westmorland at the age of 18. When mildly rebuked by her mother, who pointed out she had better matches in mind, the high-spirited girl replied, 'A bird in the hand is worth two in the bush.' The father forgave his only child, but altered his will to leave Osterley and most of his fortune to Sarah Anne's second son, or eldest daughter, thus cutting out the Westmorland heir.

Overbeck's, Sharpitor DEVON

1½ miles south-west of Salcombe, signposted from Malborough and Salcombe [442 D8]

The rolling country of south Devon lies far from any major road, crossed by a network of often steep and winding lanes. One such narrow artery leads up from the little port of Salcombe to this elegant Edwardian house set on a steep slope overlooking the sea. Like the small Victorian villa it replaced, it was known as Sharpitor after the prominent craggy line of rocks just offshore, but it now bears the name of the scientist, Otto Overbeck, who lived here from 1928–37 and who filled the house with his individual collections.

Everything is laid out in some half-dozen homely rooms. Shipbuilding tools and exquisitely detailed models reflect Salcombe's heyday in the 1870s, a replica of the *Phoenix* built here in 1836 which disappeared with all hands on a voyage to Barcelona, and photographs of the stricken Swedish vessel *Herzogin Cecilie*, wrecked off this coast in 1936, poignant reminders of the hazards faced by those who put to sea. The nautical collection also includes sailors' snuffboxes and marine paintings, one of them almost certainly showing *Phoenix* in full sail in the background.

Natural history exhibits illustrate local wildlife and British shells, birds' eggs and insects, several species among the cases of butterflies now very rare. A cabinet devoted to Otto Overbeck himself contains his popular rejuvenator, patented in 1924, which was said to inject new life into the old and tired by passing electricity through the body. Perhaps clients were also urged to consume Mr Overbeck's non-alcoholic beer, another of his many inventions. A secret room under the stairs, full of dolls and toys, has been specially created for children, room settings from doll's houses which once belonged to the Overbeck family including some diminutive bamboo furniture.

The 2.5-hectare (6-acre) garden, which enjoys the mildest of microclimates, is the most Mediterranean in

is in the Etruscan dressing room, where ochre-coloured dancing figures and urns set beneath trellis-like arches look as if a series of Greek vases has been flattened on the walls. In contrast, and despite its Adam ceiling, the antechamber has a French flavour. All claret and gold, it is hung with richly coloured Gobelins tapestries and lined with ornate gilded sofas and chairs by John Linnell.

Red-brick Tudor stables just north of the house, with original staircase turrets in the angles of the building, survive largely intact, apart from some alterations to doors and windows and the addition of a clock tower in the eighteenth century. Behind are the eighteenth-century pleasure grounds, where a Doric temple and Adam's semicircular garden house are set off by lawns, serpentine gravel paths and a recreation of a Regency flower garden, planted with roses, pinks and sweet peas. The park stretches away, with majestic cedars planted in the eighteenth century shading a lake and cattle grazing beneath the trees in the Great Meadow to the west. Despite the proximity of Heathrow and the M4, Osterley still feels like a country estate.

Adam was employed by Francis Child, whose grandfather had purchased the estate in 1711 after rising from obscurity to prominence as founder of one of the first banks in England (now subsumed in The Royal Bank of Scotland). After Francis's early death at the age of 28, his brother Robert completed Osterley, but he also died the Trust's care. Apart from the upper lawn around the house, most of it slopes steeply towards the sea in a series of sunny, sheltered terraces, where many rare and tender species thrive, among them agapanthus, mimosa, a camphor tree, olives, a Japanese banana and the ginkgo, and hundreds of fuchsias and hydrangeas. Palms, pines and cypresses flourish, the palms even seeding themselves, there are fruiting oranges in the conservatory, and pots and urns planted with agaves are placed around the garden. In March a mass of flamingo-pink blossoms visible from far beyond the garden marks the magnificent *Magnolia campbellii* for which Overbeck's is famous, one of a number of fine trees planted in the early twentieth century when the bones of the garden, including the terraces, were first established. And far below there is the constant backdrop of the sea, often speckled with little boats. Cliffs across the bay run south to the dramatic headland of Prawle Point, while inland there are views to Salcombe and up the wooded reaches of the Kingsbridge estuary.

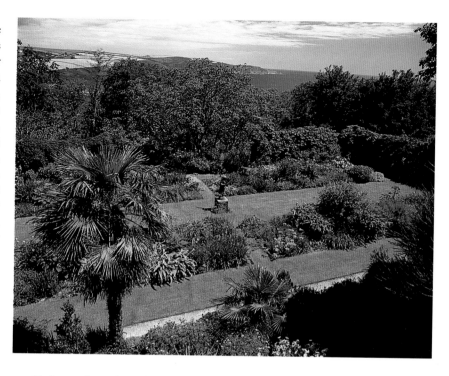

Several palms are among the many exotic plants which give the garden at Overbeck's a tropical flavour. The deep blue of the sea in Salcombe Bay can be seen in the distance.

Owletts KENT

1 mile south of the A2, at west end of village of Cobham, at junction of roads from Dartford and Sole Street [443 J5]

This red-brick, two-storey Charles II house, with dormer windows peering over the parapet added in 1754, was built for a prosperous Kentish farmer, Bonham Hayes. His initials and those of his wife Elizabeth adorn the tall chimneys rising from the steeply pitched hipped roof and also figure prominently in the plasterwork over the staircase, the finest original feature of the interior and very unusual in such a modest house. Probably the work of Italian craftsmen, realistic, three-dimensional flowers and fruit crowd the roundels carrying the date – 1684 – and the initials of the Hayes. Bunches of grapes hanging from the ceiling suggest the figs and peaches ripening above neat rows of vegetables in the walled garden to the east of the house.

A bird-bath formed of Corinthian capitals from the old Bank of England recalls the architect Sir Herbert Baker, who was born at Owletts in 1862 and was largely responsible for the historic atmosphere of the present interiors. Known today for his imperial London buildings – India House, South Africa House and the Bank of England – and for his collaboration with Sir Edwin Lutyens in the design of New Delhi, Sir Herbert also had a successful early career in South Africa, where he built Groote Schuur for Cecil Rhodes in 1890.

Owletts reflects the architect's travels and his talents, from his carved dining room chairs delightfully decorated with creatures symbolising the family and the house, to the Dutch grandfather clock and chest he brought back from Cape Town and his strip cartoon of the journey from Delhi to Owletts, with an early frame showing Sir Herbert and Lutyens together on an elephant. Sir Herbert also introduced the blue and gold wall-clock ingeniously devised to show the time in the countries of the Empire and a prominent feature in the airy sunny room looking over the garden, where broad lawns and a tennis court emphasise that this is a family house.

Oxburgh Hall NORFOLK

At Oxburgh, 7 miles south-west of Swaffham, on south side of the Stoke Ferry road [443 J2]

This romantic moated house is set on what was once an island in the East Anglian fen. The land around is now criss-crossed with drainage dykes and cultivated, but when Edward IV gave Sir Edmund Bedingfeld a licence to crenellate his manor house at Oxburgh in 1482, the site was on a raised promontory in the marsh. The Bedingfelds were to remain at Oxburgh for the next 500 years, the gradual impoverishment of the estate that resulted from their adherence to the Catholic faith also ensuring that the house survived unaltered through the sixteenth and seventeenth centuries.

Even in this remote corner of England, which still feels isolated today, Sir Edmund was more concerned with display and comfort than defence. The house is heralded by a piece of early Tudor showmanship: a seven-storey gatehouse with battlemented turrets and stone-mullioned windows rising sheer from the moat. This virtuoso status symbol is the best-preserved part of the fifteenth-century house. Flemish-style stepped gables and twisted terra-cotta chimneys on the brick ranges to either side which contribute so much to the romantic character of the place seem to be all of a piece; in fact they were added by J. C. Buckler as part of extensive restorations in the mid-nineteenth century. Buckler was also responsible for the beautiful oriel window which fills two storeys of his authentically medieval battlemented tower in the south-east corner, looking out over the florid French-style parterre flowering in swirls of blue and yellow on the grass beyond the moat.

The interior of the house includes both Tudor survivals and atmospheric Victorian rooms. The brick-walled King's Room in the gatehouse tower with its great fireplace was where Henry VII slept when he came to Oxburgh in 1487. A priest's hole in the floor of a former garderobe off this room is an evocative reminder of the family's religious sympathies. Oxburgh's most prized possession, needlework

by Mary Queen of Scots which she worked at while she was in the custody of the Earl of Shrewsbury after her flight to England, is displayed in a darkened room nearby. These richly embroidered panels set onto green velvet, mostly delightful representations of beasts, birds and fishes ranging from the unicorn to the garden snail, are very rare specimens of the queen's skill.

The nineteenth-century interiors, with designs by J. C. Buckler and J. D. Crace, are among the few examples of Catholic High Victorian taste in Britain. Crace's heraldic ceiling in the drawing room incorporates delicately painted foliage and flowers in blue, pink and green. More heraldic devices – crimson fleurs-de-lis – are woven into the carpet of the low-ceilinged library, picking up the red in the flock wallpaper. A neo-Tudor fireplace dominating this room has a carved overmantel made up of medieval fragments from continental churches, including some delicate fan vaulting. The small dining room is another rich Victorian interior, still looking exactly as it did in a watercolour of the early 1850s, the dark lustre of the panelling and of the elaborate sideboard with its crest of writhing birds relieved by vivid blue, orange and red tiles round the fireplace.

In the little chapel warmed with light cast through the great red Bedingfeld eagle in the south window, Victorian and medieval craftsmanship are again combined. The splendid altarpiece is crowned by a sixteenth-century carved triptych, purchased by the Bedingfelds in Bruges in about 1860.

Apart from the nineteenth-century Wilderness Walk to the west of the chapel and mown grass around the moat, most of the garden lies to the east of the house. A yew hedge beyond the parterre fronts a colourful herbaceous border. Behind is the fanciful, turreted wall of the Victorian kitchen garden, now planted as a formal orchard with plums, medlars, quinces and gages, and with roses, clematis and other climbers on the walls. There is also a 2-mile park walk to one of Oxburgh's old shelter belts.

Packwood House WARWICKSHIRE

2 miles east of Hockley Heath on the A34, 11 miles south-east of central Birmingham [443 G2]

Packwood's fame rests on an evocative arrangement of trees. Across the large sunken lawn to the south of the house, a semicircular flight of brick steps leads up to a terrace walk and into the famous Yew Garden, traditionally thought to represent the Sermon on the Mount. Smoothly mown grass is dotted with clipped yews, most rising well

The core of the house is a timber-framed building constructed by John Fetherston at the end of the sixteenth century. Although now rebuilt in brick and rendered over, its Elizabethan origins are still evident in the gabled roofline, massive chimneys and mullioned windows of the main block. Unlike their staunchly Catholic neighbours, the Ferrers of Baddesley Clinton (*see* p.31), the Fetherstons were politic in their allegiances. During the Civil War they seem to have offered shelter and succour as seemed expedient. Cromwell's general, Henry Ireton, slept here the night before the Battle of Edgehill in 1642 and there is a family tradition that Charles II was given food and drink at Packwood after his defeat at Worcester in 1651. Later in the century another John Fetherston added the extensive outbuildings in a rich dark-red brick, particularly fine examples of their kind.

Sold by the last of the Fetherstons in the late nineteenth century, Packwood was bought in 1905 by the wealthy industrialist Alfred Ash, also known for his fondness for the turf. Graham Baron Ash used his father's fortune to restore the house in the 1920s and 1930s, sweeping away Georgian and Victorian alterations and painstakingly acquiring features which would give Packwood a period feel, rescuing leaded casements, floors, beams and chimneypieces from other old houses. He also added the splendid long gallery and fashioned the great hall, complete with oriel window, out of an existing barn to complete his romantic vision of a Tudor house. He filled Packwood with period furnishings, including fine Jacobean panelling and an exceptional collection of tapestries, such as the seventeenth-century Brussels hanging depicting a cool terraced garden with splashing fountains and urns filled with orange trees. A long oak refectory table in the great hall and a Charles II oak cupboard inlaid with mother of pearl in the dining room are two of the many pieces obtained from Baddesley Clinton when the finances of the Ferrers family were at a particularly low ebb.

above the heads of visitors and the tallest flanking the raised walk at the far end of the garden. Here twelve of the great yews are known as the Apostles, with the Evangelists represented by four very big specimens in the middle. From the terrace a tight spiral path edged with box ascends a hummock known as the Mount, crowned by a single yew tree. Although many of the 'multitude' were planted to replace an orchard in the mid-nineteenth century, the Master and his disciples were part of the seventeenth-century garden laid out by John Fetherston. He may also have enjoyed the sunken garden immediately in front of the house, with its delightful gazebos at each corner. One of these, dating from the time of Charles II, is ingeniously designed so that its fireplace can be used to warm fruit trees ripening on an adjacent wall. A vivid mixed herbaceous border flowering red, purple, yellow and blue near the house and crimson blooms in the box-edged rose garden act as a foil for the green of grass and trees. An intriguing sunken bath in a corner of one of the yew-hedged enclosures on the west side of the house dates from 1680. Sadly, water no longer gushes from the dog's-head spout in the little waterworks building adorned with the Fetherston arms.

Patterson's Spade Mill CO. ANTRIM

On A6, 2 miles south-east of Templepatrick [444 C3]

This unusual relic of Ireland's agricultural past is the last water-driven spade mill in the country. Founded in 1919 to produce a range of implements, from light tools for flower beds to heavy-duty spades for cutting turf, Patterson's Mill was run as a family business for over 70 years. It was acquired by the Trust with all machinery and fittings intact and spades are once again being made here.

Spades nearing completion at Patterson's Spade Mill.

Trials of War

All over the British Isles, and often set in peaceful countryside, are many reminders of a far from tranquil past. Sometimes the threat came from overseas. The long war with France which fizzled and flared for much of the fourteenth and fifteenth centuries, the so-called Hundred Years War, brought raids on south-coast ports and a constant fear of invasion, fuelled by folk memories of the Conqueror and his men a few hundred years before. A similar fear of France in the mid-nineteenth century was met with new coastal defences, among them the little fort guarding the approaches to the Solent which sits high above the sea on the Isle of Wight.

Sometimes the threat was closer to home. For centuries, in the border country of what is now Northumbria and Cumbria, men looked north to a foreign and often unfriendly power, while life in the Welsh Marches was marked by campaigns to subdue and hold the wild hill country to the west, the territory of warlords and princelings. Ireland had a frontier too, between the lands of the Anglo-Irish settlers and the Gaelic territories. Sometimes the country tore itself apart. Two periods of civil war, one in the fifteenth century, the other two hundred years later, cast their shadows far and wide. In the first, the Wars of the Roses, the conflict was about who should be king. In the second, which climaxed with the execution of Charles I, it was about the limits of royal power. Some associations, such as the deliberate destruction of Corfe Castle, Dorset, are obvious, others less so. For those who backed the wrong side, or refused to temper principle with self-interest, the consequences could be devastating. Estates were left impoverished, brother was sometimes fighting brother, and those who took a leading part in the hostilities risked execution when the tables were turned or they found themselves in the hands of vengeful forces.

One of the greatest building projects ever undertaken by the Romans snakes across the wild and beautiful country-side of Northumbria. Running nearly 75 miles from the Tyne to the Solway Firth is the great wall ordered by the Emperor Hadrian in AD122 to define the province of Britannia. To the north lay the Picts, whom the Romans never managed to subdue. Up to 45.7 metres (15 feet) high and 3 metres (10 feet) wide, the wall takes advantage of the craggy outcrop of the Whin Sill, whose natural ramparts face north. Provided with forts and turrets and fully garrisoned, it was a formidable line of defence, but it was a psychological as much as a military barrier, marking the limits of the civilised world and the point where the expansion of the empire ground to a halt. For centuries the wide belt of border country between Scotland and England was

HADRIAN'S WALL
170

insecure and contested. Since the 10th century the frontiers of the infant Scottish kingdom had been pushed slowly southward but then, between 1296 and the mid-14th century, Edward 1 and his successors staged a series of assaults aiming at conquest. After fifty years, almost nothing had been achieved but the legacy of these hostilities lived on in the border country

CHIRK CASTLE
91

The great castles of the north, where powerful magnates maintained private armies, long played a role in the defence of the realm and in internal power struggles.

The romantic ruins of Dunstanburgh Castle, perched high on a basalt cliff on the lonely Northumbrian coast, were once a stronghold of the house of Lancaster. A troop of horsemen rode out from here to help Edward II in his invasion of Scotland in 1322; this was the seat of John of Gaunt and his son, who usurped the throne as Henry IV, and in the mid-15th century Dunstanburgh was embroiled in the conflicts and changing fortunes of the Wars of the Roses. By now, the Yorkists were in the ascendant, and in 1462 Edward IV marched north to besiege the rebellious strongholds of the north-east.

Dunstanburgh was surrendered, only to be handed back to the Lancastrians by its constable, but in 1464, much damaged, it was taken again, and by Tudor times it was a ruin.

SIZERGH TOWER
346

for the next two hundred years. To protect themselves and their local communities, influential landowners gradually established a line of castles and towers from coast to coast. The heart of Sizergh in Cumbria is one of these pele towers. Built in c.1350, it has massive walls of limestone rubble rising almost 18.3 metres (60 feet) and an additional turret on one side. Almost half a century earlier, a Strickland of Sizergh was knighted by Edward I for his services to border warfare. While no medieval English king managed to hold the kingdom of the Scots by force, the smaller principality of Wales was a more realistic target. Following a series of campaigns between 1276 and 1295, Edward I set out to impose his authority with a chain of massive

castles. Some were royal strongholds, others were entrusted to loyal followers such as Roger Mortimer of Chirk in Clywd, who was made Justice of Wales in 1308. His castle (**above, right**), now set in glorious pastoral countryside, was begun in c.1295, possibly to a design by James of St George, the master castle-builder whom Edward I had brought back from the Crusades. Like the royal castles, Chirk's strength was in the great drum towers which projected from the curtain wall. This stronghold never played an active role in subduing the Welsh but in the Civil War, by which time it had passed to the Myddelton family, it was besieged by Parliamentary forces and much damaged. Sir Thomas rebuilt, but the drum towers, which had once projected above the wall, were reduced to their present height.

DUNSTANBURGH CASTLE
132

SCOTNEY CASTLE GARDEN
332

The civil wars of 1639–60, which involved the first legalised execution of an anointed king, cast long shadows. Families were divided, estates impoverished and religious divisions accentuated. Some parts of Britain saw little fighting, but others were continually marched over and occupied by both sides, with all the violence and destruction that war brings. At Corfe in Dorset (**right**), the great Norman castle crowning a steep chalk hill had been lived in by the Royalist Bankes family since 1635. A loyal garrison withstood a siege in 1643 but in 1646, by which time this was the only remaining Royalist stronghold between Exeter and London, a 48-day siege was ended by treachery. The castle was deliberately ruined and the little village at its feet was also badly damaged, and the church stripped of its lead roof.

Further west, just across the Tamar into Cornwall, another drama was being played out by the Carews of Antony (**opposite, left**). Where one son wavered in his allegiance, shifting from Parliament to the king, the other, a staunch republican, was one of those who sat in judgement on Charles I in 1648 and signed his death warrant. Both brothers died on the block, but still at Antony is the powerful portrait of the king (**opposite, far right**) made at his trial by Edward Bower.

A mere three years later, Royalist hopes finally died at the decisive battle of Worcester. The young Charles II, on the run, tried to flee into Wales but found all the crossing points of the Severn were guarded. Turning back, and travelling in disguise, he found refuge in a series of safe houses before

CORFE CASTLE
109

eventually reaching the Continent about six weeks later. Just a few days after the Worcester battle he had been escorted to Moseley Old Hall in Staffordshire, home of the Catholic Whitgreave family. Here he concealed himself in a hiding place below a cupboard when soldiers came to the house, watching from an upper room as scattered remnants of his army passed by on their way back to Scotland. At Moseley, Charles asked the family chaplain, John Huddlestone, to escort him to the little chapel at the

top of the house (**right**), then open to the rafters and without its present decoration. It was Huddlestone who, at the king's request, administered the last rites when Charles lay dying in 1685.

BODIAM CASTLE
54

Scotney and Bodiam castles, only some ten miles apart and a day's march from the south coast, were built in response to fear of the French. In the changing fortunes of the Hundred Years War, control of the Channel was of vital importance and by 1375 the French had the upper hand. Scotney was started in 1378, the year after Rye and Winchelsea, about twenty miles away, had been sacked. More a fortified house than a castle, its main defence lay in the lake-like moat formed by diverting the little River Bewl. Seven

years later, in 1385, the French gathered an invasion fleet. It never sailed, but this may have been the catalyst for the building of Bodiam by Sir Edward Dalyngrigge, an opportunist who had made a fortune in France. Guarding an important crossing of the Rother and not far from its mouth, Bodiam was much more of a front-line defence than Scotney but, even so, the defensive carapace surrounded a lordly residence.

SIR ALEXANDER CAREW BT

Across the centuries, Britain has been protected from her Continental enemies by the Channel, her natural moat, and from Roman times onwards coastal defences have played an important part in strategic thinking. From the 1850s until the Second World War, the Isle of Wight, well placed to survey passing ships and guarding the approaches to the great harbour of Portsmouth, played a frontline position. Gun batteries were built at the eastern and western ends, the one on the west set on the exposed cliff-top right above the Needles rocks. Here, reached by tunnels in the cliff, searchlights were installed to watch for torpedo boats in the 1880s, and then in the Second World War, when the threat from the air was greater than that from the sea, to help pinpoint enemy aircraft.

THE SEARCHLIGHT EMPLACEMENT
THIS OBSERVATION POST WAS BUILT IN 1899.
ENEMY SHIPPING WHICH TRIED TO SLIP PAST
UNDER COVER OF DARKNESS WOULD BE PICKED
UP BY THE BEAM FROM THE SEARCHLIGHT.

Paxton's Tower CARMARTHENSHIRE

7 miles east of Carmarthen, 1 mile south of Llanarthney
[442 C4]

This lonely triangular folly crowns a prominent grassy rise above the valley of the Tywi, its castellated outline, with two round turrets framing the central tower, a familiar sight to those following the A40 to Carmarthen on the other side of the river. The tower was built between 1805 and 1808 by Sir William Paxton, a wealthy banker, as a memorial to Nelson, and originally had a banqueting room on the first floor from which the views over the valley could be enjoyed in comfort.

Paycocke's ESSEX

On south side of the A120 West Street, the road to Braintree, about 275 metres from centre of Coggeshall, next to the Fleece Inn, 5½ miles east of Braintree [443 J4]

The wealth generated by the East Anglian wool trade in the fifteenth and sixteenth centuries produced some of the most beautiful churches in the British Isles. It also enriched the homes of the merchants themselves, many of them using their fortunes to build fine half-timbered houses advertising their enhanced status. Paycocke's, a product of the early sixteenth century, is a splendid example of these buildings, its long pink and white, brick and timber street façade incorporating carpentry and carved woodwork of the highest quality.

An intricately decorated wooden beam running the width of the house beneath the five oriel windows of the projecting upper storey carries a series of delightful cameos, such as a dragon depicted upside down and a small person apparently diving into a lily. Larger naturalistic figures frame the fine oak gates through which a carriageway leads to the back of the house. Closely spaced vertical timbers limewashed a silvery-grey, with brick filling the spaces that would once have been packed with wattle and daub, form the pink and white stripes that give the façade its distinctive appearance. As indicated by the four family tombs still to be seen in the parish church, the Paycockes were people of substance, the house John Paycocke built on the occasion of his son Thomas's marriage to Margaret Harrold (indicated by the initials TP and MP carved on both interior and exterior woodwork) standing out from its more modest neighbours along West Street.

Inside, it is clear that Paycocke's was a place of work and business as well as a home. Peg holes in the studs of the walls were once used to hold the warp thread of the looms, wool was stored in the roof space and the lengths of cloth were probably stretched out to dry in the garden. A display of Coggeshall lace includes a device which used water-filled flasks to magnify candlelight, thus allowing four lace-makers to work by the light of one candle.

The Peak District DERBYSHIRE, STAFFORDSHIRE, SOUTH YORKSHIRE

Between Manchester, to the west, and Sheffield, to the east
[445 I8–J7]

Completely surrounded as the Peak District is by the great industrial cities of the North and the Midlands, it is surprising that the Trust was not involved here until 1930, when Alport Height, a hilltop near Wirksworth in the south-east corner of the area, was given anonymously. By 1940 the Trust's foothold had grown to 809.5 hectares (2,000 acres) and it now owns over 14,568.5 hectares (36,000 acres). By far the largest holding is to the north of the A625 in the heart of the High Peak: 12,949.5 hectares (32,000 acres) of wild landscape which is largely heather and grass moorland on the brown sandstone and black shales of the millstone grit, lying in a great horseshoe known as the Dark Peak round the much smaller area of limestone country known as the White Peak.

The Derwent estate, acquired in 1952, partly in South Yorkshire – 2023.5 hectares (5,000 acres) – and partly in Derbyshire – 566 hectares (1,400 acres) – includes all the Howden Moors to the east of the great Howden and Derwent reservoirs which so altered the Upper Derwent Valley in the years before 1914. To the west lie the 6,475 hectares (16,000 acres) of Hope Woodlands which came to the Trust with Hardwick Hall (*see* p.175) in 1959. These great moors, Ronksley, Bleaklow and Ashop, mile upon mile of pale grass and dark brown peat, run in a semi-circle round the valleys of the Rivers Westend, Alport and Ashop which drain the watershed into the Derwent. It was to capture the water of the two latter rivers that the vast Ladybower Reservoir was completed in 1945.

The plantations of the water companies and the Forestry Commission cover the lower slopes round the reservoirs and up into the valleys. They are less obtrusive than similar plantings in Wales or the Lake District and are not wholly coniferous; one-fifth of the 1,214 hectares (3,000 acres) of publicly owned woodland is broadleaved.

In the valleys, therefore, the reservoirs and plantations serving the need for water of the great cities of Sheffield,

Opposite: The art of late medieval timber-framing is well shown at Paycocke's, where both the lavishness of the carved decoration and the close studding suggest the builder was a man of means. Above: Figures carrying shields are carved on the gateposts at one end of the house.

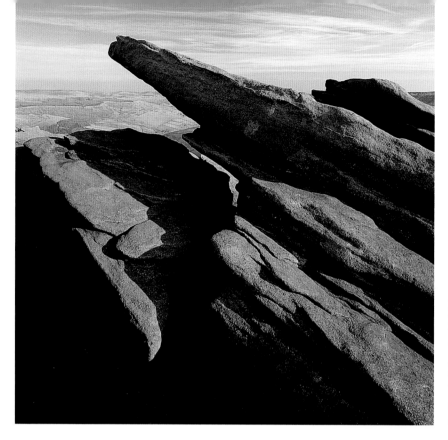

A rock outcrop on the dramatic Kinder Scout massif.

with the 647.5 hectares (1,600 acres) of Park Hall Moor adjoining to the west. The acquisition, made between 1982 and 1988, with the recent addition of Hill House Farm, embracing Kinder Head, was financed by means of a public appeal, bequests, and grants from the Countryside Commission and the National Heritage Memorial Fund. Management problems have been considerable.

The natural vegetation on the Kinder plateau has been degraded, in places eroded away altogether, due in part to atmospheric pollution, accidental fires and over-use of popular areas by walkers, but above all to overgrazing by sheep encroaching from adjoining moors. The 'hefting' of flocks, whereby ewes instinctively keep to their native moors, had broken down and the results had been disastrous. Although the Trust put in hand a vigorous programme of gathering trespassing sheep which were penned, identified and collected by their owners at regular intervals, the problem continued, so a long-term, and expensive, campaign was begun to rebuild the miles of gritstone dry walls, fence some other boundaries, and experiment with restoration of eroded areas. It is a slow business, for the soil is thin and poor, but progress is being made as techniques improve, and it is certain that eventually Kinder can be brought back to its former state.

To the south, in Edale, the Trust has built up a 809.5-hectare (2,000-acre) estate of hill farms, mainly on the south side of the valley and centred on Mam Tor, 518 metres (1,700 feet) high. Called the 'shivering mountain' because of continual landslips over the centuries, its east face, though entirely natural, resembles a gigantic quarry. A mile to the south the narrow limestone gorge of the Winnats Pass winds steeply up from Castleton; the name is a corruption of 'wind-gates' and to be caught here in a gale confirms its aptness. The grim character of this country is not to everyone's taste, although the views north to Kinder Scout and the High Peak are superb.

Longshaw, only 10 miles south-west of the centre of Sheffield, contrasts with the High Peak. Mostly acquired by the Trust in two bursts, during the 1930s and the 1970s, its 688 hectares (1,700 acres) are more varied and, although still on the millstone grit, softer in character than the great open moors.

The B6251 runs through Padley Gorge, which is cut by the Burbage Brook, sometimes just a small stream in summer but a rushing torrent in winter. Here are some of the best surviving ancient oak woodlands in the Peak District, together with the special flora and fauna which this habitat supports. There is some valley-bottom farmland, and in the great abandoned quarries at Bolehill, the

Nottingham, Derby and Leicester have made a new landscape in this century, but above 305 metres (1,000 feet) – where the Trust's moors lie – the old landscape remains unchanged. The beautifully named hill sheep – White-faced Woodland, Derbyshire Gritstone and Dalesbred – are based in the valley farms, but graze for much of the year on the high moorland. The herbage – mat grass, purple moorgrass, cotton grass, bilberry and heather – suits both the sheep and the red grouse (providing there aren't too many sheep). Careful burning of the heather is necessary to give the grouse a patchwork of differently aged plants: young shoots for food, mature plants for nesting under and over-mature heather for cover. Co-operation between the National Park and landowners, of which the Trust is the largest, allows farming and grouse shooting to co-exist happily with adequate access to all these great uplands.

South of Black Ashop Moor lies the massif of Kinder Scout, rising to over 610 metres (2,000 feet) and including the great bowl between Kinder Edge and the Downfall where the Kinder stream spills dramatically over the cliff from its source in the flat peaty moors above. The moorland stretches over Swine's Back to Edale Head and Jacob's Ladder, over 1,416.5 hectares (3,500 acres) of wild country, source of millstones for the local water-powered mills for centuries, numerous worked or half-worked stones remain. From Surprise View above the quarries there is a panorama over the Derwent and Hope valleys.

To the east of the gorge, in an attractive landscape of mixed woodland, heather and coppice, stands Longshaw Lodge, built in the 1820s as a shooting box for the Duke of Rutland, now converted into flats with a Trust shop, tea-room and information room next door. Hay Wood, to the south, was once oak but clearance in the last century has allowed the invasion of self-sown birch. Tumbling Hill above the wood is the best place from which to view the whole. In the south of the National Park Derbyshire joins Staffordshire, and the landscape changes into the very different limestone valleys of the so-called White Peak. Ossoms Hill and Wetton Hill stand on either side of the narrow wooded valley of the River Manifold west of Alstonfield, where the Trust owns 364 hectares (900 acres) of peaceful hill-farming country. Below Wetton Mill the river bed is dry during periods of low rainfall, when the river vanishes underground to reappear 6 miles further on below Ilam Hall. Dr Johnson refused to believe this until he had proved it to his satisfaction with marked corks!

Below Beeston Tor the Manifold is joined by the River Hamps, which also runs dry when the water level drops, flowing underground into porous limestone to re-emerge at Ilam. For 2 miles along the eastern bank of the Hamps the wooded slopes of Old Park Hill, Old Soles Hill and part of Little Wood belong to the Trust.

At Ilam the Manifold turns one of its many loops through Ilam Park. Ilam Hall, a Gothic extravaganza of the 1820s, was partly demolished a century later and what remains is now a youth hostel and a Trust visitor centre. The park and the hanging Hinkley Wood on the far bank of the river are pleasant places to walk, with views to Thorpe Cloud and Bunster Hill, the 'Portals of Dovedale'.

Built up since 1934, the Trust's holding in Dovedale is now over 566.5 hectares (1,400 acres), and is particularly important in terms of its beauty and popularity. The 'silver shining Dove' – with its west bank in Staffordshire, its east in Derbyshire – has been a place of pilgrimage for anglers since the middle of the seventeenth century when Charles Cotton eulogised it in his poetry and, with his friend Izaak Walton, wrote the *Compleat Angler* (1653). It is fishermen who have given the river its present character, with weirs to slow down and oxygenate the water providing a better habitat for trout and grayling.

Tourists as well as anglers began to include Dovedale in their itineraries, and the building of the railways made

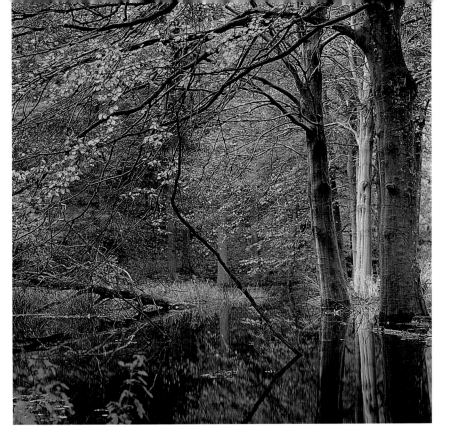

access to it easy. The hills are gentle and rolling, the dry-stone walls dividing them into jigsaw pieces, and the steep gorge of the Dove provides a vivid contrast. The river has carved its way through the soft limestone over the centuries, leaving caves, arches and pinnacles of harder rock as remnants of its former courses and tributaries. A footpath runs beside the river past the extraordinary limestone outcrops weathered into strange shapes. Like all such rocks in beauty-spots, most of them are named: Lion Face, Lover's Leap, Dovedale Castle, Jacob's Ladder, the Twelve Apostles, Tissington Spires. With the decrease in sheep grazing, these rocks had become obscured by encroaching trees and scrub. The Trust has now cleared enough of the scrub away, revealing the rock formations. Judging the right level of clearance is a delicate matter, especially in an area so rich in nature conservation interest.

Although the dale is inaccessible by car, being crossed by a road only at Milldale, it attracts some 2 million visitors a year, with the 3 miles from Thorpe to the Milldale access point being especially popular. The hamlet of Milldale has a medieval packhorse bridge, and, next to it, a small Trust information barn. The Trust's property ends 4 miles north beyond Milldale, past the dry Biggin Dale at the north end of Wolfscote Dale.

The tranquil shores of the Ladybower reservoir.

Peckover House and Garden
CAMBRIDGESHIRE

On north bank of River Nene, in Wisbech [443 J2]

Fluctuations in the coastline of the Wash have removed Wisbech further and further from the sea. Now some 12 miles distant, only 250 years ago the River Nene was navigable into the heart of the town and a substantial port developed on the basis of a thriving trade with the Netherlands. Although the sea traffic has long since died, imposing red-brick merchants' houses still line the river, giving this sleepy little town an elegance and importance out of all proportion to its present status. The influence of trading partners across the North Sea shows in the recurring Dutch gables and hipped roofs and also perhaps in the Friends Meeting House on the banks of the river, a testimony to the religious toleration which marked both countries and which fostered a substantial Quaker community in the town, many of whom, as elsewhere in East Anglia, played prominent roles in local affairs.

One such was Jonathan Peckover, who has given his name to the elegant three-storey Georgian town house overlooking the Nene which he bought in 1777. Five years later, in association with the Gurneys, another leading Quaker family, he established the local bank of Gurney, Birkbeck and Peckover in a wing adjoining the house, from where the business was run for almost a century until the bank merged with Barclays in 1896.

In contrast to the rather plain exterior, the panelled rooms have fine Georgian fireplaces and a wealth of elaborate wood- and plasterwork by local craftsmen. The decoration includes both Neo-classical motifs and more exuberant rococo features, such as the magnificently fluid carving surrounding the mirror above the drawing-room fireplace, with festoons of drapery suspended from an eagle with outstretched wings.

After the built-up river frontage, the spacious 2-acre garden comes as something of a surprise. Extending well back from the house and also running behind several other buildings along the Nene to the west, this outstanding Victorian survival is an example of the 'gardenesque' style, in which the display of individual plants is as important as the overall effect achieved. An imposing flight of steps with a stone balustrade leads on to a spacious lawn shaded by a number of fine specimen trees, including a ginkgo, a tulip tree, redwoods, a Chusan palm and a monkey puzzle. A dark and bosky wilderness walk marking the eastern perimeter winds through laurels, hollies, box and yew, the bank of unrelieved foliage very different from the bright colour schemes backed by warm red brick in the formal walled area in the middle of the garden. Here matching borders edged with pinks and planted with cones of roses and clematis flank the central path leading up to a little pool overlooked by a green and white summerhouse. Two topiary peacocks perch on the yew hedge dividing the garden.

Flowering pot plants fill the orangery at the other end of the path in summer and three old orange trees regularly bear fruit. Nearby is the cool green corridor of a fern house, and to the east climbing roses are trained over a series of metal arches; the most spectacular, known as the Bandstand, carries three varieties mingled with honeysuckle. A second lawn fills the western third of the garden. Across it, hidden in the trees, is a cats' cemetery, with a recently restored thatched reed barn beyond.

A virtuoso display of rococo carving frames the mirror over the fireplace in Peckover's elegant 18th-century drawing room. The blue and white colour scheme may be original.

Pembrokeshire Coast PEMBROKESHIRE

[442 B3–B4]

Pembrokeshire's lovely coast has a National Park of its own, and within it the Trust is strongly represented. West of the Colby estate adjoining Carmarthen Bay (*see* p.104), the coast turns south-west. Overlooking Caldey Island is Lydstep Headland, an impressive limestone promontory where the Trust's 22 hectares (54 acres) protect seabird nesting sites, cliff-top grasslands and a disused limestone quarry, colonised by lime-loving plants. Less than 2 miles further along the coast are the red sandstone cliffs of Manorbier Bay, where the Trust owns 19.5 hectares (48 acres), with views west to St Govan's Head. These two properties are footholds compared with the extensive coastal estate of Stackpole, south of the Milford Haven estuary, where 809.5 hectares (2,000 acres) of beautiful and very varied country, formerly part of the Cawdor estate, were conveyed to the Trust in 1976. Whilst the core of the property, with about 8 miles of coastline, is centred on Stackpole, there is also a very fine sand-dune system, one of the best in Pembrokeshire, at Freshwater West.

Stackpole Court (rebuilt in the 1730s on the site of an earlier house and demolished in 1963) was no great loss, as the superb landscape which surrounded it, part manmade, part natural, has survived. At the end of the eighteenth century the valley below the house was dammed to make a freshwater lake over a mile long, and a noble eight-arched bridge was built to cross it. A generation later, the two Bosherston valleys were also dammed. The three lakes meet above the great sandy beach at Broadhaven and the sea is approached through a man-made wooded landscape, much of it planted 200 years ago. With its lakes and network of paths, the estate is comparable only to one remarkably similar property also in the Trust's care: Penrose in the south of Cornwall (*see* p.351).

Broadhaven, surrounded by low cliffs, has dunes behind and hard yellow sand before, so there is always shelter from the wind, making it ideal for family outings. To the east is the limestone-based Stackpole Warren, part-covered in blown sand. The close-cropped turf, with some very rare lime-loving plants and lichens, was originally enclosed as a rabbit warren. The warren runs out to Stackpole Head, where the sweep of the Trust's cliffs to the north-east opens to view, stretching as far as Trewent Point above Freshwater East. Stackpole Warren and the Freshwater Lakes now fall within a designated National Nature Reserve.

Barafundle Bay, tucked in to the east of the headland, is very like Broadhaven but less frequented because it is a longer walk from the car park. It approaches near perfection, forming a delightful sandy bay. At Stackpole Quay the rock changes from limestone to red sandstone. The little stone pier was used to bring in coal for the estate and for shipping limestone when the quarries were active, and the former farm buildings are now holiday cottages. A disused quarry nearby has recently been developed as a recreational area for mixed-user groups.

The great stretch of sand at Broadhaven is part of an extensive coastal mosaic of turf-topped limestone cliffs and sheltered bays backed by sand dunes, tree-fringed lakes and mature woodlands.

Opposite: Looking over Whitesands
Bay towards Ramsey Island from the
heights of Carn Llidi, a stretch of
coastal heath which is rich in
prehistoric remains.

St Ann's Head is the western bastion of Milford Haven. On its west side stands Kete, a mile of cliffs and farmland between Long Point and Little Castle Point. From here there are good views to the islands of Skomer and Skokholm and the property is now far more pleasant than it was when the Trust bought the land in 1967. Then it was covered with a mess of concrete: abandoned gun positions which guarded Milford Haven until 1945. Now the landscape is gradually healing after a major reclamation project undertaken by the National Park Authority.

Furthest to the west is the parish of Marloes, with a fine sandy beach linked at low tide to the rocky tongue of Gateholm Island. A mile of Trust-owned cliffs leads to the Deer Park, a heather- and grass-clad headland with an Iron Age fort embankment still evident. Seals breed in the caves beneath and a prostrate form of yellow broom grows on the windswept cliffs. From Martin's Haven, to the north, there are boats to Skomer, passing Midland Island on the way.

Virtually all the north side of St Bride's Bay is owned by the Trust or protected by means of legal covenants. The walk from Newgale to Solva, broken into mile-long sections by the rocky promontories of Dinas Fach and Dinas Fawr, can be hard-going.

The peaceful shores of Solva Harbour are succeeded by three more rocky miles to Penpleidiau, with a gap south of St David's, then round the steep Porth Clais inlet (the harbour for the great monastery of St David), west to Porthllysgi Bay and out to the headland of Pen Dal-aderyn, with Ramsey Island half a mile offshore. The views across to the precipitous coast of Ramsey are exciting, with the tide racing through Ramsey Sound around the treacherous rocks disparagingly known as The Bitches. The Trust owns the whole of this Treginnis peninsula, but thereafter only small pieces of cliff until the massive St David's Head (Penmaen Dewi) which is overlooked by the rocky outcrop of Carn Llidi. The Treginnis peninsula is a rich site, with archaeological remains that include a Neolithic promontory fort, a chambered tomb and old copper workings as well as much that is masked by vegetation, and with a wide variety of both common and rarer grasses, heath and cliff plants. From Carnedd Lleithir, to the east, there are good views: on a clear day north to Snowdon.

Between Abereiddi, 4 miles to the north-east, and Porthgain is something quite different: a landscape of industrial archaeology. There are slate and stone quarries, an abandoned brickworks, the line of the railway which served them, and, at Porthgain, substantial remains of the harbour from which the products of these works were exported. It is all part of the 81-hectare (200-acre) Ynys Barry Farm, acquired in 1985.

Two miles further east is Longhouse Farm, another splendid headland, with a promontory fort, a burial chamber with a great capstone (not National Trust owned) and, tucked in on the east side (just as Porthgain is tucked under Ynys Barry), the tiny harbour of Abercastle.

Beyond a stretch of private land is the beach of Aber Mawr, with a freshwater marsh behind its pebble ridge and a submerged forest, exposed at low tide. The Trust's land here includes the wooded Aber Mawr Valley, rich in birdlife, and Tregwynt home farm, with fields running out to the coast.

Sheltering Fishguard Bay from the west is rocky Strumble Head, where the prominently placed Treseissylt Farm embraces the beaches of Aber Bach and Pwl Crochan. To the east lies the 40.5-hectare (100-acre) farm of Good Hope, with its craggy cliffs and small fields bounded by old turf and stone hedgebanks.

Across Fishguard Bay itself lies Dinas Island, almost circular in shape and not in fact an island but seeming so, for it is virtually separated from the mainland by a glacial overspill channel which ends as a beach on either side of the headland. Dinas Island Farm sits in the middle of its 3 miles of lovely coast, with Dinas Head rising 142 metres (465 feet) above it.

Penrhyn Castle GWYNEDD

1 mile east of Bangor, at Llandegai on the A5122 [444 F7]

From the long upward climb off the Bangor road there is a sudden view of Penrhyn's great four-storey keep rising above the trees, with battlemented turrets at each corner. The rest of the creeper-clad building stretches away across a bluff for over 183 metres, pierced by round-headed windows and with an impressive array of towers, battlements and crenellations. The interior is even more overwhelming, with long stone-flagged corridors, high ceilings, heavy doors and panelling and a wealth of carved stone surrounding arches and doors and forming bosses, corbels, friezes and capitals. A strange population looks down from the forest of slender pillars creating blind arcades on the walls of the extraordinary staircase. Each head is different. Here is a bearded wild man, there an elf with pointed ears, somewhere else a gargoyle with interlocking teeth. Look carefully and what appears to be writhing foliage becomes a contorted face. At the foot of the staircase a semicircle of hands echoes the curve of the

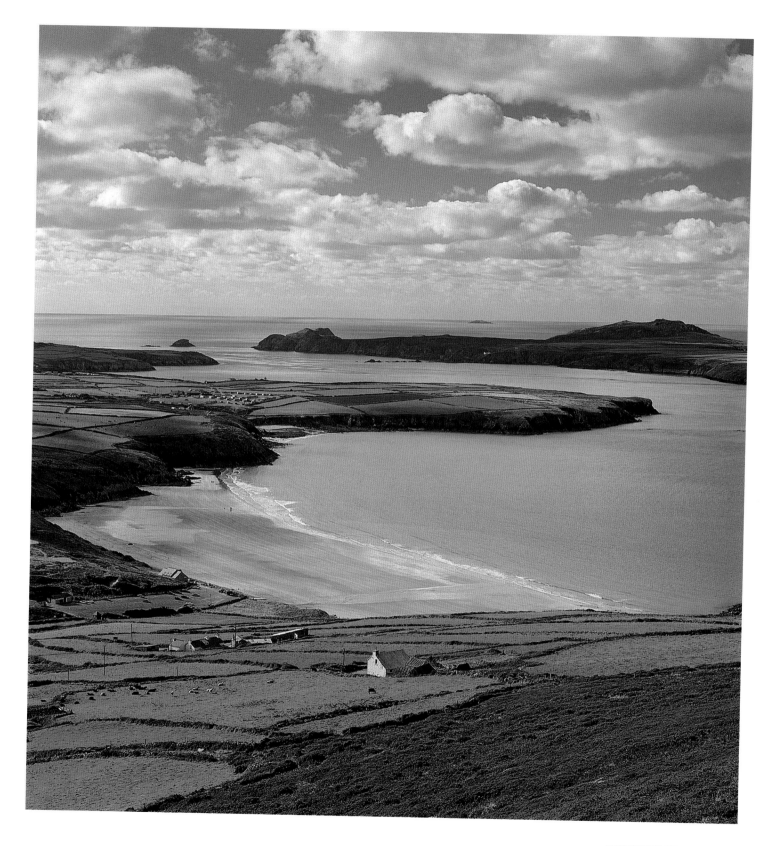

Right: Richly-carved stonework adorns Thomas Hopper's vision of a grand Norman staircase at Penrhyn. This feature of the castle has no historical precedent as Norman fortresses were built with spiral stairs, but Hopper made up for this in his use of period motifs, among them a feast of deliciously carved capitals (below). Hopper also designed much of the furniture in the house. This enormous gilt-bronze candelabra in the drawing room (bottom) is said to have been based on a piece by Cellini, but nothing comparable has been found among the 16th-century goldsmith's work.

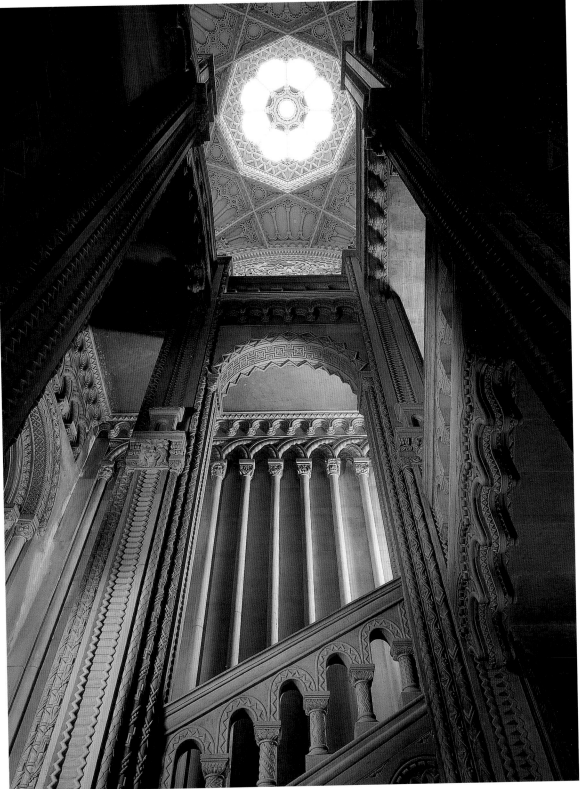

door into the drawing room. Another opening leads into the galleried great hall, where Romanesque arches soar heavenwards like the transept of a cathedral. In the evening the polished limestone flags of the floor are warmed by pools of multicoloured light from the recessed stained-glass windows.

Penrhyn is a late Georgian masterpiece, the outstanding product of a shortlived neo-Norman revival. Designed by Thomas Hopper, a fashionable architect who had been employed by the Prince Regent to build a Gothic conservatory at Carlton House, it was commissioned in 1820 by G.H. Dawkins Pennant to replace the neo-Gothic house by Samuel Wyatt he had inherited from his uncle. Whereas Richard Pennant had the benefit of a fortune made from Jamaican estates (as a result of which he strongly opposed the abolition of the slave trade), his nephew built lavishly on the profits of the Penrhyn slate quarries, exporting over 12,000 tons a year by 1792. A slate billiard table with cluster-column legs in the library and the grotesque slate bed weighing over a ton echo the basis of his prosperity.

G.H. Dawkins Pennant seems to have allowed his architect ample funds for building the castle and also for decorating and furnishing the rooms. As a result, Penrhyn is uniquely all of a piece. In the oppressive Ebony Room, original green and red curtains and upholstery and faded red damask wall-hangings give some relief from the black ebony furniture and the black surrounds to the fireplace and doorways. Huge plantain leaves on the firescreen recall the Jamaican estates. Here, too, is Dieric Bouts's (d.1475) delightful painting of St Luke sketching the Virgin and Child, the arches behind the apostle framing a sylvan landscape with a walled city. In the much lighter drawing room next door, mirrors at either end reflect two immense metalwork candelabra.

The house was greatly enriched in the mid-nineteenth century by the Spanish, Italian and Dutch paintings collected by Edward Gordon Douglas, 1st Baron Penrhyn, including a Canaletto of the Thames at Westminster, Rembrandt's portrait of a plain, middle-aged merchant's wife, and Palma Vecchio's *Holy Family*. His son commissioned the elaborate brass King's Bed for a visit by Edward VII when Prince of Wales in 1894.

This visit, over three days in July, saw the house staff at full stretch, required to produce gastronomic dinners of eight or nine courses and to attend to 35 house guests. At this date, Lord Penrhyn employed some 40 servants, including the men in the stables, which was a by no means lavish establishment for the period. The servants' quarters,

shown as they were after rebuilding in 1868, illustrate what went into keeping the household going.

A warren of rooms giving onto an inner courtyard is centred on the kitchen, presided over by a French chef in the late nineteenth century, and still with its roasting range, pastry oven and original ash-topped table. Penrhyn slate forms cool work surfaces in the pastry room and dry larder, and tops the butter table in the dairy larder where milk, cream, butter and eggs were delivered from the home farm every morning. Fitted cupboards are stacked with fine china; candlesticks and oil lamps are ready for cleaning and trimming in the lamp room; and there are top hats for sprucing up in the brushing room. In the outer court, close to the back gate, is the Ice Tower, where a deep pit in the basement was packed with ice in the winter, some of it cut from a lake high in Snowdonia, for use in the warmer months.

Beyond the back gate is the sizeable stable block, designed for 36 horses, and with Penrhyn slate between the stalls and used for the mangers. Part is now given over to a collection of dolls from all over the world; a museum of industrial locomotives associated with the slate industry also accommodated here includes *Charles*, a saddle tank engine that once worked the railway serving the Penrhyn family's quarries, and *Fire Queen*, built in 1848 for the Padarn Railway.

The siting of Penrhyn is superb, with views south to Snowdonia and the slate quarry like a great bite out of the hills and north over Beaumaris Bay to Anglesey. A west-facing terraced walled garden sloping steeply into a valley

The Brushing Room in the servants' quarters at Penrhyn, where woollen garments and accessories would be laid out on a long table.

below the castle shelters many tender shrubs and plants, including magnolias, camellias and azaleas and the fuchsias smothering a pergola halfway down. Tasmanian ferns, palms and huge patches of gunnera grow luxuriantly in the bog garden created in the 1930s at the lowest level, and a metasequoia and a maidenhair tree are two of the fine specimen trees seen throughout the grounds, with several examples of the large evergreens popular in the nineteenth century mixed with mature beeches and oaks. A carpet of daffodils covering the slope above the drive to the entrance lodge in spring is matched by the display of snowdrops on the grass above the walled garden. From here one of the paths back to the castle passes a ruined Gothic chapel placed as an eye-catcher on a prominent knoll, a row of headstones in the dogs' cemetery at its feet commemorating Annette, Suzette, Wanda and other pets.

Penshaw Monument TYNE & WEAR

Halfway between Sunderland and Chester-le-Street, east of the A183 [445 J3]

Conspicuously sited on a hilltop, and visible for miles around, this roofless classical temple surveys the landscape of Tyneside, its honey-coloured sandstone blackened and sombre. Some 30.5 metres (100 feet) long and 15 metres (50 feet) wide, this impressive eye-catcher was the work of local architects John and Benjamin Green and was erected from 1844 to commemorate the radical statesman John George Lambton, 1st Earl of Durham, one-time Governor General of Canada, who had died four years earlier.

The Pepperbox WILTSHIRE

5 miles south-east of Salisbury, on north side of the A36 [443 G6]

A steep rutted track off the A36 leads to the long tongue of Brickworth Down and this red-brick octagonal three-storey tower, with a weathervane crowning the pyramidal slate roof. Built by Giles Eyre in 1606, the Pepperbox may be the earliest folly in England, or it may have been intended as a viewpoint from which ladies could follow the hunt in comfort. The windows of the room at the top of the tower have now been bricked in – and so have the open arches on the ground floor – but the views are still magnificent, the vista north-west taking in the soaring spire of Salisbury Cathedral.

Petworth House WEST SUSSEX

In centre of Petworth [443 I6]

A luminous landscape by Turner in the Red Room at Petworth shows the park at sunset. Dark clumps of trees throw long shadows over the lake and a stag drinks from the water in the foreground, its antlers silhouetted against the dying sun. Turner was inspired by 'Capability' Brown's masterpiece, one of the greatest man-made landscapes created in eighteenth-century Europe. Over a thousand deer graze beneath Brown's clumps of beeches, chestnuts and oaks, now seen in their splendid maturity and still impressive despite the fact that some 600 trees were brought down in the freak storm in the autumn of 1987. Trees still frame Brown's serpentine lake dominating the view from the west front and crown the ridges shading imperceptibly into Sussex downland. Far in the distance on the north-west horizon is the outline of a turreted Gothick folly, possibly designed by John Soane.

Brown's sublime landscape encloses a jewel of a house, a magnificent late seventeenth-century baroque palace filled with an exceptional collection of works of art, including fine furniture, *objets* and sculpture as well as paintings. Seen from across the park, Petworth's great west front, some 91.5 metres (300 feet) long, looks as if it could have been modelled on a French château. It was the creation of the unlikeable Charles Seymour, 6th Duke of Somerset (the Proud Duke), who set about remodelling the manor house of the earls of Northumberland on his marriage to the daughter of the 11th and last Earl's. The Seymour family symbol – a pair of angel's wings – is ostentatiously displayed over every window. Although only two seventeenth-century interiors survive intact, these fully reflect Charles Seymour's vanity and self-importance. The major feature of the florid baroque chapel is the family pew filling the west end. Supported by classical columns, it is surmounted by carved and painted drapery on which angels bear the Duke's arms and coronet to heaven. By contrast, the coldly formal marble hall with its black and white chequered floor must have quelled the spirits of the few thought worthy to set foot in the Proud Duke's house.

As well as remodelling the house, Charles Seymour added to the art collection established by the earls of Northumberland, which included a series of portraits by Van Dyck and works by Titian and Elsheimer. And he commissioned Grinling Gibbons to produce the limewood carvings of flowers, foliage, birds and classical vases which now cascade down the walls of the Carved Room, and Louis Laguerre to paint the Grand Staircase.

On the Proud Duke's death, the estate passed by marriage to the Wyndham family, and it was Charles Wyndham, 2nd Earl of Egremont, who employed Brown to landscape the park. A cultivated man who had profited from the Grand Tour and time in the diplomatic service, he was largely responsible for Petworth's collection of Italian, French and Dutch Old Masters. He also amassed the wealth of ancient sculpture from Greece and Rome, now of particular importance as one of only three such collections of the period to have survived intact. It includes the sensitive sculptured head fashioned in the fourth

century BC known as the Leconfield Aphrodite and some good Roman portrait busts and copies of Greek originals. His son, the philanthropic and benevolent 3rd Earl, who presided over Petworth for 74 years, from 1763 to 1837, left his stamp on almost every room, enriching them with his purchases of contemporary art and sculpture and altering and rearranging furnishings and picture hangs in the pursuit of the perfect scheme. Best known as the patron of Turner, for whom he arranged a studio at Petworth, the 3rd Earl also acquired works by Gainsborough, Reynolds, Fuseli and Zoffany. And he augmented his father's sculpture collection, for which he twice extended the existing gallery, with works by English contemporaries such as Sir Richard Westmacott and John Rossi, and the Irish sculptor J.E. Carew. One of the most striking pieces is the vividly fluid representation of St Michael and Satan by John Flaxman, finished in 1826, the year in which the sculptor died. Except for the spear which St Michael is about to plunge into his grovelling adversary, this powerful work, which cost the 3rd Earl £3,500, was all carved from one piece of marble.

Despite a family tradition that paintings should be left as the 3rd Earl had them, much was rearranged by Sir Anthony Blunt, then Honorary Adviser on paintings, when Petworth came to the Trust in 1947. In recent years, helped by generous loans of pictures from the present Lord and Lady Egremont, the Trust has been recreating the spirit of the 3rd Earl's crowded and eclectic

Petworth's palatial grand staircase, created for the 6th Duke of Somerset in the early 18th century, is painted with murals by Louis Laguerre. The bronze statue, bought by the 3rd Earl of Egremont, is a copy of a marble original from ancient Rome.

A corner of the kitchen at Petworth, showing the early gas range and copper *batterie de cuisine*.

Philipps House WILTSHIRE

In Dinton, 9 miles west of Salisbury, on north side of the B3089 [442 F6]

This severe Neo-classical house in the Vale of Wardour was designed by Jeffry Wyatt (later Sir Jeffry Wyatville), better known for his work in the neo-Gothic style and particularly for his alterations to Windsor Castle. Philipps House, built between 1814 and 1817, does not show this versatile architect at his most inspired. Built of local Chilmark limestone, from the same quarry that had produced the stone for Salisbury Cathedral 600 years previously, it is a plain two-storey rectangle with rows of sash windows and a parapet concealing the hipped roof, the only notable feature being a pedimented portico rising the height of the building on the south façade. A curved kitchen wing curling away from the house adds a welcome touch of asymmetry.

Wyatt's interiors are similarly austere and unadorned, the fine mahogany doors and marble chimneypieces restrained and stylised. His coolly elegant staircase, top-lit from a circular lantern, rises through the heart of the house, the grand lower flight sweeping imperiously upwards from the centre of the hall to divide at a half-landing into two parallel stairs to the first floor. Brass outlets in the flags of the hall below are remnants of the original underfloor heating system, installed in the 1820s.

The house was created for William Wyndham IV, whose family had been at Dinton since 1689 and were to live here until 1917. The undulating parkland landscaped in the eighteenth century contains some magnificent specimen trees, including a noble Spanish chestnut that was mature in 1700.

arrangements. In some cases it has been possible to recreate the hangs as recorded in watercolour gouaches which Turner did when he was living here. Thus, on the south wall of the square dining room, a large canvas by Reynolds is now framed on three sides by columns of small paintings and crowned by a Reynolds self-portrait, just as it was some 200 years ago. At the same time, again with loans from Lord and Lady Egremont, additional contents have been brought in, such as the copper *batterie de cuisine* in the impressive service quarters.

Brown's pleasure grounds to the north-west of the house, also extensively damaged in 1987, are a striking contrast to the park. Serpentine paths wind through a thickly wooded rectangle planted with rare trees and shrubs, including tender rhododendrons, a handkerchief tree, a tulip tree and purple-leafed maples, its boundaries echoing a vanished Elizabethan layout. A little Doric temple was probably moved here when the pleasure grounds were created, but the Ionic rotunda, perhaps designed by Matthew Brettingham, was introduced by Brown. Here, too, are some of the carved seventeenth-century urns on pedestals which the 3rd Earl placed strategically in the gardens and park.

Pitstone Windmill BUCKINGHAMSHIRE

½ mile south of Ivinghoe, 3 miles north-east of Tring, just west of the B488 [443 I4]

This fascinating little building bearing the date 1627 is Britain's oldest post mill, an example of the earliest form of windmill that was developed in the Middle Ages. Unlike later mills, such as those at Bembridge or High Ham (*see* pp.43 and 184), the sails are brought into the wind by turning the building as a whole, rather than by simply revolving the cap on the top of the mill.

Pitstone's two-storey timber body, reached by a ladder, is perched some 2.5 metres (8 feet) above the ground on a massive wooden post, the lower half of which is enclosed in a brick roundhouse. The building projects alarmingly on either side of its support, as if it might topple over at any moment. The tail pole sweeping down to the ground – a long beam with a wheel on the end – acted as a lever for turning the mill.

Two pairs of grinding stones, one pair used for producing coarse meal, the other for fine white flour, are now in working order, but the mill cannot at present be turned into the wind.

Plas Newydd ANGLESEY

1 mile south-west of Llanfairpwll and the A5 on the A4080; 2½ miles from the Menai Bridge, 5 miles from Bangor [444 F8]

'I tried repeatedly in vain … to get some use made of my drawing.' So Rex Whistler explained his decision to join the Welsh Guards in 1940. Four years later he was dead, at the early age of 39. Fortunately for all who visit Plas Newydd, the house is full of works by this talented artist, who spent some of his happiest and most creative hours here. His epic mural dominating the dining room, a dramatic view across choppy waters to an Italianate town 'bristling with spires, domes and columns' set at the foot of wild and craggy mountains, echoes Plas Newydd's own romantic position, looking over the Menai Strait to Snowdonia and north up the water to Robert Stephenson's Britannia Bridge.

Reproductions of Whistler's massive work never capture the sweep and scale of the composition or the wealth of detail it contains, with plentiful allusions to buildings the artist had seen on his continental travels and to the family of his patron, the 6th Marquess of Anglesey. Every corner is meticulously executed. At the far end of the *trompe-l'oeil* colonnade on the left-hand side people are going about their business in a steep street running up from the water. Two women gossip; an old lady climbs slowly upward with the help of a stick; a boy steals an apple from a tub of fruit outside a shop; a girl leans out of an upstairs window to talk to a young man below. The artist himself appears in the colonnade sweeping up leaves.

The exhibition of Whistler's work in the room next door shows the range of his talent. Here are his illustrations for *Gulliver's Travels*, examples of costume and stage designs, bookplates and caricatures, and rebus letters he sent to the 6th Marquess's young son. Here, too, are drawings he did as a child, the horror of those inspired by the First World War heralding his own experiences some twenty years later. A painting of Lord Anglesey's family grouped informally in the music room is one of many examples of Whistler's skill at portraiture, his sensitive studies of the Marquess's eldest daughter Lady Caroline, eight years Whistler's junior, suggesting a particular sympathy between artist and sitter.

Whistler's mural was part of Lord Anglesey's extensive changes to Plas Newydd in the 1930s. He and his wife converted the house into one of the most comfortable of their day, following the 6th Marquess's maxim that 'every bathroom should have a bedroom', and employed Sybil Colefax to create Lady Anglesey's feminine pink and white bedroom, furnished with a white carpet, muslin curtains and bed-hangings and with a pink ribbon setting off the white bedspread. The long saloon with a view over the Menai Strait to Snowdon is also much as the 6th Marquess and his wife arranged it, with two large comfortable settees either side of the fire and four pastoral landscapes by Ommeganck dominating the pictures.

Architecturally, Plas Newydd is an intriguing and uncompromising mixture of classical and Gothick, largely the result of late eighteenth-century alterations by James Wyatt and Joseph Potter of Lichfield for the 1st Earl of Uxbridge. The classical staircase leading to a screen of Doric columns on the first floor and Wyatt's bold white friezes set against blue and red in the ante-room and octagon are a world apart from the fan vaulting in the hall, with elaborate bosses at the intersection of the ribs. This

Rex Whistler's close friendship with the Pagets of Plas Newydd in the 1930s is reflected in several family portraits in the house, such as this intimate study of Lady Caroline (above) and in the panoramic mural painted on the walls of the dining room (left), where a figure sweeping up leaves in an arcade at one end is a self-portrait of the artist.

Plas Newydd is gloriously sited, looking east over the Menai Strait to the mountains of Snowdonia.

Plas-yn-Rhiw GWYNEDD

16 miles from Pwllheli, on south coast road to Aberdaron
[444 E8]

The long Llŷn peninsula sheltering Cardigan Bay from the full force of the Atlantic is a windswept claw of craggy moorland and tiny fields. Only in the far south-east is there shelter enough for woodland to thrive, protected by the 305-metre (1,000-foot) tor of Mynydd-y-Graig (*see* p.227). Below the hill, looking east over the bay, is Plas-yn-Rhiw, with a Georgian frontage which hides a much older building behind and views to Cadair Idris and south along the coast to Fishguard. On clear nights the lights of Aberystwyth beckon across the water. Even when there is a gale in the little village up the hill, it is quiet here, with a range of native and exotic plants flourishing in the mild maritime climate.

Granite walls 2.1 to 2.4 metres (7 to 8 feet) thick in the tiny parlour and the remains of a stone spiral staircase are survivals of a Tudor building on this site. As the date stone on the front of the house proclaims, it was first extended in 1634; two wings built into the hillside, Georgian sash windows and the slate-floored Victorian verandah were additions of the early and mid-nineteenth centuries, turning the farmhouse into a gentleman's residence.

Plas-yn-Rhiw's homely interiors reflect the three forceful and indomitable Keating sisters, Eileen, Lorna and Honora, daughters of a successful Nottinghamshire architect, who bought the property in 1938 and lovingly restored it after almost twenty years of neglect. A white hat and gloves lie neatly on the patchwork quilt covering one of the simple wooden beds. A shoe rack is filled with Honora's fashionable footwear from her days in London and a successful career in the social services. Elegant Georgian chairs, fur coats and a stole speak of comfortable gentility, and an extensive collection of popular classics suggests many evenings spent listening to the old gramophone in the parlour. Gentle watercolours hanging three and four deep on the stairs, their muted colours recording local views and landmarks, recall Honora's days at the Slade and her youthful ambition to be an artist.

The little terraced garden sloping down towards the sea, with thickly planted beds framed by box hedges, dates from the 1820s. Organically managed, it is a mix of tender and exotic species and indigenous wild flora. Tree-like magnolias flower pale pink at the end of March and in summer the garden is crimson with a profusion of fuchsias, a source of pollen for the bees which traditionally nest under the eaves. Rough meadow grass and woodland

stately room rising through two storeys with a gallery at one end opens into the even more splendid Gothick music room, probably on the site of the great hall of the original sixteenth-century manor built by the powerful Griffith family and the largest room in the house.

An early artificial limb and mud-spattered Hussar trousers recall the 1st Earl's son, created 1st Marquess of Anglesey for his heroism at the Battle of Waterloo, where he lost a leg, and also remarkable for his eighteen children and 73 grandchildren. Other members of the family gaze down from a wealth of portraits, including works by Hoppner, Romney and Lawrence and a Grand Tour painting of the 1st Earl, a rather plump young man in a salmon coat. Many of these came from Beaudesert, the family's Staffordshire house dismantled in 1935, which was also the source of some of the superb furniture.

Plas Newydd is first seen from above, when the path leading down from the car park suddenly reveals the Gothick west front covered in red creeper and magnolia. The house is set off by sweeping lawns and magnificent woodland, many of the fine sycamores, beeches and oaks predating the planting undertaken with Humphry Repton's advice. Exotics thrive in the mild, wet climate and fertile soil, belts of trees to the south of the house sheltering azaleas, magnolias, Japanese maples and rhododendrons, including a number of hybrids introduced from Bodnant (*see* p.55). Formal terraced gardens are adorned with a Venetian well-head and Italianate urns, suggesting a warmer sun than that which reddens the peaks on the far side of the water in the evening.

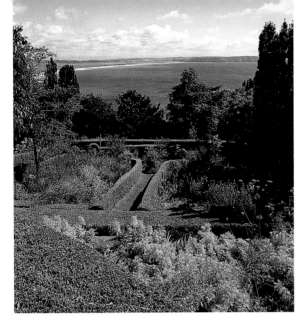

behind the house are bright with snowdrops and bluebells in the early months of the year.

Still a legend in the neighbourhood, the sisters worked tirelessly to protect the natural beauty of the peninsula. They were often seen wrapped up warmly against the Atlantic gales, tramping the lanes to check on rubbish tips and illegal caravan sites. Fiercely outspoken in defence of their beliefs, the Keatings were personally self-effacing, little realising that the words with which they chose to honour their parents – 'there is no death while memory lives' – would serve as their own memorial.

Plym Bridge Woods DEVON

3½ miles north-east of Plymouth [442 C7]

From Shaugh Bridge the River Plym runs south for 5 miles to Plym Bridge. The upper part of this section, Bickleigh Vale, is dominated by the sprawling modern barracks of the Royal Marines at Bickleigh. The lower part, for a mile and a half above Plym Bridge, is owned by the Trust, and a recent acquisition has extended this ownership for a further half mile below the bridge.

As on the high moor (*see below*), and again at Goodameavy (*see* p.164), the steeply wooded slopes of this very beautiful valley are packed with archaeological remains, most of them relics of the industries carried on here from the seventeenth century onwards.

Slates from Cann Quarry, like all long-abandoned quarries a lovely place, were used to roof Plympton Grammar School in 1664, where Sir Joshua Reynolds was

later educated. Early in the nineteenth century a canal was made from here to Marsh Mills at the head of the Plym estuary. It was quickly superseded by a railway built on its towpath, and it is to trace the remains of three railways that industrial historians swarm here. The Plymouth and Dartmoor Railway was opened in 1823 to take lime, coal, timber and sand up to the moor, returning with stone and peat. The Cann Quarry Railway followed in 1834. The tracks of both these railways were removed for scrap in 1916, though many granite and slate sleepers remain. Finally the line from Plymouth to Tavistock opened in 1859 and closed as recently as 1962. Its great Cann viaduct, far too solid to demolish, still strides across the narrow Plym Valley.

Plym Head to Cadover Bridge DEVON

Along the River Plym, between Plym Head and Cadover Bridge [442 C7]

The Trust owns land in four sections of the delightful River Plym, each very different in character. The river rises at Plym Head, 457 metres (1,500 feet) up, below Great Gnat's Head on the high ground which dominates this southern part of Dartmoor. It runs south-west off the moor and nearly all the moorland on its left bank, 1,335.5 metres (3,300 acres), belongs to the Trust for 5 miles down to Blacka Brook Foot, near Cadover Bridge. The rock is granite except in one place, at Shavercombe, where a shaley slate has intruded, creating a step in the stream and a waterfall.

At a casual glance this is simply peaty moorland,

Left: A large and varied plant collection thrives in the sheltered garden at Plas-yn-Rhiw, from which there are glorious views over the bay below.

Below: The tidal estuary of the River Plym winds down to the sea past the wooded banks of the Saltram estate.

covered with heather and purple moorgrass, and in the wetter places with bog cotton, sphagnum moss, bog pimpernel, bog asphodel, sundew and lesser spearwort. The common birds are the birds of high open ground – meadow pipit, wheatear, skylark – and in the rougher places stonechats with ravens and crows quarrelling overhead. But all is not as it seems, for three 'warrens' into which the area is divided, Hentor Warren, Willings Walls Warren and Trowlesworthy Warren, have preserved a historic landscape of the greatest interest and rarity.

The reason for its survival is twofold. Man began to live and farm here in about 2500BC. The climate then was kinder, and he preferred to live on the uplands rather than in the dangerous undrained wooded valleys below, with wild animals and unhealthy conditions. By the time the climate became less hospitable the inhabitants possessed sufficient knowledge to move down into the valleys, clear and drain them, and cultivate their better soils. The moor was then left largely unoccupied until medieval times, perhaps from the twelfth century, when the three great rabbit warrens were constructed. This productive use of otherwise unproductive land continued well into this century, the warrener at Trowlesworthy being the last in a very long line.

Mounds of soil and stone were thrown up, drained by a perimeter ditch, to make buries in which the rabbits lived and bred, being harvested for their flesh and fur. The warrener's chief job was to protect them from their natural enemies, weasel and stoat, and substantial traces remain of stone vermin traps, operated with a sliding shutter on the principle of the modern cage trap and surprisingly effective.

The use of land for rabbit warrens left the traces of prehistoric man largely undisturbed, as does its present use as rough grazing for sheep, cattle and ponies. The lay visitor may need help to recognise the several concentrations of ruined huts, burial chambers, cairns, small enclosures and the long stone rows whose purpose is still uncertain. Overlying these are the patterns of later land boundaries, marked by reeves, banks stretching for miles over the moor.

The best way to see this remarkable place is to organise two cars, leaving one at Cadover Bridge and driving another to White Works, an abandoned china-clay pit south-east of Princetown. From here it is 2 miles of rough walking to Plym Head, skirting Fox Tor Mire. The walk is down the valley, with detours into the side valleys, the Langcombe, Shavercombe and Hentor Brooks, and past the romantically named Spanish Lake.

Polesden Lacey SURREY

5 miles west of Dorking, 1½ miles south of Great Bookham, off the A246 Leatherhead–Guildford road [443 |5]

Polesden Lacey is alive with the spirit of Mrs Ronald Greville, captured so well in the vivacious portrait which now greets visitors in the hall. Those invited to the famous weekend parties held here from 1906 until the outbreak of the Second World War included Indian maharajahs, literary figures such as Beverley Nichols, Osbert Sitwell and Harold Nicolson, and prominent politicians. Edward VII was a close friend of the elegant society hostess, and the future George VI and Queen Elizabeth were lent Polesden Lacey for part of their honeymoon in 1923.

Polesden Lacey is a comfortable two-storey building sprawling round a courtyard, its large white sash windows standing out attractively against yellow stucco. The flavour of the Regency villa built in the 1820s by Joseph Bonsor to the designs of Thomas Cubitt still lingers on the south front with its classical colonnade, but the house was subsequently much enlarged and the interior transformed after 1906 by the architects of the Ritz Hotel, an essential step in the realisation of Mrs Greville's social ambitions. Here she displayed her outstanding collection of paintings, furniture and other works of art, the nucleus of which she had inherited from her wealthy father, William McEwan, founder of the Scottish brewery which still bears his name.

The range and richness of the collection, including Flemish tapestries, French and English furniture, English, continental and oriental pottery and porcelain, and European paintings from the fourteenth to the eighteenth centuries, gives Polesden Lacey its extraordinarily opulent atmosphere, vividly evoking the charmed life of the Edwardian upper classes. Some of the finest pieces were intended for very different settings. In the sumptuously decorated drawing room glittering mirrors reflect carved and gilt panelling that once adorned an Italian palace. A richly carved oak reredos in the hall, a masterpiece by Edward Pearce, was originally intended for Sir Christopher Wren's St Matthew's just off Cheapside in London, demolished in 1881. From her father Mrs Greville inherited some Dutch seventeenth-century paintings, but she herself acquired most of the English portraits in the dining room, such as Raeburn's charming study of George and Maria Stewart as children, the little girl holding a rabbit in the folds of her dress, and much of the cream of the collection in the corridor round the central courtyard. The pictures hanging here include an exquisite early fourteenth-century triptych of the Madonna and Child

Polesden Lacey (left) conjures up an affluent Edwardian lifestyle. French furniture in the opulent drawing room includes this 18th-century clock and candelabra (above) and Sir Henry Raeburn's *George and Maria Stewart as Children* is one of a collection of portraits in the dining room.

among several early Italian works, sixteenth-century portraits in the style of Corneille de Lyon and a number of atmospheric Dutch interiors and landscapes, such as Jacob van Ruisdael's skyscape of the Zuider Zee, diminutive figures on the shore dwarfed by wintry grey clouds piled overhead.

Invitation cards, scrap albums and other mementoes in the billiard room and smoking room conjure up the world in which Mrs Greville lived. The menu book records the salade niçoise and orange mousse on which Ramsay MacDonald dined on 17 October 1936, and the aubergines provençales given to the Queen of Spain the following day. The same names appear again and again in the visitors' book and the same faces recur in the photographs, statesmen and royalty, such as Grand Duke Michael of Russia and Kaiser Wilhelm II, rubbing shoulders with figures from the worlds of entertainment and literature, a memorable shot showing Mrs Greville in Hollywood with Wendy Barrie and Spencer Tracy.

The atmosphere of the house extends into the garden,

where spacious lawns shaded with fine beeches, cedars and limes suggest long idle summer days. Although much of the layout is a twentieth-century creation, the impressive long terraced walk, with magnificent views across the valley to the heights of Ranmore Common (*see* p.319), is a legacy from the years when Polesden Lacey was the home of the playwright Richard Brinsley Sheridan. A series of more intimate walled and hedged enclosures in what was the old kitchen garden to the west of the house include an iris garden filled with varieties popular in Edwardian times and a collection of lavenders. The rose garden centred on an Italianate marble well-head is much larger, planted with over 40 traditional and more modern varieties and with Edwardian ramblers shading the pergola walks between the beds. Mrs Greville's garden ornaments are everywhere, from the griffins on the terrace in front of the house to vases, urns and sundials placed as eye-catchers at strategic points and the statue of Diana crowning the rock garden. Mrs Greville herself lies in a yew-hedged tomb near the rose garden.

Craftsmanship

Before the age of the machine and of standardisation and synthetics, buildings and everything in them were created by hand using natural materials such as wood, clay and stone. For a large house, a wide range of skilled craftsmen was required – masons, joiners, glaziers, painters etc – quite apart from the labour force involved in just coping with the problems of shifting materials. Sometimes suitable stone, timber and other essentials could be found nearby, but often they had to be brought by sea or river to within a few miles of the house and taken the last leg by cart.

Up to the seventeenth century, and later in some areas, the master-craftsman was the key figure in creating a building of any size or pretension. These highly skilled men would have served a seven-year apprenticeship and a period as a journeyman before setting themselves up as masters of their craft, and they combined their trade with designing, administration and business skills. The most successful, usually stonemasons or carpenters, were effectively architects and builders, with status to match. Some, such as the master-mason Robert Smythson, travelled round England with a team of men; others, such as the Somerset mason William Arnold, established a local reputation. Alongside would work other skilled craftsmen, carving door surrounds or chimneypieces, or creating an intricate plaster ceiling. Until the age of the architect, and the straitjacket of imposed style, each man was his own master, working to an agreed design but with room for individuality.

Craft skills were still needed into the eighteenth century, but there was increasing use of a standard visual vocabulary, and the kind of repetitive plaster motifs found in classical interiors could be created using wooden moulds. Gradually, the unselfconscious craftsmanship and soft beauty of the older house were replaced by firmer lines which reflected the prevailing stylistic fashion, however unsuitable for an English setting, and, into the ninteenth century, the harder colours of machine-made bricks and synthetic pigments.

From the eighteenth century, too, foreign craftsmen were a familiar presence in England. The accession of William of Orange in 1688 encouraged a taste for Dutch fashions, the revocation of the Edict of Nantes in 1685 brought an influx of skilled Huguenots fleeing persecution, such as Daniel Marot, and the Italianate tastes of the eighteenth century led to the employment of architects such as Leoni and stuccadores Artari and Pietro Lafranchini. The Arts and Crafts movement of the later nineteenth century, with William Morris as its guiding light, attempted to recapture the spirit of medieval craftsmanship, with its use of local materials and hand-crafted furnishings. Today, although some traditional skills have not been practised for over a century, they can be revived, as those involved in restoring Uppark in Sussex after the fire of 1989 have demonstrated, creating freehand lime plasterwork and carved wood to rival what was lost.

LITTLE
MORETON
HALL
226

The exuberant timberwork of Little Moreton Hall in Cheshire, typical of the decorative effects popular among the gentry in the timber-rich Midlands and Welsh borders in Elizabethan times, was the work of local craftsmen of some calibre. Richard Dale and his son, another Richard, both worked on the house in the later 16th century. In the medieval tradition, these two were businessmen as well as skilled carpenters. They would have chosen the oak trees to be used and prepared scale drawings, and it is clear the elder Richard Dale, who had been brought in to modernise and extend a 15th-century building, discussed the work with his patron. The glazing of the windows is also exceptional, with patterns varying from room to room. The work of itinerant craftsmen from Staffordshire, the glass was cut with a glazing iron and inserted without any kind of cement, with just the lead to hold it in. Far to the south, in a quiet Cornish valley, is the small manor house of Trerice, which dates from received 5s 6d a square yard. One of the best examples of his work is in what was the Great Chamber of the 17th-century house, where the exuberant decoration consists of richly patterned strapwork studded with prominent pendants, all done in slow-setting lime plaster which could be worked *in situ*.

The grander the house, the higher the standing of the craftsmen employed. When Charles Seymour, 6th Duke of Somerset, set about remodelling Petworth in Sussex in the late 17th century he employed the virtuoso woodcarver Grinling Gibbons to produce a room decorated with his work. Gibbons, who was born in Rotterdam and probably trained

the same period. Unusually for such a remote place, two of the rooms are decorated with fine plasterwork (**above**). The plasterer is not known but it seems likely that he was also responsible for some other local decorative schemes of this period, such as the plasterwork in the hall at Buckland Abbey in Devon. Communications were poor and the roads bad, but nevertheless the West Country squirearchy were always visiting each other and very probably, as they sat over a good dinner, they passed on the names of gifted and reliable craftsmen.

The Jacobean remodelling of Blickling Hall in Norfolk involved a contract with a team of master-craftsmen for the masonry, carpentry and brickwork. A separate contract was made with the plasterer Edward Stanyon for the decorative ceilings which are such a feature of the house, and for which he

in Holland, was in England by 1668, and his genius was quickly recognised and led to commissions from Charles II and Sir Christopher Wren. At Petworth, working in his preferred medium of limewood, which is soft and malleable and responds well to the chisel, he produced delicate crestings and festoons to set off a series of full-length family portraits. Carved almost in the round, these compositions include sheaves of musical instruments (**above**), complete with a couple of scrolls of music, as well as more

conventional subjects such as flowers and fruit. Almost in the same league as the work by Grinling Gibbons is the carving at Beningbrough Hall, 7 miles outside York, where intricate carved decoration in the pine-panelled principal rooms (**above**) dates from the first decades of the 18th century, when the house was rebuilt. Executed in pine which, like limewood, was easily worked, and originally painted, it stands out in high relief on overmantels and overdoors, as here, and forms ornate friezes. Most probably the carvers were French Huguenot craftsmen, among the many who fled France after the crackdown on Protestants following the Revocation of the Edict of Nantes in 1685. There was a flourishing school of such craftsmen in northern England in the early 18th century and Beningbrough's presiding architect, William Thornton, had a close association with the group, whom he drew on for work elsewhere. Another virtuoso woodcarver, but with a genius bordering on madness, was employed by the 2nd Earl Verney to oversee the grandiose rebuilding of Claydon House in Buckinghamshire between 1757 and 1771. As an administrator and cost-controller, Luke Lightfoot was a disaster, but his work in the one surviving wing is in a class of its own. Rising gently to the first floor is an elegant mahogany staircase (**below**), its treads and risers inlaid with box and ebony. On the lower flights there are also tiny discs of ivory. This work of art is completed by a delicate ironwork balustrade which quivers when anyone uses the stairs.

The Marble Hall at Clandon Park, rising through two floors and conceived in shades of white, is one of the grandest of 18th-century interiors. This Surrey masterpiece was created by a team of foreign-born craftsmen. The architect, Giacomo Leoni, was Venetian, the stuccadores were also Italian, and the marble chimneypiece (**detail, left**) was by Michael Rysbrack, who came from an Antwerp family of artists. Rysbrack, who settled in England in c.1720, trained as a sculptor and built up an extensive practice in portrait busts. His skill with figurative images and other in-depth carving is shown at Clandon, where his fireplaces, seen throughout the house, include reliefs of classical subjects and three-dimensional garlands and other motifs. The professional architect, increasingly part of the country-house scene, was well-established by the 18th century and often brought a package of preferred craftsmen to a new project. At Wallington in Northumberland, the lavish rococo plasterwork, completed in c.1743, was created by the Italian Pietro Lafranchini. The brother of Paolo and Filippo Lafranchini, who were working in Ireland, Pietro was patronised by Daniel Garrett, who was responsible for remodelling the house and who introduced the stuccadore to several of his other clients. In the Saloon (**below**), the cove was raised to give the Italian greater scope, and a feature of his decoration is the way he has concentrated it around frames, and produced work of great liveliness and fluency. The ethos of the Arts and Crafts movement comes through strongly at

Standen in West Sussex. Designed by Philip Webb, one of William Morris's closest friends and colleagues, it reflects a love of fine craftsmanship and of the forms and materials of vernacular architecture, in this case the traditional Wealden house. Webb's garden front (**above**) shows this clearly. The creamy sandstone used for the ground floor was quarried just up the hill, the first floor is hung with handmade clay tiles in the traditional way, and the weather-boarding of the gables is of local oak, weathered to a silvery grey. The overhang which shades the bedroom windows below is also a local motif. Inside, the house is similarly of a piece. All the wallpapers came from the company Morris set up to produce hand-crafted furnishings. The papers (**right**) were printed from wooden blocks in a process which, in contrast to machine printing, was very laborious, but which allowed the use of richer, slower-drying inks.

In caring for its stable of historic houses, the Trust has had to rediscover lost skills. Rebuilding 18th-century plaster ceilings at Uppark in Sussex after the fire of 1989 involved determining the original mix for the plaster as well as finding suitable craftsmen to produce the decoration that needed to be hand-modelled, and working with them to master the necessary techniques. In the 18th century plaster was made with lime, with the addition of sand, and goat or cow hair, and moulded repetitive patterns were mixed with bold free-hand designs, whereas modern plaster is cast and gypsum based. The Trust was able to obtain lime putty from one of the works it had already established to meet its needs, while advertising and word-of-mouth recommendation produced a crop of potential free-hand plasterers, most of whom were sculptors. Designs for the ceilings were first drawn up on polythene sheets and then transferred to the ceiling by pouncing, pricking through the outlines and dusting them with powder. Decorative elements such as these rococo swirls of foliage in the staircase hall (**above**) were then worked up by hand.

Top: The massive sandstone walls of Powis Castle rise high above a flight of grand garden terraces created in the 17th century. The doorway to the orangery on the lowest level was once the castle's main entrance. Above: Inside, the romantic, portrait-hung long gallery has an original plasterwork ceiling and elm floor dating from 1593.

Powis Castle POWYS

1 mile south of Welshpool, on the A483 [442 E2]

Some time around 1200 the Welsh princes of Powis began building their new stronghold on this splendid defensive site, a great outcrop of limestone plunging steeply to the south with panoramic views over the River Severn to the hills of Shropshire. Although long since converted to a country house, Powis still has the trappings of a castle. Seen from across the valley, a massive Norman-style keep with three projecting towers rises to a battlemented skyline. To the left stretches the curtain wall which defended the inner bailey, now the ballroom range flanking the entrance court. In front of the castle grand baroque terraces blasted out of the rock fall to a vast expanse of lawn.

A wide flight of steps closely guarded by twin drum towers leads up from the entrance court to a Gothic archway. The front door opens into another world, with magnificent interiors fitted out for William Herbert, 3rd Lord Powis, 1st Earl, Marquis and titular Duke, a staunch supporter of the Stuart cause who spent his last years in exile with James II. The most remarkable of his formal apartments, possibly designed by the gentleman-architect William Winde, is the state bedroom, decorated with a profusion of gilt in the 1660s and 1680s. A deep alcove is almost filled with the canopied state bed adorned with rich red hangings and gilt cresting and separated from

the rest of the room by a finely carved balustrade. The only one of its kind in Britain, this barrier is a direct link with the formal etiquette of Louis XIV's Versailles, closely imitated by the English aristocracy. Velvet-covered furniture, a painted ceiling and rich tapestries contribute to the opulent effect. A huge and much more accomplished ceiling by Antonio Verrio, based on Veronese's *Apotheosis of Venice*, with an assembly of deities seated on clouds, dominates the 1st Marquis's grand staircase.

No hint of this pomposity permeates the beautiful T-shaped long gallery, the only surviving Elizabethan interior dating from Sir Edward Herbert's acquisition of the castle in 1587. Young trees and tendrils of foliage branch across the plasterwork ceiling above the rather indifferent family portraits set against early seventeenth-century *trompe-l'oeil* panelling and the polished silver sconces forming pools of light down the room. A table carries a more than life-size marble cat, crouched aggressively over the body of a snake, ears pricked as it looks back over its shoulder, teeth bared, muscles rippling beneath its fur. This remarkable ancient Roman sculpture, perhaps modelled on a wild animal, came to Powis through the marriage of the daughter of the house to the eldest son of Clive of India in 1784. The Clive Museum now adjoins the curiously elongated ballroom (originally almost twice as long), commissioned from T.F. Pritchard in 1775, in the range flanking the courtyard. Exotic cases filled with glittering gold suggest immense wealth, Indian curiosities acquired by the Great Nabob and his son, who was Governor of Madras, including jewelled slippers that once adorned the feet of Tipu Sahib, Sultan of Mysore, a gold tiger's head from his throne, a jewelled hookah encrusted with rubies, diamonds and emeralds, and sumptuously decorated padded armour. The tone is set for this exotic display by the richly coloured mid-seventeenth-century tapestry filling one wall of the ballroom, showing an embassy to Cairo or Istanbul. A potentate on a gold couch greets the ambassador against the backdrop of an eastern city peppered with onion domes, trees peeping over the walls suggesting hidden gardens.

Powis's splendid Italianate terraces, hanging over the valley below, are a fine example of late seventeenth-century taste. Who designed them and when is not known for certain, but it is likely they date from 1680s and were the inspiration of William Winde, who created similar features at Cliveden (*see* p.101), with some of the work being carried out by the French gardener Adrian Duval in the early years of the eighteenth century. Sadly, nothing remains of a contemporary water garden. Decorated with lead statues

Priest's House NORTHAMPTONSHIRE

In Easton on the Hill, 2 miles south-west of Stamford, off the A43 [443 I2]

This little two-storey stone building, with fireplaces to warm the chambers on both floors, predates the mid-sixteenth-century Reformation which turned the Church upside down. Originally intended for celibate clergy, it would have been lived in by married priests after the Reformation and was superseded by the handsome Georgian rectory standing nearby. A small museum illustrating past village life is housed on the upper floor.

Priest's House SOMERSET

In Muchelney, 1½ miles south of Langport [442 E6]

The Somerset hamlet of Muchelney, once on an island in the Sedgemoor marshes, boasts a clutch of medieval buildings. On one side of the fine fifteenth-century church are the remains of the abbey of Muchelney, perhaps founded as early as the seventh century and the oldest in the county after Glastonbury. On the other, facing the church across a small green, is this thatched stone cottage, built by monks of the abbey in 1308 to house the vicar of the parish. Like Alfriston (*see* p.20), which it resembled in plan, this priest's house was no mean dwelling, even before it was modernised in the early sixteenth century. Although the interior is much altered and the hall that once rose to the roof in the centre of the house is now floored over, the exterior still displays original features: a Gothic doorway, mullioned windows and the magnificent two-tiered window to the hall, with trefoil heads to the upper lights.

Princes Risborough Manor House
BUCKINGHAMSHIRE

Opposite church, off market square in Princes Risborough town centre [443 H4]

Sir Peter Lely, court painter to Charles II, once owned this elegant late seventeenth-century L-shaped red-brick house across a lane from St Mary's church. A little walled courtyard sets off the dignified five-bay entrance façade, with brick pilasters separating the long sash windows, a pedimented central doorway and three dormers in the roof. A Jacobean staircase with an openwork balustrade cut from solid oak rises from the entrance hall and there is good eighteenth-century panelling in the drawing room.

and urns and planted with clipped yews clustered closely below the castle, some lapping the terraces as if about to flow downhill, the three levels form a giant staircase descending the rock. Rare and tender plants flourish on the south-facing walls, which are hung with wistaria, magnolia and roses. These lime-tolerant species contrast with those planted in the wilderness laid out in the eighteenth century on the ridge across the valley, where the soil is acid. Here there are panoramic views of the castle from winding wooded walks through oaks, yews, rhododendrons and cedars. The formal garden by the Edwardian dower house below the castle, bordered with pyramid apple trees and crossed by a vine-covered pergola, dates from the early years of this century, when Violet Lane-Fox, wife of the 4th Earl, did much to improve the grounds. At the lowest point clipped yews like crinolined ladies look over the pond and sundial in the Fountain Garden.

The castle is surrounded by a magnificent wooded medieval deer-park, its naturalistic contours and planting partly reflecting alterations by 'Capability' Brown's disciple, William Emes, who was engaged to landscape it in 1771 and diverted a public road away from the castle. Although most of the great beeches, sycamores and limes were planted between 1800 and 1850, some of the massive ancient oaks for which Powis has long been famous – and which Admiral Rodney insisted were used for the navy at the end of the eighteenth century – may be as much as 800 years old.

Looking down the valley at Prior Park, with the Palladian bridge set amongst a chain of lakes at the foot of the slope, and a view of Bath over the trees.

Prior Park BATH & NE SOMERSET

Ralph Allen Drive, Bath [442 F5]

On the south-east edge of Bath, within walking distance of the city, is a secluded pastoral valley, rising with dramatic steepness to the heights of Claverton and Combe Downs. Just below the crest of the hill, strung out along the skyline, is a Palladian mansion (not National Trust) of impressive size designed by John Wood, with a porticoed central block linked by low balustrades to equally weighty pavilions on either side. When built, in 1740, this was the longest house in England. Below, a gentle curve of meadow following the contours of the combe sweeps down to a chain of stepped ponds, with a serene Palladian bridge sitting above the first of the cascades that links one level to another. Woodland on the slopes to either side, a mosaic of beech and yew, ash and larch, fences the valley in. This is a composition that works on two scales. The valley itself is small and intimate, but its dramatic setting, high above Bath, gives views out over a much wider landscape, looking across the Avon to the curving Georgian terraces which are contemporary with the house.

Developed between 1734 and 1764, the landscape garden at Prior Park is one of the most important survivals of eighteenth-century art, showing, in just 30 years, the evolution from an earlier taste for more formal layouts to the kind of highly contrived naturalism favoured by 'Capability' Brown, one of the two major figures linked with the scheme, and the artful use of a borrowed landscape. It was the creation of Ralph Allen, one of the big men of Georgian Bath. A Cornishman who made a fortune in postal distribution, Allen used his wealth to buy land around Bath, including the Combe Down quarries which provided stone for the Georgian city. The story goes that his great house at the top of the combe, for 'all of Bath to see and to see all of Bath', was partly a statement, an advertisement for the golden limestone which his quarries produced.

The valley garden below the house became more extensive as the years passed. Allen's first layout, extending only about halfway down the combe, was a formal design, with a gradually narrowing, straight-sided stretch of grass framed by urns and hedges focusing on a round pond. Beyond the hedge to the east there was probably a kitchen garden; to the west, with the help of the poet Alexander Pope, who had a similar feature in his garden at Twickenham, then a fashionable Thames-side retreat outside London, Allen laid out a wooded Wilderness area, with shady serpentine paths running through thick shrubbery past a series of surprises, among them a serpentine lake curving round the hillside, a grotto (for Mrs Allen), a sham bridge, and a fine cascade.

In the 1750s, Allen extended the garden down the combe, damming the stream to create the three ponds and adding the Palladian bridge. Now one of only three surviving in England, the bridge was probably designed by Richard Jones, Allen's Clerk of Works, as a direct copy of the earlier one at Wilton House (the third is at Stowe, *see* p.374). Trees were planted to frame a new cascade below the pond, a Gothic temple was built on the edge of the

Wilderness, and there was a general softening of the woodland outline. Only ten to fifteen years later, before the new plantings would have had time to grow up, let alone mature, the naturalisation was taken a step further. On the advice of 'Capability' Brown, who visited Prior Park in the early 1760s, the formal pond and its setting were swept away and the woods given their present, gently swelling contours. The Wilderness, though, hidden away in its wood, was left alone.

Apart from the drive which was carved through the Wilderness in 1834 by the then owner, Bishop Baines, who also added the double flight of urn-studded steps descending from the portico, and the filling in of the serpentine lake and its replacement with a *sotto voce* pond, later owners (the house became a Catholic seminary and then a co-educational public school, which it is today) left the valley largely untouched, although allowing structures to decay and woods and paths to become overgrown.

When Prior Park came to the Trust, in 1993, it was in an advanced state of decay. Since then, much restoration has been done and the programme is ongoing. With the exception of the elms that would have featured strongly in the original woodland, the aim is to return the landscape to its appearance in 1764, when Allen died.

A circular walk takes visitors round the combe along footpaths of limestone quarry waste, as Allen had them. Except where it descends at the foot of the valley, the path is high level, giving shifting views down into the combe and out across Bath, with the tower of ancient Widcombe church as a focal point just beyond the lower boundary, as it was in the eighteenth century. The meadow is being grazed again as it was in Allen's day, and above the woods the park runs into the borrowed landscape of the fields and leafy hedgerows of the Trust's Bath Skyline properties (*see* p.41).

The Quantocks SOMERSET

Off A39, half a mile south of West Quantoxhead [442 D6–E6]

North-west of Taunton, these hills form a fine ridge of open moorland running 12 miles to the Bristol Channel. At the northern end of the ridge, rising to 305 metres (1,000 feet), is the Trust's main holding, the 253.5 hectares (626 acres) of Beacon Hill and Bicknoller Hill. Open heather and grass moor on the summits is cut by three east-west running combes with bracken-covered slopes. This is red deer country, and there is exhilarating walking, with fine views to Exmoor and over the Bristol Channel.

Quarry Bank Mill CHESHIRE

1½ miles north of Wilmslow off the B5166, 2 miles from the M56, exit 5, 10 miles south of Manchester [445 I7]

In 1769 Richard Arkwright started a revolution in the textile industry when he invented a machine that could spin cotton using water power. In the 1780s there was another watershed when the patents protecting his invention were challenged and overthrown, opening the way for a huge expansion in factory-produced yarn. One of the first to take advantage of the new opportunities was the young Samuel Greg, who in 1780 had inherited one of the largest textile businesses in Manchester. He found a suitable site for a water-powered mill in the isolated Bollin Valley some 10 miles south of the city and had built his first mill here by 1784. As the mill prospered, it was enlarged, and a little village complete with school, shop and two chapels was built in the early nineteenth century to house the growing labour force.

This early industrial complex now lies at the centre of over 121.5 hectares (300 acres) of well-wooded park following the River Bollin, and some exotic trees and shrubs, a legacy of late nineteenth-century landscaping. The surroundings seem delightfully rural, with grass and trees setting off the red-brick four-storey mill with its cupola, tall chimney and impressive rows of windows. Samuel Greg lived in the elegant white Georgian house next to the mill, and a smaller but no less comfortable residence on the upstream side was inhabited by the mill manager, who controlled the flow of water powering the

In its day, the 18th-century Quarry Bank Mill was a new kind of functional building, with rows of generous windows lighting working space on every floor.

factory. Later generations of Gregs moved to a grandiose Victorian house high up on the side of the valley.

Although their approach was tempered by self-interest, the Gregs had an enlightened attitude to the care of their workers and this comes through in the design and layout of the village. Behind each red-brick cottage are the remains of a privy, a great luxury at a time when such facilities were usually shared between several families. The long gardens, now mostly given over to flowers, were once allotments where tenants could grow their own vegetables. Some thatched, half-timbered buildings, including the impressive Oak Farm which once provided the village with fresh dairy produce, are remnants of a medieval settlement.

Close to the mill is the Apprentice House, built in 1790 to accommodate the children who then made up about a third of the workforce. By the 1830s, this double-gabled three-storey building was home to up to a hundred pauper apprentices brought in from workhouses, most of them on seven-year contracts to work twelve hours a day, six days a week. Neat rows of vegetables in the organic garden, including the red-veined leaves of cottagers' kale, illustrate the traditional produce the children grew in their spare time, although their diet largely consisted of bread, milk, porridge and potatoes. On Sundays, they went twice to church, walking across the fields to Wilmslow.

Although none of the original machinery survives, Styal has been restored as a working museum of the cotton industry. At its heart is a giant iron water-wheel, the most powerful in Britain, which drives spinning machines and looms, part of the demonstrations showing how cotton was transformed, first by hand, later by machine, into spun yarn and calico cloth. The noise in the weaving shed and the lack of space round the flying machinery give some idea of what conditions must have been like during the mill's heyday, when tired children could be disfigured for life if they nodded off over their work.

Quebec House KENT

At east end of the village of Westerham, on the north side of the A25, facing junction with the B2026 Edenbridge road [443 J5]

A high brick wall on a sharp corner on the road from Westerham to Sevenoaks conceals the unpretentious gabled façades of Quebec House, where James Wolfe spent the first eleven years of his life. His parents rented the house, then known as Spiers, in 1726, and James was born a year later. The house was subsequently extensively altered

but has now been returned to its seventeenth-century appearance. Basically square, it is built of a pleasing mixture of brick and Kentish ragstone and has three distinctive gables on each façade. This is a homely, welcoming place, its character signalled by the fact that visitors ring the bell for admittance, as if paying an afternoon call.

The low-ceilinged, panelled rooms contain many mementoes of General Wolfe and his victory at Quebec in 1759, when he defeated the French by scaling the Heights of Abraham above the town. A pencil sketch of Wolfe to the left of the fireplace in the Bicentenary Room was drawn by his aide-de-camp on a page torn from a pocket book while they were in the field. The curiously pointed profile, a cartoonist's dream, is easily recognisable in a number of other paintings in the house.

Wolfe's travelling canteen in a corner of the Bicentenary Room gives a glimpse of the comforts enjoyed by an officer on campaign in the mid-eighteenth century. Clearly the finer things in life were not entirely discarded, as the canteen contains a cruet and glass decanters as well as more mundane objects, such as a griddle and a frying-pan. In the same room is the finely quilted dressing-gown in which Wolfe's body was brought back to England from Quebec. A seventeenth-century staircase leads up to a tranquil panelled drawing room on the first floor, furnished with William and Mary and Queen Anne pieces and a 1788 Broadwood square piano, and warmed by an open fire on cold afternoons. An imaginatively staged exhibition in the old coach house across the walled garden describes the Quebec campaign and its background and gives details of Wolfe's life. Three niches in the south wall of this building are thought to be bee boles where bees were kept in old-fashioned straw skeps, or hives, possibly to aid the pollination of fruit trees on the wall.

Rainham Hall ESSEX

The Broadway, just south of the church, 5 miles east of Barking [443 J4]

This elegant Georgian house, set back from the road behind beautiful wrought-iron gates and railings, was completed in 1729 for the merchant and shipowner John Harle. In the domestic Dutch style, with red-brick façades and stone dressings and dormers in the hipped roof, the main feature of the exterior is a fine carved wood porch with Corinthian columns. Inside, the house has been little altered, original doorcases, fireplaces and softwood panelling helping to convey a strong sense of period.

Ramsey Abbey Gatehouse
CAMBRIDGESHIRE

Abbey School, at south-east edge of Ramsey, at point where the Chatteris road leaves the B1096, 10 miles south-east of Peterborough [443 I2]

In 969 St Oswald, Archbishop of York, and Ailwyn, foster brother of the Saxon king Edgar, founded a Benedictine abbey on a remote island in the Fens. Only fragments survive, the remains of an ornate late fifteenth-century gatehouse with a richly carved oriel window above the entrance doorway suggesting how sumptuous the abbatial buildings must once have been. A small room to the right of the gateway is filled with an impressive mid-thirteenth-century marble tomb, with a time-worn effigy clutching a huge key in its right hand. An intriguing mystery surrounds the identity of the frost-damaged figure, which was once taken to represent Ailwyn.

Ranmore Common SURREY

2 miles north-west of Dorking, adjoining the south boundary of the Polesden Lacey estate [443 I5]

Running along the ridge of the North Downs north-west of Dorking and forming the attractive backdrop to the view southwards from Polesden Lacey (*see* p.308) are the 190 hectares (470 acres) of Ranmore Common. On each side of the road from Dorking to East Horsley there are grassy strips much used by families out for an afternoon, but it is the old wood pasture sloping north which provides good walking and exploring territory, for very varied vegetation grows on these clay caps and chalky slopes. Below Denbies, the country house of Thomas Cubitt, the early nineteenth-century developer of Belgravia, a further 101 hectares (250 acres) of steep hillside with varied chalk downland flora and fauna make up with the Polesden estate a fine stretch of beautiful landscape.

Red House KENT

Red House Lane, Bexleyheath [443 J5]

In the midst of the sprawl of south London, behind an undulating brick wall, is a tranquil, leafy garden and the small house in the country which Philip Webb (1831–1915) designed for his friend William Morris (1834–96), who was just starting out on married life. It was finished in 1860, in what was then a gentle Kentish countryside of orchards, fields and meadows. An unpretentious L-shaped building of deep-red brick with a steep tiled roof, also startlingly red, it is part Kentish farmhouse, part sleepy French manor, part medieval monastery. Gothic porches shelter heavy wooden doors, sash windows are topped off with brickwork arches, a buttress is corbelled out to carry an oriel window, and the roofline is broken by two massive brick chimneystacks, by the steep pyramidal roof with a finialled cap which marks the staircase tower, and by gables and dormers. Everything is at different levels, and the sashes are mixed with casements and round bulls-eye windows. This individual place, so different from the stuccoed villas favoured by his contemporaries, embodied Morris's yearning for a pre-industrial world and his romantic ideas about the good life and the value of hand-craftsmanship. Morris stayed here only five years, but the house and the way it was fitted out were to have an enduring influence on later approaches to domestic architecture and ideas of good taste. This was the birthplace of the Arts and Crafts Movement, of which both Morris and Webb were leading figures.

When the Red House was built, Morris was only in his twenties. He had met Webb during a short stint in the offices of the Gothic Revival architect G.E. Street, and he had also become friendly with two of the leading figures of the Pre-Raphaelite movement, Edward Burne-Jones, whom he had met while a student at Oxford, and Dante

William Morris's Red House (top). The well-lit first floor studio is at the end of the wing on the right, the staircase tower is in the crook of the L and in front of it, topped off by a steep conical cap, is the original well. In the welcoming hall (above) is the tall green settle which Webb designed for the house and which Morris painted with Arthurian scenes, turning his characters into portraits of his wife and closest friends.

Above: This delightful duck is one of several stained-glass animals in medieval style by Philip Webb in the Red House.

Opposite: At Rievaulx, a little Ionic temple sits at one end of the long, grassy terrace set high above the river and the ruins of the Cistercian abbey.

Gabriel Rossetti. It was Rossetti who, on the look-out for models with the kind of unconventional beauty valued by the Pre-Raphaelites, had spotted Janey Burden, whom Morris married in 1859. Both Burne-Jones and Webb were closely involved in the fitting out of Red House, which was decorated with rich embroidered hangings, medieval-style stained glass and tiles, and specially made furniture, designed by Webb to be both practical and in tune with Morris's vision. Weekend visitors, collected from the nearest station by horse-drawn wagon, were put to work painting ceilings and furniture and the textiles, too, were all produced in the house, to Morris's designs. In 1861, some half-dozen of these friends became the core of the firm of decorators and designers which Morris founded, and which took his romantic ideals and artist-craftsman principles to a much wider audience.

The house has long since lost most of the furniture made for it but some important pieces remain and sympathetic later owners, in particular Ted and Doris Hollamby, who lived here for half a century, have preserved other original features and introduced Morris and Co. wallpapers and innovations in keeping with the house. Although now largely unfurnished, it is welcoming and well lit, centred on the sturdy oak staircase set in the angle of the L. There are abstract painted ceilings (that over the stairs darkened by smoke); richly coloured Persian carpets on the floors; exposed brick fireplaces in every room; painted panelling and a selection of Morris papers in cool greens and blues, their designs shaped by the flowers growing outside in the garden. The hall, where the family and their many visitors occasionally ate, and where Morris would appear from the door to the cellar clutching several bottles of wine, still has the tall settle designed by Webb, with painted panels by Morris showing his wife and friends in medieval dress, and the dining room to one side houses Webb's massive dresser, topped off with a gothic canopy. Unusually, two of the main rooms are upstairs. The beautiful drawing room, with a high barrel ceiling going up into the roof, has an oriel window looking onto the garden, with a window seat where the ladies of the house sat to work on their embroidery. One wall is covered with the Hollambys' books and there are three paintings on a medieval theme by Burne-Jones, all that he completed of the cycle of seven that was commissioned. At the end of one wing is Morris's airy L-shaped studio, lit by windows on three sides. Ted Hollamby, who worked as an architect, designed the desk which fills the bay window looking onto the garden, and there are examples of the blocks used for printing Morris wallpapers.

The garden was designed by Webb as a natural extension of the house and is compartmental. Narrow brick paths border overflowing beds and patches of lawn, an ancient rose pergola is a long shady tunnel on a hot day, and there are the remains of the former kitchen garden and a sweeping drive leading to Webb's red-brick stables and the later coach house. Summoning up the Kentish countryside which once surrounded the house, apples and pears are trained on the house, and there is an evocative gnarled orchard. Sadly, Morris did not enjoy his dream for very long. With the practicalities of his work requiring him to spend more time in the capital, and his marriage failing, Morris moved back to London in 1865, and he never visited Red House again. Many of the furnishings ended up at Kelmscott Manor, the Oxfordshire farmhouse which he rented with Rossetti as a country retreat, and his idealism contributed to the founding of the Society for the Protection of Ancient Buildings, which directly inspired the formation of the National Trust.

Rievaulx Terrace and Temples NORTH YORKSHIRE

2½ miles north-west of Helmsley on the B1257 [445 J5]

Like Fountains Abbey 30 miles away to the south-west (*see* p.154), the Cistercian abbey of Rievaulx (not owned by the Trust) was established in a secluded valley where the monks could pursue their vocation untroubled by the world. Today their great monastery at the head of Ryedale is an evocative ruin, the walls of the mid-thirteenth-century church rising powerfully from the valley floor, the three tiers of windows in the nave still remarkably untouched by time. Above the abbey, Rievaulx Terrace winds like a serpent across the side of the hill, a gently curving walk giving changing vistas over the valley below. Sometimes there are glimpses through the trees to the three-arched bridge crossing the River Rye, sometimes branches frame a stone farmhouse or cottage on the far hillside. And then the ruins of the abbey are gradually visible, culminating in a view down the length of the great nave. In the same way, John Aislabie had devised his garden at Studley Royal a few years before to focus on the abbey ruins which lay just beyond his boundaries (*see* p.376).

Little Palladian temples punctuate either end of the terrace. To the south there is a delicate domed temple, its circular form completely enveloped in a colonnade. Inside, a richly decorated white plaster trellis, possibly the work of Giuseppe Cortese who was employed at Studley, stands

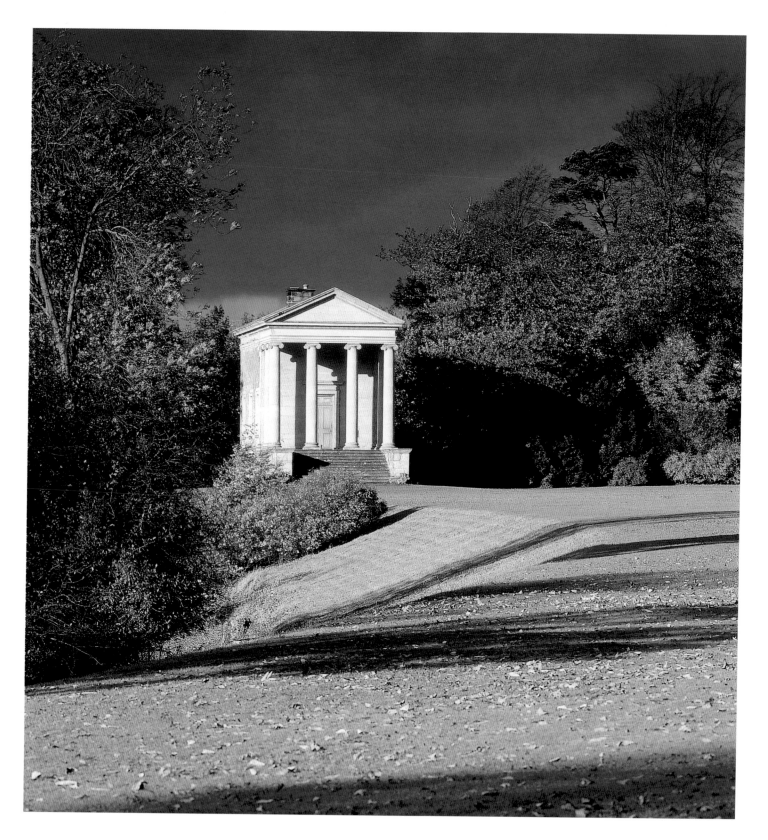

out vividly against the blue of the dome. The interior of the porticoed and pedimented rectangular Ionic temple is yet more magnificent, with brilliantly coloured frescoes by Giuseppe Borgnis and carvings covered in gold leaf. It was intended as a banqueting house, and the central table is improbably set for a meal. Both temples may be the work of the gentleman-architect Thomas Robinson, who was more spectacularly involved in Claydon House (*see* p.96).

With its two temples set on a thickly wooded hillside and its views over the ruined abbey in the valley below, Rievaulx is a romantic Italian landscape brought to life, as if a canvas by Claude or Poussin had been translated into a Yorkshire setting. This idealised creation was the vision of Thomas Duncombe III. He had inherited both Rievaulx and the adjoining Helmsley estate from his father in 1746 and must have wanted to complement, if not surpass, the more formal terrace his father had laid out in front of his house on the other side of the valley. Like William Aislabie's additions to his father's garden at Studley, Thomas Dunscombe's terrace is a product of the eighteenth-century taste for the informal and the picturesque and of a new appreciation of the drama in a natural landscape. As the agriculturalist and travel writer Arthur Young said in the late eighteenth century, 'This is a most bewitching spot.'

The River Wey and Godalming Navigations SURREY

Running between Godalming and Weybridge [443 I5]

Although bridged by the M25 and close to London's sub-urban sprawl, this tranquil waterway snaking 20 miles through Surrey from Godalming north to the River Thames is still remarkably rural, with cows grazing placidly in meadows on either side, views to church towers and wooded hills and whitewashed lock-keepers' cottages fringing the towpath. The 15½-mile stretch along the River Wey from Guildford to Weybridge was opened for navigation in 1653 on the initiative of Sir Richard Weston, who introduced the principle of the lock, but the remaining 4½ miles upstream to Godalming were not completed until about a hundred years later. When finished, there were sixteen locks to negotiate between Godalming and the Thames.

Once crowded with barges loaded with agricultural produce and timber for London, the river lost its importance with the coming of the railways, although the waterway continued to be used commercially until about 1960. Walkers now enjoy the 20 miles of towpath running alongside and a disused railway line and there are pleasure boats for hire. With its tranquil backwaters, the canalised river is also an important wildlife corridor in a heavily populated area.

59 Rodney Street, Liverpool CHESHIRE

[445 H7]

This substantial Georgian terrace house, with a long garden behind, was for years both home and workplace of Edward Chambré Hardman (1898–1988), Liverpool's leading portrait photographer from the 1920s to the 1960s. In the era before a less posed approach became fashionable and every family had the equipment to produce their own photographs, there was a demand for formal portraits which was met by commercial studios. E.C. Hardman catered for this market, photographing anyone who was anyone in Liverpool as well as a stream of distinguished visitors, among them Ivor Novello and Margot Fonteyn. He was also a skilled landscape photographer, capturing the Liverpool of his day and more distant places and countrysides. Working in the pictorial tradition, with much use of soft focus, retouching and other manipulative devices, Hardman's images are moody and atmospheric. Many of them are also now of documentary interest. He never set out to make a record of the changes in the city around him, but his evocative images of the now-vanished Liverpool shipbuilding industry, such as photographs showing the use of wooden scaffolding in the yards, and of other aspects of the urban scene, are of great historical value. His achievements were fully recognised in his lifetime: he was one of only four photographers to receive a special medal to mark the London Salon's Golden Jubilee in 1959, and he was awarded an Honorary Fellowship of the Royal Photographic Society in 1980.

Hardman was born in southern Ireland and, following the example of his father, who was a keen amateur photographer, began taking photographs seriously as a child, winning his first competition at the age of fourteen. After serving in the army in India from 1917–22, he decided to set up a photographic studio with a fellow officer, Kenneth Burrell, who seems to have been of value largely for his social connections and was not involved in the day-to-day running of the business (initially based in Bold Street). Soon, anyone of any pretensions or importance in the area was being photographed by Burrell & Hardman and

Hardman began a series of portraits of actors appearing at the Liverpool Playhouse, among them, over the years, Richard Todd, Robert Donat, Patricia Routledge, Michael Redgrave and Beryl Bainbridge. With his future wife Margaret, who had joined the studio as an employee and whom he eventually married in 1932, he set off by train and bicycle into the countryside to photograph landscapes, many of which were commissioned as covers for *Cheshire Life* or the back page of the *Daily Post*.

The business prospered. Hardman opened a second studio in Chester and in 1948 moved to Rodney Street. But little more than a decade later the tide turned. With demand for formally posed portraits declining, he worked less and less, becoming virtually a recluse after Margaret died in 1970. On his death the house and its contents passed to the E.C. Hardman Trust, which in turn gave everything to the National Trust in 2001.

Still as it was when Hardman lived and worked here, 59 Rodney Street is a complete example of a period photographic studio and is full of furnishings and ephemera from the 1930s, '40s and '50s. At the front of the house are the clients' waiting room and changing room and Hardman's studio, the latter fully equipped with backdrops, cameras, lights, props and even drawers of toys to entertain younger sitters. Three darkrooms and areas for printing, cutting and mounting were where Hardman manipulated and finished his images, and the Hardmans themselves lived in the cramped and relatively frugal quarters at the back. The furniture includes some pieces in the style of Sir Gordon Russell, who was a pioneer of the Modern Movement in English furniture design, and there is a strong period feel, with many everyday items such as tins of food, and packets of soap and silk stockings in the condition they were purchased 50 years ago.

The Studio at Rodney Street, in a photograph taken by Chambré Hardman himself.

Bottom: The long, leafy drive which leads to Rowallane is lined by cairns of round boulders like giant marbles and the bones of the countryside, as throughout the garden, keep breaking through in exposed outcrops. But the climate is mild and wet, and the planting, which includes these Himalayan blue poppies in the walled garden (below), lush and rich.

Ros Castle NORTHUMBERLAND

12 miles north-west of Alnwick, south-east of Chillingham [445 I1]

Rising out of the moors to the east of Chillingham Park is the conical hill of Ros Castle, where the Trust holds 3 hectares (7½ acres). There are no castle ruins, only vestigial remains of the Iron Age hill-fort, but the view from this remote property is memorable: seaward to Holy Island, Bamburgh and the Farnes (*see* p.146), south to the rich land between the hills and the sea, west to the Cheviot Hills and Scotland.

Rough Tor CORNWALL

Off A39, 3 miles south-east of Camelford, access via Jubilee Drive [442 B7]

Prominent in the view south from the A39 is this bleak and rocky granite tor on the northern edge of Bodmin Moor. Rising to 395 metres (1,296 feet), it is the second highest point in Cornwall after Brown Willy, which lies a quarter of a mile away across the moor. The Trust's 70 hectares (173 acres), its only foothold on Bodmin Moor, protect the summit of the tor and include a Bronze Age settlement site with hut circles and fields and a Second World War memorial.

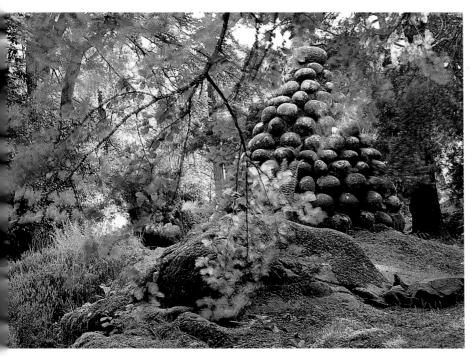

Rowallane Garden CO. DOWN

11 miles south-east of Belfast, 1 mile south of Saintfield, west of the A7 Downpatrick road [444 D4]

The drumlin landscape of Co. Down, with outcrops of basalt scraped bare by glaciers long ago and stony moraines left as the ice retreated, is harsh farming country, where little fields formed on the thin soil are edged by dry-stone walls built up from material laboriously cleared by hand. Features which would defeat most cultivators are the very essence of Rowallane. Established on the fields of a hill farm, the informal planting follows the lie of the land, banks of shrubs turning back on themselves round a hillock and natural rock gardens formed on craggy basalt outcrops. Areas known as the Paddock and the Spring Ground conjure up the flocks and herds which once grazed here, and a network of dry-stone walls still traces the skeleton of the farm, those marking the boundaries of the holding nicely coursed.

Although started by the Rev. John Moore in the late nineteenth century, this unique tree and shrub garden is largely the creation of his talented nephew who inherited the property in 1903. Hugh Armytage Moore's particular genius lay in his ability to choose a plant for a setting, enhancing the natural landscape rather than adapting it to his own designs. The garden is particularly known for spectacular displays of rhododendrons and azaleas, which flourish on the acid soils in the mild wet climate; a large clump of bright red rhododendrons by the little pool contrasts with a bank of trifoliate varieties flowering in twilight colours – pink, mauve and blue – or with the tiny yellow flowers of *Rhododendron lutescens*. Many rare and exotic species, some sent back by E.H. Wilson, G. Forrest, F. Kingdon-Ward and other collectors from the Far East and the southern hemisphere, include the Chilean fire bush, the handkerchief tree and magnificent southern beeches. This is a garden where the beauty and subtle variety of foliage can be fully appreciated, every hue and tone of green seeming to contribute to the woodland framing the open area of grass known as the pleasure ground, setting off the gay blue bandstand moved here in the 1860s.

A long drive lined with rhododendrons and specimen conifers and punctuated with tall stone cairns erected by John Moore leads up from the Belfast road. Rare bulbs, tender shrubs and climbing plants shelter in the walled garden beside the house, including the chaenomeles, viburnum, hypericum and primula named after Rowallane, a scented magnolia, fuchsias, hostas, colchicums, vivid blue

Royal Military Canal KENT AND EAST SUSSEX

3½ miles of canal bank between Appledore and Wareborne [443 K6]

Like the Needles Old Battery (*see* p.260), the Royal Military Canal running for 28 miles between Hythe and Rye along the inner edge of Romney Marsh was built in anticipation of enemy action which never came. Dug in 1804–7 to a width of 18.5 metres (60 feet) and a depth of 2.75 metres (9 feet), it was intended as a line of defence against a landing by Napoleon's forces and the military road behind it for moving troops rapidly along the coast. It is now considered one of the most important surviving examples in Europe of a linear military defence system. Once the danger of a French invasion had passed, it was very quickly made suitable for commercial traffic, which only ceased in 1909. The Trust owns a beautiful 3½-mile stretch between Wareborne and Appledore. Walkers heading west along the sometimes tree-lined towpath see the Isle of Oxney swelling out of the landscape ahead, while to the left the marsh stretches away to the sea.

Rufford Old Hall LANCASHIRE

7 miles north of Ormskirk, in village of Rufford on east side of the A59 [445 H6]

Like his father, grandfather and great-grandfather before him, Sir Thomas Hesketh married an heiress. Certainly no expense was spared on the half-timbered manor house he built in *c.*1530, establishing the family seat for the next 230 years. Although only the great hall survives in its original form – the west wing being now no more than marks in the grass and the east wing having been extensively rebuilt – what remains speaks eloquently of wealth and position. The great hall, 14 metres (46 feet) long and 6.5 metres (22 feet) wide, was built to be admired, crowned by a fanciful hammerbeam roof in which each massive timber is fretted with carved battlements. Angels – all but one now wingless – look down from the ends of the supporting beams while carved roof bosses display the arms of the great Lancashire families with which Hesketh was allied.

A massive, intricately carved movable wooden screen with three soaring finials like a pagoda takes the place of the more usual partition in houses of this date, separating the hall from the traditional screens passage. This deliberately theatrical set piece, backed by blind quatrefoils lining the upper wall of the passage and placed within a wooden

and purple drifts of the Himalayan blue poppy, and a collection of penstemons. To the east is the Spring Ground, the rocky pastures on which it was created being known for producing the first new grass of the year. Rhododendrons and azaleas backed by maples, birches and other trees line a grassy glade leading gently downhill, yellow with daffodils in spring. At the bottom a massive basalt outcrop harbours a wide range of alpines and heathers. Blue gentians cling to pockets of soil, primulas flower in shady corners and the rock is bright with dwarf rhododendrons and daffodils early in the year. Up a little clearing from here is the natural whinstone outcrop shaped like a bishop's chair, known as the Bishop's Rock.

Rowallane is spectacular in March, April and May, and again when there is autumn foliage and berries encrust trees and shrubs in the Paddock. And this was the land once judged 'not fit to graze a goat' by the Rev. John Moore.

The large 16th-century great hall at Rufford (right) survives almost unaltered and still has its ornate movable screen and elaborate hammer-beam roof, decorated with carved angels. The half-timbered hall is all that remains of the original manor and is now joined to a brick wing dating from the 1660s (opposite).

arch supported by beautifully decorated octagonal pillars, must have delighted William Shakespeare if there is truth in the legend that he performed here while in Sir Thomas's service. A canopy of honour curves over the far end of the room, where the lord and his guests would have sat at high table, their special status further emphasised by the great bay window looking north. A long refectory table, richly carved oak chests, and pieces from the Hesketh collection of arms and armour add to the house's atmosphere. The exterior is similarly fine, an impressive display of studding, quatrefoils and wood-mullioned windows greeting visitors as they come up the drive.

A Carolean wing juts out at right-angles to the medieval great hall, its symmetrical gabled façade built of warm red brick contrasting strangely with the black and white timbering. A castellated tower peering over the angle between the two ranges is a later addition, a feature of the nineteenth-century building which joins the great hall to the Charles II wing and which was added after the eldest son of the 3rd Baronet returned to the Old Hall in the 1820s. Partly formed out of the old medieval east range, this wing of the house includes a spacious drawing room stretching the full length of the first floor, with a sixteenth-century open timber roof and a spy-hole looking down into the great hall below. As elsewhere in the house, richly carved court cupboards, spindle-backed rush-seated chairs and oak settles of the seventeenth and eighteenth centuries demonstrate the skills of local craftsmen.

Outbuildings house the Philip Ashcroft Museum of Rural Life, a unique collection of objects and implements illustrating village life in pre-industrial Lancashire. Relics of the local cheese- and butter-making industries are displayed alongside a man-trap and an unusual water-filter made from local red sandstone.

Runnymede SURREY

On the Thames, ½ mile above Runnymede bridge, on south side of the A308 [443 |5]

These sleepy water-meadows beside the River Thames are where King John sealed Magna Carta on 12 June 1215, ending nine days of negotiations with his rebellious barons. Subsequently regarded as a fundamental statement of human rights, the libertarian principles thought to be enshrined in Magna Carta formed the basis of English law and were eventually incorporated into the constitutions of many other countries, including the United States. Appropriately, therefore, this peaceful spot was also chosen to honour the American President John F. Kennedy after his assassination in 1963 and to commemorate 20,455 airmen lost without trace in the Second World War.

Monuments to Magna Carta (erected 1957) and John F. Kennedy (1965) stand on the wooded slopes rising steeply from the meadows, while the crest of the hill, from where there are magnificent views towards London, is crowned by the extensive Commonwealth Air Forces Memorial (1953). Two bungalow-like lodges with deep hipped roofs bordering the road to Windsor and two kiosks at the Egham end of the property by Sir Edwin Lutyens were erected in memory of Urban Halon Broughton, father of the 1st Lord Fairhaven (*see* p.20), whose widow presented the meadows to the Trust. Lutyens also designed the pairs of memorial pillars flanking both sets of buildings with inscriptions recording Lord Fairhaven's bequest and the charter granted in 1215.

The 1957 monument to the signing of Magna Carta, in a sylvan setting on the wooded slopes above the Thames at Runnymede.

St Cuthbert's Cave NORTHUMBERLAND

10 miles north-east of Wooler [445 I1]

St Cuthbert's Cave, situated in the wooded Kyloe Hills on the mainland opposite Holy Island, is believed to have been used as a hermitage by St Cuthbert in AD674, or, alternatively, as a temporary resting place for the saint's body during its century-long journey through the country to Durham. It is a remote, tranquil spot with exceptional views over some of the most outstanding scenery in Northumberland.

St George's Guildhall NORFOLK

In King's Lynn, on west side of King Street close to the Tuesday Market Place [443 J1]

Medieval King's Lynn was a market town and port of considerable importance, trading in wool and agricultural produce across the North Sea and to Scandinavia. The Guild of St George was one of the largest of the 60 or so that flourished here in late medieval times, and this substantial building by Tuesday Market, the biggest surviving medieval guildhall in England, is a graphic illustration of the wealth and status of the fraternity.

Although the 32.5-metre (107-foot) great hall on the first floor has since been converted into a theatre and the building as a whole is an arts centre, many original fifteenth-century features survive, such as the five massive buttresses against the north wall and the open timber roof. There are also traces of the Georgian theatre constructed here in 1766. An adjoining Tudor house and the long row of medieval warehouses running down to the River Ouse from the west end of the guildhall are also owned by the Trust.

St John's Jerusalem Garden KENT

3 miles south of Dartford at Sutton-at-Hone, on east side of the A225 [443 J5]

After the noise and traffic of Dartford, this cool, secluded garden moated by the River Darent appears as an oasis of peace and serenity. Undulating lawns planted with a broad avenue of chestnuts stretch away from the house to where limes and willows edge the moat. Spring and summer flower borders are bright with bulbs and herbaceous plants and there are a number of fine specimen trees, including a descendant of one of the St Helena willows under which Napoleon was buried.

Approached down a short drive from the village of Sutton-at-Hone, the first view of St John's, a pleasant two-storey stuccoed building with dormers in the steeply pitched roof, is framed by the branches of a huge Cedar of Lebanon. This magnificent tree was probably planted by Abraham Hill in the late seventeenth century at the same time as he made alterations to the house. Sash windows and rich plasterwork inside the house were later additions by Edward Hasted, the eminent local historian, who lived here from 1755–76.

The oldest part of St John's is the former chapel, with buttressed flint walls and tall lancet windows, all that remains of the former Commandery of the Knights Hospitallers of the Order of Saint John of Jerusalem. Established here in 1199, they live on in the name of this delightful property.

St Michael's Mount CORNWALL

½ mile south of the A394 at Marazion [442 A8]

St Michael's Mount rises from the sea off the Cornish coast as if a spiny sea monster were arching its back below the waves, its dramatic profile crowned by Arthurian battlements and towers. When the skies are grey and an Atlantic gale is sending breakers crashing onto the rocks, it is easy to imagine that the Archangel St Michael did indeed do battle with the Devil here. On still summer evenings the island is another world, floating serenely in a crystal-clear sea.

This strange hybrid is part religious retreat, part fortress, part elegant country house. Associated with Christianity since the fifth century, when St Michael is said to have appeared to some local fishermen, it became an important place of pilgrimage in the Middle Ages, when the attraction of the saint's shrine was enhanced by the charms of the jawbone of St Appolonia of Alexander, said to cure toothache. The heart of the castle today is a little fourteenth-century granite church built on the highest point of the island, the major survival from the Benedictine priory established here in the twelfth century, daughter house of the much grander Mont St Michel set on another rocky outcrop some 150 miles across the Channel. Two beautiful fifteenth-century rose windows light the building, angels in flowing robes forming swirls of olive-green, blue, red and orange in that at the west end.

What was probably the monastic refectory is now the impressive Chevy Chase Room, called after the prominent

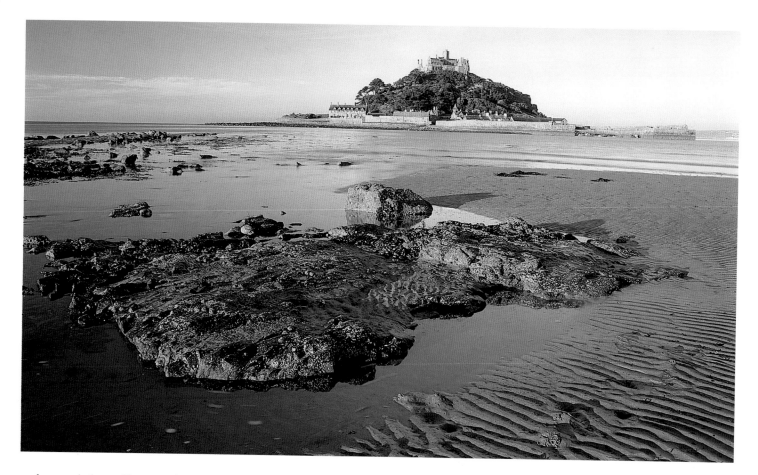

and unusual plaster frieze on which rabbits, boars, stags, a bear and a fox are being pursued by men with spears and guns. Some of the hunters' dogs have got away from the pack and are perched mischievously on top of the frieze. Appropriately furnished with a gleaming seventeenth-century refectory table, the room is dominated by the royal coat of arms picked out in gold and red over the fireplace, set up here in celebration of Charles II's restoration to the throne. The massive granite walls are probably those built in the twelfth century but the arching timber roof dates from 300 years later.

The guardroom in the entry range, the garrison room embedded in the rock, an old sentry box overlooking the steep cobbled path up to the castle and gun batteries point-ing out to sea recall the 200 years when the Mount was a manned fortress, a major link in England's defences against the Spanish Armada (a beacon lit on the church tower in 1587 heralded the approach of the fleet) and a Royalist stronghold in the Civil War until the castle's surrender in 1646. The last military governor, the Parliamentarian Colonel John St Aubyn, began the conversion of the

fortress into a private house and his descendants continued to live here for the next 300 years. Sir John St Aubyn, 3rd Baronet, transformed the ruined lady chapel into the elegant blue drawing room, early rococo Gothic plaster-work picked out in white against the blue walls, niches filled with pink Italian vases in jasper and alabaster and fine Chippendale furniture upholstered in blue conjuring up the cultivated world of Georgian England.

Far below, on the steep exposed lower slopes of the rock, is the St Aubyn family's terraced rock garden and eighteenth-century walled garden. Despite the sea gales, rare tropical and subtropical plants flourish here.

From the castle terraces there are magnificent views over Mount's Bay along the Cornish coast and inland to rolling granite moors, while far below a thread of ant-sized people crossing the causeway leading back over the sands to Marazion at low tide could be medieval pilgrims. A row of whitewashed cottages huddles above the claw-like harbour on the sheltered north side of the island, where sailing ships once loaded Cornish tin and copper for the Continent.

Romantic St Michael's Mount crowns a steep rocky island just off the south coast of Cornwall. A huddle of attractive cottages along the quay at the foot of the rock is all that remains of a once prosperous little port, used for the export of Cornish tin and copper.

Salcombe DEVON

On the south coast; about 9 miles of coastline on either side of the harbour [442 D8]

This is one of the Trust's longest stretches of coastline, running from Prawle Point, 3 miles east of Salcombe, to Bolt Tail, 6 miles to the west, 9 miles in all.

Prawle is the southernmost tip of Devon. The name means the look-out hill, and it has been used for this purpose since early times, through many wars, and is manned today by HM Coastguard. Elender Cove, to the west, does not belong to the Trust, but immediately beyond it is the beautiful sandy Maceley Cove, and from here the Trust's ownership is continuous to Salcombe.

The shapely Gammon Head shelters Maceley Cove from the west, an easy scramble out to its tip, and from here there is a wonderful view: westwards over the bay to Bolt Head, inland to the neat fields of the South Hams, and seawards where ships pass up and down the Channel.

The path runs west past the promontory of the Pig's Nose, where a delightful valley leads up to the village of

East Prawle, past Moor Sands and along Decklers Cliff, once farmed as the field hedges show but now overgrown. Rickham Sands, below the Gara Rock Hotel (converted from a row of former coastguard cottages), is a good beach. The little whitewashed and thatched building above it was the coastguard's look-out.

Overhead glide kestrels, buzzards and ravens, while seabirds and waders frequent the rocks and beaches below the cliffs. From Gara Rock there are paths at two levels along Portlemouth Down and past Limebury Point into Salcombe harbour. Below the low cliffs are little sandy coves, sheltered, wholly delightful, until the large beach of Mill Bay where the Trust's property ends.

At the head of the harbour South Pool Creek strikes off to the north-east and, on the opposite bank, where the Kingsbridge estuary continues to the north, is Snape's Point. These 61 hectares (150 acres) of farmland with 2 miles of estuary coast are important because the Trust's ownership will stop the expansion in this direction of Salcombe, a former shipbuilding town and commercial harbour, now wholly devoted to the boating fraternity.

West of the harbour entrance the Trust's land starts again above South Sands, at Overbeck's (*see* p.284). The Courtenay Walk (Courtenay being the family name of the Earl of Devon who formerly owned this land) leads steeply upwards above Stink Cove – the stink due to seaweed which collects here – to Sharp Tor 122 metres (400 feet) above the sea. There is a topograph showing what there is to see in the wide prospect to east and north. The path follows round Starehole Bay, all that a cliff path should be: craggy outcrops of rock, brackeny slopes, tidy fields inland, the sun glittering on the sea far below.

In 1936 the four-masted barque *Herzogin Cecilie*, one of a fleet of grain ships trading out of Mariehamm in Finland, struck the Ham Stone, a rock offshore round Bolt Head to the west. The damage was thought to be slight and she was towed round and beached here in Starehole Bay to be unloaded. Before this could be done a storm blew up and broke her back. On a still day the ghostly outline of her hull can be seen on the bottom of the bay.

Bolt Head is marginally higher than Sharp Tor and, because the coast turns sharply west at the opening of the harbour, it is very impressive when seen from a boat immediately below. The Warren stretches for a further 2½ miles of excellent walking to Soar Mill Cove, with its good sand and rock pools at low water, perfect for family picnics. Eighteen miles to the west, beyond Plymouth, stands the Eddystone Light, just visible from the higher ground in daylight, unmistakable at night.

Cathole and West Cliffs follow, some of the fields above the cliff bounded by upright slabs of a local mica schist, a slaty stone produced by volcanic pressure. Then the path leads across Bolberry Down, high above Slippery Point and Fernyhole Point, evocative names, far below. Whether in summer or winter the air is sparkling, the walk exhilarating, the views of cliffs, sea and ships, and inland across the South Hams to Dartmoor, unsurpassed.

Finally the path goes past Ramillies Cove, named not after the battle but the ship, a 90-gun second-rate ship of the line wrecked here in 1760, and round Bolt Tail to the picture-postcard village of Hope Cove, tucked inside the headland, a walk to remember.

Saltram DEVON

2 miles west of Plympton, 3 miles east of Plymouth city centre, between the A38 Plymouth–Exeter road and the A379 Plymouth–Kingsbridge road [442 C7]

Anyone who has travelled by train from Plymouth to London will know the pleasure of seeing the Saltram estate shortly after leaving the city, when the line suddenly emerges on the banks of the River Plym and the wooded slope of the park rises on the other side of the estuary. With a view over Plymouth Sound to the trees of Mount Edgcumbe, this is a perfect position for a house, and the building created here lives up to its setting. Saltram is essentially a product of the eighteenth century, the rooms with their original contents summing up all that was best about this elegant and civilised age.

The remodelling of the house was the work of John and Lady Catherine Parker, who wrapped three classical façades round a Tudor core and the three-storey seven-teenth-century block which John's father had purchased in 1712. But it was their son, John Parker, 1st Lord Boringdon, who invited Robert Adam to Saltram and who amassed the outstanding collection of pictures. Already at work on Kedleston Hall (*see* p.200) and Osterley (*see* p.283), Adam was at the height of his career and his rooms at Saltram, in which he designed everything, including the door knobs, are exceptional examples of his style. In the great Neo-classical saloon, delicate plasterwork attributed to Joseph Rose stands out white against the eggshell-blue and burnt-yellow of the coved ceiling. Blue damask lines the walls, setting off the four great looking-glasses and the paintings hung as Adam intended. A magnificent Axminster carpet echoes the design of the ceiling and gilded chairs and sofas line the walls.

Another aspect of the eighteenth century is reflected in the morning room, far more intimate and relaxed than the saloon, where a quartet of cloud-based cherubs makes music in the rococo plaster ceiling. Paintings hang triple-banked in the fashion of the day, their gilded frames glowing against red velvet.

The picture collection is still virtually as Lord Boringdon left it, including ten paintings by his close friend Sir Joshua Reynolds. During their long association, Reynolds not only portrayed Lord Boringdon and his family but also advised him on his other acquisitions, among them works by Angelica Kauffmann and a number of Italian, Dutch and Flemish paintings. Other delights at Saltram are the eighteenth-century Chinese wallpaper, some of it depicting those curiously elongated figures so familiar from Japanese prints, and an essentially eighteenth-century kitchen, with a battery of gleaming copper pans.

A pleasant Victorian informal garden lies to the west of the house, a soothing mixture of lawns, wooded glades and shrubs, with grass walks bordered by magnolias, camellias, rhododendrons and a number of good specimen trees. A long lime avenue is ribboned with daffodils in spring and bright with patches of cyclamen in September. An octagonal mid-eighteenth-century Gothic belvedere at the end of this walk was probably built by Harry Stockman, the estate's talented carpenter, as was the

Saltram's plain Palladian west front (above) looks out over the wooded park surrounding the house. Magnificent interiors include a Chinese bedroom lined with painted silk and hung with Chinese mirror paintings in English giltwood frames (below).

elegant pedimented orangery of 1775 by the house, still full of citrus fruits which are set out round a fountain pool in summer. Stockman also created the chapel nearby, adding battlements, buttresses and pointed windows to what was originally a barn. The extensive deer-park formed in the mid-eighteenth century was landscaped in the style of 'Capability' Brown, but the magnificent views depicted by William Tomkins's delightful landscapes in the garden room have been ruined by Plymouth's urban sprawl. Recently planted shelter belts help to hide this intrusive reminder of the twenty-first century, but passengers on the main Plymouth to London line will still be able to enjoy a glimpse of the amphitheatre, a mid-eighteenth-century folly nestling in the woods on the other side of the Plym estuary.

Sandham Memorial Chapel HAMPSHIRE

4 miles south of Newbury, ½ mile east of the A34 [443 H5]

The Spencer murals at Sandham Memorial Chapel are dominated by his resurrection scene on the altar wall, which took the artist nearly a year to complete. It is based on an intricate pattern of crosses, some of which frame soldiers emerging from their graves.

Service in Macedonia and in a military hospital during the First World War inspired the visionary and touching paintings by Stanley Spencer which fill this chapel. These are not horrific, tortured scenes of trench warfare but cameos of everyday activities which convey a sense of human companionship rarely found in civilian life. Soldiers in Macedonia are shown filling their water bottles, dressing under mosquito nets, cooking breakfast in the open and picking bilberries. In the hospital they sort

laundry, polish taps and make beds. Spencer's greatest work, the *Resurrection of the Soldiers*, entirely fills the altar wall. A stream of white crosses leads towards Christ seated in the middle distance, gathering crosses from the fallen in his arms. Soldiers emerge from their graves, shake hands with their comrades, clean buttons and wind puttees. Here, as throughout this powerful cycle, everyday life is touched by the immortal.

The 1920s red-brick chapel was built to Spencer's instructions by Mr and Mrs Behrend specially to house the paintings, which were created, on large seamless canvases, between 1927 and 1932. It is dedicated to Mrs Behrend's brother Lieutenant H.W. Sandham, who served in Macedonia during the First World War and died of an illness contracted there.

Sand Point and Middle Hope BATH & NE SOMERSET

5 miles north of Weston-super-Mare [442 E5]

Weston-super-Mare is all that a Victorian resort ought to be, its genteel stone villas ranked above its rather muddy beach with a pier and all the attractions that such places provide. Immediately to the north of the town is something quite different. Weston Woods, with deciduous trees and sunny glades, overlook Sand Bay. One and a half miles across the beach is the Trust's Sand Point, a limestone cliff with attractive outcrops of rock and fine views across the Bristol Channel. On its north side, at Swallow Cliff, there is a good example of a raised beach, formed in the distant past when the sea level was higher. Trust land extends a further half mile east along the low cliffs of Middle Hope, where a loop walk takes in the buildings of Woodspring Priory, recently restored by the Landmark Trust.

Scotney Castle Garden and Estate KENT

1½ miles south of Lamberhurst on the A21 [443 J6]

Like Sissinghurst only a few miles to the east (*see* p.341), much of Scotney's charm derives from the romantic buildings incorporated in the garden. A rich variety of flowering shrubs and trees laid out on the steep slopes of a bluff overlooking the little River Bewl provide a charming backdrop to the picturesque moated ruins in the floor of the valley. Now serene and peaceful, with roses, ivy and other climbing plants encrusting the ancient stonework, the castle was originally built during the troubled decades

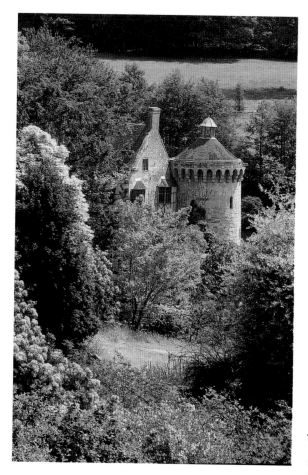

to advise on the creation of its surroundings. In view of the dramatic nature of the site, this was an inspired choice. Gilpin was a disciple of Richard Payne Knight and Sir Uvedale Price, the leading exponents of the Picturesque style, in which the naturalistic but carefully manicured landscapes of the 'Capability' Brown school were rejected in favour of the illusion of the beauty of nature untamed, as in a painting by Salvator Rosa. Scotney offered considerable potential, with its genuine ruin backed by a steeply rising slope and the added interest of a deep quarry left where the stone for the new house had been extracted. To make the castle even more romantic, and focus the eye on the oldest remains, parts of the seventeenth-century range were taken down.

The first view of the garden is one of the best. Standing on the semicircular bastion below the new house, the visitor looks down over the quarry and the slope of the valley, thickly planted with trees and shrubs, to the moated remains of the old castle. On the other side of the river the park rises gently to woodlands of sweet chestnut and oak. Walking along the top path from here, different vistas and perspectives open up, with glimpses of the seventeenth-century tower of Goudhurst church away to the north.

In April the magnolia in the quarry is in bloom and the Japanese maples are unfurling their leaves. Early summer brings a blaze of yellow, orange, purple and red from azaleas and rhododendrons on the slope above the moat, and later in the year pink, white and mauve roses bloom on the old walls of the castle, where a little formal herb garden has been created round an Italianate carved well-head. Luxuriant vegetation almost smothers a red-tiled boathouse, with pinnacles and bargeboards adorning the gable ends.

Carefully preserved by later generations of the Hussey family, the only modern note in the garden is the Reclining Figure by Henry Moore hidden away on a little isthmus in the lake, a tribute to the memory of Christopher Hussey who greatly enhanced the beauty of Scotney and gave it to the Trust.

Footpaths beyond the garden lead across the park and mixed woodland of the estate, with rare lichens on the older trees. Sweet chestnuts are coppiced to provide poles for the estate hop farm, one of the few still working in what used to be a major hop-growing area, as the views of former oast houses confirm. There are the remains of the huts that housed hop-pickers from London until the 1950s and a carpenter's workshop still operates in the estate timberyard.

of the Hundred Years War when men of substance needed to protect their property. Although not as vulnerable to French raids as Bodiam on the River Rother to the south, where Richard II gave Edward Dalyngrigge licence to fortify his estate (see p.54), Scotney was strategically sited where the road from Rye and Hastings crossed the valley of the Bewl. A massive round tower rising picturesquely from the lake-like moat, with a projecting parapet at roof level, and a ruined gatehouse are the remnants of the fortified house Roger Ashburnham constructed here in c.1378–80. A brick Elizabethan range adjoining the tower is all that survives of the sixteenth-century additions, and jagged walls with gaping windows mark a substantial seventeenth-century wing.

The magical 8-hectare (20-acre) garden which now sets off these striking remains was created from 1837 by Edward Hussey III, whose grandfather purchased the estate. As well as commissioning Anthony Salvin to build a neo-Tudor house on the bluff above the valley, he engaged William Sawrey Gilpin, the artist and landscape gardener,

Segontium GWYNEDD

On the A4085 Llanbeblig road, on south-east outskirts of Caernarfon [444 F8]

Edward I's great castle at Caernarfon was partly built of dressed stone plundered from a much earlier stronghold, the Roman fort of Segontium on the top of a hill about half a mile east. One of over 30 forts built to control the rebellious tribes in the valleys west of the Rivers Severn and Dee, Segontium was sited in a commanding position on the Menai Strait, within easy reach of the Snowdon massif and the Llŷn peninsula and with routes inland to the much larger garrisons based at Chester and Caerleon. Founded in AD78, it was held until about 390, longer than any other Roman fort in Wales, probably a reflection of its strategic importance. The perimeter defences were strengthened over the years, a ditch and clay rampart pierced by four wooden gateways being gradually replaced in stone.

The 2.2-hectare (5½-acre) site is crossed by the Caernarfon to Beddgelert road and only the ground plan of part of the northern half is excavated. The fort was of the usual playing-card shape and laid out to a standard design, with barracks for the men in tidy rows either side of the commander's house and the headquarter's building in the middle of the compound, the latter displaying the remains of an underfloor heating system. There are no visible signs of the two large granaries which housed a year's supply of corn for the garrison (up to 1,000 strong), but a rather basic bath suite added in the late third or early fourth century shows facilities here were less lavish than at Letocetum (*see* p.224). A site museum covers Roman military life in general, as well as the history and interpretation of Segontium itself.

Selborne Hill HAMPSHIRE

4 miles south of Alton, between Selborne and Newton Valence, west of the B3006 [443 H6]

Gilbert White (1720–93), the greatest of so many parson-naturalists, lived for most of his life at Selborne, recording his detailed observations of local wildlife and the natural scene in his classic *Natural History and Antiquities of Selborne*. The landscape is still much as he knew it. Above his house – now the Wakes Museum (not National Trust) – the chalk escarpment of Selborne Hill rises steeply 76 metres (250 feet) above the village. White's zig-zag path to the top cuts through the beech hangers clothing the slope and leads to Selborne Common on the plateau above, where there are old pollarded trees amongst a mix of wood and scrub. Butterflies are attracted to woodland glades, and ground cover includes yellow archangel, wood anemone, bird's nest orchid and other woodland plants.

Selworthy SOMERSET

On the Holnicote estate, astride the A39, between Minehead and Porlock [442 D5]

At first glance the thatched, cream-washed stone cottages climbing the hill to the fifteenth-century church of All Saints seem typical of this area. Unlike neighbouring villages, however, Selworthy was largely rebuilt in 1828 by Sir Thomas Acland of Killerton (*see* p.202), who designed a group of cottages in a local idiom set loosely round a long green. A philanthropist who wished to provide housing for the pensioners on his Holnicote estate (*see* p.187), Sir Thomas was probably inspired by his friend John Harford, who had commissioned Nash to design Blaise Hamlet for his aged retainers twenty years earlier (*see* p.50).

Both settlements are examples of the cult of the Picturesque, but they could hardly be more different. Whereas Nash's cottages are self-consciously flamboyant and exaggerated, those at Selworthy are gentle variations on the vernacular, with tall chimneys, deep thatched eaves, eyebrow dormers and projecting ovens. They are magnificently set, in a steep wooded valley on the northern fringes of Exmoor. The view from the church at the top of the village looks over a patchwork of thatched roofs and neat cottage gardens to the heather- and bracken-covered heights of Dunkery Beacon, the highest point on the moor. Whether the pensioners thought their surroundings worth the red cloaks they had to wear on Sundays is not recorded.

Shalford Mill SURREY

1½ miles south of Guildford, on east side of the A281 [443 I5]

This large eighteenth-century water-mill sits confidently astride the Tillingbourne, a tributary of the River Wey. Two timber-framed upper storeys attractively hung with warm red tiles are built on a brick ground floor, with three brick arches on the upstream side channelling the water of the river through the mill. A prominent projecting gable at third-floor level housed the hoist which once raised sacks of grain for storage in the large bins running the length of the attic.

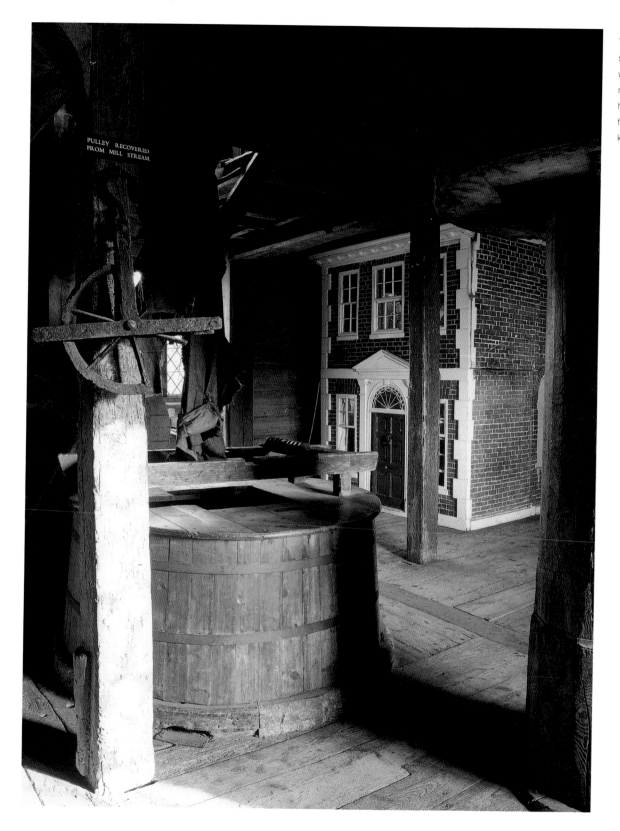

PULLEY RECOVERED
FROM MILL STREAM.

The grinding floor of Shalford Mill, showing one of the wooden casings which enclose the three pairs of millstones. Grain was reduced to meal here and fed into sacks or bins on the floor below. A doll's house is now also kept here.

All the principal machinery is still intact, but the mill can no longer be worked as only the top half of the 4.5-metre (14-foot) water-wheel remains. This is a breastshot wheel, driven by the water hitting the paddles halfway up the wheel rather than falling from above as in the more efficient overshot design (*see, for example*, Nether Alderley Mill, p.260). A vertical shaft made from a single pine trunk transmitted power from the wheel to three pairs of millstones, one of which is still complete, and to the hoist in the attic and winnowing and grading machinery on the second floor.

Shalford Mill is of particular interest because it is one of the properties that were presented to the Trust by the anonymous band of conservationists known as Ferguson's Gang, who used to meet here in the 1930s. Part of the building is now converted into a house and is privately let.

Shamrock CORNWALL

Cotehele Quay, on west bank of the Tamar; 1 mile west of Calstock by footpath (6 miles by road), 14 miles from Plymouth via Tamar Bridge, 2 miles east of St Dominick [442 C7]

Until the 1920s when competition from road and rail transport killed off the use of sail, a fleet of sturdy barges worked the coasts of Devon and Cornwall and the many river estuaries reaching into the heart of the peninsula. Everything was carried by water – from brick, limestone and coal to general provisions – loaded and landed on beaches or at one of the many old stone quays found on the rivers Fal, Dart, Tamar and Lynher.

Built in 1899 in a Plymouth yard, *Shamrock* is one of the last Tamar barges, a ketch-rigged (two-masted) 17.5-metre (57-foot) cargo boat typical of those which once crowded the river. Originally designed for inland waters and used to carry fertiliser and other bulky cargoes, she would have been a regular visitor to the little quay at Cotehele (*see* p.112) on the Tamar where she is now permanently berthed. She was later modified for work in the open sea, ending her days in the 1960s prospecting for tin in St Ives Bay and as a salvage vessel and diving tender. Reduced to a rotting hulk by 1974, she has now been fully restored.

In a nearby building on Cotehele Quay, an exhibition mounted in conjunction with the National Maritime Museum tells the story of Shamrock and of the once-flourishing local shipping industry.

Shaw's Corner HERTFORDSHIRE

At south-west end of the village of Ayot St Lawrence, 2 miles north-east of Wheathampstead [443 I4]

This rather undistinguished Edwardian villa is where the Irish dramatist and critic Bernard Shaw moved in 1906 at the age of 50 to enjoy a full and fruitful old age. Apart from the museum room, which shows such gems as the Oscar Shaw was awarded in 1938 for the screen play for the film version of *Pygmalion*, the old-fashioned steel-rimmed spectacles he wore in his later years and his membership card for the Cyclists' Touring Club dated 1950, the year in which he died, the house is still arranged very much as it was in his day and is filled with echoes of his individuality and genius. It is almost as if the great man has just gone out for the afternoon, taking a hat from the collection in the hall. In the study his typewriter sits waiting on the desk, with his pens to one side and the pocket dictionaries he used for immediate reference ranged below the window on to the garden. Perhaps his secretary Miss Patch is away, as her little desk in the corner of the room is unnaturally tidy. One of the drawers of the filing cabinets behind where she sits carries a characteristic Shavian label: 'Keys and Contraptions'.

In the drawing room next door a bronze bust by Rodin perfectly captures the craggy head, with its rather prominent nose and full beard. Shaw hardly used this room after his wife died in 1943, preferring to sit in an armchair by the fire in the dining room after eating an early vegetarian dinner. Photographs of Gandhi, Lenin and Stalin above

G. Bernard Shaw (below left) on the front steps of Shaw's Corner, the Edwardian house in the leafy village of Ayot St Lawrence where he lived for 44 years. The house is still largely as he had it, with his tweed suits and plus fours still hanging in the oak wardrobe in his bedroom (below right).

the fireplace reflect Shaw's socialist views and the room is dominated by Augustus John's glowing oil portrait. From here Shaw used to step out into the garden for his regular evening walks, or to bury himself in the little shed where he did much of his writing, safe from interruptions, sitting in the wicker chair which is still pulled up to the table at which he worked.

Sheffield Park Garden EAST SUSSEX

Midway between East Grinstead and Lewes, 5 miles north-west of Uckfield, on east side of the A275 [443 J6]

This peaceful 40.5-hectare (100-acre) landscape garden set on the edge of the Sussex Weald is large enough to accommodate a flood of visitors in the summer months without losing its character. Focused on a chain of lakes, the garden is criss-crossed by gravel and grass paths which weave and loop through the trees, sometimes bordering the water, sometimes veering away from it. It is possible to wander for an afternoon here without discovering the full range of the planting or retracing one's steps.

The garden is the creation of Arthur G. Soames, who acquired the estate on the death of the 3rd Earl of Sheffield in 1909 and devoted the next 25 years to transforming and extending the landscape park which 'Capability' Brown had laid out for the 1st Earl at the end of the eighteenth century. The neo-Gothic mansion (not owned by the Trust) which James Wyatt designed in 1775 to crown the 1st Earl's new property rises like a fairy-tale palace at the top of the garden, a great tracery window prominent in the end façade.

The 3rd Earl extended Brown's original two lakes to create a T-shaped chain, with picturesque cascades joining one level to another. From the top bridge over the first cascade, one can look back at Wyatt's pinnacled and battlemented fantasy mirrored in the waters of the first lake or down the impressive 7.5-metre (25-foot) drop to the length of the second, where palms flourishing on grassy islands immediately below the rocky falls add a suggestion of tropical luxuriance. Rafts of water lilies dot the surface of the upper lakes in summer, flowering white above the dividing cascade, red and pink below the falls. An impressive range of trees and shrubs lines the shores of the lakes, each species added and placed in an inspired planting scheme which has resulted in one of the finest woodland gardens in the British Isles.

Sheffield Park is said to be at its best in the autumn, when deep-blue water on crisp sunny days sets off turning

The extensive ornamental landscape laid out round a chain of lakes at Sheffield Park is at its best in the autumn. Here, the rust red of maple foliage is set off by pampas plumes on the shores of the Middle Lake.

leaves, a number of tupelo trees (*Nyssa sylvatica*) providing particularly spectacular displays. In spring there are wild daffodils and bluebells, and the flowers of the Japanese magnolia, like a cloud of exotic butterflies against the bare March twigs. A couple of months later the garden is ablaze with flowering shrubs, including an important collection of Ghent azaleas with honeysuckle-like blooms and banks of rhododendrons flowering blue, purple, yellow and wine-red, many of them sweetly scented. Spotted orchids appear in the long grass fringing the Queen's Walk circling one of the lower lakes, now a conservation area for wild flowers.

Although the freak storm in the autumn of 1987 thinned the trees framing and sheltering the garden, many exceptional mature specimens survived and these are being augmented by ongoing and extensive replanting. Established survivals include ancient chestnuts and oaks old enough to rival those at Croft Castle (*see* p.119) and already full grown when William of Orange landed in 1688, and conifers planted by the 3rd Lord Sheffield at the end of the nineteenth century. Exotics from the Far East are also well represented, such as the dawn redwood from east

Sheringham's sweeping parkland, framed by wooded hills, is one of Humphry Repton's best preserved landscapes. This little temple crowning a knoll in the park was designed to enhance the views from the hall in the distance but, although part of Repton's plan, it was not built until 1975.

Asia, at one time thought to be extinct, the feathery Chinese honey locust and *Pinus armandii* and the rare Nikko maple. A shady stream garden created over the last ten years is now well established, primulas, hostas, lilies and other water-loving plants flowering in a strip of pink, white and blue beneath the trees.

Sheringham Park NORFOLK

2 miles south-west of Sheringham, 5 miles west of Cromer, 6 miles east of Holt [443 K1]

The 311.5 hectares (770 acres) of Sheringham Park, mostly lying tucked behind the coast road near the holiday town of Sheringham, are what Humphry Repton called his 'most favourite work'. The parkland landscape was conceived for Abbot Upcher to whom Repton presented a Red Book in 1812. The woodlands contain magnificent displays of rhododendrons and azaleas of many varieties and the rolling parkland is adorned with an ornamental temple, suggested by Repton but actually built in 1975. North of the coast road, the land slopes gently down to soft eroding cliffs of glacial clays, sands and gravels. This part includes half a mile of coast, a dramatic section of north Norfolk coastal path, and is designated a Site of Special Scientific Interest for its exceptional geological deposits.

In 1994 the Trust's holding here was extended by the 40.5-hectare (100-acre) Weybourne Woods, adjoining the park.

Shropshire Hills SHROPSHIRE

Northern extremity extends from the Severn gorge to Montgomery on the Welsh border, and the southern extremity from Cleobury Mortimer to Knighton [442 E2–F2]

Among the glorious hills of Shropshire, including Brown Clee, Titterstone Clee and the Stiperstones, is the great Long Mynd. West of the A49 lies Church Stretton, its hotels and boarding houses starting to climb up the hill behind but petering out as if the effort were too much, and with good reason, for the mynd, from the Welsh *mynydd*, or mountain, has always been a real barrier, shielding the Welsh from the forays of the Marcher barons.

The great ridge, running for 10 miles from south-west to north-east and 3 or 4 miles wide, is broken by steep valleys known as hollows or batches, and for centuries was a wilderness of heather and grass, grazed only by sheep and ponies. Early in the morning the valleys are sunlit; as the sun moves they fall into shadow. The light can be dramatic: in stormy weather the clouds race across the hills, shafts of sunlight suddenly striking a distant spur. Along the spine runs the Portway, a Bronze Age ridgeway which later became a route for cattle drovers from Wales to the Midlands.

All this beauty seemed quite safe right up until the Forestry Commission turned its acquisitive eye towards these border hills. Here was cheap land to buy and plant, much easier to afforest than the true mountain land in north and central Wales. The great Mortimer and Clun

Forests began to blanket the hills and crept up from the south on to Long Mynd itself; the contrast at Minton Batch, where the Trust's open hills join the dark conifers, is an object lesson.

In 1965 an appeal was launched and 1,930 hectares (4,700 acres) were bought, with over 445 (1,100) since. About half the high land, which rises to over 335 metres (1,100 feet), now belongs to the Trust. It is superb for walking – up one hollow, along the ridge, back down another, or from Church Stretton up and over the top to Ratlinghope or Asterton, hamlets buried in the broken country stretching into Wales. The lie of the hills means that only from the 669.5-metre (2,197-foot) summit at Pole Bank can one see the whole panorama over Wales, the Marches and the West Midlands. On a clear day the view is from Cadair Idris to the Cotswolds, from the Brecon Beacons to Beeston Castle, near Chester.

Five miles across the A49, to the east, is a very different ridge, the narrow limestone escarpment of Wenlock Edge, running for 15 miles on the same south-west to north-east alignment as the Long Mynd. Approached from the east it is undramatic: farmland rising gently to a scrubby skyline, with an occasional view down into Hopedale below giving a sense of height. From the west it rears up as a harsh cliff, hacked about by quarry men and lime burners for centuries, menacing in certain lights.

The Wenlock limestone, formed in the Silurian period some 420 million years ago, developed as a barrier reef on the edge of a continental shelf when a deep ocean covered what is now land to the west. Built up largely from the skeletons of small marine creatures, the rock is full of fossils. The overlying thin soil has a rich flora of orchids, quaking-grass, yellow-wort, carline thistle and bushes of yew and spindle smothered in old-man's beard.

The Trust owns some 8 miles of Wenlock Edge, from Much Wenlock south to Easthope, including two viewpoints: Major's Leap, from where the Royalist Major Smallman jumped to elude his Parliamentarian pursuers (*see* p.430), and the crag of Ippikin's Rock. They lie either side of the road which slithers down the Edge to the village of Hughley, celebrated by A.E. Housman.

Contrasting with the harshness of Wenlock Edge and the magnificence of the Long Mynd is Hopesay Hill, lying north of Aston-on-Clun in the peaceful hilly country west of Craven Arms. The hill, a gentle ridge with paths leading to modest views, is used as a sheepwalk. Housman's quatrain sets the scene perfectly: 'In valleys of springs of rivers, By Ony and Teme and Clun, The country for easy livers, The quietest under the sun.'

Shugborough STAFFORDSHIRE

6 miles east of Stafford on the A513 [442 F1]

The two Anson brothers born in the 1690s took very different paths in life. George, who went to sea at the age of twelve, rose to be 1st Lord of the Admiralty and gained both fame and fortune on an epic four-year circumnavigation of the globe in the 1740s, during which he captured a treasure-laden Spanish galleon. Much of the Admiral's wealth went to help his cultivated elder brother Thomas improve the three-storey, late seventeenth-century house on the banks of the River Sow which he had inherited in 1720, financing the charming domed pavilions with the semicircular bay windows by Thomas Wright of Durham which now frame the central block. The massive two-storey portico dominating the entrance front was a later addition, part of Samuel Wyatt's alterations for the 1st Viscount Anson at the end of the century. Similarly, Wyatt was responsible for the central bow on the garden façade, and for the verandahs fronting the links to the pavilions on either side.

The interior reflects the interest in the ancient world

The wild, open ridges of Long Mynd are home to buzzard and curlew and offer glorious walking, with views to Wales and north into Cheshire.

of Thomas Anson, a leading spirit of the Society of Dilettanti which promoted the art of classical Greece. Six sombre Piranesi-like paintings of classical ruins by Nicholas Thomas Dall adorn the dining room, large and imposing enough not to be overshadowed by Vassalli's arresting plasterwork gently curving overhead. The low-ceilinged library, with a shallow arch set on Ionic columns dividing the room, is more welcoming, the apparently classical marble busts set along the bookcases including a nineteenth-century study of one of the family with a rabbit as well as likenesses of Plato and Hercules.

Neo-classical motifs also mark Wyatt's interiors. Giant yellow scagliola columns punctuate the walls of his curiously elongated saloon, their reflections in the pier glasses on the end wall making the room seem even larger than it is. Joseph Rose the Younger's coved ceiling in Wyatt's impressive Red Drawing Room is decorated with delicate compositions reminiscent of a Wedgwood vase. This room also displays remnants of Thomas Anson's famous picture collection, mostly dispersed with the rest of the contents in the 1842 sale precipitated by the extravagance of the 2nd Viscount, created 1st Earl of Lichfield. A number of paintings connected with the estate have also survived, including two portraits of Corsican goats, noble-looking beasts with corkscrew horns, part of a herd of this rare breed established by Thomas Anson. Magnificent French furniture in the principal rooms was acquired by the 2nd Earl when he set about rescuing the house in the 1850s.

A gold repeater, a snuffbox made of wood from one of his ships, Spanish coins and his commission from George III are among several mementoes of the gallant Admiral. One of his officers designed the little Chinese house by the Sow, set off by a pagoda tree and other oriental shrubs, but the rococo plaster ceiling and superb Chinese painted mirrors which once adorned it are now in the house, complementing the oriental porcelain and other chinoiserie acquired by the brothers.

Formal terraced gardens punctuated by cones of golden yew and classical urns lead down to the river, arches and pillars trailing roses and clematis partly screening the Victorian-style rose garden round a central sundial. The long loop of the Ladies' Walk meanders through the wild garden to the south where daffodils and bluebells beneath the trees in spring are followed by the dark-purple and creamy-yellow blossoms of groups of rhododendrons and azaleas. Thomas Wright's Picturesque ruin on the banks of the Sow, a crumbling array of columns and walls topped by the statue of a druid, is outclassed by the classical monuments based on buildings in ancient Athens in the park which Thomas Anson commissioned from James 'Athenian' Stuart. A triumphal arch stalks across the grass on a rise above the drive like a creature from outer space. Two pedimented porches with fluted columns project from the octagonal Tower of the Winds in the valley below and a shady knoll is crowned with the Lantern of Demosthenes, a cluster of columns topped by three dolphins supporting a tripod and bowl. No later development dulls the impact of these re-creations, only a gentle roar and tremors in the ground betraying the presence of the Stafford to Stoke main railway line buried in a tunnel beneath the triumphal arch.

The west front of Shugborough, dominated by Samuel Wyatt's projecting bow, looks out over terraced lawns to an arm of the River Sow. Almost obscured by the trees close to the water on the left is a contrived ruin, one of a series of monuments and eye-catchers which enrich the garden and park.

Sissinghurst Castle Garden KENT

2 miles north-east of Cranbrook, 1 mile east of Sissinghurst village on the A262 [443 J5]

The beauty and charm of this exceptional garden set high on a ridge above the Vale of Kent owe much to the Tudor buildings around which it was created and which form a romantic backdrop to the planting. The focal point of the garden is a four-storey red-brick Elizabethan prospect tower with two octagonal turrets, a remnant of the great, brick-built mansion built by Sir Richard Baker in the mid-sixteenth century, so magnificent that it was chosen by Elizabeth I for a three-day visit during her Progress through the Weald in 1573. Across what was the outer courtyard, the long entrance range of an earlier house is pierced by a gabled archway, crowned with three slender Tudor chimneys. On the other side of the tower two arms of an ancient moat are still filled with water and elsewhere in the garden are remains of Tudor walls, a cottage which was once part of the south wing of the Elizabethan mansion and a sixteenth-century priest's house. Despite over 200 years of neglect and decay, these romantic remains inspired the novelist and biographer Vita Sackville-West to purchase the property in 1930 and with the help of her husband, Sir Harold Nicolson, the diplomat and literary critic, to create one of the greatest gardens of the twentieth century.

Like Hidcote (*see* p.182), Sissinghurst was conceived as a series of intimate open-air rooms, bounded with red-brick walls or with hedges of yew, rose or hornbeam and with long linking walks stretching across the garden. The design, which has the happy effect of making the whole seem larger than it is, was Harold Nicolson's achievement, but it was his wife who devised the inspired planting schemes, using colour and texture to build the effects which make Sissinghurst so individual. As Vita Sackville-West herself observed, there is a southern feel about the place, perhaps partly conjured up by the lush Kentish country-side. Faint echoes of a Mediterranean villa are strengthened in the profuse planting of figs and vines, and in the terracotta Tuscan pots which adorn the lime walk. In the cottage garden even the dreariest English weather cannot subdue the tangle of tulips, columbines, irises, tiger-lilies and dahlias planted here, flaming yellow, orange and red against the paving stones and old bricks of the paths. A prolific white rose cascades over the cottage at one end. A different tone is set by the tranquil grassy walk leading down to the moat, flanked on one side by a border of azaleas, on the other by the old brick moat wall, dotted

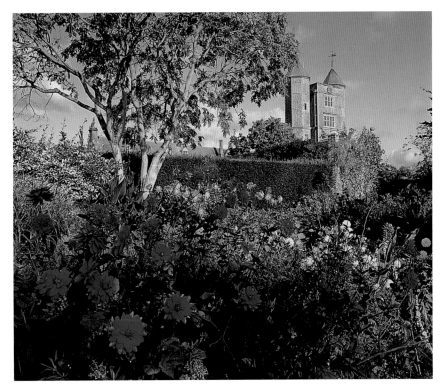

with wild flowers clinging to the mortar in spring. The nuttery beyond the azaleas ends in a yew-enclosed herb garden, crowded with aromatic, medicinal plants, camphor, woad, rue, lovage and apothecary's rose among them.

One of the best places to appreciate Sissinghurst is from the top of the tower, reached by a spiral staircase which leads up past the cluttered room where Vita Sackville-West wrote, its walls lined with books reflecting her special interests – gardening, literature, history and travel. From the roof there is a view down on to the rose garden, planted with old-fashioned species grouped round a little lawn. The rich colours when the bushes are in flower contrast vividly with the ghostly, surreal tones in the tangled White Garden on the other side of the tower, where all the blossoms are white and much of the foliage is grey. White lavender, clematis and the white double primrose echo the planting described in one of Vita's letters on display in the tower, where there is also a plan by Harold Nicolson detailing daffodils, narcissi and forsythia for the end of the lime walk.

Beyond the borders of the garden, the tower looks out over woods, fields and oast houses to a distant ridge of the North Downs, with the spire of Frittenden church in the middle distance. Perhaps Elizabeth I was taken up the tower to admire the view when she was entertained here.

Warm colours and controlled untidiness are the hallmark of the cottage garden at Sissinghurst. In the background is the Elizabethan tower, part of the framework of old walls and buildings which add so much to the character of the garden.

Water as Ornament

From the time of ancient Egypt and Mesopotamia, water has been a key ingredient in garden design. Sometimes, as in the courtyard gardens of the Islamic world, with their cool pools and canals, it is used to foster serenity and the sense of a soothing retreat, whether from the searing heat of the desert or the bustle of the world outside. Sometimes, as in the great gardens of the Italian Renaissance, water is used for drama and effect, channelled into cascades, and spouting from fountains and grottoes. More than almost any other ingredient, water affects mood. In the British Isles, sea-girt and moist, water has been used freely. A few gardens are survivals of the seventeenth-century canal garden, as developed in France and, much more modestly and intimately, in the Netherlands. These are geometric compositions focused on water, grass and trees, with reflections – of the sky, a statue, or a garden pavilion – adding to the sense of stillness and serenity. On a much larger scale are the painterly landscapes, centred on artfully sinuous lakes, which were products of the eighteenth-century landscape movement. Improvers such as 'Capability' Brown treated water as something to be manipulated and moulded, damming valleys, widening rivers and altering the contours of existing lakes. Cascades were part of the vocabulary but fountains, regarded as unnatural, were not.

More recent approaches to the use of water reflect a range of influences. The opening up of Japan in the late nineteenth century inspired a number of Japanese water gardens, adorned with temples, lanterns and other oriental touches. Other garden designers drew on the past, reinterpreting and adapting to suit the site and reflect new approaches to planting and the use of colour. At Bodnant Garden in north Wales five Italianate terraces descend below the house. Steps leading from the topmost level curve round a baroque fountain and water flows from one terrace to the next, through rills and into pools. And the enclosed, room-like nature of the Islamic garden reappears in the many compartmental twentieth-century layouts, with hedges enclosing intimate spaces. Often one room, as at Hidcote in Gloucestershire and Tintinhull in Somerset, will be filled with a still garden pool. Where all these gardens use water within, some look out to water beyond. There are glimpses of the Fal, often with a tanker at anchor, from the tranquil garden of Trelissick in Cornwall, views of Strangford Lough in Northern Ireland from Castle Ward and of the sea from Coleton Fishacre in Devon.

WESTBURY COURT
423

The formal canal gardens developed in France and the Netherlands in the 17th century spread to other countries of Europe. In England, the intimate Dutch approach, mixing water, hedges, fruit trees and flowering plants in serene, ordered compositions that were characteristically small in scale, inspired the garden at Westbury Court in Gloucestershire. Developed on a flat, low-lying site close to the Severn estuary, Westbury is laid out round two long canals bordered with yew hedges and box spires. One canal is punctuated by a tall brick pavilion, the other by a statue showing Neptune sitting astride a dolphin. The formal garden at Erddig in Wrexham is a similarly rare survival of an early 18th-century layout. Here, a broad central walk leads to a long rectangle of water. Clipped mushrooms of Portugal laurel and double avenues of pleached limes reflect the 17th- and 18th-century fashion for trained plants, and this garden, like Westbury, is both small and simply planned. Studley Royal in Yorkshire, by contrast, is a garden on the cusp. Dating from the early 18th century is a serenely simple layout of water and turf, with a round moon pond flanked by two crescent-shaped ponds and by the canal which channels the River Skell along this quiet valley.

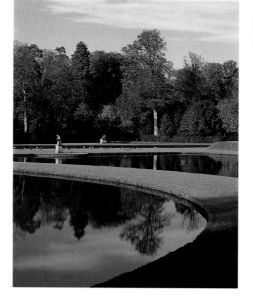

STUDLEY ROYAL
376

The ponds are mirrors, reflecting statues, a little temple and the ever-changing sky. As a backdrop, though, there are steep wooded hillsides threaded by meandering paths, and an unexpected opening in the canopy reveals the ruins of Fountains Abbey in the valley below. While the water garden looks backwards, the rest of the layout is in tune with the English landscape garden and the taste for the romantic and picturesque.

rocks and a reclining statue of a river god, a baroque composition that was toned down later in the century to leave only two piers supporting nymphs. Across the grass is the great portico on the east front of the house, designed to act as an eye-catcher in the landscape.

ERDDIG
143

STOURHEAD
366

PRIOR PARK
316

WEST WYCOMBE PARK
425

During the 18th century, changes in taste led to a more natural approach to laying out the grounds around a house. Increasingly, these were viewed with a painter's eye as compositions in trees, grass and water, perhaps punctuated by a little temple or some other architectural eye-catcher, and were allowed to merge visually with the countryside around rather than being set apart behind high brick walls. At Stourhead in Wiltshire, Henry Hoare II transformed the downland valley below his house into an idealised landscape, centred on the islanded lake formed by the damming of the River Stour. This enormous undertaking involved predetermining the level to which the water would rise and strengthening the banks with stone edging. Hanging woods and a series of temples and other features, such as the stone bridge crossing the north arm of the lake, complete the composition. More intimate and small scale, but offering the same kind of ingredients, is Prior Park, a landscape garden laid out in a combe above Bath in the mid-18th century. Framed by woods and steep grassy slopes is a gently curved chain of ponds, like a watery staircase, with cascades taking the water from one level to the next. A Palladian bridge crossing the uppermost dam provides a central focus. At West Wycombe in Buckinghamshire, an apparently naturalised landscape, with grassy slopes and woodland sweeping down to a sizeable lake, is a veneer on a semi-formal layout dating from the early 18th century. The cascade taking the outflow from the lake was originally more dramatic, with water pouring through an arch in a huge mound of

The end of the 19th century was marked by a revived interest in the great gardens of Renaissance Italy and by a new fascination with things Japanese, sparked off by the opening of Japan to foreigners mid-century. At Buscot Park in Oxfordshire, the designer Harold Peto threaded an Italianate water garden through the woodland between the house and the lake, providing a long, cool corridor of stone, grass and water, framed by box hedges and focused on a little temple on the further shore. At Cliveden in Buckinghamshire, the American sculptor Thomas Waldo Story, steeped in the street sculpture of Rome where he had been living, designed this voluptuous marble fountain for the 1st Viscount Astor. An unrestrained composition with life-size female figures attended by cupids standing around a giant shell, it dominates the approach to the house. Where Waldo Story's creation shouts at visitors, the serene Japanese garden created in a dell at Tatton Park in Cheshire is a place of tranquillity, with stone lanterns, an arched bridge and other oriental features reflected in still water.

A feature of garden design in the 20th century was the concept of the garden as a series of outdoor rooms, each with its own character. Often, a hedged compartment will be filled with a pool, or centred on a fountain or rill. From the upper windows of Tintinhull House in Somerset (**opposite, top right**) there is a view across the garden rooms aligned with the west front, with a vista through to the fountain garden with its lily pond at the end of the axis. A series of yew-hedged gardens at Knightshayes Court in Devon, where the layout has largely been created since the 1930s, includes this serene

pool garden, with a Victorian statue set in a niche in the hedging. At Hidcote Manor Garden in Gloucestershire, where water is never far away, the pine garden pool holds rafts of water lilies. Water is a pervading theme at Bodnant Garden in north Wales. Used to punctuate the great Italianate terraces which descend below the house, it is the centrepiece of the woodland garden created in the gorge-like valley of the River Hiraethlyn below. Always, there is the noise of falling water from the curtain-like cascade where the stream has been dammed and bridged.

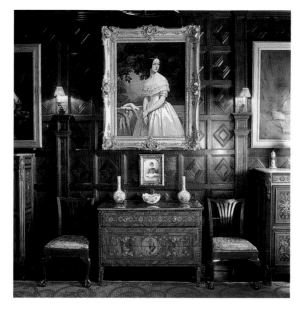

Sizergh Castle CUMBRIA

3½ miles south of Kendal, north-west of the A6/A591 interchange [445 H5]

Sizergh is dominated by the fourteenth-century fortress at its heart. The Stricklands who have lived here for 750 years were one of the great military families of the north, and the house they constructed in about 1350 reflects both their status and the vulnerability of these acres within reach of the Scottish border, part of the lowland corridor leading south between the Lakeland hills and the inhospitable North Yorkshire moors. The once-moated stronghold rises almost 18 metres (60 feet) to the battlements, its limestone rubble walls still formidable despite the later mullioned windows and the softening blanket of Virginia creeper.

Tudor and Elizabethan additions, partly hidden by a Georgian veneer, adjoin the tower. Low Elizabethan service wings with soaring chimneys flank the entrance courtyard. Double doors that once opened into the great hall now access a carriageway running through the castle, with a grand stone and oak staircase rising from one side.

Early Elizabethan woodwork in several of the rooms gives Sizergh its special flavour. The superb panelling in the Inlaid Chamber was sold to the Victoria and Albert Museum in 1891 but was returned in 1999 and can once again be seen in its former glory. Craftsmanship of similar quality is displayed in the five intricately carved armorial chimneypieces, four of which date from 1563–75. The rest of the panelling is also very fine, the oldest in the house

being the oak linenfold work dating from the reign of Henry VIII in a passage room. Intriguingly, a lozenge design on the woodwork in the old dining room and a bedroom reappears on the backs of three Elizabethan oak chairs in the tower. Here, too, there are carved oak benches with unusually rich, mid-sixteenth-century decoration.

A number of Stuart portraits and personal royal relics advertise the Stricklands' adherence to the Catholic faith and their loyal devotion to the Stuart cause. Refusing to desert the royal family after 1688, Sir Thomas Strickland and his wife accompanied James II into exile in France where Lady Strickland was governess to his young son.

Terraced lawns, their retaining walls softened with shrubs and climbers, lead down from the south front to the lake created out of the former moat. Orchids and Lent lilies (wild daffodils) flowering in the grass of the meadow above the lake are part of a native limestone flora which reflects the rock outcropping all over the estate in screes, cliffs and pavements, but the extensive rock garden covering an acre was constructed of Westmorland stone in 1926 by Hayes of Ambleside, who arranged the little stream tumbling across it into the lake in a series of pools and falls. The crevices between the water-worn stones support a wide variety of plants, including primulas, astilbes, impressively large dwarf conifers, Japanese maples and an exceptional collection of hardy ferns, examples of the grey and maroon *Athyrium nipponicum* 'Pictum', *Dryopteris erythrosora* and *Adiantum venustum* among them. A good herbaceous border beside the rock garden gives colour throughout the season and there is a rose garden beyond the gates, with a yew avenue setting off shrub roses, hydrangeas, eucryphias and other flowering shrubs.

Skenfrith MONMOUTHSHIRE

6 miles north-west of Monmouth, 12 miles north-east of Abergavenny, on north side of the B4521 Ross road [442 E4]

The remains of some 80 castles scattered across South Wales recall the drawn-out conflict between the Welsh and the English following the Norman Conquest. The little early thirteenth-century fortress of Skenfrith, set on low ground by the River Monnow, is one of the more important survivals, part of a trio (with White Castle to the south and Grosmont to the north) protecting a natural routeway into Wales. Washed by the river on one side, the castle is protected by a wide moat – now a dry ditch – on the other three. Above these defences rise the remains of the massive curtain wall, best preserved along the river, ruined circular towers, from which attackers could be subjected to deadly raking fire, projecting boldly from the four corners. A large round keep in the style of those being built by the French king at this period rises 12 metres (40 feet) from the centre of the enclosed court, constructed on a mound which probably formed part of a more primitive fortress established here in the decades after the Conquest.

Skenfrith is the work of Hubert de Burgh, Earl of Kent, who was granted the 'Three Castles' by King John and may have been influenced in his design by what he had seen while imprisoned in France. Like the builder of Bodiam away to the east (*see* p.54) two centuries later, the Earl of Kent was concerned with acquiring a nobleman's residence as well as a castle, the foundations and lower walls of his hall range still to be seen against the west curtain wall. Little changed since it was built, Skenfrith is a splendid example of the castles which foreshadowed the formidable symmetry of Edward I's great fortresses.

Smallhythe Place KENT

At Smallhythe, 2 miles south of Tenterden, on east side of the Rye road [443 K6]

This modest half-timbered sixteenth-century farmhouse belonged to the legendary actress Dame Ellen Terry for nearly 30 years, from 1899 until her death here on 21 July 1928. Appropriately, she first saw Smallhythe in the company of Henry Irving, the manager of the Lyceum Theatre in London's Covent Garden, with whom she created a famous theatrical partnership that lasted for 24 years.

Her attractive house stands at one end of the straggling hamlet, with a steep, red-tiled roof and sturdy brick chimneys outlined against the Kentish marshes on all sides. With the sea 10 miles away as the crow flies and the once sizeable stream bordering the garden shrunk to a narrow ditch, it is difficult to believe that the farm was formerly Port House to a thriving shipyard, catering for a procession of boats unloading at the wharves along the creek. A duckweed-covered pool marks the site of the repair dock used for some 400 years until the seventeenth century.

The house is now preserved as a theatrical museum, full of mementoes of Ellen Terry's long and eventful life and of the world in which she moved. In the large beamed kitchen which she used as a dining room, with traditional wheel-back chairs ranged round the walls, a refectory table in the middle of the warm red-brick floor and a high-backed settle by the fire, two walls are devoted to David Garrick and Sarah Siddons. Other exhibits connected with

famous names from the past include an affectionate message from Sarah Bernhardt – '*Merci*, my dearling' – written with a flourish on the cover of a dressing-table, Sir Arthur Sullivan's monocle, with his autograph on the glass, a chain worn by Fanny Kemble and a visiting card from Alexandre Dumas, whose *La dame aux camélias* inspired Verdi's *La Traviata*. A letter in Oscar Wilde's languorous scrawl in an adjoining room begs Ellen Terry to accept 'the first copy of my first play', adding 'perhaps some day I shall be fortunate to write something worthy of your playing'. Here, too, is her make-up box; a sponge, a mirror and a large swatch of grey hair are prominent among the notably sparse contents, which seem barely adequate for someone of Terry's stature.

Upstairs there are displays of the lavish silk and velvet costumes which Irving created for Terry, much criticised for their extravagance, including the famous moss-green beetle-wing dress she wore as Lady Macbeth in 1888. The more private face of the great actress is revealed in her simple, low-ceilinged bedroom, still as she left it, with brightly patterned rugs on the bare boards of the floor, rotund pottery pigs on the mantelpiece and a view out over the marshes from the casement windows. Kate Hastings's pastel portraits of Terry's mother and of her two children, Edith and Edward Gordon Craig, offspring of her liaison with the architect and theatrical designer Edward Godwin, hang above the bed with its theatrical curved Empire ends. The wooden crucifix Gordon Craig made for his mother stands on the bedside table, next to a worn copy of the Globe Shakespeare annotated in her distinctively generous hand. Something of the great actress's integrity and resolution also emerges in a much-read edition of Robert Louis Stevenson's 'Christmas Sermon', one of the many underlined passages exhorting 'If your morals make you dreary, depend upon it they are wrong.'

Below left: Half-timbered Smallhythe Place, the 16th-century farmhouse which the actress Ellen Terry bought in 1899 as a retreat and to which she eventually retired. The photograph (below right) shows her in her twenties, during the period she was living with Edward Godwin.

Snowshill Manor GLOUCESTERSHIRE

3 miles south-west of Broadway, 4 miles west of junction of the A44 and the A424 [443 G3]

Above: Javanese masks collected by the eccentric Charles Paget Wade at Snowshill. Wade lived in a cottage next to the main house, sleeping in a cupboard bed in the upstairs room (below).

The old lady who showed her grandson the family treasures hidden away in her Cantonese cabinet on Sunday afternoons could not have known that this would inspire one of the most extraordinary collections ever assembled by one person. Charles Wade, born in 1883, was clearly an unusual little boy and he grew up to be a most exceptional man. A talented artist, craftsman and professional architect, once he had inherited the family sugar estates in the West Indies he devoted his life to restoring the Cotswold manor house he bought in 1919 and to amassing the wide-ranging exhibits now displayed here.

Snowshill is an L-shaped building of warm Cotswold stone, with a warren of rooms on different levels leading off one another. The Tudor hall house of *c*.1500 at its heart, still evident in the huge fireplace on the ground floor and in two ceilings upstairs, was substantially rebuilt in about 1600 and altered again in the early eighteenth century, when the oddly attractive south front was added. Here Georgian sash windows on the left side of the pedimented main entrance contrast with mullioned and transomed casements to the right, giving the house a rakish air.

Every inch from ground floor to attics is devoted to Charles Wade's acquisitions, most of the rooms christened

with bizarre names such as Dragon, Meridian, Top Gallant and Seraphim. Mr Wade did not set out to accumulate things because they were rare or valuable, but saw his pieces primarily as records of vanished handicrafts. As a result, the Snowshill collection is unique, displaying an unclassifiable range of everyday objects, from tools used in spinning, weaving and lacemaking to baby minders (one for use on board ship), prams, early bicycles, exquisite bone carvings made by French prisoners of war, eighteenth-century medicine chests cunningly contrived to carry a mass of little bottles and gaily painted model farm wagons. One room is devoted to pieces connected with the sea, such as compasses, telescopes and ship models, another to musical instruments, arranged as a playerless orchestra, and yet another (his Seventh Heaven) to many of the toys Mr Wade had as a child. Perhaps the most remarkable spectacle is in the Green Room, where suits of Japanese Samurai armour topped with ferocious masks threaten visitors in a theatrically staged display. A sense of order everywhere shows that this is no random, magpie collection but a reflection of a serious purpose.

The steeply sloping terraced garden was largely designed by Wade's friend, M.H. Baillie Scott, a fellow architect with whom he had worked when employed by Raymond Unwin in London before the First World War, but Wade altered and adapted the original structure. It is laid out as a series of interconnecting but separate garden rooms, with arches and steps leading from one to another and with roses and other climbing plants trailing over the dividing walls. Flagged paths, carefully contrived vistas down and across the slope, many features and centres of interest and Wade's old-fashioned planting schemes reflect the influence of the Arts and Crafts movement, with its preference for cottage-garden styles. A long path bordered with pillars of clipped Irish yew leads past the grassy Armillary Court, dominated by a tall sundial, to the medieval dovecote, where birds roosting on the steeply pitched roof stand out brilliantly white against the stone flags. A Venetian well-head at one end of a lower terrace balances the small water-lily pool at the other, with colour from a bracelet of crowded borders.

This garden is ideally suited to the Cotswold house it sets off, the blue, mauve and purple of delphiniums, larkspur and lavender blending beautifully with the honey-coloured stone. Garden seats, tubs and other woodwork are also blue, painted the dark shade with a hint of turquoise which Charles Wade used as a foil to grass and foliage. And always there is the backdrop of a far wooded hillside across the valley.

Only metres from the manor house is the little cottage where Charles Wade lived without electricity and with a fireplace with two bread ovens as the only means of heating and cooking, the walls and even the ceiling of his kitchen/living room covered with a multitude of useful objects, from bowls and tankards to farm tools. Seeing these spartan conditions and the workshop where he spent so many happy hours, it is easy to believe, as Queen Mary said after visiting Snowshill in 1937, that the most notable part of the collection was Mr Wade himself.

Souter Lighthouse TYNE AND WEAR

2½ miles south of South Shields, on A183 [445 J3]

Just south of the Tyne estuary, overlooking a stretch of unspoilt limestone coastline owned by the Trust (*see* The Leas, p.273), is a prominent cliff-top lighthouse, its 23-metre (76-foot) tower painted in bold red and white stripes. Built in 1870, it was the first lighthouse to be powered by an alternating electric current and could be seen from some 19 miles out to sea. A focal point on a stretch of open grassy cliff-top, the lighthouse dominates a row of nineteenth-century coastguard cottages and other ancillary buildings. A nearby array of limekilns is a reminder of former quarrying along these cliffs, and there was once a colliery village here too.

South Cornish Coast

[442 A8–C7]

A few miles south of Land's End, St Levan church, vicarage and farm lie back from the coast in a sheltered valley. Seawards, the headland of Pedn-mên-an-mere commands the view across the bay to the superb headland of Treryn Dinas, owned by the Trust since 1933. As the sun goes down in the west, or as the water sparkles in the moonlight, the view is unforgettable. A steep path descends to Porthcurno, one of Cornwall's finest beaches, and also a place of significance in the history of communications. Given to the Trust by Cable & Wireless plc in 1994, it was the landing point for cables linking Britain to the world telegraph network. More than 2 miles of Trust coastline runs on from here past Pedn-vounder Beach (pronounced Pedneyfunder) beneath Treen Cliff to the east, where a steep path gives access to a curving strand of the finest sand. The bathing is good if the sea is calm, but care should be taken of the sand bar which builds up offshore

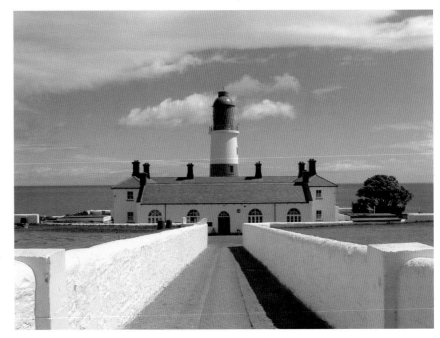

in some seasons and can cause currents.

The granite here is in blocks, cube piled on cube, for all the world like a child's bricks. Arrows painted on the rocks lead the way to the Logan Rock (the Cornish verb *log* means 'to heave', 'to move'; the name of the rock is pronounced 'loggan'). There were formerly many such in Cornwall, formed by weathering over an immensely long period, and this celebrated specimen has been visited by tourists since the eighteenth century. It is said to weigh 62 tons and to have rocked easily before 1824 when Lieutenant Goldsmith, nephew of the poet, landed with a party of sailors and with a good deal of effort and ingenuity succeeded in dislodging it. A fine old row ensued. Petitions were dispatched to the Admiralty and the Lords Commissioners sent a peremptory order to Goldsmith to replace the rock. This needed much greater effort, and spars, cables and sheaves were sent from Devonport Dockyard at Goldsmith's expense. At last all was made ready and with a long, strong heave the rock was reset. Half the county attended the occasion and Goldsmith became a hero.

Beyond Treryn the path leads across Cribba Head and steeply down to Penberth, the most perfect of Cornish fishing coves. The Trust owns most of the valley behind the cove and its policy is to let the little granite cottages to those who earn their living here, fishing and growing violets and narcissi for the early markets, though this latter trade has largely ceased due to competition from flowers

Souter Lighthouse was built in 1870 to warn shipping away from the rocks along the north-east coast, which had claimed more and more vessels as coastal traffic steadily increased in the 19th century.

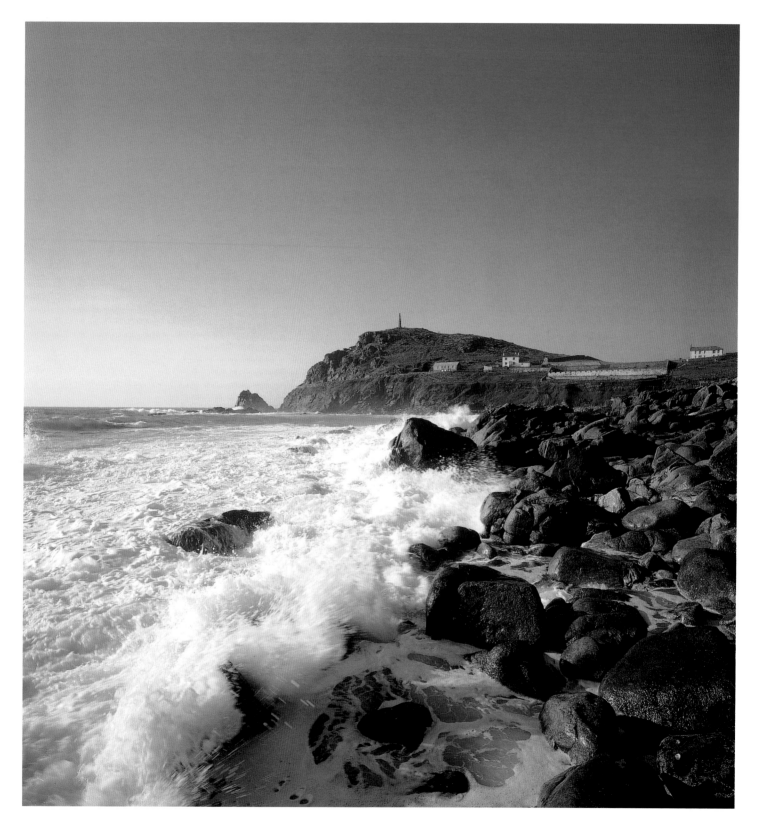

grown under glass. The fishermen have formed a co-operative society and fishing flourishes. Crab and lobster pots are no longer made from withies grown in the valley, for they last for only two seasons whereas the modern steel and plastic pots last for eight or ten. The boats are small, up to 5 metres (16 feet), because of the limited space available for pulling up clear of high water. This is an inshore fishery, boats going 5 or 6 miles out to sea, from St Michael's Mount to the Wolf Rock 12 miles to the south-west, or sometimes round Land's End to the Brisons, a group of rocks off Cape Cornwall. Fish are caught by hand-lining, three-quarters of the catch being mackerel, with some pollack and colefish. The shell fishery is for lobster and crab and high prices are given by buyers from France. In 2000, Tregiffian Cliff, a half mile stretch of the rugged and lonely coast between Penberth and Lamorna, was given to the Trust by David Cornwell, better known as the thriller-writer John le Carré. An important addition to the Trust's limited holdings on the south coast of Penwith, Tregiffian Cliff includes the deep gash of Zawn Gamper and the rocky headland of Tater-du, where Cornwall's newest lighthouse, constructed in response to the foundering of a Spanish coaster on Boscawen Point nearby, was built in 1965.

St Michael's Mount (*see* p.328), even more beautiful than its French namesake, presides grandly over Mount's Bay. To the west the view from the island looks over the expanse of Penzance, but to the east it is closed by Cudden Point, a miniature version of Gurnard's Head in shape (*see* p.271), with the low, open fields of Trenow in the foreground. Five miles to the east there is Trust land on either side of the privately owned Rinsey Head. Lesceave Cliff, west of the headland, seals off the scattered development of Praa Sands, a wilderness of caravans, chalets and bungalows where the Trust preserves a patch of scrub above the beach. To the east Rinsey Cliff surrounds a delightful cove and sets off the roofless engine house and stack of Wheal Prosper (*see* p.112), a copper-mining venture which closed in about 1860. Beyond Rinsey lies the bold Trewavas Head, only part of which the Trust owns, and the coast is also privately owned from there to Porthleven, once busy with shipbuilding and fishing, dying since the 1950s but now reactivated by a purchaser of the harbour and shipyard who has injected fresh capital and new ideas.

The 647.5-hectare (1,600-acre) Penrose estate, the largest gift ever made to the Trust in Cornwall, stretches for 6 miles south-east to Gunwalloe. The freshwater lake of the Loe (from *logh*, the Cornish word for a pool) runs inland for over a mile, cut off from the sea by the great shingle beach of Loe Bar. Carminowe Creek forms a branch of the lake to the east. The wooded banks are utterly peaceful and the Trust owns the whole of the surrounding landscape. It was a far-sighted condition of this princely gift that cars should be kept well away and the lake should remain free of boats and waterskiers. So the Trust has made a number of small car parks set back from the water, linked by a network of footpaths which provide delightful walks. Cliffs, shingle beach, sea and freshwater, with woodland, reed marsh and farmland, make up an unforgettable whole.

The Loe was not originally a lake but the estuary of the River Cober, with the port of Helston at its head, but by the thirteenth century the shingle bar had formed, cutting the town off from the sea. The shingle is nearly all of flint and where it comes from is an unsolved mystery, possibly a seabed deposit offshore. Extensive tin and copper mines on the high ground above Helston drained into the Cober Valley, bringing down vast quantities of silt which have gradually filled the upper end of the lake to form Loe Marsh, a large area of willow and alder, with reeds lower down, reminiscent of a tropical mangrove swamp. After heavy rain the water level rises rapidly, often flooding the lower parts of Helston in the past. The mayor of the town then paid three halfpence to the lord of the manor of Penrose, who allowed a channel to be cut through the bar, which none the less soon closed again. The latest channel had to be cut in 1984 and it remains to be seen whether the improvements will avoid future flooding.

The Loe is probably the most important place in Cornwall for wintering wildfowl. Widgeon, teal, mallard, shoveller, pochard, tufted duck and coot appear each year, while a few mallard, coot, moorhen and mute swans nest here. Herons and cormorants can always be seen and rarer birds, particularly migrants in season, stay for a few days. In high summer the lake sometimes suffers from the phenomenon known as eutrophication. An algal bloom turns the surface of the water green and de-oxygenates it, which is harmful to the fish and other creatures living in the lake. The bloom has become worse with the use of modern fertilisers on the land draining into the pool, not to speak of sewage effluent seeping into the lake from Helston and the large naval aerodrome at Culdrose. The recently formed Loe Pool Forum is working to improve the water quality and taking positive steps to reduce the level of pollutants.

The woods are largely mixed hardwoods, with Monterey cypress and Monterey pine near the sea. Beside the drive at Bar Lodge, at the north end of the bar, is a

Opposite: The rocky headland of Cape Cornwall is on the most exposed and windswept stretch of the Cornish coast, open to the full force of Atlantic gales and seas.

colony of an exotic plant from Chile, a member of the pineapple family, *Fascicularia pitcairniifolia*, with long spiky leaves, red at the base, and blue flowers. On the cliff below the lodge flourishes the Hottentot fig, *Carpobrotus edulis*, with brightly coloured flowers from May to August.

South of Loe Bar the beach, and most of the cliff, belongs to the Trust as far as Gunwalloe Fishing Cove. The rusting winches above the cove came from ships wrecked on this coast and were used by local fishermen to haul their boats clear of the surf. From the cove a lane leads the weary walker to refreshment at the Halzephron Inn nearby. After a short gap the Trust's land starts at Halsferran Cove and runs over the high Halzephron Cliff to Dollar Cove, then past the church to Gunwalloe Church Cove.

For some years Church Cove was degraded, visually and environmentally, by parking on the beach and dunes. The Trust had long owned Gunwalloe Towans east of the stream but could not control what happened to the west. The gift of the Penrose estate in 1974 brought the cove into one ownership and it became possible to make a car park behind Winnianton Farm. Some people protested at losing what they looked upon as a right to park on the beach and dunes; others applauded the Trust's initiative. There were some lively scenes. The benefit has been incontestable; visitors can now sit in comfort round the cove clear of cars.

The church of St Winwaloe, tucked under the cliff beside the beach, is sited on the very edge of its parish because – from about the sixth century – there was an important settlement here which later became a royal manor. The Cornish section of the Domesday Book begins 'the King holds Winneton'. The Towans were bought by the Trust in 1956 to avert the very real threat of development as a major caravan site. The golf club, started in 1890, was in financial difficulties and the course was to be sold. The Trust was able to raise the funds, buy the land, let it for grazing for some years, and then lease it to a reconstituted golf club for this very suitable use.

Beyond the Towans, Poldhu Cove, with fine hard sand and safe bathing, is dominated by the massive bulk of the former Poldhu Hotel, built in 1899 and now a residential home. When the railway arrived at Helston a series of large hotels was built round the Lizard coast, served by the Great Western Railway's motor-bus service, a trailblazer in its day. South of the hotel the monument at the cliff edge commemorates Guglielmo Marconi, who in 1901 received here the first transatlantic wireless message, sent to him from Newfoundland. In 1923 he successfully tested his short-wave beam system which revolutionised long-distance communication. Marconi came here because the geology of the Lizard peninsula provides a stable base for wireless reception. It is no coincidence that at Goonhilly Downs, 3 miles to the south-east, there now stand the great saucers of the Satellite Earth Station, beaming messages round the world day and night.

Mullion Cove is a picture-postcard place, and deserves its fame, but the once beautiful approach leading down to it has been much spoilt in recent years by bungalows and caravans. The harbour walls, built in 1893–5 by Lord Robartes of Lanhydrock (*see* p.219) to provide shelter for

Evening serenity at Lizard Point, with the buildings of the lighthouse set against the sky. The Trust's holdings of cliff and farmland on this dramatic, geologically complex coast include the most southerly part of mainland Britain.

the fishermen's boats in the open cove, are made of local greenstone, a basalt-like rock of great hardness which strikes fire with flint. The picturesque Winch House at the head of the slipway is older, built for the capstan used to haul boats clear of the sea before the harbour was constructed, and now housing a modern motor winch. This coast faces directly into the Atlantic gales and the Trust has to spend substantial sums in keeping the quays in repair. At low water a tunnel dries out to lead through the cliff to a secluded sandy beach to the south.

Predannack Cliff runs with the three small farms of Predannack Wollas, two of which belong to the Trust. The Cornish suffix *wollas* means lower and is always found, as here, in conjunction with the suffix *wartha*, meaning higher. This is a typical medieval farming settlement, the three farms huddled together with their own enclosed fields nearby, each grazing the unenclosed moorland and cliff 'in common'. However, no farmer can today afford a boy to look after grazing animals and the common grazing had become neglected, overgrown with scrub which smothered the cliff flowers. The Trust has therefore erected unobtrusive fencing to enable grazing to start again. The rarer flora is rapidly recovering: hairy bird's-foot trefoil, prostrate dyer's greenweed and fringed rupturewort, with sheets of blue-flowered squill in spring.

Heading eastwards, the Trust unusually owns half of Predannack airfield, the other half being owned by the Ministry of Defence. From 1939–45 Spitfires and Hurricanes were based here and the airfield is now used for training pilots from the naval air station at Culdrose. The reason for the Trust's acquisition is that some of the best areas of the unique Lizard heath grow within the perimeter fence.

Two miles to the south lies Kynance Cove, which has long been a place of pilgrimage. The hard yellow sand, the crystal-clear water, the rocky islets offshore and the mottled brown, red and green serpentine rock made Kynance a Victorian watercolourist's dream. Until 1987 the surroundings were marred by a large car park with commercial buildings on the skyline; these have since been acquired by the Trust, eyesores removed and the landscape restored. The Trust also owns the historic café in the cove. Even more popular as a tourist attraction is Lizard Point, the two-pronged prow of the peninsula, where the Trust now owns the furthest tip, the most southerly point of mainland Britain. There has been remedial work here too, with half a mile of dry-stone wall, known in Cornwall as a hedge, built along the access route. The Trust restored the former Polbrean Hotel, in a prominent position

alongside the Lizard lighthouse, and it is now run as a youth hostel by the YHA. The coastal footpath which links all these holdings runs on past the former Lloyd's Signal Station, on Bass Point, and north up the Lizard's eastern flank. Here is Landewednack Church Cove, with an abandoned and beautiful cliff-edge quarry to the north and, half a mile beyond, Inglewidden, with the spectacular collapsed cave known as the Devil's Frying Pan.

The steep slope leading down to Cadgwith Cove is covered with a dwarf wood of wind-clipped elms, apparently unique in Britain for this species. Limewashed cottages cluster round the beach, some of them still thatched, and a small community of fishermen work from the cove, mainly in the shellfish fishery. On the headland to the north is a little stone building, formerly the coastguard's watch-house, and from here there is a lovely cliff walk, all on the Trust's land, past Kildown Cove and Enys Head down to Carleon Cove. The shingle on the beach is of many colours, much of it sea-washed pebbles of serpentine, and the curved capstan house and three-storey warehouse which now stand so picturesquely above the beach are all that remains of the substantial works of the Lizard Serpentine Company (1853–93), where machinery driven by waterpower cut and polished objects made of this colourful rock: fonts and pulpits, tombstones, chimneypieces, urns and ornaments, even complete shop

Top: A shingle bar separates the fresh-water lake of Loe Pool from the sea. The largest natural lake in Cornwall, it is an important habitat for many kinds of water birds, including the tufted duck, red-throated diver and red-necked grebe.

Above: Inglewidden, south of Cadgwith, is one of many delightful places on the Lizard peninsula.

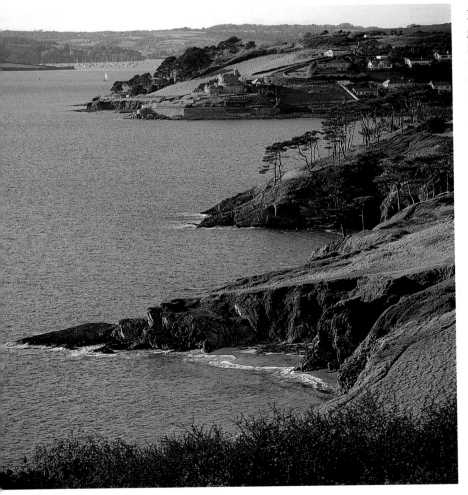

fronts. A few miles beyond, the Trust owns Black Head and a stretch of coastal farmland and cliff running south from the rocky promontory of Chynhalls Point

The estuary of the Helford river has suffered from development above Helford Passage and particularly at Port Navas, both on the north bank, but the greater part of it is beautiful to a degree, the upper reaches wooded, remote, peaceful, a place to drift in a boat with only the occasional dip of one's oars. On the south bank, where it broadens into Falmouth Bay, the Trust now owns the low promontory of Nare Point. Of historic interest as a decoy site in the Second World War, when a display of lights and other simulations were designed to draw bombers away from Falmouth and its docks, the point also carries the stark concrete remains of a 1950s structure used to track torpedoes launched by aircraft from RNAS Culdrose. The Trust owns a short length of the cliff running west from here and woodland around the tapering inlet of

Gillan Creek. About 2 miles upstream is Helford village and beyond it the sheltered Penarvon Cove, cradled by low wooded cliffs, almost like a scene from Treasure Island. Here the Trust owns 16 hectares (40 acres) and the cottages in the valley and on the bluff opposite Helford Passage. Half a mile or so further west is the entrance to Frenchman's Creek, a wooded inlet leading south from the estuary and becoming ever narrower until the tree branches meet overhead. Merthen Wood, on the north shore, a great bank of wind-trimmed oak coppice, is privately owned, but opposite lie the 20 hectares (50 acres) of the Trust's Tremayne Wood, surrounding the boathouse and quay which served Trelowarren, a romantic Tudor house hidden away in a wooded valley 2 miles to the south. The wood is of beech, ash, oak and sweet chestnut, with a good ground flora in the leaf mould below, in early spring carpeted with wood anemones, the flowers varying from purest white to a clear Cambridge blue.

On the north bank of the estuary is the hamlet of Durgan, where the Trust owns half the cottages and the garden of Glendurgan (see p.162) in the valley rising above it. Early traders from the Mediterranean called here for tin which was exported from Cornwall long before the arrival of the Romans. There is still some fishing, but Durgan's chief function today is as a sheltered base for the fleet of small boats which ride at their multi-coloured buoys, the wooded cliffs rising above them. The best approach is by water, for the non-resident visitor has to park his car half a mile before reaching the hamlet.

Bosloe lies to the east, the substantial and seemly house built as a rich man's holiday retreat in 1880, and now divided into three holiday houses by the Trust. With it runs farmland sloping down to the water's edge and joining Durgan with the Carwinion Valley, then a short privately owned gap before the bold headland of Mawnan Shear at the estuary's mouth. This formed part of the glebe of the vicar of Mawnan whose church tower peers out of the trees at the top of the cliff, with Parson's Beach beneath. From the headland the views over the estuary to Nare Point, and 3 miles up it to Merthen Wood, remain in the memory. Rosemullion Head juts eastward as Falmouth Bay sweeps in towards the Helford river. The Trust owns the coast on both sides of the headland for more than a mile, with little coves and nearby rocks which are good for bathing.

The grandest harbour in the English Channel, Falmouth has a long history. The newer town, behind the big beach of Gyllyngvase, has a proper seafront. Pendennis Castle, on the headland above it, built by Henry VIII, guards the entrance to the old town inside the estuary.

Pendennis was the last fortress, but for Raglan, to hold out for King Charles in the Civil War, and the parish church is dedicated to King Charles the Martyr. As well as the old quays and warehouses there is a modern ship-repair yard with an immense dry dock, big enough to take supertankers. The three parts of the town – the seaside resort, the old port, the ship-repair yard – hang together and make a walk through the streets and alleys in the higher part of old Falmouth an exciting experience, with views of all these activities over the chimneypots, and the broad sweep of the great estuary running up to the deep water of the Carrick Roads at its head. Overlooking the Roads, where the River Fal opens into its estuary, is the dignified façade of Trelissick House, standing high above the water and looking down over its park the full length of the harbour and out to sea. A lovely circular walk leads from the garden (see p.398) through the waterside woods to King Harry Ferry, the quiet Lamouth Creek beyond it, and then back through further woodland and park.

In contrast to the settled western bank of the estuary, the eastern shore is unspoilt and undeveloped. Part of the remote Roseland peninsula, it offers a beautiful coastline of cliffs, creeks and headlands backed by a tranquil patchwork of fields and woodland. The Trust owns nearly 4 miles of this eastern shore between Turnaware Point, opposite Trelissick, and St Anthony Head at the furthest point of the peninsula. The headland of Turnaware Point, a pleasant place for picnics and blackberrying with a safe beach, was the first piece to be acquired, coming to the Trust in 1955 as part of the Trelissick estate. South of here, the most recent addition to the Trust's holdings, bought in 1999 with the aid of a substantial bequest, is Messack Farm, which adds 77.5 hectares (191 acres) of farmland, wooded clefts, little valleys and more than a mile of shoreline running down to St Just. South again, the Trust owns virtually all the farmland between St Just and St Mawes, with a long clear stretch of cliff and a waterside walk between the two villages. This beautiful coastline is crossed by miles of paths and from several points there are breathtaking views over the Fal and far up the estuary. Always the water is alive with the busy traffic of the river: small cargo boats bound for Truro, river trips to and from Falmouth, fishermen and dinghy sailors and, from October to March, the stoutly built oyster boats which here continue the only fishery where no boats with engines are allowed, as decreed by Truro Corporation. Whenever the weather is favourable in the winter months the 'working boats' can be seen beating up and down the estuary trawling the oysters from the bottom.

At the very tip of the peninsula is St Anthony Head, protecting Falmouth from the east. The lighthouse at its foot shines a white beam to mark the entrance to the harbour, the light flashing through a red sector to warn of the dangerous Manacle Rocks across the bay. The headland was fortified at least from the year of Trafalgar in 1805 and further strengthened in 1853 and 1885. It continued to be manned by a coastal artillery unit until 1957. By that time not only had it been cut off by a high iron fence but it was covered in Nissen huts and with gun and searchlight positions erected during the Second World War. With generous help from local people, the Trust was able to buy the land, remove the concrete and the hutments (though the underground magazine remains) and encourage the natural vegetation to recover, a major piece of landscape restoration. From here there are magnificent views over Falmouth Bay and much of this part of Cornwall, with a topograph to name the places one can see.

From Porth, at the peninsula's north end, where there are hidden car parks, a circular walk runs for 3½ miles round the north end of the parish, and this can be doubled in length by making an extra circuit on the public path round the privately owned farm of Place Barton. The paths run partly on the cliff-top, partly along the creek sides, partly through woodland, a wonderfully varied walk with water and boats always in sight, and seabirds and estuary birds to be seen. Porthbeor and Towan beaches on the sea coast provide good bathing with sand, sun and shelter. It is hard to imagine now how the latter beach, a curving strand with fields sloping gently down to the sand, was disfigured by up to 150 summer caravans before the Trust acquired the land and brought this use to an end.

To the north of St Anthony much of the coast of this large bay, 3 miles across but 6 miles as the shore runs, belongs to the Trust. The sandy beach of Porthcurnick is sheltered by the low green headland of Pednvadan. It was bought because the land behind the beach had become over-commercialised and was a mess. Caravans, huts and cars were scattered higgledy-piggledy and could be seen for miles. Removal of this clutter, realignment of fences and planting of trees showed that the landscape was quite easily restored, given initiative and local support.

Treluggan Cliff continues the walk northwards, covered with blackthorn, bracken, furze and willow, good cover for small birds, with little sandy coves on the rocky foreshore below and the Trust's farmland above running back to the coast road. The beach at Pendower is popular with people from Truro, Cornwall's county town. Sand dunes behind the beach screen the car park and the few buildings, and on a hot day the Trust's path up the wooded Pendower Valley behind the beach gives a shady walk.

The Trust owns the farmland behind the coast for the next few miles and has thus been able to remove many eyesores which had accrued there. Once the ugly buildings and overhead wires had gone it is hard to imagine how they got there in the first place, for to allow such things now would cause an outcry. The Trust's long campaign to preserve the coast has caused a radical change in public opinion on these matters over the last 40 years.

Nare Head is one of Cornwall's great headlands and can be reached either by the coast path, from east or west, or by car as far as the car park hidden in an old quarry on the spine of the headland. The road there leads past the spreading new buildings of Penare Farm, which sit in a hollow in what is now a substantial holding made up from five small (and now uneconomic) farms. The homestead provides an example of how large-scale farming can be made to fit into a beautiful landscape without harming it.

The contrast between this south coast of Cornwall and the more exposed north coast is apparent. The views from the coast inland show the country to be prosperous and smiling, very different from the barer, bleaker land a comparatively few miles away. The panoramas over Gerrans Bay to the west, and the even larger Veryan Bay to the east, take in a series of small headlands, cliffs and beaches, the slopes all covered with the typical shrub cover of this coast, hawthorn, blackthorn, bramble, willow, bracken, ivy and good cliff flowers where there are more open patches. Half a mile off Nare Head the Gull Rock rises steeply out of the sea, the rocky island a nesting place for hundreds of seabirds, given by a former member of the Trust's staff to complete its ownership here.

The Trust's land runs most of the way to the fishing hamlet of Portloe, its harbour a narrow inlet in the cliffs, but the coast is privately owned for 3 miles thereafter, most of it by the Caerhays estate, presided over by a picturesque castle, designed by the architect John Nash in 1808, its towers and turrets backed by a steep wooded slope where there is a famous shrub garden.

The east side of Veryan Bay is closed by the unmistakable profile of the Dodman, its mighty Roman nose standing out bold and proud. The visitor can drive to the car park in the hamlet of Penare, which lies in a hollow on the Dodman's spine, but the better approach is along the coast. From Porthluney Cove, below Caerhays Castle, the path runs past the Trust's remote Lambsowden Cove and the privately owned Greeb Point to Hemmick Beach. Here are pebbles of many different colours, worn smooth by the action of the waves. The rock is 'mineralised' with veins of white, pink, green and brown, and these veins give each pebble its own character. A rock arch leads west to the smaller Percunning Cove. To the east a path made by the Trust climbs steeply up to the Dodman, the Point itself a promontory fort cut off by the deep ditch known as the Balk. The high granite cross on the summit was erected in 1896 by a rector of Caerhays to act as a mark for fishermen and as a reminder of the all-seeing eye of Providence. When the work was finished the rector consecrated it and spent the night at its foot. Some way back from the cross is a tiny watch-house for the coastguard, apparently the only survivor of features that were common in the early nineteenth-century, in the great days of sail, when every yard of the coast was patrolled twice daily, originally in an attempt to stop smuggling and later as a safety measure, for there is scarcely a mile of these coasts that has not had its wreck. There have been many wrecks on the Dodman itself; the currents are notorious and vessels which overran Falmouth at night in dirty weather have ended their days here. In 1897 the destroyers *Thresher* and *Lynx* went ashore in thick fog, and in 1957 the pleasure boat *Darlwin*, returning from Fowey to Falmouth with a full load of holiday visitors, sank with all on board.

East of the Dodman the gently curving sweep of Vault Beach leads out to Lamledra where the Trust owns most of the farm and the headland of Maenease Point. The path down to the beach is easy and the fine gravel of which it is composed is as pleasant as sand. Round Maenease the cliffs run down to Gorran Haven. The harbour, beach, church and old village are delightful.

St Austell Bay, 4 miles across, is the seaward face of Cornwall's only large industry, the production of china clay, based on the granite ridge rising to over 305 metres (1,000 feet) at Hensbarrow behind the town of St Austell. From here clay is dug, by computer-controlled water cannon, settled out, purified, dried and exported all over the world, a very large industry but nowadays almost wholly automated and employing far fewer people than in the past. The clay is exported in deepwater ships, up to 15,000 tons in size, from the port of Fowey, in shallow draught coasters from Par, the industry's own port in the north-eastern corner of the bay, but no longer from the early nineteenth-century port at Charlestown, in the north-western corner of the bay.

On either side of this developed coast, however, two great headlands run southward to contain the bay to east and west; on the west side Black Head, on the east The Gribbin, both backed by substantial agricultural estates. In the 1960s the three hereditary owners, with great foresight, agreed to a scheme proposed by the Trust to keep these long arms of St Austell Bay inviolate. As a result the Trust now owns the headlands on each side of the bay, and holds protective covenants over 6 miles of adjoining farmland and cliff. These protect the coast from Gamas Point, near Pentewan, round Black Head to include the west side of St Austell Bay, and, on the east side, from Polkerris round The Gribbin to Polridmouth on its east flank. Thanks to three people, St Austell Bay can continue in its invaluable commercial use while still retaining its beauty.

In misty weather The Gribbin's 79-metre (260-foot) snout can be confused with the Dodman, 9 miles to the south-west. For this reason it carries a 'day mark', a slender 24.5-metre (80-foot) stone tower erected by Trinity House in 1832 and now owned by the Trust. The three seaward faces of the tower are painted in broad red and white stripes, the effect more handsome than bizarre. On either side crouch wind-pruned plantations of sycamore, ilex, beech and *Rhododendron ponticum*. They survive tenaciously in the teeth of winter gales. On the western cliff is probably the one station in Cornwall of the sea buckthorn, *Hippophaë rhamnoides*, a grey-leaved prickly shrub with bright orange berries in autumn. Below the cliff on the eastern side there are small sandy coves, the preserve of those who scramble there across the rocks beneath.

More easily accessible is Polridmouth (called Pridmouth), a beautiful beach surrounded by the woods of Menabilly, the seat of the Rashleigh family since the sixteenth century. Pridmouth is reached by paths from Coombe to the east, or from Menabilly Barton to the west. Menabilly appears as Manderley in Daphne du Maurier's *Rebecca* (1938) which begins 'Last night I dreamt I went to Manderley again', and in which the woods, the beach and the coast are faithfully recorded. The path from the beach leads up through a little wood, along the cliff-top fields and down again after a mile to Coombe Haven, on Trust land all the way. The farm at the valley head takes its name from the place and was once a dower house of the Rashleighs. Beyond Coombe Haven is a former golf course, now grazed by sheep, and the Trust's woodland behind St Catherine's Point at the entrance to Fowey. There are exciting views up the harbour, always busy with small boats, and several times a day the deep blast of a siren can be heard heralding a large ship arriving with a pilot to creep up the harbour to the jetties upstream and load china clay destined for ports all over the world.

The curious object surrounded by iron railings on top of St Catherine's Point is the mausoleum erected in 1867 by William Rashleigh of Menabilly in honour of himself and his family. Above the harbour mouth is St Catherine's Castle, one of the many coastal forts built by Henry VIII

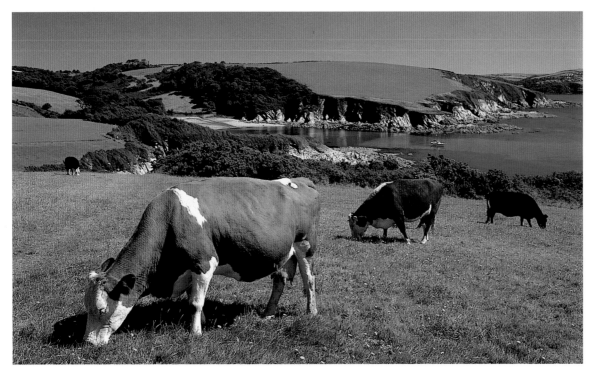

Between the deep bite of St Austell Bay and the long inlet of the River Fowey is the substantial promontory of Gribbin Head, part of some 5 miles of unspoilt coast protected by the Trust.

to protect the growing shipping trade at the dawning of the first Elizabethan age. Fowey has a long and stirring history as a seaport, and in the French wars of the fourteenth and fifteenth centuries its ships were in the van of the English fleet.

Fowey is closely associated with 'Q' (Sir Arthur Quiller-Couch), who died in 1944 and is commemorated by a great monolith of granite on Penleath Point where the beautiful creek of Pont Pill branches off east of the main estuary. Almost all this side of the harbour is owned by the Trust. Hall Walk, below the ancient vehicular ferry at Bodinnick, is celebrated for an incident in the Civil War when Charles I narrowly missed decapitation by a Parliamentary cannon ball lobbed across the water from Fowey.

The Walk was the promenade of the ancient house of Hall behind the cliffs, seat of the Mohun family who owned the parish of Lanteglos, and is held by the Trust in memory of the men of this parish and of Fowey who gave their lives in the Second World War. The path leads from Hall Walk along the north bank of the wholly unspoiled creek of Pont Pill and descends through a wood to the delightful hamlet of Pont, where the Trust has rebuilt the quays and restored the footbridge connecting them. The path continues along wooded slopes on the south bank, with lovely views over the harbour, to reach the passenger ferry at Polruan which takes pedestrians across the estuary back to Fowey.

From Townsend Farm on the edge of Polruan eastwards lie 8 miles of quiet and peaceful coast, not rugged or wild, though the cliffs are high and the spray flies in winter gales, but a smiling land of good farms, centred on the two beautiful churches of Lanteglos and Lansallos. Except for the farms of Raphael and Lizzen west of Polperro, all now belongs to the Trust.

A path from Pont leads up a bosky valley to Lanteglos church, mainly of the late fourteenth century and dedicated to St Wyllow. It lies in a hollow behind Pencarrow Head, 2 steep miles away from its village of Polruan inside the mouth of Fowey harbour. As with so many Cornish churches, the 'churchtown' is in the middle of the parish whereas the population lives elsewhere. The Trust owns Churchtown Farm beside the church, which has been well restored and is flooded with light from windows of clear glass. At the east end of the south aisle there is a beautiful brass of Thomas de Mohun from the first decade of the fifteenth century. From the church Saffron Lane leads up to the coast where a footpath runs out to Lantic Bay, the sheltered cove west of Pencarrow Head. A precipitous path

descends to the big curving beach, with small coves beyond giving excellent bathing. At the back of the beach grow several plants at home in the shingle: sea holly (*Eryngium maritimum*), sea kale (*Crambe maritima*) and the beautiful pink sea bindweed (*Calystegia soldanella*), an exotic cousin of the common bindweed found in gardens.

Pencarrow Head is on two levels. From its crown at 136 metres (447 feet) the views are enormous. To the east Rame Head marks the end of Cornwall; far beyond it Bolt Tail in south Devon reaches out into the Channel. Westward the noble Roman profile of the Dodman on the far side of St Austell Bay is backed by the Lizard peninsula, curving away to the south, a panorama of some 70 miles. Beneath this high point the headland steps down in a series of giant strides to 45.5 metres (150 feet) above the water, with the wholly unspoilt Lantic and Lantivet Bays on either side. While Lantic has its one big beach, Lantivet is quite different, with a series of little beaches, each guarded by reefs largely covered at high water, below cliffs of no more than 30 metres (100 feet). Many of Lantivet's beaches can be reached from the cliff path, though the more inaccessible may call for a bit of rock climbing. Lansallos Beach, at the foot of West Coombe below Lansallos church, is a perfect semicircle, guarded by rocks and approached through a track cut in the cliff face just wide enough for a horse and cart. The place is the epitome of a smugglers' cove and it is not so long ago that contraband was landed here. The track runs steeply up to the fifteenth-century church of St Ildierna, one of those shadowy female saints with whom Cornwall is richly endowed. The church has a fine wagon roof, many of its original pews, simple slate floors, and an atmosphere of peace. Its tower alone is visible from the cliffs and seems to ride in the sky as it appears and disappears from view.

From West Coombe the path is cut halfway up the cliff, with rocky crags jutting out above. Ravens, kestrels and peregrines wheel and float above these cliffs which run unbroken to Polperro with not a single house in sight. At all times of year there are interesting flowers, for in the kind Cornish climate autumn runs into spring with no perceptible break. Centaury, both in its common form and the rarer *Centaurium pulchellum*, can be recognised by its bright pink flower from June to September. Great mats of thyme abound in the cliff turf. Mallow grows near the base of the cliffs and, hugging the ground closely, the inconspicuous but beautifully named orchid, lady's tresses (*Spiranthus spiralis*), flowers in August and September. Walk here on Christmas Day and a dozen plants will be in bloom.

As the path approaches Polperro little hedged enclosures begin to appear, now overgrown. So closely are the cottages of the village packed into the narrow coombe in which it lies that there is no room for gardens. In the past some 50 little plots were dug in the cliffs, closely hedged with veronica and escallonia, to enable cottagers to grow flowers and vegetables. The Net Loft, wedged into a cleft behind the Peak Rock at the harbour entrance, has been restored by the Trust. Built of local stone and slate, it appears to grow out of the rock. Polperro harbour and the huddled cottages of the old village are undeniably picturesque but the village has been prostituted by the tourist trade and is best avoided in the height of the visitor season. Beyond lies the Warren, a mile of cliff bequeathed to the Trust by Angela Brazil, writer of stories for schoolgirls, and a pleasant breezy place it is. The Trust's land stops at Talland Bay, with another fine church standing high over the sea, but then starts again to round Hore Point and the sweep of coast eastwards to the hotels of Looe, giving another mile and a half of good walking. (*See also* North Cornish Coast, p.263.)

South Downs SUSSEX

Between Winchester, to the west, and Eastbourne, to the east
[443 H6–J6]

Gilbert White (*see* p.334), visiting Sussex in 1773, described the South Downs as 'that chain of majestic mountains'. Although only rarely above 244 metres (800 feet), these rolling chalk hills running 150 miles from Beachy Head to the Hampshire border are one of England's most evocative features. Rising from the south to steep, north-facing scarp slopes, cut by characteristic dry valleys, traditionally grazed to a botanically rich, close-cropped turf and rich in remains of early man, this is a treasured and vulnerable landscape in the most densely populated part of the country, where new by-passes and other developments are continually eroding what countryside remains. Partly due to the relaunching of the South Downs appeal in 1991, the Trust's holdings of fragile downland landscapes are now substantial, amounting to well over 3,035 hectares (7,500 acres) and including some of the region's most prominent viewpoints and landmarks. The emphasis has been on acquiring ancient escarpment landscape, where the Trust is encouraging a continuance of sheep grazing and where areas ploughed in recent years are being returned to grass.

Most of the Trust's land lies in West Sussex. The 1,424.5-hectare (3,520-acre) Slindon estate, 6 miles north of Bognor Regis, offers a large expanse of sweeping downland, with hanging beech and ash woods on steep scarp slopes, a flint and brick village with seventeenth-century cottages, and a substantial section of Stane Street, the Roman road from London to Chichester, with traces of its ditch-flanked, rammed chalk and flint surface running for 3¾ miles across the downs. To the north of Slindon park the ruined arch against the skyline is Nore folly. Above it lie Coldharbour Hill and Glatting Beacon, with breathtaking views south across the Channel and north over the Weald. Some 11 miles north-west, on the crest of the Downs near Uppark (*see* p.405), is the expanse of Harting Down, where, as elsewhere, the small hummocky mounds of the yellow wood ant show that the grassland has not been ploughed for a long time, and also close to the border with Hampshire is the 445-hectare (1,100-acre) Woolbeding estate, near Midhurst, which includes a hanging wood above the River Rother.

Further east, Trust properties ring the sprawl of

Sweeping downland with hanging beech woods and dry valleys is characteristic of the extensive Slindon estate, which is crossed by the South Downs Way.

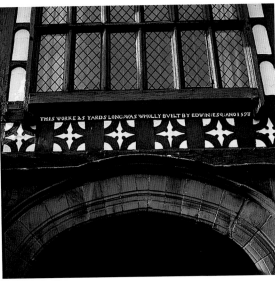

Above: Speke Hall is an outstanding example of the timber-framed manor houses built in the north-west of England in medieval and Tudor times. Set round a cobbled courtyard, the house was built over more than a century by successive generations of the Norris family, the last of whom, Edward Norris, left the inscription over the entrance (right) recording the completion of the north range in 1598.

Brighton and Hove. Overlooking Shoreham at the western end is Southwick Hill on the dip slope of the Downs, with the Brighton by-pass carried in a tunnel under the hill. Further north, Fulking escarpment, Devil's Dyke and Newtimber Hill offer over 243 hectares (600 acres) of open downland and magnificent north-facing scarp, with a series of dry combes furrowing the landscape. The most spectacular of these, Devil's Dyke, is the largest chalkland dry valley in England. The grassland flora includes orchids and the rare red star thistle and, from the top of Newtimber Hill, which can be reached by a shady walk through a hanging ash wood on the north side, there are views seaward and across the Weald, and also into the curving valleys of the large downland estate of Brighton and Hove which adjoins the property.

Two more viewpoints along this stretch of the Downs are in Trust hands. Less than a mile away, north across the busy A23, is the 206.5-metre (677-foot) Wolstonbury Hill, 81 hectares (200 acres) of open downland and the site of an extensive Iron Age hill-fort, while over the border into East Sussex, 6 miles north of Brighton, is the prominent 248-metre (813-foot) summit of Ditchling Beacon, with traces of another hill-fort and views over the mouth of the River Ouse. West of Lewes, the Black Cap estate straddles the South Downs Way, and the 141 hectares (348 acres) of Frog Firle Farm, between Alfriston and Seaford, includes some water-meadow along the River Cuckmere and a fine white horse cut into the downland turf.

Most of these properties lie within the Sussex Downs Area of Outstanding Natural Beauty, and many are skirted or crossed by the South Downs Way. This is life-enhancing country, with a sense of space and distance, sheep dotted on springy turf, skylarks singing overhead, and perhaps a glimpse of a chalkhill blue or marbled white butterfly (*see also* Cissbury Ring, p.93; Highdown Hill, p.184).

South Foreland Lighthouse KENT

3 miles east of Dover, between St Margaret's Bay and Langdon Cliffs [443 L5]

The Trust's string of properties along the White Cliffs of Dover (*see* p.202) includes this lighthouse set on downland on South Foreland Point. Sited to guide mariners past the shifting shoals and banks of the notorious Goodwin Sands, the lighthouse dates from 1843, when the light was an oil lamp. Marconi used the 21-metre (69-foot) tower for his first successful trials in radio navigation, making contact with the East Goodwin lightship, 10 miles away, on Christmas Eve 1898. There are views over Dover docks and the Channel from the balcony round the light, and walkers along the cliffs between here and Dover can take a zig-zag path down to the shore and the wreck of the sailing ship *Preussan*, which ran aground here in 1910.

4 South Quay NORFOLK

In Great Yarmouth [443 L2]

The elegant early nineteenth-century brick frontage of this three-storey house, with a classical portico sheltering the front door and ironwork balconies decorating the sash windows on the first floor, is only a façade. Behind lies an Elizabethan building dating from 1596 in which many original features, such as oak panelling, carved chimney-pieces and moulded plaster ceilings, survive. The house is now a museum of domestic life run by Norfolk Museums and Archaeology Service.

Speke Hall MERSEYSIDE

On north bank of the Mersey, 8 miles south-east of the centre of Liverpool, 1 mile south of the A561, on west side of Liverpool airport [445 H7]

A carved overmantel in the great parlour depicts the three generations of the wealthy gentry family largely responsible for this magical half-timbered moated manor house. Henry Norris to the left, accompanied by his wife and five children, carried on the building started by his father on inheriting the estate in about 1490. In the centre sits Sir William, whose considerable additions in the mid-sixteenth century may be explained by the nineteen children grouped at his feet (the son killed in battle is accompanied by a skull and bones). To the right is Edward, who recorded his completion of the house with an inscription dated 1598 over the entrance and is shown with his wife and two of their children.

These men built conservatively, each addition merging perfectly with what had gone before and with no hint of the Renaissance influences that were becoming evident further south. Four long, low ranges enclose a cobbled courtyard, jettied gables topped with finials projecting unevenly and apparently haphazardly from the façades, and the rough sandstone slabs covering the roof contributing to a charmingly crooked effect. Leaded panes appear dark in the riot of black and white timberwork, among the finest in England. An Elizabethan stone bridge crosses the now grassy moat to the studded wooden doors which give access to the interior. Walking through is a surprise: two huge yews known as Adam and Eve shadow the courtyard, their branches rising above the house.

Surviving Tudor interiors live up to the promise of the exterior. In the light and airy T-shaped great hall rising to the roof, a series of plaster heads looks down from the crude Gothic chimneypiece stretching to the ceiling. The naive decoration here contrasts with the sophisticated carving on the panelling at the other end of the room, with busts of Roman emperors set between elegant, fluted columns represented in high relief. In the great parlour next door, panels in the superb early Jacobean plaster ceiling are alive with pomegranates, roses, lilies, vines and hazelnuts; bunches of ripe grapes and other fruits dangle enticingly and rosebuds are about to burst into flower. A spy-hole in one of the bedrooms and hiding places throughout the house reflect the Norrises' Catholic sympathies which brought them to the edge of ruin in the seventeenth century, culminating in the loss of the family estates after the Civil War.

After years of neglect following the death of the last of the family in 1766, the house was rescued in the late eighteenth century by Richard Watt, whose descendants introduced the heavy oak furniture in period style which contributes to Speke's unique atmosphere. The more intimate panelled Victorian rooms in the north and west wings were created by the shipping magnate F.R. Leyland, who leased the house and carried on Watt's restoration after his early death. A noted patron of the arts, Leyland was responsible for hanging the early William Morris wallpapers which are now a feature of Speke and he also entertained the painter James McNeill Whistler here.

The house lies buried in bracken woodland only a stone's throw from Liverpool airport, a green oasis in the heart of industrial Merseyside. A wide ride leads to the great embankment which shelters the property to the south. Those who struggle up the steep grassy slope are rewarded by a panoramic view of the River Mersey stretching away in a shining sheet of water to the smoking stacks of Ellesmere Port on the other side of the estuary.

Springhill CO. LONDONDERRY

1 mile from Moneymore on Moneymore–Coagh road [444 C3]

Four flintlocks used to defend Londonderry when it was besieged by James II's forces in 1688–9 are among many mementoes of the Protestant military family who built this modest manor house and lived here for 300 years. Although the Conynghams acquired the estate in 1658, the house dates from the end of the seventeenth century, when 'Good' Will Conyngham's marriage articles required him to build for his bride (a copy of the contract now hangs in the hall).

First seen at the end of a long straight avenue, Springhill could well be a French manoir transported miraculously to Ulster. Long sash windows march across the simple whitewashed façade under the steeply pitched slate roof, those either side of the central front door only two panes wide. Hexagonal one-storey bays added in the

Bottom: Atmospheric Springhill, showing the hexagonal bays added in the mid-18th century and the long, low outbuildings where the servants lived, the senior staff in the building on the left, the more junior in the range on the right.

Below: A display of costume in what was the old laundry includes this beautiful dress decorated with formalised poppies, forget-me-nots and ears of corn. Made of a silk brocade woven at Spitalfields, it is typical of the formal dress that would have been worn at court in the 1760s and '70s.

eighteenth century extend the house on either side, as if they have snuggled up to it for warmth, and long, low buildings once used as servants' quarters flank the entrance courtyard. Old yews shade the house, the remnants of an ancient forest which once stretched for miles along the shores of Lough Neagh, clothing the ridge on which the estate stands.

Springhill's eighteenth- and nineteenth-century interiors are redolent of the Conyngham family and their connections. In the library to the right of the hall, Kneller's portraits of William and Mary were presented by the king to Sir Albert Conyngham, who commanded the Inniskilling Dragoons, for his services to the Protestant cause. The medicine chest full of bottles and drawers in this room also has military associations, used by the 3rd Viscount Molesworth, connected to the Conynghams by marriage, during the War of Spanish Succession (1701–14), when he was the Duke of Marlborough's aide-de-camp. The exceptional collection of books, mostly acquired in the eighteenth century, includes a very early edition of Gerard's *Herbal* and first editions of Hobbes's *Leviathan* (1651) and Raleigh's *History of the World* (1614). Walnut William and Mary fiddleback chairs surround an Irish table in the dining room on the other side of the house, from where there are views over the park to the tower at the end of the beech walk.

A gateway from the entrance court leads into the laundry yard, with its original seventeenth-century slaughterhouse and turf shed. A changing exhibition of costume over the last 200 years is on show in the old laundry building: the Trust's collection includes important eighteenth-century garments, a wide range of nineteenth-century costume and flimsy evening dresses of the 1920s and 1930s. The little walled garden beyond the outbuildings, where herbs surround a tiny camomile lawn, is overlooked by a two-storeyed seventeenth-century barn, its interior spanned by roughly hewn oak beams.

Sprivers Garden KENT

2 miles north of Lamberhurst on the B2162 [443 J5]

An unpretentious mid-eighteenth-century house attractively hung with red tiles, the brick façades embracing an older building behind, stands at the centre of a small formal garden with walled and hedged compartments very similar to those depicted on an eighteenth-century print. Although mostly devoted to grass, with clipped yew and box seen against a backdrop of fine trees, there is also an extensive herbaceous border, spring and summer bedding and a walled rose garden.

Standen WEST SUSSEX

2 miles south of East Grinstead [443 I6]

Standen is a most unusual house, built in 1892–4 and yet not at all Victorian, designed all of a piece and yet seeming to have grown out of the group of old farm buildings to which it is attached. This peaceful place on the edge of the Weald was designed by Philip Webb for the successful London solicitor James Beale, who wanted a roomy house for his large family for weekends and holidays. It was one of Webb's last commissions and is also one of the few unaltered examples of the work of this talented architect, so much less well known than his flamboyant contemporary Richard Norman Shaw. A lifelong friend and associate of William Morris, Webb shared Morris's views on the value of high-quality materials and craftsmanship. His aim was to design good, plain buildings, with comfortable interiors that could be lived in (*see* Red House p.319), an ambition which Standen fulfils in every respect.

As shown in Arthur Melville's delightful watercolour, painted when he visited the Beales for a weekend in 1896, Standen sits on a terrace facing south over the long lake of the Weirwood reservoir to the wooded hills of Ashdown Forest. It is part-built of stone from the hill behind, with upper storeys weather-boarded and tile-hung in the Wealden fashion to produce red and white façades. An attractive arcaded conservatory stretches away from the five-gabled garden front, with its tall chimneys reminiscent of Norman Shaw rising almost to the height of the tower holding the water tanks.

The rooms are light and airy, furnished with Morris's wallpapers and textiles, with richly coloured William de Morgan pottery, such as the red lustreware in a cabinet in the stairwell, and with a pleasing mixture of antiques and beautifully made pieces from Morris's company. The house was lit by electricity from the beginning, and many original fittings still exist. Webb's delicate wall lights in the drawing room hang like overblown snowdrops, casting soft pools of light on the blue and red hand-knotted carpet and the comfortable chairs covered in faded green velvet supplied from Morris's workshops. Engraved sunflowers on the burnished-copper plates supporting the light brackets echo the design of the wallpaper and complement the swirls of foliage and tulips on the brass cheeks of the fireplace. A view through to the conservatory from this room shows cane furniture set enticingly amidst a profusion of plants. All the rooms reflect Webb's meticulous concern with every detail. The dining room at the end of the south front, its distinctive grey-green panelling setting off blue and white Chinese porcelain, has an east-facing breakfast alcove, where the little round table flanked by oak dressers lined with china is flooded with sunshine in the early morning. Curiously, the first floor reveals that the Beales were expected still to rely heavily on washstands and hip baths, with only one bathroom provided for twelve bedrooms.

The south-facing, steep garden which falls away from the house reflects changes over several decades by a number of different hands. A fussy, gardenesque layout by London landscape gardener G.B. Simpson, who was employed before Webb and planned his design to focus on a differently sited house, was then modified by his successor, who favoured a simpler approach concentrating on grass and trees. The planting, on the other hand, was undertaken by James Beale's wife Margaret, who established a wide collection of colourful and unusual plants at variance with the quiet restful vistas Webb hoped to achieve.

The end result, although based on no coherent overall plan, is both individual and charming, with many changes of level linked by flights of steps and magnificent views across the valley. Webb's terraces, with a summerhouse set on the topmost level, descend the hill in giant leaps, their outlines followed by stepped yew hedges. Hydrangeas, azaleas, kalmias and rhododendrons surround several areas of grass, such as the upper lawns with their spangling of ladies' tresses orchid in September, and fine trees include

Above left: Philip Webb took immense care with every detail of Standen, such as the design of the dining-room fireplace, with its decorative metal-work, painted panelling and stands for blue and white porcelain. Furnishings by Webb's friend William Morris include this medieval-style tapestry panel (below right) and there are many examples of William de Morgan's richly-coloured tiles (above right) and other ceramics.

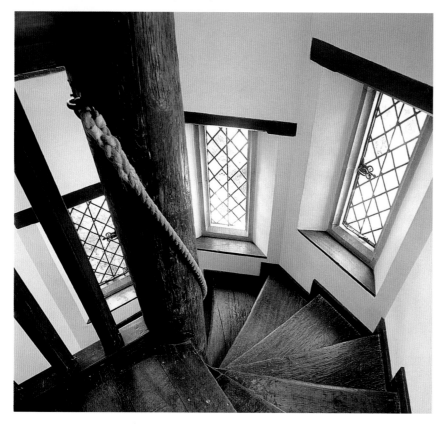

the Monterey pine, a tulip tree, a weeping holly and a handkerchief tree. The little quarry which supplied the stone for the house is now attractively leafy and overgrown, supporting a colony of royal fern, primulas, anemones and the pale-yellow hoop-petticoat daffodil.

Staunton Harold Church
LEICESTERSHIRE

5 miles north-east of Ashby-de-la-Zouch, west of the B587 [443 G1]

Sir Robert Shirley, 4th Baronet, must have been a very brave if rather foolhardy young man. The splendid church he built in 1653, one of very few erected between the outbreak of the Civil War and the Restoration, was an open act of defiance to Cromwell's Puritan regime, showing Sir Robert's identification with the High Church Anglicanism of the martyred king and advertising his wealth. The incensed Cromwell retaliated by demanding money for a regiment of soldiers, throwing Sir Robert into the Tower of London when he refused to comply. There he died, aged only twenty-seven.

Staunton Harold is this ardent Royalist's memorial. Built in the revived Gothic style which symbolised continuity with the old Church, its prominent pinnacles, embattled parapets and imposing tower are reminiscent of a medieval building.

Fine carved woodwork by a joiner named William Smith survives unaltered inside. Double rows of oak box pews fill the nave, lit by single-armed candlesticks attached to the divisions. Oak panelling lines the walls and faces the columns of the nave and a magnificent Jacobean screen supports the organ loft at the west end. The organ itself, which predates the church, is one of the oldest English-built instruments still in its original condition. Swirls of blue, black and white representing the elements in chaos draw the eye high overhead to a wonderfully abstract version of the Creation dated 1655. The Puritans would have regarded both this display and the fixed altar in the chancel as idolatrous.

The only two later features in the church are Robert Bakewell of Derby's early eighteenth-century ornate wrought-iron screen in the chancel arch and the marble tomb to Robert Shirley's great-grandson, who died of smallpox in 1714. The young man lies propped on his right elbow, as if eagerly surveying the world he has left.

Stockbridge HAMPSHIRE

At the junction of the A30, the A272 and the A3057 [443 G6]

The Trust is lord of the manor of Stockbridge and administers the common marsh, where ancient rights of grazing are still exercised, and the manorial waste, which includes the wide verges of the A30 which runs through the neat Georgian main street. A mile to the east is Stockbridge Down, where the Trust's 65 hectares (160 acres) are grazed by sheep and cattle to maintain the rich, butterfly-attracting downland flora. Both marsh and down are designated Sites of Special Scientific Interest.

Stoneacre KENT

At north end of Otham village, 3 miles south-east of Maidstone, 1 mile south of the A20 [443 J5]

Prosperous yeomen farmers and other men of moderate means in the late Middle Ages built their houses to a standard pattern that endured for generations. The core of these houses was a central hall open to the rafters, with two floors of smaller chambers on either side, a layout which reconciled increasing pressures for individual privacy with the traditional communal life.

This attractive half-timbered Wealden house, dating from about 1480, was typical of its time, following the plan already established in the little Alfriston Clergy House built over a century earlier (*see* p.20). But Stoneacre's individual character, created by Aymer Valance in the early twentieth century, sets it apart. Impressive timberwork spans the great hall, with a rare and beautiful king-post, devised as a cluster of columns, supporting the ridge of the roof from the gigantic tie beam which stretches the length of the room. A massive brick chimney built in the 1920s rises the height of the hall from the fifteenth-century fireplace introduced by Mr Valance on the south side, a collection of warm-toned Hispanic plates along the chimney breast enhancing the soft pinks of the brickwork. Morning and evening sun pours through the leaded panes in the two twelve-light windows facing east and west.

This fifteenth-century core with its solar block to the south is now the centrepiece of a much larger building. Half-timbered wings in complete harmony with the medieval work were created by Mr Valance using timber, windows and furnishings from dilapidated Tudor houses, some of which were acquired as complete buildings. Badly neglected before he began his restoration of the property, Stoneacre is a fascinating exercise in the fruits of inspired scholarship.

Stonehenge Down WILTSHIRE

1–3 miles west of Amesbury, at junction of the A303 and the A360 [443 G5]

Few visitors to the world-famous monument (not owned by the Trust) on Salisbury Plain realise that the surrounding windswept downland contains numerous other prehistoric remains, many of which are on Trust land. To the north of Stonehenge, parallel banks and shallow ditches about 30 metres (98.5 feet) apart define the enigmatic late Neolithic feature known as the Cursus, a great sweep of grass which has been variously interpreted as a racecourse and as a processional way. Running for 1¾ miles from west to east across a shallow valley, it is now largely ploughed out in its eastern half but rises impressively to a barrow silhouetted on the horizon in the other direction. Roughly parallel, on a line a few hundred metres to the north-west, is a smaller cursus, the Lesser Cursus, which is about 400 metres (1,312.5 feet) long by 60 metres (197 feet) wide. Now almost obliterated by

ploughing, only the external ditch of what was a bank and ditch formation survives. Far more indistinct – indeed, practically invisible on the ground for most of its length – is the processional way known as the Avenue. Dating from *c*.2000BC, it extends 1½ miles from Stonehenge to the River Avon. The western half, running north into the shallow valley crossed by the Cursus and then turning east to climb uphill to the skyline, is Trust property. Shallow banks and ditches are just discernible on the bend and two young beeches planted on the ridge usefully flag the outer edges at the top of the slope.

Far more impressive are the Beaker and Bronze Age barrow cemeteries dating from *c*.2500–2000BC which crown the low ridges ringing Stonehenge at distances of half a mile to a mile. One of the most prominent, flanking the southern edge of the Cursus, lies in open grazing land, the grassy mounds swelling on the skyline looking like a row of hats or upturned bowls. The New and Old King barrows extending for over half a mile along the ridge crossed by the Avenue were in open country when recorded by the antiquary William Stukeley in the early eighteenth century, but now appear as dark shapes in beech woods on the crest of the hill (trees growing actually on the barrows, obscuring their outlines, have recently been cleared). The impressive mounds here – over 30 metres (100 feet) across and 2.5 to 3.5 metres (8 to 12 feet) high – are almost all bowl barrows, the earliest and simplest form of these features, but the Cursus group contains fine examples of bell barrows, in which a flat platform, or berm, separates the central mound from the encircling ditch. Both these types and the rarer pond, saucer and dish barrows can be seen in the Winterbourne Stoke cemetery in the angle between the A303 and the A360 to the west. Just off the roundabout where the two roads intersect is a fine Neolithic long barrow dating from *c*.3000BC, its irregular profile, partly concealed by scrub, probably mistaken for a dump of waste material by many passing motorists.

Several of the cemeteries are illustrated in William Stukeley's *Stonehenge*, published in 1740, and most of the barrows were excavated by Sir Richard Colt Hoare of Stourhead (*see below*), who set out to record the prehistoric remains of Wiltshire in 1803–10. His considerable finds, many of which are now displayed in Devizes Museum, included both skeletons and cremated remains interned in coffins and urns and a variety of grave goods – amber beads, bronze daggers, pins and tweezers, various jars and cups and work in gold.

Many more barrows stud the rolling countryside round about, some hidden in woods, others isolated prominently in fields or on the crests of ridges. An even greater number have probably been ploughed out, together with the remains of field systems and settlements. Although we see the barrows grassed over, it is likely they were originally bare chalk mounds, appearing startlingly white in a green and brown landscape. Each marked the grave of a Wessex chieftain or of a member of his family, the upper echelons of a sophisticated society which profited from trade in tin, copper and gold with the Continent and which had mastered skilled metalworking techniques.

The extensive prehistoric landscape in the Trust's care was recently extended by the acquisition in 1999, as part of Countess Farm, of the western half of the late Neolithic henge of Durrington Walls, which lies astride the A345 north of Amesbury. A much eroded bank and ditch enclose a large area with a maximum diameter of about 500 metres (1,640.5 feet) and post holes excavated when the route of the road was changed indicate that there were at least two timber buildings here. In a field south-west of the henge, a single sarsen stone known as the Cuckoo stone is thought to be a fallen late Neolithic or early Bronze Age standing stone. Scattered across Countess Farm are clumps of trees reputedly planted to commemorate the Battle of the Nile in 1798, with each clump representing a French or British ship, but the original planting date is disputed.

To enhance the setting of this whole group of monuments, the Trust aims to return much of the arable land to grass in due course, and the impact of the prehistoric landscape will benefit greatly from current plans to bury the A303, which at present carries heavy streams of traffic within sight of Stonehenge, in a tunnel, and to make the A344 into a track.

Stourhead WILTSHIRE

At Stourton, off the B3092, 3 miles north-west of Mere
[442 F6]

The fine house on a ridge of the Wiltshire Downs is over-shadowed by the magical garden created in a steep-sided combe which falls away to the west. Sheltered and enclosed by windbreaks planted along the rim of the valley, the perfect eighteenth-century landscape preserved here looks inward, with views over wooded slopes to the serene artificial lake in the depths of the combe. A number of little classical temples along the shore are seen framed against the trees in a sequence of contrived vistas which shift and change according to the viewpoint on the path round the lake. Stourhead is as much a work of art as the

idealised landscapes it imitates, designed as a series of experiences and never the same however often it is visited. In spring, a carpet of tiny wild daffodils is mirrored in the water and the magnolias are in bloom. In summer, silvery-white willows along the shore appear iridescent against the darker foliage behind and patches of deep-crimson and purple rhododendrons mark the upper slopes. In autumn, Japanese maples bring flashes of fire to the russet-brown and fir-green of the woods. The trees are a mix of beeches, oaks and other native species and exotics, among them the Norwegian maple, tulip trees, cedars, the dawn redwood and the Japanese *Pinus parviflora*.

Stourhead is primarily the creation of Henry Hoare II, son of the London banker who built the Palladian house (*see below*), although later members of the family, in particular Sir Richard Colt Hoare (*see below*), enriched the garden by widening the range of species, introducing flowering shrubs and exotic trees, and also made some more fundamental changes. Perhaps turned in on himself by the tragic loss of both his wives, the garden was to be Henry's absorbing interest for 40 years from 1741, its design a direct expression of the eighteenth-century taste for the world of ancient Greece and Rome and of the reaction against the formal landscapes of the preceding century typified by Versailles. Henry's model could well have been one of Claude Lorraine's romantic and atmospheric paintings of the countryside around Rome, with little temples set in a leafy arcadian paradise.

The only professional engaged in the creation of the garden was the architect Henry Flitcroft, who designed the classical eye-catchers. His dignified Pantheon, with a broad flight of steps leading up to a pedimented portico, crowns a rounded slope above the lake, the curve of the dome continuing the contours of the grass. His tall, circular Temple of Apollo enclosed in a continuous colonnade sits high up on a knoll, looking imperiously out over the island-studded water. Across the valley, steps lead down through a leafy tunnel to the dripping grotto on the edge of the lake, its sombre rock-shadowed pools adorned with sculpture. John Cheere's hoary long-haired river god sits half in and half out of the water, one arm raised as if to welcome visitors, his flesh unhealthily white in the gloom of the cavern. His companion, a nymph of the grot, circles her head protectively with her left arm as she sleeps, oblivious of the cascade streaming down from her bed. Close by on the path above is a fantasy from another century, the Gothic cottage added by Sir Richard Colt Hoare in 1806, its prominent traceried windows and rough slab tiles almost buried in vegetation.

Although Henry Hoare originally hid the estate village on the edge of the valley behind a screen of trees so that it would not intrude on his design, the row of tiled cottages with mullioned windows stretching down to the Palladian bridge over an arm of the lake adds to the charm of his creation. Opposite is the medieval parish church, picturesquely crowned with fretwork parapets and filled with monuments to the Hoares and their predecessors, the Stourtons. Just beyond the churchyard, dominating the view over the lake to the Pantheon, rises the slender column of the medieval cross which Henry acquired from the City of Bristol in the 1760s, its tapering length suggesting the spire of a buried church.

The garden was intended to be seen from above, approached by the shady walk from the house which suddenly emerges on the edge of the combe to give a view of shining water through the trees. Visitors taking this upper route rather than following the road through the village catch a glimpse of the entrance front of Henry Hoare I's austere Neo-classical house facing east over the park to distant wooded hills. The son of Sir Richard Hoare, the founder of the family bank, Henry had purchased the estate in 1717, three years after it had passed out of the hands of the Stourton family who had lived here for 700 years. He immediately demolished the existing house and employed Colen Campbell, a leader of the fashionable

Neo-classical revival, to build this replacement, one of the first Palladian houses in England. The square main block, with its pedimented portico rising the height of the building, is flanked by pavilions added in the 1790s to house a picture gallery and library, the rather severe lines of the façade softened only by two flights of steps rising to the entrance, their end pillars supporting stone basins surmounted by the Hoare eagle, and by the three lead statues set above the portico.

Sadly, the original decoration was destroyed by the fire which gutted this central block in 1902. More or less faithful Edwardian reconstructions of Campbell's intentions by the local architect Doran Webb and the more prestigious Sir Aston Webb who replaced him are now sandwiched between the Regency rooms in the pavilions, both of which survived virtually unscathed. The contents, a rich collection of family heirlooms with finely crafted furniture by Thomas Chippendale the Younger, reflect the interests of several generations of the Hoares and the addition of pieces from Wavendon, the family's house in Buckinghamshire, in the nineteenth century.

The nucleus of paintings, sculpture and *objets d'art* acquired by Henry Hoare II to embellish his father's new house was greatly extended by his grandson Sir Richard Colt Hoare, who inherited in 1785. This eminent antiquary, scholar and county historian was an omnivorous collector,

Above: The antiquarian and historian Sir Richard Colt Hoare with his son in a portrait by Samuel Woodforde at Stourhead. Although some of the finest paintings in the house were sold in the late 19th century, the collection still includes Cigoli's *Adoration of the Magi*, which Colt Hoare acquired, and Poussin's *The Choice of Hercules* (above right). The ornate Pope's Cabinet (right) was bought from a convent in Rome by Henry Hoare II, Colt Hoare's grandfather, and arrived at Stourhead in 1742. There is a story that the cabinet belonged to Pope Sixtus V, but it is too late in date for this to be possible.

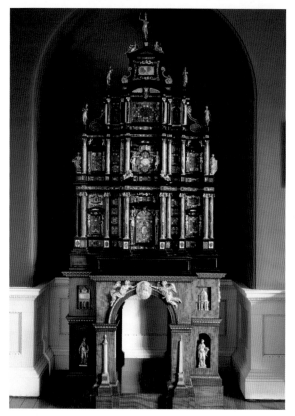

amassing a magnificent library in one of his purpose-built extensions and displaying the pick of his grandfather's collection together with his own acquisitions of works by Italian and British contemporaries in the other. Although some of the finest were sold in the late nineteenth century, the paintings still hang triple-banked against pea-green walls, simple gilt frames contrasting with florid rococo creations on the end wall. Cigoli's *Adoration of the Magi* dominates the room, an expression of great tenderness lighting the face of the grizzled king in an ermine-fringed cloak who kneels at the Virgin's feet.

Similarly, although many of his books have now been dispersed, Colt Hoare's evocative green and white library is one of the most beautiful surviving Regency rooms in England, the arch of the high barrel-vaulted ceiling echoed in the curved alcoves lined with books. Thomas Chippendale's rich mahogany furniture (including massive staircase-like library steps), gilded calf bindings and the deep-green and ochre carpet all contribute to a feeling of luxurious opulence, while the muted tones are lifted by flashes of colour from the painted glass high up in the lunettes at either end of the room. Of the other treasures in the house, perhaps the most memorable is the seventeenth-century 'Pope's cabinet' designed like the façade of a Renaissance church, a framework of ebony and bronze setting off a multicoloured inlay of marble, porphyry, jasper and other ornamental stones.

Stourhead Estate WILTSHIRE

At Stourton, off the B3092, 3 miles north-west of Mere on the A303 [442 F6]

To most people Stourhead means the finest landscape garden in the south of England and a great house with a fine collection (*see above*), but its estate of 817 hectares (2,019 acres) has much to show the walker.

The wooded escarpment between Warminster and Wincanton forms the western edge of the chalk country centred on Salisbury Plain. It is divided between three estates: Longleat to the north, Maiden Bradley in the middle reach, and Stourhead to the south. Each of these overlooks the pastoral country to the west with its market town of Shepton Mallet. Stourhead's share of this lovely country provides three very different walks.

First a woodland walk. South of the chain of lakes in the landscape garden, the River Stour winds its way through a steep wooded valley towards Gillingham, passing the hamlet of Gasper. A circular walk from

This watercolour by C.W. Bamfylde shows the landscape garden at Stourhead in *c*.1770, when the view was much more open than it is now.

Stourton leads via Bonham to the footbridge over the river below Gasper Mill, now a private house. In the woods above there are several thousand minuscule quarries, named Pen Pits. Archaeologists have shown that they were dug from about 1800BC to extract lumps of greensand which were then made into grindstones and whetstones. The path runs up through the woods, past the Pen Pits, to Pear Ash and then turns north to return to Stourton past the former hound kennels between New Lake and Turner's Paddock Lake.

The second walk is through a more contrived landscape, north of the garden. It starts past the east entrance front of Stourhead House and continues west into Long Lane, a disused road which formerly carried traffic running west from Salisbury. The lane becomes a tarred road and one is conscious of fine planting, an avenue of beeches on the ridge.

Then, on the left, Six Wells Bottom plunges southwest to the lake far below. The woods on either side of this grassy combe give it great beauty. Near the top St Peter's Pump collects the springs at the head-waters of the river to serve the chain of lakes. A mile and a half to the west is one of the Trust's finest follies, the great red-brick mass of the three-sided Alfred's Tower, 49 metres (160 feet) high, perched on the edge of the escarpment. Alfred is said to have rallied his troops here against Danish invaders in AD879. The tower was started in 1762 and stood unharmed until 1942 when it was hit by an aircraft, knocking off the spire which was eventually replaced in 1985. The views from the top of the tower, across the whole of Somerset, are superb, and it is usually open in the summer when the weather is fine. From Hilcombe Farm, some way below the tower, the walk returns to Stourton through the woods to the west of the garden.

The third walk is very different. East of Stourton one leaves the wooded country for the open, not to say very exposed, upland and takes lanes and field paths north of Search Farm up to White Sheet Down, and from there up White Sheet Hill, 244.5 metres (802 feet) high. There are Neolithic and Iron Age earthworks, almost obligatory on these West Country hills, but the visitor has much else to appreciate for this is the best sort of chalk grassland, springy underfoot, skylarks trilling overhead, and the views are superb: west back to Stourhead and Alfred's Tower, south-west over the Blackmore Vale, north-east towards the Deverills.

Visionaries and Eccentrics

The enquiring spirit of the sixteenth century, which led intrepid explorers into uncharted territory, took other men on more inward journeys. There was a break with the theological straitjacket of medieval education and, following Caxton's printing revolution only decades earlier, a flood of new books and pamphlets reflecting the new vistas of the Renaissance. This was the age of the gifted, self-taught amateur. Learning became the mark of the gentleman, going hand in hand with an Elizabethan love of wordplay and symbolism, and with dabbling on the wilder shores of astrology and alchemy. Expanding horizons of a different kind marked the Industrial Revolution of the late eighteenth and nineteenth centuries, when the vision and intuition of a select band of men helped create the underpinnings and mindset of the modern industrial economy. And always there were men who, for one reason or another, turned their back on the mainstream; the world of the country house, where families presided over little fiefdoms, gave ample scope for eccentricity. Others were visionaries, pursuing personal odysseys in which they reinterpreted general experience in a highly individual form.

LYVEDEN NEW BIELD
237

For those in a position to direct their own lives, the 16th and early 17th centuries, with their religious and political divisions and uncertainties coupled with broadening intellectual horizons, presented new challenges and opportunities. This was the age of the Renaissance man, dabbling in learning and building up libraries stuffed with literary classics as well as works on architecture, science, geography and other cutting-edge topics. Among them was Henry Percy, 9th Earl of Northumberland (1564–1632), who, following a dissolute and debauched youth, became bookish and learned. His collection of books, huge for its day, reflects an impressive range of interests, from abstract philosophy to practical matters such as breeding horses and building forts. In 1605, although a Protestant, he was sentenced to life imprisonment in the Tower for alleged involvement in the Gunpowder Plot. Here, housed in luxurious and spacious apartments, and wreathed in tobacco smoke, he pursued his interests, gaining a

reputation as a scientist, astrologer and alchemist and the nickname of the Wizard Earl. As well as being able to sharpen his wits on Walter Raleigh, a fellow prisoner and tobacco addict, the earl had the services of three scholars, one an expert on algebra, another a scientific geographer and the third a mathematician and astronomer. Appropriately, his portrait by Van Dyck (**above**) shows him in academic dress and in the melancholy pose of a learned man. The Earl's contemporary Sir Thomas Tresham (1545–1605), a committed Roman Catholic, lived more closely on the edge, spending fifteen years of his life in prison or under house arrest, and suffering crippling fines for his refusal to attend Church of England services. Nonetheless, he managed to produce three original buildings, all of which combined practicality with symbolism. The unfinished shell of Lyveden New Bield, intended as a garden house for the family manor, stands isolated among the fields and woods of deepest rural Northamptonshire. Rich in religious

allusions and number play, it is designed as a cross and carries emblems of the Passion, such as the sponge and spear, and biblical inscriptions. It has been devised so that the faces of each wing and the letters of the inscriptions are a play on three, five, seven and nine, all of which have religious significance.

The groundwork for the Industrial Revolution was laid in the 17th century, when methodical work in a series of

WOOLSTHORPE MANOR
436

disciplines led to a new understanding of natural laws and the physical sciences, as well as a dismantling of old superstitions and mysteries. William Harvey discovered the circulation of the blood just before the Civil War, Francis Bacon worked out principles of observation, measurement and inductive reasoning, and Robert Boyle did groundbreaking research on the properties of gases and vacuums.

Towering above them all was Isaac Newton (1642–1727), the yeoman farmer's son from Woolsthorpe, an obscure Lincolnshire hamlet, who became a Cambridge professor and President of the Royal Society. His many contributions to mathematical and scientific understanding included revolutionary work on gravitation, the refraction of light, differential calculus and the properties of fluids, with applications that included proof of the elliptical orbits of the planets round the sun. Although most of his adult life was spent away from Woolsthorpe, he returned there in 1665 to escape the plague. In an upstairs room in the little manor house where he was born can be seen a copy of his seminal *Principia Mathematica* (**opposite, above**), first published in 1687 and the basis of scientific understanding for the next two hundred years. Also here is a copy of the reflecting telescope which he developed (**opposite, below**) using his knowledge of metals to produce a superior mirror.

THE NEEDLES OLD BATTERY
260

The transformation of Britain from an agricultural to an industrial economy started in the mid-18th century, and gathered pace over the next hundred years. It was a complex and multi-faceted process which generated all kinds of challenges for the small group of engineers and scientists who grappled with problems and together laid the foundations of a new world. In Cornwall, the expansion of tin and copper mining was initially held back by the need to import quantities of coal from south Wales to feed fuel-hungry steam pumps. When a crucial patent expired, the Cornish engineer Richard Trevithick (1771–1813) developed a vastly improved, high-pressure steam engine. It was this invention which powered the great Cornish beam engines and underlay the huge expansion of the mining industry in the mid-19th century, as the numerous ruined engine houses in the far south-west –

many of them poised on cliff-tops – still attest. Generally, for most of this period, machinery was still being run on waterpower. William Armstrong (1810–1900), who was to become one of the greatest innovators and industrialists of his day, started his meteoric career by grappling with the problems of applied waterpower, but after the Crimean War, which exposed the limitations of the British army's heavy guns, he turned his attention to armaments. From 1859 to 1863, the Armstrong works became the government's sole supplier of heavy ordnance, and during these years six Armstrong guns (**below left**) were installed in the newly built Needles Point Battery on the Isle of Wight, guarding the approaches to Portsmouth. In later years the 1st Lord Armstrong, as he became, exercised his inventive powers on his new house, Cragside, in Northumberland, and the surrounding estate.

Among many other innovative features, he built the dramatic steel footbridge which arches 46 metres (150 feet) over the Debdon Burn below the house. Other minds tackled the need for an improved transport network to support the growing industrial economy. The great engineer Thomas Telford (1757–1854) worked on both canals and roads, surveying well-graded new routes and designing a number of innovative bridges, such as the 305-metre (1001-foot) -long cast-iron Pontcysyllte aqueduct over the River

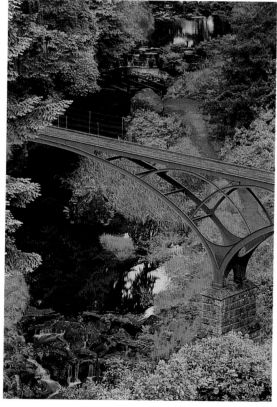

CRAGSIDE
116

Dee. His Conwy Suspension Bridge, opened in 1826, was designed to take the coastal road from Chester to Holyhead over the estuary of the River Conwy, which was a major natural barrier.

The bridge was both old and new. It was designed with Gothic turrets to blend with the medieval castle which dominates Conwy, but the engineering challenges of the suspension bridge, in particular the oscillations caused by crosswinds, were still being worked out. The bridge has a 100-metre (327-foot) span and was built to exacting standards, as is shown by the fact that the original cast-iron chains still survive. In 1825, the year before the Conwy bridge was completed, the railway age was heralded by the opening of the Stockton to Darlington railway. The line had been engineered by George Stephenson (1771–1848), who went on to construct the Liverpool to Manchester line and his revolutionary *Rocket*, which was the first of the pioneer locomotives to show the potential of the railways. The self-taught son of an impoverished colliery worker, Stephenson was born in this

18th-century stone tenement beside the Tyne (**below**). The valley around is now green and rural, but in his day it was a place of coalpits, ironworks and slag-heaps.

Those insulated by money and estates could choose to ignore the world around them and pursue idiosyncratic lifestyles and interests, often to the point of eccentricity. Until the late 18th century, the Harpurs of Calke Abbey in Derbyshire were noteworthy not only for their vast estates and great wealth, but also for the number of reclusive and singular individuals that presided

CONWY SUSPENSION BRIDGE
108

GEORGE STEPHENSON'S BIRTHPLACE
157

CALKE ABBEY
69

over it. One of the most unsociable and eccentric was Sir Vauncey Harpur Crewe (1846–1924), 10th and last Baronet. Little seen outside his estates, he sometimes would only communicate with his children by letter, and he made visitors leave their cars at the park gates, from where they would be fetched by carriage. Passionately interested in birds, butterflies and other aspects of natural history (**opposite, above and below**), he treated the park as a private bird sanctuary, and insisted

hedges were left untrimmed to provide cover for nesting birds. He added considerably to the cases of stuffed birds and other exhibits inherited from his father, building up a huge collection of butterflies, moths, birds' eggs and other specimens, and going off on shooting expeditions with his head gamekeeper to obtain more birds for stuffing.

A similarly obsessional collector, but in a different mould, was Charles Paget

SNOWSHILL MANOR
348

Wade (1883–1956). In his mid-thirties, cushioned by inheriting the family sugar plantations in the West Indies, he bought Snowshill Manor in the Cotswolds and spent the rest of his life filling it with a curious and unusual collection. An architect and talented woodworker, Wade was interested in craftsmanship and, among some more exotic items, acquired examples of all kinds of household and rural objects, many of them once very common but now rare. In one room is a collection of spinning wheels (**left**), and the skein-winders, spinning chairs and bobbin frames that went with them; in another is a collection of early bicycles (**above left**), from an age

when these would have been made by the village blacksmith.

Individuality of a different kind comes through in the work of Stanley Spencer (1891–1959), whose art expresses a purely personal vision. Known for his religious painting in which episodes from the Bible are set in the everyday surroundings of Cookham in Berkshire, where he lived, his idiosyncrasy is also evident in the paintings which reflect his experiences in Macedonia during the First World War, and which he executed in 1927–32 for a specially built memorial chapel at Burghclere in

SANDHAM MEMORIAL CHAPEL, BURGHCLERE
332

Hampshire. Scenes of everyday army routines, such as map-reading and burning off grass round the camp to create a firebreak, are depicted with his characteristic mix of realism, distortion and emphasis (**above**).

Stowe Landscape Gardens
BUCKINGHAMSHIRE

3 miles north-west of Buckingham, off A422 [443 H3]

Laid out over some 226.5 hectares (560 acres) of undulating Buckinghamshire countryside is a vast eighteenth-century landscape, with sweeping tree-framed vistas to distant arches, temples and other eye-catchers, a chain of lakes crossed by a Palladian bridge, the model for that at Prior Park (*see* p.316), and a central focus on an impressive classical house (not National Trust). Conceived on a heroic scale, its various buildings the size of houses rather than ornaments, this is more a private world than a garden, with a bucolic naturalism that has architectural jewels rising out of rough grassland and emerging from belts of woodland. A grand note is struck right from the start, with an approach down a straight 2½-mile avenue from Buckingham and glimpses of an 18.5-metre- (60-foot-) high Corinthian arch on the skyline ahead. The arch over-looks a valley and Stowe's stunning north-south main vista, running gently down to the lakes and up a broad sweep of grass to the house crowning the opposite slope. Always impressive, this romantic Claudian view is magical in the low sun of a summer's evening or a winter's afternoon, when shadows etch the sculptural façade of the house and fall long over the grass.

Stowe has an important place in the history of landscape design. Leading landscapers, architects and sculptors, among them Charles Bridgeman, Sir John Vanbrugh, William Kent and James Gibbs, were employed here and the layout, gradually developed over some 80 years, pioneered the eighteenth-century swing away from formality to the kind of artful naturalism practised by 'Capability' Brown. The young Brown, still in his twenties, was head gardener here for a decade from 1741 and was married in 1744 in the little medieval church enveloped in the garden, all that remains of the former village.

Stowe is the work of three generations of the upwardly mobile, politically ambitious Temple-Grenville family, who enshrined their Whiggish prejudices in the garden architecture. The transformation of what had been a formal terraced garden began with Richard Temple (1675–1749), later Viscount Cobham, who, funded by marriage to a brewery heiress, devoted periods in the political wilderness to extending his house and garden. Of his earlier formal design, only the innovatory encircling ha-ha by Charles Bridgeman, with military-style bastions at the southern corners, survives unaltered, but the garden still boasts Vanbrugh's domed rotunda and his lakeside pavilions, which now frame the vista to the Corinthian arch.

An increasingly naturalistic approach from the 1740s, with the addition of temples and other monuments by Kent and Gibbs, most of them classical but one a turreted, triangular Gothic fantasy faced in orangey ironstone which now graces a sheep-grazed meadow, was continued by Cobham's nephew, Earl Temple (1711–79). As arrogant and self-important as his uncle, Temple was also a man of taste, who used continental artists such as Giovanni Battista Borra and Vincenzo Valdrè to alter and embellish existing buildings, gave the house its magical south front and created the glorious main vista to the Corinthian arch. Both arch and house were the work of his architect cousin Thomas Pitt, 1st Baron Camelford, who designed the former to be lived in, tucking windows into the sides, and based the latter on designs commissioned from Robert Adam. The final touches were added to Stowe by Earl Temple's nephew, George Grenville (1753–1813), created Marquis of Buckingham in 1784 for services in Ireland, but, to his chagrin, never Duke (an honour achieved by his son).

Growing financial difficulties in the nineteenth century, when the 2nd Duke ran up huge debts, resulted in the sale of most of the estate and the family collections in 1848. In 1921, the house became a public school, which it is today. Despite valiant efforts, the designed landscape and its monuments continued to decay and in 1989, thanks to an anonymous benefactor and the National Heritage Memorial Fund, the gardens were handed over to the National Trust, which has now begun a massive, long-term restoration programme.

The extensive visitor tour is partly a feast of changing vistas, like a series of landscape paintings, partly a window onto the classical, literary and political world in which Stowe is embedded. A little valley below the house is named for the Elysian fields of classical mythology, with a dammed stream to imitate the serpentine River Styx and a curved screen by Kent, like a wayside shrine, carrying portrait busts of Whig-approved heroes, from King Alfred and Shakespeare to the now-forgotten MP Sir John Barnard, who supported Lord Cobham in voting against Walpole's excise bill; an island carries a monument to the dramatist William Congreve, Cobham's friend and drinking companion; and there are direct historical references too, such as the 30-metre (100-foot) column erected in 1759 to commemorate General Wolfe's death on the Heights of Abraham. Despite the golf course laid out below the house, surrounding Vanbrugh's rotunda with a patchwork of greens and fairways, this is one of the most memorable of planned landscapes.

Strangford Lough CO. DOWN

Stretches from Strangford inland to Newtownards [444 D4]

This great tidal inlet, 23 miles from Angus Rock at its mouth to its headwaters at Newtownards, is not only very beautiful, dotted with 120 little islands, but immensely rich in wildlife. On each tide millions of gallons of water flow through the Narrows, creating a turbulent current which ensures an even mix of nutrients and food and forms a series of differing habitats throughout the lough. Soft corals, sponges and anemones, mussels, sea squirts and brittle-stars live on the bottom, feeding on the food suspended in the water. Crab and starfish eat these filter-feeding animals, while octopus and fish take crabs, shrimps and worms, themselves being preyed on by seals and porpoises. On the shore and on the islands there is a rich resident bird life, made richer by the several migrations. Wildfowl and waders pass through on their way north in early spring, while terns arrive from Africa in order to breed. As the terns leave to go south, the waders return at the end of summer: black-tailed godwit, curlew, golden plover. In autumn more waders arrive – knot, turnstone, lapwing, Brent geese from Arctic Canada – to feed on the mud-flats and in some cases to rest before going further. In really cold weather they are joined by great-northern divers, bar-tailed godwit and other birds driven by storm. Big flocks of wintering wildfowl include widgeon from Russia, whooper swans from Iceland, teal and pochard.

This great natural reserve was at risk from uncontrolled shooting, from disturbance by a population made mobile by cars and by lack of management. The Trust already owned Castle Ward (*see* p.77), overlooking the Narrows, but the rest of the shore and the islands belonged to numerous individuals and there was no chance of acquiring the whole. In 1966, however, the Trust took the lead by making an agreement with the several wildfowling clubs, working out management plans with many of the owners, and, later on, acquiring a number of islands and stretches of foreshore. Following the purchase, with funds donated by *Daily Mail* readers, of 12 miles of shoreline along the Narrows and the southern end of the Ards peninsula in 1990, most of the foreshore is now in Trust hands. The plan has largely been achieved. Strangford Lough is now managed in the interest of its wildlife, and those who use the lough for their enjoyment can still do so.

Studley Royal NORTH YORKSHIRE

2 miles west of Ripon, off the B6265 to Pateley Bridge [445 J5]

The Studley Royal estate hides an enchanting formal water garden, with mirror-like moon pools – one round and two crescent-shaped – set in smoothly mown grass reflecting classical statues and the Tuscan columns of a pedimented temple. Laid out in the steep-sided valley of the River Skell, the water garden is framed and contained by the foliage of beeches, yews and Scots pine on the slopes above. More sculpture, a grotto and a rustic bridge provide points of interest on the walk circling the garden, while a pinnacled Gothic tower and a domed rotunda perched high up on the side of the valley were designed as eye-catchers to highlight a series of views across the glassy ponds. This is a serene and peaceful place, a restful combination of still water with green grass and trees. At one end of the garden the canalised Skell cascades into a lake, while upstream the river has been dammed to form a half moon of water curving round the mound known as Tent Hill towards Fountains Abbey (*see* p.154).

This rare survival was the inspiration of John Aislabie, who inherited the Studley Royal estate in 1699. An able, ambitious politician who rose to be Chancellor of the Exchequer, his meteoric career was brought to a sudden end in 1720 by his involvement in the South Sea Bubble, which led to his expulsion from Parliament. Returning to Yorkshire in the same year, he devoted himself to the garden he had started in 1716, perhaps regarding it as a

A serene pastoral landscape at Strangford Lough. The gently rounded islands are formed by glacial deposits from the last Ice Age.

refuge from the world. A beautiful naturalistic park surrounding his creation, with deer grazing beneath mature oaks, beeches, chestnuts and limes, reflects late eighteenth- and early nineteenth-century landscaping, but it also bears traces of the seven great intersecting avenues which John Aislabie designed to focus on features of the estate, on the tower of Fountains Abbey, or on a distant view of Ripon Minster. The house which he built to replace the medieval manor in the park, probably with advice from Colen Campbell whose enchanting banqueting house crowns the Coffin Lawn, has disappeared. Like the earlier building, this was extensively damaged by fire and only the impressive stable block (not owned by the Trust) remains.

Below the lake the Skell plunges into a natural gorge, rustic bridges carrying the path following the stream back and forth over the river. Beech woods tower over the valley, accentuating the drama of the steep cliffs outcropping on either side. Although only one of the eye-catchers built on prominent crags survives, this intentionally wild landscape is still largely as conceived by Aislabie's son William, one of the first examples of the Picturesque style in England and a direct contrast with the formality of his father's water garden. William was also responsible for purchasing the Fountains Abbey estate in 1768, and for the great sweep of grass framed by woods on the valley sides which now leads up to the ruins (*see* p.154). And he engineered what is probably Studley's most memorable feature, the surprise view of the abbey from high up on the east side of the valley, the culmination of the vista path which winds past the octagon tower and domed temple.

The only major subsequent addition to the estate was the High Victorian Gothic church built in the park in 1871–8 for the 1st Marquess and Marchioness of Ripon. The masterpiece of William Burges, its highly ornate interior includes a painted multitude of richly coloured angelic musicians on a gold background thronging the sanctuary and stained-glass windows representing the Book of Revelation. This magnificent building is seen impressively silhouetted on the horizon at the far end of the majestic lime avenue which climbs slowly to the skyline through the gate into the park from the estate village of Studley Roger.

Studley Royal is not only a remarkable survival but a unique illustration of the development of landscape gardening during the course of the eighteenth century, the formality of the early years of the period being gradually rejected in favour of the kind of naturalistic landscapes seen in the park, below the lake and in the setting of the abbey.

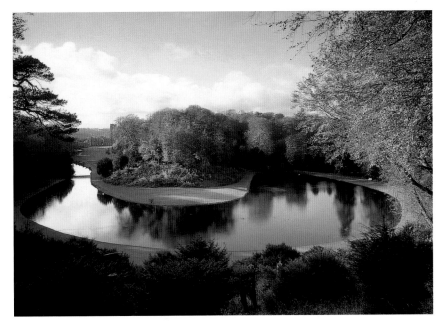

Sudbury Hall DERBYSHIRE

6 miles east of Uttoxeter at the crossing point of the A50 Derby-Stoke and the A515 Lichfield–Ashbourne roads [443 G1]

Sudbury is the most idiosyncratic of the many great houses created during Charles II's reign, built to a consciously outdated plan incorporating a great hall and long gallery and yet fashionably decorated. The message of the exterior is similarly contradictory. Diapered brickwork and an array of mullioned and transomed windows suggest a Jacobean house, but the hipped roof and gleaming central cupola, visible for miles around, are characteristic of the age. George Vernon, who started his new house the year after he inherited the Sudbury estate in 1659, seems to have acted as his own architect and to have adapted his original ideas over some 40 years as knowledge of London fashions gradually filtered through to remote Derbyshire.

Competent but uninspired early work by local men contrasts with the skills displayed by the London crafts-men Vernon employed as time went by, such as Edward Pierce, Grinling Gibbons and the plasterers Bradbury and Pettifer. The balustrade of Pierce's carved pine stair-case, one of the finest of its date, is a mass of writhing foliage, with baskets of fruit set on the newel posts. Pettifer's plasterwork overhead is similarly rich, garlands of fruit and flowers and acanthus scrolls forming three-dimensional encrustations. And yet twenty years after this work was finished Vernon employed Louis Laguerre

At Studley Royal, a bend in the River Skell was transformed into the Half Moon Pond, the largest of the pools making up the formal water garden. Wooded banks are reflected in the water and in the distance is a glimpse of Fountains Abbey.

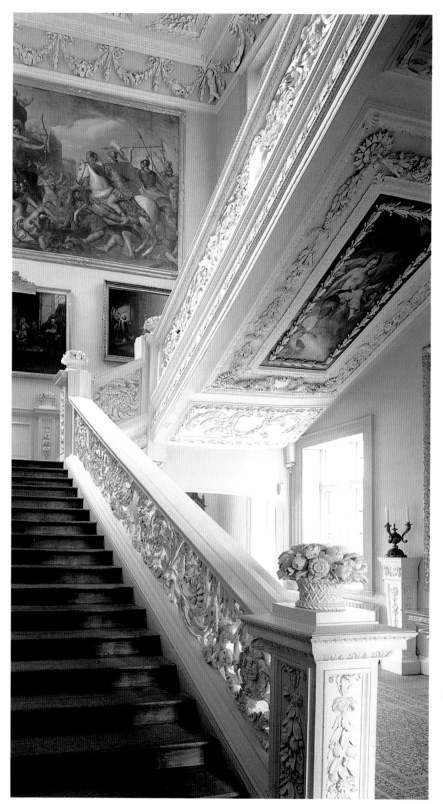

to paint mythological scenes in the plasterwork panels, a taste of the exuberant baroque style popular at court.

Another painting by Laguerre fills a plaster wreath on the ceiling of the saloon, one of the richest of Sudbury's interiors. Here, Pierce's pedimented and gilded woodwork panels displaying full-length family portraits, strongly reminiscent of his contributions to Wren's city churches. But even his work is outclassed by the Grinling Gibbons carving over the fireplace in the drawing room next door, in which fruit, flowers, dead game and fish are all depicted with lifelike realism.

After so much unrelieved grandeur, the decoration of the sunny 42-metre (138-foot) long gallery running the length of the south front is unexpected. At first glance Bradbury and Pettifer's intricate plasterwork appears to repeat established motifs. But all is not what it seems. The classical busts portrayed along the frieze are humorous caricatures, while a lion, a horse, a boar and other animals leap gaily out of the swirls of foliage on the ceiling and grasshoppers dance playfully round the sunflower rosette adorning the central window bay.

The small family rooms at the east end of the house contrast with the magnificence elsewhere. Lady Vernon's cosy sitting room, with its leaf-green walls and tranquil view over the lake below the south front, has a communicating door to her husband's study. It is easy to imagine them talking through it, and walking together across the passage to eat in the small dining room.

Although Sudbury has lost some of its original contents, there are family portraits in almost every room, including works by Lawrence, Hoppner and J.M. Wright, and several other outstanding furnishings remain. In the long gallery, a seventeenth-century Flemish ebony cabinet is enchantingly decorated with scenes of the Creation by Frans Francken the Younger. The first panel shows a purple- and red-robed god hovering above an endless expanse of ocean, brooding on what he is about to unleash.

Sugar Loaf, Park Lodge Farm and Skirrid Fawr MONMOUTHSHIRE

3 miles north-west and 3 miles north-east of Abergavenny
[442 E4]

North of Abergavenny, between the rivers Usk and Honddu and on either side of the A465, are two prominent outliers of the sandstone mass of the Brecon Beacons (*see* p.60). West of the road is the cone-shaped 594.5-metre (1,950-foot) Sugar Loaf, given to the Trust in 1936. Its

Welsh name is Pen-y-fâl, but its English name, a reference to the way sugar was once sold, has survived in this English-speaking part of Wales. To the east is the 486.5-metre (1,596-foot) Skirrid Fawr, where the Trust has held 83 hectares (205 acres) of the summit since 1939.

The hills are areas of open heather and bilberry moor, coarse tussocky grassland, bracken and ancient oak woodland, with some crags and scree. The easiest way up both is from the south, with views from the summits of the Usk Valley, the Black Mountains and across the Bristol Channel.

Sunnycroft SHROPSHIRE

200 Holyhead Road, Wellington [442 F2]

This substantial red-brick house set in 2 hectares (5 acres) of grounds on the outskirts of Wellington is a rare survival of a way of life that lasted from *c*.1850 to the Second World War and which is now largely lost. The family who lived here, the Landers, were not gentry. Rather, they belonged to the prosperous upper middle classes, the bankers, solicitors, industrialists and businessmen who had grown wealthy on the commercial and industrial expansion of the nineteenth century. These men were tied to their places of work, which meant living within easy reach of the town, but they aspired to a landed-gentry lifestyle. The solution, for thousands of them, was to have a suburban mini-estate, with a house large enough to pursue a version of gracious living and with enough land to keep livestock and grow produce for the table. Many such suburban villas were built round towns all over England, but the way of life which supported them did not survive the Second World War, and some became institutions, had their grounds sold for building land, or were demolished. Largely because it was in the same family from 1899 to 1997, Sunnycroft survived. The house still has many original features and contents and the mini-estate is still worked, with productive areas set around and dovetailed into the ornamental gardens.

Sunnycroft sits on the northern side of a squarish plot, looking south towards the wooded humps of the Wrekin hills. Built of strident red brick, it is a plain, almost austere house, with large plate-glass windows, a gabled roofline and a turret over the entrance porch. A long verandah dotted with potted plants shades the main rooms and on the west side, so close to the house as to seem part of it, is an enchanting Victorian glasshouse. The earliest part, where the rooms are more modest, was built in 1880 for J.G. Wackrill, who founded the Shropshire Brewery. He

sold the house to the widow of a wine and spirit merchant and in 1899 she extended Sunnycroft, adding the staircase hall and the larger reception rooms and creating the present entrance. The first of the Landers, John Vernon Thomas, a Wellington solicitor who used to walk into work wearing a white bowler hat and a carnation from the glasshouses, bought the property in 1912. His son, Offley, who was a founder-director of an ironworks at Coalbrookdale, acquired the house on J.V.T.'s death in 1943, and then, in 1973, it was inherited by his daughter Joan, who left the estate to the Trust.

The interior is both a period piece and a reflection of a formal and ordered way of life, with regular meal times, socialising among fellow villa owners and a concern with etiquette. There is much sombre decoration, and substantial late-Victorian and Edwardian furniture, windows and archways are hung with heavy curtains, and the house still has original parquet and decorative tiled floors, ornamental gas brackets, its Victorian rooflight with tinted glass, and a series of cast-iron radiators, part of the up-to-the-minute technology installed in 1899. Servants are kept apart in separate quarters, and the men of the house have their own domain.

All rooms lead off the central staircase hall, now hung with an array of nineteenth-century Lander portraits in place of the stuffed animals and other baronial trophies which J.V.T. favoured. A pretentious Jacobethan staircase, of pitch-pine and mahogany, leads to the bedroom floor. The two grandest reception rooms lie either side of the entrance lobby. To the south, with French windows onto the verandah, is the stately dining room where the Landers hosted five-course dinners round the long mahogany table, and where lunch was held punctually at one. Dark green

Left: The cone of the Sugar Loaf from the north-west. This extensive upland includes some ancient oak woodland as well as great stretches of open moor.

Opposite: The staircase at Sudbury Hall is one of the finest of its date. The ornate pine balustrade was carved by the talented Edward Pierce, who also supplied woodwork for several of Wren's London churches, and the similarly spectacular plasterwork is by James Pettifer. The paintings by Laguerre were added some twenty years after the rest of the work was completed.

Above: Sunnycroft was lit by gas until 1947, when the elaborate fittings were converted to electricity.

Opposite: The rounded hills and dry valleys of the South Downs meet the sea in the turf-topped cliffs of the Seven Sisters, here seen in a view from near Cuckmere Haven.

walls set off a couple of late nineteenth-century landscapes and a rare painting, of a group of card players, by the sculptor Alfred Gilbert, who modelled Eros at Piccadilly Circus. To the north is the large billiard room with a full-size table. This would have been essential in a Victorian country house and for Sunnycroft to have one shows the family's considerable social aspirations. With a gentleman's cloakroom next door, it was a male sanctuary, which could be separated off from the rest of the house with heavy curtains. A finely stitched needlework picture in the feminine drawing room across the hall, with its built-in cosy corner and a pianola for the family's Sunday evening gatherings, is one of many accomplished pieces by Joan Lander, who trained as an embroiderer after the Second World War and was chosen to work on Queen Elizabeth II's coronation dress. There is a display of her work upstairs, and the uniform she wore as a Red Cross nurse during the war is part of a collection of family clothing. A coat and leather gloves strewn across a bed were worn by Offley every day when he drove to work in the black Daimler, with the number plate AW1, which is still in the garage outside.

The grounds, combining ornamental gardens with what is essentially a smallholding, are as fascinating as the house. Despite the relatively confined nature of the plot, Sunnycroft has a grand approach, with a drive framed by majestic Wellingtonias leading from the mock-Tudor lodge on the road. Just off the avenue to the east, behind a hedge, is an extensive kitchen garden, with tidy rows of vegetables. A strip of soft fruit bushes is squeezed in on the other side, between the Wellingtonias and the spacious lawn where family and guests played tennis and croquet, and a rose garden and shrubbery are within earshot of the chickens and assertive cockerel which scratch around in the orchard behind a laurel hedge.

Red-brick outbuildings, out of sight, but only metres from the entrance porch, include pigsties and stables, and tomatoes and grapes are grown under glass. At its height, when the livestock included a pair of Jersey cows and the grounds were extended with additional grazing, Sunnycroft was largely self-sufficient in food, and any surplus was salted down, bottled, made into jams and pickles, or sold locally. One of the more poignant sights in the house is the array of jars in the larder filled with the preserves which Joan made in the last year of her life. Poignant too is the way this proud house, once a status symbol and a mark of success, now has the feel of a retreat from the world, hidden behind walls of trees and towering hedges.

Sussex Coast

[443 J6]

Like the North Downs (*see* p.272), the South Downs meet the sea in a spectacular cliffline, with a long, undeveloped stretch running out to the knob of Beachy Head between Eastbourne and Seaford. The Trust owns over 283 hectares (700 acres) here, including three and a half of the turf-thatched humps known as the Seven Sisters. This is a switchback landscape of chalk hills and dry valleys, much cultivated during the Second World War and so with a rich flora only along the cliffline and in untouched pockets. There are prehistoric remains too, and the buildings at Birling Gap, being refurbished by the Trust, include a row of nineteenth-century coastguard cottages set end on to the shore, and gradually disappearing as the sea eats into the soft and friable cliffs. The Trust's two other holdings along this coast are quite different in character. The coast east of Hastings, where the Trust owns Fairlight Cliff and adjoining farmland, is known for its geologically interesting, fragile mudstone cliffs; while westwards, guarding the mouth of Chichester harbour, is the claw-like spit of East Head, a tongue of dunes, saltings, and sand and shingle beach which is one of the most important sites in western Europe for overwintering waders and wildfowl.

Sutton Hoo SUFFOLK

Off B1083, Woodbridge to Bawdsey Road [443 K3]

In 1939 this bleak and sandy heath high above the Deben estuary was the setting for a spectacular discovery. Excavation of the largest of a cluster of gently swelling mounds uncovered the impression of a huge and elegant ship, some 27 metres (88 feet) long. Within it was an array of treasures: silver bowls and spoons, intricate work in gold and enamel, weapons, armour, fragments of textiles and much else. A great man had been buried here, but the acid soil which had reduced the wooden ship to impressions in the sand had dissolved his skeleton too. This ship burial and its treasures, most of which are now in the British Museum, together with other finds from Sutton Hoo, have made a massive contribution to our understanding of the pre-literate and pagan Dark Age society from which they came. This tract of heath, with at least eighteen mounds on an area some 170 metres (558 feet) long by 77 metres (252.5 feet) wide, was once a royal cemetery. Here, over about sixty years, from the late sixth to the early seventh century, the local ruling elite were buried, together with grave goods

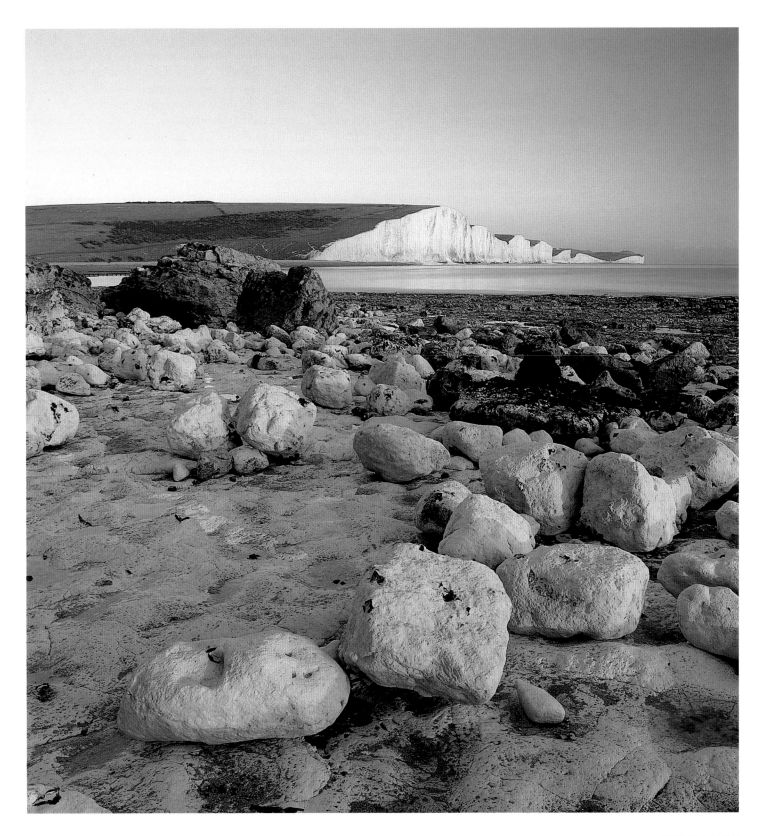

of great magnificence and fine craftsmanship. These Suffolk aristocrats lived at a time when Britain, no longer held together by the unifying might of Rome, had been colonised by Germanic peoples from across the North Sea and was divided into rival kingdoms. Both politically and culturally, it was a fluid period. To the south, across the Thames estuary, was the kingdom of Kent, where the powerful King Ethelbert had converted to Christianity following a mission from Pope Gregory I. Although some Christian objects were found in the graves, the Sutton Hoo nobility were pagans, with a culture and way of life which looked east to the tribal lifestyles of Scandinavia and the continental coastlands.

Most probably, the man in the ship was the East Anglian King Raedwald, who died in c.625. Raedwald had been baptised as a young man but had been persuaded to revert to paganism by his wife. Nonetheless he allowed Christian teaching at his court and maybe the objects with Christian associations, such as bowls inscribed Saulos and Paulos, show he was hedging his bets. Certainly, he seems to have been an astute man, something of a politician, who extended his power over Northumbria and the middle England kingdom of Mercia. The finds at Sutton Hoo illustrate the great wealth of this seventh-century king, his far-ranging contacts, and the way of life of his court, infused by a code of loyalty and honour and by a heroic warrior ethos. There were cauldrons and drinking horns for feasting, a lyre for accompanying the epic recitations by which courageous deeds and battles were remembered and passed from one generation to the next, and in one of the mounds a young warrior had been buried with his horse, sacrificed to accompany its master and with a harness and bridle richly decorated with Celtic motifs. Via

the tidal Deben and the other inlets of this coast, there was trade with the Franks across the Channel, north to Sweden and south to the Mediterranean and beyond. Gold was inset with Indian garnets, a silver bowl carries a Byzantine stamp, and there was a scatter of Frankish gold coins, prized not for their monetary value but as a source of the precious metal which goldsmiths would transform into intricately wrought jewellery, buckles and other ornaments. Raedwald presided over the last pagan East Anglian kingdom. After his death, his successor introduced Christianity and the old ways and rites were abandoned. In Scandinavia, though, where there are mound cemeteries and ship burials very like those at Sutton Hoo, they lived on in the lifestyles of the pagan Vikings.

The burial site is a short walk along the crest of the heath, with views over wooded and bracken-covered slopes to the Deben estuary, busy with sailing boats, and the red roofs of Woodbridge on the opposite bank. Inland, where once there was heath to the horizon, there are now fields and crops, but the huge East Anglian skies still lend drama and atmosphere. The mounds, ploughed and reploughed over the centuries as later generations struggled to make a living from this ungrateful soil, are now no more than swelling undulations in the turf, but one, rearing 4 metres (14 feet) from the grass, has been reconstructed to its original seventh-century size. Posts mark where the great ship lay after it had been hauled up from the estuary below, and some shallow ditches running across the site are anti-glider trenches, dug during the Second World War, when the heath was used for training tanks and armoured vehicles. Often, the turf is being grazed by Norfolk horn sheep, traditional to this area. Looking over the site but separated from it by a combe running down to the estuary is the substantial Edwardian house which was the home of Mrs Pretty, who owned the estate and initiated the investigation of the mounds in the 1930s. A permanent exhibition includes a reconstruction of the ship burial, a selection of finds from the site and much in the way of historical context and interpretation.

This fine Tudor interior at Sutton House is lined with linenfold panelling of Baltic oak and has an original fireplace, of Reigate stone.

Sutton House LONDON

At the corner of Isabella Road and Homerton High Street, Hackney [443 I4]

An inner-city borough in East London is the setting for one of the few surviving examples of a Tudor red-brick house. At the west end of Homerton High Street, where it starts to swing north, is a three-storey H-shaped house set back from the road across a paved yard, with diamond diapering marking the west wing. Dating from 1534–5, Sutton House was built for the high-flying courtier and statesman Sir Ralph Sadleir (1507–87) in what was then desirable countryside on the edge of Hackney village, with open fields between here and London. Right-hand man to Thomas Cromwell, Sadleir survived his patron's fall in 1540, and was one of those who tried the ill-fated Mary Queen of Scots in 1586. His house has had a more chequered career. Remodelled in *c*.1700, when the Tudor gables and mullioned windows were replaced with the present elegant sashes and roofline parapet, divided into two in *c*.1750, partly faced in heavy stucco in the mid-nineteenth century, reunited in 1904, Sutton House has served as school, working men's institute and offices as well as one or more private dwellings. After a recent period of uncertainty and decline, it has now been restored by the Trust.

The restoration has exposed original features hidden behind later alterations and, apart from the great hall that once filled the bar of the H, the basic Tudor plan also survives, with staircases in the wings and a few cupboard-like garderobes. The parlour in the west wing is one of the finest Tudor interiors in London, with oak linenfold panelling running from floor to ceiling and a fireplace of carved Reigate stone, and on the first floor, above what was the great hall, is the airy, high-ceilinged great chamber, lit by windows to both north and south. As in the parlour, the panelling here has been rearranged, and some of it is Jacobean rather than Tudor, but this is a striking room, its effect enhanced by Sadleir family portraits, an oak refectory table and a Charles II dresser. Other features reflect later history. There is painted Jacobean strapwork imitating what richer folk would have had executed in stone or wood, a panelled Georgian parlour in a delicate mint green and Georgian barley-twist balusters on the east staircase, and a Victorian study. There is also one surviving leaded and mullioned Tudor window, looking out on to the secluded, flagged court at the centre of the house. None of the sparse contents is original but all is in keeping, including a couple of reproduction seventeenth-century harpsichords.

'Finds' on display – thimbles, bobbins, scissors, pins, the odd shoe – date from the school years, and a squatter has left a sinister red and black eye on the wall of an attic room. The Wenlock Barn closing the court, a balconied hall with an open timber roof built by Lionel Crane, son of Arts and Crafts designer Walter Crane, is now a function room and the house is a showcase for Hackney's sizeable community of artists, said to be the largest in Europe, whose work is often shown in a first-floor gallery.

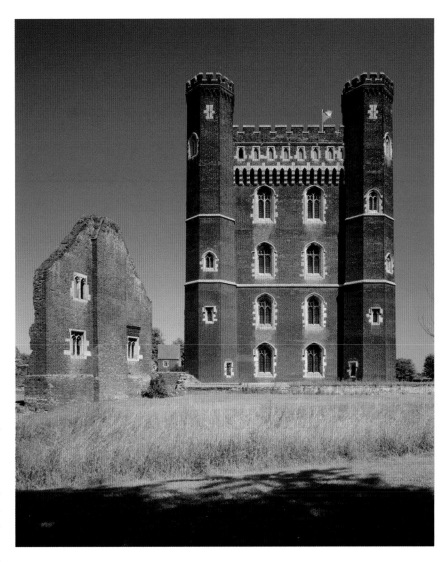

Tattershall Castle's large windows and the ornamental machicolations topping off the turrets suggest this was a display house, designed to be seen from afar, as much as a stronghold.

Tattershall Castle LINCOLNSHIRE

On south side of the A153, 15 miles north-east of Sleaford, 10 miles south-west of Horncastle [445 L8]

Ralph, 3rd Baron Cromwell, was an ambitious man, reaching the climax of his career as Treasurer to Henry VI in 1433–43. His sturdy brick tower, rising prominently from the Lincolnshire Fens and visible for miles around, is one of the most striking monuments of the later Middle Ages, all that survives of the great castle he created here.

Tattershall looks both forwards and backwards. By 1430, when Cromwell started on the extensions to the existing buildings at Tattershall, keeps had gone out of fashion in England, but were to be built for another century

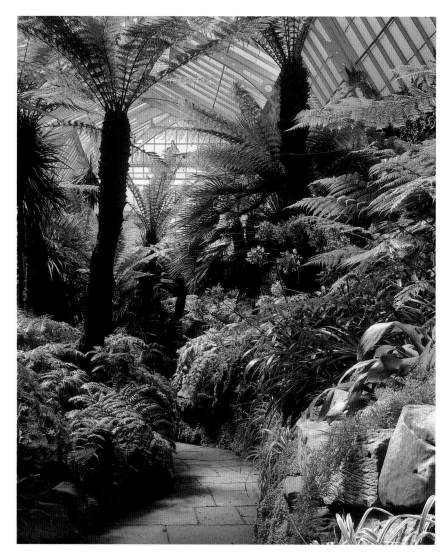

In Tatton's impressive Victorian fernery, mature tree ferns tower above a carpet of the giant fern *Woodwardia radicans* and other foliage plants.

each of the four floors above the vaulted basement, with the Treasurer's personal bedchamber at the top of his tower-house. Carved stone chimneypieces displaying the purse of his office and elaborate window tracery point to luxuriously fitted interiors.

Tattershall is as significant for its material as its design. Although bricks were used in the eastern counties in the thirteenth and fourteenth centuries, they were usually concealed under plaster. Tattershall is one of the earliest examples of the deliberate choice of this material, with its decorative possibilities exploited in the rows of corbels at the top of the façades. Inside, the skill of the craftsmen Cromwell employed shows particularly in the spiral staircase that fills one of the corner turrets, with its finely moulded stone handrail fashioned in the wall, and in the brickwork of the decorative vaults.

Cromwell was a man of the world, acquiring large estates across the East Midlands and building manor houses elsewhere as well as constructing his lavishly appointed tower-house at Tattershall. He was also a creature of his age, concerned for his fate in the next world as much as his comfort in this one. Like other great men of his time, he anticipated the Last Trump by endowing a memorial college, set only a few metres from his castle. Apart from a ruined, two-storey brick building, possibly offices and lodgings, only the beautiful collegiate church, with its armorial stained glass and mutilated brass commemorating Cromwell and his wife, survives, the attractive row of almshouses having been rebuilt in the seventeenth century (neither is owned by the Trust).

In the late Middle Ages this considerable complex of buildings, rising like an island of the civilised world from the sea of the Fens, tellingly revealed the self-importance and aspirations of the man who created them.

Tatton Park CHESHIRE

3½ miles north of Knutsford, 4 miles south of Altrincham, 3½ miles from the M6 at Manchester interchange [445 H7]

The 4th Lord Egerton was a restless man who not only travelled in Africa and India, but once lived with a tribe in the Gobi Desert, experimented with short-wave radio and had his own aeroplane. His 1900 Benz proudly displaying the number plate M1 was the first car to be registered in Cheshire.

The 4th Lord's inquiring mind seems to have been an inherited trait. In all the Wyatt family's plans for the remodelling of the house, for which they were employed

or so in France. The magnificent products of Franco-Burgundian culture, so exquisitely illustrated in the *Très Riches Heures* of the Duc de Berry, may well have inspired the young nobleman, who would have had ample opportunity to see them while serving with the English army in the Hundred Years War. Like its French counterparts, Tattershall has an air of unreality, as if it too had stepped from a contemporary manuscript. In the years that followed, many other men of substance were to reach skywards in buildings which were essentially status symbols.

Although outwardly defensive, with machicolated fighting galleries underneath the battlements and girdled by two moats, this is in fact a domestic country mansion masquerading as a fortress, with large and plentiful windows and several entrances. One great chamber fills at Tatton between 1774 and about 1825, the library is most prominent. A comfortable room filling the centre of the garden front, it was designed to be used, not admired. Books lie companionably on the reading chairs and stands, leather-padded armchairs are drawn up by the fire and a library ladder invites inspection of the topmost shelves. There is something for everyone here, including Jane Austen first editions, volumes of music, and illustrated works on the arts and classical antiquities, mostly finely bound. The nucleus of the collection is the sixteenth-century library acquired by Thomas Egerton, founder of the family fortunes, who rose from unpromising beginnings to become Lord Chancellor of England.

Lewis Wyatt's formal drawing room hung with cherry-coloured silk is much grander, with a relentless coffered ceiling and with gilt-framed chairs and sofas carved in a sinuous rococo style by Gillows of Lancaster that would not seem out of place in a Venetian *palazzo*. Van Dyck's *Martyrdom of St Stephen* seems curiously appropriate in these unrelaxed surroundings, cherubs hovering overhead to receive the saint's soul. Two moody Venetian views by Canaletto are full of delightful detail, the scene on the quay in front of the Doge's Palace including a little white dog with a jaunty tail trotting purposefully along among the figures going about their business.

Lewis Wyatt was also responsible for the inspired treatment of the staircase in the centre of the house, giving a vista through a colonnade-like series of arches on the first floor. The Regency lifestyle for which Tatton was designed emerges strongly here, every bedroom except one sporting a dressing room. Each suite was originally distinguished by the colour of its textiles and the wood of the furniture, the pieces in the principal apartment being of mahogany inlaid with ebony.

The Wyatts' exterior is a pure Neo-classical design, with a giant pedimented portico dominating the south front, a low-pitched roof and almost no decoration except for the chaste swags in panels over the sash windows. Only the dining room remains from the eighteenth-century house that, in his time, William Tatton Egerton so ruthlessly swept away. In it, green walls set off superb rococo plasterwork.

The atmosphere of opulent grandeur extends into the gardens, where herbaceous borders face across sweeping lawns. Flower-filled urns look down on Sir Joseph Paxton's grassy terraces on the south front, with shallow flights of steps descending to a fountain surrounded by an Italianate parterre. The classical conservatory, now furnished with nineteenth-century plants, is Lewis Wyatt's; Paxton

designed the fernery, but the roof has been raised to allow for the huge New Zealand tree ferns which now reach to the glass. Beyond are the vast kitchen gardens, built to service the great house in its heyday and now restored to working order again, with many of the glasshouses rebuilt. More informal planting – azaleas, rhododendrons, a collection of conifers and many other shrubs – surrounds the artificial lake known as the Golden Brook, almost concealing the Japanese garden laid out here in 1910, a mosaic of water and islands authentically planted with Japanese maples, dwarf conifers, Kurume azaleas and evergreens, and dotted with stone lanterns. A mound crowned with white stones simulates snow-capped Mount Fuji. Another surprise is the small beech maze hidden behind a bank of rhododendrons beside the long avenue known as the Broad Walk, one of only three such features in the Trust's care (*see* Glendurgan and Greys Court, pp.162 and 169).

The Home Farm at Tatton Dale was once the heart of the extensive Egerton estates, with pig sties, stockyards and stables surrounding the office from which nearly 1,000 tenant properties were administered, and workshops where everything needed on the estate would be produced, from coffins to horseshoes. Humphry Repton produced a Red Book for the extensive park, but most of the landscaping probably dates from William Emes's work in the mid-eighteenth century, with some early nineteenth-century modifications by John Webb. Flocks of Soay and Hebridean sheep mingle with the red and fallow deer beneath the trees, and the remains of the medieval manor house are used to introduce visitors to the realities of pre-modern life.

The Teign Gorge DEVON

3 miles north-east of Moretonhampstead, on both sides of the B3212 [442 D7]

The River Teign rises at Teign Head below Whitehorse Hill in the north of Dartmoor and runs north and east past Gidleigh and Chagford, gathering side streams as it goes until in the parish of Drewsteignton, where its bed is at about 152.5 metres (500 feet), it has to pierce the range of hills, 122 metres (400 feet) higher, which run parallel to the north-east side of the moor and which are outliers of it. From this point, far below Lutyens's masterpiece of Castle Drogo (*see* p.76), the Teign follows a wooded gorge for some 7 miles east, to Steps Bridge at Dunsford.

The Trust owns two substantial lengths of the gorge. At the upper end its property extends from Dogmarsh Bridge below Chagford down to Fingle Bridge, with paths on both sides of the river. On the north bank there are paths at two levels. The Hunter's Path runs along the side of the gorge above Sharp Tor and Hunter's Tor and here, below Castle Drogo, a weir across the river dams water to serve the turbine which makes electricity for the castle. The Fisherman's Path, beside the river, is also easy walking, though the granite gives way to the crumbling rock of the culm shales below Hunter's Tor.

The south bank is different. Opposite Castle Drogo Whiddon Park rises sharply from the river up to 228.5 metres (750 feet). Here is an unaltered Tudor deer-park, made by Sir John Whiddon in about 1570. There are no deer today, but the great wall built to contain them, constructed from immense blocks of granite, still stands 2.5 to 2.75 metres (8 to 9 feet) high. The park is wonderfully picturesque, with granite outcrops, groves of ancient oak, ash and rowan, broom and gorse, bracken and bilberry, and a lichen and invertebrate community that has survived from pre-Neolithic woodland. The Trust owns Whiddon Wood, to the west of the park, and also the conifer plantations between here and Fingle Bridge.

From this latter bridge down to Clifford Bridge the gorge is privately owned, but on the north bank the beautiful hanging oaks of Dunsford Wood belong to the Trust, and then continuously to Steps Bridge. On the opposite bank the woods on either side of the Doccombe stream belong, including St Thomas Cleave and running up to the B3212, as does Bridford Wood to the south of this road. Miles of paths traverse these steep woods, with peeps far down to the river below, and because oak woods let in much more light than, say, beech or conifers, there is an interesting flora beneath the trees.

Templetown Mausoleum CO. ANTRIM

In Castle Upton graveyard, Templepatrick [444 C3]

The graveyard at Castle Upton outside Templepatrick is dominated by this perfect Neo-classical temple, erected by Sarah Upton in 1789 in memory of the Hon. Arthur Upton who had died twenty years earlier. On the dignified entrance façade, urns in niches flank a rusticated arch and three more crown the parapet above the simple inscription. Coade stone plaques commemorate other members of the Upton family. One of the finest monuments ever designed by Robert Adam, the mausoleum is also one of the few examples of the architect's work in Ireland. Adam was commissioned to give a new look to Castle Upton (not owned by the Trust), but the house was subsequently remodelled and only his castellated stables near the graveyard have survived.

Theatre Royal SUFFOLK

In Westgate Street, Bury St Edmunds, on south side of the A134 from Sudbury [443 K3]

This delightfully intimate theatre, seating an audience of just under 300, is one of only three surviving Georgian playhouses. Built in 1819, it dates from an era when Bury was a provincial capital and farmers and gentry from miles around crowded into the town for the short autumn season. Comfortable red plush seats have replaced the benches in the pit, but original boxes still fill the dress circle and the stalls are steeply raked towards the stage. This little jewel is the creation of William Wilkins (1778–1839), an experienced theatre designer and one of the leading Neo-classical architects of his day, who was later to produce the National Gallery and the screen at King's College, Cambridge. Winged sphinxes and griffins decorate the dress circle and another classical frieze adorns the proscenium arch.

The pink, white and grey façade on Westgate Street, with a projecting glazed portico, is dwarfed by the huge buildings of the Greene King brewery, an ever-present reminder of the years the theatre lay forgotten. The coming of the railways in the 1840s, which transported those in search of good entertainment speedily to Norwich or London, hastened a decline which had set in a decade or so earlier and which could not be halted even by the staging of the world première of *Charley's Aunt* here in 1892. Greene King & Sons, who used the theatre as a barrel store, also played a prominent part in its revival in 1965.

Tintinhull SOMERSET

5 miles north-west of Yeovil, ½ mile south of the A303,
on east outskirts of Tintinhull [442 E6]

Formal pools, varied borders and secluded lawns in this tiny, entirely satisfying walled garden are divided by clipped hedges and seen against the backdrop of an unpretentious seventeenth- and early eighteenth-century house built of warm Ham stone. The west façade added in *c.*1722, where mullioned and transomed windows glow like liquid gold in the evening sun, overlooks one of Tintinhull's most charming features, a grassy, walled forecourt guarded by stone eagles set high on gate piers. Domes of box like vast green hedgehogs line the central path, and roses and clematis climb the walls. A flight of steps leads into the court from the central porch flanked by Tuscan columns, its curved pediment echoed in the shallow triangle breaking the roofline above.

A yew- and box-fringed path punctuated by shallow flights of steps runs gently downhill from here, past an apse-shaped lawn which is dominated by a huge *Quercus ilex* and through a thicket of azaleas to the fountain pool which closes the vista. An opening in the hedge over to the right gives a view of smoothly mown grass which frames a tranquil sheet of water, with the classical columns of a little stone loggia overlooking the far end of it. The Mediterranean feel is further enhanced by terracotta pots marking the corners of the pool, but the springy turf and the thickly planted borders on either side are quintessentially English.

The garden is still largely as created by Mrs F. E. Reiss, who moved here with her husband in 1933. This inspired plantswoman used flower and foliage, colour and texture to make pictorial compositions, setting them within an architectural framework defined by yew and box hedges and linked by axial paths, a series of outdoor rooms in the style of Hidcote (*see* p.182). She knew the value of alternating sunlight and shade in creating the spirit of a garden and how blue can be used to light dark corners. Most of the borders are mixed, mingling small trees, flowering and foliage plants, grasses and bulbs. Schemes and patterns are never repeated. Whereas one of the long beds flanking the rectangular water-lily pool is planted in deep bright colours, mostly yellow, orange and red, the other is a subtle blend of softer shades – pink, violet, and blue – with silver and grey foliage. There are many individual species here to delight the keen plantsman, but Tintinhull is above all a garden where the overall effect amounts to far more than the sum of its parts.

Townend CUMBRIA

3 miles south-east of Ambleside at south end of Troutbeck
[445 H4]

Townend is a rare and remarkably intact survival of the house of a family of yeoman farmers. Largely dating from the seventeenth century, with limewashed walls, mullioned windows and a slate roof topped with six round chimneys, it is one of the finest examples of domestic Lake District architecture. Just across the lane, dating from the same period as the house built on a much grander scale, is the homestead's stone-and-slate galleried barn, with a ramp up to the granary floor and the date 1666 carved on one of the lintels.

The Browne family who lived here for over four centuries were sheep farmers, who seem to have gradually risen in society through careful management of their affairs and judicious marriages. Much of Townend's attraction derives from the fact that its contents reflect slow accretion by several generations of the Brownes. In the little library, Milton rubs shoulders with Clarke's sermons, Walton's *Compleat Angler*, a history of England and volumes of farming periodicals. None of the books is very rare or valuable, but the collection as a whole gives a unique insight into the interests and preoccupations of a rural middle-class family.

The preservation of the house and its contents owes much to the last George Browne (1834–1914), who was both a noted antiquary and a gifted joiner and woodcarver. The rooms are filled with ornate examples of his work,

Opposite: The inviting kitchen garden at Tintinhull, as seen through the arch in the hedge from the pool garden.

Below: The kitchen at Townend. The last George Browne carved the child's chair by the fire and also decorated some of the cupboards and drawer fronts on the wall to the left. What looks like a gold-fish bowl is a device for focusing candle-power: when filled with water, the bowl concentrates light from a candle placed behind it, so enabling someone to see well enough to carry out detailed work.

from the richly carved chairs in the firehouse, the oldest part of the building, to the little spindle-fronted cupboard in one of the bedrooms, in which no two spindles are alike. Such minor masterpieces speak of long winter evenings by candlelight round the fire.

The wealth of heavy oak furniture displayed at Townend also includes the long seventeenth-century dining table in the firehouse, undoubtedly assembled *in situ*, where the Brownes would have taken meals with their farmhands and servants. From the kitchen next door, an early seventeenth-century spiral staircase winds steeply upwards to the austere quarters for the housekeeper and maids, with a pair of clogs set out ready for the morning by one of the beds.

Among many other treasures is a series of charming naive paintings of the family's sheep by local nineteenth-century artist William Taylor Longmire. Perhaps he took his models from the ancestors of the beasts which still graze the fells rising behind the house.

George Browne's notebooks have enabled the Trust to re-create the small garden as it was in the Edwardian era. Roses and a traditional mixture of cottage-garden flowers, such as delphiniums and sweet peas, fuchsias and potentillas, crowd the beds, rhododendrons and damsons are planted on the banks and there is fruit from apples, gages and plums.

These oast houses are part of a fine range of traditional buildings at Outridge Farm on the Toys Hill estate.

Town Walls Tower SHROPSHIRE

Overlooking the River Severn on the south side of Shrewsbury [442 E2]

Despite Edward I's conquest of Wales in the late thirteenth century, towns in the Welsh Marches still needed to be defended against the possibility of insurrection in the west. Of Shrewsbury's walls studded with twelve watchtowers only fragments now remain, including this four-storey fourteenth-century tower overlooking a great loop of the River Severn on the south side of town.

Toys Hill KENT

2½ miles south of Brasted, 1 mile west of Ide Hill [443 J5]

A mile and a half east of Sir Winston Churchill's beloved Chartwell (*see* p.81) lies Toys Hill, which was once part of the commons of Brasted Chart. Its 147 hectares (363 acres), rising to over 244 metres (800 feet) and including the highest point in Kent, have been built up from a tiny beginning in 1898. Local people no longer graze pigs and cattle, quarry stone, or cut peat or firewood, but the old pollarded beeches provide fascinating relics of a former land use. Sadly, only a few of these survived the Great Storm of 1987, but the Trust is now actively managing regenerating woodland and seeking to conserve aspects of the historic landscape, such as pockets of heath and wood pasture.

Treasurer's House NORTH YORKSHIRE

In Minster Yard, York, on the north side of the minster [445 J6]

Treasurer's House borders a narrow medieval cobbled street in the shadow of York Minster, only a stone's throw from the east end. Once attached to one of the wealthiest and most sought-after benefices in England, successive treasurers of the cathedral lived here from 1100 until the office was abolished under Henry VIII. Little remains of the medieval building or of the earlier structures suggested by the Roman column in the cellars.

The present elegant and roomy town house has had many and varied owners, including John Aislabie of Studley Royal (*see* p.376) and Dr Jacques Sterne, whose novelist-nephew Laurence Sterne, despite becoming a prebendary of the minster in 1741, satirised the inward-looking society of the cathedral set in his *A Political*

Romance (1759). Sterne's savage attack on local ecclesiastical courts provoked the banning of the book.

The attractive garden front, with its classical central entrance bay, dates from about 1630. The charming curved Dutch gables adorning the projecting wings on either side are also seventeenth century, but the Venetian windows in the façades below were added about a hundred years later. Although the entrance from the garden leads into a galleried hall with a medieval flavour, most of the interior dates either from the seventeenth century or early in the eighteenth. The thin, beautifully carved balusters on the stairs, possibly the work of the highly skilled local carpenter-architect, William Thornton, whose magnificent woodcarvings are the chief glory of Beningbrough Hall (*see* p.43), date from the later period, as does the airy, panelled drawing room looking over the garden.

Subsequently divided into three separate dwellings, the house was rescued by the wealthy industrialist and aesthete Frank Green, who acquired it in 1897. Removing all nineteenth-century alterations and additions, Green carefully restored the house to what he thought was its original appearance, creating a huge hall out of the two-storey central block, with a half-timbered gallery supported on classical columns. Appropriate antiques were used to form a sequence of period rooms. Furniture reflecting the craftsmanship of two centuries includes a fine oak refectory table of *c.*1600, a marquetry grandfather clock of 1680 and three early eighteenth-century tester beds in the rooms where Edward VII, then Prince of Wales, his wife Alexandra and their daughter Victoria slept when visiting the house in 1900. Three pairs of ornate early eighteenth-century giltwood mirrors make the drawing room seem even larger than it is and an exquisite walnut secretaire-bookcase of the same period stands in the staircase hall. The house is further enriched by collections of china, pottery and glass and by a number of English and Flemish portraits from the sixteenth to eighteenth centuries.

The formal walled garden fronting the principal façade was established between 1897 and 1900 by Frank Green and is largely as he left it. A central sunken lawn is bordered on one side by a pollarded plane-tree avenue and there are raised terrace walks running along the south-west and south-east walls. Nothing in the garden can compete with the view of the Minster towering above it.

Treasurer's House SOMERSET

Opposite church in middle of village of Martock; 1 mile north-west of the A303 between Ilminster and Ilchester [442 E6]

Of the clutch of late medieval priests' houses owned by the Trust (*see, for examples,* p.315), this comfortable building of mellow Ham stone, marked by a traceried two-light window and set back from the street through an archway, is perhaps the grandest. Across a spacious courtyard is a late thirteenth-century great hall, open to an arch-braced timber roof dating from the fifteenth century and with windows of *c.*1350. A screens passage divides the hall from the earlier solar block set at right angles to the south, in fact a hall house of *c.*1260 with a first-floor hall above what was originally an undercroft. In what would have been a private chamber is a wall painting of the crucifixion. A kitchen block tacked on at one corner was built in the fifteenth century. All three buildings can be seen from a second courtyard west of the great hall.

This substantial medieval survival has been linked to the village church since at least the thirteenth century, when the Treasurer of Wells Cathedral lived here and acted as Martock's rector and patron. In later years the house and associated farmland were tenanted, but a succession of Treasurers continued in the same roles until 1840.

Left: The elegant 18th-century staircase at the Treasurer's House in York. Other interiors here have been recreated to form a sequence of period rooms and furnished with appropriate, finely-crafted pieces, such as the carved oak chair in the Great Hall (above) and the walnut bidet dating from the 18th century (top) in a room fitted out as a bedroom.

Romantic Recreations

Alongside the interest in the classical world which was such a pronounced feature of the eighteenth century ran a more romantic strain. Partly this was allied to the period taste for the landscape garden, with its soft outlines and carefully composed vistas, but there was also a curiosity about anything old, which led to a new appreciation of medieval Gothic. This was the architecture of a thousand parish churches, of pointed arches, vaulting, pinnacles, tracery and gargoyles, and of manor houses with oriel windows, half-timbering, great halls and twisted brick chimneys. The methods employed were still very much alive in rural areas, where traditional building practices, unchanged for hundreds of years, were the norm.

From the late eighteenth century, Gothic began to be used self-consciously, for pictorial effect and for its romantic possibilities. Instead of classical temples, some landscapers punctuated their compositions with a freshly built Gothic ruin, or even, where opportunities allowed, incorporated vistas to genuine medieval remains, such as the ruins of the great abbeys dissolved by Henry VIII. Some treated Gothic as a decorative style, embellishing their houses with castellations or adding playful interior details. Another approach was to draw on the traditional vernacular of an area and reproduce it self-consciously in estate villages, using eyebrow dormers, porches, tall chimneys and other features for picturesque effect.

The Victorians took this borrowing from the past much further, broadening the stylistic repertoire to cover some five hundred years, from Norman to Elizabethan, and building anew in historic idioms as well as drawing on the vernacular. Often, styles and periods were mixed in the interests of an arresting composition. This approach spawned houses masquerading as castles, houses that were a riot

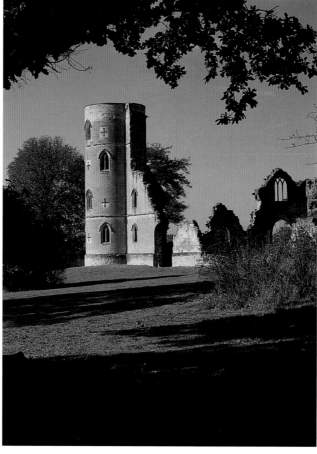

WIMPOLE HALL
431

of half-timbering, gables, and moulded arches and chimneys, and houses with richly coloured and carved interiors. At the same time, there was a serious and scholarly side to the Gothic Revival and, partly as a reaction to the Victorian machine age, a romanticised appreciation of medieval lifestyles and craft skills. In mid-century, this interest flowered in the Arts and Crafts Movement, centred on William Morris, who believed passionately in the superiority of traditional techniques and crafting objects and pieces by hand. Houses built under the influence of the movement tend to be unassertive, using local materials and vernacular styles that blended naturally with their surroundings, as do unpretentious farmhouses and cottages all over the country.

The romantic vein which fired interest in the old and in the ruins of monasteries and other medieval buildings in the 18th century fed a vogue for Gothic eye-catchers in the newly fashionable landscape garden. At Wimpole Hall in Cambridgeshire, a formal layout was gradually softened and destroyed from c.1750, when Sanderson Miller, who had begun building sham castles in the 1740s and who was acting as adviser on the landscaping, submitted designs for a Gothic ruin (**left**). Ten years later, this was built under the supervision of Capability Brown, who was now working on the park. Set in sweeping parkland amongst clumps of trees and grazed turf, it provides an intriguing focus for the view from the north front.

From the same period is the castellated and pinnacled triangular fantasy brooding over a stretch of turf in Stowe Landscape Gardens, Buckinghamshire. Designed by James Gibbs and built between 1744 and 1748, this is an eye-catcher of some weight and pretension, conceived as part of an ideological programme at Stowe and deliberately contrasted with the otherwise classical garden buildings in creamy limestone. Much more modest is the Gothic cottage at Stourhead in Wiltshire, half hidden by trees and flowering shrubs. Here, in 1806, the antiquarian Sir Richard Colt Hoare indulged his leanings towards the Picturesque and Gothic by employing the architectural draughtsman John Carter to add a Gothic porch and a bay with traceried windows and a stone seat to an existing cottage by the lake. He also built Tudor-style lodges and added parapets to cottages in the village to match those on the church. Other landowners incorporated genuine Gothic ruins in their garden views. John Aislabie, creator of the early

18th-century water garden at Studley Royal in Yorkshire, tried to buy the remains of the great Cistercian abbey which adjoined his property but was turned down. His son completed the deal, and devised the high path which suddenly opens out to a surprise view of Fountains in the valley below, with its great tower soaring heavenward.

With the help of books on its ornamental possibilities, Gothic was first applied to houses as a form of decoration. One of the earliest examples of this kind of embellishment is at St Michael's Mount in Cornwall, where a former chapel was converted into a drawing room and boudoir in the early 18th century and fitted out with plaster vaulting and other Gothic touches (below). Some time after it had become popular in England, the fashion for this kind of spidery decoration crossed the Irish Channel. Castle Ward was one of the first Gothicised houses in Ireland. Here, one side of the house has castellations, pinnacles and pointed windows, and some Gothic interiors include a boudoir (opposite, **below**) with a fan-vaulted ceiling, executed in plaster, and a dado carved with Gothic motifs.

The early Gothic Revival included an interest in artefacts and literature as well as buildings. This fine casket, with carved ivory panels illustrating a medieval romance, is one of the prize exhibits at Tyntesfield in Somerset. It was long considered to be a 14th-century treasure from Flaxley Abbey in Gloucestershire but in 1968 it was shown to date from no earlier than the late 18th century. In other words, it is an early example of a beautifully crafted fake.

TYNTESFIELD
402

CASTLE WARD
77

When Sir Thomas Acland of Killerton decided to provide housing for the pensioners on his Holnicote estate in Somerset in the 1820s, he opted for a self-conscious and picturesque use of the local vernacular. Selworthy village climbs the hill to a 15th-century church, but the thatched cottages with their tall chimneys, eyebrow dormers, deep eaves and projecting ovens were largely created by Sir Thomas.

SELWORTHY
334

CHARLECOTE PARK
80

The Victorians' interest in pictorial effect and their often romantic view of the past led to recreations of Tudor, Elizabethan and other styles, some built anew, others blended with the genuinely old. Charlecote Park in Warwickshire dates back to the 1550s and still has its Elizabethan gatehouse but the long east front, although at first glance of a piece, is largely a creation of 1829–67, when the exterior was rebuilt and its pictorial qualities improved. Octagonal corner turrets, romantic chimney pots, the pierced parapets and other details were all

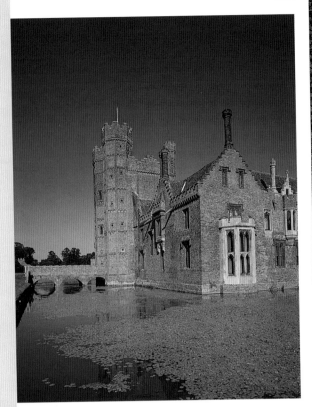

added to give a livelier effect. Similarly, at Oxburgh Hall in Norfolk, the moated late-medieval house was extensively restored by J.C. Buckler in 1830–70. The exterior was made more interesting by adding oriels and twisted terracotta chimneys, and a new suite of neo-Tudor rooms was created. The Library fireplace, with its coats of arms, was probably designed by Buckler. Above it, the Gothic oak overmantel was put together from fragments of wood taken from churches on the Continent. Cragside, set on the side of a Northumbrian valley, was built anew for the 1st Lord Armstrong from 1869. The architect

KNIGHTSHAYES COURT
206

Richard Norman Shaw drew on both the Gothic, realised in stone, and the traditional timber-framing of areas such as the Sussex Weald to produce a house which is startlingly picturesque, with deep Gothic arches (**opposite, below**), stone-mullioned windows, and black-and-white, half-timbered gables. At the same period, in the gentle Devon countryside far to the south, the arch-medievalist William Burges was commissioned to build Knightshayes Court for a *nouveau riche* entrepreneur. Although his planned interiors were toned down, the exterior is boldly Gothic, and includes a series of striking gargoyles (**above**), which look as if they might have come from an abandoned medieval church.

BADDESLEY CLINTON
31

The spirit of Victorian Romanticism is well caught in this 1885 self-portrait by Rebecca Dulcibella Orpen, whose paintings recorded life at Baddesley Clinton, the moated medieval manor in Warwickshire shown on her easel. Genuinely old, Baddesley Clinton displays many of the features – a castellated gatehouse, mullioned windows, towering chimneys and timber-framed gables – which were employed to give other houses a suitably picturesque appearance.

The sprawling, half-timbered Wightwick Manor in the West Midlands, built under the influence of the Arts and Crafts movement in the late 19th century, is also a recreation, based on the Tudor buildings of the Midlands and Welsh Marches. The Great Parlour is a pseudo-medieval great hall, with an open timber roof, a deep plaster frieze like the one in the Great Chamber at Hardwick Hall in Derbyshire, a minstrel's gallery and a deeply recessed fireplace. Hand-crafted textiles, wallpapers and other furnishings from Morris and Co. throughout the house blend well with the much more ancient, such as the Chinese vases and walnut William and Mary chairs in the Parlour.

WIGHTWICK MANOR
428

Trelissick CORNWALL

4 miles south of Truro, on both sides of the B3289 above King Harry Ferry [442 B8]

Trelissick is set in the kind of country which evokes Daphne du Maurier. The estate stands at the head of the estuary of the River Fal, a ribbon of deep water running far inland with smaller creeks and inlets branching off on either side. Woods of oak with areas of beech and pine clothe the slopes leading down to the water, hanging over the tidal mud-flats in the creeks. It is easy to imagine smugglers coming into these lonely inlets under cover of darkness. Below the house the romantically named King Harry Ferry is the only connection across the water to the Roseland peninsula on the other side. The estuary itself is still a major deep-water harbour, where huge oil tankers and cargo ships ride at anchor only metres offshore.

Although there was an ornamental woodland area on the slopes leading down to the Fal from the house remodelled by Peter Frederick Robinson in 1825 (not open to the public), the present garden was largely created by Mr and Mrs Ronald Copeland after Mrs Copeland inherited the property in 1937. Mr and Mrs Copeland planted many of the species that flourish in the mild Cornish air, including the rhododendrons and azaleas which are now such a feature of the garden, hydrangeas, camellias and flowering cherries, and exotics such as the ginkgo and various species of palm. They also ensured that the blossoms they nurtured had a wider, if unknowing audience. Mr Ronald Copeland was chairman and later managing director of his family's business, the Spode china factory, and flowers grown at Trelissick were used as models for those painted on ware produced at the works. The Copelands' family crest, a horse's head, now decorates the weathervane on the turret of the stable block, a pair to the Gilbert squirrel on the splendid Victorian Gothic water tower, an echo of the family who lived here in the second half of the nineteenth century (their ancestor, Sir Humphrey Gilbert, was lost at sea in his tiny ship *Squirrel* after discovering Newfoundland; *see* Compton Castle, p.107).

The feeling of the garden is intimate and small scale, with beeches, conifers and other trees sheltering and enclosing the valley and many changes of level and perspective. Paths bordered by high hedges suddenly open out into an area of grass, such as the spacious main lawn shaded by a large Japanese cedar. Although there are glimpses of the estuary through the trees, views are generally inward, across the valley and down to the dell at the heart of the garden, thickly planted with species hydrangeas, large-leaved rhododendrons and other exotic plants, including a banana, the Chilean fern and the Australian tree fern, and dotted with yellow and pink patches when the primulas are in flower. A narrow path leads to the rustic bridge over the Ferry Road, a green canyon through the heart of the garden. Beyond lies the wide slope of Carcadden, planted informally with conifers and a collection of choice shrubs, including hydrangeas, camellias, flowering cherries, rhododendrons and magnolias and with orange azaleas grouped round some purple-leaved nuts and maples. Near the entrance are the Trust's only fig garden, in a small enclosure, and a recently created scented garden.

Only by the house does the view open out, where Robinson's imposing columned portico rising the height of the south front looks out across a great sweep of grass to Carrick Roads. On a clear day Pendennis Castle can be seen silhouetted on one of the promontories that guard the entrance to the estuary, while across the water little boats like outsize gulls ride at anchor off Mylor harbour. Much of the woodland hugging the shores of the estuary was planted by Thomas Daniell, Robinson's patron, whose father had bought the estate in 1800 with an inherited fortune from tin-mining interests. The carriage drives Thomas laid out in the park are now leafy woodland walks, an attractive adjunct to the tree-shaded lawns and paths in the garden itself.

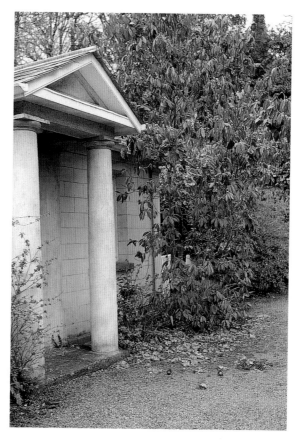

Opposite below: Trelissick on the banks of the Fal is primarily a shrub and woodland garden, mild and moist enough for tree ferns to flourish in sheltered corners and with great banks of rhododendrons and hydrangeas, among them the delicately coloured *R. macabeanum* (opposite above). Only a few miles away is Trengwainton, the second of the Trust's trio of lush Cornish gardens, where *R. macabeanum*, brought back to England by the plant-hunter Kingdon-Ward, flowered for the first time. Left: A camellia on the gatehouse heralds the drifts and banks of this plant in the garden beyond.

Trencrom Hill CORNWALL

3 miles south of St Ives, 4½ miles north-east of Penzance, 2 miles west of junction of the A30 and the A3074 [442 A8]

A single wall following the contours of the hill and incorporating natural outcrops of granite traces the irregular outline of this small Iron Age hill-fort dating from the second century BC, superbly sited on a gorse-covered tor in the far west of Cornwall. The remains of over seventeen hut circles have been found in the enclosure. To the north the fort looks over a typically Cornish patchwork of tiny stone-walled fields towards the blue expanses of St Ives Bay and the Atlantic beyond.

Trengwainton CORNWALL

2 miles north-west of Penzance, ½ mile west of Heamoor on the B3312 Penzance–Morvah road [442 A8]

This exotic garden climbing gently uphill for about a third of a mile following a little stream was largely created after 1925 by Lieutenant Colonel Sir Edward Bolitho, who inherited the rambling Victorian mansion (not open to the public) looking down the valley. Like the secluded gardens of Glendurgan and Trelissick a few miles east (*see* pp.162 and opposite), Trengwainton is particularly favoured climatically, well watered and rarely experiencing severe frosts. A remarkable collection of tender and half-hardy trees, shrubs and other plants has been established here, many of which could only be grown under glass elsewhere in the country.

The skeleton of Trengwainton is much older. The tall beeches and oaks along the stream and sheltering the house, without which the little valley would be open to the full force of the westerly gales, were planted in the early nineteenth century by Rose Price, the son of a rich West Indian sugar planter. A considerable income from the Jamaican plantations was also responsible for the unusual walled garden at the foot of the drive, expensively constructed with brick, a warmer material than the native granite. Designed as a series of compartments, the garden's dividing walls have a steeply sloped bed of banked-up soil on their western side, a rare survival of a practice that was common in the late eighteenth and early nineteenth centuries. Like vineyards on south- and west-facing slopes, these beds reap the full benefit of the sun, producing

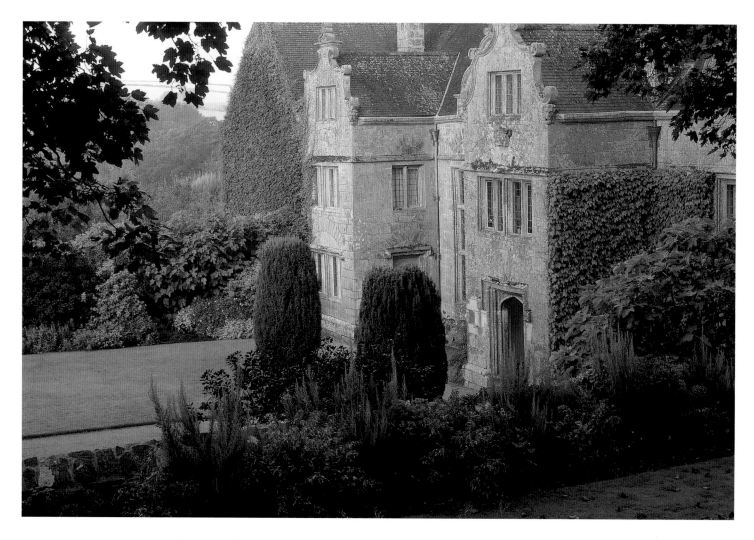

early crops of vegetables and succouring tender plants. Currently, there are ambitious plans to reinstate the original kitchen garden in this area.

Five varied compartments on the south side of the walled area suggest the back of a row of town houses, with handkerchief-sized lawns dominated by a magnolia or some other large species and with borders filled with a variety of plants – camellias, eucalyptus, the Chatham Island forget-me-not, the snowy-yellow *Azara dentata* from Chile, the passion flower, a climbing hydrangea from Japan or *Cassia corymbosa* from tropical America, with golden-yellow flowers which last through the autumn months. In late spring the air is filled with the fragrance of sweet-scented tender rhododendrons, many of them, such as *Rhododendron macabeanum*, *R. elliottii*, *R. taggianum* and *R. concatenans*, raised from seed brought back from the foothills of the eastern Himalayas in 1927–8 on an expedition partly financed by Colonel Bolitho.

The walk up to the house from here leads through the jungly stream garden beside the drive. Woodland glades are coloured by massed banks of rhododendrons, flowering scarlet, white and purple, and by a pale blue wash from hundreds of hydrangeas in late summer. Wooden bridges lead over the stream, primulas, lilies and other water-loving plants hug the banks, and Australian tree ferns and graceful feathery bamboos overhang the water.

Past a pond shadowed by tree ferns, the path leads on to the terrace fronting the house, with its two summer-houses. Most of the garden is inward-looking, with walls and thick vegetation giving a sense of enclosure. But on the terrace the vista suddenly opens out, giving a memorable view of St Michael's Mount (*see* p.328) rising like a fairy castle in the bay far below, with the long shadow of the Lizard beyond.

Trerice CORNWALL

3 miles south-east of Newquay, via the A392 and the A3058
[442 B7]

Trerice is not grand. A small but quite sophisticated Elizabethan house built of local buff-coloured limestone, it escaped later alteration in the prosperous eighteenth and nineteenth centuries, the heyday of the Cornish mining industries, perhaps because its owners chose to live elsewhere. Belonging to the Arundells, one of the great families of Cornwall, for over 400 years, in 1802 it passed to the Aclands, whose principal estates were in Devon and Somerset (*see* Killerton, p.202).

The nature of the house is heralded in an approach down a narrow winding lane, with hedges high on either side. An unpretentious gateway leads into a small grassy walled garden in front of the house, where two granite Arundell lions guard the path to the front door. Trerice faces east, its traditional E-shaped façade with a central porch surmounted by decorative scrolled gables in the Dutch style; unusual in Cornwall, their presence here perhaps reflects Sir John Arundell's service in the Low Countries for Elizabeth I. The bay to the left of the porch is entirely filled by the two-storey window lighting the great hall, original sixteenth-century glass still composing many of the 576 panes supported by a lattice of mullions and transoms.

On the first floor is the sunny, south-facing great chamber which Sir John Arundell probably created out of a medieval solar. The room is richly decorated with bold Elizabethan plasterwork over the fireplace and on the splendid barrel ceiling, one of the best of the period in the West Country. Although, apart from the 6-metre (20-foot)

table in the hall, made for the house in the early eighteenth century, none of the furniture is original, there are some good oak and walnut pieces, including a longcase clock by Thomas Tompion, a Queen Anne escritoire and an eighteenth-century travelling case fitted out with bottles for wines and spirits, and also some fine Chinese and English eighteenth-century porcelain and glass. Paintings by John Opie, who was born at Trevallas, only 15 miles away, add an appropriately Cornish flavour, among them portraits of his two wives, Mary and Amelia. There are also many reminders of the Arundells' devotion to the royal cause in the seventeenth century. The hall is filled with Stuart portraits and a haunting picture of Charles I by Henry Stone hangs in the court chamber upstairs. The face is careworn, the eyes withdrawn and watchful. Also in the house is an enchanting Jacobean embroidery panel, believed to depict Charles and his queen, showing Henrietta giving the king a bunch of flowers while a large snail crawls between them and a long-eared rabbit looks on.

Across the cobbled, walled courtyard behind the house lies a magnificent great barn of a size and age – it probably dates from the fifteenth century – rarely seen in Cornwall. A ramp from the flat lawn above, where the Home Guard drilled in the Second World War, leads to the unusual lawn-mower collection in the hayloft of the former stable. Some very early machines here were produced after Mr Budding's initial invention of 1831.

Few traces remain of the small, old-fashioned enclosed gardens known to have surrounded Trerice until 1915. Steps from the grassy court in front of the house lead up onto what was the bowling-green and another flight from there to an upper lawn, from where there is a roof-level view of the gables on the east front. The garden to the south has vanished completely and the grass here is now planted with fruit trees set out in the quincunx pattern used in the seventeenth century, where every tree is in line with its neighbour from wherever it is viewed. An early fifteenth-century chapel has also disappeared, although its site lives on in the field name Chapel Close.

Treryn Dinas CORNWALL

4 miles south-east of Land's End, 7 miles south-west of Penzance [442 A8]

The jagged granite headland of Treryn Dinas juts into the sea at the southern end of the Penwith peninsula, an inhospitable jumbled mass of rock exposed to the full

Opposite: The chapel at Tyntesfield, rich with carved stone, stained glass and glittering mosaics, was the last addition to the house and reflects William Gibbs's deep religious faith.

Below: Set in the little valley of the Wybrnant, Tŷ Mawr is typical of the rough-walled old farmhouses found in this part of Wales and is still almost as remote as it was in the 16th century.

force of westerly gales and battered by Atlantic breakers. Several Iron Age forts were built on promontories such as this, all round the coasts of Wales and Cornwall, the need to defend only one approach presumably compensating for the bleakness of the sites. At Treryn Dinas the headland is cut off by four parallel banks and ditches, the outermost, probably dating from the first century BC, an earthwork of immense size. The famous 66-ton rocking boulder known as the Logan Rock is contained within the defences.

Tudor Merchant's House
PEMBROKESHIRE

Quay Hill, Tenby [442 B4]

Like Aberconwy House (*see* p.17), this narrow late fifteenth-century three-storey building looking down Bridge Street only metres from the harbour is typical of the prosperous medieval dwellings that would have crowded the lanes of this little town when it was a thriving port in the fourteenth and fifteenth centuries. Sturdily built of lime and sandstone rubble, the house still retains a garderobe turret rising the height of the building, its original jointed roof trusses and a circular chimneystack characteristic of this part of Wales. Although the interior has been much altered, a late medieval trailing flower pattern painted in red, black and yellow on wet plaster emerged from beneath no fewer than 23 coats of whitewash on the only surviving original partition.

Tŷ Mawr GWYNEDD

At the head of the little Wybrnant Valley, 3½ miles south-west of Betws-y-Coed, 2 miles west of Penmachno [444 F8]

This little sixteenth-century farmhouse hidden away on the eastern edge of the Snowdon massif, with its rough stone walls, slate roof, massive chimneys and deep-set windows, is typical of Wales's scattered upland dwellings. This isolated spot was the birthplace of Bishop William Morgan (*c*.1541–1604), whose translation of the Bible into Welsh is still in use today. Realising that the Welsh had no alternative to the Latin service after the Reformation, in 1563 Elizabeth I ordered the four Welsh bishops and the Bishop of Hereford to produce a translation of the Prayer Book and the Bible within three years. The New Testament published in 1567 was a stilted, pedantic text, bearing no comparison to William Morgan's triumphantly

fluid masterpiece produced in Armada year (1588) with a dedication to his queen. Alas, although the bishop was born and grew up in this remote valley, the farmhouse almost certainly post-dates him.

Tyntesfield SOMERSET

Off B3130, 3 miles west of Nailsea [442 E5]

This romantic High Victorian Gothic mansion is set on steeply rising ground, with woods behind it and a panoramic view south over parkland and the valley of the Yeo to the distant ridge of the Mendips. Still all of a piece with its original furnishings, decorative schemes and the accumulated possessions of the family which lived here for four generations, this memorable place is an unspoilt and largely unaltered example of a Gothic Revival country house. Windows are stone-mullioned and traceried, there are pepper-pot turrets, huge chimneystacks and fanciful Gothic dormers, and window bays and rooflines are finished off with carved friezes, pierced parapets, finials and gargoyles. Rising over the house is the steeply-pitched roof of a spectacular chapel, with finialled buttresses between the Gothic windows and a west-end stair turret.

Together with 200 hectares of gardens, park and estate, Tyntesfield was acquired by the National Trust in 2002 after a whirlwind campaign to save the property from being sold on the open market, which required the Trust to raise over £20 million in 50 days. This was only made possible by a huge public response, and a measure of the brinkmanship involved is that the contents had already been ticketed and sorted for sale by auction. Much conservation and restoration needs to be done, but, in a break with past policy, visitors are being shown around while this is in progress and, where feasible, introduced to challenges and discoveries.

Tyntesfield is predominantly the creation of the entrepreneurial William Gibbs (1790–1875). Involved in the family firm, which had business interests in Spain and Latin America, from a young age, by 1842, when he was in his early fifties, William was in charge. In the same year, the firm's South American agent concluded the deal which was to make him a fortune, giving Gibbs and Sons a virtual monopoly in the shipment of Peruvian guano, then a fertiliser of prime importance. A growing family may have encouraged William and his wife Blanche, 28 years his junior, to look for a place out of London, and in 1843 William bought what was then a Georgian country house

The eventful west front of Tyntesfield, with a skyline of chimneystacks, turrets and finialled gables. Buried in the middle of the façade is a surviving section of the Regency house which was remodelled to create this Victorian Gothic fantasy.

in changes made by George Gibbs, 1st Lord Wraxall (1873–1931), who was a prominent politician and socialiser and invited members of the government down for country-house weekends. Again, though, with the exception of the drawing room, the essential character of the place was retained.

The 2nd Lord Wraxall (1928–2001) succeeded to the title when he was only three, and his mother Ursula, Lady Wraxall ran Tyntesfield for many years. At the end of his life, Lord Wraxall was living at Tyntesfield alone and many of the main rooms were shut up, but he maintained a keen interest in the gardens and estate and kept the fabric of the place in good order. Most importantly, although he sold some items, he did not follow the reaction against High Victorian art which led to other houses being stripped of their contents, and he added pictures and other objects to the collection

The interior is of a piece, combining original decorative schemes with much surviving Victorian furniture, some of it, such as a richly ornamented rolltop desk, by the Warwickshire cabinet-makers Collier and Plucknett, who supplied the family with furniture later in the century. Wood and stone has been used profligately: there are open timber roofs, decorative panelling and parquet floors; monumental fireplaces, stone arches and doorways and pillars of polished marble. The main rooms are arranged around the toplit staircase hall, with clerestory windows beneath an open roof of English oak. Paintings hung thickly on the walls include a portrait of William, with white hair and side whiskers, and a seascape by Sir Augustus Wall Callcott, all steely sky and blue-grey sea.

William's spirit is strong in the spacious library which fills one of the wings on the entrance front. A comfortable, welcoming room rising to an open oak roof, it has the original carpet, in deep reds and blues, by the fashionable decorators J.G. Crace and Son and this company also provided the deep-buttoned armchairs and sofa. William's seven children staged theatricals here, and the bookcases round the walls, carefully numbered in Latin numerals, are stuffed with the gilded bindings of his library. William's religious sympathies lay with the Oxford Movement, launched in the 1830s to return ceremony and ritual, and thus elements of beauty and mystery, to the Church of England. The main texts of the movement are here, and so too are key works on the Gothic Revival, with which it went hand in hand, including the writings of Pugin and Ruskin. Above the bookcases and arranged along the mantelpiece are displays of Imari porcelain – blue and white, green and red.

with some decorative Gothic touches. Twenty years later he commissioned the architect John Norton, who had learned his trade from a pupil and friend of Augustus Welby Pugin and so had direct links with the most influential figure of the Gothic Revival (*see* p.91), to remodel Tyntesfield.

The house is built of golden Bath stone, with roofs covered partly in tiles, partly in heavy stone slabs quarried in Wiltshire. Carved stone decoration enlivens every façade, including some finely detailed, three-dimensional work by a certain Mr Beates, who realised the plants and creatures of the gardens and estate in stone. There are primroses, cobnuts and strawberries carved on corbels in the porch, and a capital carries a dormouse, bees and a lizard. As throughout the house the craftsmanship is of the highest quality.

William's son Antony (1841–1907), an art collector and highly skilled amateur craftsman rather than a businessman, moved into Tyntesfield in 1890 after the death of his mother. He embarked on alterations, but his chosen architect, Henry Woodyer, also worked in the Gothic Revival style and Woodyer's changes, including the substantial verandah which he had added on for Blanche in 1883, were all in keeping with the earlier work. By the next generation, a shift in taste was reflected

The dining room, entered through a flamboyant carved stone doorway and lined with wallpaper imitating Spanish leather, is Antony Gibbs's. But the drawing room was altered and refurnished by his son George and his first wife Via and has a Renaissance-style fireplace and crimson damask on the walls, and original Crace carpet dyed to match. On display is a pair of intricately-turned ivory candlesticks made by Antony, and the Flaxley casket, also of carved ivory. Once though to be medieval, the casket is in fact an intriguing early Gothic Revival fake. Much more relaxed in spirit is the capacious billiard room, with an array of antlered heads on the walls, skins casually thrown over ageing sofas, and a centrally heated table with an electric scoreboard.

Beyond the extensive servants' quarters is William's chapel, designed by Arthur Blomfield and only just finished when William died; the family entered via a bridge from the first floor. Provided with a chancel and ornate screen and richly fitted out with gleaming mosaics, stained glass and an inlaid floor it proclaims William's commitment to High Church principles. A silver chalice and flagon were designed for the chapel by William Butterfield in 1876.

The layout of the garden is still very much as it was when William died in 1875, and the plantings are lushly mature. Close to the house, billowing hollies lap the marble urns set along the lower terrace, and bright displays of bedding plants reflect the taste of the 2nd Lord Wraxall. A lone palm and luxuriant magnolias and camellias outside the billiard room mark the site of John Norton's huge conservatory, with an onion dome and gilded cupola, that was demolished in 1917. A formal walk lined by mushroom domes of holly stretches away from the west front; above it, sheltered by trees, is the former rose garden, with a central pergola, a couple of dilapidated summer houses, and a rocky fernery to one side. Another long walk, marked by clipped Irish yews, echoes the line of the terraces, with views over the sadly waterless lake. Architectural stone Gothic seats punctuate the ends of the walks.

Everywhere in the landscaped grounds are huge specimen trees, among them redwoods, maples, chestnuts, cedars of Lebanon and copper beeches, and a ha-ha allows uninterrupted views right across the park and the valley beyond it. Hidden from the house are the impressive walled kitchen gardens, with greenhouses that are still very much in use, and a splendid half-ruined classical orangery, of brick and stone. Cut flowers and fresh vegetables are still supplied to the house from these gardens as they always have been.

Ty'n-y-Coed Uchaf CONWY

1½ miles south of Betws-y-Coed on B4406 [444 F8]

This small upland farm is spread along the Afon Machno in the beautiful hill and valley country on the north-east fringes of the Snowdonia National Park. The walk from the car park leads south up the river for three-quarters of a mile, through small stone-walled pastoral fields. Traditionally managed so as to conserve a rich flora and related wildlife, these meadows are full of wild flowers. Several orchid species include the Greater Butterfly and Northern Marsh orchid, and there are areas of dry grassland and rush which attract Common Blue and Small Pearl Bordered Fritillary butterflies. The small stone-built, nineteenth-century farmhouse sits amongst outbuildings at the upper end of the farm a little way back from the Machno and is shown with the furniture and fittings acquired by generations of tenants.

Uppark WEST SUSSEX

5 miles south-east of Petersfield on the B2146, 1½ miles south of South Harting [443 H6]

The serene two-storey house built in about 1690 for Lord Grey, Earl of Tankerville, owes its existence to his grandfather's invention of an effective method of pumping water to great heights, without which the commanding site on a crest of the South Downs would have been impractical.

The amoral and duplicitous Lord Grey is one of many colourful characters connected with the estate, emerging remarkably unscathed from his involvement in the Duke of Monmouth's rebellion against James II, perhaps because he turned king's evidence. His new house, whose architect is uncertain, was in the latest Dutch style. Standing four-square like a giant doll's house, it is built of red brick with weathered, lichen-tinted stone dressings and dormer windows in a hipped roof. A pediment crowns the south front and detached mid-eighteenth-century stable and kitchen blocks balance the composition on either side.

The rich interior is mostly the work of Sir Matthew Fetherstonhaugh, who bought Uppark in 1747. This cultivated man, heir to the vast fortune of a distant relative, redecorated most of the principal rooms and enriched the house with a magnificent collection of carpets, furniture and works of art, much of it, such as portraits by Batoni and four harbour and coastal scenes by Joseph Vernet, purchased on a Grand Tour with his wife Sarah in 1749–51. The couple were responsible for the hauntingly beautiful

Sir Matthew Fetherstonhaugh, who extensively remodelled the interior of Uppark, in a portrait by Pompeo Batoni. This picture was painted in Rome in 1751, while Sir Matthew and his wife were on an extended Grand Tour and the baronet was one of the first of a stream of British gentry and nobility who were immortalised by Batoni.

Since the disastrous fire in 1989, Uppark's interiors (right and above) have been brilliantly restored, with plasterwork, fabrics and woodwork made to match what has been lost. Opposite: Some details, such as the serpent on this doorcase, have been left unfinished to show what was involved.

white and gold saloon, with its delicate plaster ceiling and ivory silk brocade curtains framing the long south-facing windows, and with paintings set into fixed plasterwork frames in the Adam style. Fireplaces inlaid with Sienese marble warm both ends of the room, one of them carved with the Sienese wolf suckling Romulus and Remus. Sarah also introduced the highly-crafted doll's house of c.1740, with a pedimented façade opening to reveal three floors. Every detail is accurate. Diminutive landscape paintings hang on the walls, hallmarked silver and glass gleam on the dining-room table and there are fire irons of silver and

brass. Meticulously dressed dolls people the mansion, those representing the family identifiable by their wax faces, the lower orders depicted in wood.

Matthew's only son Harry inherited his parents' good taste and enriched their collection. But in other respects he was a prodigal young man, with a love of hunting and the turf which is echoed in his sporting pictures and silver-gilt cups. His close friend the Prince Regent was a frequent guest at the lavish house parties staged at Uppark, with superb meals produced by Harry's French chef Moget. It was on one of these occasions that the fifteen-year-old

Emma Hart, the future Lady Hamilton, is said to have danced on the dining-room table. Sir Harry's liaison with Emma, whom he had discovered in London, was only brief, and the letters she wrote to him after she had been sent away, six months pregnant, went unanswered. Decades later Sir Harry caused another stir when, in his seventieth year, he married young Mary Ann Bullock, his head dairymaid. Largely because of this girl and her sister Frances, who joined the household, Uppark was to survive the nineteenth century little changed.

In the basement is an extensive range of service rooms, full of echoes of life below stairs. There is an authentically laid out butler's pantry, and the sunny room where H.G. Wells's mother presided as housekeeper from 1880–93 has easy chairs drawn up by the fire and tea laid on a tray. Long whitewashed tunnels, down which the young Wells chased the maids, lead to the eighteenth-century pavilions flanking the house. One was a stable block, the other a laundry and greenhouse where, in *c*.1815, Sir Harry installed a new kitchen. During most of the nineteenth century the present kitchen, with a long scrubbed table and gleaming pots and pans, was probably a still room, used for making cakes and drinks and for giving final touches to the dishes for upstairs after their long journey through the tunnel.

Much of Uppark's charm derives from its setting, with a great stretch of downland turf planted with mature trees sweeping away from the house and leading the eye across a rolling landscape to the sea. Humphry Repton, who added the pillared portico to the north front, was probably also responsible for Mary Ann's elegant dairy, its white tiles decorated with a blue and green frieze of clematis, and for the little Gothic summerhouse.

One of the more traumatic events in the Trust's recent history was the fire at Uppark in 1989, from which most of the furniture and paintings were rescued but which largely destroyed their eighteenth-century setting. Restoration took 5½ years, and required the re-learning of traditional skills. Plasterwork was re-created, intricate mouldings and architraves re-carved, new curtains woven and wallpaper printed. From the outset, the Trust aimed to maintain the air of faded elegance which makes the house so attractive. New was carefully matched to old, even to the extent of imitating picture-protected patches of wallpaper and time-darkened white paint, but almost every room has also been left with scorched floorboards and chimneypieces and other reminders of the fire, or with unfinished, newly created detail, such as an ungilded ornamental cherub. Wherever possible, fire-mangled and shattered fittings were put back together: lanterns and

chandeliers that had been reduced to twisted metal shapes and fragments of glass were painstakingly reconstructed and a scagliola table-top was pieced together, bit by bit.

All this, and much else, is conveyed in an extensive highly visual exhibition on the fire (fought with water piped from the main at the foot of the Downs) and the whole restoration process. At the house itself, all drama has gone. As before, the most enduring memory is of mellow pink brick and lichened stone against a life-enhancing view. And martins have returned to nest under the eaves.

Pastoral Upper Wharfedale, with field boundaries and buildings made of local limestone.

Upper Wharfedale NORTH YORKSHIRE

North-west of Kettlewell, on B6160 [445 I5]

This extensive Pennine estate in the well-wooded pastoral valley of the upper Wharfe includes some of the finest countryside in the Yorkshire Dales National Park. This is an ice-smoothed, limestone landscape, with a broad, glacier-moulded valley floor walled by steeply rising slopes soaring 305 metres (1,000 feet) to the high fells. Farms and bridges are built of the local stone, and dry-stone walls edge the fields, carving the valley floor into a geometric patchwork and running up the hillsides to the acid moorland on the tops. In places the limestone shows through, outcropping in white scars on steeper slopes and in the bed of the river.

The Trust's estate includes eight upland farms, a former deer-park and substantial stands of ancient oak woodland on the valley sides. Most of the farms are being run in the traditional way and there are over a hundred of the sturdy roughwalled field barns, as big as houses, which are such a distinctive feature of this landscape. Each set in its own meadow, they were used to house cattle and their fodder over the winter. The Yockenthwaite stone circle, the remains of a Bronze Age burial mound, is a reminder of how long this country has been settled. Norse pastoralists, moving their stock from valley to fells in the summer months, gave the landscape its evocative names, such as gill, scar, tarn and beck, and in the Middle Ages Wharfedale was part of the great monastic sheepwalks which fed the riches of Fountains (*see* p.154) and Bolton Abbeys. The walls criss-crossing the farmland are relatively recent additions, most of them dating from the Enclosure Acts of the late eighteenth and early nineteenth centuries, when the field barns were also built.

Now this is walking country, traversed by the long-distance Dales Way which follows the valley and with a network of other footpaths. There are dunlin and golden plover on the heights, waterfalls on the gills tumbling into the Wharfe, and long views over a soft green and grey landscape.

Upton House WARWICKSHIRE

1 mile south of Edge Hill, 7 miles north-west of Banbury, on west side of the Stratford-upon-Avon road [443 G3]

People reveal themselves in how they choose to live. Walter Samuel, 2nd Viscount Bearsted, had the great good fortune to inherit the wealth acquired by his father, who built up the Shell organisation from very small beginnings in the late nineteenth century to an international corporation. Innumerable bequests to charities, hospitals and schools are eloquent testimony to the 2nd Viscount's humanitarianism, but those who did not know of his activities would gain a sense of his benevolence towards his fellow men by visiting Upton.

Many of the outstanding works of art which fill every room are concerned in one way or another with human beings. Among a number of works by fifteenth- and sixteenth-century masters is El Greco's *El Espolio* (the Flagellation of Christ), the spears of the soldiers grouped behind Our Lord suggesting a crown of thorns. In another strongly atmospheric work, Brueghel's *Dormition of the Virgin*, Our Lady is shown receiving a lighted taper from St Peter in a dimly lit room. The use of grey and black alone gives the picture a ghostly quality as if both the radiant figure in the bed and the shadowy, hooded women crowding round are not of this world. Serene Dutch interiors and landscapes with diminutive figures set against immense skies include Saenredam's cool study of St Catherine's Church, Utrecht, in which beetle-like clerics and two men inscribing a stone set into the floor are dwarfed by the soaring arches of the nave. A little dog is silhouetted against the magnificent tiered screen enclosing the east end, and the central pulpit proclaims that this is a Protestant church.

Dogs feature more prominently in the sporting pictures in the dining room. Here, too, hang Stubbs's *Haymakers*, *Reapers* and *Labourers*, the weariness evident in the horses about to take away a laden cart as real as the chill of Hogarth's early winter morning in front of St Paul's, Covent Garden, one of the paintings for his engraved series, *The Four Times of Day*.

Lord Bearsted's collection of china and porcelain is similarly wide-ranging. Here, again, figures feature prominently, among the most memorable being two Chelsea pieces in the long gallery depicting a wet nurse suckling a swaddled baby and a shepherd teaching his shepherdess how to play the flute, holding the instrument for her as she blows. People even adorn the eighteenth-century furniture in this room, embroidered with scenes of weaving, grape-treading and other occupations.

Architecturally, Upton is a mongrel. A baroque broken pediment on the long entrance façade advertises the modest Restoration house, now overwhelmed by additions made during the eighteenth century and later. Percy

Morley Horder's comprehensive reworking for Lord Bearsted transformed the interior into one of the most luxurious houses of the 1920s, though it has the impersonality of a hotel or liner of the period. In contrast, the gardens are full of character, descending steeply from the cedar-framed lawn and broad double terrace fronting the south façade to a chain of ponds in the valley below. A collection of asters flourishes on the warm dry terrace banks and cascades of wistaria and sprays of roses overhang the Italianate balustraded stairway added in the 1930s, its lichen-stained steps leading into the depths of the combe. The mellow brick wall of the old kitchen garden on the slope of the valley still carries espaliered fruit trees as it did in the seventeenth century, and sets off borders of lavender, hollyhocks and lupins among the rows of vegetables.

Orderly planting here, and in the little yew-enclosed rose garden, contrasts with the wilder bog garden in a natural amphitheatre to the west of the house where another combe joins the first. Sheep graze on the other side of the valley and over a mile away, just visible from the terrace, a lake reflects the columns of a little eighteenth-century Tuscan temple.

The outstanding collection of art and 18th-century porcelain at Upton House includes Hogarth's *Morning* (left), set in London's Covent Garden, and the Chelsea figures known as *The Music Lesson* (below), part of a large display of early English porcelain in the house.

The valley of the River Dwyryd as it winds slowly down to the sea.

Vale of Ffestiniog GWYNEDD

Running from Blaenau Ffestiniog to Porthmadog [442 C1–D1]

Above Penrhyndeudraeth, the Dwyryd river curls placidly up the Vale of Ffestiniog's water meadows for 5 miles. On the north bank are the hanging oak woods which make the valley so lovely. When they were threatened with conversion to conifer woodland in the 1960s, Coeddyd Maentwrog, in the upper part of the vale, was acquired intact, while Coed Cae Fali, lower down, had already been partially replanted. Now some 190 hectares (470 acres) are in the Trust's hands and the oak woods are being revitalised. Plenty of paths and the Ffestiniog railway above the tree line make access easy.

The Vyne HAMPSHIRE

4 miles north of Basingstoke, between Bramley and Sherborne St John [443 H5]

This long U-shaped red-brick house with purple diaper-work lacing the façades is set low in a hollow. There is a pedimented portico on the garden front and the original mullions have been replaced with mid-seventeenth-century sash windows, but the E-plan is that of a Tudor house. Dating from some time between 1500 and 1520, The Vyne was built for William, 1st Lord Sandys, whose long career in the service of Henry VIII culminated in his appointment to the office of Lord Chamberlain in 1526.

Seen from the other side of the lake bordering the spacious, shady lawns on the north side of the house, Sandys's battlemented chapel juts out conspicuously on the far left. One of the most perfect private oratories in England, this lofty room rising the height of two storeys is still largely as it was built in 1518–27. Intricately carved canopied stalls facing across the chapel are fringed by richly coloured blue, yellow, orange and green early sixteenth-century Italian tiles that were found in the grounds. Morning sunlight streams in through the three magnificent stained-glass windows above the altar apse, rivalled only by those of similar date in King's College, Cambridge. The depictions of Henry VIII and Catherine of Aragon, the queen accompanied by a little dog, would have been hidden from view when the king came here with Anne Boleyn in 1535.

The Oak Gallery stretching the length of the west wing on the first floor is another survival from the Tudor house, one of the finest examples of its date in Britain. The delicate pale linenfold panelling which lines the walls from floor to ceiling carries a wealth of carved badges and devices, including the Tudor rose and Catherine of Aragon's pomegranate and the curious portcullis-like hemp bray used in the separation of flax fibres, crest of Sir Reginald Bray, uncle of Lord Sandys's wife. The white marble of a seventeenth-century classical fireplace in the middle of the east wall is echoed in a series of portrait busts set down the room, a mixed company in which portrayals of Shakespeare, Milton and Mary Queen of Scots rub shoulders with a typically arrogant Nero and a world-weary Seneca.

Lord Sandys's service to Henry VIII was rewarded at the Dissolution of the Monasteries with the gift of Mottisfont Abbey (*see* p.254) and it was here that the family retired when impoverishment in the Civil War forced the sale of The Vyne in 1653. The new owner was another successful and astute politician, Chaloner Chute, shortly to be Speaker in Richard Cromwell's parliament, who reduced the size of the house and added the classical portico on the north front, thought to be the earliest on a domestic building. His grandson Edward acquired the Queen Anne furniture and Soho tapestries now displayed in the house, such as the hangings depicting oriental scenes in the room next to the gallery, full of gay spotted butterflies and darting birds and with a monkey sitting in a palm tree. Chute's great-grandson John, friend of Walpole, made notable alterations in about 1750, creating the theatrical classical staircase, with its moulded ceiling in pale blue and white, a first-floor gallery fringed with ornate fluted columns and busts of Roman emperors on the newel posts.

John Chute was also responsible for the tomb chamber off the chapel, built in honour of his distinguished ancestor. Here the Speaker lies immortalised in Carrara marble on the top of a box-like monument loosely disguised as a Greek temple. His lifelike effigy rests on an unyielding plaited straw mattress, his head supported on his right arm, one finger extended along the curve of his brow.

Waddesdon Manor BUCKINGHAMSHIRE

6 miles north-west of Aylesbury, on the A41, 11 miles south-east of Bicester [443 H4]

The great châteaux of the Loire Valley made such an impression on the young Ferdinand de Rothschild, grandson of the founder of the Austrian branch of this famous banking family (*see* p.26), that he determined to model any house he might build on what he had seen in France. This magnificent palace designed by Gabriel Hippolyte Destailleur fulfilled the young Baron's dreams, its pinnacles, mansard roofs, dormer windows, massive chimneys and staircase towers reproducing the characteristic features of Maintenon, Blois and other French Renaissance châteaux. The 45-year-old Ferdinand purchased the hill on which Waddesdon is set from the Duke of Marlborough in 1874, carving out a platform for his mansion and importing half-grown trees to clothe the slopes. Building materials were brought up by cable, while the timber was hauled laboriously up the hill by teams of horses.

The classical monument to Speaker Chaloner Chute (left), who bought The Vyne in 1653, fills the chamber off the Tudor chapel, where period fittings include some delightful Italian floor tiles (above).

An aerial view of Waddesdon Manor, a French château in all but name. The magnificent house is set off by an elaborate parterre on the south front.

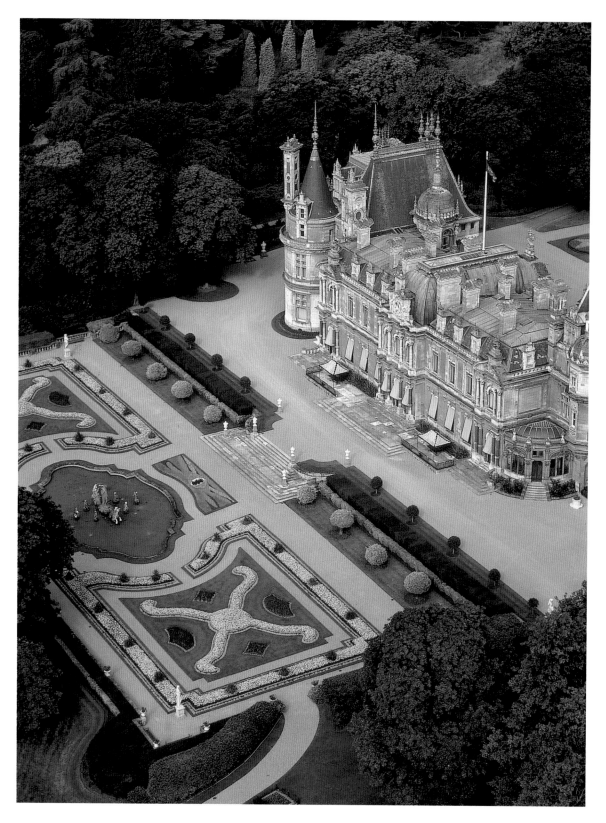

The French-inspired interiors are similarly extravagant, with a procession of high-ceilinged reception rooms re-creating the elegant splendour of the pre-Revolutionary regime. Profiting from Baron Haussmann's remodelling of Paris for Napoleon III, Ferdinand was able to obtain panelling from the great eighteenth-century houses destroyed to form the city's new boulevards, and this elaborately carved woodwork can be seen in almost every room. Royal fleurs-de-lis feature prominently on the Savonnerie carpets, a representation of the Sun King himself appearing on one from a set which Louis XIV commissioned for the long gallery of the Louvre. Eight pieces of furniture were made for the French royal family by the great Jean-Henri Riesener, the leading cabinetmaker of his day, including a marquetry writing-table created for Marie Antoinette and a drop-front secretaire ordered for the queen by Louis XVI. Elegant little tables with delicate gazelle-like legs contrast with the Baron's massive cylinder-top desk that once belonged to the dramatist Beaumarchais and a monumental black and gold secretaire surmounted by a clock and crowned by a huge gilt eagle. Teardrop chandeliers are reflected in mirrors with ornate gilt frames and every surface is crammed with clocks, Sèvres and Meissen porcelain and *objets d'art*, such as a gold snuffbox that once belonged to Louis XV's mistress, Madame de Pompadour, with her pet dogs, Ines and Mimi, shown cavorting on the lid. Paintings by Watteau, Lancret, Boucher and Greuze help to create a sense of pre-Revolutionary France.

These French pieces are harmoniously combined with a fine collection of English eighteenth-century portraits by Gainsborough, Reynolds and Romney, and with a number of seventeenth-century Dutch paintings, such as Jan van der Heyden's tranquil view of an Amsterdam canal, with stepped red-brick gables reflected in the still waters, a garden scene by de Hooch, and Rubens's dreamy *The Garden of Love*. One of the two galleries leading from the main entrance is dominated by two huge canvases of Venice by Francesco Guardi, one a view to Santa Maria della Salute and San Giorgio Maggiore, two gilded and canopied gondolas gliding across the water between them, the other looking towards the Doge's Palace from across the lagoon.

The extensive programme of restoration undertaken by the Rothschild family to mark the centenary has returned Waddesdon's Bath stone to its original striking yellow and opened new rooms to visitors. Oenophilists are now tantalised by a 'library' of Rothschild vintages on view in the wine cellars; there is a display of Sèvres porcelain;

and a tower room is hung with panels commissioned by the late James de Rothschild from the stage designer Léon Bakst, who incorporated portraits of the family and their friends in paintings illustrating the story of Sleeping Beauty. Also shown is the Bachelor's wing, complete with smoking and billiard rooms, where Ferdinand entertained his male guests. A silver dinner service made in Paris for George III which is laid out in the White Drawing Room was only recently acquired for the house.

Waddesdon is set off by a fine Victorian garden. South of the house, where there are wide views over the Vale of Aylesbury, a broad flight of steps leads down to the parterre. Ribbon beds edged with green and golden yew set off an ornate Italian fountain and sculpture acquired by Baron Ferdinand. Beyond, as the hillside falls away, is the wooded park, part of the extensive grounds designed by the French landscape gardener Lainé. There are rich plantings of specimen trees such as the blue Atlas Cedar and some contemporary sculpture, including a piece in travertine by Stephen Cox from 1999. Artificial rockwork by Pulham and Sons bordering the approach north of the house shelters an enchanting aviary in eighteenth-century style, its presence heralded by whoops, twittering and chirruping from the exotic inhabitants, among them the Rothschild mynah and peach-faced lovebirds. Many of these creatures were bred at Waddesdon. The aviary is the heart of the west garden as Baron Ferdinand conceived it, with flamboyant mounded beds and hedges giving way to tranquil glades.

A collection of French furniture and porcelain inside Waddesdon includes these 18th-century pot-pourri Sèvres vases, the middle one of which, dated 1761, is a rare example of a ship vase.

This delightful statue is a feature of the walled gardens beside the Elizabethan mansion at Wakehurst Place. Most of the extensive layout lies beyond the house, where an ever-deepening valley, with rock outcrops standing high above, is the setting for an outstanding collection of trees and shrubs.

Wakehurst Place WEST SUSSEX

1½ miles north-west of Ardingly, on the B2028 [443 I6]

Only a few miles from the sprawl of Crawley and the noise of Gatwick airport, a deep secluded valley of the Sussex Weald has been transformed into one of the most magical of woodland gardens. The valley doubles back on itself in a great 2-mile horseshoe, with steep wooded slopes walling it in on either side. Miles of footpaths thread its length, and a stream has been dammed and channelled to create cascades, ponds and a lake.

This private world, conceived on the grand scale, is primarily the creation of Gerald Loder, later Lord Wakehurst, who bought the estate in 1903 and devoted the next 33 years to improving it, but previous owners also contributed by planting the now mature wellingtonias and other exotics. Now home to some 7,500 kinds of plants, Wakehurst is leased to the Royal Botanic Gardens, Kew, forming a valuable, virtually pollution-free addition to their London acres.

The most formal part of the garden lies around a weatherbeaten Elizabethan mansion (there are no displayed interiors), its mellow sandstone walls, mullions and finialled gables forming an attractive backdrop to views across smooth lawns. To one side are two walled gardens. Clipped yew surrounds an ornamental fountain and round beds planted for spring and summer colour in The Pleasaunce, with a yew arch framing a vista through the more extensive cottage garden created in memory of Sir Henry Price, who continued Gerald Loder's work. Here clumps of sweet peas, clematis, phlox, roses, hydrangeas and other soft-coloured plants flower purple, white, blue and pink.

Elsewhere, Wakehurst is less restrained and more exotic. Near the house, descendants of many of the original Australasian and South American species introduced by Gerald Loder still flourish, such as the Tasmanian waratah, with its distinctive red claw-like flowers, and hoherias from New Zealand, a mass of white in summer, and paths lead on to a lushly planted water garden, with giant Himalayan lilies. Deeper into the valley, the garden becomes wilder. Sandstone outcrops along the southern rim, with great blocks heaped up into craggy tors giving views across wooded slopes fading into the distance.

The storms of 1987 and 1990 wreaked havoc at Wakehurst, bringing down over 15,000 trees and devastating the rock walk leading from one outcrop to another along the top of the valley, where stricken trees dislodged boulders as they fell. The hard work of clearance and restoration is now complete: the rhododendron walk near the house, which was torn apart by the storms, has been replaced by an Asian heath garden, to display shrubs found naturally above the tree line, and the replanted tree collections have been arranged geographically, so as to imitate natural forest. Trees to be seen here include the North American redwood, Monterey pine and hickory, species from the Mediterranean and Near East, and a collection of southern beech, as well as groves of oak, beech and birch and other native species. There are still fine rhododendrons deep in the valley, and Wakehurst is also known for bluebells and Lent Lilies carpeting the woodland floor in spring, and for autumn colour.

Wallington NORTHUMBERLAND

12 miles west of Morpeth on the B6343, 6 miles north-west of Belsay on the A696 [445 I2]

Many country houses are hidden behind walls or screens of trees, but there is nothing secluded about Wallington. The pedimented south front of this square stone building crowns a long slope of rough grass, in full view of the public road through the park. Nor is there a lodge or an imposing gateway. The pinnacled triumphal arch built for the house was found to be too narrow for coaches and now languishes in a field.

Wallington is largely the creation of Sir Walter Calverley Blackett, who in *c.*1738 commissioned the Northumbrian architect Daniel Garrett to remodel his grandfather's uncomfortable house. Garrett's cool, Palladian exteriors are no preparation for Pietro Lafrancini's magnificent rococo plasterwork in the saloon, where delicate, feminine compositions in blue and white, with winged sphinxes perched on curling foliage, garlands of flowers and cornucopias overflowing with fruit, suggest an elaborate wedding cake.

Oriental porcelain in the alcoves on either side of the fireplace is part of a large and varied collection, much of it the dowry of Maria Wilson, who married into the family in 1791 just a few years after the house had passed to Sir Walter's nephew, Sir John Trevelyan. A bizarre Meissen tea-set in the parlour features paintings of life-size insects nestling in the bottom of each cup. Even more extraordinary is Wallington's Cabinet of Curiosities, which Maria also introduced, its strange exhibits ranging from a piece of Edward IV's coffin to stuffed birds set against painted habitats and a spiky red porcupine fish like an animated pin cushion.

The hall rising through two storeys in the middle of the house reflects another era. Created in 1853–4 out of what was an internal courtyard, this individual room was the inspiration of the talented Pauline Trevelyan, whose vivid personality attracted a stream of artists and writers, including Ruskin, Swinburne and Rossetti. Under her influence Rossetti's friend William Bell Scott was commissioned to produce the eight epic scenes from Northumbrian history, with panels illustrating the death of the Venerable Bede and Grace Darling in her open boat rescuing the men of the *Forfarshire*. In the canvas showing the landing of the Vikings, savage heads on the prows of the silent fleet emerge out of the gloom over the sea like an invasion of prehistoric monsters. Ruskin and Pauline herself, among others, painted the delicate wild flowers – purple foxgloves, brilliant-red poppies, yellow columbine – on the pillars between the panels. The family's later connection with the Macaulays brought associations with scientists and politicians as well as artists and writers, and Lord Macaulay wrote his monumental history of England here, working at the desk in the study.

Sir Walter Calverley Blackett's spirit lives on in the 5,261-hectare (13,000-acre) estate which he transformed, laying out roads, enclosing fields, building cottages, planting woods and devising follies. His formal pleasure grounds, with straight-edged ponds and woods and radiating avenues, were later converted into a naturalistic landscape park, possibly with the advice of the young 'Capability' Brown, who was born nearby and went to school on the estate and who, in about 1765, was employed to design the setting for the ornamental lake at Rothley. But Sir Walter himself was responsible for damming the River Wansbeck and for James Paine's imposing three-arched bridge below the house.

Sir Walter also laid out the walled garden half a mile east of the house in the sheltered dell running down to the river; what was a vegetable garden with fruit and flower borders is now an unexpected delight of lawns and mixed herbaceous beds following the lines of the valley. The shady path to the gate leads past two wooded ponds, the slope above the second still crowned with a long brick wall that sheltered an earlier kitchen garden and with the porticoed, pedimented façade of what was the gardener's house. Flights of steps sweeping down from the terrace at the head of the present garden embrace Lady Mary Trevelyan's pond in a stone niche created in 1938, the source of the little stream that runs down the valley, its course marked by dwarf shrubs, herbaceous plants and alpines.

To one side a raised terrace walk carries a little brick

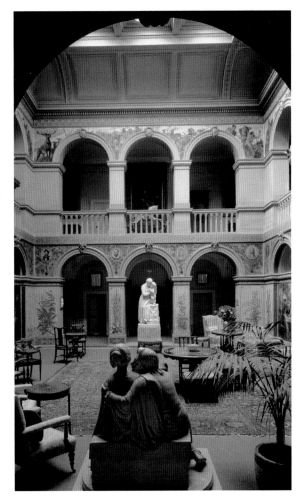

Wallington's central hall was originally an internal courtyard. It was roofed over in the mid-19th century at the instigation of the artistic Pauline Trevelyan, who commissioned William Bell Scott to paint scenes from Northumbrian history on the walls and marshalled other friends, including John Ruskin, to decorate the pillars with flowers and plants.

pavilion, surmounted with the owl of the Calverley crest, and Sir George Otto Trevelyan's 1908 conservatory. A hedged nuttery on the slopes below marks the site of the former vegetable patch, while across the valley a broad sloping mixed border includes phlox, lilies, hostas and fuchsias among a selection of bulbs, shrubs and herbaceous plants chosen for colour effect. Although this must be one of the Trust's coldest gardens, roses, honeysuckles, clematis and sun-loving plants thrive against the south-facing walls. There is also a national collection of elders here, their scarlet and purple-black berries conspicuous in late summer and autumn.

Most of the estate is enclosed farmland, but there are lovely walks through the woods near the house and along the Wansbeck. There is also a 7-mile route making use of two disused railway lines, the Rothbury line (closed in 1963) and the Wannie line (closed in 1966), with way-marked paths across fields linking sections of grassy track.

Washington Old Hall TYNE & WEAR

5 miles west of Sunderland, 2 miles east of the A1, south of Tyne tunnel [445 J3]

Two nineteenth-century watercolours in the parlour show Washington Old Hall as it once was – a modest manor house on the edge of Washington village, just below the church on its wooded hill and with cornfields stretching away behind it. Although the village has now been swallowed up by Washington New Town, the house looks over a little green valley to the red-brick mansion which was the home of the Bell family, connected by marriage to the Trevelyans of Wallington (*see* p.414), and it is still possible to shut out the twenty-first century here.

Washington Old Hall is not a grand house. Rebuilt on twelfth-century foundations in the early seventeenth century, its rough unornamented sandstone walls suggest a family of moderate means. The interior was conventionally designed on an H-plan, with a great hall occupying the centre of the building. Two arches from the original house lead from the hall into the kitchen.

This unpretentious building was the ancestral home of George Washington, elected first President of the USA in 1789; his direct ancestors lived here for five generations and the property remained in the family until 1613. Mementoes of the American connection and the struggle for independence can be seen throughout the house. A portrait of George Washington executed on drum parchment while he was on campaign as leader of the rebel forces hangs alongside a letter from Percy, 2nd Duke of Northumberland, who served with the British troops. A lottery ticket signed by Washington is displayed upstairs, by a uniform of the Washington Greys in a glass case.

Although none of the furniture is original, it is all in tune with the house and includes some interesting pieces, such as the seventeenth-century baby-walker in the bedroom and the beautifully embroidered stumpwork cabinet in the parlour.

A print of Mount Vernon, given by President Jimmy Carter when he visited the house in 1977, symbolises the importance of a more recent American connection. Washington Old Hall was divided into Georgian tenements and during the nineteenth century became increasingly dilapidated. Its condition was so bad by the 1930s that demolition was seriously considered and only a concerted effort saved the building. Generous gifts from across the Atlantic made restoration possible and the people of the USA continue to offer much-needed help, many of them visiting the Old Hall every year.

The Weald SURREY

Between the North and South Downs [443 I5–J6]

The Trust's properties in the Weald lie on the chalk hills of the North and South Downs and the sandstone ridges between them. They provide easy walking and picnicking in lovely surroundings and, above all, views over a wooded prosperous countryside which, despite the continual pressure of development, is still very beautiful indeed.

On Leith Hill, at 294.5 metres (967 feet) the highest ground in south-east England, Richard Hill of Leith Hill Place built the comparatively modest 19.5-metre (64-foot) tower (*see* p.221) so as to get the full benefit of the view from this sandstone ridge. The Trust owns nearly 364 metres (900 acres), partly to the north but mainly to the south of the ridge, and much of it is woodland, running eastwards to Coldharbour Common, with its modest village. Although the estate is fragmented, it ties in with the commons of Wotton and Abinger nearby and provides a wonderful 'lung' only 40 miles from central London.

The Weir HEREFORD & WORCESTER

5 miles west of Hereford on the A438 [442 E3]

Steep south-facing banks fringing one of the great bends on the River Wye as it meanders slowly eastward are the site of the Parr family's unusual garden created in the 1920s, informally planted with trees and shrubs and improbably held in place by masses of reinforced concrete which prevent it tumbling into the water. A walk through beech woodland high above the Wye leads to the much-altered eighteenth-century villa (not open to the public) at the top of the garden, from where paths criss-cross the slopes at all levels, sometimes punctuated by flights of steps. Yew, privet and laurel grow well on the grassy banks, with willow along the river itself, and there are also a number of exotic trees and shrubs, such as the Japanese maple. Spectacular displays of daffodils and bluebells in spring are followed by a carpet of the brilliant-yellow rose of Sharon in summer, when butter-coloured flowers completely smother the slopes at one end of the garden. A small rockery of Cheddar limestone hides a shaded lily pond fed by a trickling stream. The views over the river are spectacular, across a wooded pastoral patchwork grazed by sleepy cows to the slopes of the Black Mountains, with the tips of the Brecon Beacons beyond.

Wellbrook Beetling Mill CO. TYRONE

4 miles west of Cookstown, ½ mile off the A505 Cookstown–Omagh road [444 B3]

Like the wool industry in medieval England, linen manufacture was of major importance in eighteenth-century Ireland, particularly in the north, where new landowners from England and Scotland were anxious to maximise the return on their estates. Official encouragement included the setting-up of a Linen Board in 1711, the removal of duty on Irish linen imported into England, and

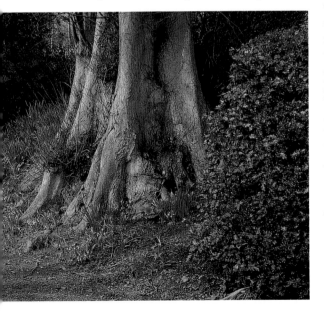

a body to fund development. Although some spinning and weaving continued to be done in the home, the industry was increasingly mechanised, with many mills established on the rivers around Belfast. Beetling was the last stage in the process, in which the cloth was pounded with heavy hammers for up to two weeks to give it a gleaming sheen.

This functional isolated building in a remote valley west of Cookstown is the only surviving part of the once-extensive Wellbrook linen works. Built in 1765 and modified in the nineteenth century, it continued operating until 1965, although the main bleaching mill closed about a hundred years earlier. Seven beetling engines, their hammers resembling rows of organ pipes, were powered by a 5-metre- (16-foot-) diameter breastshot water-wheel set against the eastern gable of the long two-storey mill. Water for the wheel was brought from a weir on the Ballinderry river a few hundred metres away, an impressive wooden aqueduct on brick piers transporting it the last 15 metres (50 feet) or so. After beetling, the cloth was hung to dry on the upper floor where the airing racks and louvred windows still survive, and was then folded on a special table for dispatch.

Now restored to working order, the mill once again reverberates to the heavy pounding of the beetling hammers. There is also a display illustrating the Irish linen industry.

The waterwheel set against one end of Wellbrook Beetling Mill once powered the hammers which gave the Irish linen produced here its gleaming sheen.

The Adam Touch

Robert Adam (1728–92), architect, interior decorator and furniture designer, was the transforming genius of the Neo-classical country house. Son of a leading Scottish architect, and with two elder brothers who also went into the profession, he grew up steeped in the business, but his individuality only emerged after a Grand Tour in the 1750s, most of which was spent studying classical remains in Rome. Commissions to remodel the interiors of old houses, often following on from other architects, saw his genius emerge.

While several of his contemporaries also worked in the newly-fashionable classical idiom, based on a return to the principles and motifs employed by the ancient Greeks and Romans, Adam created his own style. He offered a fresh interpretation of the Neo-classical approach, lighter, more delicate and more colourful than his rivals, and devised a repertoire of ornament which drew on a range of historic sources. Then, too, his designs were all-inclusive. When given the opportunity, he worked on every detail of a room scheme: plasterwork, mirrors, furniture, chimneypieces and door handles. And often he would use the same team of craftsmen to execute his designs, in particular the plasterer Joseph Rose the Younger, the decorative painter Antonio Zucchi and the cabinetmaker Thomas Chippendale.

Some commissions involved the design of new wings or a façade, and Adam was called on to plan park buildings and entrances. On the whole, however, his work on the English country house did not involve building anew. In Scotland it was different, and here, at the end of his life, Adam built sham castles in a new bold style well suited to often dramatic settings.

Adam's remodelling of Osterley in Middlesex (**above**) from 1761 transformed the Tudor courtyard house and gave it an exterior in the fashionable classical idiom. His masterstroke was the giant pedimented double portico with which he closed the courtyard on the east side and created a new entrance front.

At Kedleston in Derbyshire (**below**), where Sir Nathaniel Curzon had commissioned a grand new Palladian mansion from two more conventional architects, Adam was originally invited to turn his attention to the park. Among other features, Adam designed the three-arched bridge which carries the main drive across the lake.

With his usual ingenuity, he devised it so that approaching visitors were treated to a grandstand view of the north front while, from the house, the bridge appears as an eye-catcher in the park.

The eating-room at Osterley (**below, left**) has a carved cornice from an earlier refurbishment, but otherwise is very much as Adam envisaged it. The stucco panels and ceiling plaster-work are his designs, his carved and gilt sideboard flanked by vases on pedestals stand against the far wall, and his set of lyre-back chairs is still here. As was the fashion in the 18th century, the chairs are against the walls; when the room was used they would be set around a table brought in from the passage outside.

The Saloon at Saltram (**below**), created between 1768 and 1772, is one of the most complete surviving Adam interiors. Intended for balls and other entertaining, it was to be the grandest room in the house and to be largely free of furniture, apart from the sofas and chairs round the walls. Adam designed all the fixtures and fittings, including the huge Axminster carpet which echoes the pattern of the ceiling plasterwork, the looking-glasses between the windows, and the gilded door handles. His plan for the walls included positions for paintings, and he even suggested suitable subjects. The seat furniture is not to his design but it is by his trusted collaborator Thomas Chippendale, who supplied pieces for many of his interiors.

When working on interiors, Adam's approach, if given a free enough hand, was to design as much as possible himself, so the different elements would contribute to a unified scheme. At Kedleston, where he was working on the house from 1760, he was able to carry through many of his plans.

In the Library (**above, top**), he prepared drawings for walls and ceiling, and marked the door to the Saloon, a huge domed rotunda rising through the house, with a monumental Doric doorcase. He designed the large mahogany desk and the bookcases, both made by estate carpenters.

HATCHLANDS PARK
177

Another strand of the Adam approach was to include references to the occupations or interests of his clients. His plasterwork at Hatchlands in Surrey (**above**) for Admiral Boscawen, for example, points up the distinguished maritime career of Pitt's 'great admiral'. While Adam always paid meticulous attention to detail, as his

NOSTELL PRIORY
278

surviving drawings show, and stamped his strong artistic personality on all his commissions, the design as well as the realisation of some fittings and furnishings was left to others. At Nostell Priory, Adam only specified the furniture that was essentially part of the decorative scheme; the rest was both designed and made, in his London workshops, by Chippendale. The little drawing table

NOSTELL PRIORY
278

One of the hallmarks of the Adam touch was the delicacy and lightness of his ornamental repertoire and the wide range of influences on which he drew. Elegant plasterwork in the Top Hall at Nostell Priory in Yorkshire (**above**) was executed in a half-classical, half-Etruscan style, there is a restrained stone chimneypiece to Adam's design by a Doncaster craftsman, and the fragile oval-backed hall chairs are also part of his original scheme.

Adam's favourite plasterer, Joseph Rose, was employed on all the interiors remodelled in the house. Rose charged most for his work in the Top Hall with its endless 'foliage, husks, scrolls, ogees, vases'.

The elegant vase on a pedestal which Adam designed in 1780 for the Dining Room at Saltram in Devon (**right**) is very much in the same spirit.

SALTRAM
331

(opposite, below) is one of the pieces
made for the Library. At Kedleston
delays in completing Adam's grandest
interior, the Marble Hall (right),
probably for financial reasons, led
to a less austere decorative scheme
than originally intended, based on new
drawings by his chief draughtsman
George Richardson. The chimneypieces
are by Richardson, and he designed
some elegant plasterwork, with inset
paintings attributed to the Scottish
artist William Hamilton, who was one
of Adam's protégés.

Occasionally, too, those executing
the original designs did not follow
Adam's intentions. The cabinetmaker
John Linnell, for example, radically
altered the drawings for four great
sofas for the Drawing Room at
Kedleston. His sea nymphs (above)
and other watery creatures echoed
the theme of the ceiling but were also
strongly reminiscent of the enthusiastic
ornamentation on George III's
coronation coach.

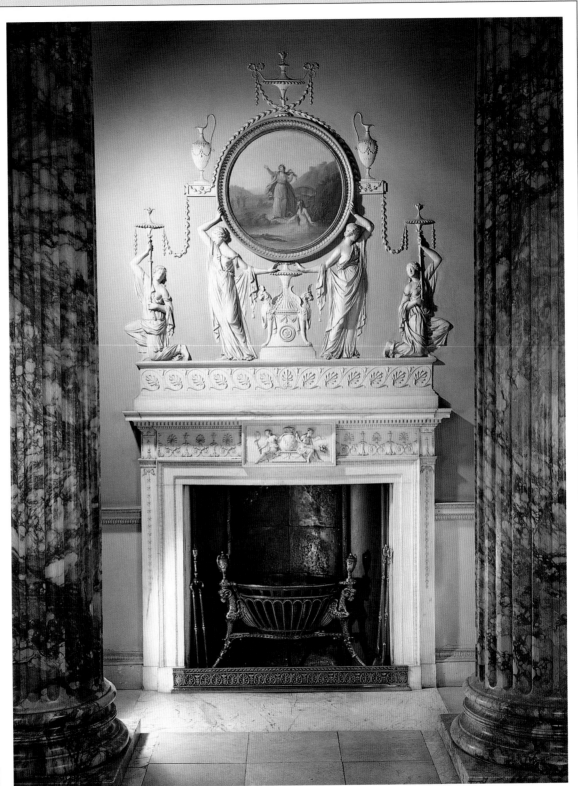

Wellington Monument SOMERSET

2 miles south of Wellington on the A38, just west of the Wellington–Hemyock road [442 D6]

Anyone travelling south-west along the M5 or by train from Taunton to Exeter will recognise this stark stone obelisk, rearing 53.5 metres (175 feet) from the Blackdown Hills on the Devon–Somerset border. Designed in 1817 by Thomas Lee, the architect of Arlington Court (*see* p.25), it was commissioned by a group of local gentry to commemorate the achievements of the Duke of Wellington, whose victory at the Battle of Waterloo was no doubt still fresh in their minds. The Iron Duke would probably have appreciated the military advantages of such a splendid position, with breathtaking views in all directions, but this is not a place to be visited in cold weather, when the wind whistles ferociously round the tiny room reached by a spiral staircase at the top of the monument.

Wembury and the Yealm Estuary DEVON

On the south coast, 5–6 miles east of Plymouth [442 C8]

To the south of Plymouth, where the grim heights of Staddon overlook the great breakwater at the mouth of the Sound, the coast is somewhat unattractive. But east round the headland into Wembury Bay there is a change.

The church of St Werburgh stands above the beach, a narrow valley curving inland behind it, the now much enlarged village mercifully hidden from view by the lie of the land. The rocky island offshore is the Great Mew Stone. As the ruined cottage by its shore suggests, it was once inhabited. It is now owned by the Ministry of Defence, as it falls within the area of *HMS Cambridge*, the gunnery school which operated until recently from near Heybrook Bay.

The Trust has owned the valley pastures and the south-facing cliffs running east to Warren Point since 1939, a most timely gift as it prevented development of a prime coastal site at a time when planning control was minimal. In 1975 it became apparent that the beauty of the Yealm estuary, which runs into Wembury Bay, was seriously at risk. The villages of Newton Ferrers and Noss Mayo were much sought after as places to retire to and the improvement of the A38 from Exeter to Plymouth was set to make the estuary much more accessible, increasing existing pressure for moorings and accommodation from the boating fraternity. The planning authority would have found it hard to contain this pressure by itself and welcomed the Trust's initiative in launching an appeal for funds to buy as much as possible of the unspoilt estuary and the coast. The appeal was a resounding success, partly because it transpired that many people then in their sixties and seventies had spent their honeymoon on the estuary, had fond memories of it, and sent handsome cheques.

The Trust was able to buy nearly 3 miles of magnificent coast from Noss Mayo, well up the estuary, round Gara Point at its mouth, and then eastwards to Saddle Cove beyond Blackstone Point, and – equally important – the farmland behind and above it, some 178 hectares (440 acres) in all. The waterside woods along the Yealm are peaceful and sheltered, with glimpses of water and brightly coloured boats below. In Passage Wood, and again in Brakehill Plantation, the path is at two levels and emerges from the latter wood onto the open cliff above Mouthstone Point. From here there is a breezy coastal walk with wonderful views: east across Bigbury Bay to Bolt Tail, west to Rame Head and for many miles along the Cornish coast to the great headland of the Dodman (*see* p.356). The walk is along the Revelstoke Drive, well graded because it was built for horsedrawn carriages towards the end of the last century by Lord Revelstoke of Membland Hall. His large estate here enabled him to build this drive for 9 miles round his property and very proud of it he must have felt. Sadly, as a member of the Baring family, he was involved in the 1890 crash of the family's bank and had to sell up to meet the bank's creditors. It is nice to be able to record that Baring Brothers made a generous contribution to the Trust's appeal to buy this land.

The attractive Warren Cottage above Blackstone Point was originally occupied by the warrener for, like so many places in similar situations on the coast, there was a large rabbit warren here well into the nineteenth century. The cottage was later enlarged for the Baring family, who used it as a base on a summer's day. It is now privately occupied.

In 1987 the Trust was able to buy a further 2 miles, some 145.5 hectares (360 acres), of the very similar cliffs running eastwards from Saddle Cove, round Hilsea Point to Stoke Point, making a superb stretch of wholly unspoilt coast. And in the early 1990s these holdings were further extended when a generous legacy allowed the purchase of nearly 202.5 hectares (500 acres) of farmland on the north bank of the Yealm estuary.

Wensleydale NORTH YORKSHIRE

1 mile south-east of Bainbridge on the A684 [445 I5]

The Trust owns two properties in Wensleydale. East Scar Top Farm, south-east of Bainbridge, runs from a valley to the top of Addleborough which, at 476.5 metres (1,564 feet), gives a wonderful view down the dale on a clear day. South of Layburn, Braithwaite Hall, a hill farm of 303.5 hectares (750 acres), has a handsome late seventeenth-century farm-house (*see* p.58).

Westbury Court Garden
GLOUCESTERSHIRE

Westbury-on-Severn, 9 miles south-west of Gloucester on the A48 [442 F4]

Only a man with a passionate interest in gardens would devote all his money to creating a new one rather than modernising an antiquated house, as Maynard Colchester I, chose to do at Westbury between 1696 and his death in 1715. Even more remarkably, his formal layout in the newly fashionable Dutch style inspired by the accession of

William and Mary is still largely as planned, the only water garden of its kind in England not to be swept away under the influence of 'Capability' Brown and Humphry Repton and the vogue for 'natural landscaping'.

Westbury lies in water meadows by the River Severn, laid out on the kind of level, well-watered site that abounds in The Netherlands. Water, grass and clipped evergreens are key elements in the garden, with beautifully cut hedges fringing tranquil canals, and balls and pyramids of box and yew punctuating shady lawns and formally planted beds. Delicious red-brick pavilions peer over walls and hedges, and sheltering trees cast long ribbons of shade across the grass. The garden is ordered and serene, with the neatness and pleasing symmetry of a sampler. It is also small-scale and intimate, quite different in character from formal gardens of French inspiration with their distant vistas and grand avenues.

The route from the car park brings visitors through the high brick wall bordering the garden on the west to the edge of the long canal, a watery corridor stretching 137 metres (450 feet) to a wrought-iron screen giving tantalising glimpses of the countryside beyond. Old varieties of apples, pears and plums are espaliered against the warm brick, and the grass under the wall is thick with daffodils, crocuses and tulips in spring. A tall, dignified two-storey pavilion faces down the canal, long sash windows in the

Crisp box hedges and cones and balls of box provide a foil for softer infills of flowers and other decorative plants in the parterre garden at Westbury Court. In the background is the tall pavilion, devised to give views across the water meadows of the Severn as well as the garden spread out below.

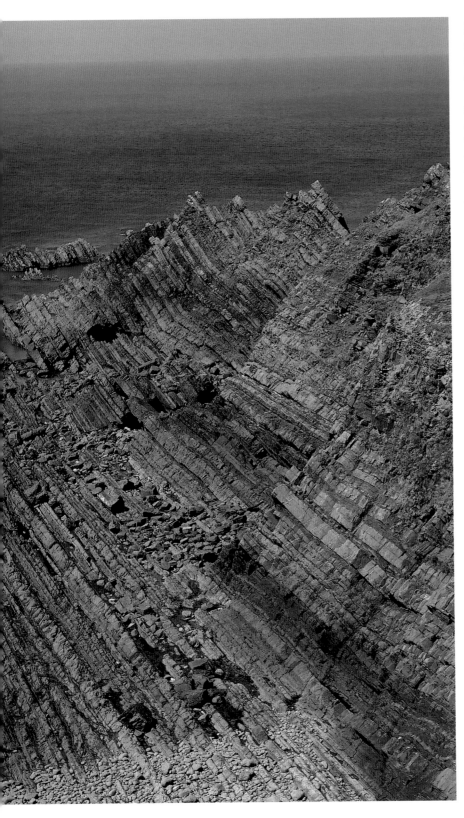

Dutch style lighting the upper room and an open loggia at ground level suggesting the building is on stilts. On fine days the sun draws flashes of fire from the gilded ball crowning a little cupola.

Another delightful brick building, its pyramidal roof concealed by a parapet ornamented with stone balls, overlooks a second T-shaped canal paralleling the first, with a statue of Neptune riding a dolphin adorning the arm of the T. On the other side of this gazebo is a small walled garden, with shady arbours rounding the corners and box-edged beds planted with old roses and a rich variety of other plants known in England before 1700, including humble cottage-garden flowers such as the primrose, violet and lily of the valley. Quinces, medlars and other old varieties of fruit tree arranged in a quincunx pattern in roughly mown grass close by partly surround the geometrical beds of a simple parterre, its smooth lines and curves echoing the design shown in Kip's engraving of Westbury executed in c.1707.

Although the garden was the inspiration of Maynard Colchester I, the T-shaped canal and some other features, such as the gazebo, were probably added by his nephew, Maynard Colchester II. Unlike his uncle, the younger Maynard turned his attention also to the house, although no traces now remain of the Palladian mansion with which he replaced the Elizabethan manor or of the nineteenth-century building which succeeded it. The garden itself was neglected for some 150 years and almost disappeared in recent times. It has been re-created by the Trust, which has planted it with species listed in Maynard Colchester I's original documents or which are known to have been in cultivation at the time. Although few original trees survive, an evergreen oak at the end of the T-canal is thought to be the oldest in the country, planted in the early 1600s.

Westward Ho! to Hartland Point
DEVON

On the north coast, 4 miles east of Hartland on the B3237
[442 C6]

Beyond the caravans and chalets of Westward Ho! rises the gorse-covered hill given to the Trust in memory of Rudyard Kipling. From its slopes there is an unspoilt view west to Hartland Point.

In 1988 the Trust acquired from the Pine-Coffin family a major section of this coastline, the seaward part of the Portledge estate, running for 5 miles from Green Cliff to Bucks Mills and including the Peppercombe Valley.

Clovelly is justly celebrated, and its long ownership by one estate has kept this most picturesque of all coastal villages largely unspoilt. The village and the park of Clovelly Court are surrounded by woods, and the Trust's property starts where these woods end, a mile and a half to the west. From here a glorious 3 miles of coast runs almost to Hartland Point.

Windbury Head, at the east end, has an Iron Age hillfort on its 148-metre- (486-foot-) high summit. Below it is the wooded Beckland Combe, down which Beckland Water rushes to plunge over the cliff in a waterfall which is a dramatic sight after heavy rain.

The Trust owns much of the farmland behind the cliffs and cars can be parked at Brownsham, East Titchberry and Exmansworthy. The cliffs are high, running from 106.5 metres (350 feet) up to over 152.5 metres (500 feet) at Fatacott, and bleak except in the few places where trees can grow. The rocks are shales, slates and carboniferous sandstones, exposed in a spectacular rockfold at Shipload Bay at the west end, where the only access to the beach is found.

The fragile nature of the rock here means that the undercliff tends to slip away, and on this slipped area are thickets of stunted oak, ash and sycamore, with thorn, gorse and sally willow giving good cover for small birds. Buzzards, kestrels and fulmars all nest in the vicinity.

Westwood Manor WILTSHIRE

1½ miles south-west of Bradford-on-Avon, in Westwood village [442 F5]

The sixteenth century was a golden age for the west of England, when men amassed considerable fortunes in the profitable cloth trade with Antwerp and built the many fine but unpretentious houses which are such a feature of towns and villages in this part of the country. One of these men was Thomas Horton, who acquired a little fifteenth-century manor built by a prosperous Wiltshire farmer and transformed it into a house more fitting for someone of his status and position. Further embellishment in the early seventeenth century resulted in the fine plasterwork and panelling now found in many of the rooms.

Westwood is both dignified and welcoming. A modest L-shaped building of warm local stone, its low ranges frame a grassy court crossed by flagged paths, with a great medieval barn just a stone's throw away. One of the most satisfying rooms is the parlour over the hall, with its unusual interior porches, an elaborate plaster ceiling and

a show of early keyboard instruments. The long, low window giving on to the courtyard from this room has a beautiful view of the little village church and over the valley of the River Frome beyond.

West Wycombe Park
BUCKINGHAMSHIRE

At west end of West Wycombe, south of the Oxford road [443 H4]

Everything about West Wycombe bears the stamp of the man who created it, the mercurial dilettante Sir Francis Dashwood. Armed with the fortune his father had made in trade with Africa, India and the East, Sir Francis interleaved several visits to Italy with tours as far afield as Russia and Turkey. Months of foreign travel not only gave him opportunities to indulge in his fondness for practical jokes but also an appreciation of art and a depth of learning that were to led him to be a founder member of the Dilettanti Society in 1732, an important influence on English taste. Now remembered chiefly for his connection with the notorious Hellfire Club, which met in caves burrowed into the hill rising steeply to the north, the more serious side of his character is demonstrated in a successful political career. Although disastrous as Chancellor of the Exchequer in 1762, he proved himself a more than able joint Paymaster General in the years that followed.

Sir Francis was largely his own architect, aided by Giovanni Servandoni, Nicholas Revett and the draughtsman John Donowell. Between 1735 and 1781 the square Queen Anne building he inherited was transformed into a classical mansion and filled with paintings and furniture acquired on his Grand Tours. In his remodelling, Sir Francis was no more than a man of his time; it is the detail and mix of decorative styles which give West Wycombe its highly individual character. An unusual double colonnade rising to roof height stretches almost the full width of the long south front, rivalling the huge porticoes decorated with frescoes which dominate the short sides of the house. The interior is a mixture of the old-fashioned and the innovative, the voluptuous and the restrained, with artfully placed gilt mirrors reflecting glittering vistas through the house. Sensual baroque painted ceilings by the Italian Giuseppe Mattias Borgnis, brought specially to England for this commission, adorn some of the principal rooms, his *Triumph of Bacchus* and *Ariadne* in the Blue Drawing Room a riot of overweight cherubs, heavily muscled bodies and flowing drapery. Elsewhere Sir Francis opted for delicate rococo plasterwork or classical compositions by William Hannan. Innovative ceilings in the hall and dining room by Giuseppe's son Giovanni herald the Neo-classicism of the late eighteenth century.

Hardly altered since Sir Francis's death, the house still displays his fine eighteenth-century furniture and his catholic collection of lesser Italian masters. Superb chimneypieces in many of the rooms include work by Sir Henry Cheere, such as the elaborate pink and white marble fireplace carved with birds in high relief in the music room, billing and cooing doves on one side balanced by an owl devouring a small bird on the other. Sir Henry was probably also responsible for the deceptively simple plaque in the study, showing cherubs warming themselves by a fire, two naked figures stretching out their hands to the blaze while their companions fetch wood. The mahogany staircase inlaid with satinwood and ebony is similarly fine, one of very few examples of work of this kind (*see also* Claydon House, p.96).

The naturalistic pleasure ground is also Sir Francis's creation, a remodelling of his own earlier, more formal layout, with a series of classical temples and follies forming eye-catchers in contrived vistas. From the north front of the house the ground falls away into the wooded valley which hides the village (*see below*), rising again to the church Sir Francis rebuilt inside a prehistoric earthwork on the top of the hill opposite, its massive golden ball glinting in the sun on fine days. A sweep of grass stretches to the shores of a lake, where the colonnade of a classical temple on one of the islands shows white against the surrounding foliage. Garden buildings by Nicholas Revett include a cottage disguised as a church and a colonnaded circular dovecote with a pyramidal roof known as the Round Temple. John Donowell was responsible for the Temple of Apollo next to the house, a gigantic grey arch of flint and stone with the motto of the Hellfire Club engraved on an inset panel. The domed classical temple on a grassy mound in the woods to the west of the lake, with an open colonnade enclosing a statue of Venus, is one of three eye-catchers commissioned from Quinlan Terry in recent years.

West Wycombe Village
BUCKINGHAMSHIRE

2 miles west of High Wycombe, on the A40 [443 H4]

For centuries the principal route from London to Oxford, the Midlands and Wales passed through West Wycombe, nurturing the creation of this exceptional village, its long main street lined by timber-framed, flint and brick cottages, many of which date from the sixteenth century or earlier. One of the oldest buildings, the fifteenth-century Church Loft, was originally a rest house for pilgrims. Later travellers were catered for by several coaching inns, three of which survive, and there are also some more gracious façades among the traditional cottage frontages, such as the Queen Anne Steps House.

The village was acquired by the Dashwood family, as part of the West Wycombe estate, in 1698, and is situated just outside the gates of Sir Francis Dashwood's great house (*see above*).

White Mill DORSET

Off B3082 north of Sturminster Marshall [442 F6]

This substantial brick and tile corn mill, in a peaceful setting on the banks of the sluggish River Stour, is one of the most important vernacular buildings on the 3,559-hectare (8,795-acre) agricultural estate attached to Kingston Lacy (*see p.204*). Largely rebuilt in 1776, but

Giuseppe Borgnis, who painted the frescoes on the staircase at West Wycombe (left) and was also responsible for other decorative schemes in the house, was specially brought over to England from Italy by Sir Francis Dashwood.

probably marking a mill site recorded in Domesday Book, the mill still has its original highly crafted elm and applewood machinery, now very rare.

White Horse Hill OXFORDSHIRE

6 miles west of Wantage, 2 miles south of Uffington, on south side of the B4507 [443 G4]

Whoever outlined the famous white horse set 244 metres (800 feet) up on the scarp of the Berkshire Downs had an eye for his work. With only a few well-placed lines he created the impression of a proud and powerful animal, eternally prancing above the vale which bears its name. Closely resembling the tiny stylised animals depicted on coins of the first century BC, the White Horse may well have marked the territory of a local Iron Age tribe, either the Dobunni, who were centred on Cirencester, or the Atrebates, who had their capital at Silchester.

Just above the horse is the Iron Age hill-fort of Uffington Castle, its powerful earth ramparts a familiar landmark to those walking the prehistoric track known as the Ridgeway along the crest of the downs. The prominent

Right: Wichenford Dovecote is a charming example of the type of vernacular building that would once have been found in every village. The hundreds of birds housed here would have been an important source of fresh winter meat as well as providing eggs and fertiliser.

Below: Looking along one of the reed-fringed drainage ditches of Wicken Fen towards a wind-pump, the only one in Cambridgeshire that is still working.

natural knob of Dragon Hill just below the chalk figure is where St George is supposed to have slain the dragon.

Wichenford Dovecote HEREFORD & WORCESTER

5½ miles north-west of Worcester, north of the B4204 [442 F3]

Perhaps built at the same time as the adjoining farmhouse was given its elegant late seventeenth-century façades, this tall timber-framed black and white dovecote strikes a similarly domestic note, mown grass surrounding the sandstone plinth on which it stands. A lantern crowning the steeply pitched roof admitted birds to some 550 nesting boxes stacked on short brick piers.

Wicken Fen CAMBRIDGESHIRE

Access south of the A1123 at the village of Wicken, 3 miles west of Soham, on the A142; 17 miles north-east of Cambridge, via Stretham on the A10 [443 J2]

Scientifically one of the most important wetland nature reserves in Western Europe, Wicken Fen is virtually all that remains of the once-vast area of undrained fen which covered 2,500 square miles from Lincolnshire to Suffolk, now called the Fens of the Great Level. The small population which lived here was a law unto itself, and

bitterly resented the progressive draining of the Fens by rich entrepreneurs, foremost among them the 1st Duke of Bedford, whose forebears had grown immensely rich with plunder from dissolved monasteries. The Duke employed the Dutch engineer Cornelius Vermuyden to drive what is now called the Old Bedford River through the area, to join the River Great Ouse at Downham Market and from there drain to The Wash.

What the Duke began continued apace, and the reclamation took place of what became some of the richest farmland in the country, now well below sea level and kept dry by immense pumping stations, for once drained the peat contracts and the level of the soil falls.

Because the Sedge Fen at Wicken has never been drained, it now stands as an island several feet above the surrounding land, and water has to be pumped up into it to maintain its character. The boundary banks have been sealed to prevent water escaping down on to surrounding arable land. If left to itself the fen would dry out, the aquatic plants would die and clog the open water which would subsequently be invaded first by reeds, then by willows and buckthorn, changing finally into oak and ash woodland. So very careful management is needed to keep a balance between reed and sedge beds, 'carr' – as the scrub is known – and open water.

Wicken Fen is rich in plant and bird life, and particularly in that of insects, with over 5,000 species, including 1,000 moths and butterflies, over 200 spiders, of which some are unique to Wicken, over 300 species of flowering plants and a long list of birds, including marsh and Montagu harriers, bittern, great-crested grebe, bearded tit, black tern, duck, owls, and many waders and small marshland species.

Wightwick Manor WEST MIDLANDS

3 miles west of Wolverhampton, up Wightwick Bank, beside the Mermaid Inn, just north of the A454 Bridgnorth road [442 F2]

In 1848 seven young men barely out of their teens – including Holman Hunt, J.E. Millais and Dante Gabriel Rossetti – founded the Pre-Raphaelite Brotherhood, a revolt against the artistic establishment and what they perceived as the emptiness and artificiality of contemporary art. The group was short-lived, but its ideals were enormously influential, feeding into the reaction against mass production and return to pre-industrial techniques which became identified with William Morris and the

Arts and Crafts Movement. Rossetti, Madox Brown and Burne-Jones were among the founders of Morris's design and furnishing company, which started life as an artist's co-operative in 1861.

Wightwick Manor is one of only a few surviving examples of a house built and furnished under the influence of the Arts and Crafts Movement. Morris wallpapers, textiles, and carpets and William de Morgan tiles and Benson metalwork supplied by his company, set off paintings and drawings by Ford Madox Brown, Holman Hunt, Millais, Burne-Jones and Ruskin. The Jacobean furniture, oriental porcelain and Persian rugs with which the house is also furnished complement rather than compete with the nineteenth-century work, demonstrating Morris's appreciation of good craftsmanship from any period.

Built in two stages in 1887 and 1893, Wightwick was commissioned by the industrialist Theodore Mander, a paint and varnish manufacturer, from the Liverpool architect Edward Ould, and was designed in a traditional, half-timbered idiom. The later, eastern half is more richly decorated and is clearly inspired by the Tudor buildings of the Welsh Marches. Decorative black and white timbering, in stripes, swirls and quatrefoils, rises from a plinth of local stone, with banks of spiral Tudor-style chimneys crowning the gabled roofline.

In keeping with the late-medieval character of the exterior, the heart of the house is a great parlour in the form of a feudal hall, with an open timber roof painted by the talented Charles Kempe. A minstrels' gallery across one end, a deeply recessed fireplace alcove and extensive use of panelling add to the period atmosphere. Kempe was also responsible for the glowing colours in the painted windows and the deep plaster frieze telling the story of Orpheus and Eurydice that may well have been inspired by that in the High Great Chamber at Hardwick (*see* p.176). Orpheus sits with his harp in a forest, enticing a whole menagerie of beasts with his music, from a trumpeting elephant to a kangaroo and a peacock with a golden tail. Morris's last woven fabric design – white and pink blossom on a deep-blue ground, like a meadow full of spring flowers – hangs below the frieze. The gallery end of the hall is dominated by Burne-Jones's romantic *Love Among the Ruins*, his tendrils of briar rose entangling the ardent couple recalling those in his masterpiece at Buscot Park (*see* p.68). This eclectic mix of antique and Victorian appears throughout the house, as in the drawing room, where an Italian Renaissance chimneypiece is inset with rich green tiles by William de Morgan featuring a

bestiary of mischievous creatures. Photographs of the Pre-Raphaelites and their associates on an upstairs landing include one showing William Morris and Burne-Jones with their families; only Mrs Morris looks straight at the camera.

The attractive 7-hectare (17-acre) garden takes full advantage of the site, which slopes away from the house into a little valley with a stream and two pools, and is shielded by trees and tall hedges from the suburbia around. First laid out on the advice of the painter Alfred Parsons, it was largely redesigned by the Edwardian landscape architect Thomas Mawson, who married strongly architectural formal gardens round the house, marked out with terraces, walls and clipped yew hedges, with an increasingly informal and natural approach to the layout and planting of the valley, which has orchards and paddocks and winding mown paths. Below the broad stone terrace with an oak balustrade which he added to the south front, barrels of clipped yew frame a narrow path across a lawn and further formal walks edged by yew and golden holly lead to a rose garden overlooked by topiary peacocks and to a thatched summerhouse, beyond which the land falls away. Wistaria and other climbers flower on the house, there is a show of rhododendrons and azaleas round the two pools in the valley and bluebells and daffodils flower in rough grass. Several trees associated with royalty and political figures include a gnarled old beech which was planted by Queen Mary when Duchess of York in 1900,

Wightwick Manor is a showplace of furnishings designed by William Morris and others of his circle. In the restful Oak Room (left), a chair covered in a Morris fabric and printed cotton curtains in his Cray design complement the Dutch tiles lining the fireplace. Morris wallpapers in the house include the Leicester design (below) by J. H. Dearle in the Morning Room.

and there is a wooden bridge over the road up to the house which was inspired by the Mathematical Bridge over the River Cam at Queens' College, Cambridge.

Wilderhope Manor SHROPSHIRE

7 miles south-west of Much Wenlock, 7 miles east of Church Stretton, ½ mile south of the B4371 [442 E2]

This gabled, unspoilt Elizabethan manor stands on the south slope of Wenlock Edge (*see* p.339), deep in the remote wooded Shropshire landscape evoked so vividly in the work of the local novelist Mary Webb, who used Wilderhope Manor as her model for Undern Hall in *Gone to Earth* (1917). Built of local grey limestone with tall brick chimneys and a stone-tiled roof, this is a delightfully asymmetrical house, with a curious detached pediment marking the off-centre entrance in the south-east front. Mullioned windows in the varied three-storeyed gables on this side of the house look out over the River Corve deep in the valley below.

Apart from the notable circular wooden staircase capped by a conical roof which ascends right through the house, the main feature of the interior is its unexpected plasterwork ceilings, executed with such skill that they were once thought to be the work of Italian craftsmen rather than by a provincial team. The initials of Francis and Ellen Smallman, who built Wilderhope in about 1586, recur frequently in the moulds punctuating the plaster ribs, alternating with standard motifs such as the Tudor rose, the fleur-de-lis and the portcullis.

The spot known as the 'Major's Leap' on Wenlock Edge nearby commemorates Francis and Ellen's descendant, Thomas Smallman, a supporter of the Royalist cause in the Civil War, who was imprisoned at Wilderhope. Escaping into the garden, probably by means of an old garderobe flue, he evaded his pursuers by riding his horse over Wenlock Edge. Although his unfortunate mount was killed, the major's fall is said to have been broken by a crab-apple tree.

Willington Dovecote and Stables BEDFORDSHIRE

4 miles east of Bedford, just north of the Sandy road [443 I3]

The serrated roofline of this imposing sixteenth-century dovecote built by Sir John Goshawk, Cardinal Wolsey's Master of the Horse, can be seen for miles across the flat Bedfordshire countryside. Built on a scale commensurate with the large mansion to which it was once attached, the dovecote's kidney-shaped nesting boxes set into the thickness of the stone walls could accommodate some 1,500 birds. Stepped Dutch-style gables are supported on thirteenth-century corbels, probably filched from local priories at the Dissolution of the Monasteries. Across the road is a contemporary barn-like building with late Gothic windows where the young John Bunyan, born at Elstow only 5 miles to the west, once stayed, leaving his signature and the date, 1650, etched on a stone fireplace.

2 Willow Road LONDON

Near junction of Willow Road and Downshire Hill,
Hampstead [443 I4]

Next to Victorian villas on the western edge of Hampstead
Heath is an unobtrusive three-storey, brick and concrete
rectangle with a flat roof and an uninterrupted expanse of
glass lighting the first floor. Compact and all of a piece,
what appears to be one house is in fact a terrace of three,
with a hidden basement giving on to gardens behind.

This piece of pre-war modernism was the work of the
anglophile Austro-Hungarian architect Ernö Goldfinger
(1902–87), who designed the central house for his artist
wife Ursula Blackwell and their children and lived here
from 1939 until his death. The first example of modern
architecture to be acquired by the National Trust, 2 Willow
Road still has its original fixtures and fittings, including
some of Ernö's prototype furniture, and the Goldfingers'
important collection of contemporary art, reflecting their
close links with the avant-garde. The couple met in Paris,
where he had trained with Auguste Perret, known for his
innovative use of reinforced concrete, and she was a student
of the painter Amédée Ozenfant, who reacted to Cubism
by advocating a return to a minimalist representational
art, in which forms are reduced to 'pure' outline. The
Goldfingers came to London in 1934, but in these pre-war
years Ernö's designs, apart from some work for the toy
firm Abbatt, were largely unexecuted. After the war, he
was responsible for some of London's now controversial
developments, notably the large office complex at Elephant
and Castle and high-rise housing in north Kensington.

Willow Road probably sees Ernö at his best. Number
2 is by no means large, but there is a sense of both space
and light, with the glass walls of the main rooms drawing
the eye out over the heath in front and on to the south-
facing balcony and gardens behind. Ernö's hand is in every
detail. A spiral staircase is the backbone and main artery
of the house, carrying the concrete frame. Wrapped round
it on the first floor is a versatile space, with movable
partitions and a change in floor level indicating dining
room, studio and living room. Above is the nursery and
bedroom floor, with compact internal bathrooms lit
through the flat roof. Built-in wardrobes are flush with
the wall, study bookshelves are recessed into a room
partition, and the studio has a tall cupboard for Ursula's
canvases. The furniture too is functional, with upturned
anglepoises either side of the low double bed in the master
bedroom, a lino-topped dining-table on a lathe base, and
dining-chairs made out of tubular metal and plywood.

The main floor of 2 Willow Road is a
well-lit, versatile space, walled in glass
front and back, and with movable
partitions between rooms.

But this is not an austere house. On the walls are some
of Ursula's surreal anatomical studies, abstract and
figurative works by Ozenfant, Delaunay, Max Ernst and
Bridget Riley and a strong portrait of Ursula by the
Goldfingers' close friend Man Ray. The living-room area
has a parquet floor and oak-veneer panelling, and there
are gay scarlet doors and areas of deep crimson paint. With
Willow Road, Goldfinger was also envisaging a particular
lifestyle. The basement was designed with accommodation
for two servants, and his house is the only one in the terrace
to be provided with two garages, one of which has an
inspection pit.

Wimpole Hall CAMBRIDGESHIRE

8 miles south-west of Cambridge, 6 miles north of Royston
[443 I3]

When Rudyard Kipling visited his daughter Elsie here, a
few months after she and her husband Captain George
Bambridge took up residence in 1936, he was moved to
remark that he hoped she had not bitten off more than
she could chew.

Two years later the Bambridges embarked on the
restoration and refurnishing of the largest house in
Cambridgeshire, whose red-brick and stone façades, three
and four storeys high in the central block, stretch nearly
91.5 metres (300 feet) from end to end. From the double
staircase leading up to the entrance set beneath a pediment
on the south front, a 82.5-metre- (270-foot-) wide avenue
lined with young limes runs over 2 miles into the distance.

Immediately in front of the house urns and busts on pedestals flank the courtyard like guards standing rigidly to attention.

The largely eighteenth-century façades added to the original mid-seventeenth-century core date from Wimpole's golden age. From 1713–40 the house was the property of Edward Harley, 2nd Earl of Oxford, who entertained Swift and Pope among a brilliant circle of writers, scholars and artists, and whose household included a Master of the Horse, a Groom of the Chamber and a Master of Music. Perhaps it was for the latter and his orchestra that Lord Harley commissioned James Gibbs's baroque chapel, Bavarian in its opulence, which is a principal feature of the house. In Sir James Thornhill's *trompe-l'oeil* decoration, statues of Saints Gregory, Ambrose, Augustine and Jerome stand in niches between pairs of classical columns, their shadows etched sharply on the stone behind. Gregory leans eagerly forward with a book in his hand, as if about to escape his perch, while half-naked St Jerome displays a splendidly muscled physique. The east wall is filled with Thornhill's *Adoration of the Magi*, in which the Three Kings are accompanied by a sizeable retinue of armed men and Mary herself sits amid a romantic classical ruin, her ruddy-faced, bearded husband watching quietly in the background.

Gibbs also designed the long library to house Harley's collection of books and manuscripts, the largest and most important ever assembled by a private individual in England, later to form the nucleus of the British Library. An oak and walnut pulpit on castors gives access to the upper shelves and a brown, pink and beige carpet picks up the subdued tones of the plaster ceiling. This room is reached through a 16-metre (52-foot) gallery, created by Henry Flitcroft for Wimpole's next owner, Philip Yorke, 1st Earl of Hardwicke, as a setting for his finest paintings. Now used to display pictures particularly associated with the house, such as *The Stag Hunt* by John Wootton, who frequently visited Wimpole in Lord Harley's time, the room's long sash windows framed by red curtains and the grey-green walls help to create an atmosphere which is both restful and warm.

Wimpole's most individual interior, John Soane's Yellow Drawing Room, was added 50 years later for Philip Yorke's great-nephew, the 3rd Earl. Running from the north front into the centre of the house, Soane's domed oval at the inner end is lit from a lantern in the roof above. With semicircular apses set either side of a central fireplace on the far wall and a large painting of playing cherubs above the chimneypiece, the effect is to suggest a chapel transformed into a room of exceptional elegance and grace, with the yellow silk on the walls setting off blue silk upholstery on the gilt chairs and long settees curved round the apses.

Soane's indulgent bath house, with a grand double staircase sweeping down to a tiled pool which holds over 2,000 gallons, is a delightful reminder of another side of eighteenth-century life.

Wimpole's setting, an extensive 141.5-hectare (350-acre) wooded park, fully matches the grandeur of the house and reflects the influence of some of the most famous names in the history of landscape gardening. The great lime avenue running 2¼ miles to the south, its unyielding lines striking through a patchwork of fields like a grassy motorway, was created by Charles Bridgeman, employed by Lord Harley in the 1720s to extend an elaborate formal layout which already included the much smaller east and west avenues to either side of the house. Originally elm, all three have been replanted, the south avenue using limes grafted and budded from mature trees Bridgeman established elsewhere in the park.

Remarkably, these remains of what was once an extensive scheme of axial avenues, canalised ponds, ha-has and bastions survived the attentions of 'Capability' Brown and his disciple William Emes later in the century, both of whom set about 'naturalising' the park. The view from the north front, artfully framed by the clumps of trees with which Brown replaced a felled avenue, looks over his serpentine ornamental lake to the three-towered Gothick ruin by Sanderson Miller which he erected as an eye-catcher on a hillock.

Brown's belts of trees defining and sheltering the park were thickened and extended by Humphry Repton, who produced a Red Book for the 3rd Earl in 1801, but Repton also re-introduced a touch of formality, creating the small flower garden enclosed by iron railings on the north side of the house. A recently reinstated parterre here is planted with *Anemone blanda* in spring and hardy fuchsias and violas later on in the year.

Sir John Soane's home farm to the north of the house, built in a pleasing mixture of brick, wood, tile and thatch, was also commissioned by the 3rd Earl, who was passionately interested in farming and agricultural improvement. Gaily painted wagons and carts now fill the thatched barn, but the surrounding paddocks and pens make up Wimpole's rare breeds farm. Unusual farmyard livestock here include the bright chestnut Suffolk Punch, once the workhorse of choice on nearly every farm in East Anglia.

The parish church only a few metres from the house, substantially rebuilt to Flitcroft's design in 1749, is all that remains of the village swept away to create the park. In the north chapel, the only part of the medieval building not demolished in the mid-eighteenth century, the recumbent effigy of the 3rd Earl with his coronet at his feet dominates a number of grandiose monuments to successive owners of the palatial house, sleeping peacefully in the midst of all they once enjoyed. Banks and ditches in the grass to the south mark the house plots of medieval villagers who tilled the land centuries ago, the ridge and furrow they created still visible on a slope of old pasture.

Win Green Hill WILTSHIRE

5 miles south-east of Shaftesbury, ½ mile north-east of the B3081 [442 F6]

South-east of Shaftesbury and north-east of Blandford lies the high ground of Cranborne Chase. At 277.5 metres (911 feet), Win Green Hill is the highest point of the chase, with a circular clump of trees at its summit. The views stretch from the Quantock Hills, to the west, to the Isle of Wight far away to the south, but it is the country nearer at hand which is so well worth exploring once one has surveyed it from this little-visited Trust outpost.

Winkworth Arboretum SURREY

Near Hascombe, 2 miles south-east of Godalming on east side of the B2130 [443 I5]

Although only a few miles south of Guildford, Winkworth feels as if it is in the depths of the country. The sweeping views across the valley from the steep hillside on which it is planted are to green fields with sheep grazing on the skyline against the blue of distant ridges. Waterfowl trek with determination across the still waters of two lakes; sometimes there is a boat apparently becalmed on the water, a rod and line over the side.

Winkworth is largely the creation of one man, Dr Wilfrid Fox, who started work on clearing and planting the

Winkworth Arboretum is at its most colourful in autumn.

Above: Heaths such as Witley Common, where animals were grazed and turf cut for fuel and other uses, once played a vital part in the local economy.

Opposite: Woodland presses close round one of the secluded lakes at Woodchester Park.

neglected woodland thickly blanketing the slopes soon after he acquired the land in 1937. Ancient oaks, clumps of hazel and belts of old pines are remnants of the original vegetation, now forming useful cover and windbreaks for young plants and more tender species. Unlike the more cultivated and continued landscapes of Sheffield Park (*see* p.337), Winkworth is naturalistic and unmanicured, with long grass and bracken under the leaf canopy. Some 1,300 different shrubs and trees are now established here, including important collections of maples, hollies, birches, cherries, whitebeam, mountain ash, rhododendrons and azaleas.

Sandy paths lead along the contours of the hill or plunge precipitously downwards. An impressive narrow corridor of over a hundred steps leads up from the boathouse at the end of the lower lake known as Rowe's Flash, the azaleas planted thickly either side providing an unforgettable display in the spring. Floral attractions also include pink and white blossoms in the magnolia wood (where there are species in flower from March to the end of September) and the rich colours of the rhododendrons massed near the car park. A stretch of woodland along the lower lake, left more or less in its natural state as a reserve for wildlife, is a carpet of bluebells in spring, and several specimens of *Eucryphia nymanensis* are smothered in drifts of white in high summer, two of them standing watch over Sir Hugh Casson's memorial to Dr Fox.

But Winkworth is at its most spectacular in autumn, with the rich scarlet, orange and yellow foliage of the maples, tupelo trees and Japanese cherries showing in brilliant patches against more sober greens and browns, and the blue of conifers. Berries – red, yellow, pink and purple – adorn the stands of whitebeam and ash, and the azalea steps are again showy with colour.

The lakes and varied habitats are a magnet for birds, the company of resident coots, moorhens, tufted ducks and Canada geese often swelled by herons and kingfishers. Tree-creepers scurry up and down the oaks in the wood fringing the upper lake, also a haunt of woodpeckers and nuthatches. Hearing the birds in full song on a warm summer's evening brings home the extent to which bird life has been impoverished elsewhere.

The Wirral MERSEYSIDE

9–18 miles north-west of Chester [445 G7–H7]

The Wirral peninsula divides the mud-flats of the Mersey from the sands of Dee, two great rivers conditioned by their very different hinterlands. At low water Caldy Hill provides views over 5 miles of islands, bars and spits to Point of Air lighthouse across the mouth of the Dee. From the gorsy Thurstaston Common, and from Harrock Wood behind it, there are similar views across the estuary to the Clwydian Hills.

Witley and Milford Commons SURREY

7 miles south-west of Guildford, 1 mile south-west of Milford between the A3 London–Portsmouth and the A286 Milford–Haslemere roads [443 H5–I5]

The 162 hectares (400 acres) of Witley and Milford Commons have changed their spots during the Trust's ownership. Before 1914 they were much as they had always been: open heath grazed by cattle and horses, with bracken cut for bedding of stock, areas of birch and some pine.

During the First World War the commons were requisitioned as army camps (Aldershot and Bordon are each within 10 miles) and much cut up, but after the Trust acquired them in the 1920s this damage largely healed over, although grazing was never fully resumed.

In 1940 the army came again. Roads and sites for buildings were gouged out with bulldozers, and alien materials were brought in, damaging the natural drainage and destroying the vegetation. When the army left, roads and foundations were removed and soil was brought from elsewhere to make good. Since then invasion by bracken and scrub has been the biggest management problem and the Trust has carried out much work to ensure that dry heath and boggy areas remain open, while retaining some woodland areas and scrub. There is an interpretation centre, with nature trails and exhibitions which take advantage of the unusual recent history of this open-air schoolroom.

Woodchester Park GLOUCESTERSHIRE

4 miles south-west Stroud off B4066 Stroud–Dursley road [442 F4]

In a deep, wooded combe in the Cotswolds are the remains of an extensive landscape park, dating from the late eighteenth and early nineteenth centuries. Conceived on the grand scale, and centred on a chain of five lakes running down the valley, the park extends for some 2 miles east of the Dursley road. Steep wooded slopes wall in the valley and near its head, set against the hill, is a great Gothic

mansion (not National Trust) built of creamy-golden local limestone. Gabled and buttressed and with prominent gargoyles carrying the water from the stone-flagged roof, the house seems complete, but viewed close up, it is clear it is empty and unfinished, with unglazed windows in the upper storeys and shafts of sunlight striking bare interior walls. This evocative place, designed by the young Benjamin Bucknall with the help of drawings by the arch-gothicist Augustus Welby Pugin, was left incomplete in 1870, sixteen years after it was started. Bucknall's client was William Leigh, a wealthy ship-owner from Liverpool who had bought the property in 1845 and demolished the substantial Georgian seat of the Ducie family who had owned Woodchester for some two hundred years.

It was to complement this earlier house that the park and grounds were laid out. In their day, both Humphry Repton and 'Capability' Brown visited the property and it may be that they advised on the landscaping of the valley and on the formal gardens which once climbed the hillside. The garden terraces are now just crumbling walling in the woodland, and nothing can be seen of the canals and fishponds that were once here, but the wider landscape, although now more wooded than it once was because of commercial planting in the nineteenth century, can still be appreciated. Original carriage drives and walks thread the woodland, the lakes offer a shimmering ribbon along the valley floor, and there are panoramic vistas from a series of viewpoints. The valley, where the Trust is returning some areas to pasture, is a haven for wildlife. Buzzards, owls,

woodpeckers and badgers breed here, and greater horse-shoe bats roost in the mansion, flitting in and out of the window openings.

The valley is approached by a gravel track which plunges downwards into the combe, with beech woodland pressing close on either side. A stretch of open parkland beside the drive is grazed by cattle and sheep and then, round a corner, is the mansion, an enigmatic presence in this idyllic place. Waymarked paths, leafy tunnels dappled with sunlight, lead deep into the park, some following a lower route down-valley, one climbing steeply upward into the woods to contour round the hill. The two longer routes lead across the great banks damming the lakes, with tree-framed vistas up and downstream. There are rafts of white water lilies, the silver trails left by moorhens, coots and other waterbirds as they trek across the water, and a little early nineteenth-century stone-built boathouse, with decorative bargeboards, a porch carried on tree trunks, and a projecting bay looking down the lake. A casement window is left open for the bats that roost in the roof space, emerging at dusk to swoop over the water. Near the mansion is a crumbling brick-lined ice house, the remains of the coach-house and stables which served the Georgian house, and some great oaks and other specimen trees, planted in what was then more open parkland to give interest to the views from the house and carriageways. There are still arresting vistas here, glimpsed fleetingly through the leaf canopy or enjoyed from one of the set viewpoints. One of the best is reached by a stiff climb up to the shoulder of the valley, where a stone bench, dated 1749, has been placed to give a view back up the combe. Far below, rising out of the encircling woodland like a Bavarian fantasy, is the mansion, a vision of buttresses, gables and huge stone-mullioned windows.

Woolsthorpe Manor LINCOLNSHIRE

At Woolsthorpe, 7 miles south of Grantham, ½ mile north-west of Colsterworth, 1 mile west of the A1 [443 H1]

The premature and sickly boy born in this modest lime-stone house on Christmas Day 1642 came into a world which believed that the Earth was the centre of the Universe. He grew up to be the leading scientist of his day, whose work was to lay the foundations of modern scientific thought and to show that our planet is merely a satellite of the Sun. The boy was Sir Isaac Newton, the offspring of a prosperous Lincolnshire farmer who died two months before his son's birth. While his mother raised a second family nearby, Isaac spent an isolated and introverted childhood at Woolsthorpe, cared for by his grandmother. Although he left to pursue his studies in Cambridge in 1661, he returned to Woolsthorpe again in 1665 when the university was closed by the plague. That year was to see some of Newton's most fruitful work, including the discovery of the principle of differential calculus.

With its mullioned windows and simple T-shaped plan, Woolsthorpe is a typical early seventeenth-century manor house, and was bought by Isaac's grandfather, Robert Newton, in 1623. Its plain rooms are sparsely furnished, reflecting the inventory of Newton's mother and illustrating how simply even a moderately wealthy yeoman family would have lived. The young Newton is evoked in some scribbled drawings on the kitchen wall, among them a sketch of a post windmill and a rough outline of a church that may be a building he knew in Grantham, where he went to school. Upstairs is the room which Isaac used when he came back from Cambridge to see his mother, now hung with a portrait of the great man by Thornhill and prints of other famous scientists of the day, many of whom fell out with their brilliant but difficult contemporary. Also here is a copy of the third edition of Newton's major work, the *Principia Mathematica*.

The original apple tree that helped Newton with his work on gravity is said to have blown down in 1820, but a gnarled old specimen in the current orchard is thought to have grown from a surviving part of the trunk. Newton's major scientific concepts are put across through some hands-on activities in the seventeenth-century threshing barn, and there is an exhibition on his life in the house.

The entrance hall of Wordsworth House, where the poet spent his formative years.

Wordsworth House CUMBRIA

Main Street, Cockermouth [445 G4]

Three men born in the early 1770s and known as the Lake Poets did much to change contemporary views of landscape, their appreciation of the wild beauty of nature suggesting new ideals for people seeking an escape from the realities of the Industrial Revolution. Of the three, William Wordsworth was the most innovative. Although he followed Robert Southey as poet laureate, Wordsworth's best work permanently enlarged the range and subject matter of English poetry, outclassing Southey's more pedestrian creations and the products of Samuel Taylor Coleridge's wayward genius. Wordsworth's love of the Lakes shows above all in the fact that he chose to live here all his life.

Although the adult Wordsworth is mainly connected with the southern Lakes, his formative years were spent in the north, in the little market town on the River Derwent where his father was agent to Sir James Lowther. The Georgian house where he was born on 7 April 1770, almost two years before his sister Dorothy, stands at the west end of the main street, its garden stretching down to the river and only a stone's throw from the ruined castle from which William derived so much inspiration.

Seven of the modest family rooms are furnished in eighteenth-century style, as the Wordsworths might have had them, and include some pieces which belonged to the poet in later life – his painted bookshelves, his sofa, his early nineteenth-century longcase clock and his white and gold porcelain inkstand. Southey's fine Georgian walnut chairs grace the drawing room, which is hung with early prints of the Lake District. And the terrace above the

Derwent at the end of the garden is where Wordsworth spent so many happy childhood hours with his beloved sister Dorothy. Sadly, the death of their father when Wordsworth was only thirteen resulted in the break-up of the family home.

The Workhouse, Southwell
NOTTINGHAMSHIRE

8 miles from Newark on A617 and A612 [445 K8 and 443 H1]

On the eastern edge of Southwell, sitting well back from the road at the top of a gentle grassy slope is a striking early nineteenth-century building of mellow red brick. Three storeys tall with rows of regularly spaced iron-framed windows, massive chimneystacks, and a grey slate roof, it is solid and functional, typical of the many institutional buildings of the period. It was built as a workhouse in 1824, as part of a pioneering approach to poor relief instigated by the Rev. J. T. Becher, a local magistrate. By the early nineteenth century, the existing system, based on the 1601 Poor Law that made each parish responsible for its destitute, was breaking down. Some parishes had banded together to provide workhouses, but the accent was on helping the poor to live in their own homes and this was no longer viable, partly because the scale of the problem had escalated, fuelled by agricultural

depression, the return of soldiers from the Napoleonic wars and a rising population, partly because there was concern about a system which provided no incentive to work.

In Southwell, the Rev. Becher came up with a new approach which was designed to deter as well as provide relief. He tried it out first in a small workhouse just for Southwell parish, and then, in 1823, proposed a much larger institution to serve a group of neighbouring parishes. The workhouse was built on what were then open fields outside the town, with a plan which reflected the Rev. Becher's ideas on how denizens should be treated. Intended to house both able-bodied and the aged and infirm, men, women and children, it was designed so each group would be segregated, day and night. Wives were separated from husbands, children from their parents. Inmates were made to wear a uniform, were fed the plainest of diets, and treated to a daily regime which involved hours of hard and monotonous work – breaking stones, unpicking old rope, digging the garden, or endlessly cleaning the interior and repainting the walls. Above all, they were strictly supervised. It was a narrow and comfortless existence. All this is reflected in the plan of the workhouse, which has separate day rooms for each group on the ground floor, with segregated dormitories above. Inmates passed from one to the other by separate staircases, set side by side, and each day room gives onto a brickwalled yard, for work and exercise and with an open privy, just a hole in the ground,

					TOTALS OF STOCK BROUGHT FORWARD AND NEW STOCK.	CONSUMED			REMAINING IN STORE.	TOTALS CONSUMED AND REMAINING IN STORE.
No.	ARTICLES.	STOCK BROUGHT FORWARD.	NEW STOCK.	No. of Invoice.		By the Paupers.	By the Officers and Servants of the Workhouse.	On the Workhouse.		
1	Bath Bricks...	8			8			1	7.8	8.8
2	Blacking	.8			.8		.4		4.12	5
3	Blacklead ... lbs.	5			5		.2		.11	.13
4	Blue ... lbs.	.13			.13					.13
5	Brimstone ... lbs.								3	3
6	Brooms... ...	3			3		2		10	12
7	Brushes ...	12			12				6	6
8	Hand Brushes	6			6		1		8	9
9	Kit Brushes	9			9				23	23
10	Candles ... lbs.	23			410	40		30	340	410
11	Coals ... cwts.	410			10	5			5	10

Southwell UNION. NECESSARIES AND MISCELLANEOUS ACCOUNT *for the* 3rd *Week of the Quarter ending* Michaelmas — W. Fryer *Master of the Workhouse at* Southwell

(Master No. 20.)—Printed and Published by HADDEN, BEST & Co., West Harding set behind a wall in the corner. From the yard, nothing can be seen of the outside world apart from the tops of the trees in the workhouse orchard.

The interior is shown unfurnished, as a succession of bare rooms with painted and whitewashed brick walls and stone-flagged or lime-ash floors, and the building explained through an audio guide. Each room has a small fireplace. There are no cupboards or other fittings, just pegs in the walls for the paupers to hang their clothing. In the middle of the main range, marked by a projecting bay with a grand pedimented entrance, are the quarters for the master and the administration of the workhouse. Here the walls are plastered, with a hierarchy of other refinements which peaks with picture rails, skirting boards and a wooden floor in the master's office. There are cupboards, and the airy committee room where the workhouse guardians met and where families could see each other briefly on Sundays, has a mantelpiece and a fender in front of the fire. From his rooms, the master could look down on paupers in the exercise yards, but there were some corners out of his sight, one of which has what may well be a gaming board scratched into the brickwork.

The Southwell Workhouse was studied by a Royal Commission looking into poor relief and became the prototype for a nationwide system as laid down in the New Poor Law of 1834. Hundreds of workhouses were built, 15 to 20 miles apart, each serving a group of parishes, and each operated on Becher principles. As the years passed, the focus shifted away from deterrence towards helping those who needed shelter and nursing, and the numbers needing relief declined. A red-brick building behind Southwell Workhouse was built in 1871 as an infirmary, the introduction of pensions in 1908 and national insurance in 1911 did much to alleviate the poverty of the old and unemployed, and children were moved to separate homes. Despite all this, the workhouse continued to be used into the 1990s and there is a room fitted out as a 1970s interior that would have housed an entire family.

Ysbyty Estate GWYNEDD

South of Betws-y-Coed, astride the B4406 and the B4407 and on the south side of the A5 and the A470 [445 G8]

Another great block of land besides the Carneddau (*see* p.74) which came to the Trust with Penrhyn Castle (*see* p.298) is the 8,498-hectare (21,000-acre) Ysbyty estate. This is very different in character from the Carneddau, for, although the latter is farmed, Ysbyty has many more

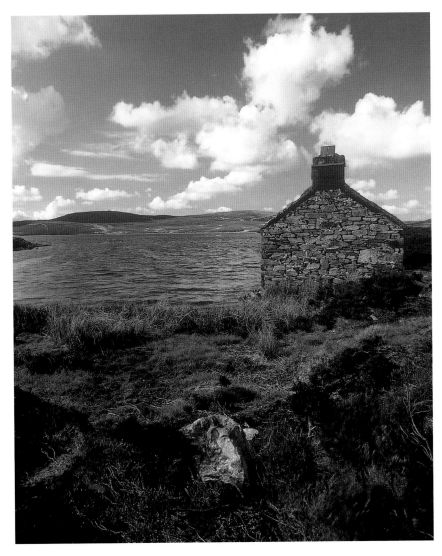

holdings and it has always been the Trust's policy to help its tenants maintain their traditional way of life, hard though this can often be. Many of the farms are remote and in some the same families have farmed for generations. Visitors must remember to stick to the tracks, to shut every gate and keep dogs very strictly under control.

The southern part of the estate is largely open moorland, with the beautiful Llyn Conwy set in its midst. The northern section is mostly farmland interspersed with woodlands on the middle slopes, with the hills above. Just outside the village of Penmachno, visitors can see Ty'n-y-Coed (*see* p.405), a nineteenth-century farmhouse and smallholding illustrating the traditional Welsh way of life; 4 miles north-west, in the Wybrnant Valley, is the equally emotive Tŷ Mawr (*see* p.402).

The extensive Penrhyn estate includes a great stretch of upland country, some of it farmed, some of it glorious open moorland around Llyn Conwy.

Maps

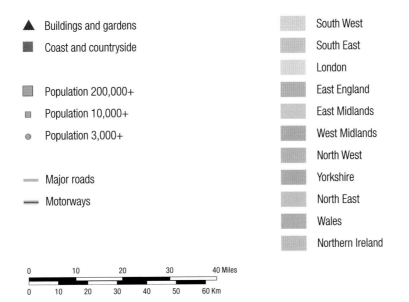

▲ Buildings and gardens

■ Coast and countryside

▣ Population 200,000+

▪ Population 10,000+

● Population 3,000+

— Major roads

▬ Motorways

South West

South East

London

East England

East Midlands

West Midlands

North West

Yorkshire

North East

Wales

Northern Ireland

0	10	20	30	40 Miles

| 0 | 10 | 20 | 30 | 40 | 50 | 60 Km |

The white chalk cliffs of Whitepark Bay
in Country Antrim, the first part of
Northern Irish coast to be bought by
the Trust.

Dovedale
Ilam Park
Hawksmoor
Kedleston Hall
The Old Manor
Sudbury Hall
Calke Abbey
Staunton Harold Church
Wall Roman Site (Letocetum)
Ulverscroft Nature Reserve
The Workhouse
Belton House
Grantham House
Woolsthorpe Manor
Tattershall Castle
Stiffkey Marshes
Blakeney Point
Sheringham Park
West Runton & Beeston Regis Heath
Brancaster
Morston Marshes
Felbrigg Hall
Blickling Hall
Horsey Windpump
Horsey Mere
4 South Quay

Back to Backs
Packwood House
Baddesley Clinton
Coughton Court
Kinwarton Dovecote
Charlecote Park
Middle Littleton Tithe Barn
Hidcote
Dover's Hill
Chipping Camden Market Hall
Chastleton House
Hailes Abbey
Chedworth Roman Villa
Sherborne Park
Lodge Park
Priest's House
Lyveden New Bield
Canons Ashby
Farnborough Hall
Stowe Landscape Gardens
Buckingham Chantry Chapel
Claydon House
Peckover House
Oxburgh Hall
Darrow Wood
Dunwich Heath
Angel Corner
Theatre Royal
Ickworth
Melford Hall
Lavenham Guildhall
Ramsey Abbey Gatehouse
Wimpole Hall & Home Farm
Wicken Fen
Houghton Mill
Anglesey Abbey
Willington Dovecote & Stables
Upton House
Coggeshall: Paycocke's & Grange Barn
Thorington Hall
Flatford: Bridge Cottage
Pin Mill
Dedham Vale
Kyson Hill
Sutton Hoo
Orford Ness

Whipsnade Tree Cathedral
Ascott
Dunstable Downs
Shaw's Corner
Pitstone Windmill
Ashridge Estate
King's Head
Waddesdon Manor
Boarstall Duck Decoy & Boarstall Tower
Long Crendon Courthouse
Coombe Hill
Princes Risborough Manor House
Bradenham
Hughenden Manor
West Wycombe
Watlington Hill
Maidenhead & Cookham Commons
Cliveden
Hatfield Forest
Blake's Wood
Copt Hall Marshes
Northey Island
Blackwater Estuary
Danbury & Lingwood Commons
Bourne Mill

Buscot Park & Old Parsonage
Badbury Hill
Great Coxwell Barn
Coleshill Estate
White Horse Hill
Ashdown House
Lardon Chase & The Holies
Basildon Park
Greys Court
Dorneywood Garden
2 Willow Road
Fenton House
Sutton House
Eastbury Manor House
Rainham Hall
Rayleigh Mount

Avebury Manor
Lockeridge Dene & Piggledene
Falkland Memorial
Sandham Memorial Chapel
The Vyne
West Green House Garden
Finchampstead Ridges
River Wey & Godalming Navigations
Runnymede & Ankerwycke
East Sheen Common
Ham House
The Homewood
Carlyle's House
Gray's Monument
Osterley Park
Roman Bath
Blewcoat School
Lindsey House
Morden Hall Park
George Inn
Red House
Roman Bath
St John's Jerusalem
Owletts
Coldrum Long Barrow
Oldbury
Old Soar Manor
Stoneacre
South Foreland Lighthouse
White Cliffs

Cherhill Down
Stonehenge Down
Figsbury Ring
Stockbridge Down
Winchester City Mill
Selborne
Ludshott Common
Hindhead Common
Black Down
Frensham Common
Witley & Milford Commons
Oakhurst Cottage
Hatchlands Park
Clandon Park
Dapdune Wharf
Shalford Mill
Polesden Lacey
Ranmore Common
Winkworth Arboretum
Leith Hill
Box Hill
Holmwood Common
Bookham Commons
Watermeads
Selsdon Wood
Headley Heath
Limpsfield Common
Quebec House
Knole
Chartwell
Toys Hill
Emmetts
Ightham Mote
Sprivers Garden
Scotney
Smallhythe Place
Sissinghurst
Royal Military Canal
Standen
Chiddingstone
Wakehurst Place
Nymans
Sheffield Park
Bateman's
Bodiam Castle
Lamb House

Little Clarendon
Mompesson House
Pepperbox Hill
Mottisfont Abbey
Hinton Ampner
Uppark
Harting Down
Petworth
Bramber Castle
Devil's Dyke
Cissbury Ring
Highdown Hill
Bramshaw Commons
Hale Purlieu
Frog Firle Farm
Chyngton Farm
Monk's House
Alfriston Clergy House
Birling Gap
Crowlink

White Mill, Lodge Farm
Ibsley & Rockford Commons
Brownsea Island
Studland
Spyway Farm
Needles Old Battery
Tennyson Down
Mottistone Manor Garden
Brighstone
Old Town Hall, Newtown
Bembridge Windmill

© MAPS IN MINUTES™ 2002

1

2

Larrybane & Carrick-A-Rede
Whitepark Bay
Dunseverick Castle
North Antrim Cliff Path
& Murlough Bay
Giant's Causeway
Portstewart
Strand
Downhill &
Mussenden Temple
Hezlett House
Bar Mouth &
Grangemore Dunes

Portrush

Ballyconagan
Rathlin Island
The Manor House

Fair Head
Murlough Head
Cushleake Mountain

Cushendun

Coleraine

Limavady

Ballymoney

Cushendall

LONDONDERRY

Dungiven

Strabane

Gray's
Printing Press

Maghera

Ballymena

Larne

3

Castlederg

Newtownstewart

Magherafelt

Randalstown

Whitehead

Moneymore

M22 M2

Antrim

Ballyclare

Patterson's Spade
Mill

Newtownabbey

Lighthouse
Island

Omagh

Springhill

Cookstown

Templetown
Mausoleum

Crumlin

BELFAST

Holywood

Ballymacormick Point
& Orlock Point

Wellbrook Beetling Mill

Coalisland

Coney Island

Crown Liquor
Saloon

Bangor

Newtownards

Mount Stewart
House & Garden

4

Enniskillen

Dungannon

Lurgan
Craigavon

M1

Portadown

Lisburn

Minnowburn Beeches,
Killynether & Collin Glen

Strangford
Lough

The Argory

Ardress House

Armagh

Tandragee

Dromore

Ballynahinch

Rowallane
Garden

Castle Ward &
Strangford Lough
Wildlife Centre

Castle Coole

Lisnaskea

Banbridge

Downpatrick

Kearney &
Knockinelder

Florence
Court

Crom Estate

Keady

Ballymoyer

Derrymore House

Rathfriland

Castlewellan

Newcastle

Murlough Nature
Reserve

Slieve Donard

Mourne
Coastal Path

5

Newry

Crossmaglen

Warrenpoint

Rostrevor

Kilkeel

Blockhouse &
Green Islands

6

7

M4

M50

Amlwch

Holyhead

M7

M11

Conwy
Suspension
Bridge

Llandudno

Llangefni

Aberconwy House

Conwy

Beaumaris

Bangor

Penrhyn Castle

Plas Newydd

Bodnant
Garden

Glan Faenol

Carneddau

Caernarfon

Segontium

Tŷ'n-y-Coed Uchaf

Tŷ Mawr
Wybrnant

Hafod y Llan

Craflwyn

Blaenau
Ffestiniog

8

Bwthyn Llywelyn

Aberglaslyn

Ffestiniog

Yst

Porthdinllaen

Pwllheli

Criccieth

Porthmadog

Porthor

Llanbedrog

Plas Yn Rhiw

Abersoch

© MAPS IN MINUTES™ 2002

Photographic credits

Useful Addresses

For all general enquiries including information about books published by the National Trust:

National Trust Membership Department
PO Box 39
Warrington WA5 7WD
Tel: 0870 458 4000
Email: enquiries@thenationaltrust.org.uk

National Trust for Scotland
Wemyss House
28 Charlotte Square
Edinburgh EH2 4ET
Tel: 0131 243 9300

The Royal Oak Foundation
26 Broadway
Suite 950
New York
NY 10004
USA
Tel: 001 212 480 2889 Fax: 001 212 785 7234

The Hall at Osterley Park, Surrey,
which was designed by Robert Adam
in 1767.

Index

Page numbers in *italics* refer to illustrations